DATABASE PROCESSING

Fundamentals ·
Design ·
Implementation

FOURTH EDITION

DATABASE PROCESSING

Fundamentals · Design · Implementation

David M. Kroenke

Macmillan Publishing Company
New York

Maxwell Macmillan Canada
Toronto

Maxwell Macmillan International
New York   Oxford   Singapore   Sydney

Editor: Vernon R. Anthony
Developmental Editor: Peggy H. Jacobs
Production Editor: Ben Ko
Art Coordinator: Lorraine Woost
Cover Designer: Robert Vega
Production Buyer: Patricia A. Tonneman
Illustrations: Tech-Graphics

This book was set in Caledonia by Graphic Typesetting Service, Inc., and was printed and bound by Arcata Graphics/Halliday. The cover was printed by Lehigh Press, Inc.

Macmillan Publishing Company
866 Third Avenue
New York, New York 10022

Macmillan Publishing Company is part of the Maxwell Communication Group of Companies.

Maxwell Macmillan Canada, Inc.
1200 Eglinton Avenue East, Suite 200
Don Mills, Ontario M3C 3N1

Library of Congress Cataloging-in-Publication Data

Kroenke, David.
  Database processing : fundamentals, design, implementation / David M. Kroenke.—4th ed.
    p.   cm.
Includes bibliographical references and index.
ISBN 0-02-366875-X
1. Data base management.   I. Title.
QA76.9.D3K76   1992
005.74—dc20   91-24765
                                                        CIP

Printing: 3 4 5 6 7 8 9   Year: 3 4 5

Photo credits: pp. 294, 298, 583 by Allen Zak/ Macmillan.

Several years ago I listened to conversations on the customer support telephone line at Microrim—the vendor of the R:BASE family of DBMS products. An amazingly wide variety of calls was received. One customer had purchased a copy of R:BASE and had been using it to keep track of people and activities. "I struggled a bit, but I finally got a table with all the data I need. But, now I'm stuck. . . ." In fact this customer needed to represent two entities having a many-to-many relationship but had stored all of his data in one table. The support representative, who was talking to a stranger two thousand miles away over the telephone, attempted to explain the essence of normalization, the need for an intersection table, and the ways of using the resulting tables to produce reports.

On another occasion I heard a conversation with a frustrated small business owner who wanted to use R:BASE to keep track of sales-orders. She had looked in the documentation index under *S* for sales-order and found no entry. (She found SELECT and SORT BY, instead.) So, she looked under *I* for invoice and again found no entry (she found INDEX though). "Is this a rare problem? Don't a lot of your customers want to keep track of sales-orders? What do I do next?" The support representative explained how to represent the sales-order with a set of five tables. Her comment: "You must be kidding!"

A third customer had installed R:BASE on a LAN server and was attempting to process a shared database with multiple single-user versions of the product. Here, the support representative explained the need for a multi-user version of R:BASE that would support resource locking, etc. The customer refused to buy; he skeptically assumed an overzealous employee was attempting to sell him a product he didn't need.

Course Objectives

These and other experiences have convinced me of the need for a database course that is broader than teaching dBASE, Paradox, SQL, or any other specific product or language. The course needs to teach database *development:* a term that includes data modeling, database design, and database implementation. These concepts need to be taught with examples that are robust enough to be realistic and yet not so complicated that the course is consumed by the details of the applications.

Increasing the scope of the course this way, however, presents another problem. How broad should the course be? Database technology overlaps into so many areas that it is difficult to know where to place the boundaries. How much systems analysis and design? How much computer science? How much enterprise modeling and information systems strategic planning?

Over the years, I have come to the conclusion that the course should include the material necessary to teach students how to create and administer multi-user databases starting from user requirements. Specifically, this book addresses the following objectives:

- Learn the purpose and appropriate application of database technology
- Understand the components of DBMS products
- Develop skills to model users' data requirements:
    Entity-relationship (top-down)
    Semantic-object (bottom-up)
- Transform users' data models into normalized designs
- Understand the structural coupling between database design and application design
- Implement normalized designs with
    Relational DBMS products
    Network DBMS products
    Hierarchical DBMS products
- Understand the role of data and database administration
- Know the essentials of distributed database processing at two levels:
    Practical application (client-server architecture)
    Critical understanding (issues and problems we need to solve)

Several aspects of these objectives need amplification. In my experience, the most difficult and the *crucial* aspect of database design is the first step: developing the users' data model. Although we can teach tools and techniques, the process of interviewing users and transforming the users' statements, forms, reports, and so forth into a data model is artistic and non-algorithmic. It is also crucial because the quality of all the work that follows depends on the accuracy of the data model.

I teach both entity-relationship and semantic-object modeling techniques. E-R modeling is, in my opinion, better used for top-down modeling approaches. Semantic objects are better used when proceeding from requirements expressed in terms of specific forms and reports, in bottom-up fashion. Both modeling tools are important for the student to learn to use.

One problem I've encountered is that the database and systems development courses overlap considerably. In particular, there is a close relationship between database design and application design. The structure of the data determines not only the structure of the forms and reports that are based on that data, but also the structure of application programs. In the database course, I believe it is important for students to understand the impact that database design decisions have on application design.

In 1991, it may seem inappropriate to include implementation using network and hierarchical products. There are two justifications. For one, there are still hundreds of applications based on these models that graduates may be asked to support. Second, as Bill Korn of the University of Wisconsin–Eau-Claire has said, "Many students will be asked to convert database applications from non-relational to relational products. To do this, they need to know all of these models."[1]

Observe also the two-level goal for distributed databases. On the practical side, distributed applications are currently in use on local area networks using the client-server, and to a lesser extent, the resource-sharing architectures. These systems, however, are not truly distributed *databases* and I believe students need to know why and what needs to happen before they can become truly distributed.

Overview of This Text

The structure of this text mirrors the objectives set out above. The first part concerns fundamental concepts. Chapter 1 introduces database processing and discusses its nature, advantages, disadvantages, and so forth. Chapter 2 discusses the components and functions of database management systems. This chapter is important not only because it shows the student what we have to work with, but also because it describes what a DBMS ought to be. This chapter will help students understand that what is sometimes marketed as a DBMS is a far cry from what a DBMS needs to be. The introductory part is concluded with a short application module in which students process queries against an existing database. The goal of this module is to show the forest before descending into the trees.

The second part concerns database modeling. Chapter 3 presents an overview of the database development process. This chapter is a summary of the systems development process as it pertains to the development of databases in particular. Then Chapter 4 describes the entity-relationship model and applies that model to two examples. Chapter 5 concludes the data modeling part with a description and application of the semantic object data model.

Part III addresses database design. Chapter 6 formally introduces the relational model and explains normalization. This text uses the relational model in two ways. In Chapter 6, we consider this model as a design tool. We use it to express logical (or DBMS-independent) designs. Later, in Chapters 9, 10, and 11, we consider the implementation of databases using DBMS products based on the relational model.

Chapter 7 applies the concepts from Chapters 4, 5, and 6 to teach students how to perform database design. The chapter shows how to transform user data models

---

[1] Speech to the International Association of Information Management, Boston, December 3, 1989.

expressed in terms of both the entity-relationship and the semantic object models into relational DBMS-independent designs. Chapter 8 concludes the design part with a discussion of database application designs. Menu, form, and report design are discussed in the context of database objects. This chapter also discusses the application's role in the implementation of data constraints and shows the coupling between application program structure and database structure.

The next two parts consider database implementation. Part IV describes and illustrates database implementation using the relational model. Chapter 9 presents an overview of the role of the relational model in database implementation and presents important relational algebra commands. Chapter 10 presents SQL. These two chapters set the stage for Chapter 11, which illustrates the implementation of a database using SQL using DB2. This particular DBMS was chosen for two reasons. First, as a mainframe DBMS, it raises important implementation issues that microcomputer DBMS products do not raise, such as storage allocation. Second, DB2 is popular and students are likely to encounter it in the course of their careers.

Non-relational implementation is considered in Part V. Chapter 12 describes the nature and characteristics of transaction processing and develops an example of a transaction-oriented database design that is then implemented using DL/I—a hierarchical data model that has seen wide use in industry as the basis of IMS/DB. Chapter 13 presents the network model and defines the fundamental concepts of the CODASYL DBTG model.

Data and database administration are the subjects of Chapter 14. Data administration is defined as an organization-wide function whereas database administration is defined as specific to the management of a particular database and its applications. The discussion of database administration includes the management of concurrent processing, security, and backup and recovery.

The last part of this text addresses distributed processing. Chapter 15 presents distributed application processing and describes the fundamentals of resource sharing and client-server architectures on local area networks. Chapter 16 concludes the text with a discussion of the major issues in true distributed database processing. Chapter 15 is pragmatic and concerns what is being done today. Chapter 16 is theoretical and concerns issues that need to be solved for the future.

Two appendices, which carry over material from earlier editions, are also included. Appendix A describes input/output processing and Appendix B summarizes data structures. An updated glossary and bibliography follow the appendices, containing definitions of important database terms and critical database readings.

New to This Edition

There are a number of important differences between this edition and previous ones. For one, this edition presents a balanced treatment of the entity-relationship and semantic object data models. Both of these models are important and useful. They approach database design from different directions and can support one another. Students, I believe, should learn to use both.

The third edition of this text was heavily biased toward the semantic object model. That bias reflected my experience in the microcomputer industry. Conversations with others having different experiences, in particular with Jim Fry at the University of Michigan and Constance Knapp at Pace University, have convinced me that the entity-relationship model provides important benefits not provided by the semantic object model.

Another important difference is the introduction of material on the client-server architecture. The rise in use of local area networks and the need for workgroup computing means that the lion's share of growth in the number of multi-user databases will occur using this and related technologies.

This edition also reflects a change in my personal philosophy with regard to the purpose and role of a database. I used to believe that databases were models of things in the world. To be sure, a database is limited and impoverished, but still, I thought, it represents the structure of things in reality.

In their book *Understanding Computers and Cognition*[2] Winograd and Flores present a radically different orientation. Using their orientation, I believe that databases are not models of reality, but rather are models of people's models. Thus, the important question in designing a database is not "How well does this database represent reality?" but rather, "How well does this database represent the users' model of their world?"

The implications of this change in philosophy are subtle but crucial and pervade this edition. When I make the statement "My design is a better reflection of reality" I am actually making the statement "My design is a better reflection of my model." It is both presumptuous and arrogant for me as a database designer to claim that my design is a better model of reality than the users'.

Effective databases are accurate models of people's models, not of reality. My job as a database designer is to determine how people understand their world and build an appropriate model of that understanding. The task is challenging and can be quite difficult because often no single individual possesses all of the user's model in his or her head. The users' model is often shared in several different minds and the design of a multi-user database is sometimes the first place in which the users' model has been integrated in a single concept. Furthermore, there is no guarantee that the separate users' models are logically consistent. If not, the inconsistencies will have to be resolved before the database can be developed. Obtaining such resolution is also full of challenge.

This orientation helps too, in selecting among design alternatives. For example, what are the possible relationships between a CUSTOMER and an ORDER? There are dozens, if not hundreds, of possibilities. All of the possibilities reflect some version of *reality*, and arguments as to which is the better version of reality lead only to frustration and long meetings. Rather, the question must be, "How do the users view the relationships between CUSTOMER and ORDER?"

Again, the difference is subtle and may seem pedantic. Taking this orientation, however, greatly simplifies the task of database design.

---

[2] Winograd, Terry and Fernando Flores. *Understanding Computers and Cognition.* Addison-Wesley, 1986.

Supplementary Materials

In addition to this text, a number of other components are available to support the instructor:

- **Cases:** Terresa Kann has developed a casebook that parallels the structure of the text. The cases present opportunities for students to practice their modeling and database implementation skills.
- **Instructor's Guide:** A comprehensive instructor's guide is available to instructors that includes sample course syllabi, lecture outlines, overhead transparency masters, and answers to questions.
- **Computerized Test Bank:** Arthur Rasher at the University of Tulsa has developed a comprehensive computer-based test bank to support the use of this text.
- **Electronic Transparencies:** Elody Krieger developed an electronic version of the transparencies. A diskette is available with the instructor's guide that presents all of the overheads via a personal computer. No additional software is needed to run the electronic transparencies.

Macmillan has a wide range of microcomputer-based software modules that can be used with this text. They include:

dBASE III +	"Information Systems Literacy . . . dBase III + " by Bidgoli (ISBN 0–02–309428–1)
dBase IV	"Hands On Computing Using dBase IV" by Hobart et al. (ISBN 0–675–22384–9)
Paradox	"Hands On Computing Using Paradox" by Hobart et al. (ISBN 0–675–22378–4)
SQL	"Select . . . SQL" by Newcomer (ISBN 0–02–386693–4)
Fox Pro	"Hands-on Computing Using Fox Pro" by Hobart et al. (ISBN 0-675-22376-8)
Programming	"Business Programming Using dBase IV" by Duggal (ISBN 0–675–21137–9) "Business Programming with Fox Pro" by Duggal

Acknowledgments

I am grateful for the assistance and advice provided by the reviewers of this edition: Kirk Arnett, Mississippi State; Barbara Beccue, Illinois State University, Normal; Linda J. Behrens, Central State University; Walter J. Briggs, University of Alaska; Alan Duchan, Canisus College; Gary Kern, University of Notre Dame; Constance A. Knapp, Pace University; Henry C. Lucas, Jr., New York University; Scott McIntyre, University of Colorado; Arthur A. Rasher, University of Tulsa, OK; Richard Scamell, University of Houston; Hung Tang, Bowling Green State University; James Teng, University of Pittsburgh; Mike Vanacheck, University of North Texas; John Winsor, University of North Texas; and Ama Zaki, College of William and Mary.

Thanks to Kathy Dolan for her help with the third edition of this text and for her friendship and assistance in the preparation of this edition. I am especially grateful to Mr. Guy DeCorte of General Research Corporation with whom I have shared many enjoyable conversations on semantic object modeling.

I also thank Mary Konstant for her help both with the initial plan and for her comprehensive and careful copy editing. I also am grateful to Vern Anthony for his unvarying support for this project at Macmillan and for his seasoned and calm professionalism throughout. Finally, I am especially grateful to Peggy Jacobs, who took a publishing-company-acquisition-process ravaged text and author and brought us happily to the light of day!

David M. Kroenke
Seattle, Washington

CONTENTS

||||||||||||||||||||||||

PART I

Introduction

Part I introduces the subject of database processing. We begin, in Chapter 1, by describing the need for databases and differentiating them from file processing systems. Then, the term *database* is defined and the role of databases in organizations is summarized. Finally, a short survey of the history of database processing is presented.

Chapter 2 describes the components of a database processing system. It begins by introducing a case study of a small organizational database. The basic components of a database processing system are illustrated in the context of this case. Next, we discuss database applications and the types of interfaces between users and databases. The last section of Chapter 2 describes the functions and structure of the database management system itself.

The part concludes with a short module that illustrates the processing of a database. The goal of this module is to help you solidify the introductory concepts with a concrete example.

Overview of
Database Processing

In this introductory chapter, we describe the need for database processing and compare and contrast the characteristics of file processing with those of database processing. Then we define the term *database* and show how databases are used at three levels of organization. Finally, we present a short history of database processing. The goal of the chapter is to give you a broad perspective before plunging into the details of the technology.

- THE NEED FOR DATABASE PROCESSING
- FILE PROCESSING SYSTEMS
- DATABASE PROCESSING SYSTEMS
- DEFINITION OF DATABASE
- DATABASES AND ORGANIZATIONAL LEVELS
- SHORT HISTORY OF DATABASE PROCESSING

The Need for Database Processing

For several reasons, database processing is one of the most important courses in the information systems curriculum. First, this technology is used at all levels of organization. Individuals use personal databases to facilitate their own work. Departments use workgroup databases to integrate the activities of individuals in the departments, and corporations use large organizational databases to blend the work of many departments. No matter what the scope of your work, you are likely to encounter database technology.

Second, databases are used to store large volumes of organizational data. Such databases become the heart of many transaction processing applications like order entry, inventory control, and general ledger accounting. The performance of these applications, which are crucial to the success of the company, depends heavily on the quality of the underlying database design.

Third, data that is stored in databases is one of an organization's most valued assets. The task of providing easy access to this asset for authorized purposes while protecting it from unauthorized uses can be vital to an organization's success. Knowing how to meet the dual need for access and protection is an important skill.

Fourth, in order to learn how to design databases, you will need to learn data modeling skills. Not only will these skills help you in designing databases, but they will also improve your general problem solving skills. Learning good data modeling skills will help you set up better spreadsheets, for example.

WHAT IS INFORMATION?

The fundamental reason that database technology is used in business today is that it facilitates the production of **information.** Before proceeding any further, we must better understand what information is and why we need it.

The word *information* comes from the Latin word *informare*, which means "to build from" or "to give structure to." Computer systems build structures from data by processing it to reveal patterns, trends, and tendencies. These patterns, trends, and so forth are the information that users need to perform their jobs. If businesspeople did not derive information from the huge volumes of data they confront, then they would be overwhelmed with details, floundering about to find the knowledge they need. They would drown in a sea of facts.

People strive to make order in their world. Think about the first time you endured the add/drop process during class registration (or the first time you went to an airport, or the first time you did anything new). If your college is like most, the registration room was large, hot, noisy, and chaotic. People were moving all around you and you didn't know quite what to do. Probably your anxiety level was high as you tried to make any meaning out of the scene before you. Unconsciously, you gathered data through sight and sound, related this data to prior knowledge (such as knowing how people line up and wait their turns or take numbers and wait to be called), compared this new data to your goal (dropping a course, for example), and decided on a course of action (to get into the line marked "drop course").

The key element in this scenario is the processing of your perceptions. As you gathered data by examining the room, you built patterns and structures in your mind and tried to relate them to structures you already had. You looked for clues in people's behavior. You might have asked somebody for help. If so, your plea was a request for information. You wanted someone who had already processed the scene and built patterns and structures to tell you what they were.

As you gained information about the add/drop process, your uncertainty decreased. When you had entered the room you did not even know in which direction to turn. Once you knew which line to join, you became more sure of yourself. Information reduced your uncertainty.

Computer systems provide a similar function for users. One of the main reasons for information systems is to reduce users' uncertainty. Let's consider that statement in the context of a business problem.

AN INFORMATION ILLUSTRATION

Suppose you work for a nationwide record club as the marketing manager in charge of rereleased albums of 1960s rock music. Near the end of your fiscal year you have $50,000 remaining in your promotion budget. You need to decide how to spend that money so that you maximize your sales per promotional dollar. In order to make that decision, you need information.

You have at your disposal many facts, such as the record club's list of all record sales during the past year. Somewhere in that mountain of data there are probably patterns that will help reduce your uncertainty about how to most effectively spend the $50,000. The task you face is to find those patterns.

Figure 1.1a is a partial list of your company's record sales. For each sale it shows the member's name and membership number as well as data about the record purchased. This is pure data—facts and figures. It is unlikely that this list will enable you to develop an effective promotional campaign because you cannot see any structures or patterns.

Suppose you eliminated from the list all but rock music purchases. Notice that you can do this because rock music is classified as product code 45. Then suppose you sorted the list by amount so you could see which customers were most active. The result of these operations is shown in Figure 1.1b.

You have gained information from these operations. You have eliminated clutter (record purchases you are not interested in), and you have organized the remaining data to reveal a pattern (how many rock music purchases were made by each member who made at least one). However, you still do not have the solution to your problem, namely, how to effectively spend the $50,000. You need to access even more data.

Your record club also maintains a list of characteristics of purchasers which it has developed through questionnaires and telephone interviews with members. You decide to somehow (we'll discuss how in the next section) combine this customer profile data with the sales data, sort the resulting data by total sales, and finally print the characteristics of customers who have purchased more than $100 worth of rock music in the past year. Among other characteristics, you print graphs of the ages, incomes, and geographic

Customer Number	Customer Name	Album Number	Album Name	Product Code	Amount	Date
100	McDonald	301	Smooth Stuff	30	1	11/30/91
410	Arnold	822	Rock Stuff	45	2	11/04/91
680	Edling	615	Classical Stuff	65	2	12/10/91
700	Mellott	987	Country Stuff	70	1	11/25/91
550	Janner	543	Oldies Vol. 1	30	1	12/05/91
360	King	833	Rock Stuff Vol. 2	45	1	11/27/91
220	Deeks	301	Smooth Stuff	30	1	12/08/91
890	Manion	763	Hard Rock	45	5	12/10/91

a. List of record purchases

Customer Number	Customer Name	Album Number	Album Name	Product Code	Amount	Date
360	King	833	Rock Stuff Vol. 2	45	1	11/27/91
410	Arnold	822	Rock Stuff	45	2	11/04/91
890	Manion	763	Hard Rock	45	5	12/10/91

b. List of rock record purchases

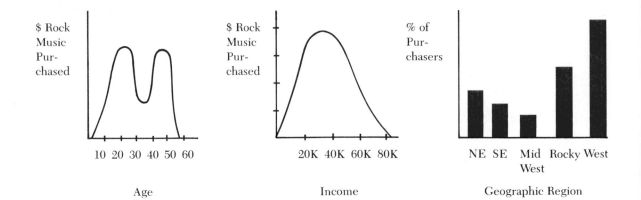

c. Characteristics of active members

FIGURE 1.1
Developing information

regions of the active members (Figure 1.1c). The result of these operations is information—information that will help you design a promotional campaign aimed at the segment of the population most likely to purchase rock music from you. Now you have some ideas on how to spend the remaining $50,000 in your budget.

Since this is not a marketing textbook, we won't consider this problem any further. The point is that in order to reduce your uncertainty you needed information. You acquired that information by processing data in such a way that you identified patterns related to the problem you needed to solve. As promised, the information you found reduced your uncertainty.

In this example we did not specify how the lists of purchases and member profiles were actually stored. They could be in manual files. Imagine how difficult and error-prone the task would be if clerks had to read receipts for all record sales (there could be thousands of them), copy the information for rock music sales only, then manually sort the selected records and match them with customer profile data (also stored on paper). Obviously, computer technology is needed to perform this process in a timely manner.

Two approaches to this problem could be taken, one based on file processing and the other based on database processing. In the next section we will consider file processing systems, and after that we will look at database processing systems.

File Processing Systems

From the start, business computer systems were developed to process business records and produce information. The early systems stored groups of records in separate files, and so they were called **file processing systems.** Figure 1.2, for example, shows two file processing systems that could be used by the record club. One system processes sales data, and the other one processes customer data.

Although file processing systems are a great improvement over manual systems, they do have limitations:

- Data is separated and isolated.
- Data is often duplicated.
- Application programs are dependent on file formats.
- Files are often incompatible with one another.
- It is difficult to represent data in the users' format.

Let's consider each of these limitations.

SEPARATED AND ISOLATED DATA

Recall that as the marketing manager you needed to relate sales data to customer data. For the system in Figure 1.2, this will be difficult. Somehow you need to extract data from both the CUSTOMER and ORDER files and combine the data into a single file for processing. With file processing, these actions will be difficult. Computer programmers must first determine which parts of each of the files are needed; then they need to determine how the files are related to one another; and then they must carefully coordinate the processing of the files so the correct data is extracted. Coordinating two files is difficult enough, but imagine the task of coordinating ten or more of them!

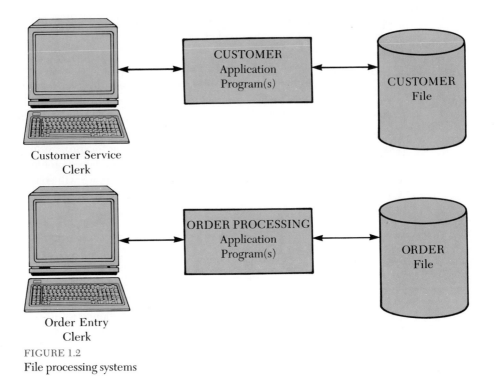

FIGURE 1.2
File processing systems

DATA DUPLICATION

In the record club example, a member's name, address, and membership number are stored in both files (CUSTOMER and ORDER). Although this duplicate data wastes file space, that is not the most serious problem. The most serious problem with duplicated data concerns **data integrity.**

A collection of data has integrity if the data is logically consistent. This means, in part, that duplicated data items agree with one another. Poor data integrity often develops in file processing systems. For example, if a member changes his or her name or address, then all files containing that data need to be updated. The danger is that all files might *not* be updated, causing discrepancies among the files.

Data integrity problems are serious. If data items differ, inconsistent results will be produced. A report from one application will disagree with a report from another application. At least one of them will be incorrect, but who can tell which one? When inconsistent results occur, the credibility of the stored data, and even the MIS function itself, come into question.

APPLICATION PROGRAM DEPENDENCY

With file processing, application programs depend on file formats. Usually in file processing systems the physical formats of files and records are part of the application code.

In COBOL, for example, file formats are written in the DATA DIVISION. The problem with this arrangement is that when changes are made to file formats, application programs must also be changed.

For example, if the customer record is modified to expand the Zip-code field from five to nine digits, all programs that use the customer record need to be modified, even if they do not use the Zip-code field. There might be twenty programs that process the customer file. Such a change means that a programmer needs to identify all the affected programs, modify them, and then retest them—time-consuming and error-prone tasks. Also, programmers find it frustrating to have to modify programs that do not even use the field whose format changed.

INCOMPATIBLE FILES

One of the consequences of program data dependency is that file formats depend on the language or product used to generate them. The format of a file processed by a COBOL program is different from the format of a file processed by a BASIC program, which is different still from the format of a file processed by a C program.

As a result, files cannot be readily combined or compared. Suppose, for example, that FILE-A contains CUSTOMER data including Customer# and that FILE-B contains ORDER data that also includes Customer#. Suppose an application requires that we combine records that have matching Customer#s. If FILE-A was processed by a COBOL program and FILE-B was processed by a C program, we will need to convert both files to a common structure before we can combine the records. This will be time consuming and, sometimes, difficult. Such problems grow worse as the number of files to be combined increases.

DIFFICULTY OF REPRESENTING DATA IN USERS' FORMAT

It is difficult to represent file processing data in a form that seems natural to users. Users build applications because they need to keep track of something. In this text, we will call such things **objects,** or frequently, **semantic objects.**

In some cases, objects can be readily represented by a single record in a file. For example, in Figure 1.2, CUSTOMER records represent customer objects and ORDER records represent order objects.

More complicated objects, however, are not so readily represented. Suppose we needed to store the representation of customer invoices for the record club. As illustrated in Figure 1.3a, invoices have a fixed-length heading and a variable-length body. The number of lines printed on the invoice depends on the number of purchases made by the record club member. Thus, the invoice is a variable-length object. Such objects are difficult to represent with files.

One approach is shown in Figure 1.3b. Here the file contains two types of records, interleaved with one another. Although this arrangement does represent the data correctly, it is difficult to write application programs to process it. Other, more complicated, objects in the business world are even more difficult to represent in file processing systems.

Database Processing Systems

Database technology was developed, in large measure, to overcome the limitations of file processing systems. To understand how this is accomplished, consider the database version of the record club's system, illustrated in Figure 1.4. A new component, the database management system (DBMS), has been added. The DBMS is a program (or set of programs) that overcomes the disadvantages of file processing: it allows stored data to be integrated, reduces data duplication, facilitates data integrity, eliminates program dependency on file formats, and allows complicated objects to be more easily represented and processed.

Notice the difference between the file processing system in Figure 1.2 and the database system in Figure 1.4. File processing programs directly access files of stored data.

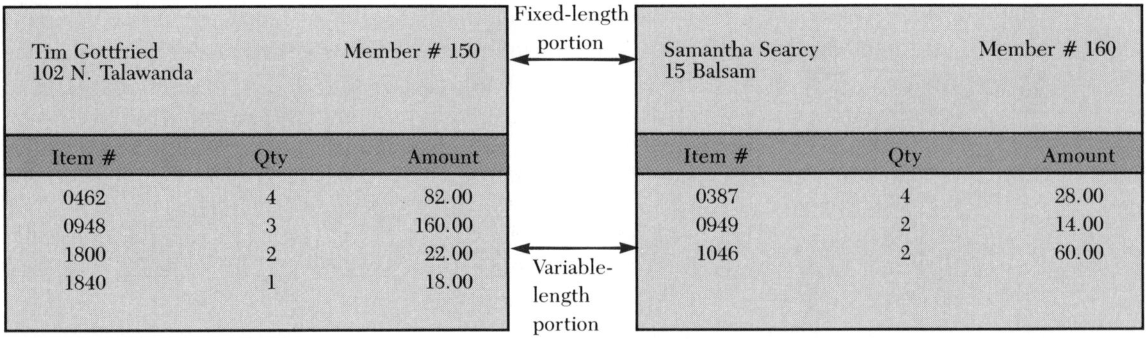

Tim Gottfried 102 N. Talawanda		Member # 150	Fixed-length portion	Samantha Searcy 15 Balsam		Member # 160
Item #	Qty	Amount		Item #	Qty	Amount
0462	4	82.00		0387	4	28.00
0948	3	160.00		0949	2	14.00
1800	2	22.00	Variable-	1046	2	60.00
1840	1	18.00	length portion			

a. Member invoices

150	M	Tim Gottfried		102 N. Talawanda		. . .
150	P	0462 4 82.00		0948 3 160.00		1800 2 22.00
150	P	1840 1 18.00				
160	M	Samantha Searcy		15 Balsam		. . .
160	P	0387 4 28.00		0949 2 14.00		1046 2 60.00

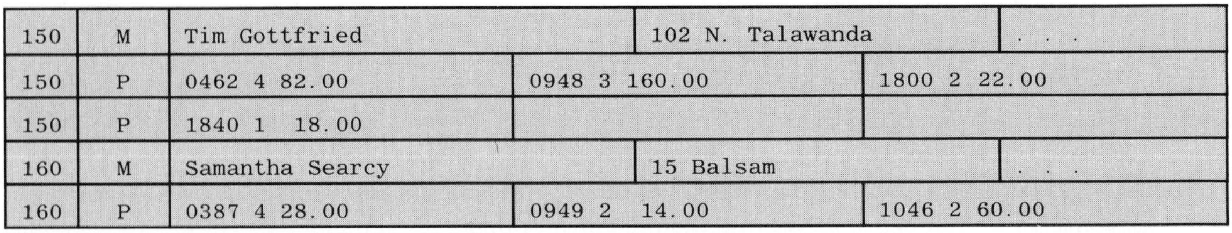

b. CUSTOMER file with Master and Purchase records

FIGURE 1.3
Using files to store complicated objects

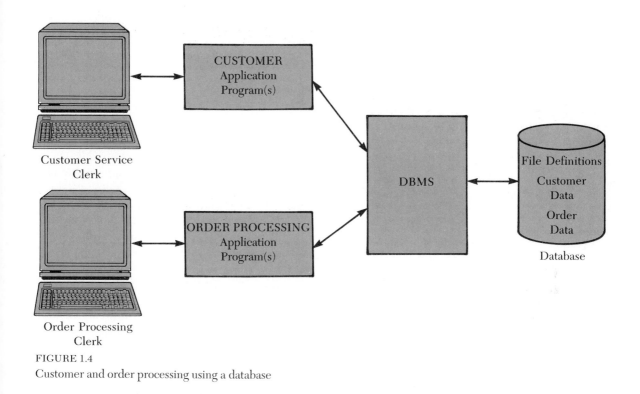

FIGURE 1.4
Customer and order processing using a database

In contrast, database processing programs call the DBMS to access the stored data. This difference is significant because it makes the application programming job easier; that is, application programmers need not be concerned with the ways data is physically stored. Rather, they are free to concentrate on matters important to the user instead of matters important to the computer system.

INTEGRATED DATA

In a database system, all application data is stored in a single facility called the **database.** An application program can ask the DBMS to access customer data, sales data, or both. If both are needed, the application programmer need only specify how the data is to be combined, and the DBMS will perform the necessary operations to combine it. Thus, the programmer is not responsible for the programming needed to coordinate the file processing system in Figure 1.2.

REDUCED DATA DUPLICATION

With database processing, duplicate data is minimal. For example, in the record club's database, the member number, name, and address need to be stored only once. Whenever this data is needed, the DBMS can retrieve it. And when it is modified, only one update need be performed. Because data is stored in only one place, data integrity problems are less frequent—there is less opportunity for discrepancies between multiple copies of the same data item.

PROGRAM/DATA INDEPENDENCE

Database processing reduces the dependency of programs on file formats. All record formats are stored in the database itself (along with the data), and they are accessed by the DBMS, not by application programs. Unlike file processing programs, database application programs need not include the format of all files and records they process. Instead, application programs need only include a definition (the length and data type) of each of the data items they need from the database. The mapping of data items into records and other similar transformations are handled by the DBMS. This is called **program/data independence.**

Program/data independence minimizes the impact of data format changes on application programs. Format changes are input to the DBMS and it updates the data it maintains about the structure of the database. For the most part, application programs are unaware that format changes have occurred. It also means that whenever data items are added, changed, or deleted from the database, only the programs that use those particular data items need to be modified. For applications consisting of dozens of programs this can represent considerable time savings.

BETTER REPRESENTATION OF THE USERS' VIEW OF DATA

As you will learn throughout this text, database technology makes it possible to represent, in a straightforward fashion, the objects found in the user's world. An invoice, for example, can be represented by a combination of data extracted from two record types. As illustrated in Figure 1.5, one record type provides data needed for the fixed-length portion of the invoice, and the second record type supplies data on purchases. There can be a different number of sales records for each member. When an invoice needs to be printed or displayed on a computer screen, the DBMS constructs it by combining the relevant data from the two record types.

Definition of Database

The term *database* suffers from many different interpretations. It has been used to refer to everything from a collection of index cards to the volumes and volumes of data that a government collects about its citizens. In this text, we will use this term with a specific meaning: *A database is a self-describing collection of integrated records.* It is important that you understand each phrase in this definition.

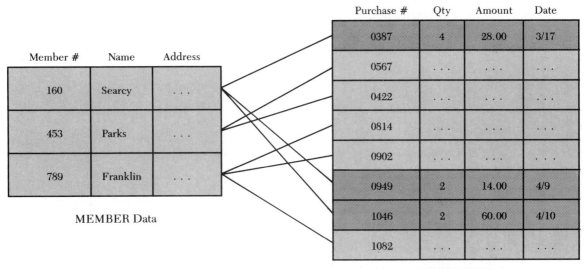

a. Storing invoice data in two record types

b. Constructed invoice

FIGURE 1.5
Representing invoices with two types of records

A DATABASE IS SELF-DESCRIBING

A database is self-describing; it contains, in addition to the user's source data, a description of its own structure. This description is called the **data dictionary** (or **data directory,** or **meta-data**). It is the data dictionary that makes program/data independence possible.

In this sense, a database is similar to your college's library. A library is a self-describing collection of books. In addition to books, the library contains a card catalog describing the books in the library. In the same way, the data dictionary (which is part of the database, just as the card catalog is part of the library) contains descriptions of the data contained in the database.

Why is this self-describing characteristic of a database so important? First, it promotes program/data independence. It makes it possible to determine the structure and content of the database by examining the database itself. We do not need to guess what the database contains, nor do we need to maintain external documentation of file and record formats (as is done in file processing systems).[1]

Second, if we change the structure of the data in the database (such as adding new data items to an existing record), we need only enter that change in the data dictionary. Few, if any, programs will need to be changed. In most cases, only programs that process the changed data items will need to be changed. In some cases, not even they will have to be changed.

If you are familiar with COBOL, you know that the structure of the data for file processing programs is described in the DATA DIVISION. Compared to database processing, this practice is inefficient. It's like putting a copy of your library's card catalog in the home or office of every library user. What happens when the library buys a new book? The card catalog needs to be changed in dozens or hundreds of places!

You may have learned in your COBOL or other programming courses that modern practice is to store the structure of files in a copy library and extract the file structure from the library at the time of compilation. A similar strategy is used with databases. The structure of the database is extracted from the database and loaded into the program prior to program compilation.

A DATABASE IS A COLLECTION OF INTEGRATED RECORDS

You probably know the following hierarchy of data structure: bits are aggregated into bytes or characters, characters are aggregated into fields, fields are aggregated into records, and records are aggregated into files. (See Figure 1.6a.) It is tempting to say that files are aggregated into databases. Although this statement is true, it does not go far enough.

A database is more than a collection of files. A database includes files of source data plus a description of the relationships among the records in the files. These relationship descriptions are stored and recalled during database processing (Figure 1.6b). For example, consider the record club with CUSTOMER and ORDER files. At various times, we may need to know the orders placed by a particular customer or the customer who

---

[1]Do not take this statement too far. The self-describing nature of the database means that we need not maintain external documentation about the physical structure of the database. We need to keep, however, external documentation about the data model, the application requirements, and so forth. Such documentation today is often maintained in CASE repositories. Perhaps some day such repositories will be integrated with database data dictionaries so that *no* external documentation is required. This is not true today, however.

a. Hierarchy of data elements in file processing

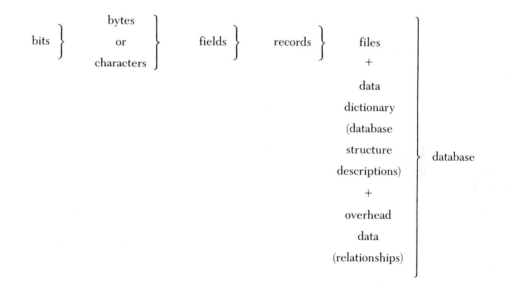

b. Hierarchy of data elements in database processing

FIGURE 1.6
Hierarchy of data elements

placed a particular order. A database is able to store these relationships. Thus, a database is a collection of **integrated records.**

In order to represent relationships, the DBMS will probably need to store some additional system data. This data, described in Appendix B, is sometimes called **overhead data.** Overhead data consists of linked lists, indexes, and similar data. So there are three fundamental parts of a database: application data, the data dictionary, and overhead data.

A DATABASE IS A REPRESENTATION OF AN ORGANIZATION

A database contains representations of facts about an organization that can be manipulated to produce information. Each byte of data is a measurement of the organization's status at some point in time. The names and addresses of employees, the names and quantities on hand of parts in inventory, and amounts of cash, receivables, and payables are measurements of the status of the company. The collection of all these measurements is a representation of the particular business unit. You have probably seen physical representations (iconic models) of buildings, boats, and other objects. A database is a data representation of an organization or part of one.

Data representations vary in their level of detail. Some are simple and crude. A list of customers and the amounts they owe is a rough and approximate representation of a retail store. A more detailed representation would include product, inventory, and accounting data. A very detailed representation would include even more data.

The degree of detail that should be incorporated into a data representation depends on the information desired. Clearly, the more information needed, the finer the level of detail should be. Which data and how much data to store in the database are key design questions we will address.

Businesses change. People come and go. Products are introduced and phased out. Money is earned and spent. As these changes occur, the data that represents the business must be altered. If not, the data representation will become out of date and be an inaccurate representation of the business unit.

Transactions are representations of events. By applying transactions to the database, we can keep the data representation current. Consider Figure 1.7, which summarizes this activity. Events occur in the business world that change the status of the company. For example, customers buy and return goods, shipments arrive, and so forth. When an event occurs, a business record, called a transaction, is created. Examples of transactions are customer invoices, credit slips, and deposit records. Transactions are data representations of events.

When events that change aspects of the business represented by the database occur, then transactions for the events must be processed against the database. To do this, someone (a data entry clerk, a salesperson, or a teller, for example) activates a transaction processing program and enters the transaction data. The program then calls on the DBMS to alter the database. Transaction processing programs usually produce displays or print responses such as order confirmations or receipts.

Databases and Organizational Levels

Database technology is applicable in many different ways throughout a company or other organization. Take a moment and imagine a very large organization, say Procter & Gamble, or IBM, or Bank of America. Think about the information systems in one of those companies. Imagine the myriad of ways in which people, groups, departments, and divisions develop, use, and share information. A truly mind-boggling picture!

In studying the application of database technology, it will be helpful at times to partition the range of applications. Daft and Steers provide a clue for such partitioning in their text *Organizations, A Micro/Macro Approach:* "As social systems, organizations are composed of systems at different levels. . . . Organizational scientists generally think of

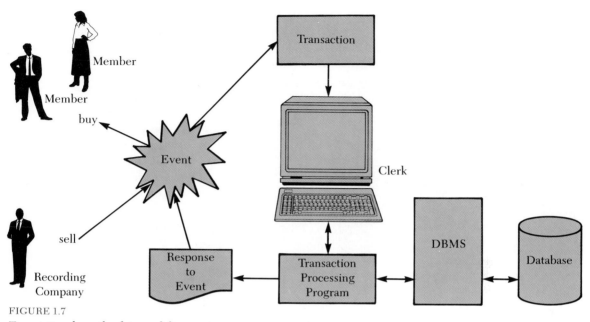

FIGURE 1.7

Transactions keep the data model current

three levels of analysis—the individual, the group or department, and the organization itself."[2]

We can use these three levels to partition our study of the application of database technology. Specifically, there are personal (individual) database applications, workgroup (group or department) database applications, and organizational database applications.

To illustrate, refer to the organizational chart in Figure 1.8, which shows a portion of the organization of the record club discussed previously. There are four departments: marketing, sales, operations, and finance. In this organization, there are applications of database technology at each of the three levels.

PERSONAL DATABASES

Consider the personal level first. Product managers, who work within the Marketing Department, need to keep track of sales projections, actual sales, characteristics of customers, details of promotional plans, and so forth. To do this, the product managers store data in personal databases—a product management database. Each product manager has his or her own database; no one else uses that database.

---

[2]Richard L. Daft and Richard M. Steers, *Organizations, A Micro/Macro Approach* (Glenview, IL.: Scott, Foresman, 1986), 7, 8.

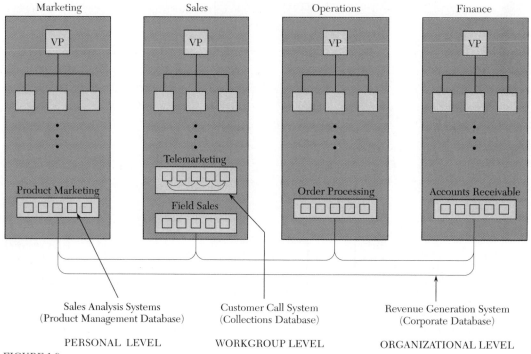

FIGURE 1.8
Three levels of database processing system

The example at the start of this chapter indicates how such a personal database could be used. The product manager manipulates the data in the database to produce information that will help him or her decide how to spend the $50,000.

Personal databases have great flexibility. Suppose, for example, the product manager decides to spend the money on advertising. He or she can further manipulate the personal database to identify characteristics of customers and thus select appropriate publications for the advertisements.

Personal databases usually have a single user who inputs and updates data, produces reports, and issues queries against the database. The sole individual is responsible for the database.

WORKGROUP DATABASES

At the workgroup level, people use database technology to store and process data that is important to a group or a department. Consider the Accounts Receivable Department in Figure 1.8, for example. Suppose that the record club has a policy of calling members who are delinquent with payments. When an account becomes overdue, the customer's data is entered into a special workgroup database, the COLLECTIONS database. Workgroup members select customers from this database and call the customers to request payment. Records of the calls are stored in the COLLECTIONS database. Comments like "The check is in the mail," "I'll mail the check today," and so forth are recorded. When payments are received, the database is modified accordingly. If payments are not received, additional follow-up calls and other actions are taken.

The workgroup uses the database to maintain a collective, group memory about who's been called and the commitments customers have made. Group members do not want to needlessly hassle a customer by duplicating calls, but at the same time, they do want to follow up on promises made. To handle follow-up effectively, each member of the group needs to know what the customer has told other members of the group.

Workgroup database applications differ from personal database applications in that they support *many concurrent users.* Whereas only one product manager uses a particular product management database, many collections agents use the COLLECTIONS database. Observe, however, that all agents do the same type of work with that database.

ORGANIZATIONAL DATABASES

The third level of organization is the corporatewide, or the organizational, level. At this level, the information system integrates the activities of many different departments and the results of those activities are stored in a shared, organizational database.

Organizational databases differ from workgroup and personal databases not only in size but also in character. Organizational databases must not only support many users, they must also support many different views of data—sometimes even different views of the same data. Consider the revenue generation system at the record club as shown in Figure 1.8.

Each business department has its own information requirements. Marketing needs information about members and past orders. Sales needs information about members and current or potential orders. Operations needs information about members, orders, and inventory. Finance needs information about members, account balances, and payments.

Even though considerable overlap exists in the information needs of these departments, not all of the departments need to process the same data. And even when they do process the same data, they process and view it differently.

Figure 1.9 shows categories of revenue generation data. No functional area needs data from every category (though, in principle, they could). In this example, different portions of the revenue data are used by different functional areas. Some of the data is shared by two or more functional areas, but in different ways.

Consider customer data. Sales needs to know the customer's name and telephone number. Operations needs to know the customer's name and shipping address. Finance needs to know the customer's name and billing address.

Additionally, the computer screens, reports, and transaction processing programs will probably be different for each of the departments. Such flexibility allows order entry clerks to employ a data entry form that is meaningful in the context of entering an order, while accounts receivable agents use a different form that is meaningful in the context of collecting a debt. Both of these forms may use the same or much of the same data.

Finally, in an organizational system, the actions of one department influence the actions of other departments. For revenue generation, when an order is shipped by oper-

FIGURE 1.9
Categories of revenue generation
data

Marketing
- Member data
- Past order data

Sales
- Member data
- Current order data
- Inventory data

Operations
- Member data
- Order data
- Inventory data

Finance
- Member data
- Account balances
- Payments

ations, a customer balance is generated for accounts receivable to collect. Thus, the shipment in operations activates an activity in accounts receivable. Organizational databases must support and facilitate these interdepartmental activities.

DIFFERENCES BETWEEN PERSONAL, WORKGROUP, AND ORGANIZATIONAL DATABASES

To summarize, a personal database application is used by an individual to keep track of entities important to him or her. A workgroup database application is used by many individuals to integrate their activities and thus keep track of entities important to the workgroup. An organizational database application is used by many departments to integrate their activities to keep track of entities important to the organization.

When we move from one type of database application to another, we cross two important boundaries. When we move from personal to workgroup database applications, we make a transition from single-user to multi-user systems. When we move from workgroup to organizational database applications, we make a transition from databases that provide one view of data to databases that provide multiple views of data. Characteristics of the three levels of database applications are summarized in Figure 1.10.

Short History of Database Processing

Database processing originated in the organizational context. It was used first to support interdepartmental processing. Then, as the microcomputer became prevalent, database technology migrated to micros and was employed in single-user, personal database appli-

FIGURE 1.10
Characteristics of three levels of
database systems

Personal Database Systems
- Single-user
- Usually single application
- Single view of data

Workgroup Database Systems
- Multi-user
- Usually single application
- Single view of data

Organizational Database Systems
- Multi-user
- Multi-application
- Multiple views of data

cations. Next, as micros were connected together in workgroups, database technology moved to the workgroup setting. Finally, attempts are being made today to integrate all of these different databases into unified and consistent distributed databases.

Unfortunately, one of the consequences of this multistage development is that different terms have been used in each of these stages. So now database technology seems more complex and complicated than it really is. Similar concepts have different names, and the same names often refer to different concepts. Be aware of this situation as you proceed through your database course.

The following short discussion of the stages in the growth of database processing places the technology in historical perspective.

THE ORGANIZATIONAL CONTEXT

The initial application of database technology was to resolve the problems with file processing systems discussed earlier in this chapter. In the mid-1960s, major corporations were producing data at phenomenal rates in file processing systems. The data was becoming difficult to manage, and new systems were becoming increasingly difficult to develop. Further, management wanted to be able to relate the data in one file system to that in another.

The limitations of file processing prevented easy integration of data, as you have seen. Database technology held out the promise of a solution to the problems, and large companies began to develop organizational databases. Companies centralized their operational data such as orders, inventory, and accounting data in these databases. The applications were primarily organizationwide, transaction processing systems.

At first, when the technology was new, database applications were difficult to develop. There were many failures. Even applications that were developed successfully were slow and unreliable: computer hardware was not fast enough to quickly handle the volume of transactions; developers had not yet discovered more efficient ways to store and retrieve data; and programmers were still new at accessing databases—sometimes their programs did not work correctly.

Companies found another important disadvantage of database processing: vulnerability. If a file processing system fails, only that particular application is out of commission. If the database fails, all of the dependent applications are out of commission.

Gradually, the situation improved. Hardware and software engineers learned how to build systems powerful enough to support many concurrent users, and fast enough to keep up with the daily workload of transactions. New ways of controlling, protecting, and backing up the database were developed. Standard procedures for database processing evolved, and programmers learned how to write more efficient and more maintainable code.

By the mid-1970s, effective organizational databases had been implemented that were in use and were efficiently and reliably processing organizational applications. With many of the early problems resolved, management turned its attention to developing new uses for this new, huge pool of organizational data.

Managers knew that somehow all of that data could provide information for both tactical (short-term) and strategic (long-term) decision making. To do this, however, users needed to access the data themselves. They could not be expected to wait weeks or months for programmers to "get the information out of the computer."

Unfortunately, most of the applications had to be developed in procedural languages such as COBOL and PL/I, and users did not have the time or resources to become professional programmers. Besides, users were interested only in getting the answers to their questions, not in learning COBOL or how to navigate through a database to extract just the right bytes of data. It seemed that users and computers were existing in two different worlds. And yet, all that data was there waiting to be put to even more good uses. This situation set the stage for the next major development in database processing: the relational representation.

THE RELATIONAL MODEL

In 1970, a computer scientist named E. F. Codd published a landmark paper[3] in which he applied concepts from a branch of mathematics called relational algebra to the problem of storing large amounts of data. Codd's paper started a movement within the database community that within a few years led to the definition of the **relational database model.** This model is a particular way of structuring and processing a database, and we will discuss it at length in Chapters 6 and 9 through 11.

Benefits of the Relational Model

The advantage of the relational model is that data is stored, at least conceptually, in a way that users can readily understand. Data is stored as tables, and relationships among rows

---

[3] E. F. Codd, "A Relational Model of Data for Large Shared Databanks," *Communications of the ACM* 13(June 1970), 377–387.

of tables are visible in the data. This approach, unlike earlier database models, made it possible for users to obtain information from databases without the assistance of MIS professionals.

Recall that databases store not only data, but also relationships among data. Consider, for example, the production of a student transcript. Figure 1.11 shows the basic data required to construct a student transcript: there is data about students and data about the courses the students have completed. But to construct a transcript, not only do we need the data, we also need to know the relationships among the data values—in this case, relationships between particular students and courses.

DBMS products vary in the way they represent such data relationships. Early DBMS products stored the relationships in overhead data, which effectively hid the relationships from anyone who did not possess some knowledge of overhead data structures. Although programmers and other MIS professionals learned these structures and how to use them to navigate through the database, the typical end-user did not know what they were and did not want to find out.

Thus, users were dependent on information systems professionals to write programs to get their information. This always took time and was often frustrating.

The relational model changed this situation. One of the keystones of the relational model is storage of relationships in user-visible data. Refer to Figure 1.11. Here, the relationship between students and courses is stored in the Student-ID field found in the COURSE record. We can retrieve a course record, and by examining its contents, determine which students took that course. We can also process the data in the other direction: given a student ID number, a relational DBMS can determine which courses he or she has completed.

With the relational model, the user need only specify which records he or she wants to process (for example, all the course records for student 100 or the names of all the students who completed course BD100). The DBMS will figure out how to navigate through the database.

Relational database management systems can be used for most applications, including transaction processing of organizational databases. But one application type has found the relational model to be particularly useful, namely, the decision-support system (DSS). Decision support applications typically address unstructured problems and involve much ad hoc, or unpredictable, processing. As one executive put it, "I know I'm doing DSS when I don't know the second question to ask until I see the answer to the first question." DSS users are typically higher-level managers (or assistants to such people) who are willing and able to learn relational DBMS tools to accomplish their goals. Because the products based on the relational model are generally easy to use, relational databases are often the heart of a DSS.

Resistance to the Relational Model

The relational model encountered a good deal of resistance initially. Relational database systems require more computer resources, and as a result, they were much slower than systems based on earlier database models. Although they were easier to use, the slow response time was often unacceptable. To some extent, relational DBMS products were

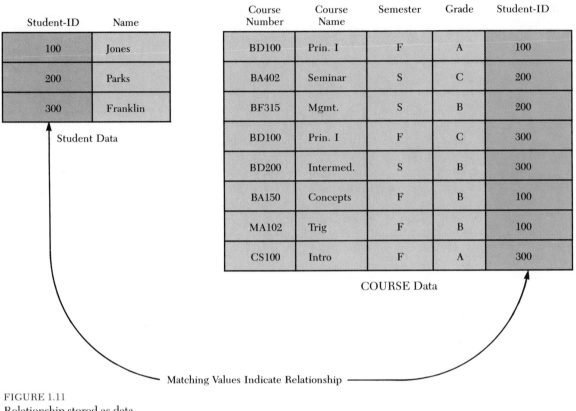

Student-ID	Name
100	Jones
200	Parks
300	Franklin

Student Data

Course Number	Course Name	Semester	Grade	Student-ID
BD100	Prin. I	F	A	100
BA402	Seminar	S	C	200
BF315	Mgmt.	S	B	200
BD100	Prin. I	F	C	300
BD200	Intermed.	S	B	300
BA150	Concepts	F	B	100
MA102	Trig	F	B	100
CS100	Intro	F	A	300

COURSE Data

Matching Values Indicate Relationship

FIGURE 1.11
Relationship stored as data

impractical until the 1980s when faster computer hardware was developed and the price-performance ratio of computers fell dramatically.

Also, the relational model seemed foreign to many programmers. They were accustomed to writing programs in which they processed data one record at a time. But relational DBMS products most naturally process data an entire table at a time. Programmers needed to learn a new way to think about data processing.

Finally, relational systems were supposed to enable a lay person to process a database with limited assistance from an MIS professional. While there is no doubt that relational processing more closely resembles the user's world than processing databases based on other models, relational DBMS products are still foreign to many users.

So the relational model had many advantages, but it did not gain true popularity until computers became more powerful. In particular, as microcomputers entered the scene, more and more CPU cycles could be devoted to a single user. Such power was a boon to relational DBMS products and set the stage for the next major stage of database development.

MICROCOMPUTER DBMS PRODUCTS

In 1979, a small company called Ashton-Tate introduced a microcomputer product called dBASE II (pronounced "d base two") and called it a relational DBMS. In an exceedingly successful promotional tactic, Ashton-Tate distributed, nearly free of charge, more than 100,000 copies of its product to purchasers of the then-new Osborne micro-computers. Many of the people who purchased these computers were the pioneering developers in the microcomputer industry. They began to develop microcomputer applications using dBASE. Sales of dBASE increased dramatically and Ashton-Tate became one of the major corporations in the microcomputer industry.

The success of this product confused and confounded the subject of database processing. The problem was this: by the definition prevalent in the late 1970s, dBASE II was neither a DBMS nor was it relational (though it was marketed as both). In fact, it was a programming language with generalized file processing (not database processing) capabilities. The systems that were developed with dBASE II appeared much more like those in Figure 1.2 than the ones in Figure 1.4. The million or so users of dBASE II thought they were using a relational DBMS, when in point of fact, they were not.

Thus, the terms *database management system* and *relational database* were used loosely at the start of the microcomputer boom. Most of the people who were processing a microcomputer database were really performing file management, and they were not receiving the benefits of database processing, though they did not know it.

Today, the situation has changed as the microcomputer marketplace has become more mature and sophisticated. dBASE III Plus is truly a *DBMS* (you will learn a definition of DBMS in the next chapter), and dBASE IV is truly a *relational* DBMS.

dBASE did pioneer the application of database technology on microcomputers. At the same time, other vendors began to migrate their products down from the mainframe to the microcomputer. Oracle, Focus, and Ingres are three examples of DBMS products that were ported down to microcomputers. They are truly DBMS programs, and most would agree they are truly relational as well. In addition, other vendors developed new relational DBMS products especially for micros. Paradox, R:BASE, Revelation, MDBS, Helix, and a number of other products fall into this category.

One impact of the move of database technology to the micro was a dramatic improvement in DBMS user interfaces. Users of microcomputer systems are generally not the traditional MIS professional, and they will not put up with the clumsy and awkward user interfaces that were prevalent on mainframe DBMS products. Thus, as DBMS products were developed for micros, user interfaces had to be simplified and made easier to use. This was possible because micro DBMS products operate on dedicated computers, and more computer power is available to process the user interface.

The combination of microcomputers, the relational model, and vastly improved user interfaces enabled database technology to move from the organizational context to the personal computing context. When this occurred, the number of sites that used database technology exploded. In 1980 there were about 10,000 sites using DBMS products in the United States; today there are well over three million such sites!

WORKGROUP DATABASE APPLICATIONS

In the middle to late 1980s, end-users began to connect their separated microcomputers using a new type of computer communications capability called **local area networks** (LANs). These networks enabled computers to send data to one another at previously unimaginable rates. The first applications of this technology shared peripherals such as large-capacity, fast disks, expensive printers and plotters, and facilitated intercomputer communication via electronic mail.

In time, however, end-users wanted to share their databases as well. This led to the development of multi-user database applications on local area networks.

The LAN-based multi-user architecture is considerably different from the multi-user architecture used on mainframe and minicomputer databases. With a mainframe or minicomputer, only one CPU is involved in database application processing; with LAN systems, however, many CPUs can be simultaneously involved with database processing. This situation was both advantageous (greater performance) and more problematical (coordinating the actions of independent CPUs). It led to the development of a new style of multi-user database processing called the **client-server database architecture.**

This client-server architecture is the basis for most workgroup database processing today. Although minicomputers could be used in the workgroup setting, this is seldom done—primarily for reasons of cost. Thus, the client-server architecture has become quite important, and we will address this architecture in detail in Chapter 15.

DISTRIBUTED DATABASE PROCESSING

Organizational database applications address the problems of file processing and allow more integrated processing of organizational data. Personal and workgroup database systems bring database technology even closer to the user by allowing him or her access to locally managed databases. **Distributed databases** combine these types of database processing. They allow personal, workgroup, and organizational databases to be combined into integrated but distributed systems. As such, they allow even more flexibility in terms of data access and processing, but, unfortunately, pose many problems yet to be solved.

The essence of distributed databases is that all of the organization's data is spread over many computers—micros, minis, mainframes, and local area networks—that communicate with one another as they process the database. The goals of distributed database systems are to make it appear to each user that he or she is the only user of the organization's data and to provide the same consistency, accuracy, and timeliness to the user that he or she would have if no one else were using the distributed database.

Among the more pressing problems with distributed databases are the problems of security and control. Ensuring that so many users actually are entitled to access the database is a difficult task (there could be hundreds of concurrent users). Further, controlling what those users do to that distributed database is also problematical.

Coordinating and synchronizing the data can be very difficult. If one user group downloads and updates part of the database and then transmits the changed data back to the mainframe, how does the system prevent another user from attempting to use the version of the data it finds on the mainframe in the meantime? Imagine this problem involving dozens of files and hundreds of users employing scores of pieces of computer equipment.

In fact, as you will learn in Chapters 15 and 16, the concept of a distributed database actually blurs the definition of a database. Supposedly a database is a centralized, controlled collection of data and relationships. But if we fragment it and copy it onto many different computers, we have altered the original database concept.

Whereas the transitions from organizational to personal to workgroup database processing were relatively easy, the difficulties facing database designers and engineers of the distributed DBMS are monumental. You will learn what they are and the current attempts to overcome them in Chapters 15 and 16.

Summary

Database processing is one of the most important courses in the information systems curriculum for several reasons: database technology is used at all levels of organization; databases are the heart of crucial applications; databases must be accessible yet protected; and, finally, database design teaches important modeling skills.

Database technology facilitates the production of information. It helps to identify patterns, trends, and tendencies. The fundamental purpose of such information systems is to reduce uncertainty.

File processing systems store data in separate files, each of which contains a different type of data. File processing systems have several limitations: it is difficult to combine data stored in separate files; data is often duplicated among files, leading to data integrity problems; application programs are dependent on file formats, causing maintenance problems when formats change; files are incompatible, requiring file conversions; and it is difficult to represent data in the users' view.

Database processing systems were developed to overcome these limitations. In the database environment, the database management system is the interface between application programs and the database. Data is integrated and duplicated data is reduced. Only the DBMS is affected by changes to the physical formats of stored data. And if data items are changed, added, or deleted, few application programs will require maintenance. With database technology, it is easier to represent objects in the users' environment.

A database is a self-describing collection of integrated records. It is self-describing because it contains a description of itself in a data dictionary. The data dictionary is also known as a data directory or meta-data. A database is a collection of integrated records because relationships among records are stored in the database. This arrangement enables the DBMS to construct even complicated objects by combining data according to the stored relationships. Relationships are often stored in overhead data. Thus, the three parts of a database are the application data, the data dictionary, and the overhead data.

A database is a data representation of an organization. The degree of detail incorporated in the representation depends on the information users need to derive. Transaction processing keeps the data in the database current, so that it is always an accurate model of the company.

Databases are used at three organizational levels: personal, workgroup, and organizational. When we move from one type of database application to another, we cross two important boundaries. When we move from personal to workgroup database applications, we make a transition from single-user to multi-user systems. When we move from workgroup to organizational database applications, we make a transition from databases that provide one view of data to databases that provide multiple views of data.

Database technology has developed in several stages. Early databases focused on transaction processing of organizational data. Then, the relational model was developed. This model, together with the microcomputer, led to the use of personal database applications. With the advent of local area networks, departments began to implement workgroup databases. Today, efforts are underway to integrate all of these different types of databases into distributed databases.

||||||||||||||||||||||||||

GROUP I   QUESTIONS

1.1   Why is database processing an important subject?

1.2   Explain how information generated by an information system can reduce uncertainty. Use an example other than one in this chapter.

1.3   List four disadvantages of file processing systems and give an example of each.

1.4   Explain how database processing overcomes each of the disadvantages of file processing.

1.5   Describe a database management system. Define *database*. Explain the difference between these two terms.

1.6   What is a data dictionary?

1.7   What is the function of overhead data?

1.8   What are the three fundamental parts of a database?

1.9   What is transaction processing?

1.10   Explain how a database is a model.

1.11   Describe the three organizational levels in which database technology is used and explain their differences.

1.12   Give an example, other than one in this chapter, of a personal database application.

1.13 Give an example, other than one in this chapter, of a workgroup database application.

1.14 Give an example, other than one in this chapter, of an organizational database application.

1.15 Explain the two boundaries crossed when moving from personal database applications to workgroup to organizational.

1.16 What were some of the weaknesses of early organizational database applications?

1.17 What is the primary advantage of the relational model?

1.18 Why was the relational model resisted initially?

1.19 Summarize the events in the development of microcomputer DBMS products.

1.20 What was the major factor that gave rise to workgroup database applications?

1.21 How does the client-server architecture differ from mainframe or minicomputer multi-user architectures?

1.22 Explain the general nature of distributed processing. What are some of the difficult problems to be faced?

GROUP II QUESTIONS

1.23 Should a database course be required for an information systems major? Give reasons to support your answer. (It might be interesting to save your reasons and review them at the end of the course.)

1.24 List some objects from a business environment. Identify those that are easy to represent as one record in a file and those that are more complicated.

1.25 Interview a salesperson at a local computer store. Ask for information on microcomputer database management systems. Does the store distinguish between file management systems and database management systems? If so, what are the differences? Determine if the store distinguishes between relational and non-relational DBMS products. If so, what are the differences?

1.26 Interview people who use a database application. What business functions are served? What information is produced? What objects are involved? Is this application a personal, workgroup, or organizational application?

Components of
Database Processing
Systems

This chapter describes the fundamental components of database processing systems. We begin by introducing a case involving a small organizational database. Then, we discuss the basic systems components of a database processing system and illustrate those components in the context of the case. Next, we discuss database applications and the means by which users interface with the database. The chapter concludes with a description of the functions and structure of the DBMS itself.

- THE CARBON RIVER BOOKSHOP
- COMPONENTS OF A DATABASE PROCESSING SYSTEM
- DATABASE APPLICATIONS
- THE DBMS

THE CARBON RIVER BOOKSHOP

The Carbon River Bookshop is a general bookstore that serves a wide variety of reader interests. As a small bookshop, Carbon River must maintain close control of its inventory. The owners of Carbon River simply do not have the capital to finance a large, slowly selling inventory.

Carbon River uses a database processing system to maintain records of its book inventory. Figure 2.1 is a data flow diagram of the four processes at the bookshop that utilize the INVENTORY database: ANSWER QUERY, SELL BOOK, ORDER BOOK, and RECEIVE BOOK. A fifth process, ACCOUNTING, does not use the INVENTORY database, but is shown to establish the context of processing.

Each of these processes operates as you would expect. In the ANSWER QUERY process, one of the bookshop employees accesses the INVENTORY database. The database shows which books are in stock and which are on back order. A record of any title ever stocked is in this database. In the SELL BOOK process, an application accesses the database and removes the appropriate books from inventory. The ORDER BOOK pro-

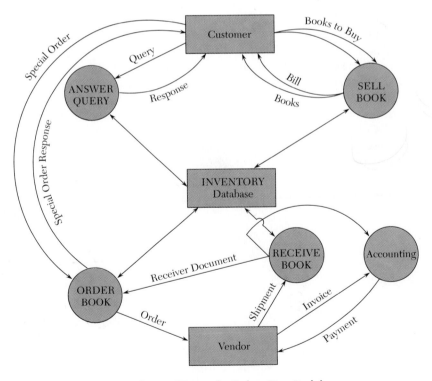

Context Diagram for Carbon River Bookshop

FIGURE 2.1
Data flow diagram for Carbon River Bookshop

cess generates orders to vendors for books. When a title is placed on order, a record of the order is stored in the database. Finally, the RECEIVE BOOK process modifies the inventory data when book shipments are received.

Each process in Figure 2.1 has its own database application and application programs. Figure 2.2 summarizes the database activities of each of these programs. The ANSWER QUERY program reads both BOOK and ORDER data files. SELL BOOK modifies BOOK data. ORDER BOOK reads or inserts new BOOK data, inserts new ORDER data, and reads or inserts VENDOR data. Finally, RECEIVE BOOK modifies BOOK data and modifies or deletes ORDER data.

We will use this example to illustrate the concepts of this chapter. For now, consider the basic components of a database processing system.

Components of a Database Processing System

A database processing system has five components. To learn these components, imagine that you are about to purchase a book at the Carbon River Bookshop. You hand the book to the clerk and he begins to enter data at a keyboard. At this moment, you can see two of the system's components: the clerk and the keyboard, or, in more general terms, people and hardware.

Now, as the clerk touches one of the keys on the keyboard, another of the system's components becomes evident—the data. When the clerk pushes the 1 key to indicate that you are purchasing one copy of the book, an element of data is transferred from the human to the machine.

Computers are general-purpose devices. We make them perform specialized functions by encoding instructions in programs. Similarly, people can perform a myriad of activities. To help them perform a specific function (such as selling a book), we encode instructions in procedures. Now we have the remaining two systems components: programs and procedures.

FIGURE 2.2
Application database activity

Application	Database Activity
ANSWER QUERY	Read BOOK data Read ORDER data
SELL BOOK	Modify BOOK data
ORDER BOOK	Read or insert BOOK data Read or insert VENDOR data Insert or modify ORDER data
RECEIVE BOOK	Modify BOOK data Modify or delete ORDER data

The five components are illustrated in Figure 2.3. On the machine side, hardware processes instructions encoded in programs. On the human side, people process instructions encoded in procedures. Data is the interface between machines and humans.

Each of these five components can be related specifically to database systems. Since this is a database course, we will begin with data and then consider programs, hardware, people, and procedures.

DATA

As you would expect, the major data component of a database processing system is the database itself. You learned in Chapter 1 that the database contains source data, the data dictionary, and overhead data. Source data are the facts stored in the database, such as book ISBNs (unique book identifiers), vendor names, order numbers, and the like. The data dictionary describes the structure of the database. Overhead data is used for lists, indexes, and other data structures that represent record relationships and serve other roles.

In most cases, different applications process different, but overlapping, subsets of the database. In Figure 2.2, all four processes access BOOK data, but not all of them access ORDER or VENDOR data.

Learning some new terminology will facilitate the discussion of database data. The structure of the entire database is called the **schema,** or the conceptual view. Figure 2.4 shows the structure of the bookshop's database—the INVENTORY database schema. There are three files (equivalently, tables) of data: BOOK, ORDER, and VENDOR. The fields (equivalently, columns) in each of these files are indicated. The fork in the line between BOOK and ORDER and between VENDOR and ORDER represents a one-to-many relationship. It simply means that a BOOK may have many ORDERs for it and a VENDOR may have received many ORDERs. Sample data for this schema is shown in Figure 2.5.

Observe that relationships are carried in the data. ISBN is stored in both BOOK and ORDER and enables data in those two tables to be related. For example, the BOOK with the ISBN of 12345 is related to the ORDERs that also have the ISBN of 12345. Vendor# is stored in both VENDOR and ORDER and enables data in those two tables to be related in a similar way.

The portion of the database structure that is processed by a particular application is called a **subschema,** or **application view.** A subschema is also known as a **logical view.**

FIGURE 2.3

Five components of a database processing system

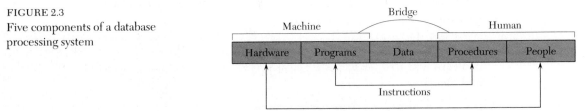

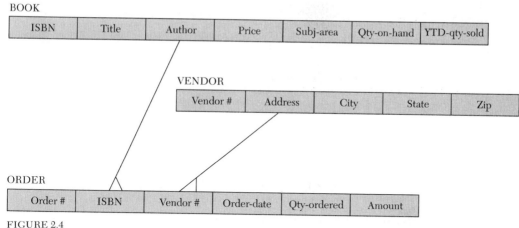

FIGURE 2.4
INVENTORY database schema

For example, the BOOK and ORDER data types together comprise the RECEIVE BOOK subschema or RECEIVE BOOK application view. (Actually, as you will learn, the application view also indicates which items of BOOK data and which items of ORDER data are visible to the application. This specification, however, is more detail than we need for our current purposes. You will learn more about this in Chapter 8.)

Application programs are aware only of data that is in their view. This fact has both an advantage and a disadvantage. The advantage is that data can be protected from unauthorized access. The user of the SELL BOOK subschema, for example, is unable to access VENDOR data.

The disadvantage concerns conflicts over shared data between programs or users of overlapping subschemas. At the bookstore, if a user who is accessing the database via the SELL BOOK application view were to delete a BOOK record, problems may result for programs that access other application views. For example, the users of the SELL BOOK subschema do not even know that ORDER data exists. They may unknowingly delete a book that has open orders, thereby creating unattached and seemingly nonsensical ORDER data.

Such potential conflicts among application views must be identified and problems prevented by properly designing the schema, the subschemas, and the application programs.

In addition to source data, meta-data, and overhead data, some DBMS products store a fourth type of data in the database: **application meta-data.** This is data about the structure of menus, screens, reports, and other application constructs. For example, some DBMS products include a report generation facility that can be used to define report formats. Such formats include the report name, names of column headings, names of data items that appear in the report, control breaks, report variable definitions, and so forth.

Once the report format is defined its structure (application meta-data) can be stored in the database. Then, when the user wants to print the report, the report generator

BOOK Data

ISBN	Title	Author	Price	Subj-area	Qty-on-hand	YTD-qty-sold
12345	New World	Smith, JB	$22.95	Art	2	1
80010	Ceramics	Jones, PM	$15.95	Art	1	2
14111	Fantasy	Laird, RD	$15.95	Fict	3	5
18722	New Poems	Fritz, AE	$29.95	Poetry	3	12
13991	Chemistry	Shultz, BF	$34.95	Sci	2	0
17101	Cats	Eliot, TS	$24.95	Poetry	1	4
89336	Physics	Hughes, M	$11.95	Sci	1	3
14892	Selling	Suit, CM	$14.95	Bus	3	4
23712	Birds	Hurd, ME	$39.95	Sci	2	2

VENDOR Data

Vendor#	Address	City	State	Zip
10	123 - 18th	Memphis	TN	22322
20	14 - 3rd Ave	New York	NY	10012
30	733 Elm	Memphis	TN	22343

ORDER Data

Order#	ISBN	Vendor#	Order-date	Qty-ordered	Amount
100	12345	10	12/11/91	3	$39.00
101	80010	10	12/11/91	1	$11.00
102	14111	20	12/11/91	1	$12.00
103	18722	30	12/11/91	7	$141.00
104	13991	10	12/11/91	2	$46.00
105	17101	20	12/11/91	1	$19.00
106	80336	30	12/11/91	1	$7.00
107	14892	10	12/11/91	1	$9.00
108	23712	10	12/11/91	3	$73.00
109	80010	20	12/11/91	1	$11.00

FIGURE 2.5
Sample bookshop data

need only examine the report's meta-data in the database to determine the report's structure. This data is called application meta-data because it pertains to application structure, not to database structure.

PROGRAMS

A variety of programs are needed to support database processing systems. As a minimum, the **operating system** and the **database management system** are required. These two alone can support simple personal database applications. In such a case, the user's interface to the data is through the forms, reports, and menus automatically provided by the DBMS. For more complicated personal database applications and for all workgroup and organizational systems, **application programs** are required.

In addition, for multi-user systems, programs are required to facilitate concurrent processing. The particular type of program depends on the system architecture. In a LAN environment, such facilities are included as part of the **LAN operating system.** In a mainframe environment, a separate program called a **communications control program** (CCP) is needed. With minicomputer systems, concurrent processing functions are usually built into the operating system.

Figure 2.6 shows the relationship of these programs on a mainframe system. Note that the database can be processed both by batch application programs and by online users via the CCP.

In almost all database processing systems, only the application programs are written by the developers. The CCP, the DBMS, and the operating system are supplied by vendors. Usually the operating system is supplied by the hardware vendor, and in many cases, the DBMS and the CCP are provided as well. It is also common, however, for the DBMS and the CCP to be obtained from independent software vendors.

Application programs fall into two major types. The first category includes applications that are written in a standard programming language such as COBOL, BASIC, or Pascal. These programs access the DBMS through subroutine calls or other, equivalent means.

A second type of application program consists of programs that are written in the DBMS product's own language. Many such languages came into existence through the backdoor. That is, the initial version of the DBMS included an interactive query/update language which users began to employ. As users became more proficient in the language, they began to do more complex tasks requiring longer sequences of instructions. DBMS vendors provided methods for storing sequences of query/update commands, and soon,

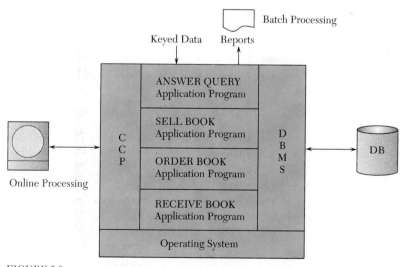

FIGURE 2.6
Relationship of programs for mainframe database processing system

these stored commands took on the complexity and capability of application programs. The use of such DBMS-unique languages is particularly common on microcomputers.

Some DBMS products include a code generation system. If the logic of the application is not too complex, programmers (and, sometimes, even end-users) can use this tool to generate application programs. The developer defines the program's features and functions to the code generator by answering a series of questions. The code generator then writes the code.

As mentioned, some simple personal database systems can be developed with no application programs whatsoever. In this case, the user employs default forms and other facilities to enter data, uses default reports and queries for displaying data, and controls the application by issuing DBMS commands.

Figure 2.7 shows the logic of a typical application program: the ORDER process at Carbon River. This program reads BOOK data from the database. If the data does not exist, then the book has not been ordered before, and the user is prompted to provide BOOK data. Then, the program reads VENDOR data from the database, and, again, if the data is not present, the user is prompted to add it. Following these actions, the new ORDER data is inserted into the database. The means by which the database is accessed varies from product to product. We will consider a number of different alternatives throughout this text.

The other programs needed by the Carbon River Bookshop depend on the type of hardware used. We will consider them after discussing the hardware component.

HARDWARE

Since they are computer systems, database processing systems require computer hardware. In general, database systems do not require any special hardware, but they do sometimes require additions to existing hardware.

```
Get ISBN from user
Read BOOK data for this ISBN
If not found
        Then get BOOK data from user
Get Vendor#
Read VENDOR data
If not found
        Then Get VENDOR data from user
Get ORDER data from user
        Verify ORDER data for correctness
        Print order documents
        If have new BOOK data then add to database
        If have new VENDOR data then add to database
        Add ORDER data to database
```

FIGURE 2.7
Logic of application program for order processing at Carbon River Bookshop

Computer hardware is required to run the DBMS, the application, and other programs. A wide range of hardware can be used. Personal database applications run on microcomputers of all types, although generally at least the power of an 80286 processor is desirable. Workgroup and organizational applications can run on local area networks, minicomputers, or mainframes. Depending on the product and its features, a DBMS can require from 256,000 to one million bytes or more of main memory.

In determining data storage requirements, it is important to remember that a database contains meta-data, overhead data, and possibly application meta-data. Consequently, the size of a database can be double or even triple the size of the user data.

Several companies have developed special-purpose computers called **database machines.** These computers, which are dedicated to the task of processing the database, are designed to provide exceptionally fast performance when processing very large databases. Database machines have not received much acceptance in the market, however, and it is unlikely that you will encounter one in the near future.

The hardware and program components used by Carbon River Bookshop are illustrated in Figure 2.8. The system, called a **client-server system,** consists of a local area network with a database server and four microcomputers. The database server processes

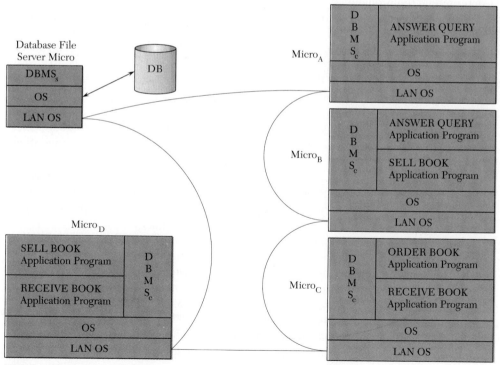

$DBMS_c$ = Client version of DBMS
$DBMS_s$ = Server version of DBMS

FIGURE 2.8
Hardware and programs for Carbon River Bookshop

the database on behalf of the microcomputers. Observe that the local operating system, the LAN operating system, and portions of the DBMS reside on all computers. Application programs, however, reside only on the users' computers. Further, not all applications reside on all computers. The ORDER BOOK application, for example, resides only on the computer that is used for order processing. Such distinctions provide greater control over user activities.

Other systems architectures, including minicomputer and mainframe computer systems, are also used for database processing. For example, the mainframe alternative shown in Figure 2.6 could be used. Realistically, however, a mainframe is too expensive for a small company like the bookshop.

PEOPLE

People are the fourth component of a database processing system. *Clientele* are the people for whom the system is developed. For example, the clientele of an airline reservation system are the airline passengers. The clientele of a payroll system are employees. Customers are the clientele at the bookshop. Since clientele do not usually have an active role in database system development or use, we will only be concerned with them when determining requirements.

Users employ the system to satisfy a business need. The users of an airline reservation system include ticket agents and travel agents. The users of a payroll system include payroll administrators, clerks, and business managers. The users of the bookshop system are sales, order, and receiving clerks.

Operations personnel run the computer and associated equipment. Typically, for an organizational system, the operations department includes computer operators, data control personnel, and data entry people.

For personal, workgroup, and small organizational database applications, there is seldom a separate group of operations personnel. Instead, users take on the operations responsibilities. For personal systems, this means little extra work (the making of backups is an example task), and users are seldom aware they are doing it. For workgroup systems, however, operations tasks can mean more work, and sometimes these tasks are assigned to a few people as part-time job responsibilities. Often these people receive special operations training.

Systems development personnel design and implement the database and its applications. They determine requirements, specify alternatives, design the five components of the system, and implement the system. Systems development personnel include systems analysts, application programmers, and systems programmers (those people who support and maintain the operating system, the CCP, the DBMS, and other similar systems support programs).

The final category of people involved in database applications consists of the *database administration (DBA[1]) personnel*. Workgroup and organizational databases are shared

---

[1]DBA refers to either the office of database administration or the database administrator (the manager of the office) depending on context.

resources. As such, their design and use must be managed with a view toward all users (sometimes called the *user community*). The functions of the DBA are to protect the database and to resolve conflicts among users. The DBA should be representative of the community as a whole, not of any particular user or group of users. In this role, the DBA must arbitrate the processing rights and responsibilities of each user. We will discuss the position of DBA thoroughly in Chapter 14.

The issues in this book are oriented primarily toward systems development people, who might work in any of the widely varying database environments. However, it is important for development people to know the roles and needs of users, operations personnel, and DBA, and a discussion of their needs will be included when appropriate.

At the bookshop, the users are the sales, order, and receiving clerks. The manager serves as a part-time operator, as does one of the clerks. Database administration tasks are accomplished by the store manager. Development is done by an outside service agency.

The personnel involved in database applications vary widely. Contrast the people component of the Carbon River Bookshop with the personnel who work at a large bank. In a bank there are hundreds of users, dozens of operations personnel, and a formal database administration staff. The bank probably has a Management Information Systems Department that includes professional systems developers to build and maintain the system.

PROCEDURES

The final component of a database processing system is procedures. Both users and the operations staff need documented procedures describing how to run the system. Users need to know how to sign on to the system, how to enter data and commands, how to operate the computer or terminal, and how to employ the system to perform the tasks they need to accomplish.

Consider again the Carbon River Bookshop. The store is staffed each day by an average of six different sales clerks, and two different people share order responsibilities. Any number of these different people can receive merchandise. They need standardized procedures for processing the database using the different applications. If every clerk, for example, has his or her own way of recording book shipments, the database would soon become chaotic.

The need for manual procedures can be reduced by building procedures into application programs. Recall the logic of the ORDER program that was illustrated in Figure 2.7. This program guides the user through the ordering process. If BOOK data does not exist, then the program forces the user to enter it. Similarly, if the VENDOR data has not been entered, the program causes the user to enter it. Constructing the program in this way reduces the need to design, document, and train personnel in manual procedures.

Either manual or programmed procedures can be appropriate. The point here is just to recognize that procedures can be programmed into application programs. Alternatively, procedures can be documented and enforced manually.

In addition to procedures for normal operation, procedures for backup and recovery operations are also needed. When a database system fails, both users and operations personnel need procedures describing what to do. Such procedures are especially important for multi-user database systems, because many people depend on the database. Users need to know what manual procedures to follow during the failure, what data to save, and what to do with business transactions that cannot be processed during the failure. When the system is returned to operation, users need to know what to do to resume processing. For example, how can a user tell how much work needs to be redone? Also, how much of the data gathered manually during the failure needs to be input before new transactions can be processed? All these issues must be considered in developing user recovery procedures, and we will look closely at them in Chapter 14.

Similar procedures are required for computer operations. When the database system fails, operations personnel need to know what to do. What action should be taken to identify the source of the problem and to correct it? What must be done to minimize damage to the database? Who should be called? Once the problem is corrected, how should the database be restored? These actions need to be carefully thought out and documented during the design and implementation of the system. Waiting until the error occurs is too dangerous.

The DBA also has procedures. Normal procedures concern changes to the structure of the database must be made very carefully. A change made to benefit one user may be detrimental to users in seemingly unrelated departments. Consequently, changes to the database structure need to be made with a communitywide view. The DBA defines and documents procedures for backup and recovery. Figure 2.9 presents a framework for organizing the procedures needed by a database processing system.

Carbon River has user procedures for each of its four major functions: ANSWER QUERY, SELL BOOK, ORDER BOOK, and RECEIVE BOOK. The procedures include actions for both normal and failure recovery operations. In addition, operations procedures are in place for the local area network. These procedures include instructions for starting and stopping the LAN, the microcomputers, and the programs on each. They also concern actions to take when errors are made in processing or when equipment malfunctions occur.

FIGURE 2.9
Categories of procedures for
database processing systems

	Normal Processing	Failure Recovery Processing
Users		
Operations Personnel		
Database Administrators		

Database Applications

So far, we have discussed the system components of a database processing system. The five components represent a broad foundation and are important to all business computing systems, including database processing systems.

In the remainder of this chapter, we will narrow our discussion and focus on database applications. A **database application** is a subset of a data base processing system that processes some or all of a database in order to meet the information needs of an individual, a department, or a functional area within an organization. An application provides a window into the database for a particular user or group. Most personal and many workgroup databases involve just a single application. Most organizational databases involve multiple applications.

At Carbon River Bookshop, the database supports four applications, one for each of the store's four functional areas. Figure 2.10 is a schematic of these applications.

Each database application has the five components of an information system. Each application has people, procedures, the database (which it may share with other applications), programs (some of which it may share), and hardware (which it probably shares with other applications).

Each database application program has three fundamental functions: to control users' activities, to provide a facility for updating data, and to supply a facility for displaying the data. The word *facility* is an awkward word. We use it here because it is generic—there are many, many ways of displaying data, for example, and we need a term that can cover all of them.

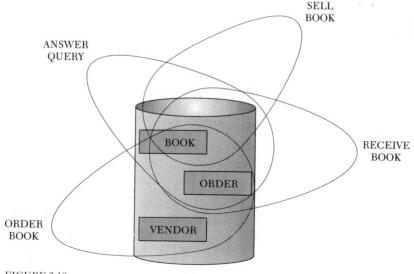

FIGURE 2.10

Database applications at the Carbon River Bookshop

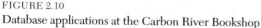

CONTROLLING USERS' ACTIVITIES

A database is a valuable resource. An application is a window to this resource. As such, the application must implement control policies established by management; these restrictions control who accesses the database, and what they do once they have accessed it.

Applications vary in the degree of control they place on the user's activities. Some applications are written with a high degree of control. In such applications, when the user signs in to the system, an application program is invoked that controls all of the user's activities. The user is asked, primarily, to enter data. All control choices about what to do next are predetermined by program logic.

At the other end of the spectrum, some applications provide little control. For example, with some applications, when the user signs in the DBMS is activated and the user is presented with a command prompt. The user then issues any DBMS command that he or she wants, or activates an application, or takes some other action.

As shown in Figure 2.11, applications control is a continuum from a high degree of programmed control to a high degree of user control. In between the extremes are menu-based systems in which the user decides actions to take from a programmed list of choices.

Figure 2.12 shows a two-level menu structure used by the ORDER process at the bookshop. In menu 1, the user is given the options of processing BOOK, ORDER, or VENDOR data. If the user chooses BOOK, then menu 2 is displayed, and so forth.

Typically, applications that support operational processing and that support many different users involve a high degree of programmed control. The bookshop, for example, wants the sale of every book to be recorded in the same way. The manager does not want clerks to be able to be creative in the way they process the database when selling a book.

On the other hand, applications that support planning and analysis tend to involve a high degree of user control. If the manager of the bookshop wants to process historical sales data to determine the most profitable publishers or subject areas, then he or she needs considerable flexibility in processing the database. A high degree of preprogrammed control would be a hindrance.

There are several principles and techniques for controlling access to the database. First, users should not be able to access data that they do not need. This means that an application view should contain only data relevant to the application purpose. A checking account application, for example, should not be able to access loan data.

FIGURE 2.11
Continuum of control

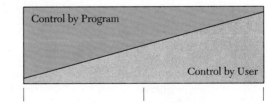

High Application Control   Menu Driven Applications   High User Control
     (Operations)   (Planning)

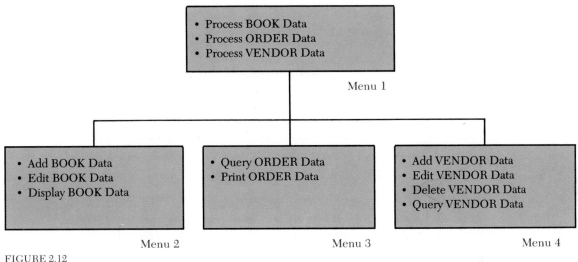

FIGURE 2.12
Sample menu structure

Second, the operating system or the DBMS should provide some means for controlling access to the application programs. Passwords and account numbers are often used to ensure that people do not use applications they are not authorized to use. Third, employees should not be taught how to use applications that they have no need to use.

Once a user has accessed a database application, processing the database must be controlled. Such controls are primarily intended to reduce the likelihood of inadvertent errors such as deleting data instead of changing it.

Menus are one form of application processing control. The structure of the menu and the options allowed restrict or hide processing options. In Figure 2.12 observe that menus 2, 3, and 4 provide different processing options. The user can Add, Edit, and Display BOOK data, but can Add, Edit, Delete, or Query VENDOR data.

Further, application programs can provide another form of processing control once a menu action is selected. For example, suppose the user selects Add BOOK Data from menu 2 of Figure 2.12. When the application program processes this choice, it can perform controls like confirming that the user truly wants to add a book and did not invoke this program by mistake. It could also check the initials of the user to determine if he or she is allowed to invoke this process. Then, after the user keys data, the program could ensure that the book data is not already present in the database. Many other controls can be incorporated into the application program as it processes the menu selection.

Another form of processing control is to reduce the command set available to the user. With some DBMS products, certain commands can be enabled and disabled on a user-by-user basis. Also, some vendors provide different versions of products. In particular, some microcomputer vendors provide run-time versions of their products. With these, developers can produce application programs that users can execute, but that they cannot modify.

- Limit database views to required data
- Limit access to application via passwords and account numbers
- Teach applications to users only as they are needed
- Restrict processing via menus
- Limit processing through design of application program
- Restrict allowable command set

FIGURE 2.13
Summary of application control mechanisms

Facilities for application control are quite important. Figure 2.13 summarizes the forms of control described here. We will discuss this topic further in Chapters 8 and 14.

PROVIDING FACILITIES FOR UPDATING DATA

A database application must provide a facility for updating data. **Updating** means entering, deleting, and editing (or changing) database data. There are two general categories of update capabilities: generic DBMS update facilities that can either be invoked from a DBMS command prompt or an application program and those that can only be invoked from within an application program.

Generic DBMS Update Facilities

Consider Figure 2.14 which shows several typical methods for updating BOOK data in the Carbon River Bookshop database. Each of these methods could be invoked from a DBMS prompt. Alternatively, they could be called from within an application program.

In Figure 2.14a, the user enters data using a **load utility program** that is part of the DBMS. This is a primitive database update method. The user is prompted with only the name of the data item—the load utility does not indicate the format or length of the data to be entered. If the user enters erroneous data, he or she will get only the most rudimentary error messages, such as "INVALID DATA. TRY AGAIN".

Figure 2.14b shows the same data being entered by means of a **data entry form.** Like the simple prompting in Figure 2.14a, this form was generated by a DBMS utility. This data entry form provides slightly better prompt text and also indicates the length of the data item to be entered. Error messages will still be rudimentary (depending on the DBMS product being used).

A third updating facility is shown in Figure 2.14c. Here, the BOOK data is displayed in **tabular format.** The user can scroll up and down the BOOK data, adding or deleting lines, and changing data by moving the cursor to the correct data item and keying the change.

The tabular format is not supported by all DBMS products, but when it is, the form generation and processing is done automatically by the DBMS. The form in Figure

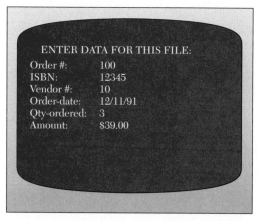

```
ENTER DATA FOR THIS FILE:
Order #:        100
ISBN:           12345
Vendor #:       10
Order-date:     12/11/91
Qty-ordered:    3
Amount:         $39.00
```

a. Entering data via a load utility

```
ORDER DATA ENTRY FORM

Please Enter Order Data:
Order #     [100]      Vendor #      [10]
ISBN        [12345]    Qty-ordered   [3]
Order date  [12/11/91]
Amount      [$39.00]


Press Enter when Finished
Press F10 for Help
```

b. Entering data with a form

Order Date	Quantity	Amount	Order #	ISBN	Vendor #
12/11/91	3	$39.00	100	12345	10
12/11/91	1	$11.00	101	80010	10
12/11/91	1	$12.00	102	14111	20
12/11/91	7	$141.00	103	18722	30
12/11/91	2	$46.00	104	13991	10
12/11/91	1	$19.00	105	17101	20
12/11/91	1	$7.00	106	80336	30
12/11/91	1	$9.00	107	14892	10
12/11/91	3	$73.00	108	23712	10
12/11/91	1	$11.00	109	80010	20

c. Entering editing data in tabular format

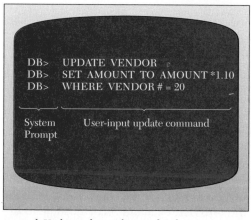

```
DB>    UPDATE VENDOR
DB>    SET AMOUNT TO AMOUNT *1.10
DB>    WHERE VENDOR # = 20

System    User-input update command
Prompt
```

d. Updating data with an update language

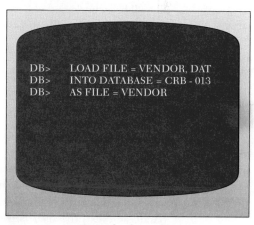

```
DB>    LOAD FILE = VENDOR, DAT
DB>    INTO DATABASE = CRB - 013
DB>    AS FILE = VENDOR
```

e. Example of mass data input

FIGURE 2.14
Update mechanisms for VENDOR data

2.14c, for example, would be generated and processed by a command like, "BROWSE BOOK DATA WHERE ISBN = 12345." Error messages for this facility are somewhat better than for the previous examples, but since they are generically produced by the DBMS, they will tend to be general.

A fourth method for updating data is to use an **interactive query/update command language.** In this mode, the user accesses a DBMS query/update program (the particulars depend on the DBMS product) and then issues a command to make the desired changes. In Figure 2.14d, the clerk is adding 10 percent to the amount of all orders from vendor number 30.

Updates like this are quite dangerous. The user is given great power, power which, when used correctly, can rapidly accomplish the task at hand; but when used incorrectly, such power can cause serious problems. In Figure 2.14d, for example, imagine what would happen if the clerk accidentally typed < instead of = ! Updating a database via interactive languages must be done carefully, if at all.

A fifth update facility allows the user to input a mass of data, such as an external file produced by another system or stored on another computer. Sometimes this process is called **importing** data. Figure 2.14e shows a sample command to import data.

Updates Using Application Programs

None of the updating facilities in Figure 2.14 require application programming. All of them are accomplished by using generic features of the DBMS product. Many of these features can be employed by users without any assistance from a professional systems developer.

The advantage of that approach is that users can often get the information they want faster than if they waited for someone to write a program. But using utilities to update data also has drawbacks. Error messages will be generic and often unhelpful. Processing is limited to features anticipated by the designer of the DBMS. Help text, if it exists at all, will be generic and of limited use.

To overcome these problems, nearly all DBMS products provide an interface between the DBMS and a standard programming language (such as COBOL), or between the DBMS and the DBMS's own programming language, or both.

Figure 2.15 shows an example of an application program performing database updates. In this figure, the program displays a screen and leads the user through the update process. The program first displays a form heading (BOOK ORDER FORM) and prompts the user for the ISBN. The program then reads the database for that book. If the data is not found in the database, the program asks the user for the BOOK data (or, and this is not shown in the figure, it could give the user a chance to enter a different ISBN in case a keying error was made).

If the user indicates that the book has been correctly identified, the program then asks for and looks up VENDOR data. It takes appropriate action if the data is not in the database. Next, the user is prompted for the ORDER data and order documents are generated. As you can see, processing is tailored to the requirements of this particular situation; no DBMS would have logic such as this as part of its basic function. The developer of this program would need to design its logic just like any other program he or she

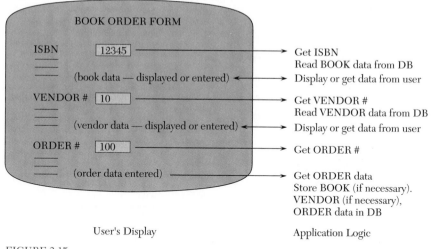

User's Display   Application Logic

FIGURE 2.15
Update via application program

would write. Although program design is not a topic in this course, the techniques you have learned in other courses should be applied to database processing programs as well.

As you can see, there are many different ways of updating data in a database. The problem for the application developer is to select the method that will meet the requirements of the application at the least cost.

DBMS command level functions, because they do not require programming, are cheaper and faster than developing application programs. However, they are also more generic (thus, less helpful to the user), and sometimes more dangerous. Update facilities are summarized in Figure 2.16.

PROVIDING FACILITIES FOR DISPLAYING DATA

Database applications provide three ways of displaying data: in reports, as responses to queries, and exported in bulk to other systems.

Reports

A report is an extraction of data from the database. Reports can be printed on paper, displayed on computer screens, and issued to other output devices. Some reports are prepared on a regular, recurring basis; others are prepared when exceptional conditions are detected; and still others are prepared only on demand.

Reports are similar to update forms. Reports, however, only display data, whereas forms allow the user to read, update, and delete data. It might be helpful to think of a report as a "display-only form."

Without Programming

- DBMS load utility
- DBMS default data entry form
- DBMS-supplied tabular form
- Query/update language
- Mass data input via command

With Programming

Form generated and processed by application program

FIGURE 2.16
Summary of update mechanisms

Reports, like forms, can be generated either by facilities built into the DBMS product or by application programs. Many DBMS products include a default report that is automatically defined for every file in the database. Figure 2.17a shows a sample default report for the ORDER file in the bookshop database. It's not attractive, but it's simple; it requires no development time because the DBMS includes this report format automatically.

Figure 2.17b is a more sophisticated report that was developed using a DBMS report writing utility. It is more attractive, and it has more meaningful column headings. Additionally, this report breaks out books by subject area and totals the revenue over each category. The production of this report required knowledge of the DBMS report generation facility, but it did not require any programming. Consequently, it could have been produced by someone who had only a few hours of instruction (and who was not a professional programmer).

A much more complex report can be produced by an application program. With the power and flexibility of programming, a report can be tailored exactly to the user's most demanding requirements. The disadvantage of writing programs to produce reports is that it takes significantly longer to develop a report with an application program than it does with a report generator feature of a DBMS. Further, report development would require the services of a professional programmer. A knowledge of systems requirements helps database systems developers to decide which report generating facilities are appropriate.

It is important to distinguish between a report and the medium of a report. The same report can be displayed on a computer screen, paper, microfiche, or some other medium. Changing the medium does not change the report. Similarly, there is a difference between report content and report format. Report content is the information on a report. The report format is the design of the report, including details like column headers, blank lines, and page numbers.

Query Response

The second major type of display facility in a database application is the response to a request made with a database query language. While there are many query languages (seemingly as many as there are DBMS products), one language, SQL (pronounced "sequel"), is quite popular and has become a national standard. We will discuss this language at length in Chapter 10.

For now, consider two SQL examples. To list all of the books for subject area poetry, a SQL user would type:

```
SELECT          *
FROMBOOK
WHERE           SUBJ-AREA = 'POETRY'
```

The result of this query is a list of all of the data items in BOOK for the indicated student.

A more sophisticated query is to list all the orders ever filled by vendors in a particular city. The following SQL statements will do this for vendors in Memphis:

```
SELECT      ORDER#
FROM        VENDOR,ORDER
WHERE       CITY='MEMPHIS'
    AND     VENDOR#.VENDOR=VENDOR#.ORDER
```

The result of this query is a list of all of the numbers of orders processed by vendors located in Memphis. Do not be alarmed if you do not understand this query. For now, just realize that query languages are one important facility for displaying data from the database.

File Export

A final way in which applications can display data is to **export files.** This is similar to importing a mass of data, except the application is generating rather than receiving the file.

Display facilities are summarized in Figure 2.18 on page 54.

The DBMS

In this section, we will describe a generic set of functions and tools that are incorporated into almost every DBMS product. Be aware, however, that products vary. Some do not include all the functions and tools described and some contain more. In almost all cases, the particular terms used to describe the features and functions will differ from the terms used here. Each product has its own vocabulary. If you focus on the nature of each feature and function, you will find great commonality among the products.

BOOK Data

ISBN	Title	Author	Price	Subj-area	Qty-on-hand	YTD-qty-sold
12345	New World	Smith, JB	$22.95	Art	2	1
80010	Ceramics	Jones, PM	$15.95	Art	1	2
14111	Fantasy	Laird, RD	$15.95	Fict	3	5
18722	New Poems	Fritz, AE	$29.95	Poetry	3	12
13991	Chemistry	Shultz, BF	$34.95	Sci	2	0
17101	Cats	Eliot, TS	$24.95	Poetry	1	4
89336	Physics	Hughes, M	$11.95	Sci	1	3
14892	Selling	Suit, CM	$14.95	Bus	3	4
23712	Birds	Hurd, ME	$39.95	Sci	2	2

a. DBMS-supplied default report format

FIGURE 2.17
Sample report forms

FUNCTIONS OF THE DBMS

A DBMS is a set of programs that is used to define, process, and administer the database and its applications. First, a DBMS is *software*. Second, this software is *used* by people or programs that need to interface with the database. Third, some DBMS programs are used to *define* and *build* both the *database* and database *applications;* other DBMS programs *process data* in the database; and still other DBMS programs provide *administrative facilities*.

A systems developer hired by the bookshop would use the *definition* features of the DBMS to establish the structure of the database (such as the formats of files and data items) and to define constraints governing the data values and processing of the database data. The systems developer would also define data entry forms and other facilities for loading, reading, and updating the database. In addition, the developer would define database applications that users can employ to process the database. Once these aspects of the system are defined, data can be loaded into the database.

With data now in the database, users can employ the applications to store, retrieve, and update it. The programs in these applications access the *processing* features of the DBMS. Concurrently, other DBMS programs *administer* the database.

Figure 2.19 lists generic DBMS functions. First, as stated, the DBMS stores, retrieves, and updates user data. The manner in which the data is processed depends on characteristics of the database application accessing the DBMS. For example, data might be retrieved and then printed in a report, displayed on a computer screen, or transmitted to another computer.

As the DBMS stores and updates source data on behalf of the application, it must also maintain the appropriate overhead data. If, for example, a database includes customer records and the DBMS keeps an index of customer numbers, then the index must be

Revenue by Subject Area

Subject Area: Art

Title	Year to Date Quantity Sold	Year to Date Revenue
New World	1	$22.95
Ceramics	2	$31.90
Total revenue for this subject area:		$54.85

Subject Area: Bus

Title	Year to Date Quantity Sold	Year to Date Revenue
Selling	4	$59.80
Total revenue for this subject area:		$59.80

Subject Area: Fict

Title	Year to Date Quantity Sold	Year to Date Revenue
Fantasy	5	$79.75
Total revenue for this subject area:		$79.75

Subject Area: Poetry

Title	Year to Date Quantity Sold	Year to Date Revenue
Cats	4	$99.80
New Poems	12	$359.40
Total revenue for this subject area:		$459.20

Subject Area: Sci

Title	Year to Date Quantity Sold	Year to Date Revenue
Chemistry	0	$0.00
Physics	3	35.85
Birds	2	$79.90
Total revenue for this subject area:		$115.75

Total bookshop revenue to date:	$769.35

b. Report prepared with DBMS report utility

FIGURE 2.17, *continued*

Reports
- Default
- Developed by utility report generator
- Generated by application program

Query
- SQL
- Other query languages

Export
- Generating a file for another system

FIGURE 2.18
Application display mechanisms

changed whenever new customers are added or deleted. Various types of overhead data are presented in Appendix A.

The second DBMS function is to store, retrieve, and update the meta-data stored in the data dictionary. Remember that the data dictionary contains descriptions of all the files and records in the database, cross-references among data items, files, records, and programs, and much other valuable information about the database. This information is particularly useful to the database administrator; it can also be accessed by users who need to know the physical formats of data items of interest to them. As you will see in the next section, except for retrieval, which is frequently done by users or the DBA, all of the manipulation of meta-data is done by the DBMS itself.

A third function of the DBMS is to enforce integrity rules and constraints. For example, for the database in Figure 2.4, the developer may define a constraint that a value of ISBN cannot be accepted for an ORDER record unless that value already exists in some record in the BOOK file. Once such constraints are established, it is the responsibility of the DBMS to enforce them.

Integrity rules are sometimes difficult to enforce. For example, one of the constraints imposed by the bookshop may be that no vendor can be used for an order if that vendor has more than $10,000 in current outstanding orders. So to determine if a vendor can be used, the sum of all orders for that vendor must be computed. Constraints like this one are difficult for the DBMS to enforce, and such constraints are usually enforced by application programs.

As a general rule, however, the greater the number of constraints that can be enforced by the DBMS, the better. If the DBMS enforces the constraint, then the constraint need only be written once. If the constraint is enforced by application programs, then every program that processes the related data must enforce the constraint. In the latter situation, there is always the possibility that a programmer will forget to check the constraint in his or her program or will check incorrectly.

The fourth function of a DBMS is closely allied with the third. The DBMS must enforce security rules and constraints. To maintain order and protect the database, com-

- Store, retrieve, and update user data (maintain overhead data)
- Store, retrieve, and update meta-data
- Enforce integrity rules and constraints
- Enforce security constraints
- Provide coordination and control facilities for multi-user processing
- Provide facilities for backup and recovery

FIGURE 2.19
Functions of a generic DBMS product

panies that use databases need to ensure that only authorized people can perform authorized database functions at authorized times. The DBMS provides facilities to define user authorization (for example, each user might be assigned a password recorded in the database), and processing rights (for example user number 123 might be allowed to sell books, but not to order books; user number 456 may receive both privileges). Once these security constraints are defined to the DBMS, it is up to the DBMS to enforce them.

The fifth DBMS function pertains to concurrent applications. When two programs attempt to process the same record at the same time, conflict can occur. If both programs only read the data, then there is no problem. But if one or both of the programs want to change the data, then errors and inconsistencies can result. The DBMS includes features such as **locks** that control concurrent access to data. For example, while one application is using a record, a lock can be placed on it preventing all other applications from accessing that record. When the lock is released, other applications can access it again. More sophisticated locks and additional techniques are employed by the DBMS to maintain order in concurrent applications. We will address this topic more fully in Chapter 14.

Finally, the DBMS provides facilities for backup and recovery. Unfortunately, in spite of everyone's best efforts, equipment can fail, programs can contain bugs, and users can make mistakes. When any of these occur, the organization must have a means for correcting the database. Sometimes this means the database must be reloaded from a backup copy, and all transactions that had been processed since the backup was done must be reapplied. In other cases, an error is corrected by backing out of the database the effects of one or more transactions. In any case, the DBMS must provide facilities for making backup copies, for logging all transactions, and for reestablishing the database to an earlier version when necessary.

We will now consider the subsystems of a typical DBMS product.

SUBSYSTEMS OF A DBMS

Figure 2.20 shows the basic subsystems of a DBMS. Refer to this figure as we discuss the nature and structure of DBMS products. No particular product's structure is exactly as shown, but all products have subsystems that are, in essence, equivalent to these.

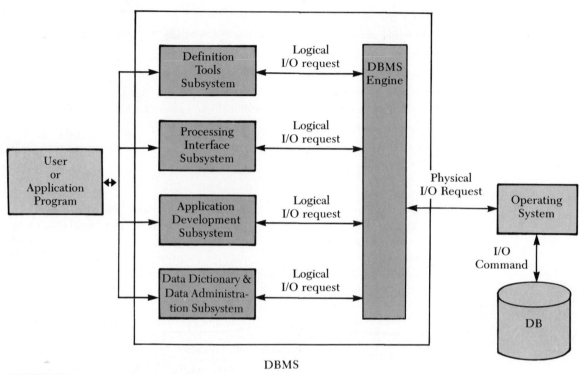

FIGURE 2.20
Functional components of a DBMS

A DBMS is a large and complex set of programs. For example, the subsystems for Paradox, a popular microcomputer database management system, require over four million bytes of storage. If you recall all of the functions a DBMS must perform, you shouldn't be surprised that it is so large.

DBMS Engine

The DBMS engine is the core of the DBMS. This subsystem receives **logical I/O requests** from other subsystems and translates those requests into reads from or writes to database files. Logical I/O requests are expressed as descriptions of the data, rather than as physical storage locations. Here is an example of a logical I/O request:

```
READ BOOK WITH ISBN 12345
```

The DBMS engine looks up the location of the requested data in the data dictionary and then issues a corresponding **physical I/O request** to the operating system. The operating system in turn executes the I/O commands. Physical I/O requests are usually expressed in terms of the storage location of the requested data, such as:

```
READ BLOCK 714 FROM FILE DBMS3.DAT INTO MEMORY LOCATION 22458
```

To appreciate the complexity of the DBMS engine, consider the following illustration. Suppose the DBMS engine receives the following request:

```
CHANGE Qty-on-hand IN BOOK with ISBN 12345 TO 1
```

To process this command, the engine must execute the following series of instructions:

1. Determine the physical file location of the data dictionary (meta-data) for BOOK records.
2. Read the meta-data.
3. Using the meta-data, determine the location of overhead data that pertains to BOOK records.
4. Read the overhead data for book 12345's record.
5. Using overhead data, determine the operating system file and block address of book 12345's record.
6. Read the block containing book 12345's data.
7. Using meta-data, determine the location of book 12345's record within the block just read, and the location of Qty-on-hand within that record (see Figure 2.21).

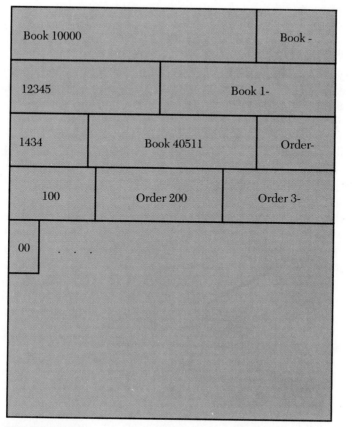

FIGURE 2.21
Structure of a block of database data

8. Change the value of Qty-on-hand.
9. Mark this block for rewriting to the file (or rewrite it now).
10. Check meta-data for overhead data that may need to be changed in light of the data change.
11. For each related index or other overhead structure, read, change, and replace overhead data as appropriate.

This is an impressive list of tasks to accomplish for a relatively simple change. There are complications, too. Before data can be read, there must be space in memory. The DBMS keeps a large buffer (section of memory) just for this purpose. But if that buffer is full, data that is in the buffer must be removed or overlaid. Thus, the DBMS engine must perform **memory management** by administering buffers, keeping track of available memory locations, and so forth.

The DBMS engine also performs disk management. When data is added to the database, the DBMS engine must find available disk space and allocate it. When records are deleted, the DBMS engine must remove the data (or mark it as deleted) and then somehow make available the newly freed space.

As all of this activity is taking place, the DBMS engine constantly *maintains both the overhead data and the meta-data stored in the data dictionary*.

Definition Tools Subsystem

Examine Figure 2.20 again. Notice that the other four subsystems in a DBMS interface with either a user or an application program. These subsystems call on the DBMS engine for services.

The first subsystem, the definition tools subsystem, consists of tools and utilities for defining and changing the database structure. The user employs this subsystem to create the structure of the database, which includes the files, fields, relationships, constraints, overhead data structures, and other components of the database. Recall that the word *schema* refers to the complete conceptual view of the database. The definition tools subsystem is used to define the schema.

As stated earlier, for security and control reasons it is undesirable to allow a program or user to have access to the entire schema. During design, the subset of the database that each program and user needs is identified. This *subschema*, or *application view*, is also defined using the definition tools subsystem.

Nothing remains the same. Business needs change, people learn more about the tasks they wish to accomplish, decisions are made that necessitate storing more data in the database. As these changes occur, the structure of the database may need to be altered. New files become necessary. New data items must be added to existing files. Overhead data structures must be added, or they become obsolete and need to be removed. All of these changes are accomplished using the definition tools subsystem.

Processing Interface Subsystem

The processing interface subsystem allows users and programs to access the database system. All of the update and display facilities described in the previous section are implemented by the processing interface subsystem. Some of the facilities can be employed directly by users, others require programming; the processing interface subsystem supports both types.

The interface to standard programming languages such as COBOL and PL/I is accomplished in two different ways. With the first, more primitive method, the DBMS product includes a program library of DBMS routines. The programmer writes calls to the appropriate routine for DBMS service. An example of such a call is:

```
CALL DBMS-READ (file, field-name, field-value, buffer, status)
```

where the parameters indicate the name of the file to be read, the name of the key field, the value of the key field, an address to place the record in, and a status flag to indicate normal or error conditions. The command would need to be expressed in proper host-language syntax.

Writing CALL statements like this one can be complex, and it is easy to make programming errors. To make the programmer's job easier, some DBMS vendors provide special DBMS commands for the application programmer to use in place of call statements. These commands, which are simpler and easier to use than the equivalent programming statements, replace the call statements in the host program. Here is an example:

```
SELECT Title INTO .tname FROM BOOK WHERE ISBN = .isbn-val
```

In this example, .tname and .isbn-val represent program variables. This command obtains the title of the book whose ISBN equals the value of the variable .isbn-val and places it in the variable .tname.

Statements like this are not part of any standard programming language, so the language compilers do not recognize them. Therefore, the application program is first translated by a precompiler (usually provided by the DBMS vendor). The precompiler replaces the database commands with standard programming language statements. Thus, for example, the SELECT command in the example would be replaced with the equivalent external program call.

The procedure for a COBOL program is illustrated in Figure 2.22. In this example, the application programmer identifies the database needed by means of an INVOKE command: INVOKE SUBSCHEMA ALPHA. INVOKE is not a COBOL instruction, so the precompiler must translate it into COBOL instructions before the COBOL compiler reads the program. The precompiler locates the subschema, ALPHA, in the data dictionary and inserts the appropriate COBOL description in the DATA DIVISION. Other DBMS instructions in the program are likewise replaced with the equivalent COBOL code. After precompilation, the COBOL compiler can be used. The particulars of precompilation are unimportant at this point. You simply need to realize that the processing interface subsystem enables programmers to include database access commands in their host-language programs by providing precompilation when needed.

Application Development Tools Subsystem

The next subsystem in Figure 2.20 concerns application development. This subsystem contains tools for developing application components such as forms, reports, and menus.

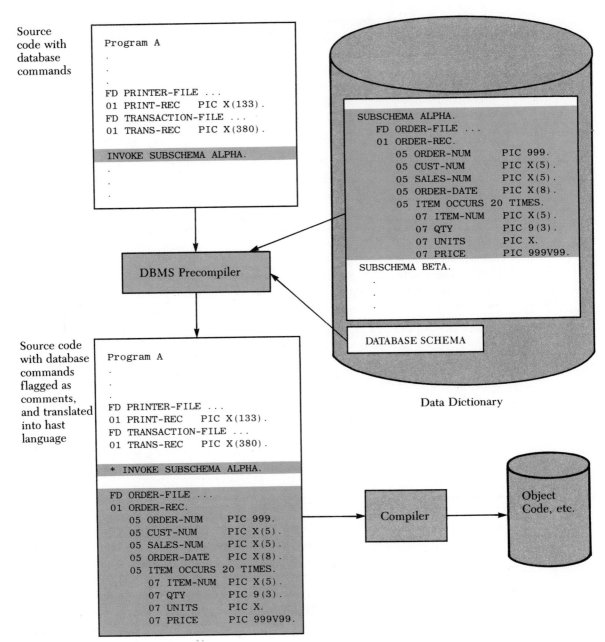

FIGURE 2.22
Illustration of use of precompiler

It may also include program code generators. Although at one time these tools were sold separately from the DBMS, the current trend is to integrate them with it. Consider the development of a data display form.

Suppose you want to define a form that has data from both BOOK and ORDER records. A form includes both constants (such as the form title, column headers, and prompts) and variables (such as the book's title and author). Defining the form is relatively easy when using a forms generator, which is part of the application development subsystem. Forms generators employ several techniques for constructing the form, but one typical way is to present the user with a blank screen on which she can "paint" the form, just the way she wants it to look.

The developer positions the cursor and enters form constants precisely where they will appear on the form. She also indicates the locations of variable data. This might be done by placing the cursor at the appropriate screen position and then pressing a function key, such as F6. This tells the forms generator that a variable will appear here. The user enters the name of the variable. Because the forms generator can access the data dictionary, it can rapidly determine the length of the field and automatically allocate enough space on the form to accommodate the field.

After positioning all of the constants and variables, the user can store the format of this form as part of the application meta-data. Thereafter, the DBMS can retrieve it whenever it is needed in an application. The form format can also be retrieved so the user can modify it.

The application development subsystem includes similar tools for developing menus, reports, and application programs. In each case, the subsystem uses the meta-data stored in the data dictionary to speed up the development process and to reduce the likelihood of errors. And it stores the results for future reference.

Data Dictionary and Data Administration Subsystem

The last DBMS subsystem shown in Figure 2.20 is the **data dictionary and data administration subsystem,** which provides query and report functions on the database meta-data in addition to its other roles. This subsystem is employed most often by the DBA. The data dictionary is a gold mine of information needed for administering the database. Because it contains complete descriptions of the database structure and all the relationships among programs and data, and because it can be queried using the same commands as users employ for source data, its value to the DBA is inestimable.

For example, suppose the format or length of a data item needs to be changed. By querying the data dictionary, the DBA can determine which records contain the data item; the forms, reports, and programs that use the data item; security considerations regarding the data item; and so forth. Such information helps the DBA to determine the extent of work needed to implement such a change, and how making such a change will affect the rest of the database system. Knowing this, the DBA is in a good position to approve the change (or not), to allocate people and other resources to implement it, and to notify all those individuals who will be affected by the change, such as data entry clerks and users.

Databases need care and maintenance. They need to be backed up, and occasionally they may need to be recovered. As time passes, obsolete data may need to be archived or purged from the database. All of these functions are handled by the data dictionary and data administration subsystem. It usually includes a collection of utility programs that perform maintenance functions on the database itself. These functions are more likely to be used by the computer operations staff or by the DBA than by users or application programmers.

Summary

A database processing system has five components: data, programs, hardware, procedures, and people. The major data component is the database. Databases contain source data, the data dictionary, and overhead data. The schema, or conceptual view, is the structure of the entire database. A subschema, or application view, is the portion of the structure that is processed by a particular application. Some DBMS products store application meta-data in the database.

A database processing system requires, as a minimum, the operating system and the DBMS. All but the simplest personal database systems require application programs. Also, a communications control program or LAN operating system is required for concurrent processing on mainframes and local area networks, respectively. Application programs can be written in a standard programming language such as COBOL or BASIC, or they can be written in the DBMS product's own language. Some products include code generation systems.

In general, database processing systems do not require any special hardware, but they may require *more* hardware. Micros, LANs, minicomputers, and mainframes can all be used. In most cases, at least the power of an 80286 processor is required to run the DBMS product. The DBMS can take from 256,000 to a million or more bytes of main memory. Database machines, which are special computers for processing a database, exist, but are rare.

Clientele are people for whom the system is developed. Users employ the system to satisfy a business need. Operations personnel run the computer and associated equipment. Systems development personnel design and implement the database and its applications. Database administration personnel protect the database and resolve conflicts among users.

Procedures for both normal and recovery processing are needed for users, operations personnel, and database administration personnel. Procedures can be manual or they can be encoded in application programs.

A database application is a business computer system that processes some or all of a database to meet the information needs of an individual, a department, or a functional area. Each application has the five components of an information system; the database, certain programs, and hardware are often shared among applications.

The three fundamental functions of a database application are to control users' activities, to provide facilities for updating data, and to provide facilities for displaying data.

Applications vary in the degree of control they provide. Some have a high degree of control and leave little discretion to the users. Others provide a wide degree of flexibility. Menu-driven systems fall in the middle ground. Applications that support operations generally provide a high degree of control; those that support planning and like functions generally have a low degree of control.

There are several principles and techniques for control. Users should not be able to access data they do not need. Access to applications should be controlled. Within an application, access to the database should be controlled. Menus restrict or hide processing options. Additional controls can be placed within the processing of the menu choice. Another control is to reduce the command set available to the user.

Database updates include adding new records, deleting unwanted ones, and modifying records. DBMS products provide a wide spectrum of facilities to update data. One category of approaches is the generic facility. Generic facilities require no program development effort, but they are not very sophisticated. However, users can employ them without the assistance of systems development personnel. The other category employs programs written by professional developers. Such programs can be tailored to meet stringent user requirements, but they take longer to develop and therefore are more expensive.

DBMS applications include facilities for displaying data, although the term *display* here includes printed reports, computer display screens, and machine-readable computer files. Reports, like forms, can be generated by DBMS utilities or by application programs. The latter is more time consuming and expensive but can accommodate complicated requirements.

In the case of displaying data in response to a database query, the user formats and enters a query command identifying the data that should be extracted from the database. The DBMS locates the specified data and formats and displays it on the computer screen. The query language SQL is popular today.

Data can also be displayed by exporting files to another computer system. This data is in machine-readable format.

A database management system provides tools to systems developers for designing and implementing a system, and to users who need to employ the system. A DBMS is a set of programs that provides facilities to define, process, and administer the database and its applications.

Major components of the DBMS are the DBMS engine, the definition tools subsystem, the processing interface subsystem, the application development subsystem, and the data dictionary and data administration subsystem.

GROUP I   QUESTIONS

2.1   Explain why the database processing system at the Carbon River Bookshop is an organizational system.

2.2   Summarize the actions of each of the database applications at the bookshop.

2.3   What are the five components of a database processing system?

2.4   Give an example of each component using the bookshop as an illustration.

2.5   What is a schema, or conceptual view?

2.6   What is a subschema, or application view? How can views be used to control access to a database?

2.7   What are four types of data in a database processing system? How are they related?

2.8   Summarize the programs required for a database processing system.

2.9   Do professional programmers develop database application programs? Do users? Do you suppose most users want to learn how to write COBOL or Pascal programs to access a database? How do you suppose their reactions have influenced the development of DBMS features?

2.10   What are the two types of languages in which applications are written?

2.11   What is a code generation system?

2.12   Summarize the hardware requirements for database processing systems.

2.13   What is a database machine? How common are they?

2.14   List the types of personnel involved with database processing systems. Summarize the role or function of each type.

2.15   Describe the basic types of procedures required for database processing systems. Use a diagram.

2.16   Summarize the procedures required at the Carbon River Bookshop.

2.17   Explain how procedures can be encoded in application programs.

2.18   Define *database application*.

2.19   Describe three functions of a database application.

2.20   Explain Figure 2.11. Why are menu-driven systems in the middle of this continuum?

2.21   What types of application require a high degree of programmed control? What types require a high degree of flexibility?

2.22   Describe three examples in which application programs can control database processing activity.

2.23   Describe the two general categories of update facilities.

2.24   Describe five generic update facilities.

2.25   Explain the advantages and disadvantages of updating the database from application programs.

2.26 Describe three ways in which database data can be displayed.

2.27 Define *database management system.*

2.28 Describe the generic DBMS functions.

2.29 Sketch the basic architecture of a DBMS product.

2.30 Describe the functions of the DBMS engine.

2.31 Describe the functions of the definition tools subsystem.

2.32 Describe the functions of the processing interface subsystem.

2.33 Describe the functions of the application development subsystem.

2.34 Describe the functions of the data administration and data dictionary subsystem.

GROUP II QUESTIONS

2.35 Interview the manager of a small business that uses a database processing system. Describe the applications installed in the system. For any two applications, identify the five system components.

2.36 Interview database administration personnel of a local company. Find out if users develop any of their own applications in that company. If so, what tools do they use? If not, who develops applications? What tools do they use?

2.37 Design the logic for an application program that would delete a vendor from the Carbon River Bookshop database. Keep in mind that the vendor may have orders in process.

2.38 What controls do you think need to be placed on processing at the bookshop? To what kinds of crime is the bookshop vulnerable? How could database applications help to prevent these crimes?

Database Query

This textbook concerns a robust and comprehensive process for developing databases and their applications. The process is effective for designing and implementing large and complicated databases. Because it is a robust process, you will need to learn a number of complicated concepts and techniques before you have an opportunity to work with an actual database. This could be frustrating: perhaps you won't be able to see the relevance of the conceptual material if you have had no database processing experience at all.

To reduce the risk of such frustration, this application module illustrates the construction and querying of a small database. The purpose of the module is to give you a taste of what a database is and how one is processed. The best way to proceed is to implement the database described here using a personal computer DBMS product like Paradox, DataEase, R:BASE, or one of the dBASE products.

- THE PROBLEM
- BUILDING THE DATABASE
- QUERYING THE DATABASE

The Problem

Suppose that you manage Carbon River Bookshop. You decide that you'd like to get away for a few days and, in a relaxed setting, consider the organization of the bookshop's departments. You have a portable computer of sufficient size and power to run a personal computer DBMS product. Suppose that such a product is already loaded on your computer.

You'd like to load data from the Carbon River Bookshop database onto your portable computer and take it to your relaxed setting—say a cabin on the beach. Then, over a several day period, you'd like to query the data and see if you can find some trend in your book selling and ordering process that suggests a better way of organizing the bookshop. You're not exactly certain what you want to do, but you suspect that there is a pattern in the BOOK and ORDER data from the INVENTORY database that would help you.

Building the Database

To accomplish your plan, you will need to perform the following activities:

1. Unload the data from the INVENTORY database.
2. Create the database structure on your computer.
3. Load the data into your database.
4. Query the database.

You will take steps 1 through 3 to build the database; in step 4 you will perform your analysis by querying the data.

Observe that you need not develop a design for your database. You are going to copy the design that has already been established for the INVENTORY database. This fact greatly simplifies your task—it makes your job nearly trivial, in fact. Once the design is determined, implementing the database is mechanical and straightforward, as you will learn. It is for that reason that the bulk of this textbook concerns a process for designing the database. But, that's getting ahead of the story. For now, you can copy the design of the INVENTORY database.

Observe, too, that step 1 is the only step that needs to be performed at the bookshop; you can take the unloaded data on diskette and perform the other steps at your retreat. Let's suppose, however, that you're uncertain that you can do steps 2 and 3 correctly on your own, so you decide to perform steps 1, 2, and 3 before you leave. In that way, if you get stuck, one of your employees can help you.

Step 1: Unloading the Data

To unload the data, you will need to access the INVENTORY database and use one of the commands or functions of the DBMS to copy the data to a diskette. The particular command that you need depends on the DBMS product. A typical command would be the following:

```
UNLOAD TABLE tablename INTO filename   {ALL
                                        DATA ONLY}
```

To use this command, you should fill in specific names for the underlined key words and pick one of the two terms within the braces. ALL means that both data structure and data will be unloaded; DATA ONLY means only data values will be unloaded.

Suppose you want to unload BOOK data into the file BOOK.DAT and ORDER data into the file ORDER.DAT. Assume you want only the data; no structure is to be unloaded. In that case, you would issue these commands:

```
UNLOAD TABLE BOOK INTO BOOK.DAT DATA ONLY
and
UNLOAD TABLE ORDER INTO ORDER.DAT DATA ONLY
```

The result of these two commands would be two character-oriented DOS files (or other operating system files, for example, Macintosh or Unix files). The files will contain tables of data similar to those shown in Figure 2.5. The records of the files will be fixed in length; each field will occupy as many characters in the file as the column occupies in the database table. For example, suppose the data items in BOOK are defined to have the following characteristics in the INVENTORY database:

BOOK Table Definition

ISBN	Numeric	10
Title	Text	10
Author	Text	10
Price	Currency	8
Subj-area	Text	8
Qty-on-hand	Numeric	6
YTD-qty-sold	Numeric	8

In this case, the file BOOK.DAT will have records that are 60 bytes in length. The first 10 bytes of each record will contain ISBN, the next 10 Title, and so forth.

Step 2: Creating the Database Structure

The particulars of the next step depend on the DBMS product that you have installed on your portable computer. This step can be easy or somewhat more difficult, depending on the product. With Paradox, DataEase, R:BASE, and similar products, the step will be very simple. With dBASE or one of its related products such as FoxPro, the process will be more complicated.

In general, you need to inform the DBMS that you want to build a database that contains two tables, and you will need to name the database and the tables. For this example, suppose that you decide to call your database STUDY1 and to call the two tables BOOK and ORDER.

As you name the tables, you will also need to define their structure. The best course of action is to define the structure of STUDY1 to mirror the structure of the INVENTORY database. In that way, the files unloaded from INVENTORY can be directly input to STUDY1.

A method that several DBMS products use for defining table structure is to display the skeleton of a table with blank fields in the name and column headings. You then type in the name of the table, the names of the columns, and type and lengths of the columns.

The following is a typical table definition display:

BOOK

ISBN	Title	Author	Price	Dept	QOH	YTDQOH
Numeric	Text	Text	Currency	Text	Numeric	Numeric
10	10	8	8	8	6	8

In this example, the user has typed in all names and column descriptions (like Numeric 10). The DBMS then creates the structure to store data for such tables.

Observe in this example that some of the column names have been changed. Column name Subj-area in INVENTORY has been changed to column name Dept in STUDY1, for instance. This is entirely possible; the only restriction is that the length of the columns be the same between the two databases.

Step 3: Loading the Database

If the previous two steps have been performed correctly, the loading step is easy. You simply have the DBMS on your portable computer load the tables using the files BOOK.DAT and ORDER.DAT. Suppose your DBMS had a load command with the following syntax:

```
LOAD tablename FROM filename
```

In this case, you would issue the following two commands to load your data:

```
LOAD BOOK FROM BOOK.DAT
LOAD ORDER FROM ORDER.DAT
```

The DBMS will respond with a message like "Load successful, 270 rows read" or some equivalent message.

At this point, your database is loaded. You might issue a command to list the first screen full of rows, or some other command, just to be sure. After that, you can drive to the beach.

ISBN	Title	Author	Price	Dept	Qty-on-hand
12345	New World	Smith, JB	$22.95	Art	2
80010	Ceramics	Jones, PM	$15.95	CB	1
14111	Fantasy	Laird, RD	$15.95	CB	3
18722	New Poems	Fritz, AE	$29.95	Poetry	3
13991	Chemistry	Shultz, BF	$34.95	Sci	2
17101	Cats	Eliot, TS	$24.95	Poetry	1
89336	Physics	Hughes, M	$11.95	Sci	1
14892	Selling	Suit, CM	$14.95	Bus	3
23712	Cat in Hat	Seuss, Dr	$39.95	CB	2

a. BOOK data imported from INVENTORY database

Order#	ISBN	ndor#	Order-date	Qty	Amount
100	12345	10	12/11/91	3	$39.00
101	80010	10	12/11/91	1	$11.00
102	14111	20	12/11/91	1	$12.00
103	18722	30	12/11/91	7	$141.00
104	13991	10	12/11/91	2	$46.00
105	17101	20	12/11/91	1	$19.00
106	80336	30	12/11/91	1	$7.00
107	14892	10	12/11/91	1	$9.00
108	23712	10	12/11/91	3	$73.00
109	80010	20	12/11/91	1	$11.00

b. ORDER data imported from INVENTORY database

FIGURE AP.1
Sample data

Figure AP.1 gives sample data for the BOOK and ORDER tables. You can use this data to verify the operations that will be shown in the next section.

Querying the Database

Like the other steps, the specific means by which you query the database will vary from DBMS product to product. It will be easier with some products and more difficult with others.

QUERY BY EXAMPLE

Some DBMS products, such as Paradox and DataEase, support a visual means for querying data. Paradox uses a method called **query by example,** or QBE. With QBE, querying a database is done by illustrating the query to be answered. The screen display is much the same as that shown in the table definition example. Instead of typing in column names and formats, however, you check the columns you want to see and specify data values that you want to use to restrict your query.

For example, suppose you want to see the Title and Price of all books sold in department code CB (children's books). To execute this query using QBE, you check the Title and Price columns and fill in the value CB in the Dept column. The DBMS responds with a display of a table having three columns: Title, Price, and Dept. The values in Dept will be equal to CB, and the values in Title and Price will show values in the database found for the CB Dept.

QUERY BY COMMAND

Other products are more difficult to use. With dBASE III and III Plus and the DBMS products that have copied the dBASE III command language, querying the database will be somewhat difficult. You will need to learn the syntax of one or more commands to accomplish the query you want. To query more than one table, you may also need to define indexes and other structures that go beyond the scope of the discussion here. (You can learn about indexes in Chapter 11 and in Appendix B.) Because of complexity, we will not consider such commands further here.

QUERY BY SQL

Another alternative is to express queries in terms of the language SQL. Many DBMS products support this language, including dBASE IV, R:BASE, Oracle, and others. We will consider several examples of SQL commands in this section. Let's begin with queries that involve only a single table and then expand the discussion to queries that involve two tables. (A more rigorous discussion of SQL is presented in Chapter 10.)

SQL Queries Involving a Single Table

1. Suppose that you want to obtain the Title and Price of all books. To do so, you would issue the following SQL query:

```
SELECT      TITLE, PRICE
FROM        BOOK
```

The result of this query for the data in the tables in Figure AP.1 is shown in Figure AP.2.

2. Next, suppose you want the Title and Price of books in the children's department (code CB in the Dept column). This can be done with the SQL query:

```
SELECT      TITLE, PRICE
FROM        BOOK
WHERE       DEPT = 'CB'
```

FIGURE AP.2
Result of query number 1

Title	Price
New World	$22.95
Ceramics	$15.95
Fantasy	$15.95
New Poems	$29.95
Chemistry	$34.95
Cats	$24.95
Physics	$11.95
Selling	$14.95
Cat in Hat	$39.95

The result of this query for the data in the tables in Figure AP.1 is shown in Figure AP.3.

The structure SELECT, FROM, WHERE is common to most SQL queries. In fact, it is the backbone of almost all SQL commands.

3. SQL includes functions, sometimes called **built-in functions,** that provide additional processing capability. For example, suppose you want a count of the number of books in the children's department. Issue the query:

```
SELECT      COUNT(*)
FROM        BOOK
WHERE       DEPT = 'CB'
```

The result of this query will be a table with a single row and a single column as shown in Figure AP.4. The value is the number of rows for which the value of DEPT equals CB.

4. Now suppose you want to know the number of books in the children's department that have a Price greater than $25.00. Here, issue the query:

```
SELECT      COUNT(*)
FROM        BOOK
WHERE       DEPT = 'CB'
    AND     PRICE > 25.00
```

FIGURE AP.3
Result of query number 2

Title	Price
Ceramics	$15.95
Fantasy	$15.95
Cat in Hat	$39.95

FIGURE AP.4
Result of query number 3

Count
3

FIGURE AP.5
Result of query number 4

Count
1

The result of this query for the data in the tables in Figure AP.1 is shown in Figure AP.5.

SQL Queries Involving Two Tables

5. Suppose you want to see a list of the Vendor#, Amount, and Dept of all books that have been ordered. This query requires data from both the BOOK and the ORDER tables. In order to answer it, rows from the two tables must be combined.

Since both BOOK and ORDER contain ISBN, it makes sense to combine rows where the value of ISBN in a row in one table equals a value of ISBN in a row in the second table. This condition can be specified in the WHERE statement as follows:

```
SELECT      VENDOR#, AMOUNT, DEPT
FROM        BOOK, ORDER
WHERE       BOOK.ISBN = ISBN.ORDER
```

The result of this query for the data in the tables in Figure AP.1 is shown in Figure AP.6.

6. Suppose that you want to see Vendor# and Amount for orders for books from only the children's department. The following query will generate the correct result:

```
SELECT      VENDOR#, AMOUNT
FROM        BOOK, ORDER
WHERE       BOOK.ISBN = ISBN.ORDER
    AND     DEPT = 'CB'
```

The result of this query for the data in the tables in Figure AP.1 is shown in Figure AP.7.

FIGURE AP.6
Result of query number 5

Vendor#	Amount	Dept
10	$39.00	Art
10	$11.00	CB
20	$11.00	CB
20	$12.00	CB
30	$141.00	Poetry
10	$46.00	Sci
20	$19.00	Poetry
10	$9.00	Bus
10	$73.00	CB

FIGURE AP.7
Result of query number 6

Vendor#	Amount
10	$11.00
20	$11.00
20	$12.00
10	$73.00

7. Finally, suppose that you want to know the average Amount for all orders for Vendor 10 for books that are sold in the children's department. This result can be obtained with:

```
SELECT      AVG (AMOUNT)
FROM        BOOK, ORDER
WHERE       BOOK.ISBN = ISBN.ORDER
    AND     DEPT = 'CB'
    AND     VENDOR# = '10'
```

The result of this query for the data in the tables in Figure AP.1 is shown in Figure AP.8.

There are quite a number of other options for querying databases using SQL, and they will be illustrated in Chapter 10. The goal here is to give you a notion of how databases are processed so that you will have a general idea of the direction that we are heading.

The difficult task is developing a database design that supports the applications' requirements. Once the design is created, implementing it using a DBMS product is straightforward. It may be complicated, but the implementation task is not fraught with the same degree of risk as is the design task. Hence, we will consider the task of designing databases in the next five chapters.

FIGURE AP.8
Result of query number 7

Average
$42.00

PART II

Data Modeling

Part II addresses the first phase of the database development process: data modeling. It presents processes, tools, and techniques for analyzing user requirements and developing a data model from them.

Chapter 3 concerns database development. First, we summarize the systems development process and develop a framework for subsequent discussion about database development. Then, the process of developing a database is summarized; the top-down and bottom-up styles of development are present.

Chapter 4 describes and illustrates the use of the entity-relationship model, a conceptual framework that is used to interpret, specify, and document database requirements. It provides constructs for showing the overall design of the database. As such, it is often used for top-down database design.

In Chapter 5, we consider a second important database model, the semantic object model. This model also can be used to document requirements for databases, but it is closer to the user and allows for the specification of more details. It is often used for bottom-up database design. Both entity-relationship and semantic object models are used to develop a specification of the users' data model, as you will learn in this part.

Database
Development

The goal of this chapter is to describe, in broad terms, the process by which databases and their applications are developed. We begin with a description of the basic stages of development that pertain to all information systems—whether database or other type of system. With this perspective, we then narrow our focus to activities that are peculiar to the development of database systems.

   The purpose of this discussion is to establish a context for the use of the concepts that are discussed throughout this text. This context will help you understand the shape of the forest as we plunge into the details of the trees.

- SUMMARY OF THE SYSTEMS DEVELOPMENT PROCESS
- DEVELOPING A DATABASE

Summary of the Systems Development Process

The systems development process is a complicated subject about which many lengthy books have been written. In this section, we will summarize the process and sketch the outline of major tasks. Our goal is to provide a framework for subsequent discussion about database design and development. Refer to Flaatten et al.[1] or Jordan and Machesky[2] or other systems development texts for more comprehensive discussions.

Developing a database and its attendant applications can be a complex task requiring the efforts of dozens of people over many months. Systems requirements arise from the users' needs to keep track of something. In Figure 3.1, the user wants to keep track of sales orders. To do this with a database processing system, sales orders and other source documents are taken as requirements. From these, a model of the users' data is developed; this model is then transformed into a database design. Once the design has been developed, it is implemented into structures on physical media. The database is then processed by one or more database applications via the DBMS.

Figure 3.1 shows the situation of a single user with a single application. The situation becomes far more complicated for workgroup and organizational systems that have many users and many applications, as you will learn.

In some cases, systems development means building a completely new system. In others, it means adding a new application to an existing database system. For example, a

[1] Per Flaatten et al., *Foundations of Business Systems* (Chicago: Dryden Press, 1989).

[2] Eleanor Jordan and Jefry Machesky, *Systems Development* (Boston: PWS-Kent, 1990).

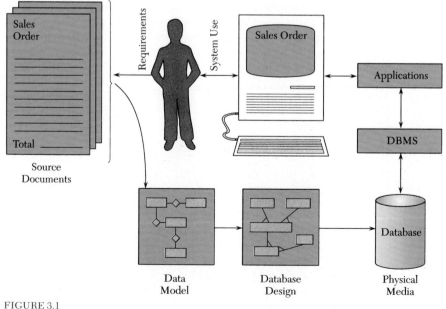

FIGURE 3.1

Development of a database processing system

year after the Carbon River Bookshop (Chapter 2) implemented its system, a need developed to expand the database to include past customer purchases. This new application required alterations to the schema of the database; it also meant that new forms, reports, menus, and transaction processing programs had to be developed. In this case, during the design phase the development team needed to design changes to the database and to the other application components.

There are many different processes for developing systems; the process we summarize here captures the essence of most development methodologies. Although people might differ with the terminology described here, most would agree with the fundamental phases, which are shown in Figure 3.2.

Definition Phase
- Form project team
- Define the problem
- Establish scope
- Assess feasibility

Requirements Phase
- Create users' data model
- Determine update, display, and control mechanisms
- Interview users
- Use prototypes

Evaluation Phase
- Select systems architecture
- Reassess feasibility
- Reassess requirements, possibly defer some

Design Phase
- Develop database design
  - Files (relations, tables)
  - Data items (attributes, columns)
  - Relationships
- Develop application design
  - Design menus, forms, reports, query facilities
  - Specify update, display, and control mechanisms
  - Design program logic

Implementation Phase
- Construct database
- Build applications
- Install database and applications

FIGURE 3.2
Summary of database and application development

DEFINITION PHASE

The first phase of an application development project is to define what the project is to do. The project may be to modify an existing application, or it might be to develop a comprehensive set of applications around an organizational database, or it might be something else. The goal of the **definition phase** is to find out what is to be done.

The first task is to form a team of people to work on the project. Once the team has been formed, it must define the problem to be solved. Problem definition often sounds easier than it is. A problem is a perceived difference between what is and what ought to be. Since a problem is a perception, different people will have different ideas about it. The team members must consolidate the various problem definitions and achieve a consensus definition that is understood and accepted by the user community.

The next task of the definition phase is to establish the scope of the project. Users, understandably, want to have systems that perform numerous functions for them. Unfortunately, systems developers are often unable to put all the features the users want into the first release of a new system. Thus, when the team determines the scope of the system, it may be limiting development to certain functions or even certain users.

The final task of the definition phase is to assess feasibility. Most developers agree on cost, technical, schedule, and political components. Each of these must be assessed before investing time and money into systems development.

In summary, the goal of the definition phase is to get organized, to determine what is to be done, and as much as possible, to determine if it makes sense to proceed. Depending on the size of the project, the definition phase should take somewhere between a few hours and one month.

At the end of this phase, the team should report to its sponsor (a company manager, a steering committee, a senior executive). The sponsor will want to be informed of progress and needs the opportunity to make corrections as the team proceeds.

REQUIREMENTS PHASE

The purpose of the **requirements phase** is to determine, as specifically as possible, what the new system must do. Prior to this phase, during definition, the team will have determined the general goals of the system. These determinations, however, are insufficient to design and implement the database and applications. More detail is needed.

Defining the requirements for a database system involves two major goals. First, the development team must develop a **users' data model,** or a **requirements data model.** This model describes the things (sometimes called entities or objects) that must be stored in the database, the structure of those things, and the relationships that those things have to one another. The requirements data model is used as the basis for the database design, as shown in Figure 3.1. Chapters 4 and 5 are devoted to data modeling.

Second, the team determines the functional components of each application that will use the database. As described in Chapter 2, each application includes update, display, and control mechanisms. These components provide the means by which the user keeps the database current and obtains information from it. We will discuss this goal in more detail in Chapter 8, Database Application Design.

The ultimate authority on application requirements is the users. The development team applies its knowledge, experience, and intuition to help the users describe their needs. These needs include outputs, inputs, and constraints on processing.

The team may develop **prototypes** of forms, reports, and menus, and show them to the users. A prototype is a quickly developed mock-up of the real thing—a working model. Prototypes provide a context for dialogue between users and the development team. When users have the opportunity to evaluate interfaces using prototypes at the early stages of systems development, the developers are much more likely to learn the real requirements.

The output of the requirements phase is a statement of requirements. This statement can take a variety of forms: a verbal description; a collection of data flow, entity-relationship, and object diagrams; one or more prototypes; or all of these. The requirements document must be reviewed and approved both by users and the sponsor of the project.

EVALUATION PHASE

The third stage of systems development is the **evaluation phase.** It consists of three tasks. First, alternative application systems architectures are identified and one is chosen. Second, the feasibility of the application is reassessed now that the requirements are known in more detail and the basic alternative solution has been specified. Third, all user requirements are reexamined within the context of the chosen alternative. If all requirements cannot be accommodated during this project, then some are deferred to future projects or are eliminated.

For database development projects, part of the assessment of requirements is to review the data model that has been developed. You will learn more about this later in the chapter.

Alternative systems architectures describe the basic structure of the system. At the Carbon River Bookshop, one such architecture is a set of microcomputers connected to a common, multi-user, multi-application database using a local area network. An alternative architecture would consist of the same type of database shared on minicomputer hardware. During the evaluation phase, one of these alternatives is selected.

At this point, system feasibility is reassessed. Can the selected alternative satisfy the requirements? Sometimes a particular approach can be feasible only if one or several of the most demanding or troublesome requirements can be deferred. In these cases, the users may agree that eliminating or deferring the requirement is the best choice.

The result of the evaluation phase is a systems architecture, a set of feasible, finalized requirements, and an improved data model. As with the definition phase, the results of this phase are presented to the system's sponsor for review and approval.

DESIGN PHASE

The goal of the **design phase** is to develop a blueprint for all five components of the information system. Both programs and procedures are designed, job descriptions are developed, and the specifications for the hardware are written.

FIGURE 3.3
Components of database design

- Names of file (or tables)
- Data items in files
    - Name of data item
    - Physical description of data item
    - Logical description of data item
- Relationships among files
- Constraints on data items or relationships

For the data component, the structure of the database is developed. To do this, the development team translates the user data model into specific data structures including a description of the files in the database, the data items within each file, and the relationships among the files. Further, constraints on data item values and relationships are specified. See Figure 3.3. We will consider database design in Chapters 6 and 7.

The design phase includes the design of both the database and applications. An application is a collection of menus, forms, reports, and programs that provide a means for data update, display, and control. During design, the specific structure of forms, reports, menus, and query facilities are defined. Also, the logic of transaction programs that will be written for the system is developed. We will consider application design in Chapter 8.

All design documents should be subjected to a thorough review before implementation begins. This is the last opportunity the team has to find errors before building the system. After this phase, errors become much more costly and difficult to repair. Such reviews are absolutely vital to the success of any project where the cost of a mistake in implementation is high.

IMPLEMENTATION PHASE

The final phase of the development process is implementation. The primary task of the **implementation phase** is to construct the system according to the design. Hardware is installed, programs are developed, procedures are documented, and personnel are hired and trained.

With regard to the data component, the details of implementation depend on the particular DBMS product in use. The database design developed in the prior phase is converted to a design that fits the structures of the DBMS to be used to process the database. Then, the definition facilities of the DBMS are used to define the schema and subschemas and other structures.

Developers use the features of the application development subsystem to build forms, reports, and menus, and also to build transaction processing programs. Other programs may need to be written in a standard programming language and linked to the DBMS via the processing interface.

Each component of each application needs to be tested. The amount and type of testing depends on the nature of the system and how the components were developed. We will discuss this issue further in the implementation chapters of this text.

Installation is the last stage of the development. User and operator procedures are documented during this final stage, and data is loaded into the database. Personnel need to be trained in the use and operation of the new system. They need to know how to follow procedures to accomplish their work. User training is so important that sometimes it is done in parallel with the design phase. Operations personnel also need to be trained in procedures, especially in those that concern backup and recovery.

PHASES AND COMPONENTS FOR DATABASE PROCESSING

The preceding section presented a brief overview of a process for developing information systems. Figure 3.4 summarizes the development phases and components of an information system. We will not consider all cells of the matrix in Figure 3.4 equally. Instead, we will focus on those that pertain most directly to the development of *database* systems.

The shaded portion of Figure 3.4 indicates the components and phases we will focus upon in this text. These include the requirements, evaluation, design, and implementation phases of the data component. From time to time, we will also focus on those same phases for the program and procedure components, though our attention will be primarily on their interface to the data component. Given the preceding broad overview of information systems development, we are ready to reconsider the phases and activities that pertain most directly to the development of a database.

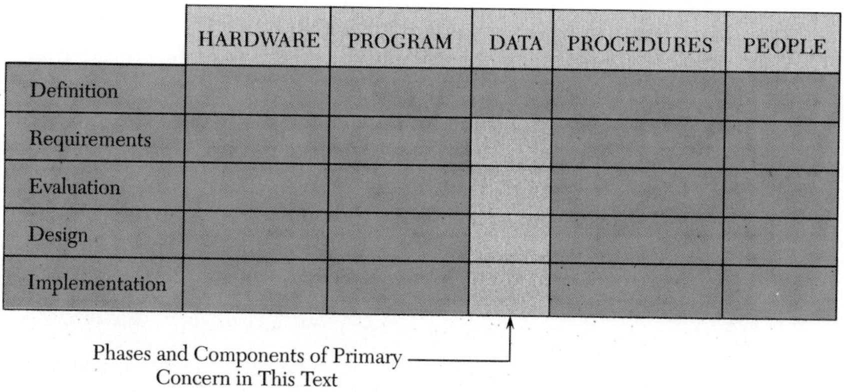

	HARDWARE	PROGRAM	DATA	PROCEDURES	PEOPLE
Definition					
Requirements					
Evaluation					
Design					
Implementation					

Phases and Components of Primary Concern in This Text

FIGURE 3.4

Summary of database development phases and components

Developing a Database

At the end of this discussion you should understand the basic phases in the development of a database as summarized in Figure 3.5. We begin in the requirements phase by building a model of the users' data. We then evaluate this model (the evaluation phase) and transform it into a database design (the design phase). Next, we implement the model using a particular DBMS product. In parallel, applications are also developed.

TOP-DOWN VERSUS BOTTOM-UP DATABASE DEVELOPMENT

There are two major styles for developing a database. **Top-down development** proceeds from the general to the specific. It begins with a study of the strategic goals of the organization, the means by which those goals can be accomplished, the information requirements that must be satisfied to accomplish those goals, and the systems that must exist to provide that information. From such a study, a data model is developed at a high level of abstraction.

Given the high-level model, the development team then progressively works downward toward more and more detailed descriptions and models. Intermediate-level models are developed and they, too, are expanded to more detail until a point is reached at which particular databases and related applications are identified. One or more of these applications is then selected for development. Over time, the entire high-level data model is transformed into lower-level models and all of the indicated systems, databases, and applications are developed.

Bottom-up development operates in the reverse order of abstraction. It begins with the need to develop a specific system. The means of selecting the first system varies from organization to organization. In some organizations, a steering committee picks the application; in other organizations, the users may pick it themselves; and in some, the loudest voice in the executive rank wins out.

By whatever means, a particular system is selected for development. The development team then obtains statements of requirements by considering outputs and inputs of any existing computer-based systems, by analyzing forms and reports for existing manual systems, and from interviews in which users describe the need for new reports, forms, queries, and other requirements.

REQUIREMENTS PHASE	EVALUATION PHASE	DESIGN PHASE	IMPLEMENTATION PHASE
Build users' data model	Evaluate data model	Transform model to DBMS-independent design	Implement DBMS-independent design

FIGURE 3.5
Systems development phases and database development tasks

From these requirements, the team develops the information system. If the system involves a database, then the team uses the requirements specifications to develop a data model. From the model, it develops a design and implements the database. When this system is finished, other projects are started to build additional information systems.

Proponents of the top-down approach claim that it is superior to the bottom-up approach because the data models (and subsequent systems) are developed with a global perspective. They claim that systems that are developed in this way have better interfaces to one another, are more consistent, and require far less rework and modification.

Proponents of the bottom-up approach claim that it is superior to top-down because it is faster and less risky. They claim that top-down modeling results in many studies that are difficult to complete and that the planning process often ends in **analysis-paralysis.** Although bottom-up modeling does not necessarily produce the optimum set of systems, it does produce useful systems quickly. The benefits of these systems begin accruing much faster than with top-down modeling, and they can more than pay for any rework or modification that will need to be done to adjust to a global perspective.

In this text, you will learn tools and techniques that can be used with either style of systems development. For example, you will learn both entity-relationship modeling in Chapter 4 and semantic object modeling in Chapter 5. Although both of these data models work with either top-down or bottom-up development, the entity-relationship approach is particularly effective with top-down development and the semantic object approach is particularly effective with bottom-up development.

REQUIREMENTS FOR DATABASE DEVELOPMENT

In terms of the database, the most important goal of the requirements phase is to create a model of the users' data. Whether this is done in top-down or in bottom-up style, it involves interviewing users, documenting requirements, and, from those requirements, building the data model. As stated previously, such a model identifies the things to be stored in the database and defines their structure and the relationships among them.

For example, consider Figure 3.6a, which is a list of orders made by a salesperson in a specific period of time. For this report to be produced by a database application, the database must contain the data shown. So the database developers need to examine the report and work backwards to the data that must be stored in the database. In this case, there must be data about salespeople (name and region) and data about orders (company, order date, and amount).

The problem in developing a database is that there is not just one requirement, but many, and the requirements usually overlap. The report in Figure 3.6b is also about salespeople, but, instead of orders, it lists commission checks. From this report, we can conclude that different types of orders occur and that each type has a different commission rate.

The orders implied by the report in Figure 3.6b somehow relate to the orders listed in Figure 3.6a, but it is not entirely clear how. The development team must determine this relationship by inference from reports and forms, from interviews with users, by drawing on the team's subject-matter expertise, and from other sources as well.

FIGURE 3.6
Example of two related reports

```
                       SALES REPORT
                     Week of March 4, 1991


   SALESPERSON: Mary Jones                     REGION: 4
   - - - - - - - - - - - - - - - - - - - - - - - - -

   Company              Order Date          Amount

   Ajax Construction      3/4/91            $2,768.55
   Beeline Delivery       3/5/91            $1,224.00
   Masterfield Tile       3/7/91            $2,898.65

                         Total Sales        $6,891.20
```

a. Sample SALES Report

```
             SALESPERSON COMMISSION REPORT
                       March 1991


   SALESPERSON: Mary Jones                     REGION: 4
   - - - - - - - - - - - - - - - - - - - - - - - - -

   Sales Category Total Sales  Commission Rate   Commission

   I              $5,898.33    3 percent          $176.95
   IV             $2,889.41    5 percent          $144.47
   VII            $9,445.85    1.5 percent        $850.13

                              Total Commission   $1,171.55
```

b. Sample COMMISSION Report

Figure 3.7 illustrates database development tasks from a different perspective. The user, on the right, states, in some fashion, the need for certain forms and reports. In their minds, users have certain models of the structure and relationship of things in their world. They cannot, however, say directly what those models are. If a developer were to ask the typical user, "What is the structure of the data model in your brain about sales-people?", the user would, at best, look quizzical. Users do not think that way.

Instead, the developers must infer, from forms and reports, the structure and relationships of the things to be stored in the database. Developers record these inferences in a data model. The data model is transformed into a database design and the design is implemented using a DBMS. Applications are then constructed that produce the reports and forms for the user.

Data Modeling

Building a data model is a process of inference. Reports and forms are like shadows projected on a wall. The users can describe the shadows, but they cannot describe the shapes that give rise to the shadows. The developers must infer, work backwards, and reverse engineer the structure and relationships of those shapes from the shadows.

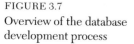

FIGURE 3.7
Overview of the database
development process

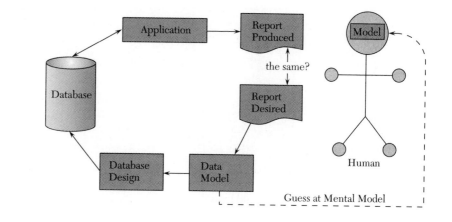

This inferencing process is, unfortunately, more art than science. It is possible for you to learn tools and techniques for data modeling; in fact, such tools and techniques are the subject of the next two chapters. But, using those tools and techniques is an art that requires experience guided by intuition. And, the quality of the data model matters.

If the documented data model accurately reflects the data model in the user's mind, then there is an excellent chance that the resulting reports will be close to the user's needs. If the documented data model inaccurately reflects the data model in the user's mind, then it is quite unlikely that the report to be produced will be close to the user's needs.

Modeling in Multi-user Systems

The data modeling process becomes even more complicated for multi-user workgroup and organizational databases. Since there are many users, there will be many individual data models. Occasionally, these data models will be inconsistent. Sometimes the inconsistencies will be resolvable; they may, for example, be only different in wording. Users may be employing the same term for different things, or different terms for the same things.

Sometimes, however, the differences will be irreconcilable. In such cases, the database developer must document the problematical differences and help the users resolve them. This usually means that some people have to change the way they view their world. A resolution must occur before the project can continue.

An even greater challenge is presented by multi-user systems in which no single user has a model of the complete structure. Each user understands a piece of the workgroup or organization's data model, but no single user understands all of it. In such cases, the database becomes the logical union of the pieces of the workgroup's or organization's model.

This text presents two alternative tools for building data models: the entity-relationship model and the semantic object model. Both models are structures for describing and documenting users' data requirements. See Figure 3.8.

User-oriented → Computer-oriented

REQUIREMENTS PHASE	EVALUATION PHASE	DESIGN PHASE	IMPLEMENTATION PHASE
Build users' data model	Evaluate data model	Transform model to DBMS-independent design	Implement DBMS-independent design
Entity-relationship model Semantic object model	Evaluation phase prototypes	Relational model	Relational model DBTG model DL/I model

FIGURE 3.8
Systems development phases, tasks, and tools

To avoid confusion, note the different uses of the term *model.* The development team analyzes the requirements and builds a *users' data model,* or *requirements data model.* This model is a representation of the structure and relationships of the things that need to be in the database to support the users' requirements.

To express the users' data model, the development team uses tools called the entity-relationship and the semantic object **data models.** These data models are representational tools that consist of language and diagramming standards for representing the users' data model. These data models play a role for database development similar to the role played by flowcharting and pseudocode for programming.

Hints for User Interviews

To build a data model, the development team interviews users of the applications and others who have expertise in the subject of the applications. Such interviews are critical throughout systems development, but they are most crucial during the requirements definition phase. Without a clear understanding of requirements, the development team will almost certainly build an inadequate and inaccurate data model. This will, in turn, lead to an inappropriate database design, which will lead to incorrect, contrived, and inefficient applications. Thus, informative interviews that produce accurate information are essential.

Since this is not a text on systems development, a comprehensive discussion of interviewing techniques is inappropriate. There are, however, several important points about interviewing users that relate directly to the development of database applications. First, the word *database* is dangerously general. When users hear it, they may expect the system to do far more than it actually will. Consequently, it is important from the outset to discuss the scope of the project with the user. Setting boundaries will help keep user expectations realistic and help keep the interview (and the project) on track.

Second, information users seem to want everything. You can expect that the answer to any question that begins "Would you like . . . ?" will be "YES!" Putting questions in that form invites serious problems. Instead, spend some time with users discussing their basic needs. After those have been identified and documented, then you might offer some other options.

Third, all users of workgroup and organizational database systems need to realize that the systems serve a community. The goal of the development project is to build applications that best satisfy the needs of the entire user community. At times, this may mean that the needs of one user or group conflict with those of another—both cannot be fully accommodated. The requirements of one user may have to be deferred in favor of the needs of another. A great deal of diplomacy is required to keep all users cooperating; often, this aspect of database systems development falls to the DBA (see Chapter 14).

Finally, keep in mind during the interview process that users interface with database *applications,* not with the database itself. Users "see" the database data through the windows of screens, menus, and reports. They do not see the database directly. Thus, when users express requirements, they are probably requirements for an application interface. Translating *application* requirements into *database* requirements is the responsibility of the development team. Users are more likely to respond effectively to questions such as "Does this sample report have all the data you need?" than to questions like "Do you need separate files for completed and uncompleted orders?"

DATA MODEL EVALUATION

So far, you have learned that data modeling is an artistic process that involves inferring mental models from a group of people who may or may not have a consistent view of the things in their environment. Reflect on that sentence and you will conclude that data modeling is a risky business. There are many, many opportunities for mistakes and few natural checks against them.

In general, the sooner a mistake is identified, the cheaper it will be to fix it. The situation is similar to that for architecture. Moving a wall on a blueprint is not too expensive. Moving the wall once it's been built is quite a bit more expensive. Moving the wall once the building has been sold and the occupants have moved in is very expensive.

So it is with database development, as shown in Figure 3.9. Fixing an error in a data model is cheap. Fixing the error after the data model has been transformed into a database design is more expensive, but usually tolerable. Fixing the error once the database

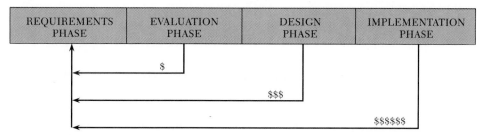

FIGURE 3.9
Relative cost of changes at systems development phases

has been implemented is more difficult. Fixing it after the applications have been constructed is quite expensive; and fixing an error after the users have begun to employ the system for their work can be exceedingly expensive.

Thus, it is quite important to exert every effort to ferret out and correct errors at the data modeling stage. This is the primary task of the evaluation phase as it pertains to database development.

A number of techniques can be used. One is to conduct data modeling review sessions. Some sessions are conducted with users who have been involved with the system as team members or interviewees. These people are asked to comment on whether the users' needs and perceptions have been adequately represented in the data model. Other sessions are conducted with people who are independent of and disinterested in the project. This group is asked to use their fresh perspective to compare the data model to the documented requirements and to identify possible inconsistencies, omissions, and errors.

A common problem, however, is that users often do not understand the concepts, language, and diagrams involved in data modeling. They have difficulty relating the model to their needs. In such cases, their review is meaningless, because it is based on factors unrelated to the problem.

In light of this situation, prototypes that illustrate questionable aspects of the data model are sometimes constructed for users' review. These prototypes are constructed in addition to those used during the requirements phase. The purpose of the evaluation-stage prototypes is to illustrate the consequences of decisions that were made when creating the data model.

Consider, for example, the process of generating a report as summarized in Figure 3.7. Suppose that the database development team has decided from the report shown as "Report Desired" that there will be a need to store SALESPERSON and ORDER data in the database. Suppose further that the team has decided that under no circumstances is an order placed by more than one salesperson.

Rather than ask the users directly whether or not this restriction is a good decision, the development team may elect to show the consequences of the decision to end-users in the form of a prototype report. The team will design this report so that only one salesperson appears per order. Then the team might ask a group of users to use the report for its intended purpose. The users might be asked, "Does the report need room for more than one salesperson?" Such a prototype illustrates the consequences of a decision about data model design.

At the end of the evaluation stage, the team produces an evaluated and approved data model—input for the design stage.

DATABASE DESIGN

During the design phase, the users' data model is transformed into a database design. As shown in Figure 3.8, a data model is closer to the user than the database design is. The data model represents the users' view of data. The database design represents the computer's view of the data.

The database design is expressed as a DBMS-independent description of the data that is to be stored in the database, the relationships among the data, and the data constraints. Keeping the description independent of particular DBMS structures ensures that the design is determined only by user requirements and not by peculiarities or limitations of the DBMS to be used.

In this text, we will express database design in terms of yet another model, the **relational data model.** Use of this model for design purposes is common practice today. The relational model is rich and general enough to represent the database structure without being so specific that it must be used with a particular DBMS. The relational model is a general stepping-stone on the way to database implementation.

An understanding of the concepts of the relational model is crucial to our discussion of database design. These concepts will be addressed in detail in Chapters 6 and 7. Then, application design will be treated in Chapter 8.

DATABASE IMPLEMENTATION

During implementation, the DBMS-independent design is converted (in truth, sometimes *contorted* is a better term) to fit the structures, peculiarities, and limitations of the DBMS that will be used to process it. The result of this conversion is a DBMS-dependent design that is then implemented using the data definition subsystem of the DBMS.

As you might guess, the nature of the conversion depends on the DBMS to be used. This is not as complicated as it might sound because, while there are dozens of different DBMS products, most of them fall into one of the three categories listed in Figure 3.8. Relational DBMS products conform closely to the relational model of data. Converting a design to this model is straightforward, because both the DBMS-independent design and the DBMS-dependent design are expressed in the same model.[3]

The second model, the DBTG model, represents a category of older DBMS products that are used, primarily, to process organizational databases. The full name of this model is the **CODASYL DBTG Model.** CODASYL, or Conference on Data Systems Languages, is the group that created the language COBOL. DBTG stands for Database Task Group—a subcommittee that defined this data model. For the most part, DBMS products based on this model are seldom used for new databases anymore, but there are many, older databases still in use that do use such products.

If you learn how to convert a DBMS-independent design into a DBTG design, you will know the essence of the conversion process for all of the DBMS products based on the DBTG model. Learning this conversion is the primary goal of Chapter 13.

The third model, DL/I, is the only survivor of a category of data models called the **hierarchical data model.** DL/I stands for data language, one, and it is part of a product called IMS/VS that was developed and licensed by the IBM Corporation. DL/I

---

[3]The term *relational model* is used in two senses here. It is a type of data model that is used to express database design. It is also a type of DBMS product that can be used to implement a database design. The dual uses are different but compatible.

is the database management portion of IMS/VS. DL/I, too, is fading from use, though there are still many organizational databases and applications in existence that are based on this model. The goal of Chapter 12 is to learn how to convert a DBMS-independent design into a DL/I design.

We will consider all three types of DBMS products for database implementation. The relational model, because it is the most common and will likely be the most popular in the future, will receive the most attention. You should also know DBTG and DL/I, however, because you may run into such systems—if for no other reason than to convert them to relational systems.

Summary

Developing a database and its attendant applications can be a complex task. It involves determining requirements, modeling data, and designing and implementing the database. Applications that process the database also need to be developed. In some cases, development means building an entirely new system. In other cases, it means adding new applications to an existing database.

There are many different processes for developing information systems. The process described in this chapter is typical; it involves five phases: definition, requirements, evaluation, design, and implementation.

During the definition phase, a development team is formed, the problem is defined, the scope of the project is established, and feasibility is assessed. The purpose of the second phase, requirements definition, is to determine, as specifically as possible, what the new system is to do. For database projects, this involves developing a model of the users' data and determining the needs for the functional components of each application that will use the database. To do this, users are interviewed to determine system outputs, inputs, and constraints on processing. Prototypes may be developed.

During the evaluation phase, various systems architectures are identified and one is chosen. Feasibility is reassessed and requirements are reviewed. The data model is evaluated for completeness and accuracy. Some requirements may be eliminated or deferred. The goal of the fourth stage, design, is to develop a blueprint for all five components of the information system. For the data component, the structure of the database is developed and includes a description of the files in the database, the data items within each file, and the relationships among the files. Constraints on data item values and relationships are specified. The design phase also includes the design of applications.

The final phase is implementation. Here, the system is constructed according to the design. The system's components are tested, and the system is installed.

Not all phases and components of an information system are relevant to a database course. Most of the discussion in this text will focus on the requirements, evaluation, design, and implementation phases of the data component.

There are two major styles for database development. Top-down development begins with the general and proceeds to the development of specific systems. Bottom-up development begins by building specific systems and works up to an overall set of systems.

Each style has strengths and weaknesses. The top-down approach is slow and expensive, but it may result in more robust and more smoothly integrated systems. The bottom-up approach is quicker and less expensive, but the systems produced may not integrate well. We will consider both approaches in this text.

The major task of the requirements phase for a database project is developing a model of the users' data. This includes identifying the entities to be stored in the database, the structure of those entities, and the relationships among them.

Building a data model is done by inference. Developers work backwards from forms and reports to infer the structure of the entities that give rise to those forms and reports. The process is more art than science. Multi-user databases are particularly challenging because the perceptions of the structure of the entities are shared among several or many people. In this text you will learn two tools, or models, for building data models: the entity-relationship model and the semantic object model. The requirements that are input to the data modeling process are most often gained by interviewing users. During these interviews, it is important for the development team to manage the users' expectations by describing the scope of the system. Users should also be encouraged to be realistic about their expectations and to understand that the database will serve a community of users. Finally, the development team should strive to talk to users in terms of the application interfaces they will see and not in terms of the structure of the database, which will most likely be hidden from them.

The major task during the evaluation phase is to evaluate the data model. Fixing errors in the data model at this phase is far cheaper than fixing them at later stages, or worse, after implementation. A number of techniques can be used. One is to conduct review sessions among team members. Another is to conduct a review by independent and disinterested personnel. Sometimes, the consequences of data model decisions need to be illustrated to users through prototypes.

During the design phase, the data model is translated into a DBMS-independent design. This design can be expressed in terms of a third model, the relational data model. During implementation, the DBMS-independent design is converted to a DBMS-dependent design. In this text we use three different models for DBMS-dependent design: the relational model, the CODASYL DBTG model, and DL/1. Finally, the DBMS-dependent design is implemented using the data definition subsystems of the DBMS.

||||||||||||||||||||||||||

GROUP I   QUESTIONS

3.1   Describe the basic tasks required to develop a database processing system. Use Figure 3.1 as an example.

3.2   List the five phases in the systems development process.

3.3   Summarize the major activities in the definition phase.

3.4   List four types of feasibility.

3.5   Summarize the purpose of the requirements phase. Describe the two major goals of this phase.

3.6   Describe the three portions of a users' data model.

3.7   What are prototypes and how are they used?

3.8   Summarize the major activities in the evaluation phase. What is the most important task during this phase with regard to a database?

3.9   What is the goal of the design phase?

3.10   What are the elements of a database design?

3.11   What is the purpose of the implementation phase?

3.12   What tasks are required for the data component during implementation?

3.13   Explain the phases and components of systems development that most concern the database.

3.14   Describe top-down and bottom-up data model building.

3.15   Compare the top-down and bottom-up approaches. Which do you think is better?

3.16   Explain how the process of developing a data model is a process of moving backwards.

3.17   Why is it inappropriate to ask users to describe the data model of their business environment?

3.18   How can users be asked about their data model?

3.19   Why is it important for the documented data model to fit the users' data model?

3.20   Describe special problems of data modeling in multi-user projects.

3.21   Name the two data modeling tools that will be presented in this text.

3.22   Describe two different uses for the term *model*.

3.23   Summarize the hints provided in this chapter for conducting user interviews during a database development project.

3.24   Describe two different methods for evaluating a data model.

3.25   How can prototypes be used to evaluate a data model?

3.26   Explain the term *DBMS-independent* database design. Why is it important to have such a design?

3.27   Name the model that we will use to express a DBMS-independent design.

3.28   Describe the nature of a DBMS-dependent design.

3.29   List the three models that you will learn in this text to express DBMS-dependent designs.

3.30   Locate a company that has developed a multi-user database system. Interview the users of this system. Determine the extent to which they are satisfied with the system. If possible, determine the process used to develop the database. To what extent did it agree with the process described here? How did it differ? Do you think the differences are an improvement over the process described in this chapter? Justify your answer.

Entity-Relationship Model

The goal of this chapter is to describe and use the first of several data models we will consider in this text. This model, called the entity-relationship model, is used to interpret, specify, and document requirements for database processing systems. It provides constructs for showing the overall structures of the users' data requirements. As such, it is often used for top-down database design.

In the next chapter, we will consider a second important data model, the semantic object model. This model also can be used to document requirements for databases, but it is closer to the user and allows for the specification of more details. It is often used for bottom-up database design.

These two models provide a language for expressing the structure of data relationships in the users' work environment. They are tools for expressing data needs. With programming, one learns pseudocode or flowcharting to express program logic; so, too, with database design, one learns data models to express data structure.

- DEFINITION OF THE ENTITY-RELATIONSHIP MODEL
- APPLICATIONS OF THE E-R MODEL
- AN IMPORTANT NOTE ABOUT DATA MODELING

Definition of the Entity-Relationship Model

The **entity-relationship model** (E-R model) was first described by Peter Chen in 1976.[1] In this paper, Chen set out the foundation of the model; it has since been extended and modified by Chen and many others. In addition, the E-R model has been made part of a number of CASE tools, which have also modified it. Today, there is no single, standardized E-R model. Instead, there is a set of common constructs from which most of the E-R variants are composed. This chapter describes these common constructs and shows how they are used. Be aware, however, that in the course of your career you may encounter variants on the approach presented here.

ENTITIES

An **entity** is something that can be identified in the users' work environment. It is something important to users in the context of the system that is to be built. Examples of entities are EMPLOYEE John Doe, CUSTOMER 12345, SALES-ORDER 1000, SALESPERSON Jane Smith, and PRODUCT A4200. Entities are grouped into **entity classes,** which are collections of entities of the same type. In this text, entity classes will be printed in all capital letters. Thus, the name EMPLOYEE is the name of a class of employee entities.

It is important for you to be able to distinguish between an entity class and an instance of an entity. An entity class is the general form or description of a thing, such as a CUSTOMER. An instance of an entity class is the representation of a particular entity, such as CUSTOMER 12345. It is common to use the terms *entity* and *entity class* interchangeably.

There are usually many instances of an entity in an entity class. For example, within the class, CUSTOMER, there are many instances—one for each customer represented in the database.

PROPERTIES

Entities have **properties,** or as they are sometimes called, **attributes,** that describe entity characteristics. Examples of properties are Employee-name, Date-of-hire, Job-skill-code, and so forth. In this text, properties will be printed with an initial capital letter. The E-R model assumes that all instances of a given entity class have the same properties.

As defined in the original E-R model, properties can be single or multiple valued. They can also be composite. For example, in SALES-ORDER, the composite property Item-data can be defined as the group {Item-description, Item-color, Item-size}. Some

---

[1]Peter Chen, "The Entity-Relationship Model—Toward a Unified View of Data," *ACM Transactions on Database Systems* 1 (March 1976), 9–36.

FIGURE 4.1
CUSTOMER—an example of an
entity

CUSTOMER
entity contains:
   Cust#
   Cust-name
   Address
   City
   State
   Zip
   Contact-name
   Phone-number

Two instances of CUSTOMER:

12345	67890
Ajax Manufacturing	Jefferson Dance Club
123 Elm St	345 - 10th Avenue
Memphis	Boston
TN	MA
32455	01234
P. Schwartz	Frita Bellingsley
223-5567	210-8896

implementations of the E-R model, however, do not allow multivalued or composite properties.

Entity instances have names that identify them. EMPLOYEE instances have Social-security-number, CUSTOMERs have Customer-number or Customer-name, SALES-ORDERs have Order-number, and so forth. The identifier of an entity instance is one of its properties. In order to find a particular entity instance, such entity names must have unique values. In cases where duplication can occur (Customer-name, for example), additional data, such as address or telephone number, is added to form a composite identifier.

Figure 4.1 shows an entity and two instances of it.

RELATIONSHIPS

Entities can be associated with one another. These associations are called **relationships;** there are relationship classes and relationship instances. Relationship classes are associations among entity classes. Relationship instances are associations among entity instances. Relationships can have properties.

As defined in the original E-R model, relationships can exist among many entities. The number of entities involved in a relationship is called the **degree** of the relationship. In Figure 4.2a, the SP-ORDER relationship is of degree 2 because each instance of the relationship involves two entity instances: a SALESPERSON entity instance and an

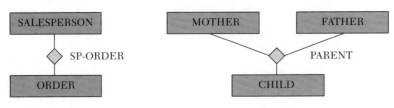

a. Example relationship of degree 2   b. Example relationship of degree 3

FIGURE 4.2
Relationships of different degrees

ORDER entity instance.[2] In Figure 4.2b, the PARENT relationship is of degree 3 since each instance involves three entities: MOTHER, FATHER, and CHILD.

Although the E-R model allows for relationships of any degree, almost all the applications of the model involve only relationships of degree 2. Such relationships are sometimes called **binary relationships.**

Three Types of Binary Relationship

Figure 4.3 shows the three fundamental types of binary relationship. In a 1:1 (read "one-to-one") relationship, a single entity instance of one type is related to a single entity instance of another type. In Figure 4.3a, the AUTO-ASSIGNMENT relationship associates a single EMPLOYEE to a single AUTO. According to this diagram, no employee has more than one automobile assigned, and no automobile is assigned to more than one employee.

Figure 4.3b shows the second type of relationship, 1:N (read "one-to-N" or "one-to-many"). In this relationship, called the DORM-OCCUPANT relationship, a single instance of DORMITORY relates to many instances of STUDENT. According to this sketch, a dormitory has many students, but a student has only one dormitory.

Observe that the positions of the 1 and the N are significant. The 1 is close to the line connecting DORMITORY. This means the 1 refers to the DORMITORY side of the relationship. The N is close to the line connecting STUDENT. This means the N refers to the STUDENT side of the relationship. If the 1 and N were reversed, and the relationship were written N:1, then a DORMITORY would have one STUDENT, and a STUDENT would have many DORMITORIES. This is, of course, not the case.

Figure 4.3c shows the third type of binary relationship, N:M (read "N-to-M" or "many-to-many"). This relationship is named STUDENT-CLUB and it relates instances of STUDENT to instances of CLUB. A student can join more than one club, and a club has many students as members.

The numbers inside the relationship diamond show the maximum number of entities that can occur on a given side of the relationship. Such constraints are sometimes called

---

[2]For brevity, we will sometimes drop the word *instance* where the context makes it clear that an instance rather than an entity class is involved.

FIGURE 4.3
Three types of binary relationship

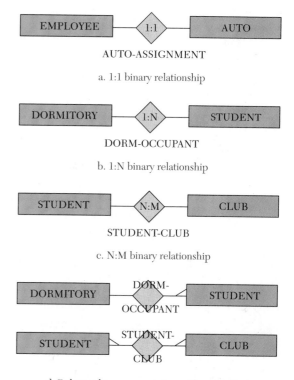

a. 1:1 binary relationship

b. 1:N binary relationship

c. N:M binary relationship

d. Relationship representation with crow's feet

the relationship's **maximum cardinality.** The relationship in Figure 4.3b, for example, is said to have a maximum cardinality of 1:N.

Relationships of the types shown in Figure 4.3 are sometimes called **HAS-A relationships.** This term is used because an entity *has a* relationship to another entity. For example, an EMPLOYEE has an AUTO, a STUDENT has a DORMITORY, and a CLUB has STUDENTs. You will learn about another type of relationship, IS-A relationships, later in this chapter.

Entity-Relationship Diagrams

The sketches in Figure 4.3 are called **entity-relationship** or **E-R diagrams.** Such diagrams are standardized, but loosely. According to this (loose) standard, entity classes are shown by rectangles, relationships are shown by diamonds, and the maximum cardinality of the relationship is shown inside the diamond. The name of the entity is shown inside the rectangle and the name of the relationship is shown nearby the diamond.

In some E-R diagrams, the name of the relationship is shown inside the diamond, but this can make the diagram look awkward since the diamonds may have to be large and out of scale to include the relationship name. To avoid this, relationship names are sometimes written over the diamond. When the name is placed inside or on top of the diamond, then the relationship cardinality is shown by placing crow's feet on the lines connecting to entity(ies) on the many side of the relationship. Figure 4.3d shows the DORM-OCCUPANT and STUDENT-CLUB relationships with such crow's feet.

As stated, the maximum cardinality indicates the maximum number of entities that can be involved. The diagrams do not indicate the minimum. For example, in Figure 4.3b, a student relates, as a maximum, to one dormitory. This diagram does not show whether a student *must be* related to a dormitory instance.

A number of different ways are used to show **minimum cardinality.** One way, illustrated in Figure 4.4, is to place a hash mark across the relationship line to indicate that an entity must exist in the relationship and to place an oval across the relationship line to indicate that an entity may or may not exist in the relationship. Thus, Figure 4.4 shows that a STUDENT must exist for a DORMITORY, but a DORMITORY may or may not exist for a STUDENT. Thus, the complete relationship restrictions are: a DORMITORY has a minimum cardinality of one STUDENT and maximum cardinality of many. A STUDENT has a minimum cardinality of zero DORMITORY and a maximum cardinality of one.

It is possible for a relationship to exist among entities of the same class. For example, the relationship ROOMS-WITH could be defined on the entity STUDENT. Figure 4.5a shows such a relationship and Figure 4.5b shows instances of entities that conform to this relationship. Relationships among entities of a single class are sometimes called **recursive relationships.**

Properties in Entity-Relationship Diagrams

In some versions of E-R diagrams, properties are shown in ellipses and connected to the entity or relationship to which they belong. Figure 4.6a shows the DORMITORY and STUDENT entities and the DORM-OCCUPANT relationship with properties. As shown, DORMITORY has Dorm-name, Location, and Number-of-rooms properties and STUDENT has Student#, Student-name, and Student-year properties. The relationship DORM-OCCUPANT has the property Rent, which shows the amount of rent paid by a particular student in a particular dorm.

For many examples that arise in business, however, there are too many properties to list them on the E-R diagram. Doing so makes the diagram cluttered and difficult to interpret. In these cases, entity properties are listed separately as shown in Figure 4.6b.

WEAK ENTITIES

The entity-relationship model defines a special type of entity called a **weak entity.** Such entities are those whose presence in the database depends on the presence of another entity. An example commonly shown for the E-R model is that between employees and their dependents. In Figure 4.7a, the entity DEPENDENT depends on the presence of the entity EMPLOYEE. This means that DEPENDENT data is stored in the database only if the DEPENDENT has a relationship to an EMPLOYEE entity.

As shown in this figure, weak entities are signified by rounding the corners of the entity rectangle. Further, the relationship on which the entity depends for its existence

FIGURE 4.4
Relationship with minimum
cardinality shown

DORM-OCCUPANT

is shown in a diamond with rounded corners. Alternatively, in some E-R diagrams (not shown here), weak entities are depicted by using a double line for the boundary of the weak entity rectangle and double diamonds for the relationship upon which the entity depends.

As originally defined in the E-R model, the concept of existence dependence is actually ambiguous. Let's compare the entity in Figure 4.7b with that in Figure 4.7a. In Figure 4.7b, APPOINTMENT has properties Client#, Date, Time, and Charge. Clearly, if the client does not exist, then no appointment entity for that client can exist. Someone must physically exist to have an appointment.

Although both DEPENDENT and APPOINTMENT are shown as weak entities, there is an important difference between them. A dependent person can physically exist even if there is no employee that claims that person as a dependent. That person's very existence does not depend on the existence of someone who claims him or her as a dependent. For APPOINTMENT, however, no entity can exist without a client. The very existence of an appointment depends on the existence of a client.

It is usually easy to tell the difference between entities like APPOINTMENT and DEPENDENT. Entities whose very existence depends on another entity usually do not have a name (identifier) of their own. Instead, their identifier includes the identifier of the entity on which they depend. The identifier of APPOINTMENT is the group (Client#, Date, Time); Client# is the identifier of CLIENT. But, the identifier of DEPENDENT is Social-security-number. That identifier does not include the name of any other entity.

FIGURE 4.5
Recursive relationship

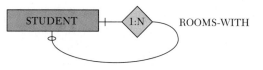

ROOMS-WITH

a. Example recursive relationship

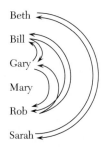

b. Example data for ROOMS-WITH relationship

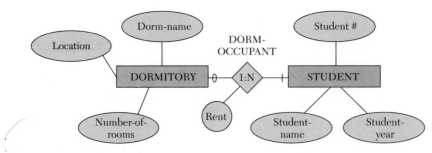

a. Entity-relationship diagram with properties shown

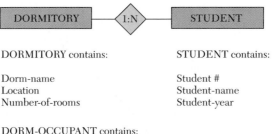

DORMITORY contains:

Dorm-name
Location
Number-of-rooms

STUDENT contains:

Student #
Student-name
Student-year

DORM-OCCUPANT contains:

Rent

b. Entity-relationship diagram with properties listed seperately

FIGURE 4.6
Showing properties in entity relationship diagrams

Entities like APPOINTMENT are sometimes called **ID-dependent entities.** Such entities are a subclass of weak entities.

For now, just note this ambiguity. We will address it again in the next chapter when we discuss semantic objects. There, the best way to model these types of existence dependence will become clearer.

FIGURE 4.7
Weak entities

a. Example of weak entity

b. ID-dependent entity

SUBTYPE ENTITIES

Some entities are not homogeneous but rather consist of an amalgamation of subgroups. Consider, for example, CLIENT with properties Client#, Client-name, and Amount-due. Suppose that a CLIENT can be an individual, a partnership, or a corporation, and that additional data is to be stored depending on the type. Assume the additional data is as follows:

INDIVIDUAL-CLIENT: Address, Social-security-number
PARTNERSHIP-CLIENT: Managing-partner-name, Address, Tax-identification-number
CORPORATE-CLIENT: Contact-person, Phone, Tax-identification-number

Now, one possibility is to allocate all of these properties to the entity CLIENT as shown in Figure 4.8a. In this case, some of the properties are inapplicable. Managing-partner-name has no meaning for an individual or corporate client, and so its value would be null or not applicable.

A closer fitting model, however, would instead define three subtype entities as shown in Figure 4.8b. Here INDIVIDUAL-CLIENT, PARTNERSHIP-CLIENT, and CORPORATE-CLIENT entities are shown as **subtypes** of CLIENT. CLIENT, in turn, is called a **supertype** of the INDIVIDUAL-CLIENT, PARTNERSHIP-CLIENT, and CORPORATE-CLIENT entities.

The ϵ next to the relationship lines indicates that INDIVIDUAL-CLIENT, PARTNERSHIP-CLIENT, and CORPORATE-CLIENT are subtypes of CLIENT. Observe that each subtype entity must belong to the supertype CLIENT. The curved line with a 1 next to it indicates that a CLIENT entity must belong to one and only one subtype. It means that the subtypes are exclusive and that one of them is required.

Subtypes are not always mutually exclusive nor are they always required. Figure 4.8c shows CLIENT-USING subtypes within CLIENT. The m indicates that CLIENT may belong from zero to many CLIENT-USING subtypes.

Structures such as this are sometimes called **generalization hierarchies** because CLIENT is a generalization of the three subtypes. Sometimes, too, this relationship type is called an **IS-A relationship** since, in Figure 4.8b, INDIVIDUAL-CLIENT *is a* CLIENT as are PARTNERSHIP-CLIENT and CORPORATE-CLIENT also CLIENTs.

A way to verify that the term *IS-A* is appropriate is to consider the identifier of all four of these entities. They all have the same identifier: Client#. Thus, they all have the same name and hence all refer to the same entity. Contrast this situation with the HAS-A relationships shown in Figure 4.3.

Generalization hierarchies have a special characteristic called **inheritance.** This means that entities in subtypes inherit properties of the supertype entity class. PARTNERSHIP-CLIENT for example, inherits Client-name and Amount-due from CLIENT. Again, for inheritance to be appropriate, both of these entity classes must have the same identifier.

FIGURE 4.8
Subtype entities

CLIENT contains:

Client #
Client-name
Amount-due
Address
Social-security-number
Managing-partner-name
Tax-identification-number
Contact-person
Phone

a. CLIENT without subtype entities

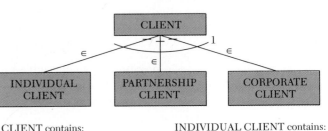

CLIENT contains: INDIVIDUAL CLIENT contains:

Client #   Address
Client-name   Social-security-number
Amount-due

PARTNERSHIP CLIENT contains: CORPORATE CLIENT contains:

Managing-partner-name   Contact-person
Address   Phone
Tax-identification-number   Tax-identification-number

b. CLIENT with subtype entities

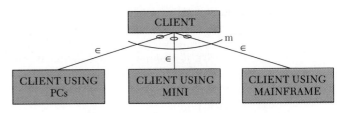

c. Nonexclusive subtypes with optional supertype

EXAMPLE

Figure 4.9 is an example E-R diagram including all of the elements of the E-R model
that we have discussed. This diagram shows the entities and relationships for an engineering consulting company that provides engineering analysis of homes and other
buildings and facilities.

FIGURE 4.9
Example entity-relationship
diagram

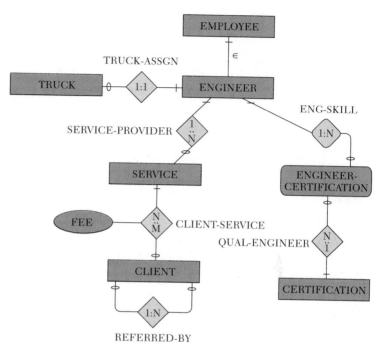

There is an entity class for the company's employees. Some **EMPLOYEE**s are ENGI-NEERs, so there is a subtype relationship between **EMPLOYEE** and **ENGINEER**. Every **ENGINEER** must be an **EMPLOYEE**. ENGINEER has a 1:1 relationship to TRUCK. Further, each TRUCK must be assigned to an ENGINEER, but not all ENGI-NEERs have a TRUCK.

ENGINEERs provide SERVICEs to CLIENTs. An ENGINEER can provide from zero to many services, but a given SERVICE must be provided by an ENGINEER and can only be provided by that ENGINEER. CLIENTs have many SERVICEs and a SER-VICE can be requested by many CLIENTs. A CLIENT must have purchased at least one SERVICE, but SERVICE need not have any CLIENTs. The CLIENT-SERVICE relationship has a property Fee, which shows the amount that a particular client paid for a particular service. (Other properties of entities and relationships are not shown in this diagram.)

Sometimes CLIENTs refer one another. This fact is shown by the recursive relation-ship REFERRED-BY. A given CLIENT can refer one or more other CLIENTs. A CLI-ENT may or may not have been referred by another client. Also, a CLIENT may be referred by only one CLIENT.

The ENGINEER-CERTIFICATION entity shows that a given engineer has passed a given certification. An ENGINEER may have many certifications. ENGINEER-CER-TIFICATION is existence dependent on ENGINEER through the relationship ENG-SKILL. CERTIFICATION is the entity that contains a description about a particular certification.

DOCUMENTATION OF PROCESSING CONSTRAINTS

Often during the creation of a data model, systems developers will discover the existence of constraints on processing. Even though finding such constraints is not the primary purpose of the data modeling activity, it is useful and important to think about and document such constraints as the model is completed. Otherwise, valuable knowledge about processing restrictions can be lost.

Examine the E-R diagram in Figure 4.9. What restrictions are there on data changes to each of the entities in this diagram? For example, consider the ENGINEER entity. Are there restrictions on adding new ENGINEERs? The diagram shows that an ENGINEER must be an EMPLOYEE, so, before the ENGINEER data can be added, the EMPLOYEE data must be added.

What about modifications to ENGINEER data? If any of the properties of ENGINEER have been propagated to other entities, then changes made to ENGINEER must be made to the propagated properties. At this stage of design, this is seldom the case.

This situation is different for deletions, however. If an ENGINEER entity is deleted, then the TRUCK, SERVICE, and ENGINEER-CERTIFICATION entities will be affected. Depending on the requirements, these other entities may be assigned to another ENGINEER entity, or they may themselves be deleted (sometimes called a cascading deletion), or the deletion may be disallowed. Any of these actions is legitimate. The choice of one depends on the nature of the application's requirements.

When processing constraints are identified, they should be documented as part of the data model. Often a list of such constraints is attached to the E-R diagram. Some CASE tools provide facilities for recording such constraints.

Applications of the E-R Model

A common application of the E-R model is for top-down database design. To do this, the development team interviews users and identifies the entities and relationships that are within the scope of the project. At the same time, properties of entities and relationships are also documented.

A number of sources of knowledge are used for the modeling process. In addition to interviews, the developers can study existing forms and reports. They can also examine the queries that users typically make of each other (or existing related databases). From all of this, a model is developed and then reviewed with the users for accuracy and relevancy. Adjustments are made as necessary.

ENTITY-RELATIONSHIP MODEL AND CASE TOOLS

Developing a data model using the entity-relationship model has become easier in recent years, because tools for building E-R diagrams are included in many popular CASE products. Products such as IEW, IEF, DEFT, Accelerator, Design/1, and others have drawing and diagramming facilities to create E-R diagrams. Such products also integrate entities with database relations that represent them. This can facilitate database administration, management, and maintenance.

We will not assume use of a CASE tool for the discussions in this text. If your university has such a tool, however, by all means use it to create E-R diagrams for exercises you are assigned. E-R diagrams created using these tools are generally more visually pleasing, and they are far easier to change and adapt.

To understand the creation of E-R diagrams more fully, consider the following two examples.

JEFFERSON DANCE CLUB

Jefferson Dance Club teaches social dancing and offers both private and group lessons. Jefferson charges $45 per hour per student (or couple) for a private lesson and $6 per hour per student for a group lesson. Private lessons are offered throughout the day, from noon until 10 PM, six days a week. Group lessons are offered in the evenings.

Jefferson employs two types of instructor: full-time salaried instructors and part-time teachers. The full-time instructors are paid a fixed amount per week. Part-time instructors are paid either a set amount for an evening or a set amount for teaching a particular class.

In addition to the lessons, Jefferson also sponsors two weekly social dances featuring recorded music. The admission charge is $5 per person. The Friday night dance is the more popular and averages around eighty people; the Sunday night dance has about thirty attendees. The purpose of the dances is to give the students an environment to practice their skills. No food or drinks are served.

Jefferson would like to develop an information system to keep track of students and the classes they have taken. Jefferson managers would also like to know how many and which types of lessons have been taught by each teacher. They'd like to be able to compute an average cost per lesson for each of their instructors.

Entities

Normally, the best way to begin an entity-relationship model is to determine potential entities. Entities are usually represented by nouns in documents or in interviews. A search of the preceding paragraphs for important nouns that relate to the information system reveals the following list:

- Private-lesson
- Group-lesson
- Teacher
- Full-time-teacher
- Part-time-teacher
- Dance
- Customer

Clearly, the nouns *private-lesson* and *group-lesson* have something in common as do the nouns *teacher, full-time-teacher,* and *part-time-teacher.* One solution is to define an entity LESSON, with subtypes PRIVATE-LESSON and GROUP-LESSON and another entity TEACHER with subtypes FULL-TIME-TEACHER and PART-TIME-TEACHER. Additional entities are DANCE and CUSTOMER.

As stated in Chapter 3, data modeling is as much art as it is science. The solution just described is one of several feasible solutions. A second solution is to eliminate LESSON and TEACHER from the list in the preceding paragraph and to have no subtypes at all. A third solution is to eliminate LESSON (since lesson was never mentioned by itself as a noun), but to keep TEACHER and its subtypes. Here, we will choose the third case because it seems to be the best fit for the data we have. Thus, the list of entities is: PRIVATE-LESSON, GROUP-LESSON, TEACHER, FULL-TIME-TEACHER, PART-TIME-TEACHER, DANCE, and CUSTOMER.

Choosing among these alternatives requires an analysis of the requirements and consideration of the design implications of each of them. Sometimes it helps to consider the properties of the entities involved. If, for example, the entity LESSON has no properties other than its identifier, then it is not required.

In Chapter 3, we discussed the evaluation phase of systems development. Sometimes, data model alternatives cannot be readily eliminated in the requirements stage. In such a case, the alternatives are carried forward to the evaluation stage and a formal analysis of alternatives is conducted.

Relationships

To begin, TEACHER has two subtype entities, FULL-TIME-TEACHER and PART-TIME-TEACHER. A given teacher must be one or the other; the subtypes are mutually exclusive.

Consider next the relationships between TEACHER and PRIVATE-LESSON and GROUP-LESSON. A TEACHER can teach many PRIVATE-LESSONs, and normally a PRIVATE-LESSON is taught by a single teacher. However, further discussion with Jefferson management reveals that, for advanced dancers, especially those preparing for competitions, there are sometimes two teachers involved in a private lesson. Therefore, the relationship between TEACHER and PRIVATE-LESSON must be many-to-many. Assume, however, that only one teacher is involved in a group lesson. The relationships just described are shown in Figure 4.10.

CUSTOMERs can take either PRIVATE-LESSONs or GROUP-LESSONs. Sometimes a lesson is taken by a single individual and sometimes by a couple. There are two ways this situation can be modeled. For one, an entity COUPLE can be defined as having a one-to-two relationship to CUSTOMER. Then either CUSTOMER or COUPLE can have a relationship to PRIVATE-LESSON. We assume that couples do not take group lessons, or if they do, it is unimportant to store that fact in the database. This alternative is shown in Figure 4.11a.

PRIVATE-LESSON is existence dependent on CUSTOMER or COUPLE. That is, a lesson does not exist unless it is given to either a CUSTOMER or to a COUPLE. Observe the horizontal line underneath CUSTOMER and COUPLE. The 1 next to this

FIGURE 4.10
Initial E-R diagram for Jefferson
Dance Club

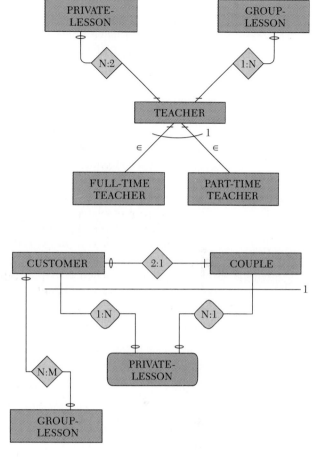

FIGURE 4.11
Alternatives for representing
CUSTOMER

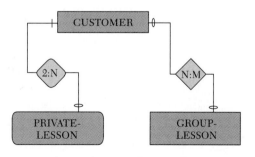

a. E-R diagram showing COUPLE entity

b. E-R diagram without couples

line indicates that PRIVATE-LESSON must have at least one CUSTOMER or one COUPLE. This makes sense since PRIVATE-LESSON is dependent on them.

Another alternative is not to represent couples. Instead, the relationship between CUSTOMER and PRIVATE-LESSON is modeled as many-to-many. More precisely, that relationship is 1- or 2-to-many. This alternative is shown in Figure 4.11b. Although the model is not as detailed as that in Figure 4.11a, it may very well suffice for Jefferson's purposes.

The last relationship possibility to consider is that between DANCE and other entities. Both customers and teachers attend dances. The developers need to decide whether it is important to store these relationships. Does Jefferson really need to know which customers have attended which dances? Do Jefferson's managers really want to record that in a computer-based information system as customers enter the door? Do the customers want that fact recorded? Most likely, this is not a relationship that needs or should be stored in the database.

The situation is different between DANCE and TEACHER. Jefferson likes some of its teachers to be present at each dance. In order to be equitable about this, Jefferson management has developed a schedule for teacher attendance at dances. Developing and recording this schedule requires that the database contain the DANCE-TEACHER relationship. It is many-to-many.

E-R Diagram for Jefferson Dance Club

Figure 4.12 is the E-R diagram for the model described in this section. We have not named the relationships in this diagram. Doing so would make the diagrams more true to form, but, for the data we have, naming relationships adds little.

FIGURE 4.12
Final E-R diagram for Jefferson
Dance Club

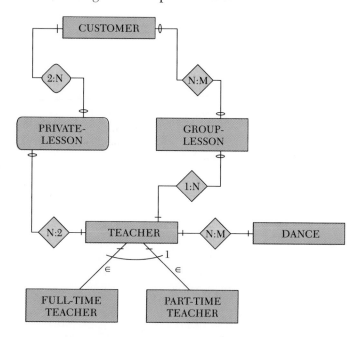

Observe that PRIVATE-LESSON is existence dependent on CUSTOMER, but GROUP-LESSON is not. This is so because group lessons are scheduled long before any customer signs up. They will be held even if no customer shows up. This situation is not true for private-lessons. They are only scheduled at the customer's request. Also observe that this model does not represent couples.

Once a model such as this is developed, it is important to verify its accuracy and completeness in the context of the requirements. This usually means verifying it with the users.

EVALUATING THE E-R DATA MODEL

As shown in Figure 3.9 in the previous chapter, it is easier and cheaper to correct errors early in the database development process rather than later. For example, changing the maximum cardinality of a relationship from 1:N to N:M in the data modeling stage is simply a matter of recording the change in the E-R diagram. However, once the database has been designed and loaded with data and application programs written to process the database, making such a change will involve considerable rework, possibly even hundreds of labor hours. It is important, therefore, to evaluate the data model before proceeding to design.

One evaluation technique is to consider the E-R data model in the context of possible queries that might be posed to a database having the structure implied by the model. For example, consider the diagram in Figure 4.12. What questions could be answered from a database that was implemented according to this design?

- Who has taught which private lessons?
- Which customers have taken a private lesson taught by Jack?
- Who are the full-time teachers?
- Which teachers are scheduled to attend the dance on Friday?

When evaluating an E-R data model, you can construct such questions and show them to the users. Users can then be asked to construct their own list of questions that they would like to ask. Their list of questions can then be posed against the design to check the design's appropriateness. For example, suppose that the users posed the following question:

Which customers attended last week's Friday night dance?

The designers of the data model in Figure 4.12 would conclude that their design was not correct, because it is not possible to answer this question from their E-R model. If that question needs to be answered, then a relationship between CUSTOMER and DANCE must be developed.

Clearly, such an informal and loosely structured process cannot be used to *prove* that a design is correct. It is, however, a pragmatic technique that can be used to verify the potential correctness of a design. And, it's far better than no evaluation at all!

Consider another example.

SAN JUAN SAILBOAT CHARTERS

San Juan Sailboat Charters is an agent that leases sailboats to customers for a fee. San Juan does not own any sailboats. Instead, it leases sailboats on behalf of boat owners who wish to earn some income when they are not using their boats. San Juan charges a fee for its service, and it specializes in boats that can be used for multiday or week charters. The smallest sailboat is twenty-eight feet and the largest is forty-four.

San Juan Operations

Each sailboat is fully equipped at the time it is leased. Most of the equipment is provided by the owners, but some is added by San Juan. Owner-provided equipment includes equipment that is fixed on the boat such as radios, compasses, depth indicators and other instrumentation, stoves, refrigerators, and so forth. Other owner-provided equipment is not installed as part of the boat. Such equipment includes sails, lines, anchors, dinghies, life preservers, and, within the cabin, dishes, silverware, cooking utensils, bedding, and the like.

San Juan provides consumable equipment, which could be considered supplies. These include charts, navigation books, tide and current tables, soap, dish towels, toilet paper, and similar items.

An important part of San Juan's responsibilities is to keep track of equipment on the boat. Much of the boat equipment is expensive, and, some of it, particularly that which is not attached to the boat, can easily be lost or stolen. Customers are responsible for all equipment during the period of their charter.

San Juan likes to keep accurate records of its customers and the charters they have made. This is done not only for marketing but also to keep a list of which customers have accomplished which trips. Some itineraries and weather conditions are more dangerous than others and San Juan likes to know which customers have what experience.

Most of San Juan's business is bare-boat chartering, which means that no skipper or other crew is provided. In some cases, however, customers request the services of a skipper or other crew member. San Juan hires such personnel on a part-time basis.

Sailboats often need maintenance. San Juan is required by its contract with the boat owners to keep accurate records of all maintenance activities and costs, including normal activities, such as cleaning or engine oil changes, and unscheduled repairs.

In some cases, repairs are necessary during a charter. A boat engine, for example, might fail while the boat is located a considerable distance away from San Juan's facility. In this case, the customers radio the San Juan dispatcher, who determines the best facility to make the repair and sends its personnel to the disabled boat. Dispatchers need information about repair facilities as well as past history of repair quality and costs to make these decisions.

Before you continue reading, you might try to produce an entity-relationship diagram on your own. Examine the foregoing statements and look for nouns that might be important to the design. Then, check the possible relationships among the entities. Finally, if you wish, list likely properties for each entity or relationship.

Entities

The data model required for San Juan Charters is more complicated than that for the Jefferson Dance Club. Potential entities are shown in Figure 4.13a. The equipment-related entities suggest possible subtypes, and defining subtypes is certainly a feasible alternative. So that we can illustrate another design approach, however, we will not define subtypes in this case.

Consider the equipment-related entities. Why does San Juan need to model them? The goal is not to keep track of their characteristics. We do not need to maintain data about the length chain on each anchor, for example. Instead, the requirement is just to

LEASE
BOAT
CUSTOMER
OWNER
EQUIPMENT
OWNER-PROVIDED-EQUIPMENT
FIXED OWNER-EQUIPMENT
REMOVABLE OWNER-EQUIPMENT
SAN-JUAN-PROVIDED-EQUIPMENT
ITINERARY/WEATHER
CHARTER
PART-TIME-CREW
SCHEDULED-MAINTENANCE
UNSCHEDULED-MAINTENANCE
REPAIRS
REPAIR-FACILITY

a. Possible entities for San Juan Charters

LEASE or CHARTER (synonyms)
BOAT
CUSTOMER
OWNER
EQUIPMENT
ITINERARY/WEATHER
PART-TIME-CREW
SCHEDULED-MAINTENANCE
REPAIR or UNSCHEDULED-MAINTENANCE (synonyms)
REPAIR-FACILITY

b. Entities selected for the E-R design

FIGURE 4.13
Entities for San Juan Charters

keep track of the items and their type. This can be done without keeping detailed records of the particular subtypes of equipment. Thus, for this design, we will place all types of equipment into the entity EQUIPMENT.

Ownership of equipment will be established by defining a relationship between EQUIPMENT and OWNER. If San Juan Charters is allowed to be an instance of OWNER, then all of the equipment that it owns can be carried by this relationship. Similarly, from the case description, there is no reason to define equipment that is attached to boats differently than that which is not attached. An accurate list can be produced without this division.

Figure 4.13b shows the final list of entities. Note that LEASE and CHARTER are synonyms; they refer to the same transaction. We show both names here so that they can be related to the case description.

It is possible that SCHEDULED-MAINTENANCE should be combined with UNSCHEDULED-MAINTENANCE. One way to decide is to examine the properties of each of these entities. If they are the same, then the two entity classes should be merged into one. Also observe that REPAIR and UNSCHEDULED-MAINTENANCE are defined as synonyms.

Relationships

Figure 4.14 is an entity-relationship diagram for San Juan Charters. For the most part, the relationships in this diagram are straightforward. The relationship between EQUIP-MENT and LEASE is arguable. One might say that EQUIPMENT should be related to BOAT and not to LEASE, or that some EQUIPMENT should be related to BOAT (the

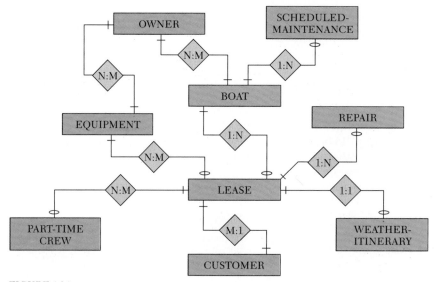

FIGURE 4.14
E-R diagram for San Juan Charters

equipment that stays with the boat) and the other equipment should be related to LEASE. These changes would be feasible alternatives to the design shown in Figure 4.14.

Observe, too, that SCHEDULED-MAINTENANCE is related to BOAT, but REPAIR (UNSCHEDULED-MAINTENANCE) is related to LEASE. This implies that no repair action is required when the boat is not being leased. Perhaps this is unrealistic.

Finally, LEASE and ITINERARY-WEATHER have a 1:1 relationship. They also have the same identifying properties. Therefore, it would be possible, and might even be preferable, to combine them into one entity class.

An Important Note about Data Modeling

As you can see, there are many different ways of modeling a given business situation. The variety becomes even greater as the complexity of the application increases. Often, dozens of models are feasible, and it can be difficult to choose among them.

Sometimes, when evaluating alternatives, project team members engage in discussions and arguments about which data model best represents the real world. These discussions are misguided. Databases do not model the real world, though it is a common misconception that they do.

Rather, databases are models of users' models of the world (or, more to the point, of their business environment). The question to ask when evaluating alternative data models is not "Does this design accurately represent the real world?" but rather, "Does this design accurately represent the users' model of his or her environment?" The goal is to develop a design that fits the user's mental conception of what he or she wants to track.

In fact, Immanuel Kant and other philosophers have argued that it is impossible for humans to build models of what actually exists. They claim the essence of things is forever unknowable by humans.[3] Extending this line of argument to computer systems, Winograd and Flores have stated that humans develop, in their societies, systems of tokens that enable them to operate with success in the world. A series of tokens is not a model of the infinitude of reality, but rather, a system that enables users to coordinate their activities in a successful way, and nothing more.[4]

Thus, computer systems need to model and represent the users' communications with one another. They do not model anything other than that system of tokens and communications.

---

[3]"We cannot indeed, beyond all possible experience, form a definitive concept of what things in themselves may be. Yet we are not at liberty to abstain entirely from inquiring into them; for experience never satisfies reason fully but, in answering questions, refers us further and further back and leaves us dissatisfied with regard to the complete solution." Immanuel Kant, *Prolegomena to Any Future Metaphysics* (Indianapolis: Bobbs-Merrill, 1950), 100.

[4]Terry Winograd and F. Flores, *Understanding Computers and Cognition* (Reading, Mass.: Addison-Wesley, 1986).

So, on the bottom line, learn to ask these questions: "Does this model accurately reflect the users' perceptions and mental models of their world? Will it help users respond consistently and successfully with one another and with their clients?" It is pointless for one analyst to claim that his or her model is a better representation of reality. Instead, the point is to develop a model that well represents the users' model of his or her business environment.

Summary

The entity-relationship model was first described by Peter Chen. With this model, entities, which are identifiable things of importance to the users, are defined. All of the entities of a given type form an entity class. A particular entity is called an instance. Entities have properties that describe their characteristics. One or more properties identifies an entity.

Relationships are associations among entities. The E-R model explicitly defines relationships; each relationship has a name and there are relationship classes as well as relationship instances.

The degree of the relationship is the number of entities that participate in the relationship. Most relationships are binary. There are three types of binary relationship: 1:1, 1:N, and N:M.

With entity-relationship diagrams, entities are shown in rectangles and relationships are shown in diamonds. The maximum cardinality of the relationship is shown within the diamond. The minimum cardinality is indicated by a hash mark or by an oval. Relationships that connect entity instances of the same class are called recursive. Properties can be shown in an E-R diagram in ellipses or in a separate table.

A weak entity is one whose existence depends on another entity. Weak entities are shown in rectangles with rounded corners; the relationship on which the entity depends is indicated by a diamond with rounded corners.

Some entities have subtypes that define subsets of similar entities. Subtypes inherit properties from their parent, the supertype. HAS-A relationships connect entities of different types; the identifiers of the entities are different. IS-A relationships are subtypes; the identifiers of the entities are the same.

Once a data model is developed, the designers should consider the possibility of processing restrictions against entities. Each entity in the model should be evaluated in light of possible data additions, changes, and deletions. Deletions, in particular, often are the source of important processing restrictions. When processing restrictions are discovered, they should be documented along with the data model.

The E-R model is an important part of many CASE products. These products provide tools for constructing and storing E-R diagrams. Some CASE tools integrate the E-R constructs with data constructs in the CASE repository.

Once they are completed, E-R models need to be evaluated. One technique is to develop a list of queries that could be answered from the data model. This list is shown to users who are asked to develop additional questions. The design is then evaluated against these questions to ensure that the model is rich enough to answer them.

Databases do not model the real world. Instead, they model the users' model of their business environment. The appropriate criteria for judging a data model is whether the model fits the users' model. Arguing about which model best fits the real world is pointless.

||||||||||||||||||||||||||

GROUP I   QUESTIONS

4.1   Define *entity* and give an example.

4.2   Explain the difference between entity class and entity instance.

4.3   Define *property* and give examples for the entity you described in question 4.1.

4.4   Explain what a composite property is and give an example.

4.5   Which property defined in your answer to question 4.3 identifies the entity?

4.6   Define *relationship* and give an example.

4.7   Explain the difference between relationship class and relationship instance.

4.8   Define *degree of relationship*. Give an example, other than the one in this text, of a relationship greater than degree 2.

4.9   List and give an example of the three fundamental types of binary relationship. Draw an E-R diagram for each.

4.10   Define the terms *maximum cardinality* and *minimum cardinality*.

4.11   Name and sketch symbols used in entity-relationship diagrams for

   a. Entity
   b. Relationship
   c. Weak entity and its relationship
   d. Recursive relationship
   e. Subtype entity

4.12   Give an example E-R diagram for the entities DEPARTMENT and EMPLOYEE which have a 1:N relationship. Assume that a DEPARTMENT need not have any EMPLOYEE, but that every EMPLOYEE has a DEPARTMENT.

4.13   Give an example of a recursive relationship and show it in an E-R diagram.

4.14   Show example properties for DEPARTMENT and EMPLOYEE (from question 4.12). Explain the two ways that properties can appear on or with E-R diagrams.

4.15   Define the term *weak entity* and give an example other than one in this text.

4.16   Explain why weak entities are ambiguous. Give examples, other than those in this text, of each type of weak entity. Explain the term *ID-dependent entity*.

4.17   Describe subtype entities and give an example other than those in this text.

4.18   Explain the term *inheritance* and show how it applies to your answer to question 4.17.

4.19   Explain the difference between a HAS-A relationship and an IS-A relationship. Give an example of each.

4.20   What are processing restrictions? How can an E-R diagram be used to discover such restrictions? How should such restrictions be documented?

4.21   What role can CASE tools play in the construction of E-R diagrams?

4.22   Describe why it is important to evaluate a data model once it has been created. Summarize one technique for evaluating a data model and explain how that technique could be used to evaluate the data model in Figure 4.14.

GROUP II QUESTIONS

4.23   Change the E-R diagram in Figure 4.12 to include an entity LESSON. Let PRIVATE-LESSON and GROUP-LESSON be subtypes of LESSON. Modify relationships as necessary.

4.24   Change the E-R diagram in Figure 4.12 to exclude TEACHER. Modify relationships as necessary.

4.25   Which of the models in Figure 4.12 and in your answers to questions 4.23 and 4.24 do you prefer? Explain the rationale for your preference.

4.26   Change the E-R diagram in Figure 4.14 to include subtypes of equipment. Assume that equipment owned by San Juan Charters pertains to LEASE. Assume that other equipment pertains to BOAT. Model the differences in BOAT-related equipment that is fixed on the boats and BOAT-related equipment that is not fixed. What benefits does the added complexity of this model bring?

PROJECT

Develop an E-R diagram for the following organization: The Metropolitan Housing Agency (MHA) is a nonprofit organization that advocates the development and improvement of low-income housing. MHA operates in a metropolitan area of approximately 2.2 million people in a midwestern city.

MHA maintains data about the location, availability, and condition of low-income housing in eleven different census tracts in the metropolitan area. Within the boundaries of these tracts are approximately 250 different buildings that provide low-income housing. On average, each building contains twenty-five apartments or other units.

MHA keeps data about each census tract including geographic boundaries, median income of the population, elected officials, principal businesses, principal investors involved in properties in that tract, and other demographic and economic data. It also maintains a limited amount of data about crime. For each building, MHA stores the name, address, size, owner(s)'s name and address, mortgager(s)'s name and address, renovations and repairs, and availability of facilities for handicapped people. In addition, MHA keeps a list of each of the units within each building. This list includes the type of unit, size, number of bedrooms, number of baths, kitchen and dining facilities, location in the building, and any special remarks. MHA would like to maintain data about the average occupancy rates for each unit, but it has been unable to collect or store such data to date. MHA does, however, keep data about whether a given unit is occupied.

MHA serves as an information clearinghouse and provides three basic services. First, it works with politicians, lobbyists, and advocacy groups to foster the development of legislation that encourages the development of low-income housing through tax incentives, developmental zoning preferences, and other legislative inducements. To accomplish this, MHA provides information about low-income housing to state, county, and city governments. Second, MHA strives to raise community consciousness about the need for low-income housing through speeches, seminars, displays at conventions, and other public relations activities. Finally, MHA provides information about the availability of low-income housing to other agencies that work with the low-income and homeless populations.

Semantic Object Model

This chapter presents the semantic object model. This model, like the E-R model in Chapter 4, is used to interpret the users' requirements and to build the users' data model. Figure 5.1 illustrates the situation. The development team interviews users, analyzes the users' reports, forms, and queries, and from these, constructs a model of the users' data. This data model is later transformed into a database design.

The particular form of the users' data model depends on the constructs used to build it. If the E-R model is used, then the model of the users' data will have entities, relationships, and the like. If the semantic model is used, then the model of the users' data will have semantic objects and related constructs that you will learn about in this chapter.

The E-R model and the semantic object model are like lenses that database developers look through when studying and documenting the users' data. Both lenses work and they both, ultimately, result in a database design. They use different images to form that design, however, and the designs they produce may not be exactly the same.

When developing a database, you will have to decide which approach to use, just as a photographer needs to decide which lens to use. Each approach has strengths and weaknesses, and we will discuss these at the end of this chapter.

The semantic object model has evolved over fifteen years. In particular, the discussion of objects and their relationship to database structures has evolved from work by Codd and by Hammer and McLeod. After you read this chapter, you may wish to consult their papers for more information.[1]

Semantic Objects

The purpose of a database application is to enable users to gain information they need about the things that are important in the work environment. The major goals of database development during the requirements phase are to build a data model that documents the things that are to be represented in the database, to determine the characteristics of those things that need to be stored, and to determine the relationships among them.

In Chapter 4, we referred to these things as entities. In this chapter, we will refer to them as **semantic objects,** or sometimes just **objects.** The word *semantic* means meaning. A semantic object is one that models, in part, the meaning of the users' data. Semantic objects attempt to model the users' perceptions more closely than the E-R model. Or, as Coad and Yourdon put it, "The primary motivation for identifying Objects is to match the technical representation of a system more closely to the conceptual view . . ."[2] We are using the adjective *semantic* with object to distinguish the objects discussed in this chapter from the objects defined in object-oriented programming languages. Other differences will be explained at the end of this chapter.

OBJECT DEFINITION

Entities and objects are similar in some ways, and they are also different. We begin with the similarities. A semantic object is a representation of some identifiable thing in the users' work environment. More formally, a semantic object is a *named collection of properties* that *sufficiently describes* a *distinct identity.*

Like entities, semantic objects are grouped into classes. An object class has a *name* that distinguishes it from other classes. The name of the class corresponds to the name of the name of the things it represents. Thus, a database that supports users who work with records of students will have an object class called STUDENT. Note that object class names, like entity class names, are shown with all capital letters.

---

[1] E. F. Codd, "Extending the Relational Model to Capture More Meaning," *ACM Transactions on Database Systems* 4 (December 1976): 397–434; Michael Hammer and Dennis McLeod, "Database Description with SDM: A Semantic Database Model," *ACM Transactions on Database Systems* 6 (September 1981): 351–386.

[2] Peter Coad and Edward Yourdon, *Object-oriented Analysis* (Englewood Cliffs, N.J.: Yourdon Press, 1990), 59.

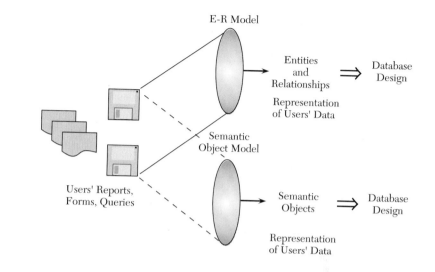

A particular semantic object is an instance of the class. Thus, STUDENT 12345 is an instance of the STUDENT class; PRODUCT ABC-12 is an instance of the PRODUCT class.

Like entities, an object has a *collection of properties*. Each property represents a characteristic of the identity being represented. For instance, an object STUDENT might have properties Name, Home-address, Campus-address, Date-of-birth, Date-of-graduation, and Major.

Further, this collection of properties is a *sufficient description*. This means that the properties represent all of the characteristics that the users need to perform their work. As stated at the end of Chapter 4, things in the world have an infinite set of characteristics; we cannot represent all of them. Instead, we represent those necessary for the community of users of the database to successfully perform their jobs.

Objects represent *distinct identities*. They are something that users recognize as independent and separate. They are also something that users want to track and report. These identities are the nouns about which information is to be produced.

To understand the term *distinct identity* better, recall that there is a difference between objects and object instances. CUSTOMER is the name of an object; CUSTOMER 12345 is the name of an instance of an object. When we say that an object represents a distinct identity, we mean that users consider each *instance* of an object to be unique and identifiable in its own right.

Finally, note that the identities that objects represent may or may not have a physical existence. For example, EMPLOYEEs physically exist. ORDERs do not. Orders are, themselves, models of the contractual agreement to provide certain goods or services under certain terms and conditions. They are not physical things but are representations of agreements. Thus, something need not be physical to be considered an object; it must only be identifiable in its own right in the minds of the users.

FIGURE 5.2
E-R model representation of
ORDER and LINE-ITEM

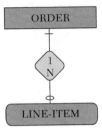

INDEPENDENT EXISTENCE OF OBJECTS

One important difference between semantic objects and entities is that objects always exist independently. There is no concept similar to weak entities in the E-R model. No object is existence dependent on another object. The circumstances that lead to the need for weak entities are handled differently with semantic objects.

Consider an order. Orders are something that users identify as distinct identities. Each instance of ORDER (ORDER 12345 and ORDER 45678, for example) is identifiable and stands on its own. Hence, ORDER can be both a strong entity and an object.

Now, consider a line item within an order. Although users talk about line items in general terms, they do not think of each line item as a distinct identity. Users do not refer to line item number 789. Rather, users refer to line items in the context of an order. They refer to the second line item of ORDER 12345.

The order is the distinct identity; line item is a part of an order. With the entity-relationship model, both an ORDER and the LINE-ITEM on an ORDER are modeled as entities. LINE-ITEM is defined as a weak entity that is existence dependent on ORDER as shown in Figure 5.2.

With semantic object models, the situation is handled differently. With semantic objects, ORDER is defined as an object, but a line item is not. Instead, line item is made a property of OBJECT, as you will learn.

To summarize, for something to be considered a semantic object, the instances of the thing must be considered unique and distinct in the minds of the users. There are no weak objects. The advantages of this restriction will become apparent later in this chapter.

OBJECT IDENTIFIERS

As stated, both object classes and object instances have names. The name of the object is the name of the entity it represents. Example object names are CUSTOMER, INVOICE, STUDENT, PROFESSOR, PAYMENT, DEPARTMENT, SHIPMENT, TREATMENT, and so forth. In a database, an object class has one and only one name.

Object instance names are the names of particular customers, invoices, students, and so on. ABC Plumbing, Kansas Flax, and Parks Printing are names of customers—they are the names of instances of the CUSTOMER class. The name of an object instance is a value of one or more of the properties of the object. The name of a DEPARTMENT instance, for example, is one value of the property Department-number. Object instances sometimes have alternative names. The name could be a value of either Department-number or Department-name.

In some cases, a single property does not suffice to uniquely identify an object instance. This may or may not be a problem. For example, a small business might not be concerned with non-unique customer names—having two John Smiths might be perfectly acceptable. Users may say that when there is a need to distinguish one from the other, they will examine other properties, such as address, to select the appropriate one. The combination {Name, Address} may serve to uniquely identify an object.

For other systems, in other environments, unique, single-property names are essential. This is frequently true for larger, organizational systems. For example, in banking systems, the possibility of confusing one customer with another is unacceptable. Here, unique account numbers are always required.

Do not confuse the concepts of composite identifiers and existence dependence. They are not the same. To see why, consider the differences between a CUSTOMER with identifying properties (Cust-name, Cust-address) and a line item with identifying properties (Order#, Line#). We have said that CUSTOMER is an object but line item is not. Both of these have an identifier with more than one property, so this is not the crucial difference.

What is the difference? Why is CUSTOMER an object but line item is not? The difference is in the way the users work with and think about customers and line items. The users, in their work environment, think of customers as identifiable, different things, having an existence of their own. The users do not think of line items in this way. A line item does not exist independent of an order. Thus, line items cannot be considered as objects.

Again, notice that the crucial difference is in the minds of the users. That is one reason that objects are called *semantic* objects. What makes a thing an object is the meaning that is ascribed to it by the users, nothing more.

OBJECT PROPERTIES

Objects have properties that define their characteristics. Properties can be simple data item values like Cust# and they can be composites like Cust-addr which consists of the group of properties {Street, City, State, Zip}. Properties, whether simple or composite, can also be single valued or multiple valued. Finally, and this is most important, *properties can also be other objects.*

To understand these statements, consider Figure 5.3, which is an example of a **semantic object diagram,** or **object diagram.** Such diagrams are used by development teams to summarize the structure of objects and to present those structures visually. Objects are shown in portrait-oriented rectangles. The name of the object appears above or beneath the rectangle. Properties are written inside of the rectangle.

In Figure 5.3, the DEPARTMENT object includes nine properties. Each property represents a characteristic of a department in this university, such as the name of the

FIGURE 5.3
DEPARTMENT object diagram

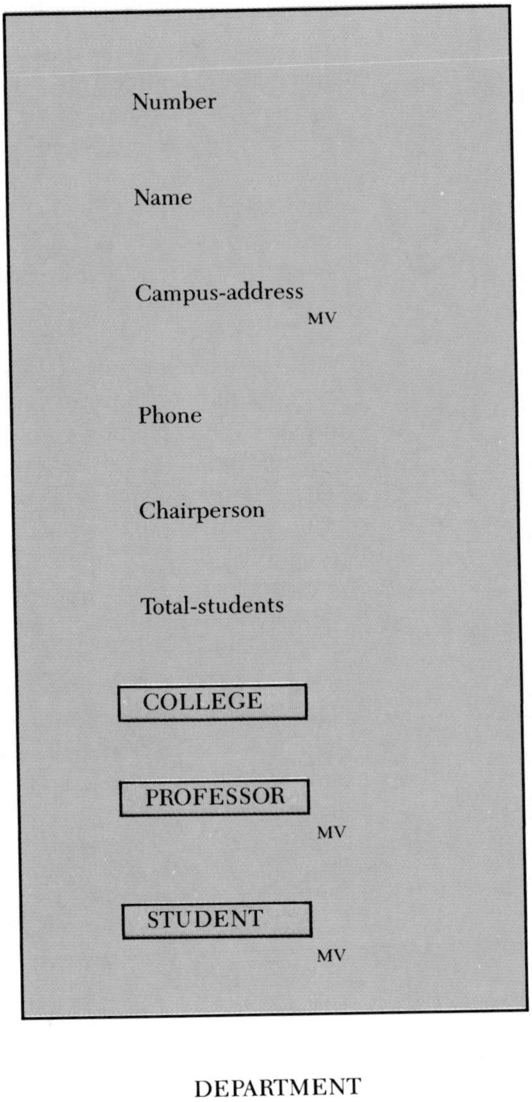

Number

Name

Campus-address
                MV

Phone

Chairperson

Total-students

COLLEGE

PROFESSOR
                MV

STUDENT
                MV

DEPARTMENT

department (Name), the name of the department chair (Chairperson), and the mailing address of the department (Campus-address). The property Campus-address has the letters MV next to it. This signifies that Campus-address is multiple valued; some departments can have more than one address.

The first six properties listed in the figure are **nonobject properties.** Their values are scalar data items. The last three properties are **object properties.** Their values are other objects. This fact is signified by capitalizing the name of the property and enclosing it in a rectangle.

In Figure 5.3, COLLEGE, PROFESSOR, and STUDENT are other objects that are contained within DEPARTMENT. According to this model, when a user thinks about a DEPARTMENT, he or she thinks not only about Number, Name, and so forth, but also about the COLLEGE, PROFESSOR, and STUDENT who work in that department.

Since COLLEGE, PROFESSOR, and STUDENT are other objects, the complete data model will contain object diagrams for them, too. The COLLEGE object will contain properties of the college; the PROFESSOR object will contain properties of faculty; and the STUDENT object will contain properties of the students.

The MV after PROFESSOR and STUDENT indicate that DEPARTMENT contains multiple values of these objects. Many professors can teach in a given department and many students can major in that department. Notice that whether a property is single or multiple valued has nothing to do with whether it is an object or nonobject property. Nonobject properties can be single valued or multiple valued; object properties also can be single valued or multiple valued. Examples of each appear in Figure 5.3.

The object diagram for DEPARTMENT shown in Figure 5.3 is a format, or general structure, that can be used for any department. An instance of the DEPARTMENT object is shown in Figure 5.4. This figure shows each property's **value** for a particular department, Information Systems. Observe that there are two values for Campus-address—the Information Systems Department has two locations on campus. Other departments might have only one value, or several more values for this property.

Further, there are multiple values for the PROFESSOR and STUDENT object properties. Each PROFESSOR instance is a complete object; it has all the properties of PROFESSOR. To keep this diagram simple, all but the name of the person has been omitted from the sketch. The ellipsis (. . .) indicates that other properties are not shown.

The object diagram is a picture of the user's perception of an object in the work environment. Thus, in the user's mind, the DEPARTMENT object includes all of the PROFESSOR properties as well. Similar comments pertain to the STUDENT object property. Each instance of STUDENT represents a complete STUDENT object. Again, the ellipsis represents properties omitted from this diagram for simplicity.

PROPERTY DOMAINS

The **domain** of a property is the set of all possible values the property can have. The description of a nonobject property domain is different from that of an object property domain. The domain of a nonobject property consists of both a physical and a semantic description. The physical description indicates the type of data (for example, numeric versus string), the length of the property, and other restrictions or constraints (such as the first character must be alphabetic, or the value must not exceed 9999.99).

The semantic description describes the function or purpose of the property—it distinguishes this property from other properties that might have the same physical description. For example, the domain of Department-name might be defined as "the set of strings of up to seven characters that represent names of departments at Eastcoast University." The phrase *strings of up to seven characteristics* is the physical description of the domain. The phrase *that represent names of departments at Eastcoast University* is

FIGURE 5.4
DEPARTMENT object instance

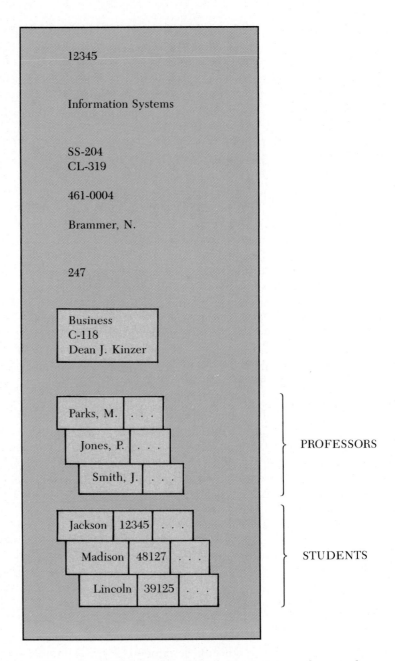

the semantic description. The semantic description differentiates strings of seven characters that represent names of departments from similar strings that represent, say, names of courses or buildings or some other property.

The domain of an object property is a set of object instances. In Figure 5.3, for example, the domain of the PROFESSOR object property is the set of all PROFESSOR object instances.

In some cases, the domain of an object property will be only a subset of the object. For example, the PROFESSOR object might include these properties: Name, Address, Marital-status, Date-of-birth, Education-history, Current-salary, Medical-history, Blood-type, Dependents, and Religious-preference. However, only some of those properties are perceived by the user as being carried to the DEPARTMENT object, such as Name, Address, Education-history, and Current-salary. This situation is common.

When describing objects, we need to specify both the properties and the property domains. Typically, the object properties and domain names are listed with the object. The domains themselves are defined separately from the objects. This helps reduce duplicate domain definitions for those situations in which one domain is used by several properties. For example, the same domain definition can be used for Employee-name, Salesperson-name, and Order-processor-name. You will study examples of this later in this chapter (in Figure 5.18).

SEMANTIC OBJECT VIEWS

Users access objects through applications. An application may or may not require access to all of the object's properties. For example, in Figure 5.5 three applications view the DEPARTMENT object. Some properties of DEPARTMENT (its Name, for example) are seen by all three applications. Other properties are seen by just one or two of these applications. For example, STUDENT is seen only by Application1, while COLLEGE is seen only by Application2.

The portion of an object that is visible to a particular application is called a **view.** A view consists of the name of the object, plus a list of all of the properties visible from that view.

Since an application's view may not encompass all the properties of an object, the development team must integrate the views of all applications in order to completely describe the object. Remember that during requirements definition the team is trying to determine what data must be stored to satisfy *all* users' needs. In the process, the team works with various users, each of whom offers his or her view of an object. The team then develops a composite picture of the object by putting together all the views. This final picture becomes the object diagram.

Creating Data Models with Semantic Objects

This section illustrates a process for developing semantic objects. The process can be done in either a top-down or bottom-up fashion. With a bottom-up approach, developers examine the application interface—primarily reports and screen displays—and work backwards (or, reverse-engineer), to derive the object structure. This approach is based on the theory that if you know how the users view their interface to the system, you can figure out what must be stored in the database.

For example, to derive the structure of a DEPARTMENT object we could first gather all of the reports, forms, and other views of DEPARTMENT. From them, we could

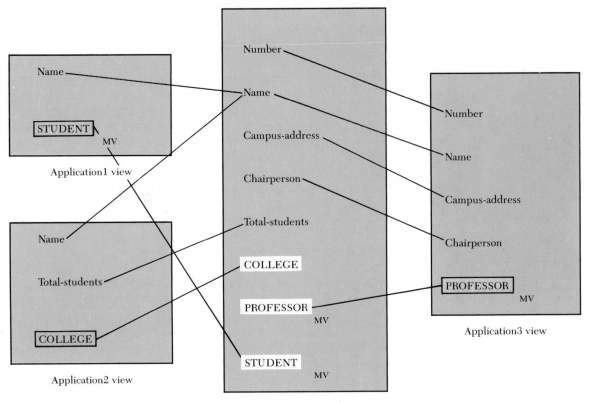

FIGURE 5.5

Three application views of DEPARTMENT object

define a DEPARTMENT object that would enable those reports, forms, and views to be constructed.

A second method for identifying and describing objects is to work from the top down. Starting with a general idea of the goals of the applications, developers ask the users what objects they need to track. Then the team and the users imagine, from the nature of the objects and the application goals, which properties need to be stored in the database.

The top-down approach requires knowledge and experience in the application domain and is risky. There is a significant chance that the imagination of even skilled database systems designers will be insufficient and that important properties or objects will be left out.

Probably the best approach is a combination of the two. Begin at the top by developing a list of potential objects by considering the general goals of the application. Then, with that list, examine available reports, forms, and other views to determine the possible structure of the initial set of objects and properties. Use the revised object diagrams to suggest to the user new reports, forms, and views in light of the goals of the application. These steps can be repeated until the users agree that the system will be able to produce the information they need.

For a totally new application there will be no reports, forms, or views to examine. In this case, the developers have no choice but to begin by discussing with users what "things" are important to them. With this data, developers can begin to develop object diagrams that can then be embellished as more details about the new system become evident. Often developers use prototypes to help users through this process.

DATA MODELING AS AN ARTISTIC PROCESS[3]

The definition of objects and views of objects is iterative. The team discusses data needs with each user and puts together several views of an object. Then the team combines the views to build a composite picture. Now the team reviews user needs again, in light of the object definition. Some adjustments often need to be made. Users might also adjust their requirements when they become aware of what data might be available. Object definition is not a straight-line process; there is considerable reiteration of the definition of views and the definition of objects.

When using the semantic object model, the goal of the requirements phase is to identify and describe objects to be represented in the database. The process of identifying objects is an artistic process. There is no algorithm that can be specified to build a consistent set of objects. There are, however, tools and techniques to be learned, and these will enable you to obtain high-quality data models. Nevertheless, two competent data modelers can arrive at two different sets of objects.

It's like any artistic process. Using similar skills and tools, two potters can create two high-quality teapots that vary in the location of their handles. The buyer or user of teapots may or may not judge one to be better than the other.

So it is with data models. Two people can use the tools and process described in this chapter and arrive at two different sets of objects for the same set of requirements. That may happen. If so, either the developers or the users will need to judge the merits of the two. Developers can judge the objects directly; users will need to be shown prototype interfaces that illustrate the difference in the object designs. The users can then judge the prototypical interfaces.

In short, do not expect data modeling to be an exact science; it is an art.

AN EXAMPLE: THE UNIVERSITY ADMINISTRATION DATABASE

In this section we will illustrate the process for object definition with examples drawn from a case study. Suppose a university wanted to keep track of department, faculty, and student major data. Without getting into the details of the applications, suppose that the

---

[3]The comments in this section pertain equally well to development of entity-relationship designs. Both modeling processes, and indeed, all of data modeling, is artistic in nature. Seldom is a correct model obtained on the first pass, and an attempt to make it so would probably slow the process down unreasonably and overly constrain the developers' thinking. Further, differences are to be expected with both techniques. We are attempting to build a model of a group of users' mental models; this will be an artistic process no matter what tool or technique is used.

```
                          College of Business
                       Mary B. Jefferson, Dean

            232-1101                                       SS-101
    -----------------------------------------------------------------

    Department            Chairperson          Phone    Total Majors

    Accounting            Seymour P. Jackson   232-1841     318

    Finance               Linda R. Smith       232-1414     211

    Information Systems    Nathaniel D. Brammer 232-4146     247

    Management            Christine A. Tuttle   236-1732     184

    Production            Jack T. Barnes        236-1914      98
```

FIGURE 5.6
COLLEGE report

system needs to produce five reports (Figures 5.6, 5.8, 5.10, 5.12, and 5.14). Our goal is to examine these reports and deduce from them the objects and properties that need to be stored to produce them. We will reverse-engineer the objects from these reports.

The COLLEGE Object

Consider the first report in Figure 5.6. What objects does this report seem to be about? This is a report about a college—specifically, the College of Business. Because this is an instance of a report, we can be sure that there will be similar reports about other colleges, such as the College of Arts and Sciences, the College of Medicine, and so forth. The fact that a user wants a report about colleges tells us that a college is an object. Remember, an object is the representation of an important entity in the user's work environment; if he or she wants a report about something, it must be important.

Examining the report, we find that there is data specific to the college, such as the name, telephone number, and office of the dean, and there are also facts about each of the departments within the college. This *suggests* that the database might contain COLLEGE and DEPARTMENT objects, with DEPARTMENTs contained within COLLEGEs.

We document these preliminary findings in the diagram in Figure 5.7. Notice that we have omitted from the object diagrams all but the nonobject property, Name, and any object properties, such as DEPARTMENT. A complete object diagram includes all properties, of course. They are not shown here to focus the example and discussion on the essentials.

In the report in Figure 5.6, groups of department data repeat underneath college data. Such repeating groups are often a signal that the repeating group is data about

COLLEGE object

DEPARTMENT object

FIGURE 5.7
Preliminary COLLEGE and DEPARTMENT object diagrams

another object. *However, this is not always the case.* The repeating group could also be composite COLLEGE data that happens to have several values. As a guideline, when you see a repeating group in a form or report, consider the possibility that this repeating group *may* represent another object.

The DEPARTMENT Object

Now examine the report in Figure 5.8. It is a report about a department, specifically the Information Systems Department. Within the report is data about the faculty members who teach in the department. Like Figure 5.6, this report suggests that DEPARTMENT is an object (there is a report about it) and that PROFESSOR might be an object contained within DEPARTMENT. These findings are documented in the adjusted DEPARTMENT object diagram in Figure 5.9.

Notice that we have not included the COLLEGE object as a property of DEPARTMENT. There is no college data in the report in Figure 5.8, so as far as we can tell from this report, there is no reason to place the COLLEGE object within DEPARTMENT. Other reports may provide a reason.

Be aware that whenever one object is contained in another, there is always the *possibility* that the second object may also be contained in the first. In this case, since COLLEGE contains a DEPARTMENT property, it is prudent to investigate whether DEPARTMENT contains a corresponding COLLEGE property.

The structure of the DEPARTMENT and MAJOR report in Figure 5.10 is similar to that of the DEPARTMENT and FACULTY report in Figure 5.8. The report in Figure 5.10 is also about a department, which reinforces the notion that department is an object. But this report lists data about students who major in the department, implying that student is also an object. Thus, the DEPARTMENT object needs to contain the STUDENT object as well as the PROFESSOR object. This is shown in Figure 5.11. The reports in Figures 5.6 and 5.8 present two different views of the DEPARTMENT object. The situation is similar to that shown in Figure 5.5.

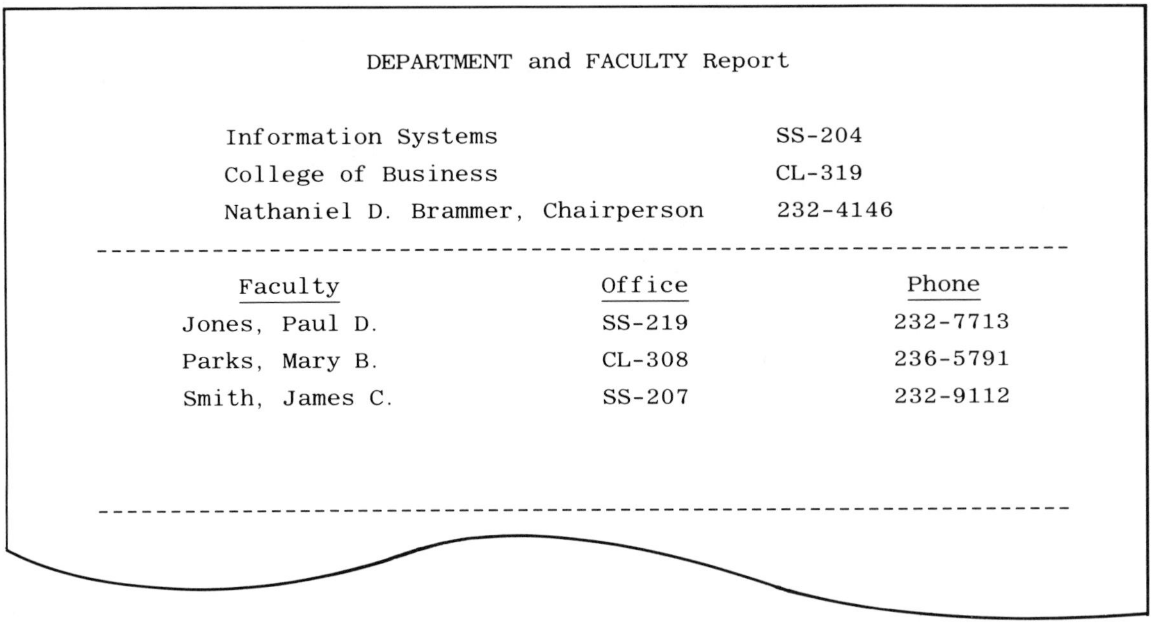

```
                    DEPARTMENT and FACULTY Report


          Information Systems                    SS-204
          College of Business                    CL-319
          Nathaniel D. Brammer, Chairperson      232-4146
     -------------------------------------------------------------

            Faculty                 Office              Phone
       Jones,  Paul D.              SS-219            232-7713
       Parks,  Mary B.              CL-308            236-5791
       Smith,  James C.             SS-207            232-9112



     -------------------------------------------------------------
```

FIGURE 5.8
DEPARTMENT and FACULTY report

FIGURE 5.9
Adjusted DEPARTMENT object
diagram

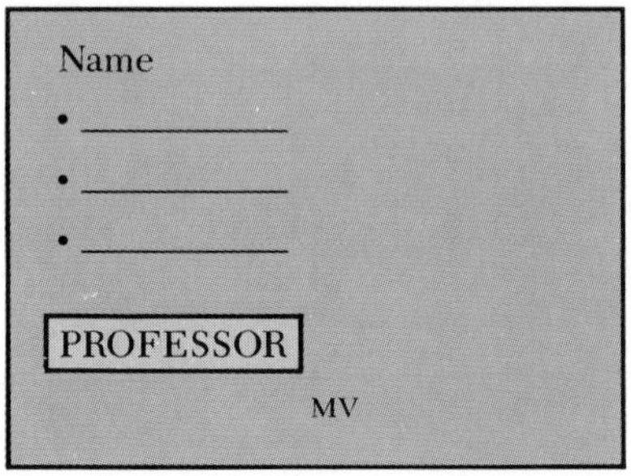

DEPARTMENT object

The STUDENT Object

Figure 5.12 is an example of the acceptance letter that the university sends to its incoming students. This is a report about a student. Data items that need to be stored in the database are shaded in this example. In addition to data about a student, the letter also contains data about the student's major DEPARTMENT and the student's PROFESSOR advisor. A sketch of a STUDENT object that could support this report is shown in Figure 5.13. In this object diagram, both DEPARTMENT and PROFESSOR are single valued. A student at this university has at most one major department and one advisor.

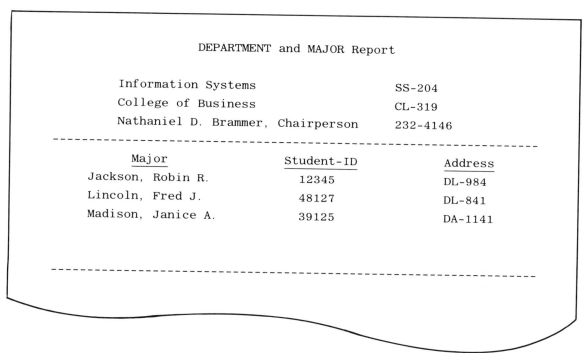

DEPARTMENT and MAJOR Report

Information Systems   SS-204
College of Business   CL-319
Nathaniel D. Brammer, Chairperson   232-4146

- -

Major	Student-ID	Address
Jackson, Robin R.	12345	DL-984
Lincoln, Fred J.	48127	DL-841
Madison, Janice A.	39125	DA-1141

- -

FIGURE 5.10
DEPARTMENT and MAJOR report

FIGURE 5.11
Further adjustment to
DEPARTMENT object diagram

Name

• _____
• _____
• _____

PROFESSOR
                MV

STUDENT
                MV

DEPARTMENT object

Figures 5.11 and 5.13 illustrate the situation in which two objects contain each other. STUDENT contains DEPARTMENT and DEPARTMENT contains STUDENT. Although at first this situation may seem infeasible, it makes sense from the users' perspectives. When one user envisions a DEPARTMENT, he sees the STUDENT as a subset of the DEPARTMENT (a department has student majors in it). At the same time, another user views a STUDENT and sees the DEPARTMENT as a property of STU-

Mr. Fred Parks
124 Elm Street
Los Angeles, CA 98002

Dear Fred Parks :

You have been admitted as a BIOLOGY major to Eastcoast State University starting the Fall Semester, 1988. The office of the BIOLOGY department is located
at SC-213 . The department phone number is 232-4101 .

Your advisor is Dr. James . Please schedule an appointment with your advisor as
soon as you arrive on campus. Your advisor's office and phone are SC-105 and 232-
7220 .

Congratulations and welcome to Eastcoast State University.

Sincerely,

James J. Saen
President

JJS/rkp

FIGURE 5.12
Acceptance letter

FIGURE 5.13
STUDENT object diagram

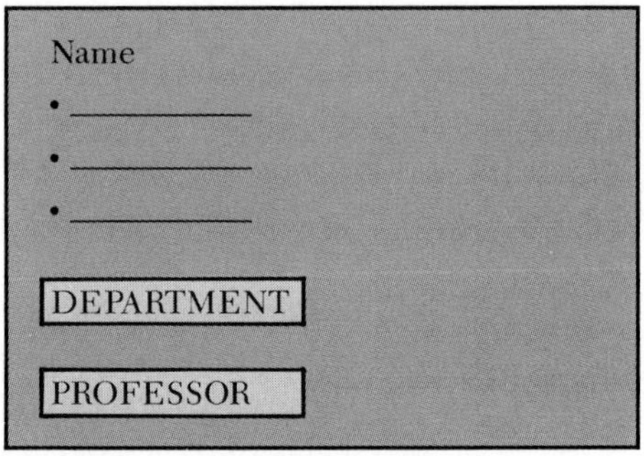

Name

• _____
• _____
• _____

DEPARTMENT

PROFESSOR

STUDENT object

DENT (this student has declared her major in a particular department). The database needs to support these different perspectives; defining objects this way will make the jobs of database and application design much easier.

The TEACHING-STAFF Object

The final report is for the university's faculty directory (Figure 5.14). This report lists faculty names sorted in alphabetical order, their offices, and telephone numbers. Though it appears to be a simple report, the directory presents a very subtle problem. What is this a report about? What is the underlying object? It is tempting to say the underlying object is PROFESSOR. However, PROFESSOR is not the underlying object. Is a directory a report about *a* professor? No. A directory is a report about a *group of professors*. It is actually a report about the university's teaching staff. Thus, the underlying object here is TEACHING-STAFF.

The words *sorted alphabetically* are an important clue. Sorting implies a group; there must be several members to sort. Thus, whenever a report is sorted by something, the underlying object is probably a collection of the things that are being sorted. Accordingly, the underlying object for the report in Figure 5.14 is TEACHING-STAFF.

The object diagram for TEACHING-STAFF appears in Figure 5.15. TEACHING-STAFF has three properties, University-name, Date, and PROFESSOR, which is a multiple valued object property.

```
                        Eastcoast University
                            June, 1990

            Name                Campus Address        Phone

      Adams,  John C.               SC-234           232-0940

      Addingting,  Jane M.          FL-2718          236-9912

      Agis,  Mary                   FL-1718          236-9003
```

FIGURE 5.14
Report for faculty directory

FIGURE 5.15
TEACHING-STAFF object

FIGURE 5.15
TEACHING-STAFF object

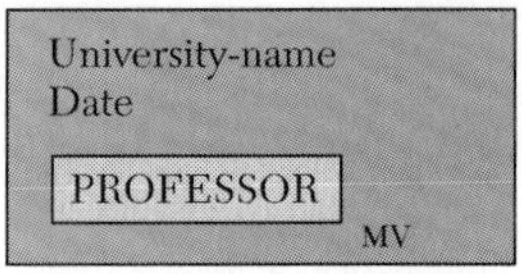

Validating Object Definitions

One technique to help you identify objects is to consider what constitutes an **instance** of a report. Imagine that a computer run has been made and a stack of continuous form paper is sitting on your desk. Suppose the stack is a group of acceptance letters like the one shown in Figure 5.12. Where will you tear the paper? What constitutes a complete report? Obviously, one acceptance letter is an instance of the report. You will tear the paper after each letter and send each one to an accepted student. This paper tearing is a physical manifestation of the fact that the underlying object is a single STUDENT.

Now consider the faculty directory. If the stack of paper on your desk is a printout of the directory, you would not tear it at all. The instance of the report is the entire stack of paper. To have copies of the directory printed and bound, you would ship the entire stack of paper to the printer, as is. This is evidence that the underlying object of the directory is TEACHING-STAFF.

Thinking about reports in this way can help you conceptualize objects. Think about the COLLEGE report shown in Figure 5.6. If this report were produced on continuous form paper, where would you separate it? To answer this question, you may need to dig deeper into user requirements. You might need to know who the users of this report are before you can be sure what the underlying objects are. There are two possibilities. If the dean of each college receives the section of the report for his or her college, then the underlying object is COLLEGE, defined as we did in Figure 5.5.

However, if the entire report goes to the university president's office, then the report is really about the university—an object that contains a multivalued COLLEGE object property. Upon discovering this, we would need to return to the object diagrams and add one for UNIVERSITY.

The PROFESSOR Object

The objects shown in Figures 5.7, 5.11, 5.13, and 5.15 contain enough data to produce the necessary reports. However, we have omitted one final detail: we have not yet defined a PROFESSOR object, though we did treat PROFESSOR as an object property of DEPARTMENT, STUDENT, and TEACHING-STAFF. We *guessed* that PROFESSOR is an object, but we encountered no report about professors. If there were, for example, a payroll check printed for each PROFESSOR, then that report would be evidence that PROFESSOR is an object.

In the absence of such hard evidence, we must ask a key question: Do users of this system have a reason to view professors as independent objects, or do they see professors only as subordinate properties of other objects? The question is not whether professors are separate from the other objects. Obviously, they are. A teacher and a department are not the same thing. The question here is whether the users of this system see them separately.

Based on the five reports we just studied, there is no reason to define professor as a separate object. If we are confident that these five reports constitute a complete requirements specification, then we do not need to define a PROFESSOR object.

In this case, the set of object diagrams that describe the data requirements for this system appear in Figure 5.16. We have replaced the object property PROFESSOR with a set of data items—Faculty-name, Faculty-office, Faculty-phone—which appear in the DEPARTMENT, STUDENT, and TEACHING-STAFF objects.

It is far more likely, however, that eventually some user will need to view professor as an object. In this case, the object diagrams in Figure 5.17 would be appropriate. The final authority, of course, is the user. But skilled database designers sometimes need to

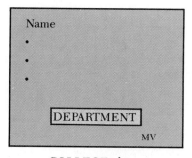

COLLEGE object

DEPARTMENT object

STUDENT object

TEACHING-STAFF object

FIGURE 5.16

Alternative objective diagrams for university administration database (no PROFESSOR object)

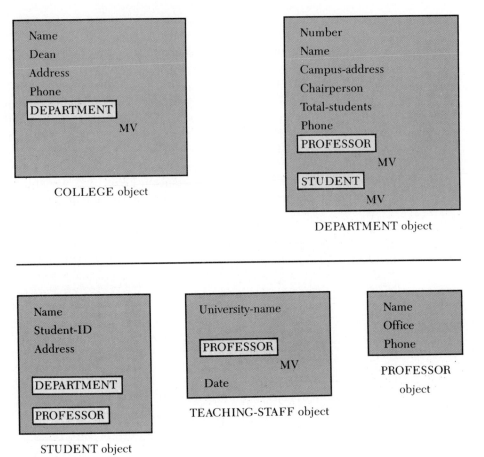

FIGURE 5.17
Object diagrams for university's database (with PROFESSOR object)

call on their experience and instincts to supplement the information given by the user. We will assume that PROFESSOR is actually an object and that the diagrams in Figure 5.17 are correct.

OBJECT SPECIFICATION

Figure 5.17 shows completed object diagrams for the university's database. The purposes of these diagrams are to show graphically the properties of each object and to indicate the relationships among objects, that is, which objects contain which other objects. Object diagrams give the overall picture of object relationships.

Figure 5.18 presents the complete object specifications for the university's database. This specification is made up of two parts: object definitions and the domain definitions. An object definition lists all the properties of an object, and it indicates the domain from which values for each property can be drawn.

Domain definitions specify formats, lengths, and special restrictions on the values of each domain. We will examine the entire object specification document in this section. Object specifications are sufficiently detailed that, once they are completed and approved, they can be used for database design.

Although there is no formal syntax for object specifications, we have adopted some standards for use in this text. Other designers may present their specifications differently. Under each object name we list all of the properties for that object. We separate the name of each property from its domain with a colon (:). If the domain is another object, and if only some of the properties of the object are to be carried to the object being specified, then we use the keyword *SUBSET* and enclose the appropriate properties of the foreign object within brackets [   ]. (A **foreign object** is the object from which the properties are being drawn. For example, in Figure 5.18 DEPARTMENT is foreign to COLLEGE.)

A domain definition describes the set of values from which an instance of a property may be drawn. As described earlier in this chapter, it consists of both a physical and a semantic description. In some cases, the physical descriptions include restrictions on the allowable values. For example, Campus-phones is a domain whose description includes a mask—or restriction—that specifies that the first two digits must be 23 and the third one must be either a 2 or a 6. Total-student-count is an example of a domain that is specified by a formula: it is computed as the count of STUDENT objects in DEPART-MENT. Such domains, called **computed values,** occur frequently in financial systems where a balance is computed as the sum of values from the local object, or even from a foreign object.

Other items in this figure are largely self-explanatory. This format is one of many acceptable formats for specifying objects. The particular format you use is not as important as being sure to clearly and unambiguously set out the structure and content of objects and to define the property domains.

Types of Objects

This section describes and illustrates six categories of objects. To do this, we will first consider a report or form that a business might use and then learn how to model it with an object. Later, in Chapter 7, you will learn methods for transforming each of these types of objects into database designs.

SIMPLE OBJECTS

A **simple object** contains only single-valued, nonobject properties. Figure 5.19a shows two instances of a report called an EQUIPMENT TAG. Such tags are applied to items of office equipment to help keep track of equipment inventory. The tags are printed, so we will call them a report.

Figure 5.19b shows a simple EQUIPMENT object that models EQUIPMENT TAG. The properties of the object include the items shown on the tag: Equip#, Description,

---

Object Definitions

COLLEGE OBJECT

Name; College-names
Dean; Faculty-names
Address; Campus-addresses
Phone; Campus-phones
DEPARTMENT; DEPARTMENT object; MV; SUBSET [Name, Chairperson, Phone, Total-students]

DEPARTMENT OBJECT

Number; Dept-numbers
Name; Dept-names
Campus-address; Campus-addresses; MV
Chairperson; Faculty-names
Total-students; Total-student-count
Phone; Campus-phones
PROFESSOR; PROFESSOR object; MV
STUDENT; STUDENT object; MV

STUDENT OBJECT

Name; Student-names
Student-ID; Student-IDs
Address; Campus-addresses
DEPARTMENT; DEPARTMENT object; SUBSET [Name, Campus-address, Phone]
PROFESSOR; PROFESSOR object; SUBSET [Name, Office, Phone]

TEACHING-STAFF OBJECT

University-name; U-names
PROFESSOR; PROFESSOR object; MV

PROFESSOR OBJECT

Name; Professor-names
Office; Campus-addresses
Phone; Campus-phones

a. Object definitions

FIGURE 5.18
Object specifications for university's database

Acquisition-date, and Purchase-cost. Note that none of these properties is multivalued and none is another object. EQUIPMENT is therefore a simple object.

COMPOSITE OBJECTS

Composite objects contain one or more nonobject multivalued properties. The HOTEL BILL shown in Figure 5.20a is a typical example of a report that gives rise to the need for a composite object. The bill has data that concerns the bill as a whole: Bill#, Arrival-date, Customer-name, and Total-due. It also contains a group of properties that

Domain Definitions

Campus-phones:

Text 8, mask 23X-NNNN,

where X is either 2 or 6, NNNN is any four digits

Number of a telephone in the university's exchange

College-names:

Text 25

Names of colleges at Eastcoast State University

Campus-addresses:

Text 6, mask BB-NNN,

where BB is building code, NNN is room number

Official campus mailing addresses

Dept-names:

Text 20

Official university department name

Dept-numbers:

Numeric 5

Unique number of a university department

Faculty-names:

Text 40: Mask:

First-name Text 15

Initial Text 2

Last-name Text 23

Names of full- and part-time professors at Eastcoast State University

Staff-date:

Date: Mask:

Month Test 9

Year NNN

Date of publication of staff directory

Student-names:

Text 40; Mask:

First-name Text 15

Initial Text 2

Last-name Text 23

Names of students who have been accepted to the university

Student-IDs:

Numeric 5

Unique and permanent student number

Total-student-count

Numeric 999; computed as count of STUDENT objects in DEPARTMENT

Number of students who have declared a major in a department

U-names

Text 30

Official university names

b. Domain definitions

FIGURE 5.18, *continued*

FIGURE 5.19
Example of a simple object

EQUIPMENT TAG:
    Equip#: 100   Description: Desk
    Acquisition-date: 2/27/90   Purchase-cost: $350.00

EQUIPMENT TAG:
    Equip#: 200   Description: Lamp
    Acquisition-date: 3/1/90   Purchase-cost: $39.95

a. Reports based on simple object

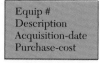

Equip #
Description
Acquisition-date
Purchase-cost

EQUIPMENT object

b. Simple object representing EQUIPMENT TAG report

are repeated for services provided to the guest. Each group includes Service-date, Service-description, and Price.

Figure 5.20b shows an object diagram for the HOTEL-BILL object. The brace around the right side of the properties Service-date, Service-description, and Price indicate that those properties repeat as a group. Such groups are sometimes called **composite groups.**

The multivalued attributes do not represent another object. The hotel does not view one line of a guest's charges as a separate thing. Line items on the guest's bill do not have identifiers of their own. No employee queries the database directly in search of a room charge on day 2 of bill number 1234. Instead, the line items are processed only in the context of a particular bill. Employees query the database in search of bill number 1234 and, then, in the context of that bill, examine the various charges.

Observe, too, that on the printed hotel bill in Figure 5.20a, the identifying number is labeled *Invoice Number.* In the object diagram in Figure 5.20b, however, this same data item is called *Bill-number.* Often, the labels attached to data items on reports and forms differ from the names given to the data items in the database. This is especially true in multi-application databases in which the same data item may be referred to by several or even many different labels.

In general, in database development projects, data items are given one official, internal name and other names and labels are mapped to this name. In this situation, Bill-number is the official internal name, and Invoice Number is the name given it on the hotel bill. Throughout this section, we will occasionally assign an internal data item name that differs from the report or form label.

A composite object can have more than one multivalued group. Figure 5.21a shows a hotel bill that has a multivalued property for customer name as well as a multivalued composite group for service charges. Each of these groups is independent of each other.

FIGURE 5.20
Example of a composite object

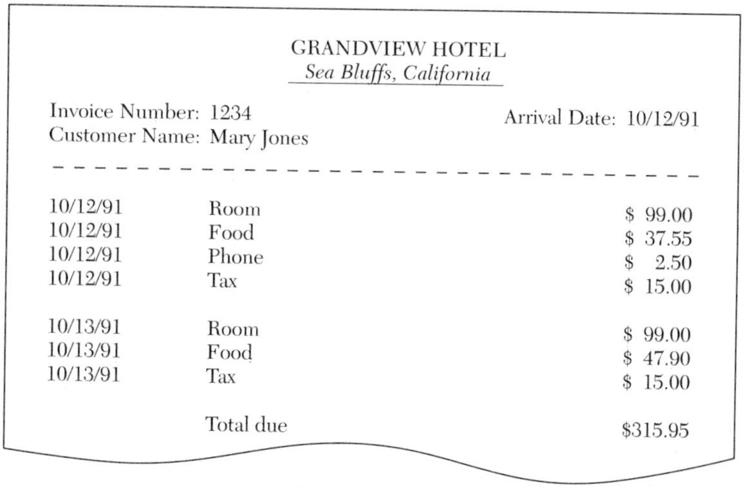

```
                     GRANDVIEW HOTEL
                      Sea Bluffs, California

   Invoice Number: 1234                      Arrival Date: 10/12/91
   Customer Name: Mary Jones

   - - - - - - - - - - - - - - - - - - - - - - - - - - - - - - - -

   10/12/91      Room                            $  99.00
   10/12/91      Food                            $  37.55
   10/12/91      Phone                           $   2.50
   10/12/91      Tax                             $  15.00

   10/13/91      Room                            $  99.00
   10/13/91      Food                            $  47.90
   10/13/91      Tax                             $  15.00

                 Total due                       $315.95
```

a. Report based on a composite object

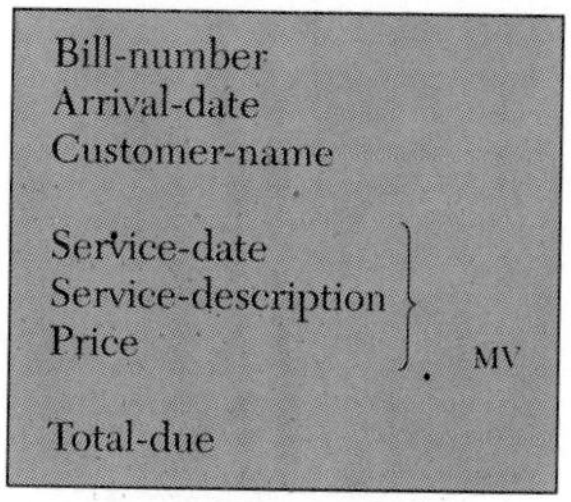

Bill-number
Arrival-date
Customer-name

Service-date
Service-description
Price . MV

Total-due

HOTEL BILL object

b. Composite object modeling HOTEL BILL report

The second instance of customer name, for example, has nothing to do with the second service charge.

Figure 5.21b is an object diagram for the hotel bill in Figure 5.21a. Customer-name is shown as a multivalued property. It is not included in the brace of service charges because the repetitions of Customer-name have nothing to do with the repetitions of services. The two are independent, as we just noted.

Composite groups can also be nested within one another. For example, suppose it is important to track each service charge to a room as shown on the hotel bill in Figure 5.22a. Since a guest can request multiple meals on the same day, room-service-charge is multivalued within the service-charge composite group.

An object diagram for this situation is presented in Figure 5.22b. As shown, any service charge can have subitems. If only room service were to have subcharges, then a different diagram would be necessary.

To repeat, a composite object is an object that contains at least one multivalued property (or composite group) and no object properties.

FIGURE 5.21

Example of a composite object with two multivalued groups

a. HOTEL BILL with multivalued customer names

HOTEL-BILL object

b. Composite object modeling HOTEL BILL with multiple name

COMPOUND OBJECTS

A **compound object** contains at least one object property. Consider Figure 5.23a which shows two different reports. One report, used by the company's motor pool, is used to keep track of vehicles. The second report is about employees and is used by the human resources department. Observe from these reports that a vehicle is assigned to one employee, and that an employee has one auto assigned.

We cannot tell from these reports whether an auto must be assigned to an employee or whether every employee has an auto. To obtain that information, we would need to ask the users in the motor pool or human resources department.

Figure 5.23b shows object diagrams for EMPLOYEE and VEHICLE. An EMPLOYEE contains VEHICLE as one of its properties. VEHICLE, in turn, contains EMPLOYEE as one of its properties. Since both EMPLOYEE and VEHICLE contain

FIGURE 5.22

Example of a composite object with nested composite groups

GRANDVIEW HOTEL
Sea Bluffs, California

Invoice Number: 1234
Customer Name: Mary Jones

Arrival Date: 10/12/91

- -

10/12/91	Room		$ 99.00
10/12/91	Food		
	Breakfast	$15.25	
	Dinner	$22.30	
10/12/91	Phone		$ 37.55
10/12/91	Tax		$ 2.50
			$ 15.00
10/13/91	Room		
10/13/91	Food		$ 99.00
	Breakfast	$15.25	
	Snack	$ 5.50	
	Dinner	$27.15	
			$ 47.90
10/13/91	Tax		$ 15.00
	Total due		$315.95

a. HOTEL BILL with nested composite groups

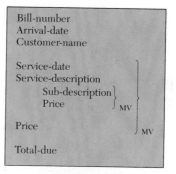

HOTEL-BILL object

b. Composite object modeling HOTEL BILL

object properties, they are both compound objects. Further, since neither property is multivalued, the relationship from EMPLOYEE to VEHICLE is one-to-one.

So far, in object diagrams, we have not recorded minimum relationships. The diagrams in Figure 5.23b, like the preceding object diagrams in this chapter, do not show whether a VEHICLE is required for an EMPLOYEE or an EMPLOYEE is required for a VEHICLE.

Since there are no weak objects, this issue occurs less frequently with semantic objects than it does for the entity-relationship model. In most compound objects, the contained objects are optional; in most cases the minimum is zero. For those less common cases in

VEHICLE DATA			
License number	Serial number		
Make	Type	Year	Color
Employee assignment			

EMPLOYEE WORK DATA			
Employee name		Employee ID	
Mailing address		Division	Phone
Pay code	Skill code	Hire date	Auto assigned

a. Example reports on two objects

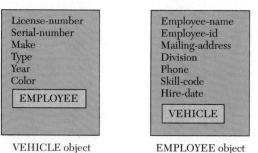

VEHICLE object   EMPLOYEE object

b. Two compund objects for the reports in Figure 5.23a

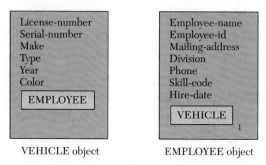

VEHICLE object   EMPLOYEE object

c. An EMPLOYEE must be assigned a VEHICLE

FIGURE 5.23
Example of compound objects

which the minimum is 1, we can document that fact by placing a 1 next to the contained object rectangle. Thus, in Figure 5.23c, the 1 indicates that an EMPLOYEE must be assigned a VEHICLE.

In Figure 5.23, EMPLOYEE and VEHICLE each contained one another. This need not always be the case; sometimes the relationship can occur in only one direction. Consider Figure 5.24a, which are reports concerning two objects: DORMITORY and STU-

DORMITORY OCCUPANCY REPORT

Dormitory	Resident Assistant	Phone
Ingersoll	Sarah and Allen French	3-5567

Student name	Student Number	Class
Adams, Elizabeth	710	SO
Baker, Rex	104	FR
Baker, Brydie	744	JN
Charles, Stewart	319	SO
Scott, Sally	447	SO
Taylor, Lynne	810	FR

STUDENT DATA FORM

Student Name		Student Number
Major	Advisor	
Class	High School	
Prior College		
Local Address		
	Phone	
Permanent Address		
	Phone	

a. Report and form with a one-way relationship

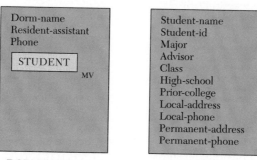

DORMITORY object

```
Dorm-name
Resident-assistant
Phone
  ┌──────────┐
  │ STUDENT  │
  └──────────┘  MV
```

STUDENT object

```
Student-name
Student-id
Major
Advisor
Class
High-school
Prior-college
Local-address
Local-phone
Permanent-address
Permanent-phone
```

b. Compound objects for the report and form in Figure 5.24a

FIGURE 5.24

Compound objects with a one-way object relationship

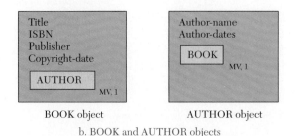

a. Forms based on compound objects

b. BOOK and AUTHOR objects

FIGURE 5.25
Compound objects with a many-to-many relationship

DENT. From the DORMITORY OCCUPANCY REPORT, we can see that users think of a dorm as having properties about the dorm (Name, Resident-assistant, Phone) and also properties about students (Student-name, Student-number, Class) who live in the dorm.

On the other hand, the STUDENT DATA FORM[4] shows only student data; it does not indicate that any dormitory data is considered part of student. (The local address might contain a dorm address, but this, if true, is apparently not important enough to document on this form. In a database development project, this possibility should be checked out with users in an interview. We assume that the STUDENT DATA FORM does not include dormitory data.)

Figure 5.24b shows semantic objects for the situation described. DORMITORY contains multiple values of STUDENT, but STUDENT does not contain any values of DORMITORY. These diagrams imply that when the users think of DORMITORY, they also think of the STUDENTs who live in the dormitory. But when they think of STUDENT, they do not think of the DORMITORY in which the student lives.

---

[4]A form is a display on a screen. We will show forms with rectangles with rounded corners; reports will be shown with square corners.

FIGURE 5.26
Nine subtypes of compound
objects

	OBJECT-1 Can Contain		
	One	Many	Unknown
OBJECT-2 Can Contain — One			
Many			
Unknown			

A third illustration of compound objects appears in Figure 5.25a. In these examples, we see that a book can be written by many authors (in the form about book stock data) and that an author can have written many books (in the form about books in stock by author). Thus, in Figure 5.25b, the BOOK object contains many values of AUTHOR, and AUTHOR contains many values of BOOK. In general, a BOOK must have an AUTHOR, and an AUTHOR (to be an author) must have written at least one BOOK. Thus, both of these objects show a 1 as the minimum required number of contained objects.

Figure 5.26 summarizes the types of compound objects. In general, OBJECT-1 can contain 1, N, or unknown OBJECT-2s. Similarly, OBJECT-2 can contain 1, M, or unknown OBJECT-1s. We will use this table to advantage when we discuss database design in Chapter 7.

ASSOCIATION OBJECTS

An **association object** is an object that relates two (or more) objects together and stores data that is peculiar to their relationship. Figure 5.27a shows three reports. The first contains data about an airline flight and data about the particular airplane and pilot assigned to that flight. The next two reports contain data about a pilot and an airplane, respectively.

In Figure 5.27b, the object FLIGHT is an association object. It associates the two objects AIRPLANE and PILOT and stores data about their association. FLIGHT contains one each of AIRPLANE and PILOT, but both AIRPLANE and PILOT contain multiple values of FLIGHT. This is a typical pattern.

Association objects are always compound objects, and, in fact, you can consider them a special case of compound object, if you wish. The particular pattern, however, of associating two (or more) objects with data about the association occurs so frequently that it is probably worth calling out separately. Association objects occur frequently in assignment situations. Systems that deal with applying an X to a Y, such as an attorney to a client or an employee to a project, give rise to association objects.

HYBRID OBJECTS

As the term implies, **hybrid objects** are combinations of objects of other types. Most frequently, hybrid objects involve the combination of a compound and composite objects in which the object property occurs in a composite group. Consider Figure 5.28a. This

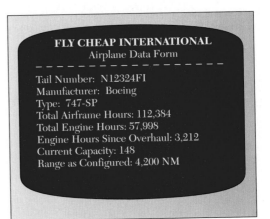

FLY CHEAP INTERNATIONAL
Flight Planning Data Report

FLIGHT NUMBER   *FC-17*   DATE   *7/30/91*
ORIGINATING CITY   *Seattle*   DESTINATION *Hong Kong*
FUEL ON TAKEOFF

WEIGHT ON TAKEOFF

AIRPLANE
    Tail Number   *N1234FI*
    Type   *747-SP*
    Capacity   *148*

PILOT
    Name   *Michael Nilson*
    Base   *Los Angeles International*
    FI-ID   *33489-Z*
    Flight Hours   *18,348*

FLY CHEAP INTERNATIONAL
Pilot Summary Data Form

FCI-ID		
Name	Social Security Number	
Address		
City	State	Zip
Phone	Emergency Phone	
Date of Last Checkout	Hours	
Date of Last Physical		

FLY CHEAP INTERNATIONAL
Airplane Data Form

Tail Number: N12324FI
Manufacturer: Boeing
Type: 747-SP
Total Airframe Hours: 112,384
Total Engine Hours: 57,998
Engine Hours Since Overhaul: 3,212
Current Capacity: 148
Range as Configured: 4,200 NM

a. Example report and forms supported by an association object and two compound objects

Flight-number
Date
Originating-city
Destination
Fuel-on-takeoff
Weight-on-takeoff

AIRPLANE

PILOT

FCI-ID
Name
Social-sec-num
Address
City
State
Zip
Phone
Emergency-phone
Date-of-last-checkout
Hours
Date-of-last-physical

FLIGHT   MV

Tail-number
Manufacturer
Type
Total-airframe-hours
Total-engine-hours
Engine-hours-since-overhaul
Current-capacity
Range-as-configured

FLIGHT   MV

FLIGHT object   PILOT object   AIRPLANE object

b. Association and compound object for FLIGHT report and forms

FIGURE 5.27
Example of association object

DORMITORY OCCUPANCY REPORT

Dormitory	Resident Assistant	Phone
Ingersoll	Sarah and Allen French	3-5567

Student name	Student Number	Rent
Adams, Elizabeth	710	$175.00
Baker, Rex	104	$225.00
Baker, Brydie	744	$175.00
Charles, Stewart	319	$135.00
Scott, Sally	447	$225.00
Taylor, Lynne	810	$175.00

a. Report requiring hybrid object

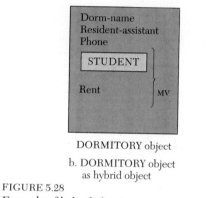

DORMITORY object

b. DORMITORY object
as hybrid object

c. Incorrect DORMITORY
object

FIGURE 5.28
Example of hybrid object

is a second version of the report about dormitory occupancy shown in Figure 5.24a. The difference in this version is that the third column of the student data contains rent instead of class. This is an important difference because rent is not a property of STUDENT; it pertains to the combination of STUDENT and DORMITORY and is a property of DORMITORY.

Figure 5.28b is an object diagram that represents this situation. DORMITORY contains a composite group of the object property STUDENT with the nonobject property Rent. Rent is paired with STUDENT in the context of DORMITORY. To be certain you understand this, examine the alternative DORMITORY object in Figure 5.28c. This is an *incorrect* model of the report in Figure 5.28a. It shows that Rent and STUDENT are independently multivalued, which is incorrect because Rent and STUDENT are multivalued as a pair.

Figure 5.29a shows a form based on another hybrid object. This SALES ORDER form contains data about itself (number, date, sub-total, tax, and total), and also data about a customer, salesperson, and items. Furthermore, the item data (item number, description, and unit price) occurs within a repeating line item of the sales order.

FIGURE 5.29
Another hybrid object

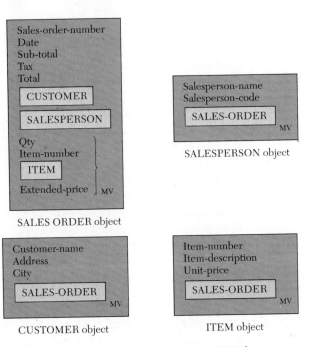

CARBON RIVER OFFICE FURNITURE
Sales Order Form

Sales Order Number 12990   Date 5/31/91

Customer   Carbon River Bookshop
Address   1145 Elm Street
City   Carbon River   State   Zip
Phone   232-0010

Salesperson Name   Elmira   Salesperson Code EZ-1

Qty	Item Number	Description	Unit Price	Extended Price
1	2304	Executive Desk	$199.00	$199.00
1	2690	Conference Table	$345.00	$345.00
4	2799	Side Chairs	$ 99.00	$396.00

Sub-total $940.00
Tax $ 47.94
Total $987.94

a. SALES ORDER form

Sales-order-number
Date
Sub-total
Tax
Total
[CUSTOMER]
[SALESPERSON]
Qty
Item-number
[ITEM]
Extended-price   MV

SALES ORDER object

Salesperson-name
Salesperson-code
[SALES-ORDER]   MV

SALESPERSON object

Customer-name
Address
City
[SALES-ORDER]   MV

CUSTOMER object

Item-number
Item-description
Unit-price
[SALES-ORDER]   MV

ITEM object

b. Hybrid object to represent SALES ORDER form

Figure 5.29b shows the SALES-ORDER semantic object. It contains nonobject properties Sales-order-number, Date, Sub-total, Tax, and Total. It also contains CUSTOMER and SALESPERSON object properties. Additionally, it contains a composite group that represents each line item in the sales order. The composite group contains nonobject properties (Item-number, Qty, and Extended-price), and it contains the object property ITEM.

In this diagram, the property Item-number is shown in both the object diagrams for SALES-ORDER and for ITEM. This is because Item-number is, indeed, a nonobject property of SALES-ORDER, and it is also a nonobject property of ITEM.

GENERALIZATION AND SUBTYPE OBJECTS

Generalization and subtype objects are used to model what we called generalization hierarchies in Chapter 4. Figure 5.30a is a report that gives rise to a generalization object. The report shows data about clients and about three subtypes of client. Note the messages shown in small print, for example, "Use for individual clients only." Clearly, the intent of the designer of this form is that different data is to be collected for different types of client.

Figure 5.30b shows objects that model this form. The generalization object is CLIENT and the subtype objects are IND-CLIENT, PART-CLIENT, and CORP-CLIENT. In CLIENT, observe the keyword *OR* between each of the subtype object properties. Each of these subtypes is an object in its own right, and each of these objects contains CLIENT. This enables the subtype objects to inherit properties from CLIENT.

It is possible for there to be multiple layers of generalization objects. Suppose, for example, that CORP-CLIENTs have divisions, and that each division has a different set of properties. Figure 5.31 shows a set of object diagrams for such CORP-CLIENTs.

Be certain you understand the role of subtype objects. They are used to represent different kinds of subcategories. In the foregoing example, a corporation can have multiple divisions and not need DIVISION subtypes. The need for subtypes arises when different DIVISIONs need to have different models, different sets of properties. If all DIVISION subtypes have the same properties, then subtypes are unnecessary.

Comparison of Semantic Objects with Object-Oriented Programming

The term *object* is used in many ways today. In this chapter, we have appended the word *semantic* to *object* to distinguish the use of this term for data modeling from the use of it in the field of **object-oriented programming.** In fact, both uses of the term are compatible with one another and, in the future, will probably merge.

Figure 5.32, an adaptation of a figure from Coad and Yourdon,[5] shows that the entity-relationship model gave rise to semantic data modeling, including the original semantic

---

[5]Peter Coad and Edward Yourdon, *Object-oriented Analysis* (Englewood Cliffs, N.J.: Yourdon Publications, 1990), 32.

FIGURE 5.30
Example of generalization and
subtype objects

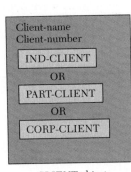

ABERNATHY INSPECTION ENGINEERS
Client Data Form

| Client Name | Client Number |

Amount due

Use for individual clients only:
Address
Social Security Number

Use for partnership clients only:
Managing Partner Name
Address
Tax Identification Number

Use for corporate clients only:
Contact Person
Phone
Tax Identification Number

a. Form indicating need for subtype object

CLIENT
Address
Social-sec-number

IND-CLIENT object

Client-name
Client-number
IND-CLIENT
OR
PART-CLIENT
OR
CORP-CLIENT

CLIENT object

CLIENT
Managing-partner-name
Address
Tax-identification-number

PART-CLIENT object

CLIENT
Contact-person
Phone
Tax-identification-number

CORP-CLIENT object

b. Generalization and subtype objects

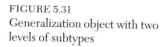

FIGURE 5.31
Generalization object with two
levels of subtypes

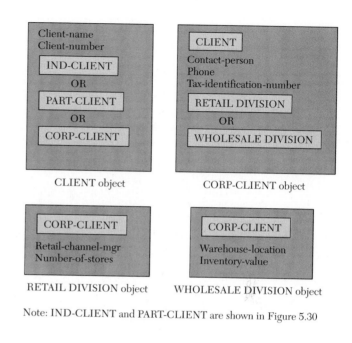

CLIENT object · CORP-CLIENT object

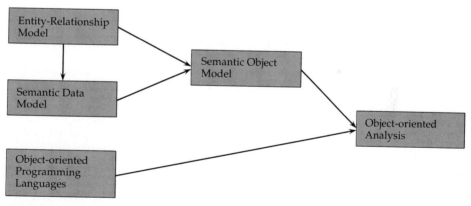

RETAIL DIVISION object · WHOLESALE DIVISION object

Note: IND-CLIENT and PART-CLIENT are shown in Figure 5.30

FIGURE 5.32
Progression of object-oriented perspectives

data model and semantic objects. In a parallel track, object-oriented programming (OOP) languages have been developed that are different from, but sympathetic with, semantic object modeling. In the future, these two streams will likely merge, and a new type of systems development process—one that involves all five components of an information system—will evolve.

To substantiate this claim, we need first to discuss some of the fundamental terms of object-oriented programming.

BRIEF SKETCH OF OBJECT-ORIENTED PROGRAMMING

An OOP object is an **encapsulated** structure having both *attributes* and *methods*. The term *encapsulated* means that it is complete to itself; programs external to an object know nothing of its structure and need to know nothing of its structure. OOP objects have *attributes* arranged in a particular structure. These are quite similar to the properties of semantic objects discussed in this chapter. Finally, and this is a crucial difference, OOP objects contain *methods* which are programs that OOP objects use to process themselves.

Thus, an OOP object might have a method (program) to display itself, one to create itself, and one to modify itself. Consider, as an example, a method that modifies a CUSTOMER object. This method, which is part of the OOP object, is a program; to modify the OOP object, this program could contain instructions to obtain the current data of itself (an instance of CUSTOMER), obtain data for the modification from the user or other source, modify itself, and then store itself back into the database.

OOP objects communicate by sending messages to one another. The modify method, for example, sends messages to other objects to obtain data, perform modifications, and to restore itself in the data. These other objects receive the messages and respond to them by executing their own methods. Since all objects are encapsulated, no object can or need know the structure of any other object. This provides clean separation of complexity and promotes effective cohesion.

Many objects have methods in common. To reduce the duplication in programming, objects are arranged in generalization hierarchies, and methods as well as properties can be inherited.

Consider CLIENT, the example we have been using for such hierarchies. Suppose OOP objects are defined for CLIENT, IND-CLIENT, PART-CLIENT, and CORP-CLIENT. These objects will have a structure of properties similar to the structure shown in Figure 5.30b. They will also have methods for executing messages they receive.

Suppose one of those methods has the function of modifying Client-name. One way to implement these objects is to define a Client-name modification method for each of the four objects. The method, however, would be the same for each object and there is no need to define it four times. Instead, the method can be defined once, in CLIENT, and subtype objects can be allowed to inherit that method from CLIENT. Thus, with OOP, subtypes inherit both data and methods from their supertypes.

A number of languages and language compilers have been developed to support object-oriented programming. The grandparent of them all is SMALLTALK, which was developed at Xerox and implemented by Apple. Another early object-oriented language includes C++, developed by Bell Labs. Both Microsoft and Borland license C and Pascal compilers that support object-oriented programming.

MERGER OF OOP AND SEMANTIC OBJECTS

As defined here, semantic objects do not contain methods. Most likely, they will evolve to do so. Furthermore, recall (from Chapter 2) the symmetry between the program and procedure components of an information system. It is likely that the methods of future semantic objects will consist of both programs and procedures.

Consider the example of the creation of a new checking account. Today, the structure and data of the checking account is recorded in a database, the programs for processing the checking account are located in many different systems in the MIS department, and the manual procedures for processing a checking account are located in procedure manuals in many departments of the bank. Portions of checking accounts and their processing are spread all over the bank, and few people, if any, know all of the activities involved.

Greater efficiency and control could be achieved if CHECKING ACCOUNT were defined as an encapsulated object with structure and methods (both programmed and manual). All methods, whether programmed or manual, would be defined within that object. The checking account would thus be able to manage its own integrity. It would send messages to other programs and to people about what they should do in reference to it. For example, suppose a customer at an ATM wants to withdraw $200. The checking account object would receive the request as a message, "Withdraw $200." The checking account object would then respond by sending messages to the central MIS department requesting data, and then send other messages back to the customer at the ATM machine. Whatever it did, all programs, procedures, and structures would be embedded (and hidden) within the object.

SEMANTIC/OOP SALES-ORDER

Currently, there are no DBMS products that process objects in the sense that is compatible with OOP. We can imagine, however, what such processing might be like. To do that, consider the SALES-ORDER object shown in Figure 5.29. Suppose that this object had, in addition to the structure shown, a set of methods (both programmed and manual) that defined the processing of that object. Call that object SO-OOP. Suppose further that one of the messages that SO-OOP responds to is "Create yourself," and that parameters are sent with this message that specify Customer-name and Date.

When SO-OOP receives this message, it sends messages to other objects to gather data. Suppose it begins by gathering CUSTOMER data. To obtain that data, SO-OOP sends a message with the Customer-name to another OOP object, CUST-OOP. The message says, "Send Address, City for CUST having Cust-name."

Now, SO-OOP knows nothing about the structure of CUST-OOP nor anything about the process that CUST-OOP goes through to obtain Address, City. In fact, there may not even be a customer with the given name, but CUST-OOP may be programmed to enter into a dialogue with the user to create a new customer with that name. CUST-OOP may, for example, open a window on the user's screen, go through a creation process, close the window, and then send the Address and City back to SO-OOP.

Alternatively, CUST-OOP may send messages to distributed computers to obtain the needed data, or it could send a voice message to a salesperson to provide the data or a fax to a forest ranger in a lookout tower in the wilderness. SO-OOP is protected from knowing any of this. SO-OOP would then continue sending messages to other objects until it had all of the data gathered and the new sales order stored in the database.

By partitioning data structure and logic in this way, interfaces among programs are much cleaner and adaptable. CUST-OOP can change the process that it uses for responding to the message, "Send Address, City for CUSTOMER Cust-name" in any way it wants without impacting SO-OOP in anyway. The benefit of this strategy is that systems of great complexity can be developed in much less time than with other approaches. Further, such systems are less prone to errors and are far more flexible and adaptable.

Encoding the structure and meaning of the users' data in semantic objects is a requisite step toward the development of such systems. In the near term, semantic objects can be considered one approach for developing database designs. In the long run, such objects may be extended to include methods and be married with OOP languages in a way that sets a new standard for database processing.

Comparison of the Semantic Object and the E-R Model

The E-R model and the semantic object model have similarities and differences. They are similar in that they both are tools for understanding and documenting the structure of the users' data. They both strive to model the structure of the things in the users' world and the relationships among those things.

The principal difference between the two models is one of orientation. The E-R model takes the concept of *entity* as basic. Entities and their relationships are considered the atoms, if you will, of a data model. These atoms can be combined to form what the E-R model calls *user views*, which are combinations of entities whose structure is similar to semantic objects.

The semantic object model takes the concept of *semantic object* as basic. The set of semantic objects in a data model is a map of the essential structure of the things the user considers important. These objects are the atoms of the users' world and are the smallest distinguishable units that users want to process. They may be decomposed into smaller parts inside the DBMS (or application), but those smaller parts are of no interest or utility to the users.

According to the semantic object perspective, entities, as defined in the E-R model, do not exist. They are only pieces or chunks of the real entities. The only entities that have meaning to users are, in fact, semantic objects.

Consider an example. Figure 5.33 shows two semantic objects, SALES-ORDER and CUSTOMER. When a user says, "Show me sales order number 2000," he or she means show all of the data modeled in Figure 5.33. That includes, among other properties, CUSTOMER data. CUSTOMER is part of SALES-ORDER. The SALES-ORDER entity includes CUSTOMER.

Figure 5.34 is an E-R model of this same data. In this model, there are SALES-ORDER, CUSTOMER, SALESPERSON, LINE-ITEM, and INVENTORY entities. The SALES-ORDER entity includes the properties Sales-order-number, Date, Sub-total, Tax, and Total. Now, if a user were to say, "Show me sales order number 2000" and be given only the properties Date, Sub-total, Tax, and Total, he or she would be disap-

FIGURE 5.33
SALES-ORDER and
CUSTOMER objects

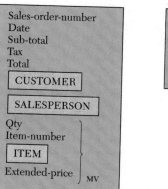

SALES-ORDER object

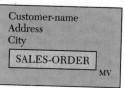

CUSTOMER object

FIGURE 5.34
Entity-relationship model of
SALES-ORDER and
CUSTOMER

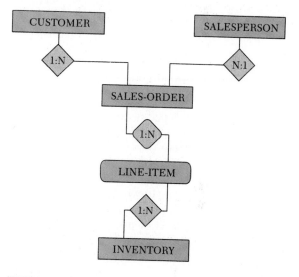

CUSTOMER contains:
 Customer-name
 Address
 City

SALES-ORDER contains:
 Sales-order-number
 Date
 Sub-total
 Tax
 Total

ITEM contains:
 Item-number
 Item-description
 Unit-price

SALESPERSON contains:
 Salesperson-name
 Salesperson-code

LINE-ITEM contains:
 Qty
 Item-number
 Extended-price

pointed. Most likely the user's response would be, "Where's the rest of the data?" The entity, SALES-ORDER, does not represent the user's meaning of the distinct identity SALES-ORDER. The entity is only a part of SALES-ORDER.

At the same time, when a user (perhaps even the same user) says, "Show me customer ABC," he or she means show all of the data modeled for CUSTOMER in Figure 5.34. That data includes Customer-name, Address, City, and data from the ORDERs that the customer has made. The entity CUSTOMER in Figure 5.34 has only the properties Customer-name, Address, and City. If the user were to say "Show me customer ABC" and be given only this data, he or she again would be disappointed. "No, that's only part of what I want."

According to the semantic object view, E-R entities are unnecessary. Semantic objects can be readily transformed into database designs without ever considering E-R model entities. They are halfway houses constructed in the process of moving away from the paradigm of the computer file to the paradigm of the user.

We will revisit this debate in Chapter 7 when we discuss database design. Before we can do that, however, we need to define the relational model and discuss normalization.

Summary

Both the E-R and the semantic object models are used to interpret requirements and to build models of the users' data. These models are like lenses through which developers look when studying and documenting the users' data. Both, ultimately, lead to a database design. The major goals of database development during the requirements phase are to build a data model that documents the things that are to be represented in the database, to determine the characteristics of those things, and to determine the relationships among them.

A semantic object is a named collection of properties that sufficiently describes a distinct identity. Semantic objects are grouped in classes. Both classes and instances of semantic objects have names. For example, the name of a class is EMPLOYEE and the name of an instance is EMPLOYEE 2000.

Properties represent characteristics of the identities being represented. The set of properties is sufficient in that it represents all of the characteristics the users need to accomplish their work. Objects represent distinct identities; they represent instances that the users view as independent and separate. The distinct identities represented may or may not be physical; they may be themselves representative, such as a contract. There are no weak objects in the semantic object model—no object is existence dependent on another.

Both object classes and object instances have names. The names of instances are carried by one or more properties. For larger, organizational systems, objects generally have single-property names, although this is not essential. The fact that an object has a composite name does not mean that it is existence dependent.

Object properties can be simple data items or they can be composite. They can also be either single or multiple valued. Finally, properties can be other objects. Simple, composite, and object properties can be single or multiple valued.

Object diagrams summarize the structure of objects. Object names are shown in all capital letters. Nonobject properties are shown with initial capitals. Multiple valued objects have the letters MV written next to them. Composite groups are indicated by braces.

The domain of a property is the set of all possible values that the property can have. For object properties, the domain is the set of all object instances the property can have. For nonobject properties, the domain is both a physical and a logical (semantic) description.

Applications process objects through users' views. A view of an object consists of the name of the object and all of the properties visible from that view. View and object definition is often an iterative process.

Semantic objects can be used in either a top-down or bottom-up fashion. With the bottom-up approach, developers work from reports and forms and reverse-engineer the object descriptions. With the top-down method, developers begin with a general idea of the goals of the applications and ask the users what objects they need to track. It is also possible to combine the two approaches.

The process of developing a set of object diagrams is an iterative one. Reports or forms are examined and an initial set of objects is documented. New reports and forms are then examined to reveal new objects and changes to existing objects. The process continues until all forms and reports have been examined.

There are six basic types of object. Simple objects have no multivalued properties and no object properties. Composite objects have multivalued properties but no object properties. Compound objects have object properties; association objects are compound objects in which one object relates the two or more other objects. Hybrid objects combine two or more types. Most commonly, hybrid objects contain a composite group that has one or more object properties in it. Finally, generalization and subtype objects represent generalization hierarchies.

In object-oriented programming, an object is an encapsulated data structure that includes attributes (properties) and methods. Methods are programs that are part of the object; both methods and attributes can be inherited. Object-oriented programming and semantic objects are compatible with one another and will likely merge in the future.

The E-R model and the semantic object model have similarities and differences. They both are tools for understanding and documenting the structure of the users' data. The principal difference between the two is one of orientation. The E-R model considers an entity as the basic building block; the semantic object model takes semantic objects as the basic building block. To the semantic object model, an entity is too small; in fact, proponents of this model claim that entities, as defined in the E-R model, do not exist.

GROUP I   QUESTIONS

5.1   Explain how the E-R model and the semantic object model are like lenses.

5.2   Define *semantic object*.

5.3   Explain two types of names that pertain to semantic objects and give an example of each.

5.4   What is required for a set of properties to be a sufficient description?

5.5   Explain the words *distinct identity* as they pertain to the definition of a semantic object.

5.6   Explain why a line item of an order is not a semantic object.

5.7   Give an example of an object and an object identifier that contains two or more properties.

5.8   Explain the difference between a composite identifier and existence dependence. Give examples of an object with a composite identifier and of a weak entity. Use examples different from those in this text.

5.9   Give an example of each of the following:

   a. a simple, single-valued property
   b. a composite, single-valued property
   c. a simple, multivalued property
   d. a composite, multivalued property
   e. a simple object property
   f.   a multivalued object property

5.10   Define *property domain*. What are the type types of property domain? Why is the semantic description necessary?

5.11   What is a semantic object view? Give an example of an object and two views, other than those in this text.

5.12   Explain top-down data modeling.

5.13   Explain bottom-up data modeling.

5.14   Refer to Figure 5.17 and explain how a STUDENT can be contained in a DEPARTMENT object and, at the same time, a DEPARTMENT is contained in a STUDENT object.

5.15   Give an example of a simple object other than the one discussed in this chapter.

5.16   Give three examples of composite objects other than those in this chapter. One of your examples should have just one composite group, one should have two independent composite groups, and the third should have nested composite groups.

5.17   Give an example of four sets of compound objects other than those in this chapter. One set should have a 1:1 relationship, one set should have a 1:N relationship, one set should have a M:N relationship, and the last set should have a 1:unknown relationship.

5.18   Give an example of one association and two compound objects other than those in this chapter.

5.19   Give an example of a hybrid object other than the one in this chapter.

5.20   Give an example of a generalization object with three subtype objects other than those in this chapter.

5.21   Define the term *object* as used in the discipline of object-oriented programming.

5.22   Summarize the major differences between objects in object-oriented programming and semantic objects.

5.23   Explain the similarities between the E-R model and the semantic object model.

5.24   Explain the major differences between the E-R model and the semantic object model.

5.25   Explain the line of reasoning that states that entities, as defined in the E-R model, do not truly exist.

5.26   Show how both the E-R model and the semantic object model would represent the SALES ORDER form in Figure 5.29a. Explain the major differences.

_____

GROUP II QUESTIONS

5.27   Collect as many forms or reports as you can about your relationship with your college or university. Examples include acceptance letters, class schedules, transcripts, bills, class-change forms, and grades. Using the E-R model, create a data model of the entities that underlie your relationship with your school.

5.28   Answer question 5.27, but use the semantic object model instead.

5.29   Compare your answers to questions 5.27 and 5.28. How are they similar? How are they different? Are the differences important? Do you think one model is uniformly superior to the other? Justify your answers.

Database and Database Application Design

The chapters in Part III address the design of databases and database applications. Chapter 6 presents the relational model and normalization. The relational model is important for design because it can be used to express DBMS-independent designs. Normalization is a technique for checking the quality of a design. Given the groundwork in Chapter 6, we then consider, in Chapter 7, the process of transforming data models into DBMS-independent, relational designs. You will see how to transform users' data models expressed in both the entity-relationship model and the semantic object model. Finally, in Chapter 8, we address application design. The purpose of this chapter is to examine the relationship between database structure and application structure and processing. You will learn several important principles for designing database applications.

Relational Model and Normalization

The relational model is important to us for two reasons. First, since the constructs of the relational model are broad and general, it can be used to express DBMS-independent designs. Second, the relational model is the basis for an important category of DBMS products. Knowing this model will help you implement databases using one of these products.

This chapter presents the basics of the relational model and explains the fundamental concepts of a topic called normalization. As you will see, not all relations are equal; some are better than others. Normalization is a process for converting a relation that has certain problems into two or more relations that do not have those problems. Even more important, normalization can be used as a guideline for checking the desirability and correctness of relations.

Considerable theoretical work has been done on the question of what is a well-structured relation. This work is called normalization because one of the pioneers in database technology, E. F. Codd, defined a variety of normal forms that relations can take. This chapter presents a survey of normalization. In it you will learn the results of theorems that are of use and significance to the database practitioner. Proofs of these theorems, and formal, more rigorous treatment of this subject, can be found in the work of Date and that of Ullman.[1]

The Relational Model

A relation is a two-dimensional table. Each row in the table holds data that pertains to some thing or portion of some thing. A row is analogous to a record in a file processing system. Each column of the table contains data; columns are like fields in file processing systems. Sometimes rows are called tuples (rhymes with "couples") and columns are called attributes. We will use the terms **table** and **relation** interchangeably and also the terms **column** and **attribute** interchangeably. We will seldom use the term **tuple.**

Certain restrictions are imposed on tables (relations). The cells of the table must be single valued; neither repeating groups nor arrays are allowed as values.[2] Entries in any column (attribute) are all of the same kind. For example, one column may contain employee numbers. If so, that column has employee numbers for every row of the table. Further, each column has a unique name, and the order of the columns in the table is insignificant. Finally, no two rows (tuples) in a table may be identical, and the order of the rows is insignificant.

Figure 6.1 is a sample table. Notice that this table has seven rows (tuples) made up of four columns (attributes). If we were to rearrange the order of the columns (say by placing Employee-number at the far left) or reorder the rows (perhaps in ascending sequence on Age), then we would have an equivalent table.

Figure 6.1 shows one occurrence, or instance, of a table. The generalized format, EMPLOYEE (Name, Age, Sex, Employee-number), is called the **relation structure,** and it is what most people mean when they use the term *relation*.

The terms *relation, tuple,* and *attribute* arose from the field of relational mathematics, which is the theoretical source of this model. MIS professionals find the terms *file, record,* and *field* more comfortable. Most users, today, find the terms *table, row,* and *column* most sensible. Figure 6.2 summarizes relational terminology.

MODIFICATION ANOMALIES

Not all relations are equally desirable. Obviously, those that satisfy users' needs are better than those that do not, but that does not mean that any relation that fits the definition established is well structured. With some relations, changing the data can have undesir-

---

[1]C. J. Date, *An Introduction to Database Systems* (Reading, Mass.: Addison-Wesley, 1987); J. D. Ullman, *Principles of Database Systems* (Computer Science Press, 1980).

[2]This does not mean that the values must be fixed length. A variable-length text field, for example, is perfectly legitimate as a value. Only *one* such value is allowed, however.

FIGURE 6.1
EMPLOYEE relation

	Attribute1 Name	Attribute2 Age	Attribute3 Sex	Attribute4 Employee-number
Tuple 1	ANDERSON	21	F	010110
Tuple 2	DECKER	22	M	010100
.	GLOVER	22	M	101000
.	JACKSON	21	F	201100
.	MOORE	19	M	111100
.	NAKATA	20	F	111101
Tuple 7	SMITH	19	M	111111

Relational Model	Programmer	User
Relation	File	Table
Tuple (Row)	Record	Row
Attribute	Field	Column

FIGURE 6.2
Relational terminology

FIGURE 6.3
ACTIVITY relation

ACTIVITY (SID, Activity, Fee)
Key: SID
Sample Data

SID	Activity	Fee
100	SKIING	200
150	SWIMMING	50
175	SQUASH	50
200	SWIMMING	50

able consequences. These consequences are called **modification anomalies.** As you will see, anomalies can be eliminated by redefining the relation into two or more relations. In most circumstances the redefined, or **normalized,** relations are preferred.

Consider the relation ACTIVITY in Figure 6.3. As you can see, the attributes are SID (student identifier), Activity, and Fee. The meaning of a row is that a student engages in the named activity for the specified fee. This relation can be used to illustrate modification anomalies.

Suppose that each activity has a fixed fee that is the same for all students. Using the data in Figure 6.3, if we delete the tuple for student 100, we lose not only the fact that student 100 is a skier, but also the fact that skiing costs $200. This is called a **deletion anomaly;** in deleting the facts about one entity (that student 100 is a skier), we inadvertently deleted facts about another entity (that skiing costs $200). We lose facts about two entities with one deletion.

The same relation can be used to illustrate an **insertion anomaly.** Suppose we want to store the fact that scuba costs $175. We cannot enter this data into the ACTIVITY relation until a student takes up scuba. This restriction seems silly. Why should we have to wait until someone takes the activity before we can record its price? This restriction is called an insertion anomaly. We cannot insert a fact about one entity until we have an additional fact about another entity.

The relation in Figure 6.3 can be used for some applications, but it obviously has problems. We can eliminate both the deletion and insertion anomalies by dividing the ACTIVITY relation into two relations, each one dealing with a different theme. For example, we can put the SID and Activity attributes into one relation (we will call the new relation STU-ACT for student activity), and we can put the Activity and Fee attributes into a relation called ACT-COST (for activity cost). Figure 6.4 shows the same sample data stored in these two new relations.

Now if we delete student 100 from STU-ACT, we do not lose the fact that skiing costs $200. Further, we can add scuba and its fee to the ACT-COST relation even before anyone enrolls. Thus, the deletion and insertion anomalies have been eliminated.

Separating the one relation into two relations has a disadvantage, however. Suppose a student tries to sign up for a nonexistent activity. For instance, suppose student 250 wants to enroll in racquetball. We can insert this new tuple in STU-ACT (the row would contain 250, RACQUETBALL), but should we? Should a student be allowed to enroll in an activity that is not in the relation ACT-COST? Put another way, should the database applications somehow prevent student rows to be added if the value of the ACTIVITY is not in the ACT-COST table?

The answer to this question lies with the users' requirements. The constraint is called an **interrelation constraint** or **intertable constraint.** If the action should be prohibited, then this constraint should be documented as part of the database design. Later, in implementation, the constraint will be defined to the DBMS, if the product in use provides such constraint checking. If not, then the constraint must be enforced by application programs.

FIGURE 6.4
Division of ACTIVITY into two relations

STU-ACT (SID, Activity)
Key: SID

SID	Activity
100	SKIING
150	SWIMMING
175	SQUASH
200	SWIMMING

ACT-COST (Activity, Fee)
Key: Activity

Activity	Fee
SKIING	200
SWIMMING	50
SQUASH	50

Suppose the user specifies that activities can exist before any student enrolls in them, but that no student may enroll in an activity that does not have a fee assigned to it (that is, no activities that are not in the ACT-COST table). We can document this constraint in any of several ways in the database design:

Activity in STU-ACT is a subset of Activity in ACT-COST
or   **STU-ACT [Activity] is a subset of ACT-COST [Activity]**
or   **STU-ACT [Activity] $\subseteq$ ACT-COST [Activity]**

In the notation above, the brackets [ ], denote a column of data that is extracted from a relation. You will learn more about the rules governing this operator in Chapter 9. These expressions simply mean that the values in the Activity attribute of STU-ACT must exist in the Activity attribute of ACT-COST. This also means that before we allow an Activity to be entered into STU-ACT we must check to ensure that it is already present in ACT-COST.

ESSENCE OF NORMALIZATION

The problem with the ACTIVITY relation in Figure 6.3 can be stated in the following intuitive way: problems occur because ACTIVITY contains facts about two different themes. It contains a theme about which students participate in which activities, and it also contains a theme about how much each activity costs. When we add a new row, we must add data about two themes at once; and when we delete a row, we delete data about two themes at once.

Remember your eighth-grade English teacher? He or she claimed that a paragraph should have a single theme. If a paragraph had more than one theme, we were taught to break the paragraph up into two or more paragraphs so that each paragraph would have only one theme.

Similar logic applies to relations. Every normalized relation has a single theme. If a relation has two or more themes, it should be broken up into relations that each have a single theme. Every time we break up a relation, however, we create the possible need for an interrelation constraint.

This process is the essence of normalization. When we find a relation with modification anomalies, we eliminate them by splitting the relation into two or more separate ones, each containing a single theme. In the remainder of this chapter, you will learn a number of rules and facts about normalization. All of this knowledge is aimed at the process just described.

CLASSES OF RELATIONS

Relations can be classified by the types of modification anomalies to which they are vulnerable. In the 1970s, relational theorists chipped away at these types. Someone would find an anomaly, classify it, and think of a way to prevent it. Each time this happened, the criteria for designing relations improved. The classes of relations, and techniques for preventing anomalies, are called **normal forms.** Depending on its structure, a relation might be in first normal form, second normal form, or some other normal form.

E. F. Codd, in his landmark 1970 paper,[3] defined first, second, and third normal forms (1NF, 2NF, 3NF). Later, Boyce-Codd normal form (BCNF) was specified, and then fourth and fifth normal forms were defined. As shown in Figure 6.5, these normal forms are nested. A relation in second normal form is also in first normal form. A relation in 5NF (fifth normal form) is also in 4NF, BCNF, 3NF, 2NF, and 1NF.

These normal forms were helpful, but they had a serious limitation. No theory guaranteed that any of these forms would eliminate all anomalies; each form would eliminate just certain ones.

This situation changed, however, in 1981 when R. Fagin defined a new normal form called **domain/key normal form** (DK/NF). In an important paper,[4] Fagin showed that a relation in domain/key normal form is free of all modification anomalies, regardless of their type. Further, he showed that any relation that is free of modification anomalies is also in domain/key normal form.

Until DK/NF was defined, it was necessary for relational database designers to continue looking for more and more anomalies, and more and more normal forms. Fagin's proof, however, simplified the situation. If we can put a relation in DK/NF, then we are guaranteed it will have no anomalies, period. The trick is to know how to put relations in DK/NF.

The next section surveys normal forms. You should strive to gain an intuitive understanding of 1, 2, 3, BC, 4, and 5 normal forms. From a practitioner's standpoint, however, the most important normal form is domain/key. You need to understand it, as domain/key normal form will become the primary design goal when constructing relations.

RELATIONSHIPS AMONG ATTRIBUTES

Earlier we defined a relation as a two-dimensional table that met certain restrictions. Any such relation is, by definition, said to be in **first normal form.** Thus, the relation in Figure 6.3 is in first normal form. As we have seen, relations in first normal form can be used, but they may have modification anomalies. We can eliminate these anomalies by changing the format of the relation: by splitting it into two or more relations. When we do this, the new relations are in some other normal form—just which one depends on the anomalies we have eliminated, as well as the ones to which the new relations are vulnerable.

To understand normalization, you must first understand two important terms: **functional dependency** and **key.** These terms concern the relationships among attributes in a relation. (A good example of how terminology in database technology can be confusing! A *relation* is a table. Don't confuse it with the term *relationship*, which is an associ-

---

[3] E. F. Codd, "A Relational Model of Data for Large Shared Databanks," *Communications of the ACM* 13(June 1970), 377–387.

[4] R. Fagin, "A Normal Form for Relational Databases that Is Based on Domains and Keys," *ACM Transactions on Database Systems* 6(September 1981) 387–415.

FIGURE 6.5
Relationship of normal forms

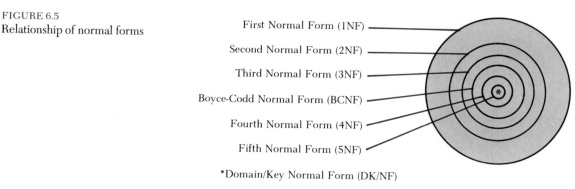

First Normal Form (1NF)
Second Normal Form (2NF)
Third Normal Form (3NF)
Boyce-Codd Normal Form (BCNF)
Fourth Normal Form (4NF)
Fifth Normal Form (5NF)
*Domain/Key Normal Form (DK/NF)

ation among things. As you will learn, relations can express relationships, but the two terms refer to different concepts.)

Functional Dependencies

A functional dependency is a relationship between or among attributes. Suppose that if we are given the value of one attribute, we can obtain (or look up) the value of another attribute. For example, if we know the value of Customer-account-number we can obtain the value of Customer-balance. If this is true, then we say that Customer-balance is *functionally dependent* on Customer-account-number.

In more general terms, attribute Y is functionally dependent on attribute X if the value of X determines the value of Y. Or, stated differently, if we know the value of X, then we can obtain the value of Y.

Equations can represent functional dependencies. For example, if we know the price of an item, and if we know the number of items purchased, then we can calculate the total price for that item as follows:

Total-price = Item-price × Number-of-items

In this case, we would say that Total-price is functionally dependent on Item-price and Number-of-items.

Usually, the functional dependencies between attributes in a relation do not involve equations. For example, suppose students have a unique identification number, SID. Further, suppose that every student has one and only one major. Given the value of a SID, we can obtain that student's major. Thus, Major is functionally dependent on SID. Or, consider microcomputers in a computer lab. Each has one and only one size of main memory. Hence, Size-of-main-memory is functionally dependent on Computer-serial-number. Unlike an equation, such functional dependencies cannot be worked out using arithmetic. Instead, they are listed in the database. In fact, the expression of the functional dependencies is one of the important reasons for having a relation.

Functional dependencies are written using the following notation:

SID → Major
Computer-serial-number → Size-of-main-memory
(Item-price, Number-of-items) → Total-price

The first expression can be read: "SID functionally determines Major," or "SID determines Major," or "Major is dependent on SID." Attributes on the left side of the arrow are called **determinants.**

A functional dependency is a relationship among attribute values. If SID determines Major, then a particular value of SID will be paired with only *one* value of Major. Conversely, a value of Major may be paired with *one or more* different values of SID.

For example, suppose the student whose SID is 123 majors in accounting. Then, any time SID and Major are found in a relation together, SID value of 123 will always be paired with the Major value of accounting. However, the opposite is not true. The Major accounting may be paired with many values of SID (many students may major in accounting). Consequently, we can say that the relationship of SID to Major is many-to-one (sometimes written N:1). In general, we can say that if A determines B, then the relationship of the values of A to B is N:1.

Functional dependencies can involve groups of attributes. Suppose the relation in Figure 6.3 were expanded to include an attribute to distinguish graduate from undergraduate students as follows: ACTIVITY (SID, Student-status, Activity, Fee). The school's policy might be to determine an activity fee by the activity itself and the student's status. Thus, the combination (Student-status, Activity) determines Fee.

In general, if $X \rightarrow (Y, Z)$, then $X \rightarrow Y$ and $X \rightarrow Z$. But if $(X, Y) \rightarrow Z$, then it is not necessarily true that $X \rightarrow Y$ or $Y \rightarrow Z$.

Keys

A key is a group of one or more attributes that uniquely identifies a row. Every relation has at least one key. Sometimes the key is one attribute. If a student were allowed to participate in only one activity at a time, then the SID attribute in the ACTIVITY relation in Figure 6.3 would be the key field: any value of SID would appear, at most, once in the table.

Sometimes a key is comprised of a group of attributes taken together. For example, if students were allowed to enroll in many activities at once, then it would be possible for one value of SID to appear more than once in the table. SID would not uniquely identify the row, then. However, the combination (SID, Activity) would be unique. Therefore, it could be the key for the relation.

As stated, a key is an attribute or group of attributes that uniquely identifies a row. If a student could only participate in one activity at a time, then SID would identify a unique row; it would identify the row of the student's single activity. Thus, SID would be the key.

Now suppose we discover that students are, in fact, allowed to participate in several activities at one time. If so, then SID will not identify a unique row. This situation is represented by the relation ACTIVITIES, shown in Figure 6.6. In this relation, SID is *not* a key. Student 100, for example, has enrolled in both skiing and golf and the SID value of 100 occurs in two different rows. In fact, for this relation, no single attribute is a key. The key must be a combination of two or more attributes.

Consider a combination of two attributes. There are three possibilities: (SID, Activity), (SID, Fee), and (Activity, Fee). Is any one of these combinations a key? If so, it must uniquely identify a row.

FIGURE 6.6   ACTIVITIES (SID, Activity, Fee)
Relation with a two-attribute key   Key: (SID, Activity)

SID	Activity	Fee
100	SKIING	200
100	GOLF	65
150	SWIMMING	50
175	SQUASH	50
175	SWIMMING	50
200	SWIMMING	50
200	GOLF	65

To help us decide, we must examine the semantics of the application. In the users' setting, what makes sense? We cannot simply depend on sample data like that in Figure 6.6 to make the decision, because the data is only one example. We must determine what will be true for all instances of this relation. For this information, we must turn to the users' data model.

Considered from the standpoint of the requirements at a typical college, does it seem likely that the combination (SID, Fee) will determine a unique row? No. It might for one instance of data, but it won't for all. Student 100 could engage in two different activities, both of which cost $200. This would mean that the combination (100, $200) occurs twice in the table. Hence this combination cannot be a key.

Can the combination (Activity, Fee) be a key? Does the combination (skiing, $200) determine a unique row? No, it would not, because many students can participate in skiing. What about (SID, Activity)? Does it seem likely that a combination of values for SID and Activity would determine a unique row? Yes. While a particular SID can appear more than once, and while a particular Activity can appear more than once, the combination of SID and Activity can appear, at most, one time. Thus, (SID, Activity) determines unique rows, and consequently, (SID, Activity) is the key for this relation.

It is very important to understand that we must consider the underlying requirements and data model when assessing functional dependencies. We cannot depend on a set of sample rows to provide us with the answer. Rather, we have to refer to the requirements and to the environment in which the application will be used. We must determine what makes sense in that environment.

Functional Dependencies, Keys, and Uniqueness

Many students confuse the concepts of functional dependencies, keys, and uniqueness. Consider each of these terms.

First, a functional dependency implies nothing about uniqueness in a relation. If A determines B, then the values of A may or may not be unique within a relation. For example, in the ACTIVITIES relation, Activity functionally determines Fee, and yet there can be many instances of a given Activity in the relation. The functional dependency just states that wherever Activity occurs with Fee, it will always occur with the same value of Fee. Skiing always costs $200, regardless of how many times the value skiing occurs in the table.

Unlike the determinants of functional dependencies, keys are always unique. A key functionally determines the entire row. If the value of the key were duplicated, then the entire tuple would be duplicated. But this is not allowed because, by definition, rows in a relation must be unique. Thus, when we say an attribute (or combination) is a key, we know it will be unique. If (SID, Activity) is a key, then, for example, the combination (100, skiing) will occur only once in a relation.

To test your understanding of these concepts, see if you can explain why in the ACTIVITY relation in Figure 6.3, SID is both a determinant and a key, but Activity is a determinant and not a key. (Keep in mind that the relation in Figure 6.3 reflects the school's policy that a student may participate in, at most, one activity at a time.)

These concepts may seem confusing. Work through them several times with examples, if you need to. A thorough understanding of functional dependencies, keys, and uniqueness will make both normalization and the expression of record relationships (in the next chapter) easier to grasp.

First through Fifth Normal Forms

We mentioned earlier that any relation is, by definition, in first normal form. All tables that meet the criteria of the definition of a relation are in first normal form. Unfortunately, as we have seen, relations in first normal form can have modification anomalies. In this section, we will examine each type of normal form and discuss the anomalies that each can have.

SECOND NORMAL FORM

The ACTIVITIES relation in Figure 6.6 has modification anomalies identical to the ones we examined earlier. If we delete the tuple for student 175, we lose the fact that squash costs $50. Also, we cannot enter an activity until a student signs up for it. Thus, the relation suffers from both deletion and insertion anomalies.

The problem with this relation is that it has a dependency involving only part of the key. The key is the combination (SID, Activity), but the relation contains a dependency, Activity → Fee. The determinant of this dependency (Activity) is only part of the key (SID, Activity). In this case, we say that Fee is *partially dependent* on the key of the table. The modification anomalies would not exist if Fee were dependent on all of the key. Therefore, we separate the relation into two relations to eliminate the partial dependency.

This situation leads to the definition of second normal form: *A relation is in second normal form if all nonkey attributes are dependent on all of the key.* Observe from this definition, that every relation that has a single attribute as its key is automatically in second normal form. Since the key is only one attribute, by default, every nonkey attribute will be dependent on *all* of the key; there can be no partial dependencies. Second normal form only pertains to relations that have composite keys. Thus, if the key is a single attribute, then the relation is automatically in second normal form.

ACTIVITIES can be decomposed to form two relations in second normal form. The relations are the same as those in Figure 6.4, namely STU-ACT and ACT-COST. These relations are in second normal form because they both have single-attribute keys.

THIRD NORMAL FORM

Relations in second normal form also have anomalies. Consider the HOUSING relation in Figure 6.7a. The key is SID, and the functional dependencies are SID $\rightarrow$ Building and Building $\rightarrow$ Fee. These dependencies arise because a student lives in only one build-

FIGURE 6.7
Elimination of transitive
dependency

HOUSING (SID, Building, Fee)
Key: SID
Functional
dependencies: Building $\rightarrow$ Fee
               SID $\rightarrow$ Building $\rightarrow$ Fee

SID	Building	Fee
100	RANDOLPH	1200
150	INGERSOLL	1100
200	RANDOLPH	1200
250	PITKIN	1100
300	RANDOLPH	1200

a. Relation with transitive dependency

STU-HOUSING (SID, Building)
Key: SID

BLDG-FEE (Building, Fee)
Key: Building

SID	Building
100	RANDOLPH
150	INGERSOLL
200	RANDOLPH
250	PITKIN
300	RANDOLPH

Building	Fee
RANDOLPH	1200
INGERSOLL	1100
PITKIN	1100

b. Relations eliminating the transitive dependency

ing and each building charges only one fee. Everyone living in Randolph Hall, for example, pays $1200 per quarter.

Since SID determines Building and since Building determines Fee, then, indirectly SID → Fee. An arrangement of functional dependencies like this is called a **transitive dependency** since SID determines Fee via the attribute Building.

Because of this transitive dependency, SID, a single attribute, is the key and the relation is in second normal form (both Building and Fee are determined by SID). In spite of this, however, HOUSING has anomalies.

What happens if we delete the second tuple shown in Figure 6.7a? We lose not only the fact that student 150 lives in Ingersoll Hall, but also the fact that it costs $1100 to live there. This is a deletion anomaly. Further, how can we record the fact that the Fee for Carrigg Hall is $1500? We can't until a student decides to move in. This is an insertion anomaly.

To eliminate the anomalies from a relation in second normal form, the transitive dependency must be removed. This leads to a definition of third normal form: *A relation is in third normal form if it is in second normal form and has no transitive dependencies.*

The HOUSING relation can be divided into two relations in third normal form. The relations STU-HOUSING (SID, Building) and BLDG-FEE (Building, Fee) in Figure 6.7b are examples.

The ACTIVITY relation in Figure 6.3 also has a transitive dependency. In ACTIVITY, SID determines Activity and Activity determines Fee. Therefore, ACTIVITY is not in third normal form. Decomposing ACTIVITY into the relations STU-ACT (SID, Activity) and ACT-COST (Activity, Fee) eliminates the anomalies.

BOYCE-CODD NORMAL FORM

Unfortunately, even relations in third normal form can have anomalies. Consider the ADVISOR relation in Figure 6.8a. Suppose the requirements underlying this relation are that a student (SID) can have one or more majors (Major), a major can have several faculty members (Fname) as advisors, and a faculty member (Fname) advises in only one major area.

Since students can have several majors, SID does not determine Major. Further, since students can have several advisors, SID does not determine Fname, either. Thus, SID cannot be a key.

The combination (SID, Major) determines Fname and the combination (SID, Fname) determines Major. Hence, either of the combinations can be a key. Two or more attributes or attribute collections that can be a key are called **candidate keys.** Whichever of the candidates is selected to be *the* key is called the **primary key.**

In addition to the candidate keys, there is another functional dependency to consider: Fname determines Major (any faculty member advises in only one major. Therefore, given the Fname we can determine the Major). Thus, Fname is a determinant. This will prove important in a moment.

ADVISOR is in first normal form by definition. It is in second normal form since any nonkey attributes are dependent on the entire key (no matter which candidate key we

FIGURE 6.8
Boyce-Codd normal form

ADVISOR (SID, Major, Fname)

Key (primary): (SID, Major)
Key (candidate): (SID, Fname)

Functional
dependencies: Fname → Major

SID	Major	Fname
100	MATH	CAUCHY
150	PSYCHOLOGY	JUNG
200	MATH	RIEMANN
250	MATH	CAUCHY
300	PSYCHOLOGY	PERLS
300	MATH	RIEMANN

a. Relation in third normal form but not in Boyce-Codd normal form

STU-ADV (SID, Fname)
Key: SID, Fname

ADV-SUBJ (Fname, Subject)
Key: Fname

SID	Fname
100	CAUCHY
150	JUNG
200	RIEMANN
250	CAUCHY
300	PERLS
300	RIEMANN

Fname	Subject
CAUCHY	MATH
JUNG	PSYCHOLOGY
RIEMANN	MATH
PERLS	PSYCHOLOGY

b. Relations in Boyce-Codd normal form

select). Further, it is in third normal form because it has no transitive dependencies. In spite of all this, however, it has modification anomalies.

Suppose student 300 drops out of school. If we delete student 300's tuple, we lose the fact that Perls advises in psychology. This is a deletion anomaly. Similarly, how can we store the fact that Keynes advises in economics? We cannot until a student majors in economics. This is an insertion anomaly.

Situations like this lead to the definition of Boyce-Codd normal form (BCNF): *A relation is in BCNF if every determinant is a candidate key.* ADVISOR is not in BCNF since it has a determinant, Fname, which is not a candidate key.

As with the other examples, ADVISOR can be decomposed into two relations having no anomalies. For example, the relations STU-ADV (SID, Fname) and ADV-SUBJ (Fname, Subject) have no anomalies.

Relations in BCNF have no anomalies regarding functional dependencies, and this seemed to put the issue of modification anomalies to rest. It was soon discovered, however, that anomalies can arise from situations other than functional dependencies.

FOURTH NORMAL FORM

Consider the STUDENT relation in Figure 6.9. It shows the relationship of students, majors, and activities. Suppose that students can enroll in several different majors and participate in several different activities. Since this is so, the only key is the combination of attributes (SID, Major, Activity). Student 100 majors in music and accounting. She also participates in swimming and tennis. Student 150 majors only in math and participates in jogging.

What is the relationship between SID and Major? It is not a functional dependency, because students have several majors. In a functional dependency, the determinant is paired with only one value of an attribute. The same statement is true of the relationship between SID and Activity.

The attribute dependency we see here is called a **multivalued dependency.** Multivalued dependencies lead to modification anomalies.

First, note the data redundancy in Figure 6.9. Student 100 has four records: each one shows one of her majors paired with one of her activities. If the data were stored any other way (say we had only two tuples: one for music and swimming and one for accounting and tennis) then the implications would be misleading. It would *appear* that student 100 swam only when she was a music major and played tennis only as an accounting major. This interpretation is illogical! Her majors and her activities are completely independent of one another. So, to prevent such a misleading conclusion, we store all the combinations of majors and activities.

FIGURE 6.9
Relation with multivalued
dependencies

STUDENT (SID, Major, Activity)
Key: (SID, Major, Activity)

Multivalued
dependencies: SID$\twoheadrightarrow$ Major
SID$\twoheadrightarrow$ Activity

SID	Major	Activity
100	MUSIC	SWIMMING
100	ACCOUNTING	SWIMMING
100	MUSIC	TENNIS
100	ACCOUNTING	TENNIS
150	MATH	JOGGING

FIGURE 6.10
STUDENT relations with insertion anomalies

STUDENT (SID, Major, Activity)
Key: (SID, Major, Activity)

SID	Major	Activity
100	MUSIC	SKIING
100	MUSIC	SWIMMING
100	ACCOUNTING	SWIMMING
100	MUSIC	TENNIS
100	ACCOUNTING	TENNIS
150	MATH	JOGGING

a. Insertion of a single tuple

SID	Major	Activity
100	MUSIC	SKIING
100	ACCOUNTING	SKIING
100	MUSIC	SWIMMING
100	ACCOUNTING	SWIMMING
100	MUSIC	TENNIS
100	ACCOUNTING	TENNIS
150	MATH	JOGGING

b. Insertion of two tuples

Suppose that student 100 decides to sign up for skiing, so we add the tuple [100, MUSIC, SKIING] (Figure 6.10a). The relation at this point implies that she skis as a music major, but not as an accounting major. In order to keep the data consistent, we must add one row for each of her majors paired with skiing. Thus we must also add the row [100, ACCOUNTING, SKIING] (Figure 6.10b). This is an update anomaly—far too much updating needs to be done to apply a simple change to the data.

In general, a multivalued dependency exists when there are at least three attributes in a relation, two of them are multivalued, and their values depend only on the third attribute. In other words, in a relation R (A, B, C) a multivalued dependency exists if A determines multiple values of B, A determines multiple values of C, and B and C are independent of each other. As we saw in the previous example, SID determines multiple values of Major, and SID determines multiple values of Activity; but Major and Activity are independent of one another.

FIGURE 6.11
Elimination of multivalued dependency

STU-MAJOR (SID, Major)
Key: (SID, Major)

SID	Major
100	MUSIC
100	ACCOUNTING
150	MATH

STU-ACT (SID, Activity)
Key: (SID, Activity)

SID	Activity
100	SKIING
100	SWIMMING
100	TENNIS
150	JOGGING

Refer again to Figure 6.9. Notice how multivalued dependencies are written: SID →→ Major, and SID →→ Activity. This is read "SID multidetermines Major, and SID multidetermines Activity."

This relation is in BCNF (2NF because it is all key; 3NF because it has no transitive dependencies; and BCNF because it has no nonkey determinants). However, as we have seen, it has anomalies: If a student adds a major, then we must enter a tuple for the new major paired with each of the student's activities. The same holds true if a student enrolls in a new activity. If a student drops a major, we need to delete each of his records containing that major. If he participates in four activities, then there will be four tuples containing the major he has dropped—each of them must be deleted.

To eliminate these anomalies, we must eliminate the multivalued dependency. We do this by building two relations, each one storing data only for one of the multivalued attributes. The resulting relations do not have anomalies. They are STU-MAJOR (SID, Major) and STU-ACT (SID, Activity) (Figure 6.11).

From these observations, we will define fourth normal form in the following way: *A relation is in fourth normal form if it is in BCNF and has no multivalued dependencies.* A more intuitive understanding of multivalued dependencies is possible after you understand domain/key normal form. Consequently, we will come back to this topic at the end of the chapter.

FIFTH NORMAL FORM

Fifth normal form concerns dependencies that are rather obscure. It has to do with relations that can be divided into subrelations as we have been doing, but then cannot be reconstructed. The condition under which this situation arises has no clear, intuitive meaning. We do not know what the consequences of such dependencies are, or even if they have any practical consequences. For more information about fifth normal form, refer to the work of Date which was mentioned earlier in the chapter.

Each of the normal forms we have discussed were identified by researchers who found anomalies with some relations that were in a lower normal form: noticing modification anomalies with relations in second normal form led to the definition of the third normal form. Although each normal form solved some of the problems that had been identified with the previous one, no one could know what problems had not yet been identified. With each step, progress was made toward a well-structured database definition, but no one could guarantee that no more anomalies would be found. In the next section we will study a normal form that guarantees there will be no anomalies of any type. Once we put relations into that form, we know that even the obscure anomalies associated with fifth normal form cannot occur.

Domain/Key Normal Form

In 1981, R. Fagin published an important paper[5] in which he defined domain/key normal form (DK/NF). He showed that a relation in domain/key normal form has no modification anomalies, and further, that a relation having no modification anomalies must be in domain/key normal form. This finding establishes a bound on the definition of normal forms. No higher normal form will be needed, at least for the purpose of eliminating modification anomalies.

Equally important, DK/NF involves only the concepts of key and domain. These concepts are fundamental and close to the heart of database practitioners. They are readily supported by DBMS products (or could be, at least). In a sense, Fagin's work formalized and justified what many practitioners believed intuitively, but were unable to express precisely.

DEFINITION

The DK/NF concept is quite simple. *A relation is in DK/NF if every constraint on the relation is a logical consequence of the definition of keys and domains.* Consider the important terms in this definition: *constraint, key,* and *domain.*

Constraint in this definition is intended to be very broad. Fagin defines a constraint as any rule on static values of attributes that is precise enough that we can evaluate whether or not it is true. Thus, edit rules, intrarelation and interrelation constraints, functional dependencies, and multivalued dependencies are examples of constraints as Fagin has defined them. Fagin expressly excludes constraints having to do with *changes* in data values, or *time-dependent constraints.* For example, the rule "Salesperson salary in the current period can never be less than salary in the prior period," is excluded from Fagin's definition of constraint. Except for time-dependent constraints, Fagin's definition is very broad and inclusive.

As defined in the last section, a key is the unique identifier of a tuple. The third significant term in the definition of DK/NF is *domain.* In Chapter 4, we said that a

[5]R. Fagin, "A Normal Form for Relational Databases that Is Based on Domains Keys," *ACM Transactions on Database Systems* 6(September 1981), 387–415.

domain is a description of the allowed values of an attribute. It has two parts: a physical description and a semantic, or logical, description. The physical description is the set of values the attribute can have and the logical description is the meaning of the attribute. Fagin's proof refers to both parts.

Informally, a relation is in domain/key normal form if enforcing key and domain restrictions causes all of the constraints to be met. Further, since relations in domain/key normal form cannot have modification anomalies, the DBMS can prohibit them by enforcing key and domain restrictions.

Now for the bad news: there is as yet no formal way of converting a relation to DK/NF, nor is it even known which relations can be converted to DK/NF. Finding, or designing, DK/NF relations is more of an art than a science.

Despite this, DK/NF can be exceedingly useful for database design. DK/NF is a design objective. We wish to define our relations such that constraints are logical consequences of domains and keys. For many designs, this objective can be accomplished. Where it cannot be accomplished, the constraints must be built into application programs that process the database. We will see more of this later in this chapter and in Chapter 8. To illustrate DK/NF we will use three examples.

DOMAIN/KEY NORMAL FORM EXAMPLE 1

Consider the STUDENT relation in Figure 6.12. It contains SID, Grade-level, Building, and Fee. Building is the building in which the student lives and Fee is the amount the student pays to live in that building.

SID functionally determines the other three attributes, so SID is a key. Assume we also know, from the requirements definition, that Building → Fee and that SIDs must not begin with 1.

If we can find a way to express these constraints as logical consequences of domain and key definitions, then we can be certain, by Fagin's theorem, there will be no modification anomalies. For this example, it will be easy.

FIGURE 6.12
DK/NF example 1

STUDENT (SID, Grade-level, Building, Fee)

Key: SID

Constraints: Building → Fee

                  SID must not begin with digit 1

Domain Definitions

SID   IN   CDDD, where C is decimal digit not = 1; D =
                 decimal digit
Grade-level IN   {'FR', 'SO', 'JR', 'SN', 'GR' }
Building   IN   CHAR(4)
Fee   IN   DEC(4)

Relation and Key Definitions

STUDENT (SID, Grade-level, Building)
Key: SID

BLDG-FEE
(Building, Fee)
Key: Building

FIGURE 6.13
Domain/key definition of example 1

To enforce the constraint that student numbers not begin with 1, we simply define the domain for student numbers to incorporate this constraint (Figure 6.13). Enforcing the domain restriction guarantees that this constraint will be met.

Next, we need to make the functional dependency Building → Fee a logical consequence of keys. If Building were a key attribute, then Building → Fee would be a logical consequence of a key. Therefore, the question becomes, How can we make Building a key? It cannot be a key in STUDENT because more than one student lives in the same building. It could be a key of its own relation, however.

Thus we define the relation BLDG-FEE with Building and Fee as its attributes. Building is the key of this relation. Having defined this new relation we can remove Fee from STUDENT. The final domain and relation definitions for this example appear in Figure 6.13.

This is the same result we obtained when converting a relation from 2NF to 3NF to remove transitive dependencies. In this case, however, the process was simpler and the result more robust. It was simpler because we did not need to know that we were eliminating a transitive dependency. We simply needed to search for creative ways to make all the constraints logical consequences of domain and key definitions. The result was more robust because, when converting the relation to 3NF, we only knew that it had fewer anomalies than when it was in 2NF. By converting the relation to DK/NF, we know that the relations have no modification anomalies whatsoever.

DOMAIN/KEY NORMAL FORM EXAMPLE 2

The next example involves the relation described in Figure 6.14. It it more complicated than the previous one. The PROFESSOR relation contains data about professors, the classes they teach, and the students they advise. FID (for Faculty ID) and Fname uniquely identify a professor. SID uniquely identifies a student, but Sname does not necessarily identify a SID. Professors can teach several classes and advise several students. A student, however, is advised by only one professor. FIDs start with a 1; SIDs must not start with a 1.

These statements can be expressed more precisely by the functional and multivalued dependencies shown in Figure 6.14. FID and Fname functionally determine each other (in essence, they are equivalent). FID and Fname multidetermine Class and SID. SID functionally determines FID and Fname. SID determines Sname.

In more complex examples such as this one, it is helpful to consider DK/NF from a more intuitive light. Recall the essence of normalization is that every relation should have a single theme. Considered from this perspective, there are three themes in PROFESSOR. One is that FIDs and Fnames are the same. Another concerns the classes that a professor teaches; the third concerns the identification number, name, and advisor of a given student.

Figure 6.15 shows three relations that reflect these themes. The FACULTY relation represents the equivalence of FID and Fname. FID is the key, and Fname is an alternate key. This terminology means both attributes are unique in the relation. Because both are keys, the functional dependencies FID → Fname and Fname → FID are logical consequences of keys.

The PREPARATION relation contains the correspondence of faculty and classes; it shows the classes a professor is prepared to teach. The key is the combination (Fname, Class). Both attributes are required in the key because a professor may teach several classes. Finally, STUDENT represents the student and advisor names for a particular SID. Observe that each of these relations has a single theme.

These relations express all of the constraints of Figure 6.14 as a logical consequence of domains and key definitions. These relations are, therefore, in DK/NF.

Note that the separation of the PREPARATION theme from the STUDENT theme has eliminated the multivalued dependencies. When we examined fourth normal form, we learned that to eliminate multivalued dependencies, we needed to separate the multivalued attributes into different relations. Our approach here is to break a relation with several themes into several relations, each with one theme. In doing that, we eliminated a multivalued dependency. In fact, we arrived at the same solution via both approaches.

DOMAIN/KEY NORMAL FORM EXAMPLE 3

The next example concerns a situation that was not addressed by any of the other normal forms, but that occurs frequently in practice. Specifically, this relation has a constraint among data values within a tuple that is neither a functional dependency nor a multivalued dependency.

PROFESSOR (FID, Fname, Class, SID, Sname)
Key: (FID, Class, SID)
Constraints: FID→Fname
                    Fname→FID
                    FID→→Class | SID
                    Fname→→Class | SID
                    SID→FID
                    SID→Fname
                    SID→Sname
                    FID must start with 1; SID must not start with 1

FIGURE 6.14
DK/NF example 2

Domain Definitions

FID	IN	CDDD, C = 1; D = decimal digit
Fname	IN	CHAR(30)
Class	IN	CHAR(10)
SID	IN	CDDD, C is decimal digit, not = 1; D = decimal digit
Sname	IN	CHAR(30)

Relation and Key Definitions

FACULTY (FID, Fname)
Key (primary):   FID
Key (candidate): Fname

PREPARATION (Fname, Class)
Key: Fname, Class

STUDENT (SID Sname, Fname)
Key: SID

FIGURE 6.15
Domain/key definition of example 2

Consider the constraints in the relation STU-ADVISOR in Figure 6.16. This relation contains information about a student and his or her advisor. SID determines Sname, FID, Fname, and Grad-faculty-status, and is therefore the key. FID and Fname identify a unique faculty member and are equivalent to one another as in example 2. Both FID and Fname determine Grad-faculty-status. Finally, the new type of constraint is that only members of the graduate faculty are allowed to advise graduate students.

Domain restrictions are that SID must not begin with a 1, SID must begin with a 9 for graduate students, FID must begin with a 1, and Grad-faculty-status is 0 for under-graduate faculty and 1 for graduate faculty.

With these domain definitions, the constraint that graduate students must be advised by graduate faculty can be expressed as a constraint on row values. Specifically, if the SID starts with 9, then the value of Grad-faculty-status must be 1.

To put this relation in DK/NF, we proceed as in example 2. What are the basic themes of this relation? There is one about faculty personnel that relates FID, Fname, and Grad-faculty-status. Since FID and Fname determine Grad-faculty-status, either of these attributes can be the key and this relation is in DK/NF. See Figure 6.17.

Now consider data about students and advisors. Although it may first appear that there is only one theme, that of advising, the constraint that only graduate faculty can advise graduate students implies otherwise. Actually, there are two themes: graduate advising and undergraduate advising. Thus, in Figure 6.17, there is a G-ADV relation for graduate students and a UG-ADV relation for undergraduates. Observe the domain definitions. GSID starts with a 9, Gfname is the Fname of a FACULTY tuple with Grad-faculty-status equal to 1, and UGSID must not begin with 1 or 9.

All the constraints described in Figure 6.16 are implied by key and domain definitions in Figure 6.17. These relations are therefore in DK/NF and have no modification anomalies.

Before continuing, you may wish to review the definitions of the normal forms. Figure 6.18 summarizes the normal forms we have discussed.

STU-ADVISOR (SID, Sname, FID, FName, Grad-faculty-status)

Key: SID

Constraints: FID → Fname
Fname → FID
FID and Fname → Grad-faculty-status
Only graduate faculty can advise graduate students
FID begins with 1
SID must not begin with 1
SID of graduate student begins with 9
Grad-faculty-status = $\begin{cases} 0 \text{ for undergraduate faculty} \\ 1 \text{ for graduate faculty} \end{cases}$

FIGURE 6.16
DK/NF example 3

Domain Definitions

FID	IN	CDDD, where C = 1; D = decimal digit
Fname	IN	CHAR (30)
Grad-faculty-status	IN	[0, 1]
GSID	IN	CDDD, where C = 9; D = decimal digit; graduate student
UGSID	IN	CDDD, WHERE C ≠ 1 and C ≠ 9; D = decimal digit; undergraduate student
Sname	IN	CHAR (30)

Additional Domain Definitions

Gfname	IN	{Fname of FACULTY, where Grad-faculty-status = 1}

Relations and Key Definitions

FACULTY (FID, Fname, Grad-faculty-status)
Key: FID or Fname

G-ADV (GSID, Sname, Gfname)
Key: GSID

UG-ADV (UGSID, Sname, Fname)
Key: UGSID

FIGURE 6.17
Domain/key definition of example 3

Form	Defining Characteristic
1NF	Any relation
2NF	All nonkey attributes are dependent on all of the keys.
3NF	There are no transitive dependencies.
BCNF	Every determinant is a candidate key.
4NF	There are no multivalued dependencies.
5NF	Not described in this discussion.
DK/NF	All constraints on relations are logical consequences of domains and keys.

FIGURE 6.18
Summary of normal forms

Rules for Composing Records

In the previous section, we approached relational design from an analytical perspective. The question we asked was, "Given a relation, is it in good form? Does it have modification anomalies?" In this section, we will approach relational design from a different perspective—a synthetic one. From this approach, we ask the question, "Given a set of attributes with certain functional dependencies, what relations can we form?"

Two attributes, say *A* and *B,* can be related in three basic ways:

1. They determine each other:

   A → B and B → A

   In this case, A and B have a one-to-one attribute relationship.
2. One determines the other.

   A → B, but B ↮ A

   Here, A and B have a many-to-one relationship.
3. They are functionally unrelated.

   A ↮ B and B ↮ A

   A and B have a many-to-many attribute relationship.

ONE-TO-ONE ATTRIBUTE RELATIONSHIP

If A determines B and B determines A, then the values of the attributes have a one-to-one relationship. Here's why: we know that if A determines B, then the relationship from A to B is many-to-one. It is also true, however, that if B determines A, then the relationship from B to A must be many-to-one. Now, how can both of these statements be true at the same time? It must be that the relationship from A to B is actually one-to-one (which is a special case of many-to-one) and that the relationship from B to A is also actually one-to-one. Hence, the relationship is one-to-one.

This case is illustrated by FID and Fname in examples 2 and 3 in the previous section on domain/key normal Form. Each of these attributes uniquely identifies a faculty person. Consequently, one value of FID corresponds to exactly one value of Fname, and vice versa.

Three equivalent statements can be drawn from the example of FID and Fname:

- If two attributes functionally determine each other, then the relationship of their data values is one-to-one.
- If two attributes uniquely identify the same thing (entity or object), then the relationship of their data values is one-to-one.
- If two attributes have a one-to-one relationship, then they functionally determine each other.

Attributes that have a one-to-one relationship must occur together in at least one relation. Other attributes that are functionally determined by these (an attribute that is functionally determined by one of them will be functionally determined by the other as well) may also reside in this same relation.

Consider FACULTY (FID, Fname, Grad-faculty-status) in example 3 in the previous section. FID and Fname determine each other. Grad-faculty-status can also occur in this relation because it is determined by FID and Fname.

Attributes that are not functionally determined by these attributes may not occur in a relation with them. Consider relations FACULTY and PREPARATION in example 2. Here, FID and Fname both occur in FACULTY, but Class (from PREPARATION) may not. There can be multiple values of Class for a faculty member, so Class is not dependent on FID or Fname. If we added Class to the FACULTY relation, then the key of FACULTY would need to be either (FID, Class) or (Fname, Class). In this case, however, FACULTY would not be in DK/NF, because the dependencies between FID and Fname would not be logically implied by either of the possible keys.

These statements are summarized in the first column of Figure 6.19. Record definition rules are listed in Figure 6.20. If A and B have a 1:1 relationship, then A and B can reside in the same relation, say R. A determines B and B determines A. The key of the relation can be either A or B. A new attribute, C can be added to R if either A or B functionally determines C.

Attributes having a one-to-one relationship must exist together in at least one relation in order to establish their equivalence (FID of 198, for example, refers to Professor Heart). It is generally undesirable to have them occur together in more than one relation, however, because this causes a needless data duplication. Often, one or both of the two attributes will occur in other relations. Fname, for example, occurs in both PREPARATION and STUDENT in example 2. Although it would be possible to place Fname in PREPARATION and FID in STUDENT, this is generally bad practice. When attributes are paired in this way, one of them should be selected to represent the pair in all other relations. Fname was selected in example 2.

Type of Attribute Relationship

	One-to-One	Many-to-One	Many-to-Many
Relation Definition°	R(A,B)	S(C,D)	T(E,F)
Dependencies	A → B B → A	C → D D $\nrightarrow$ C	E $\nrightarrow$ F F $\nrightarrow$ E
Key	Either A or B	C	(E,F)
Rule for Adding Another Attribute	Either A or B → C	C → E	(E,F) → G

° The letters used in these relation definitions match those used in Figure 6.20.

FIGURE 6.19

Summary of three types of attribute relationship

Concerning One-to-One Relationships
- Attributes that have a one-to-one relationship must occur together in at least one relation. Call the relation R and the attributes A and B.
- Either A or B must be the key of R.
- An attribute can be added to R if it is functionally determined by A or B.
- An attribute that is not functionally determined by A or B cannot be added to R.
- A and B must occur together in R, but should not occur together in other relations.
- Either A or B should be consistently used to represent the pair in relations other than R.

Concerning Many-to-One Relationships
- Attributes that have a many-to-one relationship can exist in a relation together. Assume C determines D in relation S.
- C must be the key of S.
- An attribute can be added to S if it is determined by C.
- An attribute that is not determined by C cannot be added to S.

Concerning Many-to-Many Relationships
- Attributes that have a many-to-many relationship can exist in a relation together. Assume two such attributes, E and F, reside together in relation T.
- The key of T must be (E,F)
- An attribute can be added to T if it is determined by the combination (E,F).
- An attribute may not be added to T if it is not determined by the combination (E,F).
- If adding a new attribute, G, expands the key to (E, F, G), then the theme of the relation has been changed. Either G does not belong in T or the name of T must be changed to reflect the new theme.

FIGURE 6.20
Summary of rules for constructing relations

MANY-TO-ONE ATTRIBUTE RELATIONSHIP

If attribute A determines B, but B does not determine A, then the relationship among their data values is many-to-one. In the advisor relationship in example 2, SID determines FID. Many students (SID) are advised by a faculty member (FID), but each student is advised by only one faculty member. Thus, this is a many-to-one relationship.

For a relation to be in DK/NF, all functional dependencies must be implied by keys. Thus, for a relation in DK/NF, every determinant must be a key. If A, B, and C are in the same relation, and if A determines B, then A must be the key (meaning it also determines C). If (A, B) determines C, then (A, B) must be the key. In this latter case, no other functional dependency, such as A determines B, is allowed.

You can apply these statements to database design in the following way: When constructing a relation, if A determines B, then the only other attributes you can add to the relation must also be determined by A. For example, suppose you have put SID and Building together in a relation called STUDENT. You may add any other attribute determined by SID, such as Sname, to this relation. But if the attribute Fee is determined by Building, then you may not add it to this relation. Fee can be added only if SID → Fee.

These statements are summarized in the center column of Figure 6.19. If C and D have an N:1 relationship, then they may reside together in a relation, say S. C will determine D, but D will not determine C. The key of S will be C. Another attribute E, can only be added to S if C determines E.

MANY-TO-MANY ATTRIBUTE RELATIONSHIP

If A does not determine B and B does not determine A, then the relationship among their data values is many-to-many. In example 2, Fname and Class have a many-to-many relationship. A professor teaches many classes and a class is taught by many professors.

In a many-to-many relationship, both attributes must be a key of the relation. For instance, the key of PREPARATION in example 2 is the combination (Fname, Class).

When constructing relations that have multiple attributes as keys, you can add new attributes that are functionally dependent on all of the keys. Number-of-times-taught is functionally dependent on both (Fname, Class), and could be added to the relation. Faculty-office, however, could not be added because it would be dependent only on Fname, not on Class. If Faculty-office needs to be stored in the database, it must be added to a relation about faculty, not to the relation about preparations.

These statements are summarized in the right column of Figure 6.19. If E and F have an M:N relationship, then neither E determines F nor F determines E. E and F can be put into a relation T, and if this is done, the key of T will be the composite (E,F). A new attribute, G, can be added to T if it is determined by all of (E,F). It cannot be added to T if it is determined by only one of (E,F).

Consider a similar, but different example. Suppose we add Classroom-number to PREPARATION. Is Classroom-number functionally determined by the key of PREPARATION, (Fname, Class)? Most likely, it is not. A given professor could teach a particular class in many different rooms.

The composite (Fname,Class) and Classroom-number have an M:N relationship. Since this is so, the rules in Figure 6.19 can be applied, but let E represent (Fname, Class) and F represent Classroom-number. Now, we can compose a new relation, T, with attributes Fname, Class, and Classroom-number. The key becomes (Fname, Class, Classroom-number).

In this situation, we have created a new relation, with a new theme. Consider relation T. What does it contain? It has faculty names, classes, and classroom numbers. The theme of this relation is no longer PREPARATION, but rather, WHO-WHAT-WHERE-TAUGHT.

Changing the theme may or may not be appropriate. If Classroom-number is important, then the theme does need to be changed. In that case, PREPARATION is the wrong relation. WHO-WHERE-TAUGHT is a more appropriate theme.

On the other hand, depending on user requirements, PREPARATION may be completely appropriate as it is. If so, then Classroom-number, if it belongs in the database at all, should be located in a different relation—perhaps SECTION-NUMBER, or CLASS-SECTION, or some similar relation.

Multivalued Dependencies, Iteration Two

The discussion about many-to-many attribute value relationships may make the concept of multivalued dependencies easier to understand. The problem with the relation STUDENT (SID, Major, Activity) in Figure 6.9 is that it has *two* different many-to-many relationships; one is between SID and Major and the other is between SID and Activity. Clearly, a student's various majors have nothing to do with the student's various activities. Putting both of these many-to-many relationships in the same relation, however, makes it appear as if there is some association.

Major and Activity are independent. There would be no problem if a student had only one of each. Then, SID would functionally determine Major and Activity, and the relation would be in DK/NF. In this case, the relationships from Major to SID and Activity to SID would both be many-to-one.

Another way of perceiving the difficulty is to examine the key, (SID, Major, Activity). Since STUDENT has many-to-many relationships, all of the attributes have to be in the key. Now, what theme does this key represent? We might say the combination of the studies and activities of a student. But this is not one thing; it is plural. One row of this relation describes only part of the combination; we need all of the rows about a particular student to get the whole picture. In general, a row should have all of the data about one instance of the theme of the relation. A row of Customer, for example, should have all the data we want about a particular customer.

Consider PREPARATION in example 2 in the section on domain/key normal form. The key is (Fname, Class). What theme does this represent? The fact that a particular professor is prepared to teach a particular class. We only need one row of the relation to get all of the information (the relation might include Number-of-times-taught, Average-course-evaluation-score, and so on) we have about the combination of that professor and that class. Looking at more rows will not generate any more information about it.

As you know, the solution to the multivalued dependency constraint problem is to break the relation into two relations, each having a single theme. STU-MAJOR shows the combination of a student and a major. Everything we know about the combination is in a single row. We will not gain more information about that combination by examining more rows.

Caveats on Normalization

A database design, as described in Chapter 3, consists of definitions of data items (what we have called attributes in this chapter), records, and relationships among records. The definition of each of these includes a section describing constraints. We have been discussing such constraints throughout this chapter, although we have not been explicit about it—now we will.

CONSTRAINTS

Data item (attribute) constraints are implied in domain definitions. When we say, as part of the domain definition, that UGSID must not begin with 1 or 9, we are stating data item constraints. Thus, the definitions of domains will provide much of the material for the constraints section of data item definitions.

Additionally, a key is a (relation) constraint. The statement that an attribute is a key is equivalent to stating that the attribute must be unique in the relation. Another way of explaining domain/key normal form is that if a relation is in domain/key normal form, then the only nondomain constraints will be uniqueness constraints. No other constraints will be allowed (or necessary).

Finally, there are constraints about relationships. In fact, an interrelation constraint is a relationship constraint. The statement that Fname in PREPARATION is a subset of Fname in FACULTY is a relationship constraint. Thus, interrelation constraints will provide the material for relationship constraints in the database design.

You will see how all of these concepts interplay in later chapters when we illustrate specific DBMS products. For now, just be aware that normalization indicates the identity of relations that will be needed, the attributes contained within those relations, and much information about constraints that will be required.

DENORMALIZATION

Normalization is only an aide to database design. Normalized relations avoid modification anomalies, and on that ground they are preferred to unnormalized relations. However, judged on other grounds, normalization is sometimes not worth it.

Consider this relation:

CUSTOMER (Cust#, Cust-name, City, State, and Zip)

It is not in DK/NF. The key is Cust#, and Zip functionally determines City and State. Hence, there is a constraint that is not implied by the definition of keys.

This relation can be transformed into the following two DK/NF relations:

CUSTOMER (Cust#, Cust-name, Zip)
CODES (Zip, City, State)

But why? Little is gained.

Hence, sometimes relations are purposely left unnormalized or are normalized and then denormalized. Often this is done to improve performance. This does not mean that your hard work in understanding normalization theory was wasted. You need to know how to normalize. The point is not to become slavish about it. Sometimes it doesn't make sense. Just as sometimes the rules of grammar are violated.

Summary

The relational model is important for two reasons: it can be used to express DBMS-independent designs, and it is the basis for an important category of DBMS-products. Normalization can be used as a guideline for checking the desirability and correctness of relations.

A relation is a two-dimensional table that has single-valued entries. Entries in a given column are all of the same kind, columns have a unique name, and the order of columns is immaterial. Columns are also called attributes. No two rows of a table are identical and the order of rows in the table is immaterial. Rows are also called tuples. The terms *table*, *file*, and *relation* are synonymous; the terms *column*, *field*, and *attribute* are synonymous, and the terms *row*, *record*, and *tuple* are synonymous.

Some relations, when updated, suffer from undesirable consequences called modification anomalies. A deletion anomaly occurs when the deletion of a row loses information about two or more entities. An insertion anomaly occurs when the relational structure forces the addition of facts about two entities at the same time. Anomalies can be removed by splitting the relation into two or more relations.

There are many types of modification anomalies. Relations can be classified by the types of anomaly which they eliminate. Such classifications are called normal forms.

A functional dependency is a relationship between attributes. Y is functionally dependent on X if the value of X determines the value of Y. A determinant is a group of one or more attributes on the left side of a functional dependency, for example, if X determines Y, then X is the determinant. A key is a group of one or more attributes that uniquely identifies a tuple. Every relation has at least one key; because every row is unique, in the most extreme case, the key is the collection of all of the attributes in the relation. Although a key is always unique, the determinant in a functional dependency need not be unique.

Every relation is in first normal form by definition. A relation is in second normal form if all nonkey attributes are dependent on all of the key. A relation is in third normal form if it is in second normal form and has no transitive dependencies. A relation is in Boyce-Codd normal form if every determinant is a candidate key. A relation is in fourth normal form if it is in Boyce-Codd normal form and has no multivalued dependencies. The definition of fifth normal form is intuitively obscure, and we did not define it.

A relation is in domain/key normal form if every constraint on the relation is a logical consequence of the definition of domains and keys. Constraint is any constraint on static values of attributes whose truth can be evaluated. As we have defined them, domains have both a physical and a semantic part. In the context of domain/key normal form, however, domain refers only to the physical description.

An informal way of expressing domain/key normal form is to say that every relation must have only a single theme. For example, it might be about PROFESSORs or about STUDENTs but not about both PROFESSORs and STUDENTs at the same time.

Normalization can be considered from the standpoint of the relationship among attributes. If two attributes functionally determine each other, then they have a one-to-one relationship. If one attribute functionally determines the other, but not the reverse, then the attributes have a one-to-many relationship. If neither attribute determines the other, then they have a many-to-many relationship. These facts can be used when constructing relations.

GROUP I   QUESTIONS

6.1   What is a deletion anomaly? Give an example.

6.2   What is an insertion anomaly? Give an example.

6.3   Explain the relationship of 1, 2, 3, BC, 4, 5, and D/K normal forms.

6.4   Define *functional dependency.* Give an example of two attributes having a functional dependency. Give an example of two attributes that do not have a functional dependency.

6.5   If SID functionally determines Activity, does this mean that only one value of SID can exist in the relation? Why or why not?

6.6   Define *determinant.*

6.7   Give an example of a relation having a functional dependency in which the determinant has two or more attributes.

6.8   Define *key.*

6.9   If SID is a key of a relation, is it a determinant? Can there be more than one occurrence of a given value of SID in the relation?

6.10 Define *second normal form.* Give an example of a relation in 1NF but not in 2NF. Transform the relation into relations in 2NF.

6.11 Define *third normal form.* Give an example of a relation in 2NF but not 3NF. Transform the relation into relations in 3NF.

6.12 Define *BCNF.* Give an example of a relation in 3NF but not BCNF. Transform the relation into relations in BCNF.

6.13 Define *multivalued dependency.* Give an example.

6.14 Why must multivalued dependencies exist in pairs?

6.15 Define *fourth normal form.* Give an example of a relation in BCNF but not in 4NF. Transform the relation into relations in 4NF.

6.16 Define *domain/key normal form.* Why is it important?

6.17 Transform the following relation into DK/NF. Make appropriate assumptions about functional dependencies and domains. State your assumptions.

EQUIPMENT (Manufacturer, Model, Acq-date, Buyer-name, Buyer-phone, Plant-location, City, State, ZIP)

6.18 Transform the following relation into DK/NF. Make appropriate assumptions about functional dependencies and domains. State your assumptions.

INVOICE (Number, Customer-name, Customer-number, Customer-address, Item-number, Item-price, Item-quantity, Salesperson-number, Salesperson-name, Sub-total, Tax, Total-due)

6.19 Do 6.18 again, except add attribute Customer-tax-status (0 if nonexempt, 1 if exempt). Also, add the constraint: there will be no tax if Customer-tax-status = 1.

GROUP II QUESTIONS

6.20   Using the following relation definition and sample data, answer the questions.

PROJECT (Project-id, Emp-name, Emp-salary)
Where Project-id is the name of a work project
          Emp-name is the name of an employee who works on that project
          Emp-salary is the salary of the employee whose id is Emp#

Project-id	Emp-name	Emp-salary
100A	Jones	64K
100A	Smith	51K
100B	Smith	51K
200A	Jones	64K
200B	Jones	64K
200C	Parks	28K
200C	Smith	51K
200D	Parks	28K

PROJECT relation

Which of the following statements is/are true?

a. Project-id → Emp-name
b. Project-id → Emp-salary
c. (Project-id, Emp-name) → Emp-salary
d. Emp-name → Emp-salary
e. Emp-salary → Project-id
f. Emp-salary → (Project-id, Emp-name)

Answer these questions:

g. What is the key of PROJECT?
h. Are all nonkey attributes (if any) dependent on all of the key?
i. In what normal form is PROJECT?
j. Describe two modification anomalies from which PROJECT suffers.
k. Is Project-id a determinant?
l. Is Emp-name a determinant?
m. Is (Project-id, Emp-name) a determinant?
n. Is Emp-salary a determinant?
o. Does this relation contain a transitive dependency? If so, what is it?
p. Redesign this relation to eliminate the modification anomalies.

6.21   Using the following relation definition and sample data, answer the questions.

PROJECT-HOURS (Emp-name, Project-id, Task-id, Phone#, Total-hrs)
Where Emp-name is the name of an employee
          Project-id is the name of a project
          Task-id is the name standard work task

Phone# is the employee's telephone number
Total-hrs is hours worked by the employee on this project

Emp-Name	Project-id	Task-id	Phone#	Total-hrs
Don	100A	B-1	12345	12
Don	100A	P-1	12345	12
Don	200B	B-1	12345	12
Don	200B	P-1	12345	12
Pam	100A	C-1	67890	26
Pam	200A	C-1	67890	26
Pam	200D	C-1	67890	26

PROJECT-HOURS relation

Which of the following statements is/are true?

a. Emp-name → Project-id
b. Emp-name →→ Project-id
c. Emp-name → Task-id
d. Emp-name →→ Task-id
e. Emp-name → Phone#
f. Emp-name → Total-hrs
g. (Emp-name, Project-id) → Total-hrs
h. (Emp-name, Phone#) → Task-id
i. Project-id → Task-id
j. Task-id → Project-id

Answer these questions:

k. List all of the determinants.
l. Does this relation contain a transitive dependency? If so, what is it?
m. Does this relation contain a multivalued dependency? If so, what are the unrelated attributes?
n. Describe a deletion anomaly from which this relation suffers.
o. How many themes are there in this relation?
p. Redesign this relation to eliminate the modification anomalies. How many relations did you use? How many themes are there in each of your new relations?

6.22 Consider the following relation, key, and domain definitions:

Domain Definitions

Emp-name	IN	CHAR(20)
Phone#	IN	DEC(5)
Equip-name	IN	CHAR(10)
Location	IN	CHAR(7)
Cost	IN	CURRENCY
Date	IN	YYMMDD
Time	IN	HHMM where HH between 00 and 23 and MM between 00 and 59

Relation Definitions

EMPLOYEE (Emp-name, Phone#)
Key: Emp-name
Constraints: Emp-name → Phone#

EQUIPMENT (Equipment-name, Location, Cost)
Key: Equipment-name
Constraints: Equipment-name → Location
              Equipment-name → Cost

APPOINTMENT (Date, Time, Equipment-name, Emp-name)
Key: (Date, Time, Equipment-name)
Constraints: (Date, Time, Equipment-name) → Emp-name

Modify the definitions to add this constraint: An employee may not sign up for more than one equipment appointment.

Database Design

In Chapters 4 and 5 we discussed the specification of data requirements using the entity-relationship and the semantic object models. In the previous chapter, we studied the relational model and normalization. In this chapter, we bring these subjects together and illustrate the transformation of user requirements expressed in entity-relationship and semantic object models into relational database designs. These designs will be independent of any particular DBMS.

The result of the database design phase is a set of relation definitions, a set of domain definitions, and a list of constraints. These outputs will be illustrated with data structure diagrams.

Before we begin, you need to understand the plan of the chapter. It has three major sections. In the first, we show how to transform entity-relationship data models into relational designs. Normalization plays an important role in this process because entities can contain more than one semantic theme. After showing how to represent entities, we discuss the representation of relationships using the relational model.

The second major section is, in actuality, an application of the techniques shown in the first section. In it, we apply the techniques for the transformation of entity-relationship models to the representation of four common data structures. These structures are special cases of E-R constructs. The techniques

- TRANSFORMATION OF ENTITY-RELATIONSHIP MODELS INTO DATABASE DESIGNS
- TREES, NETWORKS, AND BILLS OF MATERIALS
- TRANSFORMATION OF SEMANTIC OBJECT DATA MODELS INTO DATABASE DESIGNS
- SAMPLE OBJECTS

shown in the first section can be directly applied to represent them with relations. We give these structures special attention only because they occur so frequently. They are common patterns of entities and relationships.

In the third section, we discuss the transformation of semantic objects into relations. Here, normalization takes a less prominent role. This is so because the nature of semantic object modeling is to separate distinct themes into different objects or composite groups. Hence, the normalization is done, in essence, in the data modeling phase. In this last section, you will learn how to transform each of the six basic types of object into relations.

Transformation of Entity-Relationship Models into Relational Database Designs

In Chapter 4, you learned how to express user data requirements in terms of the entity-relationship model. With this model, the things that users want to track are represented by **entities** and the relationships among those entities are represented by explicitly defined **relationships.** As defined in the E-R model, relationships can be of any degree, but, as discussed, almost all of the relationships you will encounter in practical database management are of degree 2, or **binary relationships.** This section describes how to transform entities and binary relationships into the terms of the relational model.

REPRESENTING ENTITIES WITH THE RELATIONAL MODEL

In general, the representation of entities with the relational model is straightforward. We begin by defining a relation for each entity. The name of the relation is the name of the entity, and the attributes of the relation are the properties of the entity. Then, we examine each relation according to the normalization criteria discussed in Chapter 6. We may or may not make changes according to these criteria, as you will see.

Consider the example in Figure 7.1, which was the first entity example in Chapter 4. The CUSTOMER entity contains the following properties: Cust#, Cust-name, Address, City, State, Zip, Contact-name, and Phone-number. To represent this entity with a relation, we define a relation for the entity and place the properties within it as attributes. If we know from the data model which property identifies this entity, then that property becomes the key of the relation. Otherwise, we determine the key by examining the underlying semantics of the application. In this case, assume that Cust# is the key.

FIGURE 7.1
Representation of an entity with a
relation

CUSTOMER entity contains:
   Cust#
   Cust-name
   Address
   City
   State
   Zip
   Contact-name
   Phone-number

a. CUSTOMER entity

CUSTOMER (Cust#, Cust-name, Address, City,
               State, Zip, Contact-name, Phone-
               number)

b. Relation representing CUSTOMER entity

During the requirements phase, the only stipulation that is placed on an entity is that it be something of importance to the user. No attempt is made to determine if the entity fits any of the criteria for normalization discussed in Chapter 6. Therefore, once a relation has been defined for an entity, it should be examined according to normalization criteria.

Role of Normalization

Consider, for example, the CUSTOMER relation in Figure 7.1b. Is it in DK/NF? To find out we need to know the constraints on this relation. Without a full description of the underlying requirements, we do not know all of the constraints. We do not know all of the domain constraints, for example. But we can tell a number of requirements just from the names of the attributes and some knowledge about the nature of business.

To begin, Cust# determines all of the other attributes. Unique values of Cust-name, Address, City, State, Zip, Contact-name, and Phone-number can be determined from a given value of Cust#.

There are other constraints, however; these arise from other functional dependencies. Zip determines City and State, and Contact-name determines Phone-number. To create a set of relations in DK/NF, we need to make these additional functional dependencies a logical consequence of domains and keys. We can do that by defining the three relations shown in Figure 7.2. In this figure, as in others to follow, keys of relations are shown underlined. Thus, the key of CUSTOMER is Cust#, the key of ZIP-TABLE is Zip, and the key of CONTACT is Contact-name.

The design in Figure 7.2 is in DK/NF, and so there will be no modification anomalies. We can add new zip codes and new contacts without having to add a customer with the

FIGURE 7.2

Representing the CUSTOMER
entity with relations in DK/NF

CUSTOMER (<u>Cust#</u>, Address, Zip, Contact-name)
ZIP-TABLE (<u>Zip</u>, City, State)
CONTACT (<u>Contact-name</u>, Phone-number)

Interrelation constraints:
  Zip in CUSTOMER must exist in Zip in ZIP-
  TABLE
  Contact-name in CUSTOMER must exist in
  Contact-name in CONTACT

new zip code or contact. Further, when we delete the last customer in a given zip code, we will not lose the city and state for that zip code. But, as stated at the end of Chapter 6, this design is too pure. It is so broken up that it will be difficult to work with.

In this case, the original CUSTOMER relation may be preferable. Even though it suffers modification anomalies, these may not be too important. For example, without a CUSTOMER, it is probably not important to maintain the phone number of the contacts in another company. We do not need to know that Jones' phone number is 555-1234 if the company for whom Jones works is not a customer.

In other examples it is clearer that the DK/NF design is preferred. Consider the SALES-COMMISSION entity in Figure 7.3. If we attempt to represent this entity with one relation as shown in Figure 7.3b, the result is clearly a confused mess of attributes with many potential modification anomalies.

Clearly, this relation contains more than one theme. On examination, it contains a theme about salespeople, a theme about sales during some period, and a theme about sales commission checks. Relations in DK/NF that represent this entity are shown in Figure 7.3c. Intuitively, this design seems superior to that in Figure 7.3b; it seems more straightforward and better fitting.

To summarize the discussion so far, when representing an entity with the relational model, the first step is to construct a relation that has all of the entity's properties as attributes. Then, the relation is examined against normalization criteria. In many cases, the design can be improved by developing sets of relations in DK/NF.

DK/NF relations are not always preferred, however. If the relations are constrived and difficult to work with, a non-DK/NF design may be preferred. Also, performance can be a factor. Having to access two or three relations to get the data needed about a customer may be prohibitively time consuming.

Regardless of our decision about whether to normalize, we should examine every entity's relation(s) against normalization criteria. If we are going to sin, we should make an informed and conscious decision to do so. In the process, we will also learn the types of modification anomalies to which the relations will be vulnerable.

Representation of Weak Entities

Before turning to the representation of E-R model relationships, consider the relational representation of weak entities. Recall that a weak entity depends for its existence on another entity.

SALES COMMISSION entity contains:
  Salesperson#
  Salesperson-name
  Phone
  Check#
  Check-date
  Commission-period
  Total-commission-sales
  Commission-amount
  Budget-category

a. SALES-COMMISSION entity

SALES-COMMISSION (Salesperson#, Salesperson-name, Phone, Check#, Check-date, Commission-period, Total-commission-sales, Commission-amount, Budget-category)

Functional dependencies:
  Check# is key
  Salesperson# determines Salesperson-name, Phone, Budget-category
  (Salesperson#, Commission-period) determines Total-commission-sales, Commission-amount

b. Representing SALES-COMMISSION with a single relation

SALESPERSON (Salesperson#, Salesperson-name, Phone, Budget-category)
SALES (Salesperson#, Commission-period, Total-commission-sales, Commission-amount)
COMMISSION-CHECK (Check#, Check-date, Salesperson#, Commission-period)

Interrelation constraints:
  Salesperson# in SALES must exist in Salesperson# in SALESPERSON
  (Salesperson#, Commission-period) in COMMISSION-CHECK must exist in (Salesperson#, Commission-period) in SALES

c. Representing SALES-COMMISSION with DK/NF relations

FIGURE 7.3
Example of entity that should be represented by DK/NF relations

If the weak entity is not ID-dependent, then it can be represented using the techniques described in the last section. The existence dependency needs to be recorded in the relational design, however, so that no application will create a weak entity without its proper parent (the entity upon which the weak entity depends). Further, a processing constraint needs to be implemented such that when the parent is deleted, the weak entity is deleted. These rules need to be described in the relational design.

This situation is slightly different if the weak entity is also ID-dependent. In Figure 7.4a, LINE-ITEM is an ID-dependent weak entity. It is weak because its existence depends on INVOICE. It is ID-dependent because it has no name of its own.

FIGURE 7.4
Relational representation of a weak
entity

a. An example weak entity

LINE-ITEM (Line#, Qty, Item#, Description, Price, Ext-price)

b. Relation representing LINE-ITEM entity that has no key

LINE-ITEM (<u>Invoice#</u>, <u>Line#</u>, Qty, Item#, Description, Price, Ext-price)

c. LINE-ITEM relation with proper key (partly from INVOICE)

Consider what would happen if we merely establish a relation for LINE-ITEM and set the attributes of the relation to be the same as the properties of the entity. Such a relation is shown in Figure 7.4b.

What is the key of this relation? Because the weak entity depends on another entity, it does not have a complete key, and in fact, this relation could very well have duplicate rows. (This would happen if two invoices have the same quantity of the same item on the same line of the invoice.) The problem is that the relation in Figure 7.4b has no unique identifier.

For an ID-dependent, weak entity, it is necessary to add the key of the parent entity to the weak entity's relation. This added attribute will become part of the weak entity's key. Thus, in Figure 7.4c, we have added Invoice#, the key of INVOICE, to the attributes in LINE-ITEM. The key of LINE-ITEM is the composite (Invoice#, Line#). With relations that represent ID-dependent, weak entities, the key will always be composite.

We now turn to the representation of E-R model relationships.

REPRESENTING BINARY HAS-A RELATIONSHIPS

As you learned in Chapter 4, the E-R model explicitly models relationships. Although the E-R model allows for relationships greater than degree 2, almost all applications in the practical business world involve binary relationships. Consequently, we will constrain the discussion here to such relationships.

Further, there are two fundamental types of relationships in the E-R model: HAS-A relationships among entities of different logical types; and IS-A relationships among entities that are subtypes of a common class. In this section, we cover HAS-A relationships; later, we discuss IS-A relationships.

One-to-One Relationships

The simplest form of binary relationship is a one-to-one (1:1) relationship. For this form, an entity of one type is related to no more than one entity of another type.[1] Consider the example of EMPLOYEE and AUTO introduced in Chapter 4. An employee is assigned

---

[1]Actually, in a recursive relationship, the two entities can be of the same type. For ease of explanation, however, we will assume the entities are of different types. Otherwise, we must use awkward phrases like "the first entity in the relationship has a 1:1 relationship to the second entity in the relationship."

FIGURE 7.5
Example of 1:1 relationship

exactly one automobile, and an auto is assigned to exactly one employee. An E-R diagram for this relationship is shown in Figure 7.5.

Representing One-to-One Relationships

The representation of the 1:1 relationship with the relational model is straightforward. First, represent each entity with a relation. Then, store the key of one of the relations in the other. In Figure 7.6a, the key of EMPLOYEE is stored in AUTO. In Figure 7.6b, the key of AUTO is stored in EMPLOYEE.

When the key of one relation is stored in a second relation, it is sometimes called a **foreign key.** Thus, in Figure 7.6a, Employee# is a foreign key in AUTO; and in Figure 7.6b, License# is a foreign key in EMPLOYEE. In this figure, foreign keys are shown in italics. Sometimes you will see foreign keys shown with a dashed underline. In still other cases, foreign keys are not denoted in any special way. In this text, when there is danger of confusion, we will show foreign keys in italics. Most of the time, they will not receive any special notation.

For a 1:1 relationship, it does not matter which key is stored in which relation. We can process the relationship in either of two directions. Assume first we have an employee and want the auto assigned to that employee. Using the design in Figure 7.6a, we use Empoyee# to look up the row in EMPLOYEE having that number. From this row, we obtain the License# of the auto. We can then use this number to look up the auto data in AUTO. For the design in Figure 7.6b, we go directly to the AUTO relation and look up the row in AUTO that has the employee's number as its value of Employee#.

Now assume the other direction: suppose we have an auto and want the employee assigned. For the design in Figure 7.6a, we go directly to EMPLOYEE and look up the employee row that has the given license number as a value for License#. For the design in Figure 7.6b, we go to AUTO and look up the row in AUTO having the given License#. From this row, we extract the Employee# and use it to access the employee data in EMPLOYEE.

In this discussion, we are using the term *look up* to mean find a row given a value of one of its attributes. You will learn later, as we discuss particular DBMS models, more specifically how this is done.

Although the two designs in Figure 7.6 are equivalent in concept, they may be different in performance. If a query of one type is more common than a query of the other type, then we may prefer one design to the other. Also, if the DBMS product is much faster in lookups on keys versus lookups on nonkeys, then we might also prefer one design to another.

Suspicious One-to-One Relationships

Figure 7.7 shows another 1:1 relationship. Here, each EMPLOYEE has a JOB-EVALUATION, and each JOB-EVALUATION corresponds to a particular employee. Observe

EMPLOYEE (<u>Employee#</u>, Employee-name, Phone, . . .)
AUTO (<u>License#</u>, Serial#, Color, Make, Model, . . . , *Employee#*)

    a. Representing the 1:1 relationship by storing the key of EMPLOYEE in AUTO

EMPLOYEE (<u>Employee#</u>, Employee-name, Phone, . . . , *License#*)
AUTO (<u>License#</u>, Serial#, Color, Make, Model, . . .)

    b. Representing the 1:1 relationship by storing the key of AUTO in EMPLOYEE

FIGURE 7.6
Representing 1:1 relationships with relations

from the hash marks that the relationship is mandatory in both directions. When the relationship is 1:1 and is mandatory in both directions, there is a strong likelihood that the records are describing different aspects of the same entity, or object. If so, in most cases, the records should be combined into one relation. Sometimes, too, the keys of the relations will be the same. In Figure 7.7, both EMPLOYEE and JOB-EVALUATION have the key of Employee#. Learn to regard such 1:1 mandatory relationships with suspicion.

The separation of an entity, or object, into two relations can sometimes be justified for performance reasons. For example, one reason that a database designer might want to separate EMPLOYEE data from JOB-EVALUATION data is that JOB-EVALUATION data is lengthy and used far less frequently than other employee data. If so, better performance might be achieved by separating the two.

A second reason for separating the two records could be security. If the DBMS does not support security at the data item level, the JOB-EVALUATION data may need to be separated to prevent unauthorized users from accessing it. Or, it may be desirable to place JOB-EVALUATION in a separate table so that the table can be placed on disk media that are kept in special locked facilities.

Do not conclude from this discussion that all 1:1 mandatory relationships are inappropriate. Only those that appear to describe different aspects of the same entity, or object, are questionable. For example, the 1:1 mandatory relationship between EMPLOYEE and AUTO is quite appropriate because each relation defines a different entity.

One-to-Many Relationships

The second type of binary relationship is one-to-many (1:N). In a 1:N relationship, an entity of one type is related to potentially many entities of another type. Figure 7.8 is an E-R diagram of a one-to-many relationship between professors and students. In this

FIGURE 7.7
Suspicious 1:1 relationship

FIGURE 7.8

Examples of one-to-many relationships

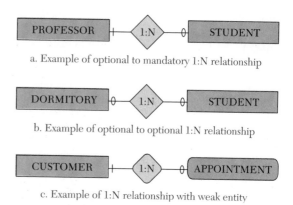

a. Example of optional to mandatory 1:N relationship

b. Example of optional to optional 1:N relationship

c. Example of 1:N relationship with weak entity

relationship, PROFESSOR is related to the many STUDENTs he or she advises.

Remember that the oval means that the relationship from PROFESSOR to STUDENT is optional; a professor need not have any advisees. The bar across the line at the other end means that a STUDENT row must correspond to a PROFESSOR row.

The terms **parent** and **child** are sometimes applied to relations in 1:N relationships. The parent relation is on the *one* side of the relationship and the child relation is on the *many* side. Thus, in the example in Figure 7.8a, PROFESSOR is the parent entity and STUDENT is the child entity.

Figure 7.8 shows two other one-to-many relationships. In Figure 7.8b, a DORMITORY entity corresponds to many STUDENT entities, but a STUDENT entity corresponds to one DORMITORY. Further, a dormitory does not have to have any students assigned to it, nor is a student required to live in a dormitory.

In Figure 7.8c, a CUSTOMER is related to many APPOINTMENT weak entities, and a particular APPOINTMENT corresponds to only one CUSTOMER. Moreover, a CUSTOMER may or may not have an APPOINTMENT and every APPOINTMENT must correspond to a CUSTOMER.

Representing One-to-Many Relationships

The representation of 1:N relationships is simple and straightforward. First, each entity is represented by a relation. Then, the key of the relation representing the parent entity is stored as an attribute of the relation representing the child entity. Thus, to represent the ADVISES relationship of Figure 7.8a, we need to place the key of PROFESSOR, Prof-name, in the STUDENT relation. This is shown in Figure 7.9.

Figure 7.9 is an example of what is sometimes called a **data structure diagram.** Such diagrams show relations in rectangles with lines representing relationships. Key attributes are underlined. A fork, or crow's foot, on a relationship line indicates a many relationship.

In Figure 7.9, the fork at the STUDENT end of the relationship line means that there are potentially many STUDENT rows for each PROFESSOR. No fork at the other end

FIGURE 7.9
Representation of ADVISES
relationship from Figure 7.8a

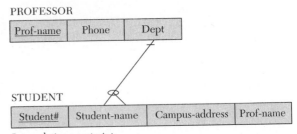

Interrelation constraint:
Prof-name in STUDENT must exist in Prof-name in PROFESSOR

means each STUDENT can be advised by, at most, one PROFESSOR. As with E-R diagrams, hash lines are used to denote mandatory relationships and ovals denote optional ones.

Notice that with Prof-name stored as a foreign key in STUDENT, we can process the relationship in both directions. Given a Student#, we can look up the appropriate row in STUDENT and get the name of his or her advisor from the row data. To obtain the rest of the PROFESSOR data, we use the professor name obtained from STUDENT to look up the appropriate row in PROFESSOR.

To determine all of the students advised by a particular faculty member, we look up all rows in STUDENT having the professor's name as a value for Prof-name. Student data is then taken from those rows.

Contrast this situation to one representing 1:1 relationships. In both cases, we store the key of one relation as a foreign key in the second relation. In a 1:1 relationship it does not matter which key is moved to the second relation. In a 1:N relationship, however, it does matter. *The key of the parent relation must be placed in the child relation.*

To understand this more fully, see what happens if we try to put the key of the child into the parent relation. Since attributes in a relation can have only a single value, there will be room in any professor's record for only one student. Consequently, such a structure cannot be used to represent the "many" side of the 1:N relationship. Again, to represent a 1:N relationship, place the key of the parent relation in the child relation.

Figure 7.10 shows the representation of the CUSTOMER and APPOINTMENT entities. Here, we represent each entity with a relation. As stated previously, the ID-dependent, weak entity, APPOINTMENT, will have a composite key consisting of the key of the entity on which its key depends plus an attribute from itself. In this case, the key will be (Cust#, Date, Time). Now, to represent the 1:N relationship, we would normally add the key of the parent to the child. In this case, however, the key of the parent (Cust#) is already part of the child. Consequently, we need not add it. The relationship is already represented. (Verify this for yourself by determining how you would look up data to process the relationship in both directions.)

Many-to-Many Relationships

The third and final type of binary relationship is many-to-many (M:N). In an M:N relationship, an entity of one type corresponds to many records of the second type, and an entity of the second type corresponds to many records of the first type.

FIGURE 7.10

Representation of weak entity
relationship from Figure 7.8c

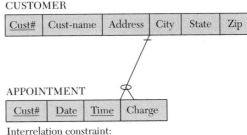

CUSTOMER

Cust#	Cust-name	Address	City	State	Zip

APPOINTMENT

Cust#	Date	Time	Charge

Interrelation constraint:
Cust# in APPOINTMENT must exist in Cust# in CUSTOMER

Figure 7.11a presents an E-R diagram of the many-to-many relationship between students and classes. A STUDENT entity can correspond to many CLASS entities and a CLASS entity can correspond to many STUDENT entities. Notice that both participants in the relationship are optional: a student does not need to be enrolled in a class, and a class does not need to have any students. Figure 7.11b gives sample data.

Representing Many-to-Many Relationships

Many-to-many relationships cannot be directly represented by relations as one-to-one and one-to-many relationships are. To understand why this is so, suppose we try to use the same strategy we did for 1:1 and 1:N relationships—inserting the key of one relation as a foreign key in the other relation.

First, define a relation for each of the entities; call them STUDENT and CLASS. Now, suppose we try to put the key of STUDENT (say Student#) in CLASS. Because multiple values are not allowed in the cells of a relation, we only have room for one Student#. What do we do with the second student enrolled in that class?

FIGURE 7.11

Example many-to-many (M:N)
relationship

a. E-R diagram of STUDENT to CLASS relationship

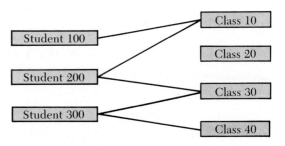

b. Sample Data for STUDENT to CLASS Relationship

SID   Other STUDENT Data

SID	Other STUDENT Data
100	. . .
200	. . .
300	. . .

STUDENT

Class#	Class-time	Other CLASS Data	SID
10	10:00 MWF	. . .	100
10	10:00 MWF	. . .	200
30	3:00 TH	. . .	200
30	3:00 TH	. . .	300
40	8:00 MWF	. . .	300

CLASS

FIGURE 7.12

Incorrect means of representing an M:N relationship with relations

The same problem will occur if we try to put the key of CLASS (say Class#) in STU-DENT. We can readily store the identifier of the first class in which a student is enrolled, but we have no place to store the identifier of the second and subsequent classes.

Figure 7.12 shows another (*but incorrect*) strategy. In this case, we have stored a row in the CLASS relation for each STUDENT who is enrolled in one class. Thus, there are two records for class 10 and two for class 30. The problem with this scheme is that we duplicate the class data and thus generate the problem of modification anomalies.

Consider that many rows will need to be changed if, say, class 10's schedule is modified. Also, consider the insertion and deletion anomalies: how can we schedule a new class until a student has enrolled? And what will happen if student 300 drops out of class 40? Obviously, this strategy is unworkable.

The solution to this dilemma is to create a third relation that represents the relationship itself. An instance of such a relation is shown in Figure 7.13. This new relation will show the correspondence of students to classes. Such relations are called **intersection relations** because each row of such a relation documents the intersection of a particular student with a particular class.

Observe in Figure 7.13b that there is one row in the intersection relation for each line between STUDENT and CLASS in Figure 7.11b. The data structure diagrams for the

STUDENT (Student#, Student-name, Campus-address)
CLASS (Class#, Class-name, Hours)
STU-CLASS (*Class#, Student#*)

a. Relations required to represent STUDENT-CLASS M:N relationship

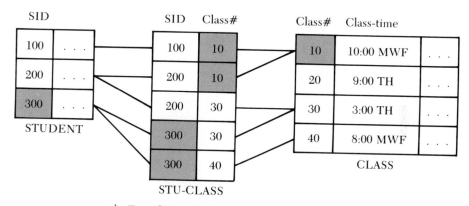

b. Example Data for STUDENT/CLASS Relationship

FIGURE 7.13
Correct means of representing an M:N relationship

STUDENT-CLASS relationship appear in Figure 7.14. Notice that the relationship from CLASS to STU-CLASS is 1:N and that the relationship from STUDENT to STU-CLASS is also 1:N. In essence, we have decomposed the M:N relationship into two 1:N relationships.

The key of STU-CLASS is the combination of the keys of both of its parents, (SID, Class#). The key for an intersection relation is always the combination of parent keys.

Representing Recursive Relationships

A recursive relationship is a relationship among entities of the same class. Fundamentally, recursive relationships are no different than other HAS-A relationships and can be represented using the same techniques. The only complication is that entities in recursive relationships have relationships to entities of their own class. As with nonrecursive HAS-A relationships, there are three types of recursive relationships: 1:1, 1:N, and N:M; Figure 7.15 shows an example of each.

Consider first, the SPONSOR relationship in Figure 7.15a. As a 1:1 relationship, one person can sponsor another person, and each person is sponsored by no more than one person. Figure 7.16a shows sample data for this relationship.

FIGURE 7.14

Data structure diagram for
STUDENT-CLASS relationship

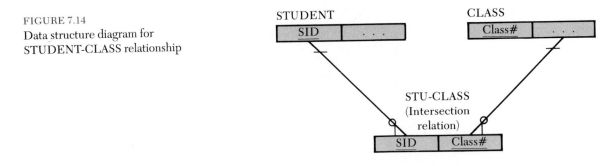

To represent 1:1 recursive relationships, we take an approach nearly identical to the approach taken with regular 1:1 relationships: We can place the key of the person being sponsored in the row of the sponsor, or we can place the key of the sponsor in the row of the person being sponsored. Figure 7.16b shows the first alternative and Figure 7.16c shows the second. Either will work, and the choice depends on issues like performance.

Observe that this technique is identical to that for nonrecursive 1:1 relationships, except that both child and parent rows reside in the same relation. You can think of the process as follows: pretend the relationship is between two different relations. Determine where the key goes, then, resolve the two relations into a single one.

To illustrate, consider the REFERRED-BY relationship in Figure 7.15b. This is a 1:N relationship as shown in the sample data in Figure 7.17a. When this data is placed in a relation, one row will represent the referrer and other rows will represent those who have been referred. The referrer row takes the role of parent and the referred rows take the role of child. As with all 1:N relationships, we place the key of the parent in the child. Thus, in Figure 7.17b, we place the name of the referrer in all the rows that have been referred.

a. Example of 1:1 recursive relationship

b. Example of 1:N recursive relationship

c. Example of N:M recursive relationship

FIGURE 7.15

Examples of recursive relationships

FIGURE 7.16
Example of 1:1 recursive
relationship

Person

⎧ Jones
⎨ Smith
⎩ Parks
⎧ Myrtle
⎩ Pines

a. Sample data for 1:1 recursive relationship

Person	Person-sponsored
Jones	Smith
Smith	Parks
Parks	null
Myrtle	Pines
Pines	null

b. First alternative for representing 1:1 recursive relationship

Person	Person-sponsored-by
Jones	null
Smith	Jones
Parks	Smith
Myrtle	null
Pines	Myrtle

c. Second alternative for representing 1:1 recursive relationship

Now consider M:N recursive relationships. Examine the TREATED-BY relationship in Figure 7.15c with sample data shown in Figure 7.18a. As with other M:N relationships, we must create an intersection table. This intersection will show all pairs of doctors; the name of the doctor in the first column is the one who provided the treatment and the name of the doctor in the second column is the one who received the treatment. This structure is shown in Figure 7.18b.

Recursive relationships are thus represented in the same way as other relationships. Rows of the tables can take two different roles, however. Some rows are parent rows and some rows are child rows. If a key is supposed to be a parent key, and if the row has no parent, then its value will be null. If a key is supposed to be a child key and the row has no child, then its value will be null.

Summary of HAS-A Relationship Representation

The three types of binary relationships are one-to-one (1:1), one-to-many (1:N), and many-to-many (M:N). For each relationship, we begin by representing each entity type by a relation. Then, to represent a 1:1 relationship we place the key of either relation in

FIGURE 7.17

Example of 1:N recursive
relationship

Customer Number	Referred These Customers
100	200, 400
300	500
400	600, 700

a. Sample data for the REFERRED-BY relationship

CUSTOMER Relation

Customer-number	Customer-data	Referred-by
100	...	null
200	...	100
300	...	null
400	...	100
500	...	300
600	...	400
700	...	400

b. Representing a 1:N recursive relationship by a relation

the second relation. To represent a 1:N relationship, we place the key of the parent relation in the child. To represent an M:N relationship we create a third relation, called an intersection relation. Each record in an intersection relation contains the keys of each of the related records in the other two relations. The key of the intersection relation is the combination of the keys of its parents.

Recursive relationships are treated in the same manner. The only difference is that keys are located in a single relation and not two.

REPRESENTING IS-A RELATIONSHIPS (SUBTYPES)

The strategy for representing generalization hierarchies and subtypes, or IS-A relationships, is similar to the strategy for representing other E-R constructs. Consider the example of CLIENT with properties with Client#, Client-name, and Amount-due. Suppose that there are a number of subtypes of CLIENT; refer again to Figure 4.8. The subtypes and their properties are:

INDIVIDUAL-CLIENT: Address, Social-security-number
PARTNERSHIP-CLIENT: Managing-partner-name, Address, Tax-identification-number
CORPORATE-CLIENT: Contact-person, Phone, Tax-identification-number

To represent this structure with relations, we define one relation for the generalization category and one relation for each subtype. Then, we place each of the properties of the generalization category into the relation that represents it, and each of the prop-

FIGURE 7.18
Example of M:N recursive
relationship

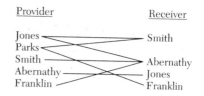

Provider   Receiver

Jones
Parks
Smith
Abernathy
Franklin

Smith
Abernathy
Jones
Franklin

a. Sample data for the TREATED-BY relationship

DOCTOR relation

Name	Other-attributes
Jones	...
Parks	...
Smith	...
Abernathy	...
O'Leary	...
Franklin	...

TREATMENT-INTERSECTION relation

Physician	Patient
Jones	Smith
Parks	Smith
Smith	Abernathy
Abernathy	Jones
Parks	Franklin
Franklin	Abernathy
Jones	Abernathy

b. Representing a M:N recursive relationship by relations

erties of the subtypes into the relations that represent them. At this point, the subtype relations do not have a key. To create a key, we add the key of the generalization category, Client#, to each of the subtypes. The final list of relations is:

CLIENT (<u>Client#</u>, Client-name, Amount-due)
INDIVIDUAL-CLIENT (<u>Client#</u>, Address, Social-security-number)
PARTNERSHIP-CLIENT (<u>Client#</u>, Managing-partner-name, Address, Tax-identification-number)
CORPORATE-CLIENT (<u>Client#</u>, Contact-person, Phone, Tax-identification-number)

Observe that with this structure, the relationship from a row in CLIENT to a row in one of the subtypes is 1:1. No client has more than one row in a subtype relation, and each subtype corresponds uniquely to one row of the generalization category. Depending on the restriction of the application, it might be possible for a row in the generalization relation to correspond to multiple rows, each in a separate subtype. But, no row of the generalization relation will correspond to more than one row in the *same* subtype relation.

It is possible for one or more of the subtypes to have a key of its own. For example, the application may call for a Corporate-client# that is distinct from Client#. In that case, the key of CORPORATE-CLIENT will be Corporate-client#. Since the relationship between CLIENT and CORPORATE-CLIENT is 1:1, it can be established by placing the key of one in the other. Most often, it is considered better aesthetics to place the key of the generalization relation in the key of the subtype. Thus, for this case, the structure of CORPORATE-CLIENT is:

CORPORATE-CLIENT (<u>Corporate-client#</u>, Client#, Contact-person, Phone, Tax-identification-number)

Example

Figure 7.19a is a copy of the E-R diagram introduced in Chapter 4 as Figure 4.9. It has all of the basic elements used in E-R diagrams. To represent this diagram with relations, we begin by establishing one relation for each entity. Doing so yields the following list of relations. We assume keys as stated:

Relation	Key
EMPLOYEE	Employee#
ENGINEER	Employee#
TRUCK	License#
SERVICE	Invoice#
CLIENT	Client#
ENGINEER-CERTIFICATION	(Employee#, Certification-name)
CERTIFICATION	Certification-name

The next step is to evaluate each of these relations against normalization criteria. The example does not tell us what properties must be represented, and so we cannot assess constraints. We will assume that these relations are in DK/NF, though, in practice, we would need to check out that assumption against the property lists and constraints. For now, we will focus on the representation of relationships. Relations and their key properties (including foreign keys) are listed in Figure 7.19b.

The relationship between EMPLOYEE and ENGINEER is already represented since the relations have the same key, Employee#. ENGINEER and TRUCK have a 1:1 relationship and so can be related by placing the key of one in the other. Since a truck must be assigned to an employee, there will be no null values if we place Employee# in TRUCK, and so we will do that.

For the 1:N relationship between ENGINEER and SERVICE, we place the key of ENGINEER (the parent) in SERVICE (the child). The relationship between SERVICE and CLIENT is M:N, and so we must create an intersection relation. Since this relationship has a property, Fee, we add that property to the intersection relation. For the 1:N recursive relationship, REFERRED-BY, we add the attribute Referred-by to CLIENT. The name *Referred-by* implies, correctly, that the key of the parent—the one client doing the referring—is being placed in the relation.

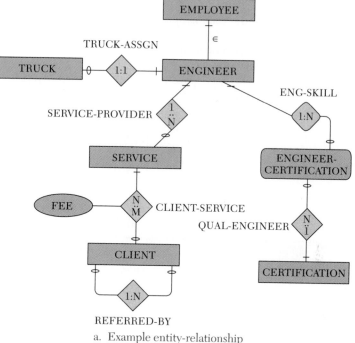

a. Example entity-relationship
   diagram (from Chapter 4)

EMPLOYEE (<u>Employee#</u>, other nonkey
   EMPLOYEE attributes . . .)
ENGINEER (<u>Employee#</u>, other nonkey ENGI-
   NEER attributes . . .)
TRUCK (<u>License#</u>, *Employee#*, other nonkey
   TRUCK attributes . . .)
SERVICE (<u>Invoice#</u>, *Employee#*, other nonkey
   SERVICE attributes . . .)
CLIENT (<u>Client#</u>, *Referred-by*, other nonkey CLI-
   ENT data . . .)
SERVICE-CLIENT (<u>Invoice#</u>, <u>Client#</u>, Fee)
ENGINEER-CERTIFICATION (<u>Employee#</u>,
   <u>Certification-name</u>, other nonkey ENGINEER-
   CERTIFICATION data . . .)
CERTIFICATION (<u>Certification-name</u>, other non-
   key CERTIFICATION data . . .)

b. Relations needed to represent the E-R diagram
   in Figure 7.19a

FIGURE 7.19
Relational representation of example E-R diagram

Since ENGINEER-CERTIFICATION is existence dependent on ENGINEER, we know that Employee# must be part of its key; thus, the key will be the composite (Employee#, Certification-name). The dependency relationship is 1:N and so will be carried by Employee#. Finally, the relationship between CERTIFICATION and ENGINEER-CERTIFICATION is 1:N and we would normally add the key of CERTIFICATION (the parent) in ENGINEER-CERTIFICATION. That key is already part of the relation, however, so we need not do this.

Study this example to ensure that you understand the various types of relationships and how they are expressed in terms of the relations. Before we turn to a discussion of the transformation of the second type of data model, the semantic object model, we need to consider four common data structures.

Trees, Networks, and Bills of Materials

Although neither the E-R model nor the semantic object model makes any assumptions about patterns in relationships among entities, there are patterns that occur often enough that they have been given special names. These patterns are trees, simple networks, complex networks, and bills of materials. We will introduce the concept of these patterns here, in the context of the E-R model. You will see how these patterns apply to particular DBMS products in Chapters 11, 12, and 13.

TREES

A **tree** is a data structure in which the elements of the structure have only one-to-many relationships to one another. Further, each element has at most one parent. Figure 7.20 is an example of a tree (sometimes also called a **hierarchy**). According to standard terminology, each element is called a **node,** and the relationships between the elements are called **branches.** The node at the top of the tree is called the **root** (what a metaphor—roots of real trees are normally at the bottom!). In Figure 7.20, node 1 is the root of the tree.

Every node of a tree, except the root, has a **parent** which is the node immediately above it. Thus node 2 is the parent of node 5, node 4 is the parent of node 8, and so on. As stated, trees are distinguished from other data structures having only one-to-many relationships, because every node has at most one parent. In fact, every node except the root has exactly one parent. The root node has no parent.

The descendants of a node are called **children.** In general, there is no limitation on the number of children a node may have. Node 2 has two children: nodes 5 and 6; node 3 has no children; and node 4 has three children: nodes 7, 8, and 9. Nodes having the same parent are called **twins,** or **siblings.**

Figure 7.21a illustrates a tree of entities. In this example, you can see several one-to-many relationships between entities in a university system. Colleges consist of many departments, which in turn have many professors and many administrative employees.

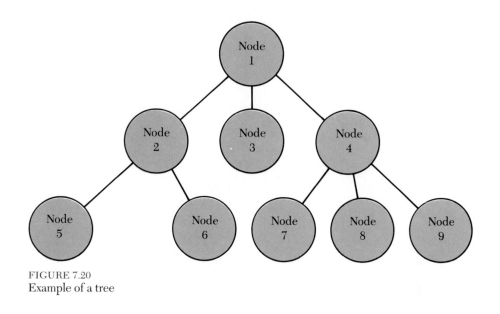

FIGURE 7.20
Example of a tree

Finally, professors advise many students who have received many grades. There are six different entity types in this structure, but all of the relationships are 1:N.

To represent a tree of entities using the relational model, we simply apply the concepts from the prior sections of this chapter. First, transform each entity into a relation. Examine the relations generated against normalization criteria, and subdivide the relations if necessary. Represent the 1:N relationships by storing the key of the parent in the child. Figure 7.21b is a relational representation of the tree in Figure 7.21a.

In summary, a tree, or hierarchy, is a collection of records organized such that all relationships are 1:N. All records have exactly one parent except the root, which has no parent. A hierarchy can be represented by a set of relations using the methods defined previously. Hierarchies occur frequently in business, especially in manufacturing applications.

SIMPLE NETWORKS

A **simple network** is also a data structure of elements having only one-to-many relationships. In a simple network, however, the elements may have more than one parent, as long as the parents are different types of element. For example, in the simple network shown in Figure 7.22, each STUDENT entity has two parents, an ADVISOR entity and a MAJOR entity. This would not be a simple network if the parents of STUDENT entities were of the same type, say both ADVISOR entities. Further, the data structure in Figure 7.22 is not a tree because STUDENT entities have more than one parent.

FIGURE 7.21
Representation of tree by relations

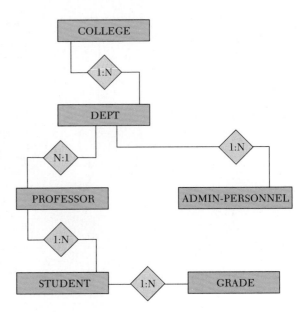

a. Tree composed of entities

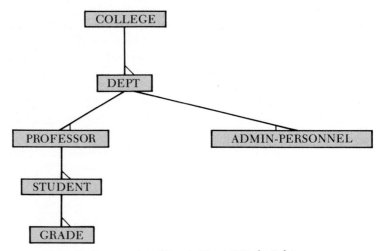

b. Represention of Tree in Figure 7.21a by Relations

Figure 7.23a shows the general structure of this simple network. Notice that all relationships are one-to-many, but that STUDENT has two parents. In this figure, the parent records are on top and the children records are beneath the parents. This arrangement is convenient but inessential. You may see simple networks depicted with parents
beside or below the children. You can identify simple networks in such arrangements by
the fact that a single record type participates as a child in two (or more) one-to-many
relationships.

FIGURE 7.22
Example of a simple network

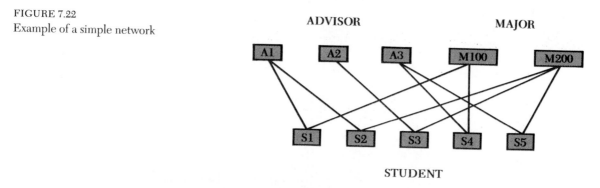

To represent a simple network of entities with the relational model, we follow the procedures described earlier. First, transform each entity into a relation and normalize the relations if necessary. Then, represent each 1:N relationship by storing the key of the parent relation in the child relation. The result of this process for the network in Figure 7.23a is shown in Figure 7.23b.

COMPLEX NETWORKS

A **complex network** is a data structure of elements in which at least one of the relationships is many-to-many. The complex network in Figure 7.24a illustrates the relationships among invoices, line items, parts, and suppliers. Two of the three relationships are 1:N, and the third is M:N. Since there is at least one many-to-many relationship, this structure is called a complex network.

FIGURE 7.23
Representation of a simple network
by relations

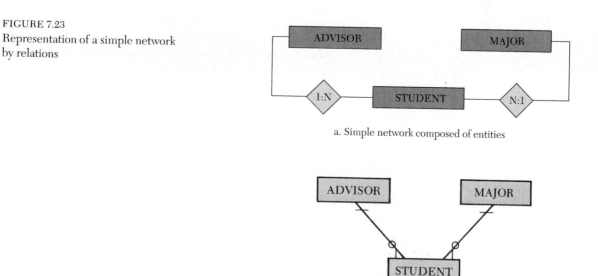

a. Simple network composed of entities

b. Represention of Simple Network in Figure 7.23 by Relations

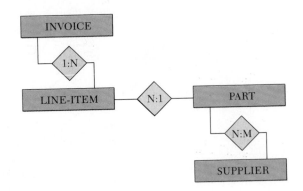

a. Complex network composed of entities

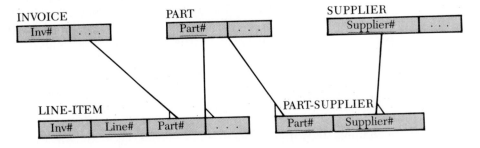

b. Represention of complex network in Figure 7.24a by relations

FIGURE 7.24
Representation of a complex network by relations

As mentioned in the previous section, M:N relationships have no direct representation in the relational model. Consequently, before this structure could be stored in relational form, we need to define an intersection relation. We have done this in Figure 7.24b. Notice that PART-SUPPLIER is the intersection relation.

BILLS OF MATERIALS

A **bill of materials** is a special data structure that occurs frequently in manufacturing applications. In fact, such structures provided a major impetus for the development of database technology in the 1960s.

Figure 7.25 is an example of a bill of materials. Basically, such structures show the parts that constitute a given product, assembly, or component. When viewed from the standpoint of a given product, this data structure is a hierarchy. But, since a part can be used in more than one product, this structure is, in actuality, a network. In Figure 7.25, the part ABC100 has two parents: product A and product B.

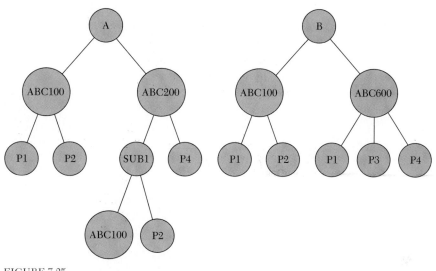

FIGURE 7.25
Example of a bill of materials

A bill of materials can be represented in relations in several ways; the most common way is to consider it as an M:N recursive relationship. A part (or product, or assembly, or subassembly, and so forth) has many elements that it contains. At the same time, there are potentially many elements that contain it.

Figure 7.26a shows the general data structure of the M:N recursive relationship; and Figure 7.26b shows an instance of the intersection relation created to represent this bill of materials.

Transformation of Semantic Object Data Models into Relational Database Designs

Chapter 5 introduced the semantic object data model and defined six types of semantic object. In this section, we present guidelines for you to follow when transforming objects into relations. Remember that after you perform these transformations, you should thoroughly review the derived relations using normalization theory. If you identify anomalies, you must change your design to eliminate them.

When working with semantic objects, you are less likely to encounter normalization problems than you are when working with the entity-relationship models. The definition of semantic objects usually partitions semantic themes into separate objects. When you represent an object with a relation, then, you are most often representing only a single semantic theme.

We will now consider the representation of each of the six types of semantic object defined in Chapter 5.

FIGURE 7.26
Representation of a bill of materials
with relations

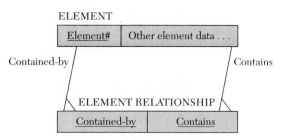

a. Relations to represent a bill of materials

Contained-by	Contains
A	ABC100
A	ABC200
B	ABC100
B	ABC600
ABC100	P1
ABC100	P2
ABC200	SUB1
ABC200	P4
ABC600	P1
ABC600	P3
ABC600	P4
SUB1	ABC100
SUB1	P2

Observe element A
contains an ABC100
and element ABC100
is contained by an A

b. Data for the ELEMENT RELATIONSHIP intersection relation

EQUIPMENT (object)

a. Example Simple Object

EQUIPMENT

Equip#	Equip-desc	Acquisition-date	Purchase-cost

b. Relation to Represent the EQUIPMENT Simple Object

FIGURE 7.27
Relational representation of example simple object

TRANSFORMATION OF SIMPLE OBJECTS

Figure 7.27 illustrates the transformation of a simple object into a relation. Recall that a simple object has no multivalued properties and no object properties. Consequently, simple objects can be represented by a single relation in the database.

Figure 7.27a is an example of a simple object, EQUIPMENT. This object can be represented by a single relation as shown in Figure 7.27b. Each property of the object is defined as an attribute of the relation. The identifying property, Equip#, becomes the key attribute of the relation.

The general transformation of simple objects is shown in Figure 7.28. Object OBJ1 is transformed into relation R1. The property that identifies OBJ1 instances is OBJ1°. It is represented by the key of R1, R1° in the database. Nonkey data is represented in this and subsequent figures with ellipses (. . .).

TRANSFORMATION OF COMPOSITE OBJECTS

A composite object is an object that has one or more multivalued properties or groups of properties, but no object properties. Figure 7.29a shows an example composite object, HOTEL-BILL. To represent this object, we establish a relation for the base object, HOTEL-BILL, and then an additional relation for the repeating composite group. This relational design is shown in Figure 7.29b.

In general, composite objects are transformed by defining one relation for the object itself and another relation for each group of properties that is contained within the object. In Figure 7.30, object OBJ1 contains two groups of multivalued properties. Each of these groups is represented by a relation in the database. Thus, the database representation of OBJ1 is a relation R1 with key R1°, a relation C1 with key (R1°, C1°), and a relation C2 with key (R1°, C2°).

TRANSFORMATION OF COMPOUND OBJECTS

The relational representation of compound objects is similar to the representation of entities. In fact, compound objects and entities are in many ways quite similar.

FIGURE 7.28
General transformation of simple
object into relation

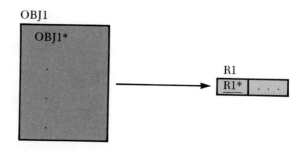

BILL

Bill#	Arrival-date	Customer-name	Total-due
1234	10/27/91	James, F.	$224.70
5678	10/30/91	Lincoln, P.	$538.28

DAILY-CHARGE

Bill#	Charge-date	Room-charge	Food-charge	Phone-charge	Misc-charge	Tax-charge
1234	10/27/91	100.00	0.00	0.00	0.00	12.35
1234	10/28/91	100.00	0.00	0.00	0.00	12.35
5678	10/30/91	90.00	55.30	10.00	5.00	11.11
5678	10/31/91	90.00	65.80	7.50	4.67	11.11
5678	11/01/91	90.00	72.18	7.50	7.00	11.11

b. Two relations representing HOTEL-BILL

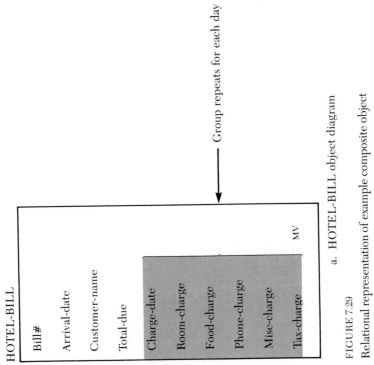

— Group repeats for each day

HOTEL-BILL

Bill#

Arrival-date

Customer-name

Total-due

Charge-date

Room-charge

Food-charge

Phone-charge

Misc-charge

Tax-charge   MV

a. HOTEL-BILL object diagram

FIGURE 7.29

Relational representation of example composite object

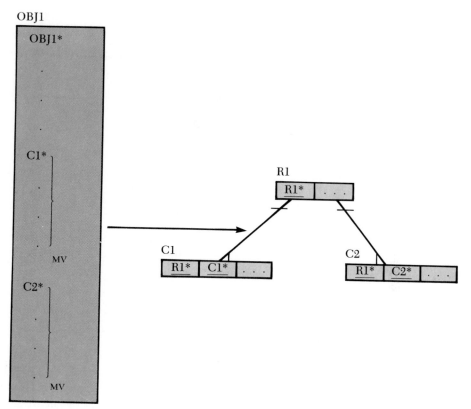

FIGURE 7.30
Transformation of object with two composite groups into relations

As stated in Chapter 5, an object, OBJ1, can contain 1, many, or an unknown number of a second object, OBJ2. Further, OBJ2 can contain 1, many, or an unknown number of the first object, OBJ1. This leads to the object types shown in Figure 7.31, which is a copy of Figure 5.26.

Setting aside the issue of the unknown relationships for a moment, all of the other relationships involve some variation of one-to-one, one-to-many, or many-to-many relationships. Specifically, the relationship from OBJ1 to OBJ2 can be 1:1, 1:N, or N:M, while the relationship from OBJ2 to OBJ1 can be 1:1, 1:M, or M:N. Thus, to represent any of these we need only to address these three types of relationship.

Representing One-to-One Compound Objects

Consider the example of the assignment of a LOCKER to a health club MEMBER. A LOCKER is assigned to one MEMBER, and each MEMBER has one and only one

FIGURE 7.31

Nine subtypes of compound objects

		OBJECT-1 Can Contain		
		One	Many	Unknown
OBJECT-2 Can Contain	One			
	Many			
	Unknown			

LOCKER. Figure 7.32a shows the object diagrams. To represent these diagrams with relations, we define a relation for each object, and, as with 1:1 entity relationships, we place the key of either relation in the other relation. Thus, we can place the key of MEMBER in LOCKER or the key of LOCKER in MEMBER. Figure 7.32b shows the situation with the key of LOCKER in MEMBER.

In general, for a 1:1 relationship between OBJ1 and OBJ2, we define one relation for each object, R1 and R2. Then we place the key of either relation (R1° or R2°) as a foreign key in the other relation, as shown in Figure 7.33.

Representing One-to-Many and Many-to-One Relationships

Now consider 1:N relationships. Figure 7.34a shows an example of a 1:N compound objects. Object OBJ1 contains many objects OBJ2, and object OBJ2 contains just one OBJ1. To represent this structure with relations, we represent each object by a relation and place the key of the parent (the object containing the multivalued object) in the child. Thus, in Figure 7.34b, the attribute R1° is placed in R2.

FIGURE 7.32

Relational representation of example 1:1 compound object

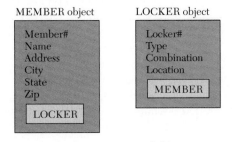

MEMBER object

Member#
Name
Address
City
State
Zip

LOCKER

LOCKER object

Locker#
Type
Combination
Location

MEMBER

a. One-to-one compound objects

MEMBER (<u>Member#</u>, Name, Address, City, State, Zip, Locker#)

LOCKER (Locker#, Type, Combination, Location)

b. Representation of one-to-one compound object in relations

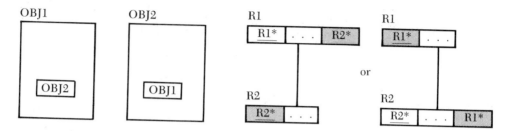

1:1 object relationship

Relational representation

FIGURE 7.33

General transformation of 1:1 compound object into relations

If OBJ2 were to contain many OBJ1s and OBJ1 were to contain just one OBJ2, then we would use the same strategy, but reverse the role of R1 and R2. We would place R2° in R1.

Representing Many-to-Many Relationships

Finally, consider M:N relationships. As with M:N entity relationships, we define three relations: one for each of the objects and a third intersection relation. The intersection relation represents the relationship of the two objects and consists of the keys of both of its parents. Figure 7.35a shows the M:N relationship between BOOK and AUTHOR. Figure 7.35b presents the three relations that represent these objects: BOOK, AUTHOR, and AUTHOR-BOOK, the intersection relation. Observe AUTHOR-BOOK has no nonkey data.

In general, for two objects that have an M:N relationship, we defined a relation R1 for object OBJ1, a relation R2 for object OBJ2, and relation R3, the intersection relation. This scheme is shown in Figure 7.36. Note the attributes of R3 will always be R1° and R2°. For M:N compound objects, R3 will never contain nonkey data. The importance of this statement will become clear when we contrast M:N compound relationships with association relationships.

FIGURE 7.34

General transformation of 1:N compound object into relations

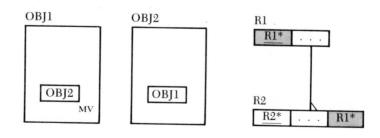

a. 1:N object relationship

b. Relational representation

FIGURE 7.35
Example of M:N compound objects

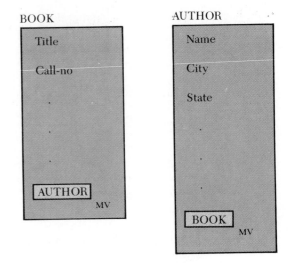

a. Object diagrams

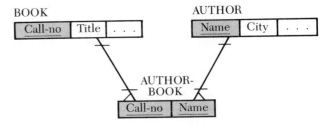

b. Relational representation

One-Way Relationships

Now consider the case where one object contains another, but there is no indication in the data model that the second object contains the first. This situation means that the relation between two objects is processed in one direction, but not in the other. There are two types of such one-directional relationships, 1:? and N:?

The dilemma is the ambiguity. A 1:? relationship can either be 1:1 or 1:N, and an N:? can either be N:1 or N:M. If the underlying relationship is 1:1, then the key of one relation is stored in the other. If the underlying relationship is 1:N or N:1, then we represent the relationship by storing the key of the parent in the child. But, if the underlying relationship is N:M, then we must create a third, intersection relation. Without more information, we do not know how to represent the data.

There are several alternative approaches. One is to attempt to gain more information about the underlying semantics of the objects. The nature of the model may dictate which type of relationship should be represented.

Without this information, one course of action is to assume the relationship is 1:N (or N:1) and design the database accordingly. If it turns out that the relationship is actually

FIGURE 7.36
General transformation of M:N
compound objects into relations

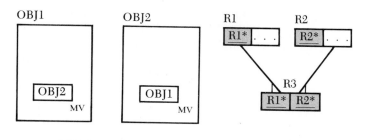

a. M:N object relationship   b. Relational representation

N:M, the database, and applications, can be subsequently modified. Another alternative is to assume M:N, since an M:N relationship (with intersection relation) can always support a 1:N relationship as a special case (there will only be one row in the intersection relation for each object on the one side of the relationship). This is the safest course of action, but it is also the most expensive because the third relation must be maintained and the logic of applications developed to process that relation. None of these alternatives can be set out as a general recommendation. Without information about the underlying semantics, the design requires a guess.

ASSOCIATION OBJECTS

An association object is an object that associates two other objects. It is a special case of compound objects that most often occurs in assignment situations. Figure 7.37a shows the FLIGHT object that associates an AIRPLANE with a PILOT.

To represent association objects, we define a relationship for each of the three objects. Then, we represent the relationships among the objects using one of the strategies used with compound objects. In Figure 7.37b, for example, one relation is defined for FLIGHT, one for AIRPLANE, and one for PILOT. The relationships between FLIGHT and AIRPLANE and between FLIGHT and PILOT are 1:N. Thus, we place the key of the parent in the child. In this case, we place the key of AIRPLANE and the key of PILOT in FLIGHT.

Observe that FLIGHT contains a key of its own. It does contain foreign keys, but these keys are only attributes and are not part of FLIGHT's key. This characteristic distinguishes relations that represent association objects from intersection relations. An intersection relation never has a key of its own; such relations always have keys that are composites of their parents' keys. Also, observe that FLIGHT contains nonkey data, for example, Fuel. The presence of nonkey data is a second distinguishing characteristic.

The second distinguishing characteristic is actually stronger than the first. Relations that represent association objects always have nonkey data. It sometimes occurs that the semantics of the application is such that the users' name for the object is the combination of the keys of the objects being associated. A query such as "How much time did James Winter spend on the Bothel project?" is an example. Here, the association object relates

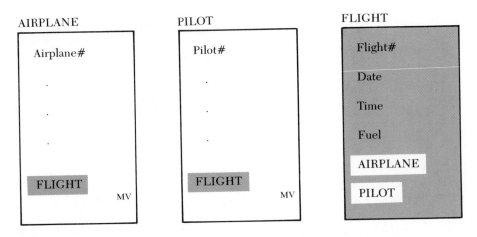

a. Object diagrams showing FLIGHT as an association object

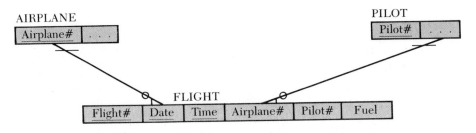

b. Relational representation

FIGURE 7.37
Relational representation of example association object

an architect (Winter) to a project and the name of the association in the users' mind is the combination of the architect and the project names.

Contrast this situation with FLIGHT. Airline personnel do not ask queries like, "What was the destination of the flight on 2/27/91 in which Winthrop flew plane N1234U?" They use a flight number, instead. They would say, "What was the destination of flight #17 on 2/27/91?" FLIGHTs have their own identification.

In general, when transforming association object structures into relations, we define one relation for each of the objects that are participating in the relationship. In Figure 7.38, OBJ3 associates OBJ1 and OBJ2. In this case, we define R1, R2, and R3 as shown. Each relation will have an independent—not composite—key: R1°, R2°, and R3°. The key of each of the parent relations, R1° and R2°, will appear as foreign key attributes in the relation representing the association object, R3.

Note the difference between the key of the association relation in Figure 7.38 and the key of the intersection relation in Figure 7.36. An association relation has a key of its own because it represents a real object in the user's work environment; an intersection rela-

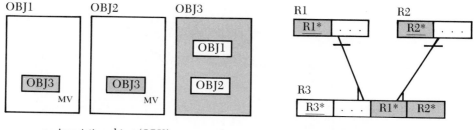

a. Association object (OBJ3)   b. Relational representation

FIGURE 7.38
General transformation of association object into relations

tion does not represent an object of any kind—it exists only to eliminate anomalies in the database.

HYBRID OBJECTS

Hybrid objects can be transformed into relational designs using a combination of the techniques for composite and compound objects. Figure 7.39a shows SALES-ORDER, a hybrid object introduced in Chapter 5, in Figure 5.29. To represent this object with relations, we establish one relation for the object itself and another relation for each of the contained objects CUSTOMER and SALESPERSON. Then, as with any composite object, we establish a relation for the composite group; but since this group contains another object, ITEM, we also establish a relation for ITEM. The result is the set of relations shown in Figure 7.39b.

In general, to represent a hybrid object with relations, establish a relation for the object itself, other relations for each object property, and still other relations for composite groups. A generalized scheme is shown in Figure 7.40.

GENERALIZATION AND SUBTYPE OBJECTS

Generalization and subtype objects can be represented with relations in the same way that compound objects are represented. To do this, we create a relation for the generalization object and another relation for each subtype object. If there are constraints such as mutual exclusion among the subtypes, those constraints can be carried forward in the design as shown in Figure 7.41.

Sample Objects

To reinforce the concepts presented in this chapter, we will now consider several objects taken from actual businesses. These objects will be presented in increasing order of complexity. We will study each form and report and determine the underlying objects and their relationships. Then we will represent them using the relational model. Your

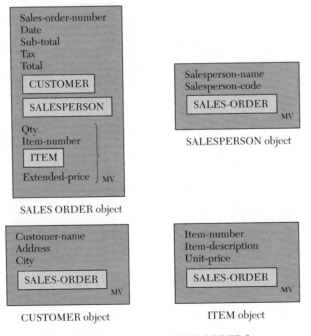

CARBON RIVER OFFICE FURNITURE
Sales Order Form

Sales Order Number 12990   Date 5/31/91

Customer   Carbon River Bookshop
Address   1145 Elm Street
City   Carbon River   State   Zip
Phone   232-0010

Salesperson Name   Elmira   Salesperson Code EZ-1

Qty	Item Number	Description	Unit Price	Extended Price
1	2304	Executive Desk	$199.00	$199.00
1	2690	Conference Table	$345.00	$345.00
4	2799	Side Chairs	$ 99.00	$396.00
			Sub-total	$940.00
			Tax	$ 47.94
			Total	$987.94

a. SALES ORDER form

Sales-order-number
Date
Sub-total
Tax
Total

    CUSTOMER

    SALESPERSON

Qty
Item-number
    ITEM
Extended-price   MV

SALES ORDER object

Salesperson-name
Salesperson-code
    SALES-ORDER   MV

SALESPERSON object

Customer-name
Address
City
    SALES-ORDER   MV

CUSTOMER object

Item-number
Item-description
Unit-price
    SALES-ORDER   MV

ITEM object

b. Hybrid object to represent SALES ORDER form

FIGURE 7.39
Relational representation of example hybrid object

FIGURE 7.40
Transformation of hybrid object
into relations

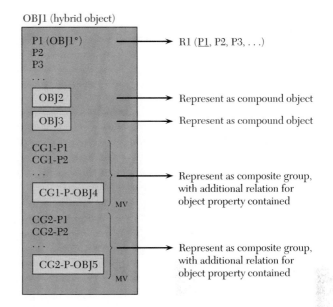

goal is to learn how to produce the object structure that underlies forms and reports and how to derive relational structures from them.

SUBSCRIPTION FORM

Figure 7.42a shows a magazine subscription form. There are at least two object structures that could underlie this form. If the publishers of *Fine Woodworking* consider a subscriber a property of a subscription, then a subscription could be a simple object, stored in the database as a single relation (Figure 7.42b).

This design is appropriate if this company has only one or a few publications and is not concerned about duplicating subscriber data across these publications. (Subscriber information to a second publication would be duplicated in the object that would represent the subscription to that publication.)

If, however, the publisher wants to build a list of customers to use when soliciting subscriptions to other publications, then the publisher will view subscriber as a separate entity. In this case, we define a SUBSCRIBER object, and establish a relationship between SUBSCRIBER and SUBSCRIPTION. This is illustrated in Figure 7.42c. Notice that SUBSCRIBER is a compound object—it contains an object property. The 1:N relationship between these objects is represented by the relations in Figure 7.42d.

PRODUCT DESCRIPTION

Figure 7.43a shows the description of a popular packaged goods product. Whereas Figure 7.42a shows a generic form, Figure 7.43a shows an instance of a specific report about a cereal product. Reports for all Kellogg's cereal products follow this format.

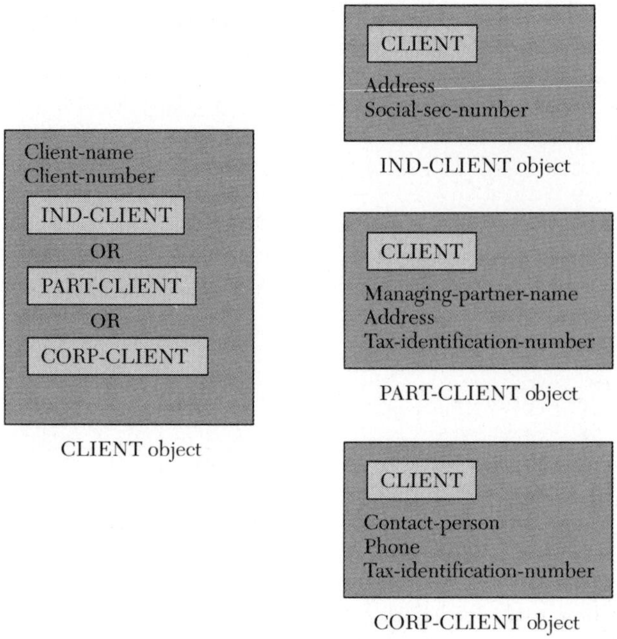

a. Example generalization and subtype objects

CLIENT (<u>Client#</u>, Client-name, Amount-due)
INDIVIDUAL-CLIENT (<u>Client#</u>, Address, Social-security-number)
PARTNERSHIP-CLIENT (<u>Client#</u>, Managing-partner-name, Address, Tax-identification-
    number)
CORPORATE-CLIENT (<u>Client#</u>, Contact-person, Phone, Tax-identification-number)

b. Relations needed to represent the E-R diagram in Figure 7.41a

FIGURE 7.41
Representing generalization hierarchies and subtypes with relations

Figure 7.43b shows a composite object that could underlie the report. We say *could* because further investigation might turn up other objects that are not apparent from looking at only one report.

The object diagram in Figure 7.43b describes cereal products with certain common properties, such as calories, carbohydrates, fats, and so forth. However, this object diagram indicates that ingredients vary with the product. For instance, some cereals contain corn, some contain wheat, some rice, and some barley; some cereals contain cane sugar, others honey, and some have both. Because of this wide variance, ingredient is shown as a multivalued property. The data structure diagram in Figure 7.43c indicates that two relations are required here—one for the product details and one for the repeating group of ingredients.

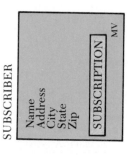

a. Subscription order form

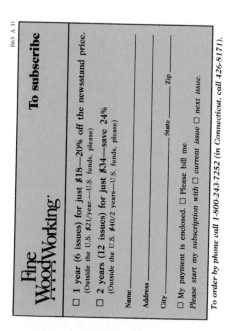

b. Subscription as one object represented with a single relation

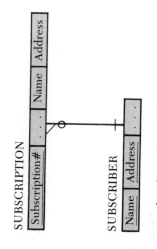

c. Subscription as two objects

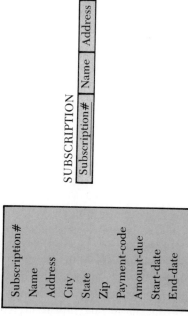

d. Relation diagram for Figure 7.42C

FIGURE 7.42

Possible representations of SUBSCRIPTION

NUTRITION INFORMATION
SERVING SIZE: 1 OZ. (28.4 g, ABOUT 1 CUP)
SERVINGS PER PACKAGE: 13

	CEREAL	WITH ½ CUP VITAMINS A & D SKIM MILK
CALORIES	110	150*
PROTEIN	2 g	6g
CARBOHYDRATE	25 g	31g
FAT	0 g	0g*
CHOLESTEROL	0 mg	0mg*
SODIUM	290 mg	350mg
POTASSIUM	35 mg	240mg

PERCENTAGE OF U.S. RECOMMENDED DAILY ALLOWANCES (U.S. RDA)

PROTEIN	2	10
VITAMIN A	25	30
VITAMIN C	25	25
THIAMIN	35	40
RIBOFLAVIN	35	45
NIACIN	35	35
CALCIUM	**	15
IRON	10	10
VITAMIN D	10	25
VITAMIN B₆	35	35
FOLIC ACID	35	35
PHOSPHORUS	4	15
MAGNESIUM	2	6
ZINC	2	6
COPPER	2	4

*WHOLE MILK SUPPLIES AN ADDITIONAL 30 CALORIES, 4 g FAT, AND 15 mg CHOLESTEROL.
**CONTAINS LESS THAN 2% OF THE U.S. RDA OF THIS NUTRIENT.

INGREDIENTS: RICE, SUGAR, SALT, CORN SYRUP, MALT FLAVORING.

VITAMINS AND IRON: VITAMIN C (SODIUM ASCORBATE AND ASCORBIC ACID), NIACINAMIDE, IRON, VITAMIN B₆ (PYRIDOXINE HYDROCHLORIDE), VITAMIN A (PALMITATE), VITAMIN B₂ (RIBOFLAVIN), VITAMIN B₁ (THIAMIN HYDROCHLORIDE), FOLIC ACID, AND VITAMIN D.
TO KEEP THIS CEREAL FRESH, BHT HAS BEEN ADDED TO THE PACKAGING.

a. Report about a product

FIGURE 7.43
Representation of product

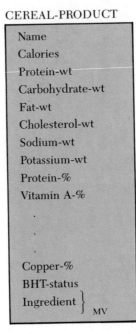

b. Object diagram

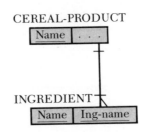

c. Relational representation

TRAFFIC WARNING CITATION

Figure 7.44a shows an instance of the traffic warning citation form used in the state of Washington. The designer of this form has given us important clues about the underlying objects of this form. Notice that portions of the form are visually divided by rounded corners, implying that different sections pertain to different objects.

Figure 7.44b is one approach illustrating the underlying objects of the traffic warning citation. Although it is not necessarily true, there are certain clues that lead us to believe that driver, vehicle, and officer are independent objects. For one thing, data about each of these subjects is in a separate section on the form. But more important, each object has its own user-defined key field: Drivers-license uniquely identifies a driver, Vehicle-license identifies every registered vehicle, and Personnel-no identifies every law officer. These key fields are obviously determinants. Consequently, we decided to treat those three entities as separate objects. The equivalent relation diagram appears in Figure 7.44c.

We could have incorporated all of the properties into one big object diagram for CORRECTION-NOTICE. Would that give us different results? Actually, with persistence, the end results would likely be the same. If we were to start with one simple object diagram, we would transform it into one relation containing many attributes. When we reviewed that relation and applied the rules of normalization to it, we would discover several modification anomalies. These anomalies exist because there would be transitive dependencies in the relation. (For example, Number → Drivers-license → Last-name | First-name | Address, and so forth) We would eliminate those anomalies by separating the relation into several relations, each of which had no anomalies. The end result would be the relation diagram in Figure 7.44c.

Summary

Data models expressed in terms of both the entity-relationship model and the semantic object models can be transformed into relational database designs.

To transform E-R data models, each entity is represented by a relation. The attributes of the relation correspond to the properties of the entity. Once the relation has been defined, it must be examined in light of normalization criteria. The relations may be adjusted accordingly.

Weak entities are transformed into relations just as strong ones are. The key of such relations, however, always contains the key of the relation upon which it is existence dependent.

There are three types of HAS-A relationships in the E-R model with which we are concerned: 1:1, 1:N, and N:M relationships. To represent a 1:1 relationship, place the key of one relation in the other relation. One-to-one relationships sometimes indicate that two relations have been defined on the same entity and should be combined into one relation. This is not always the case, however, particularly when the keys of the relations are different.

To represent a 1:N relationship, place the key of the parent in the child. Finally, to represent an M:N relationship, create an intersection relation that has the keys of the other two relations.

Recursive relationships are relationships in which the participants in the relationship arise from the same table. There are three types: 1:1, 1:N, and N:M. The types are represented in the same way as nonrecursive relationships. The only difference is that the value of the key attribute varies depending on whether the row plays the role of parent or child.

Generalization and subtype entities (IS-A relationships) are also represented by relations; one relation is defined for the generalization entity, and other relations are defined for each subtype. Often the keys of the relations are the same. If so, the relationship

FIGURE 7.44
Representation of traffic warning
citation

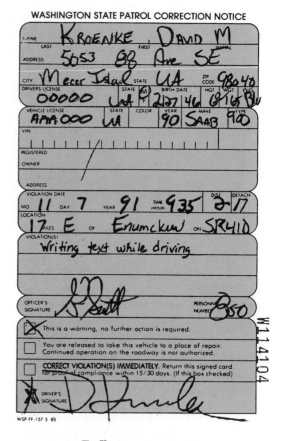

a. Traffic warning citation

among the rows is defined via the key values. If not, then, since the rows have a 1:1 relationship, the keys of the subtype relations can be placed in the generalization relation or the opposite. Most often, the key of the generalization relation is placed in the subtype relation.

Binary relationships can be combined to form three types of larger structures. A tree is a collection of record types such that each record has exactly one parent except the root, which has no parent. In a simple network, records may have multiple parents, but the parents must be of different types. In a complex network, records have multiple parents of the same type. Another way of saying this is that in a complex network, at least one of the binary relationships is M:N.

A bill of materials is a data structure frequently seen in manufacturing applications. Such structures can be represented by M:N recursive relationships.

The transformation of semantic objects into relations depends on the type of object. Simple objects are represented by a single relation. The nonobject properties are carried as attributes of the relation. Composite objects require two or more relations for their representation. One relation contains the nonrepeating properties and the second con-

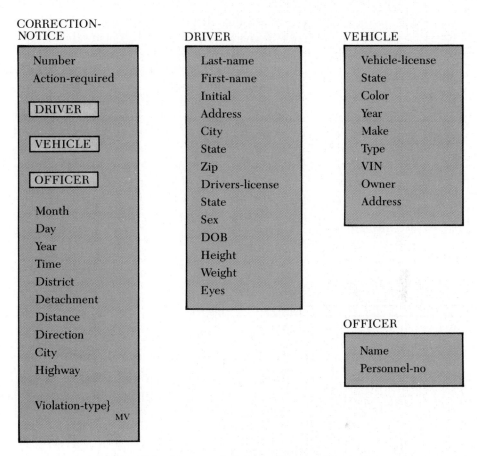

CORRECTION-NOTICE

Number
Action-required

DRIVER

VEHICLE

OFFICER

Month
Day
Year
Time
District
Detachment
Distance
Direction
City
Highway

Violation-type}
MV

DRIVER

Last-name
First-name
Initial
Address
City
State
Zip
Drivers-license
State
Sex
DOB
Height
Weight
Eyes

VEHICLE

Vehicle-license
State
Color
Year
Make
Type
VIN
Owner
Address

OFFICER

Name
Personnel-no

b. Possible objects underlying traffic warning citation

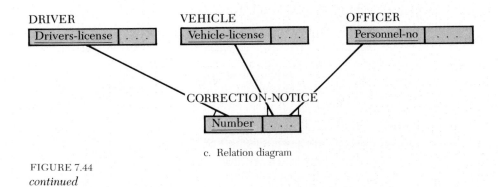

c. Relation diagram

FIGURE 7.44
continued

tains the properties of the composite group. The key of the relation that represents the repeating properties is always a composite key. It contains the key of the object plus an identifier of the composite group within that object.

At least two relations are required to represent a compound object. Each relation has its own distinct key. There are several different types of compound objects: one-to-one, one-to-many, many-to-one, and many-to-many. These are represented as entity relationships are represented. In some cases, the data model indicates that a relationship is only processed in one direction. In that case, either more information needs to be obtained about the underlying relationship or a guess must be made about the type of relationship.

Association objects require at least three relations for their representation; one is required for each of the objects involved. Each relation has its own key, and the relation representing the association object will contain the keys of the other two objects as foreign keys.

Hybrid objects are represented by a combination of the techniques used for composite and compound objects. Generalization and subtype objects are represented as compound objects.

GROUP I   QUESTIONS

7.1   Explain how E-R entities are transformed into relations.

7.2   Why is it necessary to evaluate relations transformed from entities according to normalization criteria? Under what conditions should the relations be altered if they are not in DK/NF? Under what conditions should they not be altered?

7.3   Explain how the representation of weak entities differs from the representation of strong entities.

7.4   List the three types of binary relationships and give an example of each. Use examples not in this text.

7.5   Define *foreign key* and give an example.

7.6   Show two alternative ways to represent the 1:1 relationship in your answer to question 7.4. Use data structure diagrams.

7.7   For your answers to question 7.6, describe a method for obtaining data about one of the entities, given the key of the other. Describe a method for obtaining data about the second entity, given the key of the first. Describe answers for both of your alternatives in question 7.6.

7.8   Why are some 1:1 relationships considered suspicious? Under what conditions should relations in a 1:1 relationship be combined into one relation?

7.9   Define the terms *parent* and *child* and give an example of each.

7.10 Show how to represent the 1:N relationship in your answer to question 7.4. Use a data structure diagram.

7.11   For your answer to question 7.10, describe a method for obtaining data for all of the children, given the key of the parent. Describe a method for obtaining data for the parent, given a key of the child.

7.12   For a 1:N relationship, explain why the key of the parent must be placed in the child rather than the key of the child in the parent.

7.13   Give examples of binary 1:N relationships other than those in this text for:

a. An optional-to-optional relationship
b. An optional-to-mandatory relationship
c. A mandatory-to-optional relationship
d. A mandatory-to-mandatory relationship

Illustrate your answer using data structure diagrams.

7.14   Show how to represent the N:M relationship in your answer to question 7.4. Use a data structure diagram.

7.15   For your answer to question 7.14, describe a method for obtaining the data for one entity, given the key of the other. Describe a method for obtaining the data for the second entity, given the key of the first.

7.16   Why is it not possible to represent N:M relationships with the same strategy used to represent 1:N relationships?

7.17   Explain the meaning of the term *intersection relation*.

7.18   Define three types of recursive binary relationships. Give an example of each.

7.19   Show how to represent the 1:1 binary relationship in your answer to question 7.18. How does this differ from the representation of 1:1 nonrecursive relationships?

7.20   Show how to represent the 1:N binary relationship in your answer to question 7.18. How does this differ from the representation of 1:N nonrecursive relationships?

7.21   Show how to represent the M:N binary relationship in your answer to question 7.18. How does this differ from the representation of M:N nonrecursive relationships?

7.22   Give an example of a generalization hierarchy and subtypes. Show how to represent it using relations.

7.23   Define the following: *tree, simple network, complex network*.

7.24   Give an example of a tree structure other than one in this text. Show how to represent it with relations.

7.25   Give an example of a simple network other than one in this text. Show how to represent it with relations.

7.26   Give an example of a complex network other than one in this text. Show how to represent it with relations.

7.27　What is a bill of materials? Give an example other than the one in this text. Show how to represent your example with relations.

7.28　Give an example of a simple object, other than one in this text. Show how to represent this object with relations.

7.29　Give an example of a composite object, other than one in this text. Show how to represent this object with relations.

7.30　Give an example of the following types of compound object: 1:1, 1:N, N:1, and N:M. Show how to represent each with relations.

7.31　Give an example, not in this text, of a one-way compound relationship. Describe alternatives for representing it with relations.

7.32　Give an example of an association object, other than one in this text. Show how to represent this object with relations.

7.33　Give an example of a hybrid object, other than one in this text. Show how to represent this object with relations.

7.34　Convert your answer to question 7.22 to semantic objects. Show how to represent these objects with relations.

GROUP II QUESTIONS

7.35　Transform the entity-relationship diagram for Jefferson Dance Club (Figure 4.12) into relations. Express your answer with a data structure diagram. Show interrelation constraints.

7.36　Transform the entity-relationship diagram for San Juan Charters (Figure 4.14) into relations. Express your answer with a data structure diagram. Show interrelation constraints.

7.37　Transform the objects in Figure 5.17 into relations. Express your answer with a data structure diagram. Show interrelation constraints.

7.38　Suppose you are working on a project to develop a database to support a student microcomputer lab at a university. Consider the following statements describing various objects and relationships:

　　a. Students must be enrolled in certain courses in order to use the microcomputer lab.
　　b. Students can make appointments to use the lab by reserving a certain computer for use at a certain time.
　　c. Each computer has a certain amount of memory and might also have special peripherals attached (such as a mouse, a speech synthesizer, or a special keyboard.)

FDA REPORT #6272
Date: 06/30/89
Issuer: Kellogg's Corporation
Report Title: Product Summary by Ingredient

Corn	Corn Flakes
	Krispix
	Nutrigrain (Corn)
Corn syrup	Rice Krispies
	Frosted Flakes
	Sugar Pops
Malt	Rice Krispies
	Sugar Smacks
Wheat	Sugar Smacks
	Nutrigrain (Wheat)

a. FDA report

SUPPLIER LIST
Date: 6/30/89

Ingredient	Supplier	Price
Corn	Wilson	2.80
	J. Perkins	2.72
	Pollack	2.83
	McKay	2.80
Wheat	Adams	1.19
	Kroner	1.19
	Schmidt	1.22
Barley	Wilson	0.85
	Pollack	0.84

b. Internal supplier list

FIGURE 7.45
Reports for question 7.39

Perform the following tasks:

a. Draw the object diagrams for STUDENT, COURSE, COMPUTER, PERIPHERAL, and APPOINTMENT.
b. What type (simple, composite, compound, associative, hybrid, or generalization) is each of the objects?
c. Transform the object diagrams into relation diagrams. Underline the key of each relation.
d. Identify the foreign keys (if any) in each relation.

7.39 Modify Figures 7.43b and 7.43c to add the reports shown in Figure 7.45.

7.40 Using the album cover shown in Figure 7.46 as a guide, perform the following tasks:

a. Draw the object diagrams for these underlying objects: ARTIST, ROLE, and SONG.
b. Identify the relationships among those objects. What types of objects are they (simple, composite, and so on)?
c. Define for each participant in a relationship whether it is optional or mandatory.
d. Transform the object diagrams into relation diagrams. What is the key of each relation? What foreign keys appear in each relation?

7.41 Consider the following opinion: Data models based on semantic objects seem to result in database designs that are better normalized than those based on the entity-relationship model. Do you agree with this opinion? If so, why do you think it is true? If not, why not?

WEST SIDE STORY

Based on a conception of Jerome Robbins

Book by ARTHUR LAURENTS
Music by LEONARD BERNSTEIN
Lyrics by STEPHEN SONDHEIM

Entire Original Production Directed
and Choreographed by JEROME ROBBINS

Originally produced on Broadway by Robert E. Griffith and Harold S. Prince
by arrangement with Roger L. Stevens
Orchestration by Leonard Bernstein with Sid Ramin and Irwin Kostal

HIGHLIGHTS FROM THE COMPLETE RECORDING

Maria . . . . .KIRI TE KANAWA
Tony . . . . .JOSÉ CARRERAS
Anita . . . . .TATIANA TROYANOS
Riff . . . . .KURT OLLMANN
and MARILYN HORNE singing "Somewhere"

Rosalia	. . . . .Louise Edeiken	Diesel	. . . . .Marty Nelson
Consuela	. . . . .Stella Zambalis	Baby John	. . . . . .Stephen Bogardus
Francisca	. . . . .Angelina Reaux	A-rab	. . . . .Peter Thom
Action	. . . . .David Livingston	Snowboy	. . . . .Todd Lester
	Bernardo	. . . . Richard Harrell	

[1]	**Jet Song** (Riff, Action, Baby John, A-rab, Chorus)	[3'13]
[2]	**Something's Coming** (Tony)	[2'33]
[3]	**Maria** (Tony)	[2'56]
[4]	**Tonight** (Maria, Tony)	[5'27]
[5]	**America** (Anita, Rosalia, Chorus)	[4'47]
[6]	**Cool** (Riff, Chorus)	[4'37]
[7]	**One Hand, One Heart** (Tony, Maria)	[5'38]
[8]	**Tonight** (Ensemble) (Entire Cast)	[3'40]
[9]	**I Feel Pretty** (Maria, Chorus)	[3'22]
[10]	**Somewhere** (A Girl)	[2'34]
[11]	**Gee, Officer Krupke** (Action, Snowboy, Diesel, A-rab, Baby John, Chorus)	[4'18]
[12]	**A Boy Like That** (Anita, Maria)	[2'05]
[13]	**I Have a Love** (Maria, Anita)	[3'30]
[14]	**Taunting Scene** (Orchestra)	[1'21]
[15]	**Finale** (Maria, Tony)	[2'40]

FIGURE 7.46
Album cover for question 7.40

Database
Application Design

Chapter 8 addresses the design of database applications. Since this is not a text on systems development, we will address only those aspects of application design that pertain directly to database processing and technology.

An assumption of the chapter is that the users' data model has been expressed in terms of semantic objects. This assumption is made to show more clearly how the users' paradigm (mental models of business activity), as expressed in the data model, drives application design. Even though this fact is true whether the data model is expressed in entity-relationship terms or in semantic object terms, it is more obvious when semantic objects are used.

We begin with an overview of the database application design process. Next, we discuss views and materializations of objects, and then we turn to the design of application components: control facilities, forms, reports, and finally, application programs themselves.

- NATURE OF DATABASE APPLICATIONS
- OBJECT MATERIALIZATION
- CONTROL MECHANISM DESIGN
- FORM DESIGN
- REPORT DESIGN
- APPLICATION PROGRAM DESIGN

Nature of Database Applications

There are many ways to design database applications. The subject has been discussed extensively in the literature; there are multitudes of texts on the subject. In this section, we will present an overview of an object-oriented method of designing an application.

OVERVIEW OF APPLICATION DEVELOPMENT

Figure 8.1 summarizes the general process for developing database applications. As shown, there are three major phases: requirements, design, and implementation (we omit definition and evaluation in this abbreviated discussion).

During requirements, the functions of applications are determined. As shown in Figure 8.1, data flow diagrams are constructed of business activities. These diagrams show the data flows and processes that must occur on those flows. Often, especially for organizational and large workgroup databases, requirements are divided into groups, each of which is then referred to as a particular application; for example, a personnel and payroll system might be divided into *administration, compensation,* and *benefits* applications.

Once the application functions are known, the applications are designed. The term **application design** includes more than the design of application programs' structure and logic. It also includes the design of the user interfaces: control facilities such as commands and menus, the structure and processing of forms, and the definition of reports. In this chapter, we will consider the user interface first and then the design of application program logic.

Once the application(s) has been designed, it is implemented. Implementation can be accomplished in a variety of ways, as discussed in Chapter 2. On one end of the continuum, programs may be written entirely from scratch; at the other end, the default appli-

FIGURE 8.1
Major tasks for database application development

Requirements Phase
- Interview users
- Build data flow diagrams
- Determine data flows
- Determine processes that operate on data flows
- Specify application groups

Design Phase
- Design application control facilities
- Design forms
- Design reports
- Specify program logic

Implementation Phase
- Build applications
    with DBMS application facilities
    with code generation systems
    with programming

cation facilities of the DBMS may be used. In between these extremes are applications that combine in-house programming with DBMS-provided forms and reports.

In this chapter we will be concerned only with the design phase of application development. In particular, we will show how the design of the database influences, and in large measure, determines, the design of the applications that process it.

FUNCTIONS OF A DATABASE APPLICATION

The purpose of a database application is to create, update, delete, and display objects (or views of entities) at the direction of the users while at all times protecting the security and integrity of the database. In the ideal, an application provides an easy-to-use interface for authorized users who are making authorized requests with valid and accurate data. In the ideal, it presents the equivalent of a closed door to unauthorized users, and it provides informative and helpful error messages to authorized users who are making unauthorized requests or mistakes, or who are attempting to process invalid data. Often these ideals cannot be fully realized because of limitations in DBMS products, time and budget restrictions, limits to the knowledge or abilities of the developers, or other constraints. Still, they serve as important goals.

Create, Update, Delete, and Display Objects

The first element of the database application's purpose is to *create, update, delete, and display objects*. As you know from prior chapters, objects are not stored in the database. Rather, objects are transformed and stored as sets of relations. Thus, before objects can be processed, the application must construct them from the underlying relations. Or, as is sometimes stated, the application must **materialize objects.** We will consider this subject further in the next section.

Objects are created by obtaining data from users or other sources and storing it in the database. Updating occurs by reading the object data from the relations and making appropriate changes. Deleting involves removing all object data from the underlying relations. Display can be done via reporting (on paper or other external media) or by showing object structures on video display devices.

Creating, updating, and deleting objects is the bulk of the work for the application and application developer. When objects are so modified, the data must be correctly changed while constraints are enforced. Although DBMS products should enforce many constraints automatically, in practice, few do. It often falls on the application program to enforce domain, intrarelation, and interrelation constraints.

Additionally, if the database is concurrently processed, updating must be controlled so that the actions of one user do not interfere with those of another. Finally, update processing must be structured so that in the event of failure, the database can be recovered.

Objects are seldom queried. Most DBMS products to date support the querying of *relations* not *objects*. You will study SQL, the ANSI standard query language, in Chapter 10. As you will see, this language is relation oriented. Thus, when using such a language, users themselves must compose objects from underlying relations. In practice, this means that such languages are used only for the querying of simple objects. If the objects are more complex, users invoke an application program that constructs the object from the underlying relations.

Provide Facilities for Controlling Processing

Consider the next phrase in the purpose of a database application: *at the direction of the users*. An application must provide a means for the user to direct and control the activity of the application. Two means are used. For one, the user learns a set of **commands** to issue. Here's an example:

> UPDATE CUSTOMER WHERE Cust-num = 12345
>   SET CUST-BALANCE TO 1350

The advantage of command-driven applications is that they are direct and to the point. The user need not fuss with menus or other structures. The disadvantage is that the end-user must learn and remember the commands and their syntax. Command-driven applications are used in situations where there are a few commands that are used frequently. Teller processing at a bank or airline reservation processing are situations that would likely employ command-driven applications.

The second means are application **menus.** Here, the user is provided one or more menus from which to make choices. (An example of menu for the Carbon River Book-shop will be shown when we get to Figure 8.8). The advantage of menus is that the end-user need not remember commands nor even remember which commands are appropriate in a given context. The system leads the user by the hand through the choices that are appropriate. The disadvantage of menu-driven applications is that they seem cumbersome for frequent or experienced users.

Recently, a new style of control interface has begun to emerge. This style of interface, which has been made popular by Apple Macintosh microcomputers and products like Microsoft's Windows, is an outgrowth of menu-oriented control. Called a **graphical user interface,** or GUI, such interfaces include pull-down menus, icons, dialogue boxes, mice, and other facilities that greatly enhance the applications' ease of use. Because of their intuitive nature, and because of the standardized mode of processing, such interfaces will become common for database applications in the near future. The major impediment to their use today is the lack of high-productivity development tools.

Protect Security and Integrity

The phrase *while at all times protecting the security and integrity of the database* means that the application should be designed so that only authorized users can perform authorized activities with valid data. Again, this is far easier to state as a goal than it is to accomplish in practice. Application designers, however, must be cognizant of this goal at all times.

End-users will make keystroke mistakes. The data that end-users receive (on source documents, for example) will often be incorrect. End-users will attempt to perform operations out of sequence. They will also attempt to perform invalid operations. They will try to perform operations that they are not trained, qualified, or authorized to perform. Applications should be designed to prevent as many such activities as possible.

There are several ways in which the application developer can provide protection for security and integrity. For one, passwords and other controls can be established, as will be described in Chapter 14. Additionally, the developer can encode constraint enforcement into update programs. Forms can be designed to eliminate errors as well. A twenty-five character text field can be displayed in a window of only twenty-five spaces, for example. Further, menus can be developed so that only commands appropriate to a given context can be executed in that context.

Security and integrity protection must be designed into the applications from the start. All too often such considerations are made only after problems have developed. At this point, it is usually far more difficult to implement such protection. The purposes of a database application are summarized in Figure 8.2.

A CONTINUUM OF APPLICATIONS

A database application is the interface between the user and the database. Although all applications have the functions described in the previous section, they are not all equivalent. In fact, there is a continuum of applications. On the high end, some applications provide extensive services on behalf of the user. They obtain data from several relations, combine it in accordance with an object structure, and display and manage updates to the data in a sophisticated GUI. While doing this, the application is constantly monitoring database integrity, ensuring that the user is not violating any constraints and is performing only authorized activities. All of these activities are organized and structured so as to maximize the application's performance.

At the other end of the spectrum, there are applications that do little more than list tables. In the next chapter, you will learn about SQL, which is a language that the sophisticated end-user could use as a bare bones application. Such an application would only display data in tables; there would be little formatting, no object structure, and little data integrity checking.

OBJECT MATERIALIZATION

One of the functions of a database application is to materialize objects. To understand this function, consider the object BOOK, shown in Figure 8.3a. BOOK is represented

FIGURE 8.2
Functions of database applications

- Create, update, delete, and display objects (materialize objects)
- Provide facilities for controlling processing
- Protect security and integrity of the database

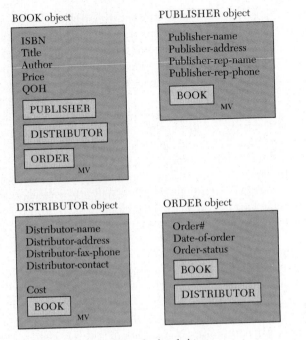

BOOK object

```
ISBN
Title
Author
Price
QOH
  PUBLISHER
  DISTRIBUTOR
  ORDER        MV
```

PUBLISHER object

```
Publisher-name
Publisher-address
Publisher-rep-name
Publisher-rep-phone
  BOOK
          MV
```

DISTRIBUTOR object

```
Distributor-name
Distributor-address
Distributor-fax-phone
Distributor-contact

Cost
  BOOK       MV
```

ORDER object

```
Order#
Date-of-order
Order-status
  BOOK
  DISTRIBUTOR
```

a. BOOK and related objects

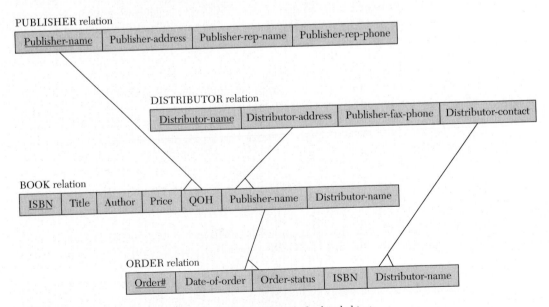

PUBLISHER relation

Publisher-name	Publisher-address	Publisher-rep-name	Publisher-rep-phone

DISTRIBUTOR relation

Distributor-name	Distributor-address	Publisher-fax-phone	Distributor-contact

BOOK relation

ISBN	Title	Author	Price	QOH	Publisher-name	Distributor-name

ORDER relation

Order#	Date-of-order	Order-status	ISBN	Distributor-name

b. Relations to represent BOOK and related objects

FIGURE 8.3
Representation of BOOK and related objects

by the four relations PUBLISHER, BOOK, DISTRIBUTOR, and ORDER, as illustrated in Figure 8.3b.

The users of an application that processes books do not want to work with these relations—they want to work with books. They want to process a BOOK as a whole unit, and they do not want to have to navigate among the four tables that are, to them, just pieces of BOOK. Most likely, the user will want to specify an identifying value, such as ISBN, and have the application obtain the appropriate data from the underlying tables. Thus, given an ISBN, the application will obtain the appropriate rows of PUBLISHER, BOOK, DISTRIBUTOR, and ORDER and assemble those rows into the distinct identity that represents that book.

In general, one of the important functions of an application is to assemble the object from underlying relations. The application brings together data from the rows of all the tables involved in the object. In this way, users can process what they know and understand (BOOKs) and need not be concerned with individual relations.

OBJECT VIEWS

Although many users may process the same object, they often do not see this object from the same perspective. For example, if they use the object to accomplish different business objectives, the particular data they need will vary.

Consider two different users at the Carbon River Bookshop. Clerks at the sales desk want to process BOOK data to determine price, remove stock from inventory, and so forth. Order clerks, on the other hand, want to process BOOK data to be able to submit an order to the correct vendor. Suppose that clerks at the sales desk need a view of BOOK that includes ISBN, Title, Author, Price, QOH, Publisher-name, Distributor-name, and Date-of-order (for books on order). The order clerks, on the other hand, want a view that includes ISBN, Title, Author, QOH, Publisher-name, Publisher-address, Distributor-name, Distributor-fax-phone, and the Order# and Date-of-order. See Figure 8.4. These two groups are processing the same object, but they want to see different attributes about that object.

An **object view,** or **user view** or **view,** is a subset of an object that is utilized by a particular user or group of users. A view is described by naming the object on which it is based and listing the attributes of the object that are visible from that view.

Often we need to give views a name. We might call the two views in Figure 8.4 the Sales and Order Views of BOOK. Another way of naming views is to number them. The Sales View could be denoted V_1(BOOK) and the Order View could be denoted V_2(BOOK).

The definition of views is especially important for security and control. With views, sensitive data can be hidden from all but authorized users. In a personnel administration system, suppose there is an object called EMPLOYEE that includes Salary. Not all users may need to work with Salary data. If this is so, then one view can be defined of the EMPLOYEE object to enable those who need Salary to see it, and another view can be defined without Salary for those who do not need its data.

FIGURE 8.4
Two views of BOOK

Sales view of BOOK
V_1(BOOK)

Order view of BOOK
V_2(BOOK)

MATERIALIZATIONS OF OBJECT VIEWS

A view is a list of visible attributes of an object. In most cases, users want more than just a list of attribute values. They want the view data to be formatted. They want labels, lines, boxes, indentations, control breaks, and the like. A view plus this formatting data is called a **materialization.** Normally, object views are processed by application programs that add the formatting data to produce the materialization. Thus, we can restate one of the purposes of an application program to be to produce materializations of views of objects.

A materialization is a view plus labels, lines, boxes, indentations, colors, and other display data. All of this formatting data is sometimes called **window dressing** since it is data that is used to improve the appearance of data, without changing the format of the data.

There can be several materializations for the same view. One materialization might be used to update data while a second is used to display the data. Consider the bookshop. Clerks at the sales desk want to process data in an easy-to-use format. Consequently, they will not process the Sales View directly, but will process a materialization of that view. Similarly, order clerks will process a materialization of the Order View. There are potentially many materializations for a given object view.

Figure 8.5 shows a materialization of the Sales View, or V_1(BOOK). This materialization is a data entry form the clerks use when selling books. Note this materialization differs from the view in that it has a defined physical appearance. It includes fixed text such as titles and column headings, borders, and specific locations where data is to be displayed or entered.

As with object views, we can name materializations with functional titles like BOOK SALES form. We can also number them. The BOOK SALES form could be called: $M_1(V_1(BOOK))$. This expression is read "the first materialization of the first view of BOOK," or simply "M sub 1 of V sub 1 of BOOK." A second materialization of the Sales View would be denoted $M_2(V_1(BOOK))$.

Now consider Figure 8.6 which is also a materialization of BOOK, but it is a materialization of the Order View, or V_2(BOOK). This figure shows the BOOK ORDER form which is used by the ordering department to determine the order status of books.

FIGURE 8.5
Materialization of the Sales View

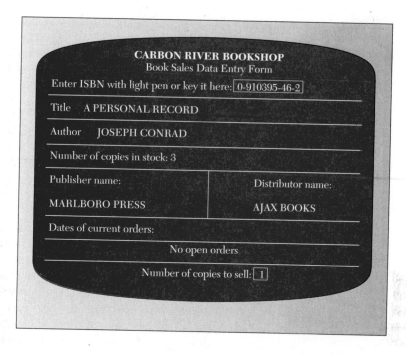

FIGURE 8.6
Materialization of the Order View

To summarize, a view is a list of attributes of an object. A materialization of a view is a view plus window dressing to present that view in a particular format. Objects, views, and materializations have a hierarchical relationship as shown in Figure 8.7. An object has, potentially, many views, and each view has, potentially, many materializations. In most cases, the application program receives the view data and constructs the materialization.

Control Mechanism Design

The design of application programs includes the design of the user interface as well as the design of program logic. The user interface consists of facilities for control, forms, and reports. We will consider each of these in turn.

With regard to control mechanisms, the design decision is whether the application is to be menu driven, command driven, a GUI, or some combination of these. Menu-driven and GUI systems tend to be easier to use, though at times they can seem cumbersome and slow to experienced users. Command-driven systems require that users remember the syntax of commands; thus, they demand more from the users. Here, we will consider the design of menu-driven and GUI control mechanisms.

Consider the needs of the users at the Carbon River Bookshop. The bookshop is staffed by many different clerks who receive little training in the application's operation, so a menu-driven application seems appropriate. The menus save the clerks from the necessity of learning and relearning commands. Figure 8.8a shows the appearance of the main menu and one path of submenus, and Figure 8.8b shows the structure of this menu and submenus.

MENU DESIGN

There are two primary strategies in structuring a menu hierarchy: **object/action** and **action/object.** With the former, the highest menu lists objects to be processed, and lower-level menus lead the user to pick the action to be performed on that object. The menus in Figure 8.8 are such object/action menus. Action/object menus, on the other hand, begin with an action, say ADD NEW DATA, and the lower-level menus lead the user to pick the object to perform the action on.

FIGURE 8.7
Hierarchical relationships of object, view, and materialization

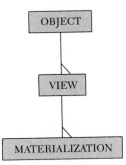

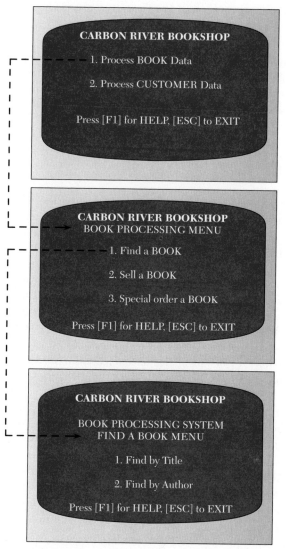

CARBON RIVER BOOKSHOP

1. Process BOOK Data

2. Process CUSTOMER Data

Press [F1] for HELP, [ESC] to EXIT

CARBON RIVER BOOKSHOP
BOOK PROCESSING MENU

1. Find a BOOK

2. Sell a BOOK

3. Special order a BOOK

Press [F1] for HELP, [ESC] to EXIT

CARBON RIVER BOOKSHOP

BOOK PROCESSING SYSTEM
FIND A BOOK MENU

1. Find by Title

2. Find by Author

Press [F1] for HELP, [ESC] to EXIT

a. Example Menu Selections for Carbon River Bookshop

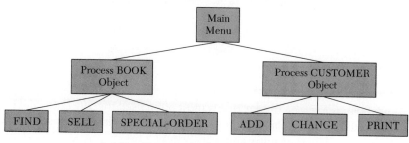

b. Menu Hierarchy for the Carbon River Bookshop

FIGURE 8.8
Menu hierarchy for the Carbon River Bookshop

In general, object/action menus are closer to the end-user's way of thinking than action/object menus are. When people start work, for example, they are more likely to think to themselves, "Now I'll process order documents; what do I want to do with them?" than they are to think, "Now I'll load some data; what data should I load?"

EXAMPLE MENUS FOR THE CARBON RIVER BOOKSHOP

To illustrate the menu design process, consider the SALES DESK application for the bookshop. From the requirements specification, the developers learned that salespeople need to work with two different objects: BOOKs and CUSTOMERs. The designers decided to use object/action oriented menus and so, at the highest level, clerks are asked to pick either of these objects to work with. The high-level menu is shown in Figure 8.8a.

Now, consider the path for BOOKs. When the user selects this path, he or she is presented with the next menu shown in Figure 8.8a. During the requirements stage, the team learned that the clerks need to perform one of three actions on books: find a book, sell a book, or special order a book. Consequently, the developers designed the second-level menu to present these three choices.

If the user selects the choice to find a book, a third-level menu is displayed. This menu presents two choices: find by title and find by author. When the user picks one of these two choices, a data entry form is then displayed.

Examine the hierarchy in Figure 8.8b to determine other paths through the Carbon River Bookshop menus. Observe in all cases that the orientation is from an object to a set of actions that become more and more specific. As stated, in most instances, this style of menu is preferred over action/object menus. Either style can work, however. An alternative that does *not* work, however, is to mix these styles on different paths; a set of menus should be consistently either object/action or action/object.

GUI applications have an additional element of sophistication (and complication). In addition to menus (which are usually of the pull-down type), **dialogue boxes** are used to help direct processing. For example, in a GUI system, if the user selects, say, the file open choice, the system will present a dialogue box to accept parameters of the open command. Because of dialogue boxes, GUI control facilities can have both menu- and command-based characteristics.

Form Design

A **form** is a screen display that is most often used for data entry and edit. Forms can also be used to report data, but, in most cases, when developers speak of forms, they mean those used for data entry and edit.

Not all forms are equal. Some seem natural, are easy to use, and result in few data entry errors. Others seem awkward and contrived and are difficult to use without creating errors. In this section, we will discuss and illustrate several principles of good form design.

FORM STRUCTURE

First, to seem natural and be easy to use, *the structure of a form must reflect the structure of the object that it materializes.* To understand this statement, consider the SALES-ORDER object in Figure 8.9. The ORDER has its own data such as Sales-order-number, Date, Sub-total, and the like, and it also contains data about CUSTOMER, SALESPERSON, and individual LINE-ITEMs. Further, ITEM data is contained within the LINE-ITEM composite group.

The ORDER relation is the **entry point** of the object. Such a relation is the first relation used when processing the object. The key of the object and the key (or at least

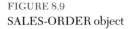

FIGURE 8.9
SALES-ORDER object

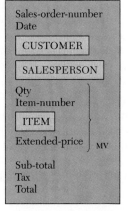

a. SALES-ORDER object

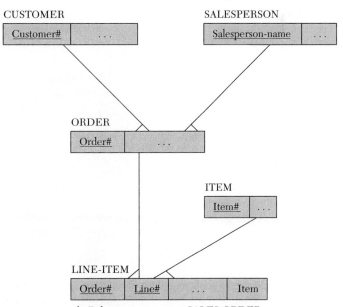

b. Relations to represent SALES-ORDER

a candidate key) of the entry point relation are always the same. For SALES-ORDER, Sales-order-number (Order#) is both the key of the SALES-ORDER object and the key of the relation SALES-ORDER.

To be easy to use, a form that materializes SALES-ORDER should reflect the structure in Figure 8.9. One such form is shown in Figure 8.10. In almost every case, it is good practice to locate data that identifies the object at the beginning of the form. This means that the key of the entry point and possibly other data from the entry point relation appear first. This serves as a title of the form and helps the user establish a mental context for the work to be done.

Thus, the first part of the form in Figure 8.10 displays data about the identity of the SALES-ORDER. Next, data about the CUSTOMER is presented, then data about the SALESPERSON, and next, a multiple-line section containing a variable number of LINE-ITEMs. Finally, more SALES-ORDER data, namely the Sub-total, Tax, and Total, is presented.

With the possible exception of the entry point relation, all of the data from a single relation should be placed in one contiguous section of the form. Assuming the database is in domain/key normal form (which it should be), each relation will pertain to a specific theme and the user will expect to have all of the data for that theme in one location. Thus CUSTOMER, SALESPERSON, and LINE-ITEM data groups are each contiguous on the form.

Observe, however, that this practice was not followed for the SALES-ORDER data. This was required because SALES-ORDER is the entry point of the object. Some SALES-ORDER data is located at the top of the form and some at the bottom.

FIGURE 8.10
SALES-ORDER form

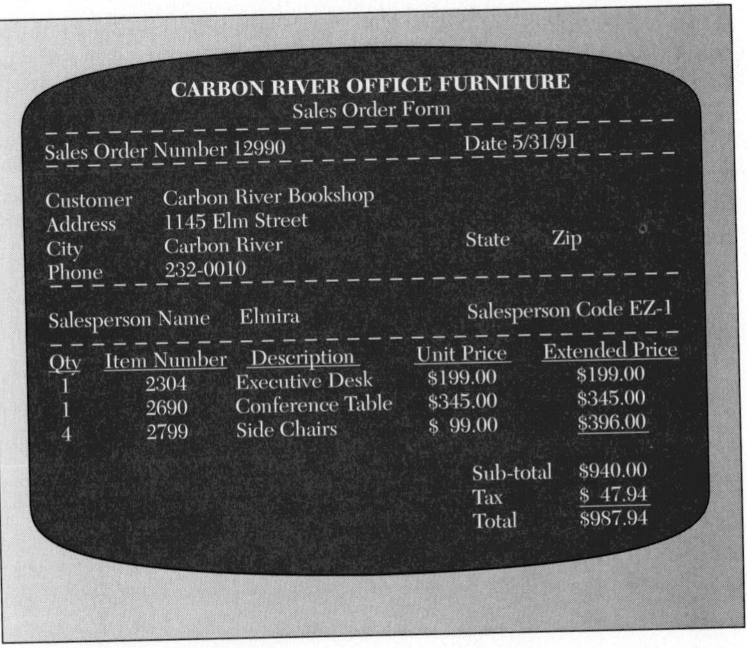

CARBON RIVER OFFICE FURNITURE
Sales Order Form

Sales Order Number 12990   Date 5/31/91

Customer   Carbon River Bookshop
Address   1145 Elm Street
City   Carbon River   State   Zip
Phone   232-0010

Salesperson Name   Elmira   Salesperson Code EZ-1

Qty	Item Number	Description	Unit Price	Extended Price
1	2304	Executive Desk	$199.00	$199.00
1	2690	Conference Table	$345.00	$345.00
4	2799	Side Chairs	$ 99.00	$396.00

Sub-total $940.00
Tax $ 47.94
Total $987.94

Such splitting is sometimes necessary for the relation that is the entry point of the object. As stated, a well-designed form will present identifying data (from the entry point relation) at the top of the form, but sometimes, particularly with objects that have composite groups (like LINE-ITEM), the rest of the data for that relation cannot appear until data from other relations has been entered or displayed. Thus, in Figure 8.10, the identifying data is presented, but the data concerning SALES-ORDER totals is not presented until after LINE-ITEM.

If we were to attempt to locate all of the SALES-ORDER data in one section, then either SALES-ORDER totals would need to appear before LINE-ITEMs, which would cause the totals to be presented out of context, or identifying data would need to be placed at the end of the form, which would make the form hard to use. Hence, in this case, a compromise is struck and the data is split. Again, such splitting is normally only appropriate for the entry point relation.

The form in Figure 8.10 is not the only acceptable one. CUSTOMER data could be presented after SALESPERSON data. Often, in a situation like this, the best strategy is to consider the manual paper forms. Users will find the computer form easier to use if data is presented in the same SALES-ORDER as on paper forms. (But don't fall into the trap of replicating a poorly designed paper form on the computer.)

Although the order of SALESPERSON and CUSTOMER seems unimportant, the order of SALESPERSON and LINE-ITEM or of CUSTOMER and LINE-ITEM probably is important. SALESPERSON and CUSTOMER data establishes a context for the SALES-ORDER; in a broad sense these data groups are semantic identifiers. It seems more appropriate to place them before LINE-ITEM. This judgment is an artistic one, however. One could argue this last point in the same sense one could argue the best location for a handle on a clay teapot. Still, such nuances are what make some forms easier to use than others. When in doubt, build prototypes of the alternatives and let the users decide.

DATA LOOKUP

A second principle of form design is that *users ought never be required (or allowed) to enter data that is already stored in the database.* The user of the form in Figure 8.10 ought not to be required to enter SALESPERSON or CUSTOMER data if that data is present in the database. Requiring such duplicate data entry is an invitation for data integrity problems.

When the user enters a new SALES-ORDER, he or she will need to enter the key of SALESPERSON and the key of CUSTOMER. The application should then obtain additional SALESPERSON and CUSTOMER data from the database. If this data is not present in the database, then, and only then, should the user be required to enter it. Further, the user should be given the opportunity to enter new SALESPERSON and CUSTOMER data only if he or she has the authority to do so. There may be important reasons for separating the authority to enter new SALES-ORDERs from the authority to add new SALESPERSONs or CUSTOMERs.

This type of data retrieval is sometimes called a **lookup.** The nonkey data is looked up in the database and displayed for the user. In this way, users can ensure they have entered the correct key value (the nonkey data on the source document and the data obtained from the database should match).

MODELESS PROCESSING

In some cases, forms are easy to use if they are **modeless.** This term means that the application determines the mode (insert, modify, or delete) from the context of activity. With modeless processing, the user of the form in Figure 8.10 would call up the form and key in Sales-order-number. The application would then search the database for a SALES-ORDER with that Sales-order-number. If no such SALES-ORDER exists, the application would assume the mode is insert and allow a new SALES-ORDER to be entered.

If the value of Sales-order-number does match a SALES-ORDER in the database, a modeless application would assume the mode is modify or delete and display the existing SALES-ORDER data in the form. The application would then give the user an opportunity to make changes to the data or to delete it (using a function key or similar means).

Modeless processing can be convenient but is not appropriate for every application. In some cases, it is important for the user to declare a mode and for the application to disallow actions that conflict with that mode. For example, if values of Sales-order-number are suspect—perhaps they are handwritten by busy clerks—then, with modeless processing, SALES-ORDER modifications may be erroneously processed as SALES-ORDER insertions. If so, over time, the same SALES-ORDER may be stored under three or four different SALES-ORDER numbers.

The issue is one of rigidity and control. Modeless processing is flexible and convenient, but errors can occur. Non-modeless processing is inflexible and rigid, but errors are less likely.

FORMS IN A GUI ENVIRONMENT

There are a number of form features that are peculiar to GUI systems. These features can dramatically improve the ease of use of database applications. We will discuss several of these important features in this section.

Unfortunately, to date, most DBMS products provide only a rudimentary application program interface to GUI systems. This means that developing GUI database applications currently requires substantial amounts of highly skilled programming labor. The productivity and visual desirability of such applications is high, however, and there is considerable pressure for vendors to create easier to use and high-productivity development tools. The creation of such tools is likely to occur in the near future.

Pop-down List Boxes

It is easier for human beings to *recognize* than to *recollect*. For example, it is easier to choose a salesperson's name from a list of salespeople than it is to remember that person's

FIGURE 8.11
Form options for GUI interfaces

name. It is also easier to recognize it than it is to spell it correctly. In light of these facts, some application forms use pop-down list boxes to present a list of choices that are appropriate in a given context.

A **pop-down list box** is a box that appears on a form when a given command is issued or a key pressed. The box lists alternatives that would be appropriate to a given context. Such boxes are most often found with GUI applications.

Consider an example. Suppose a user is keying in a SALES-ORDER using the form in Figure 8.10 and needs to supply a salesperson's name. The user cannot remember the name, but thinks he or she may recognize it if shown a list of possibilities. In this situation, a pop-down list box would be appropriate. With it, the user can press a button on the form or take other action to cause the list box, with salespersons' names, to be displayed. Figure 8.11 shows an example. From the list box, the user chooses or clicks with a mouse to select one of the names from the list.

Option Buttons

An **option button,** or **radio button,** is a display device used to enable users to select one alternative condition or state from a list of possibilities. Suppose, for example, the user of the form in Figure 8.10 needs to indicate whether the order is to be shipped by regular mail, second-day mail, or next-day mail. These choices are mutually exclusive; the order is shipped by just one method. In this case, one of the option buttons can be used. The user clicks on the appropriate button, from the list. Like a series of radio buttons, pressing a new button "deselects" any button that may already be pressed.

Behind the form, the application program must store data in the attribute that represents the radio button selected. For our example, suppose the attribute is named Shipping-mode. Two possible ways for storing the option button data are used. One is to store an integer number from 1 to the number of buttons. In this example, one of the values 1, 2, or 3 would be stored. A second option is to store a text value that describes the option chosen. Possibilities are regular, 2-day, and 1-day.

Check Boxes

Check boxes are similar to option buttons except that more than one alternative in the group may be chosen. For the SALES-ORDER form, suppose that shippers require that packages that are extra heavy, contain hazardous materials, or are delicate, be marked in special ways. Check boxes can be used to indicate these characteristics. The user can select or *check* as many of these items as are appropriate.

There are a number of feasible ways of representing check boxes. One common and simple way is to define a single character text attribute for each item in the check box list. The value of each of such attribute is binary; it can be 1 or 0, T or F, Y or N. Other possibilities, such as encoding bits in a byte, also exist, though they are unimportant for our purposes here.

CURSOR MOVEMENT AND PERVASIVE KEYS

Another consideration in forms design is the action of the cursor. The cursor should move through the form in an easy and natural manner. Typically, this means that the cursor follows the processing pattern of the end-user as he or she reads the source data entry documents. If forms are used to enter data over the telephone, the cursor controls the flow of the conversation. In this case, its movement should progress in a manner that the customer will find natural and appropriate.

Particular attention needs to be paid to the action of the cursor during and after an exception condition. Suppose, for example, that in using the form in Figure 8.10, an error is made—perhaps an invalid salesperson number is entered. The form processing should be done so that the cursor moves to a location that is logical; if a pop-up menu is presented, then the cursor should move to the start of the list of options in the pop-up menu. Once the menu has been processed, the cursor should then move back to the salesperson number, or the next appropriate space on the form.

The actions of special purpose keys such as ESC, function keys, and the like, should be *consistent* and *pervasive*. If ESC is used to exit menus, it should be used consistently for this purpose and for none other (except for actions that are logically equivalent to exiting from menus).

The actions of keys should pervade throughout the application. If ESC is used to exit from one menu, it should be used to exit from all. If F1 is used to delete data in one form, it should be used to delete data in all forms. Otherwise, habits that are formed in one portion of the application will have to be disregarded or relearned in other portions of the application. This is not only wasteful, it is frustrating and aggravating, and it generates errors.

These comments may seem obvious, but attention to such details is what makes a form easy and convenient to use.

Report Design

The subject of report design, even more so than form design, has been discussed extensively in texts on application development. We will not duplicate or even attempt to summarize those discussions here. Rather, this section will discuss several concepts that relate directly to the notion of a report as a materialization of a database object.

REPORT STRUCTURE

Principles of effective report design are similar to those for form design. In fact, it is possible to consider a report as a display-only form. As with forms, *the structure of a report should reflect the structure of the underlying object.* The name of the report, or the object the report is about, will indicate the entry relation into the object. As with forms, the key of the object will be the key of the entry point relation.

With the exception of the entry point relation, all of the data from a given relation should be located in a contiguous section of the report. Data from the entry point relation may need to be split, however, as is sometimes required with forms.

Data from relations that are parents of the entry point (or even grandparents) is looked up and displayed. Data from relations that are children to the entry point relation are shown as control breaks. For the SALES-ORDER object, LINE-ITEM data (Figure 8.9b) is listed as a repeating line under "Picking List" as shown in Figure 8.12. For this report, LINE-ITEM data is displayed in the order in which it was keyed when the SALES-ORDER was entered. For other reports, data from child relations may be sorted by a column; for this example, the data could be sorted by Item-number, Qty, Price, and so forth.

PROCESSING OF SORTED BY CLAUSES

The report shown in Figure 8.12 is a report about a SALES-ORDER as a single, individual entity. The report documents the facts about a particular SALES-ORDER for shipping, customer support, sales, and other business activities. As stated previously, when the user indicates a need for a report about semantic objects in some sorted order, then that report is not about the object, but rather about a collection of those objects, or a super-object. There are three ways in which this can occur.

FIGURE 8.12
Report based on SALES-ORDER
object

CARBON RIVER OFFICE FURNITURE
Shipping Instruction

Sales Order Number 12990   Date 5/31/91

SHIP TO: Carbon River Bookshop
            1145 Elm Street
            Carbon River   Phone: 232-0010
Our contact: Elmira

PICKING LIST:

Qty	Item Number	Description	Unit Price	Extended Price
1	2304	Executive Desk	$199.00	$199.00
1	2690	Conference Table	$345.00	$345.00
4	2799	Side Chairs	$ 99.00	$396.00

BILLING DATA:

Sub-total	$940.00
Tax	$ 47.94
Total	$987.94

Sorted by Object Key

If the report is to be sorted by a column that is a key or candidate key of the object, then the super-object is simply a collection of the objects. Thus, a SALES-ORDER report sorted by Invoice# is a report about the object SALES-ORDER-COLLECTION. With most DBMS report-writing products, a report about SALES-ORDER-COLLECTION will be no more difficult to produce than a report about SALES-ORDER.

Sorted by Nonkey Columns of the Entry Point Relation

When a user states a need for a report to be sorted by a column that is a nonkey column of the entry point relation, then the super-object is most likely an object of a totally different type. For example, suppose the SALES-ORDER relation has a column called Shipping-mode which contains a value of a code for the means by which the order was shipped. If the user requests a report of SALES-ORDERs sorted by Shipping-mode, then this report is actually a materialization of the object SHIPMENT, which contains SALES-ORDER as a multivalued object attribute. One such object is sketched in Figure 8.13a.

Often reports are sorted by a value of Date. Suppose SALES-ORDER contains two date columns: Order-date and Shipping-date. If the user requests a SALES-ORDER report sorted by Order-date, then that report is actually a report of ORDER-DATEs, not SALES-ORDERs. It is a report about certain days and the orders that were shipped on those days. Note that ORDER-DATE does, however, contain SALES-ORDER as a

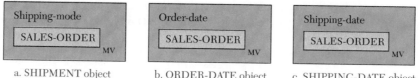

| a. SHIPMENT object | b. ORDER-DATE object | c. SHIPPING-DATE object |

FIGURE 8.13
Objects implied by sorting of SALES-ORDER

multivalued object attribute. Similarly, if the user requests a SALES-ORDER report sorted by Shipping-date, then that report is about SHIPPING-DATEs, which has SALES-ORDER as a multivalued object. These objects are sketched in Figures 8.13b and 8.13c.

Sorted by Columns Foreign to the Entry Point Relation

The third way in which reports can be sorted is by columns that are foreign to the entry point relation. A user might request, for example, that a report of SALES-ORDERs be sorted by Customer-name. In this situation, the report is actually a report about CUS-TOMER, not SALES-ORDER. SALES-ORDER is a multivalued object attribute within CUSTOMER. Thus, a request such as this changes the entry point relation from SALES-ORDER to CUSTOMER.

Understanding this switch in objects may ease the task of developing the report. Proceeding as if SALES-ORDER was the entry point relation will make the report logic contrived. If SALES-ORDER is considered the entry point, then all of the SALES-ORDERs will need to be prepared, stored on disk, and then sorted by Customer-name. On the other hand, if CUSTOMER is considered the entry point relation, then the CUS-TOMER rows can be sorted and SALES-ORDERs (and LINE-ITEMs within SALES-ORDERs) can be treated as multiple valued child rows. The second approach is much more direct.

This section has been concerned with the design of reports considered from the standpoint of object materialization. The design of the appearance of the report is also important, but it does not relate to database processing, and we will not consider that subject here.

Application Program Design

Literally hundreds of books have been written about application program design. It is not appropriate here to attempt to summarize even the basic schools of thought about such design. Instead, we focus only on aspects of program design that pertain directly to database processing.

```
Obtain Number, Date, Customer#, Salesperson-name
Using Customer# read row in CUSTOMER having that customer number
Using Salesperson-name read row in SALESPERSON having that salesperson name
Display data for of SALES-ORDER, CUSTOMER, and SALESPERSON in top of form
Obtain first LINE-ITEM data from user
Set Row# = 1
Set Sub-total = 0

DOWHILE LINE-ITEM data not-null
    Read ITEM data
    Compute new QOH
    IF new QOH >= 0
        Compute Ext-price
        Set Sub-total = Sub-total + Ext-price
        Format new LINE-ITEM row
        Display new row
        Add new row to LINE-ITEM table
        Update ITEM row
        Add 1 to Row#
        Obtain data for next LINE-ITEM
    ELSE
        Display error message indicating insufficient stock
    ENDIF
END-DO

Compute Tax
Compute Total
Display results
Write new row to SALES-ORDER table
```

FIGURE 8.14
Structure of logic for adding new SALES-ORDER

STRUCTURE OF APPLICATION PROGRAM LOGIC

Some experts, notably Michael Jackson[1] and those who have followed his line of reasoning, state that the structure of a program should mirror the structure of the data that it processes. If one adheres to that design philosophy, then the data model and database design provide rich and valuable guidelines for designing the structure of application logic.

Consider, for example, an application program that displays the SALES-ORDER object shown in Figure 8.9. The fundamental structure of the logic of such a program is shown in Figure 8.14. Observe the similarity in the structure of the object and the structure of the program. In the first section, the program obtains identifying data for the

---

[1]Michael Jackson, *Principles of Program Design* (New York: Academic Press, 1975).

entry point relation. It then accesses the database to obtain the appropriate row from the SALES-ORDER relation.

Next, the program looks up and displays SALESPERSON data, and then it looks up and displays CUSTOMER DATA. Following this, there is an iteration structure that corresponds to the multivalued composite group. Normally, composite groups require that group headings be displayed. In this program, the headings are printed before the iteration is started. Within the loop, ITEM data is looked up and displayed. Finally, the application program displays the remaining entry point relation data.

In general, any program that processes a multivalued property will need to contain an iteration logic structure for that property. If there are nested multivalued properties, then there will be nested iterations. If there are serial multivalued properties, then there will be serial iterations in the program.

It is not necessary that all of the logic to process an object be contained in a single program module. In fact, good design dictates that, for all but the simplest programs, logic be divided into submodules. If application program logic is divided along the boundaries of the object structures, then appropriate cohesion will result.

For example, the SALES-ORDER object has four major parts: the object itself, the SALESPERSON object, the CUSTOMER object, and the LINE-ITEM composite group (which contains a subsection for ITEM data). A program to process this object can be appropriately divided along these same lines. There will be a main module that makes calls to submodules to process SALESPERSON, CUSTOMER, and LINE-ITEM groups. The LINE-ITEM submodule, in turn, can make calls to an external module to process ITEM data.

RELATIONSHIP CONSTRAINT CHECKING

The processing of updates for database applications differs in one important regard from the processing of updates in nondatabase applications. Namely, when processing updates, the application must be certain to preserve the constraints defined on the database data. In this section we consider constraints that arise from relationships. In the next, we will consider other types of constraint.

Figure 8.15 depicts the relationship between MAJOR and STUDENT relations. As shown, a MAJOR must have at least one STUDENT and a STUDENT must have exactly one MAJOR. When users process updates on either of these relations, the application program must ensure that these constraints are not violated (we will assume in this section that such checking is not done by the DBMS). In Figure 8.15b, for example, if a user attempted to delete the row for student 400, the application program should disallow this request. If the request were allowed, then the row for FINANCE would not have a child row, and the mandatory constraint would be violated. Similarly, a new MAJOR, say BIOLOGY, cannot be added until there is a student who is majoring in that subject.

A row that exists inappropriately without a required parent or child is sometimes called a **fragment.** Also, child rows that exist without a mandatory parent are sometimes called **orphans.** One of the functions of an application program is to prevent the creation of fragments and orphans.

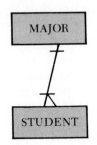

a. Sample mandatory-to-mandatory relationship

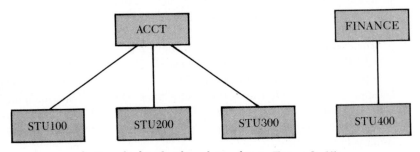

b. Sample data for the relationship in Figure 8–15a

FIGURE 8.15

Example of mandatory-mandatory constraint

Types of Relationship Constraint

The means of preventing fragments depends on the type of constraint. Figure 8.16 shows examples of the four possible kinds of constraints. They are mandatory-to-mandatory (M-M), mandatory-to-optional (M-O), optional-to-mandatory (O-M), and optional-to-optional (O-O). These constraints are shown on one-to-many relationships, but the same four constraint types pertain to one-to-one relationships. We need not be concerned with many-to-many relationships constraints, as these relationships will have been converted to one-to-many relationships by defining intersection tables.

Constraints can be violated whenever there are changes to key attributes (whether local or foreign). This can occur because changes in key values have the effect of changing the parent-child relationship. For example, in Figure 8.15b, changing the major of student 300 from ACCT to FINANCE reassigns that student to the finance department. This results in a change of parent, but does not cause a constraint violation.

Such a violation will occur, however, if the major of student 400 is changed to ACCT. When this is done, FINANCE no longer has any majors and the M-M constraint between MAJOR and STUDENT is violated. As another example, in Figure 8.16a, a change in the HOTEL-BILL Invoice# will invalidate the relationship carried by the for-

FIGURE 8.16

Examples of the four types of
relationship constraint

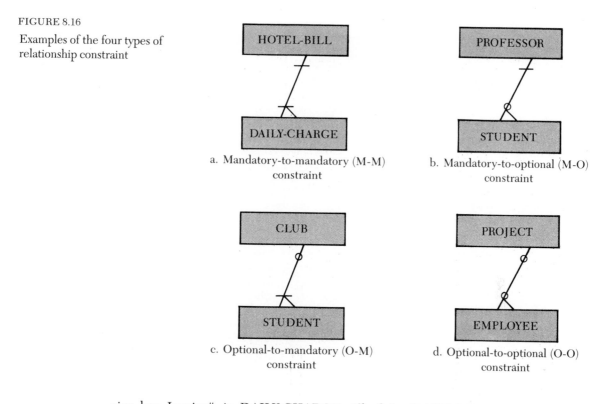

a. Mandatory-to-mandatory (M-M)
constraint

b. Mandatory-to-optional (M-O)
constraint

c. Optional-to-mandatory (O-M)
constraint

d. Optional-to-optional (O-O)
constraint

eign key, Invoice#, in DAILY-CHARGE. All of the DAILY-CHARGE rows for the changed invoice will become orphans.

Figure 8.17 presents rules for preventing fragments for each of these types of constraint. Figure 8.17a concerns actions on the parent row and Figure 8.17b concerns actions on child rows. As indicated in these figures, we are concerned with the insertion of new rows, modifications on key data, and the deletion of rows. Figure 8.17 shows rules for one-to-many relationships. The rules for one-to-one relationships are similar.

Restrictions on Updates to Parent Rows

The first row of Figure 8.17a concerns M-M constraints. A new parent row can be inserted only if at least one child row is being created at the same time. This creation could occur by inserting a new child row or by reassigning a child from a different parent (however, this later action may cause a constraint violation itself).

A change to the key of a parent can be allowed in an M-M relationship only if the values in the corresponding foreign key in the child rows are also changed to the new value. (It would be possible to reassign all of the children to another parent and then create at least one new child for the parent, but this is rare.) Thus, changing the Invoice# in HOTEL-BILL can be allowed as long as the Invoice# is changed in all the appropriate DAY-CHARGE rows as well.

Finally, a parent of an M-M relationship can be deleted as long as all of the children are also deleted or are reassigned.

Proposed Action on Parent

Type of Relationship		Insert	Modify (key)	Delete
	M-M	Create at least one child	Change matching keys of all children	Delete all children OR Reassign all children
	M-O	OK	Change matching keys of all children	Delete all children OR Reassign all children
	O-M	Insert new child OR Appropriate child exists	Change key of at least one child OR Appropriate child exists	OK
	O-O	OK	OK	OK

a. Conditions for allowing changes to parent records

Proposed Action on Child

Type of Relationship		Insert	Modify (key)	Delete
	M-M	Parent exists OR Create parent	Parent with new value exists (or create one) AND Sibling exists	Sibling exists
	M-O	Parent exists OR Create parent	Parent with new value exists OR Create parent	OK
	O-M	OK	Sibling exists	Sibling exists
	O-O	OK	OK	OK

b. Conditions for allowing changes to child records

FIGURE 8.17
Rules for preventing fragments

Considering M-O constraints, a new parent can be added without restriction since parents need not have children. Thus, for the relationship in Figure 8.16b, a new PRO-FESSOR row can be added without restriction. A change in the parent's key value, however, can only be allowed if the corresponding values in the child rows are changed. If a PROFESSOR in the relationship in Figure 8.16b changes his or her key, then the value of Advisor in all of that professor's advisees' rows must also be changed.

Finally, in a relationship having an M-O constraint, the parent row can be deleted only if all children are deleted or reassigned. For the PROFESSOR-STUDENT relationship, all of the student rows would most likely be reassigned.

For O-M constraints, a parent can be inserted only if at least one child is added at the same time, or if an appropriate child already exists. For the O-M relationship between CLUB and STUDENT in Figure 8.16c, for example, a new club can be added only if an appropriate STUDENT row can be created (either by adding a new student or by changing the value of Club in an existing STUDENT). Alternatively, an appropriate student row may already exist.

Similarly, the key of the parent of an O-M relationship may be changed only if a child is created or if a suitable child row already exists. The Ski Club can change its name to Scuba only if at least one skier is willing to join Scuba, or if a student has already enrolled in Scuba. There are no restrictions on the deletion of a parent row in an O-M relationship.

The last type of relationship constraint, O-O, is shown in Figure 8.16d. There are no restrictions on any type of update on rows in an O-O relationship. Both PROJECT and EMPLOYEE rows can be updated at will.

Restrictions on Updates to Child Rows

The rules for preventing fragments when processing updates on child rows are shown in Figure 8.17b. The rules are similar to those in Figure 8.17a. The one notable difference is that in several cases, child rows can be modified or deleted as long as sibling rows exist. For example, in an M-M constraint, a child row can be deleted as long as there are siblings in existence. (The last child never leaves home!) For the M-M constraint in Figure 8.16a, a particular DAY-CHARGE row can be deleted as long as at least one remains.

With the exception of considerations regarding siblings, the rules for avoiding fragments when processing child rows are similar to those for parents. Be certain you understand each statement in Figure 8.17b.

Many of the rules set out in Figure 8.17 provide several alternatives. In these cases, the application program developer needs to select one of them. The choice depends on the requirements of the application. The point for you to remember is that you must consider such constraints in the design and development of application programs.

OTHER TYPES OF CONSTRAINT CHECKING

There are types of constraints besides those that arise from relationships. One common constraint is uniqueness. In some cases, the values of attributes or of composites of attributes must be unique. Many DBMS products have the capability of enforcing this type of constraint, and if so, the application program is freed of the burden.

With regard to uniqueness, observe that requiring the composite (Last-name, First-name) to be unique is different from requiring the attributes (Last-name) and (First-name) to be independently unique. The second case is far more restrictive than the first. For example, in the first case, there can be only one Jill Smith. In the second case, there can be only one Jill and only one Smith. Some DBMS products do not support composite uniqueness and, as you can tell, this can be problematical.

Another common type of constraint is null values. A null value is a value that is unknown. For example, if the value of Shipping-mode is null, this means that the shipping mode is unknown. Null is not the same as zero (for numeric attributes) or a blank (for text attributes).

Nulls can arise in one of two ways. Either no value has ever been entered into the database or no value is appropriate. These two are not, logically, the same. If Shipping-mode has the value null it might mean that the mode of shipment is unknown. It might also mean that a value is inappropriate. A SALES-ORDER used for consulting services does not have a meaningful Shipping-mode.

We will consider nulls further in the following chapters. For now, realize that some DBMS products can enforce the constraint, NULLS NOT ALLOWED. Others do not, however, and in that case, the enforcement is up to the application program.

Finally, there are constraints that do not fall into any of these types. There might be a constraint, for example, that if the SALESPERSON resides in a region east of the Mississippi, then the value of Shipping-mode cannot equal 1-Day. Few DBMS products provide robust means of defining and enforcing such constraints. Today, for almost all products, such constraints must be written into the application program.

ROLE OF APPLICATION PROGRAMS IN BACKUP AND RECOVERY

We will address strategies for providing backup and recovery in Chapter 14. For now, however, you should realize that backup and recovery of concurrently processed databases requires application programs to define transaction boundaries to the DBMS. These boundaries, called **logical transactions** or **logical units of work,** define a set of atomic actions. By atomic, we mean that either all of the actions are performed, or none of them are.

To understand the need for atomicity, suppose that a user is entering data for a new SALES-ORDER and, after several line items have been filled, the computer system fails. In this case, a partial SALES-ORDER has been entered into the database. When the system is recovered and the user re-enters the SALES-ORDER, it is possible that some line items will be duplicated, thus decrementing inventory counts twice.

To prevent such an occurrence, the application program can define boundaries of atomicity for the DBMS. The means by which this is done varies from DBMS product to DBMS product, but, in general, before performing any transaction processing the application issues a command like START TRANSACTION (other terms are used synonymously). Then, the application program processes the users' requests to a logically consistent end point (the end of a SALES-ORDER, for example).

If all processing has occurred correctly, the application program then issues a command like END TRANSACTION, or COMMIT, or some other equivalent command. At this point, the DBMS makes all the changes to the database permanent. If some problem has occurred during processing, then the application program issues a command like ROLL BACK, thus telling the DBMS to remove all changes since the START TRANSACTION command. If the application program is abnormally terminated due to a system failure or unexpected program termination, then no END TRANSACTION command is received and the DBMS removes the provisional changes.

The reason for introducing this topic here is that the definition of an object provides a definition of the boundaries of the logical transaction. The start transaction is issued when the application program begins work on the object. The end transaction is issued when all object properties have been processed. You will learn more about this important topic in Chapter 14.

Summary

There are three major phases for developing database applications: requirements, design, and implementation. During the requirements phase, the application functions are determined. Data flow diagrams specify data flows and the actions that must be taken on them. For organizational and workgroup databases, requirements are divided into several applications.

During the design phase, both the user interface and the application program structure and logic are designed. The user interface includes the design of control facilities, forms, and reports. During implementation, the application development facilities of the DBMS are used in conjunction with programming languages to build the applications.

The purpose of a database application is to create, update, delete, and display objects (or views of entities) at the direction of users while at all times protecting the security and integrity of the database. Before objects can be processed, they must be constructed, or materialized, from the underlying relations. When objects are updated, the data must be correctly modified while constraints are enforced. Further, if the database is concurrently processed, updates must be controlled so that the actions of one user do not interfere with those of another.

The application must provide a means for the user to direct and control activities. Two strategies are used. With command-driven applications, the users are given a set of commands to accomplish their work. Commands are direct and to the point, but users must memorize them and their syntax. Menu-driven applications provide a list of choices from which users pick. Recently, a new style of control interface has emerged; graphical user interfaces include pull-down menus, icons, dialogue boxes, mice, and other facilities.

Database applications must protect the security and integrity of the database. They should be designed to enable authorized users to perform authorized activities, to provide accurate and helpful error messages when mistakes are made, and to prohibit unauthorized users and unauthorized activities.

Databases differ in character along a continuum. At the high end, some applications provide extensive services on behalf of the user; they materialize complicated objects and present them in a sophisticated GUI. At the other end of the continuum, some applications do little more than list tables.

Applications materialize objects by combining data from one or more relations in accordance with the defined object structure. An object view is a subset of an object utilized by a particular user or group of users. Views can be described by naming the object on which they are based and listing the visible attributes. A materialization of a view is a view plus display data such as labels, lines, boxes, and other window dressing. An object can have many views, and a view of an object can have many materializations.

The design of application programs includes the design of the user interface, which consists of control mechanisms, forms, and reports. With regard to control mechanisms, applications can be command driven, menu driven, a GUI, or some combination of these.

There are two primary strategies in structuring a menu hierarchy: object/action and action/object. In general, object/action-oriented menus are easier for users to understand and work with. With these, the highest-level menus ask users to choose objects to act upon; lower-level menus provide selections of actions to take on those objects. Menu structures that combine these two strategies are confusing to users and should be avoided.

A form is a screen display that is most often used for data entry and edit, though forms are sometimes used for display. Not all forms are equal. For a form to be easy to use, its structure must reflect the structure of the object that it materializes. The entry point of a form should be the entry point relation. With the possible exception of the entry point relation, all data from a single relation should be located in a contiguous portion of the form. Sometimes data from the entry point relation is placed at the top and the bottom of the form. Multivalued composite groups are represented by control breaks or scrolling form sections. Manual forms and prototypes can be used to evaluate the appropriateness of a form design.

Users ought never be required (or allowed) to enter data that is already stored in the database. Allowing them to do so invites data integrity problems. In some cases, forms are modeless; the mode of the form (display, insert, update) is derived by the application from the context of the user's activities. Sometimes a modeless process is inappropriate.

There are several form features peculiar to GUI systems. These include pop-down list boxes, option buttons, and check boxes. Such facilities can provide very effective ways of materializing objects. Forms should be designed so that the movement of the cursor is natural to the user—for both normal use and exception handling. Further, the meaning and use of keys should pervade the application in a consistent manner.

Reports should also be designed so that their structure reflects the structure of the object they materialize. Report sorting often implies the existence of other objects. If the sort is by the object key, then the report concerns a super-object, or collection of objects of this type. If the sort is by a nonkey column of the entry point relation, then the report concerns an object of a different type. If the sort is by a column foreign to the entry point relation, then the report is about a super-object of that other relation. The report will be easier to produce if the entry point of the object is considered to be the relation from which the sort field arises.

In the design of application programs, the structure of the application program logic should also reflect the structure of the object that it processes. Multivalued properties or groups require iteration structures.

Application programs have an important role in enforcing data constraints. There are four types of relationship constraint: M-M, M-O, O-M, and O-O. Changes to key values can alter relationships and possibly violate these constraints. Such changes need to be disallowed when necessary.

Other types of constraints include attribute value uniqueness constraints and null values constraints. In some cases, composites of attributes are constrained to be unique. Null values represent the fact that either a value is unknown or that it is inappropriate. Sometimes the constraint exists that null values are not allowed for attributes.

DBMS products are taking on more and more of the task of constraint checking. This frees the application from the burden. The type and degree of such checking varies dramatically from product to product, however.

For backup and recovery in concurrent systems, application programs must define boundaries atomically. This is done with START TRANSACTION and END TRANS-ACTION commands (or their equivalent). Object definitions can be used to establish these boundaries.

GROUP I QUESTIONS

8.1   Name the three phases of application development discussed in this chapter and summarize the basic tasks for each.

8.2   What is the purpose of a database application?

8.3   Explain the special tasks the application must perform when adding, updating, or deleting objects.

8.4   Explain why relations are frequently queried, but objects are seldom queried.

8.5   What are the three major means by which users control applications? Summarize the advantages and disadvantages of each.

8.6   What does GUI stand for and how does it relate to database applications?

8.7   Summarize the role that database applications take with regard to security and integrity.

8.8   Describe the continuum of applications discussed in this chapter.

8.9   Explain the term *materialize objects.*

8.10   Define *view*. How are views described?

8.11   Explain the difference between a view and an object.

8.12   Describe two ways of naming views.

8.13   What is a materialization of a view? How are materializations described?

8.14   Describe two ways of naming materializations.

8.15   Diagram the relationship of objects, views, and materializations.

8.16   What are the three major components of the user interface?

8.17   Name the two primary strategies for structuring a menu hierarchy. Describe the differences between them. Which does the text recommend?

8.18   Give an example of an object/action menu hierarchy. Your example should have at least two choices at the top and three levels.

8.19   Rework your answer to question 8.18 to be an action/object menu hierarchy. Describe the advantages and disadvantages of each.

8.20   Define *form*.

8.21   What characteristic makes a form seem natural and easy to use?

8.22   What is an entry point of an object? How can you determine which relation in an object is the entry point relation?

8.23   Give a general rule for determining the location of data in a form. What data should be physically contiguous?

8.24   Explain why data from the entry point relation is sometimes placed both at the top and bottom of a form.

8.25   When there are several alternative forms, what should be done to choose among them?

8.26   What is a data lookup? How does it pertain to the processing of forms?

8.27   Explain how modeless processing differs from mode-oriented processing. What are the strengths and weaknesses of modeless processing?

8.28   What is a pop-down list box? Under what conditions would one be useful for a form?

8.29   What is an option button? Under what conditions would one be useful for a form? How would the underlying data be stored?

8.30   What are check boxes? Under what conditions would they be useful for a form? How would the underlying data be stored?

8.31   Describe general design considerations regarding cursor movement on a form.

8.32   What is a pervasive key? Why are such keys desirable?

8.33   What relationship should exist between reports and object structures?

8.34   Explain how sorting implies a change to the definition of the object.

8.35   Consider the object STUDENT with key Student# and nonobject property Date-enrolled. Suppose that STUDENT contains a single-valued object property

DORMITORY that contains a property Dorm-name. Describe the object implied when producing reports about STUDENT that are sorted in the following way:

a. by Student#
b. by Student-last-name (a nonobject property of STUDENT)
c. by Date-enrolled
d. by Dorm-name

8.36 What general rule pertains to the relationship of the structure of a program and the structure of an object that it processes?

8.37 What is a fragment? an orphan?

8.38 Describe four types of relationship constraint. Give an example, other than one in this book, of each type.

8.39 Explain the use of the rules in Figure 8.17 for each type of relationship constraint in your answer to question 8.38.

8.40 What is a null value? What meaning does a null value have?

8.41 What roles does an application have in enforcing rules about null values?

8.42 What role does an application have in enforcing rules about uniqueness constraints?

8.43 How does the statement that First-name must be unique and Last-name must be unique differ from the statement that (First-name, Last-name) must be unique? Which of these two statements is the more restrictive?

8.44 What is a logical unit of work? What is a set of atomic actions? Why are these important?

8.45 What role does an application have in defining logical units of work?

GROUP II QUESTIONS

8.46 Develop a set of menus that could be used to control an application that is used to manage the access of students to a microcomputer lab at a university. Assume the system is used to schedule student appointments for equipment at the lab and also to check out optional hardware or software. Further, assume that only authorized students may use the lab, and thus students must be preenrolled in the database before they can schedule an appointment. Finally, assume that when a student schedules an appointment, he or she must indicate the class for which the appointment exists. This means class data must also be stored. Assume the objects in Figure 8.18 are to be stored.

8.47 Transform the objects in question 8.46 into normalized relations. Indicate the key of each relation. Name the entry point for each object in question 8.46.

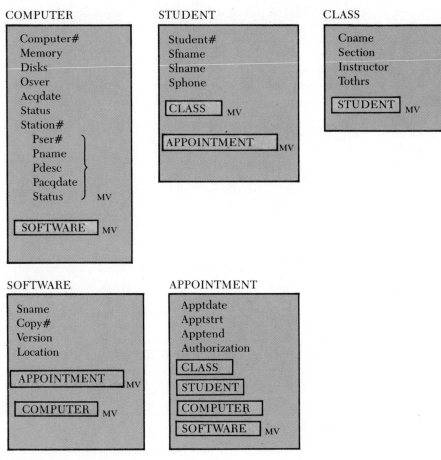

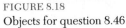

FIGURE 8.18
Objects for question 8.46

8.48 Design a data entry form for the STUDENT and the APPOINTMENT objects in question 8.46. Be certain your forms follow the design guidelines set out in this chapter.

8.49 Design a report to display the COMPUTER object in question 8.46. Be certain your report follows the design guidelines in this chapter. Explain how the underlying object changes when this report is sorted by Computer#, Acqdate, and Operating-system (a value of Sname).

8.50 Show the basic logic of an application program that creates a new APPOINTMENT. Assume all required CLASS, STUDENT, COMPUTER, and SOFTWARE objects already exist.

8.51 Modify Figure 8.17 to describe the update rules for one-to-one relationships. Explain each entry.

Database Implementation with the Relational Model

Part IV considers database implementation using the relational model. It begins, in Chapter 9, with a discussion of relational data manipulation. First, a survey of types of relational data manipulation languages and relational interfaces is presented. Then, the basic operators of relational algebra are explained and example queries are expressed in terms of relational algebra.

Chapter 10 describes Structured Query Language, or SQL. This language has been endorsed by the American National Standards Institute as the language of choice for manipulating databases. SQL is the primary data manipulation language for commercial relational DBMS products.

The concepts presented in these two chapters are illustrated in Chapter 11. Here, we discuss and illustrate the implementation of an example relational database using the DBMS product, DB2.

Implementing
Relational Databases

‖‖‖‖‖‖‖‖‖‖‖‖‖‖‖‖‖‖‖‖

Chapter 9 and the next two chapters discuss the implementation of databases using the relational-oriented DBMS. This model, which is one of the three basic models used in commercial database processing today, is the most popular and widely used of the three. Implementation using DBMS products based on the other two models, DL/I and CODASYL DBTG, will be illustrated in Chapters 12 and 13.

You have already been introduced to the relational model; we used it to express DBMS-independent designs in Chapters 6 and 7. Here, you will learn how to implement such database designs using DBMS products that are themselves based upon the relational model.

We begin with relational data definition. We review relational terminology and then explain how a design is defined to the DBMS. Space allocation and database data creation are also discussed.

The remaining sections of the chapter address relational data manipulation. First, a survey of four types of relational data manipulation language (DML) is presented, and then the three common modes of DML interfaces to the DBMS are described and illustrated. Finally, the basic operators of relational algebra are explained and example queries are expressed in terms of relational algebra.

- RELATIONAL DATA DEFINITION
- RELATIONAL DATA MANIPULATION
- RELATIONAL ALGEBRA

Relational Data Definition

There are a number of tasks to be accomplished when implementing a relational database. First, the structure of the database must be defined to the DBMS. To do this, the developer uses a data definition language (DDL) or some equivalent means (such as a graphical display) to describe the structure. Then the database is allocated to physical storage media and filled with data.

We will discuss each of these tasks in this section. First, however, we will review relational terminology.

REVIEW OF TERMINOLOGY

A **relation** is a two-dimensional table that has several properties:

1. The entries in the relation are single valued; multiple values are not allowed. Hence, the intersection of a row and a column contains only one value.
2. The entries in any column are all of the same kind. For example, one column may contain customer names, and another birthdates. Each column has a unique name and the order of the columns is immaterial in the relation. Columns of a relation are called **attributes.** Each attribute has a **domain,** which is the set of values that the attribute can have.
3. No two rows in the relation are identical, and the order of the rows is insignificant.

See Figure 9.1. Each row of the relation is known as a **tuple.**

Figure 9.1 is an **example,** or **occurrence.** The generalized format, PATIENT (Name, Age, Sex, Account-number, Physician), is the **relation structure** and is what

	Col 1 (or Attribute 1)	Col 2	Col 3	Col 4	Col 5
	Name	Age	Sex	Account Number	Physician
Row 1 (or Tuple 1)	Riley	56	F	147	Lee
Row 2	Murphy	17	M	·289·	Singh
Row 3	Krajewski	25	F	533	Levy
Row 4	Ting	67	F ·	681	Spock
Row 5	Dixon	17	M	704	Levy
Row 6	Abel	41	M	193	Singh

FIGURE 9.1
Occurrence of PATIENT relation structure

most people mean when they use the term *relation*. (Recall from Chapter 6 that an underlined attribute is a key.) If we add constraints on allowable data values to the relation structure, we then have a **relational schema.**

Although relations are defined in the formal terms *relation, attribute,* and *tuple,* the informal terms *table, column,* and *row* are often used synonymously. Sometimes, too, the terms *file, field,* and *record* are used as synonyms. Relational terminology is summarized in Figure 9.2.

FIGURE 9.2
Summary of relational terminology

Term	Meaning
Relation (or Table) (or File)	Two-dimensional table
Attribute (or Column) (or Field) (or Data-item)	Column of a relation
Tuple (or Row) (or Record)	Row in a relation
Domain	Set of values that an attribute can have
Relation structure	Format of relation
Occurrence	Relation structure with data
Relational schema	Relation structure plus constraints
Key	Group of one or more attributes that uniquely identifies a tuple in a relation
Logical key	Same as key
Physical key	A group of one or more attributes that is supported by a data structure that facilitates fast retrieval or rapid sequential access

Confusion Regarding the Term Key

The term **key** is a common source of confusion when implementing relational databases. This occurs because the term is used with different meanings between the design and the implementation stages.

During design, the term *key* means one or more columns that uniquely identify a row in a relation. As you learned in Chapter 6, every relation has a key because every row is unique; at the limit, the composite of every column is the key. In most cases, the key is comprised of one or two columns, however.

During implementation, the term *key* is used differently. To most relational products, a key is a column upon which the DBMS builds an index or other data structure so as to quickly access rows by value of that column. Such keys need not be unique, and often, in fact, they are not. They are constructed only for the purpose of improving performance. See Appendix B for information about such data structures.

For example, consider the relation ORDER (<u>Order#</u>, Order-date, Cust#, Amount). From the standpoint of relational *design*, the key of this relation is Order#, since the underline means Order# is a unique key identifier.

From the standpoint of relational *implementation*, however, any of the four columns could be a key. Order-date, for example, could be defined as a key. If this is done, then the DBMS will create a data structure so that ORDER rows can be quickly accessed by value of Order-date. Most likely there will be many rows for a given value of Order-date. Defining it as a key implies nothing about uniqueness.

Sometimes the terms **logical key** and **physical key** are used to distinguish between these two meanings for the term. A logical key is a unique identifier. A physical key is a column that has a special data structure defined for it to improve access performance. A logical key need not be a physical key and a physical key need not be a logical key.

Physical Keys

There are two common reasons for defining physical keys. One is to allow rows to be quickly accessed by value of the key. The second is to facilitate sorting rows by that key. Order-date might be defined as a key so that a report showing orders by dates can be more quickly generated. Physical keys need not be unique.

With most relational DBMS products, a column or group of columns can be forced to be unique by using the keyword UNIQUE when defining the appearance of a column in a table. The DDL statement

Order# UNIQUE in ORDER

is an example of such a definition.

IMPLEMENTING THE DATABASE

In this text, we use the relational model to express database designs. Since we have done so, we can proceed directly from database design to implementing the database. There is no need to transform the design during the implementation stage. We simply define the existing relational design to the DBMS.

The situation will be different when we implement databases using DBMS products that are based on data models other than the relational model. For example, when implementing a database for a CODASYL DBTG DBMS, we must convert the relational design into a CODASYL DBTG design and then define the converted design to the DBMS product. You will see examples of such design transformations in Chapters 12 and 13.

Defining the Database Structure to the DBMS

There are a number of different means by which the structure of the database is described to the DBMS. The particular tasks depend on the DBMS product in use.

With some products, a text file is constructed that describes the database structure. The language used to describe such a structure is sometimes called the **data definition language,** or DDL. The DDL text file names the tables in the database, names and describes the columns of those tables, defines indexes, and describes other structures such as constraints and security restrictions.

Figure 9.3 shows typical data definition language for defining a simple relational database for a hypothetical DBMS. You will see a more realistic example of such a language for the DBMS product DB2 in Chapter 11.

FIGURE 9.3
Example DDL text file for database definition

```
DEFINE DATABASE EXAMPLE1

ATTRIBUTES
    Name                Text 15
    Age                 Numeric
    Sex                 Text 1
    Account-number      Numeric
    Physician           Text 20
    Physician-phone     Text 8
    Physician-code      Text 3


RELATIONS
    PATIENT with Name, Age, Sex, Account-
    number, Physician

    PHYSICIAN with Physician, Physician-phone,
    Physician-code

PASSWORDS
    UPDATE PASSWORD FOR PATIENT IS
    BLUEBERRY

    UPDATE PASSWORD FOR PHYSICIAN IS
    CURRENT


END DEFINITION
```

FIGURE 9.4
Example of graphical relation
definition

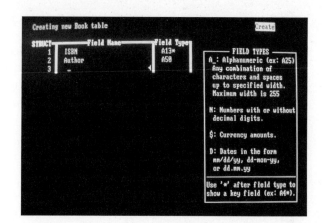

Some DBMS products do not require that the database be defined by DDL in text file format. One common alternative is to provide a graphical means for defining the structure of the database. With Paradox, for example, the developer is shown a graphical list structure and asked to fill in the table and column names in the appropriate places. See Figure 9.4.

In general, graphical definition facilities are easier to use than textual DDL. In Figure 9.4, the developer need not remember that table names are restricted to a certain number of characters. The form provides space only for the maximum number of characters that are allowed. For the text file, there is no such graphical constraint, and the developer will not find out that a mistake has been made until the DBMS definition utility reports an error message. A systems flowchart for the process of defining the database structure is shown in Figure 9.5.

Regardless of the means by which the database structure is defined, the developer must name each table, define the columns in that table, and describe the physical format (for example, TEXT 10) of each column. Also, depending upon the facilities of the DBMS, the developer may specify constraints that the DBMS is to enforce. Column

FIGURE 9.5
Processes for database definition

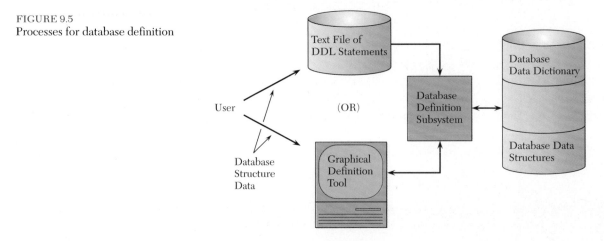

values can be defined to be NOT NULL or UNIQUE, for example. Some products also allow the definition of range and value constraints (Part# less than 10000 or Color equal to one of ['Red', 'Green', 'Blue'], for example.) Finally, interrelation constraints can also be defined. An example is Employee# in DEPT must equal Emp# in EMPLOYEE.

With many products, the developer can also define passwords and other control and security facilities. As you will learn in Chapter 14, a number of different strategies can be taken. Some strategies place controls on data constructs (passwords on tables, for example) and others place controls on people (the user of password X can read and update tables T1 and T2).

Allocating Media Space

In addition to defining the structure of the database, the developer must allocate database structures to physical media. Again, specific tasks depend on the particular DBMS product in use. For a personal database, all that need be done is to assign the database to a directory and to give the database a name. The DBMS will then allocate storage space automatically.

For multi-user databases, more work will need to be done. To improve performance and control, the distribution of the database data across disks and channels must be carefully planned. For example, depending on the nature of application processing, it may be advantageous to locate certain tables on the same disk, or, it may be important to ensure that certain tables are not located on the same disk.

Consider, for example, an order object that is comprised of data from ORDER, LINE-ITEM, and ITEM tables. Suppose in the processing of an order that the application retrieves one row from ORDER, several rows from LINE-ITEM, and one row from ITEM for each LINE-ITEM row. Further, suppose that the LINE-ITEM rows for a given order tend to be clustered together. However, the ITEM rows are not at all clustered. Figure 9.6 illustrates this situation.

Now, suppose an organization concurrently processes many orders. Further suppose the organization has one large, fast disk and a smaller, slower disk. The developer must determine the best place to locate the data. One possibility is that performance will be better if the ITEM table is stored on the larger, faster disk and the ORDER and LINE-ITEM data on the smaller, slower disk. Or, perhaps performance will be better if ORDER and LINE-ITEM data for prior months' orders is placed on the slower disk and all data for this month's orders is placed on the faster disk.

We cannot answer this question here. The answer depends on the amount of data, the processing characteristics of the DBMS and the operating system, the size and speed of disks and channels, and the application processing requirements of all applications that use the database. The point is for you to understand that the allocation of data to physical media is an important task during database implementation.

Creating the Database Data

Once the database has been defined and allocated to physical storage, then it can be filled with data. The means by which this is done depends on the application require-

FIGURE 9.6

Example data for three tables
representing an order

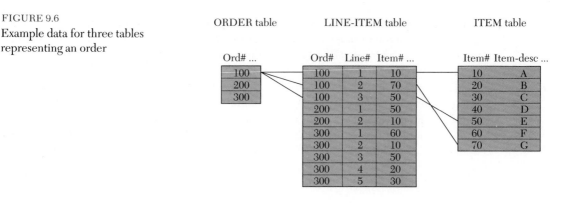

Note: For a given order, LINE-ITEM rows are clustered, but ITEM rows are not.

ments and the features of the DBMS product. In the easiest case, all of the data is already in a computer-sensible format and the DBMS has features and tools to readily facilitate importing the data from magnetic media. In the worst case, all of the data must be entered via manual keyboarding using application programs that are created from scratch by the developers. Most data conversions lie between these two extremes.

The data, once input, must be verified for correctness. Verification is a labor-intensive and tedious task. It is also very important. Oftentimes, especially for large databases, it is well worth the time and expense for the development team to write verification programs. Such programs count the number of records of various categories, compute control totals, perform reasonableness checks on data item values, and provide other verification processing.

Relational Data Manipulation

So far in this text, we have discussed the design of relational databases and the means by which such designs are defined to the DBMS. Whenever we have referred to the processing of relations, we have done so in a general and intuitive manner. This is fine for discussing designs, but to implement applications, we need clear, unambiguous languages for expressing processing logic. In this section, we will survey four types of relational data manipulation. Then, we will describe the three primary means by which users access a database.

CATEGORIES OF RELATIONAL DATA MANIPULATION LANGUAGE

To date, four different strategies for relational data manipulation have been proposed. **Relational algebra,** the first of the strategies, defines operators that work on relations (akin to the operators $+$, $-$, and so forth, of high school algebra). Relations can be manipulated using these operators to achieve a desired result. Relational algebra is hard to use, partly because it is procedural. That is, when using relational algebra we must know not only *what* we want, but also *how* to get it.

Relational algebra is infrequently used in commercial database processing. Although a few commercially successful DBMS products do provide relational algebra facilities, these are seldom used due to their complexity. In spite of this, learning relational algebra is important here; such knowledge will help you gain an intuitive understanding of the ways in which relations can be manipulated and will establish a foundation for you to learn SQL, a language which is quite important in the commercial world. Therefore, we will present the essential relational algebra operators and illustrate their use later in this chapter.

Relational calculus is a second type of relational data manipulation. Relational calculus is nonprocedural; it is a language for expressing what we want without expressing how to get it. Recall the variable of integration in calculus, a variable that ranges over an interval to be integrated. Relational calculus has a similar variable. For **tuple relational calculus,** the variable ranges over the tuples of a relation. For **domain relational calculus,** the variable ranges over the values of a domain. Relational calculus is derived from a branch of mathematics called **predicate calculus.**

Unless you are going to become a theoretician of relational technology, you will probably need not learn relational calculus. Relational calculus is seldom used in commercial database processing, and the little use it once had is declining in importance. Therefore, relational calculus will not be discussed in this text.

Although relational calculus is hard to understand and use, its nonprocedural property is highly desirable. Therefore, DBMS designers looked for other nonprocedural techniques. This led to the third and fourth categories of relational DML.

Transform-oriented languages are a class of nonprocedural languages that transform input data expressed as relations into results expressed as a single relation. These languages provide easy-to-use structures for expressing what is desired in terms of the data that is given. SQUARE, SEQUEL, and SEQUEL'S offspring, SQL are all transform-oriented languages. We will present SQL in some depth in the next chapter.

The fourth category of relational DML is the **graphical-oriented system.** Systems based on this technology, such as Borland's Paradox and IBM's QBE, provide the user with a picture of the structure of a relation. The user fills in an example of what he or she wants, and the system responds with actual data in that format. See Figure 9.7.

If you understand relational algebra and SQL, then it will be quite easy for you to use a graphical-oriented DBMS product. Consequently, we will not discuss this category further here. The four categories of relational DML are summarized in Figure 9.8.

DML INTERFACES TO THE DBMS

As described in Chapter 2, there are several different ways that users can interface to a database. They can use the default forms and reports supplied by the DBMS. They can access the database via a query/update language, and they can process the database

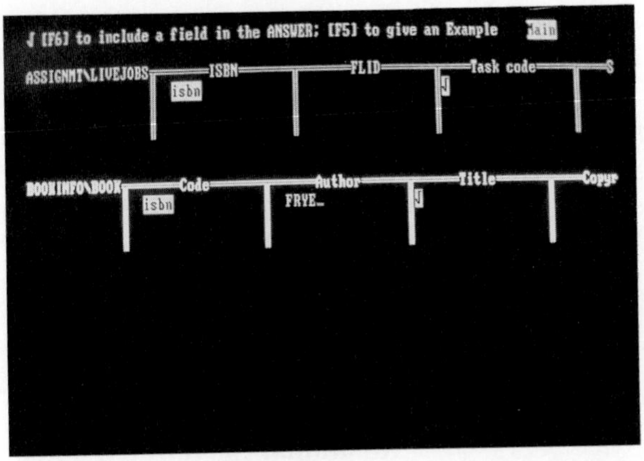

FIGURE 9.7
Example of graphical query

through application programs that access the database through DBMS commands. We will consider each of these in turn.

Data Manipulation via DBMS-Generated Forms

Most relational DBMS products include tools for building forms. Usually, when a table is defined, the DBMS will automatically define a screen form for entering and modifying the relation's data. The form may be tabular, like a spreadsheet, in which case it shows multiple rows at a time, or the form may show each row as an independent entity. Figures 9.9 and 9.10 show an example of each for the PATIENT table shown in Figure 9.1.

With some products, some flexibility is provided in the processing of the forms and reports. For example, rows can be selected for processing based on column values and they can also be sorted. The table in Figure 9.9 is sorted by Account-number.

Many of the default forms present data from only a single relation at a time. If data is required from two or more relations, then customized forms must be created using DBMS tools. Both multi-table and multi-row forms can be created using such tools. The use of such tools is very specific to the product involved, however, and we will not discuss them further here.

Query/Update Language Interface

The second type of interface to a database is via a **query/update language,** or simply **query language.** (Although most such languages perform both query and update, they

FIGURE 9.8
Four categories of relational DML

- Relational algebra
- Relational calculus
- Transform-oriented languages (such as SQL)
- Graphical systems (such as QBE)

FIGURE 9.9
Example of tabular default screen
form

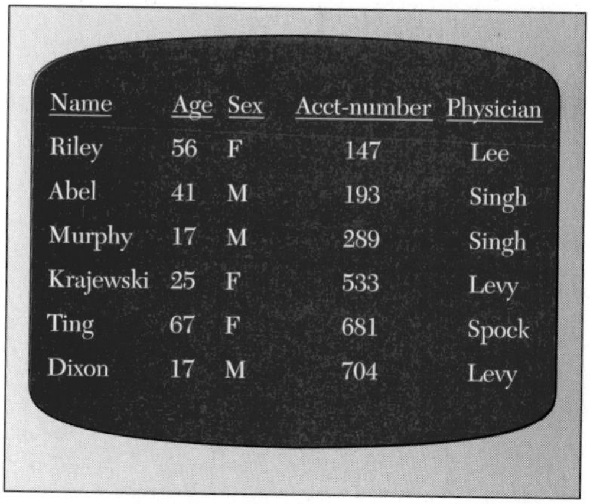

Name	Age	Sex	Acct-number	Physician
Riley	56	F	147	Lee
Abel	41	M	193	Singh
Murphy	17	M	289	Singh
Krajewski	25	F	533	Levy
Ting	67	F	681	Spock
Dixon	17	M	704	Levy

are generally referred to as query languages.) With this type, the user enters query commands that specify actions on the database. The DBMS decodes the commands and takes appropriate action. Figure 9.11 shows the programs involved in query processing.

The single most important query language is SQL. You will learn this language in detail in the next chapter. To give you an idea of the nature of query languages, however, consider the following SQL statement that processes the relation PATIENT (Name, Age, Sex, Account-number, Physician) shown in Figure 9.1:

```
SELECT    Name, Age
FROM      PATIENT
WHERE     Age > 50
```

This SQL query statement will extract all of the rows from the relation PATIENT such that the patient's age is greater than 50. It will then display the Name and Age for the qualifying rows in a second table. The results of such an operation on the data in Figure 9.1 are shown in Figure 9.12.

FIGURE 9.10
Example of single-row default
screen form

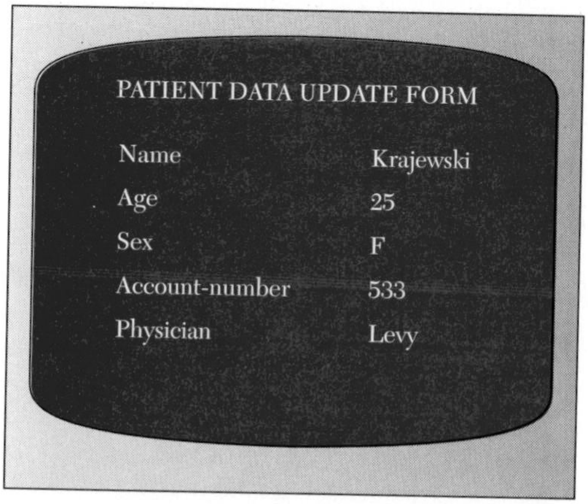

PATIENT DATA UPDATE FORM

Name	Krajewski
Age	25
Sex	F
Account-number	533
Physician	Levy

FIGURE 9.11
Programs involved in query
processing

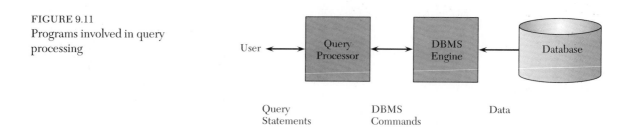

Query languages were developed to provide a robust interface to the database that does not require writing traditional computer programs in a procedural language. This was especially important prior to the advent of the microcomputer. At that time, when most databases resided on mainframes, there was not enough processing power at the users' terminals to provide the sophisticated default forms and reports that are so common today. Query languages were a way of giving the nonprogramming user access to a database.

Although query languages are simpler than computer programming languages, they have proven, by and large, to be too complicated for the average end-user. As a consequence, many end-users engage specialists to write query procedures that are stored as files. Such procedures can be written to be parameter driven thus enabling the users to execute them with changing data. As an example, the following command invokes a query procedure called BILLING and provides it with a date value:

```
DO BILLING FOR BDATE = '9/15/91'
```

Stored queries are similar in character to the BATCH files on DOS systems. The commands are processed by the DBMS, however, and not by the operating system (COMMAND.COM in DOS).

When query procedures are stored and processed in this way, there is, in fact, little difference in concept between them and stored programs that are written in a traditional programming language. The primary justification for their use is productivity. Stored query procedures are often quicker for the specialist to write.

FIGURE 9.12
Result of example query

Name	Age
Riley	56
Ting	67

There is one group of end-users who are an exception and who have found it feasible and desirable to learn a query language and develop their own queries. This group consists of business professionals working in decision support environments. A typical example is a group of financial planners who process corporate databases to develop a series of what-if financial analyses. Such end-users are generally well-educated professionals who have been given specialized training on the query language, the DBMS, and the structure of the databases they access.

Application Program Interface

The third type of data access interface is via application programs written in programming languages such as COBOL, BASIC, REXX, PASCAL, and C. Additionally, some application programs are written in languages provided by the DBMS vendors. The dBASE programming language is the best known example of this category.

There are two styles of application program interface to the DBMS. In one, the application program makes subroutine calls to routines in a subroutine library provided with the DBMS. For example, to read a particular row of a table, the application program would call the DBMS read routine, passing parameters that indicate the table to be accessed, the data to be retrieved, criteria for row selection, and other data.

Accessing the DBMS via a subroutine call can be complicated. The parameters to be passed are often complex, and often complicated shared data areas must be set up and maintained. Such programming is time consuming and often error-prone.

To overcome these disadvantages, a second style of program interface is provided by many vendors. Here, the vendors define a set of high-level data access commands. These commands, which are peculiar to database processing and not part of any standard language, are embedded in the application program code.

The application program, with embedded commands, is then submitted to a precompiler provided by the DBMS vendor. This precompiler translates the data access statements into valid subroutine calls and data structure definitions. In this process, the precompiler sets up parameter sequences for the calls and defines data areas that will be shared between the application program and the DBMS. The precompiler also inserts program logic to maintain the data areas. Subsequently, the precompiled routine is submitted to the language compiler. Figure 9.13 shows the relationships of the programs involved in this process.

In addition to its role in query processing, SQL is also used as a data access language within application programs. In this mode, SQL statements are embedded in the programs and translated into subroutine calls by a precompiler. Training costs and learning time are reduced since the same language can be used for both query and application program access.

There is one important problem to be overcome, however. SQL is a transform-oriented language that accepts relations, manipulates them, and outputs a result relation. Thus, it deals with relations-at-a-time. Almost all application programs, however, are row (record) oriented. An application program reads one row, processes it, reads the next row, and so forth. Such programs deal with a row-at-a-time.

Thus, there is a mismatch in the basic orientation of SQL and of application program languages. To correct for this mismatch, the results of SQL statements are assumed, in

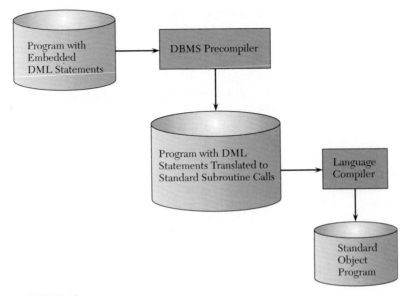

FIGURE 9.13
Processing of program with embedded DML statements

the application program, to be files. To illustrate, assume the following SQL statements (the same as those earlier) are embedded in an application program:

```
SELECT      Name, Age
FROM        PATIENT
WHERE       Age > 50
```

The result of these statements is a table with two columns and N rows. To accept the results of this query, the application program will be written to assume that these statements have produced a file with N records. Thus, the application will open the query, process the first row, process the next row, and so forth, until the last row has been processed. This logic will be the same as that for processing a sequential file. You will see examples of such application programs in Chapter 11. For now, just understand that there is a mismatch in the basic orientation of SQL (relation oriented) and programming languages (row, or record, oriented) and that this mismatch must be corrected when programs access a relational database via SQL.

Relational Algebra

Although conceptually similar, relational algebra differs substantially from the algebra you learned in high school. In high school algebra, variables represented numbers, and operators like $+$, $-$, $\times$, and $/$ operated on numeric quantities. For **relational algebra,** however, the variables are relations, and the operations manipulate relations to form new relations. For example, the operation + (or union) combines the tuples of one relation with the tuples of another relation producing a third relation.

Relational algebra is *closed*. This means that the results of one or more relational operations is, *always*, a relation. Relational algebra expressions combine relations to form new relations.

Although we have not stated it previously, relations are sets. The tuples of a relation can be considered elements of a set. Therefore, operations that can be performed on sets can also be performed on relations. We will first show four such set operators and then discuss operators that are peculiar to relational algebra. Before proceeding, however, consider the following sample relations.

SAMPLE RELATIONS

To facilitate the discussion of relational algebra and (in the next chapter) SQL, we will use a single set of relations. Six relations and their domain definitions are shown in Figure 9.14. First, observe that the attribute Name is used in several relations. When we refer to a specific attribute, we will qualify it with its relation name. Thus, Name in CLASS will at times be denoted CLASS.Name.

The format of the Ages and the Class-sizes domains is the same, yet the domains are different. Even though two domains have the same values, they are not the same, semantically, since they do not represent the same properties. The integer 21 in Ages represents 21 years; the same integer 21 in Class-sizes represents a number of people in a class. Thus the value 21 represents two entirely different characteristics.

In the following discussion, character values will be shown in single quotes. Characters not in quotes represent names. Thus, 'ROOM' differs from Room. 'ROOM' is a value, whereas Room is, say, a domain name. Concerning numeric data, numbers not in quotes refer to numeric quantities. Numbers in quotes refer to character strings. Thus, 123 is a number, '123' is a string of the characters '1', '2', and '3'.

UNION

The **union** of two relations is formed by adding the tuples from one relation to those of a second relation to produce a third relation. The order in which the tuples appear in the third relation is immaterial, but duplicate tuples are eliminated.

For this operation to make sense, the relations must be **union compatible.** This means that each relation must have the same number of attributes, and the attributes in corresponding columns must come from the same domain. If, for example, the third attribute of one relation comes from the Ages domain, then the third attribute of the second relation must also come from the Ages domain.

In Figure 9.14 the JUNIOR and the HONOR-STUDENT relations are union compatible. They both have three attributes, and corresponding attributes come from the same domain. JUNIOR.Snum and HONOR-STUDENT.Number come from the domain People-identifiers; JUNIOR.Name and HONOR-STUDENT.Name have the

1. JUNIOR (Snum, Name, Major)
2. HONOR-STUDENT (Number, Name, Interest)
3. STUDENT (SID, Name, Major, Grade-level, Age)
4. CLASS (Name, Time, Room)
5. ENROLLMENT (Student-number, Class-name, Position-number)
6. FACULTY (FID, Name, Department)

a. Relation definitions

	Attribute	Domain
1.	Snum	People-identifiers
	JUNIOR.Name	People-names
	Major	Subject-names
2.	Number	People-identifiers
	HONOR-STUDENT.Name	People-names
	Interest	Subject-names
3.	SID	People-identifiers
	STUDENT.Name	People-names
	Major	Subject-names
	Grade-level	Classes
	Age	Ages
4.	CLASS.Name	Class-names
	Time	Class-times
	Room	Rooms
5.	Student-number	People-identifiers
	Class-name	Class-names
	Position-number	Class-sizes
6.	FID	People-identifiers
	FACULTY.Name	People-names
	Department	Subject-names

b. Attribute domains

FIGURE 9.14
Examples of relations and domains used in relational algebra and SQL
a. Relation definitions
b. Attribute domains
c. Domain definitions

FIGURE 9.14
continued

Domain Name	Format
People-identifiers	Decimal (3)
People-names	Char (8) (unrealistic, but handy for these examples)
Subject-names	Char (10)
Classes	One of [FR, SO, JR, SN, GR]
Ages	Decimal from 0 to 100
Class-names	Char (5)
Class-times	Char (5) format: DDDHH, where D is one of [M, T, W, R, F, or blank], and HH is decimal between 1 and 12
Rooms	Char (5) format: BBRRR, where BB is a building code, and RRR is a room number
Class-sizes	Decimal from 0 to 100

c. Domain definitions

domain People-names; and JUNIOR.Major and HONOR-STUDENT.Interest have the domain Subject-names.

The relations JUNIOR and CLASS both have three attributes, but they are **union incompatible.** The three attributes do not have the same domain.

Figure 9.15 shows the union of two instances of the JUNIOR and HONOR-STU-DENT relations. Note that the tuple, [123, JONES, HISTORY], which occurs in both relations, is not duplicated in the union.

DIFFERENCE

The **difference** of two relations is a third relation containing tuples that occur in the first relation but not in the second. The relations must be union compatible. The difference of JUNIOR and HONOR-STUDENT is shown in Figure 9.16. As with arithmetic, the order of the subtraction matters. A − B is not the same as B − A.

INTERSECTION

The **intersection** of two relations is a third relation containing the tuples that appear in both the first and second relations. Again, the relations must be union compatible. In Figure 9.17 the intersection of JUNIOR and HONOR-STUDENT is the single tuple, [123, JONES, HISTORY]. This is the only tuple that occurs in both JUNIOR and HONOR-STUDENT.

FIGURE 9.15
JUNIOR and HONOR-
STUDENT relations and their
union

Snum	Name	Major
123	JONES	HISTORY
158	PARKS	MATH
271	SMITH	HISTORY

a. Example JUNIOR relation

Number	Name	Interest
105	ANDERSON	MANAGEMENT
123	JONES	HISTORY

b. Example HONOR-STUDENT relation

Snum or Number	Name	Major or Interest
123	JONES	HISTORY
158	PARKS	MATH
271	SMITH	HISTORY
105	ANDERSON	MANAGEMENT

c. Union of JUNIOR and HONOR-STUDENT relations

PRODUCT

The **product** of two relations (sometimes called the **Cartesian product**) is the concatenation of every tuple of one relation with every tuple of a second relation. The product of relation A (having m tuples) and relation B (having n tuples) has m times n tuples. The product is denoted A $\times$ B or A TIMES B. In Figure 9.18, relation STUDENT has four tuples and relation ENROLLMENT has three. STUDENT TIMES ENROLLMENT will therefore have twelve tuples. These tuples are shown in Figure 9.19. (Incidentally, the resulting relation in Figure 9.19 contains some meaningless tuples. Other operations, shown below, would need to be performed to extract from this relation meaningful information. This is simply an illustration of the product operator.)

FIGURE 9.16
JUNIOR minus HONOR-
STUDENT relation

Snum	Name	Major
158	PARKS	MATH
271	SMITH	HISTORY

FIGURE 9.17

Intersection of JUNIOR and
HONOR-STUDENT relations

Snum or Number	Name	Major or Interest
123	JONES	HISTORY

PROJECTION

Projection is an operation that selects specified attributes from a relation. The result of the projection is a new relation having the selected attributes. In other words, a projection picks columns out of a relation. For example, consider the STUDENT relation data in Figure 9.18. The projection of STUDENT on Name and Major attributes, denoted with brackets as STUDENT [Name, Major], is shown in Figure 9.20a. The projection of STUDENT on Major and Grade-level, denoted STUDENT [Major, Grade-level], appears in Figure 9.20b.

Note that although STUDENT has four tuples to begin with, the projection STUDENT [Major, Grade-level] has only three. A tuple was eliminated because, after the projection was done, the tuple [HISTORY, JR] occurred twice. Since the result of projection is a relation, and since relations cannot contain duplicate tuples, the redundant tuple is eliminated.

Projection can also be used to change the order of attributes in a relation. For example, the projection STUDENT [Age, Grade-level, Major, SID] reverses the order of STUDENT attributes (see Figure 9.14 for the original order). This feature can sometimes be used to make two relations union compatible.

SID	Name	Major	Grade-level	Age
123	JONES	HISTORY	JR	21
158	PARKS	MATH	GR	26
105	ANDERSON	MANAGEMENT	SN	27
271	SMITH	HISTORY	JR	19

a. STUDENT relation

Student-number	Class-name	Position-number
123	H350	1
105	BA490	3
123	BA490	7

b. ENROLLMENT relation

FIGURE 9.18

Examples of STUDENT and ENROLLMENT relations

SID	Name	Major	Glev	Age	Snum	Cname	Pnum
123	JONES	HISTORY	JR	21	123	H350	1
123	JONES	HISTORY	JR	21	105	BA490	3
123	JONES	HISTORY	JR	21	123	BA490	7
158	PARKS	MATH	GR	26	123	H350	1
158	PARKS	MATH	GR	26	105	BA490	3
158	PARKS	MATH	GR	26	123	BA490	7
105	ANDERSON	MANAGEMENT	SN	27	123	H350	1
105	ANDERSON	MANAGEMENT	SN	27	105	BA490	3
105	ANDERSON	MANAGEMENT	SN	27	123	BA490	7
271	SMITH	HISTORY	JR	19	123	H350	1
271	SMITH	HISTORY	JR	19	105	BA490	3
271	SMITH	HISTORY	JR	19	123	BA490	7

FIGURE 9.19
Product of STUDENT and ENROLLMENT relations in Figure 9.18

SELECTION

Whereas the projection operator takes a vertical subset (columns) of a relation, the **selection** operator takes a horizontal subset (rows). Projection identifies *attributes* to be included in the new relation; selection identifies *tuples* to be included in the new relation. Selection is denoted by specifying the relation name, followed by the keyword WHERE, followed by a condition involving attributes. Figure 9.21a shows the selection of the relation STUDENT WHERE Major = 'MATH'. Figure 9.22b shows the selection of STUDENT WHERE Age < 25.

Name	Major
JONES	HISTORY
PARKS	MATH
ANDERSON	MANAGEMENT
SMITH	HISTORY

a. STUDENT [Name, Major]

Major	Grade-level
HISTORY	JR
MATH	GR
MANAGEMENT	SN

b. STUDENT [Major, Grade-level]

FIGURE 9.20
Projections of STUDENT relation

SID	Name	Major	Glev	Age
158	PARKS	MATH	GR	26

a. STUDENT WHERE Major = 'Math'

SID	Name	Major	Glev	Age
123	JONES	HISTORY	JR	21
271	SMITH	HISTORY	JR	19

b. STUDENT WHERE Age < 25

FIGURE 9.21

Examples of relational selection operation

JOIN

The **join** operation is a combination of the product, selection, and (possibly) projection operations. The join of two relations, say A and B, operates as follows: First, form the product of A times B. Then, do a selection to eliminate some tuples (the criteria for the selection are specified as part of the join). Then, (optionally) remove attributes with projection.

Consider the STUDENT and ENROLLMENT relations shown in Figure 9.18. Suppose we want to know the sizes of the classes for each student. To obtain this, we need to join STUDENT tuples with matching ENROLLMENT tuples based on the SID. We denote such a join as STUDENT JOIN (SID = Student-number) ENROLLMENT. The meaning of this expression is "Join a STUDENT tuple to an ENROLLMENT tuple if SID of STUDENT equals Student-number of ENROLLMENT."

SID	Name	Major	Glev	Age	Snum	Cname	Pnum
123	JONES	HISTORY	JR	21	123	H350	1
123	JONES	HISTORY	JR	21	123	BA490	7
105	ANDERSON	MANAGEMENT	SN	27	105	BA490	3

a. Equijoin

SID	Name	Major	Glev	Age	Cname	Pnum
123	JONES	HISTORY	JR	21	H350	1
123	JONES	HISTORY	JR	21	BA490	7
105	ANDERSON	MANAGEMENT	SN	27	BA490	3

b. Natural join

FIGURE 9.22

Examples of joining STUDENT and ENROLLMENT relations

To form this join, we first take the product of STUDENT and ENROLLMENT. This operation was shown in Figure 9.19. Now, we SELECT those tuples from the product where SID of STUDENT equals Student-number of ENROLLMENT (there are only three). This operation leads to the relation in Figure 9.22a. Observe that two attributes are identical: SID and Student-number (Snum). One of these is redundant, so we eliminate it (in this case, we will choose Student-number) with projection. The result is the join in Figure 9.22b.

The join in Figure 9.22a is called the **equijoin;** the one in Figure 9.22b is called the **natural join.** Unless otherwise specified, when people say join, they mean the natural join.

In reality, forming the product of two large relations may be time consuming. Consequently, other, more efficient, methods have been devised for joining two relations. The output of these other methods is identical to the output described here.

Joining on conditions other than equality is also possible. For example, STUDENT JOIN (SID not = Student-number) ENROLLMENT, or STUDENT JOIN (SID < FID) FACULTY. The latter join would result in tuples where student numbers are less than faculty numbers. Such a join may have meaning if, say, People-identifiers were assigned in chronological order. Such a join would portray pairs of students and teachers such that the student had been at the institution longer than the teacher.

There is one important limit on the conditions of a join, however. The attributes in the condition must arise from a common domain. Thus, STUDENT JOIN (Age = Class-size) ENROLLMENT is *illogical.* Even though the values of Age and Class-size are compatible, they do not arise from the same domain. Semantically, this type of a join makes no sense. (Unhappily, many relational DBMS products will permit such a join.)

EXPRESSING QUERIES IN RELATIONAL ALGEBRA

Figure 9.23 summarizes the basic relational operations discussed. Set operations include +, −, intersection, and product. Selection picks specific tuples (rows) from a relation in

Type	Format	Example
Set operations	+, −, intersection, product	STUDENT [Name] − JUNIOR[Name]
Selection	SELECT relation WHERE condition	SELECT CLASS WHERE Name = 'A'
Projection	relation[list of attributes]	STUDENT [Name, Major, Age]
Join	relation 1 JOIN (condition) relation 2	STUDENT JOIN (SID = Student-number) ENROLLMENT

FIGURE 9.23
Summary of relational algebra operations

accordance with conditions on attribute values. Projection picks specific attributes (columns) from a relation by attribute name. Finally, join concatenates the tuples of two relations in accordance with a condition on values of attributes.

We will now illustrate how relational operators can be used to express queries. We will use relations STUDENT, CLASS, and ENROLLMENT from Figure 9.14; sample data is shown in Figure 9.24. The purpose of this demonstration is to illustrate the manipulation of relations. Although you will probably never use relational algebra in a commercial environment, these examples will help you understand how relations can be processed.

a.   **What are the names of all students?**

   STUDENT [Name]

This is simply the projection of the Name attribute of the STUDENT relation. The result is

JONES
PARKS
BAKER
GLASS
RUSSELL
RYE

Duplicate names have been omitted. The names JONES and BAKER actually occur twice in the relation STUDENT, but repetitions have been omitted because the result of a projection is a relation, and relations may not have duplicate tuples.

b.   **What are the student numbers of all students enrolled in a class?**

   ENROLLMENT [Student-number]

This is similar to query a, but the projection occurs on the relation ENROLLMENT. The result is

100
150
200
300
400
450

Again, duplicate tuples have been omitted.

SID	Name	Major	Grade-level	Age
100	JONES	HISTORY	GR	21
150	PARKS	ACCOUNTING	SO	19
200	BAKER	MATH	GR	50
250	GLASS	HISTORY	SN	50
300	BAKER	ACCOUNTING	SN	41
350	RUSSELL	MATH	JR	20
400	RYE	ACCOUNTING	FR	18
450	JONES	HISTORY	SN	24

a. STUDENT relation

Student-number	Class-name	Position-number
100	BD445	1
150	BA200	1
200	BD445	2
200	CS250	1
300	CS150	1
400	BA200	2
400	BF410	1
400	CS250	2
450	BA200	3

b. ENROLLMENT relation

Name	Time	Room
BA200	M-F9	SC110
BD445	MWF3	SC213
BF410	MWF8	SC213
CS150	MWF3	EA304
CS250	MWF12	EB210

c. CLASS relation

FIGURE 9.24
Example data for relations defined in Figure 9.14

c. What are the student numbers of all students not enrolled in a class?

STUDENT [SID] − ENROLLMENT [Student-number]

This expression takes the difference of the projection of two relations. STUDENT [SID] has the student numbers of all students. ENROLLMENT [Student-number] has the student numbers of all students enrolled in a class. The difference is the students not enrolled in a class. The result is

250
350

d. What are the numbers of students enrolled in the class 'BD445'?

ENROLLMENT WHERE Class-name = 'BD445' [Student-number]

This expression selects the appropriate tuples and then projects them onto the attribute Student-number. The result is

100
200

e. What are the names of the students enrolled in class 'BD445'?

STUDENT JOIN (SID = Student-number) ENROLLMENT WHERE Class-name = 'BD445' [STUDENT.Name]

To answer this query, data from both STUDENT and ENROLLMENT are needed. Specifically, student names must come from STUDENT, whereas the condition, "enrolled in BD445," must be checked in ENROLLMENT. Since both relations are needed, they must be joined. After STUDENT and ENROLLMENT have been joined, the select is applied, followed by a projection on student names. The result is

JONES
BAKER

As stated previously, when two or more relations are considered, attribute names can become ambiguous. Therefore, for clarity, the relation name may be prefixed to the attribute name. Thus, in the above example, the projection is on [STUDENT.Name]. This prefix was added only for clarity in this example, since all the attribute names are different. When attribute names are identical (a join involving STUDENT and CLASS will yield two attributes, both called Name), the prefix is required. Consider the following query:

f. What are the names and meeting times of 'PARKS' classes?

To answer this query, we must bring together data in all three relations. We need STUDENT data to find PARKS' student number, we need ENROLLMENT data to learn which classes PARKS is in, and we need CLASS data to determine class meeting times. One way to respond to this query is as follows:

STUDENT WHERE Name = 'PARKS' JOIN (SID = Student-number) ENROLLMENT JOIN (Class-name = Name) CLASS [CLASS.Name, Time]

This expression first selects PARKS' tuple and joins it to matching ENROLLMENT tuples. Then, the result is joined to matching CLASS tuples. Finally, the projection is taken to print classes and times. The result is

BA200	M-F9

We must specify CLASS.Name; simply specifying Name is ambiguous because both STUDENT and CLASS have an attribute called Name.

There are other, equivalent ways of responding to this query. One is

STUDENT JOIN (SID = Student-number) ENROLLMENT JOIN (Class-name = Name) CLASS WHERE STUDENT.Name = 'PARKS' [CLASS.Name, Time]

This expression differs from the first one because the select on PARKS is not done until after all of the joins have been performed. Assuming a computer performs the operations as stated, this latter expression will be much slower than the former one because many more tuples will be joined.

Such differences are a major disadvantage of relational algebra. To the user, two equivalent queries should take the same time (and hence cost the same). Imagine the frustration if one form of a query costs $1.17 and another costs $4,356. To the unwary and unsophisticated user, the cost algorithm will appear capricious. To eliminate this situation, relational algebra expressions need to be optimized before they are processed.

Summary

There are several tasks to be accomplished when implementing a relational database. First, the structure of the database must be defined to the DBMS. Then, file space needs to be allocated, and, finally, the database is filled with data.

The relational model represents and processes data in the form of tables called relations. The columns of the tables are called attributes, and the rows are called tuples. The values of attributes arise from domains. The terms *table, column,* and *row* and *file, field,* and *record* are used synonymously with the terms *relation, attribute,* and *tuple,* respectively.

The use of the term *key* can be confusing because the term is used differently in the design and implementation stages. During design, the term means a logical key, which is one or more attributes that uniquely define a row. During implementation, the term means a physical key, which is a data structure used to improve performance. A logical key may or may not be a physical key and a physical key may or may not be a logical key.

Since we are using the relational model to express database designs, there is no need to transform the design during the implementation stage. We simply define the relational design to the DBMS. Two ways of defining the design are to express it in a DDL text file or to use a graphical data definition tool. In either case, the tables, columns, indexes, constraints, passwords, and other controls are defined to the DBMS.

In addition to defining the database structure, the developers must allocate media space for the database. With multi-user systems, such allocation can be important to effective performance of the DBMS. Finally, the database is filled with data using either tools provided by the DBMS vendor, or programs developed in-house, or both.

There are four categories of relational data manipulation language: relational algebra, relational calculus, transform-oriented languages, and graphic-oriented systems. Relational algebra consists of a group of relational operators that can be used to manipulate relations to obtain a desired result. Relational algebra is procedural. The transform-oriented languages provide a nonprocedural capability to use relations to transform given data into wanted results. SQL is an example.

Three primary means exist for accessing a relational database. One is to use the default forms and reports provided by the DBMS. A second is to use a query/update, or, simply, a query language. SQL is the most common such language. A third is via application programs.

Application program interfaces can either be via subroutine call or by special-purpose database commands that are translated by a precompiler. The processing orientation of the relational model is relations, but the orientation of most programming languages is row-at-a-time. Some means needs to be devised to correct for this mismatch.

Relational algebra is used to manipulate relations to obtain a desired result. Some of the operators are union, difference, intersection, product, projection, selection, and join.

This chapter provided an introduction to the relational model. In Chapter 11, the concepts presented here will be used to develop a relational database implementation within a case study.

GROUP I QUESTIONS

9.1   Name and describe the three tasks necessary to implement a relational database.

9.2   Define the following terms: *relation, attribute, tuple,* and *domain.*

9.3   Explain the use of the terms *table, column, row, file, field,* and *record.*

9.4   Explain the difference between a relational schema and a relation.

9.5   Define *key, logical key,* and *physical key.*

9.6   Why are physical keys used?

9.7   Under what conditions is it necessary to transform the database design during the implementation stage?

9.8   Explain the term *data definition language*. What purpose does it serve?

9.9   How can database structure be defined other than via a text file?

9.10   What database design elements need to be defined to the DBMS?

9.11   Give an example, other than the one in this text, in which the allocation of the database to physical media is important.

9.12   Describe the easiest and worst cases for creating the database data.

9.13   Name and briefly explain four categories of relational DML.

9.14   Describe how relational data can be manipulated via forms.

9.15   Explain the role of query languages in relational data manipulation. How do stored queries differ from application programs? Why are they used?

9.16   Describe the two fundamental styles of application program interface to the database. In your answer, explain the role of a precompiler.

9.17   Describe the mismatch between the orientation of the SQL and the orientation of most programming languages. How is this mismatch corrected?

9.18   How does relational algebra differ from high school algebra?

9.19   Explain why relational algebra is *closed*.

9.20   Define *union compatible*. Give an example of two relations that are union compatible and two that are union incompatible.

Questions 9.21 through 9.23 refer to the following two relations:

COMPANY (Name, Number-employees, Sales)
MANUFACTURERS (Name, People, Revenue)

9.21   Give an example of a union of these two relations.

9.22   Give an example of a difference of these two relations.

9.23   Give an example of an intersection of these two relations.

Questions 9.24 through 9.28 refer to the following three relations:

SALESPERSON (Name, Age, Salary)
ORDER (Number, Cust-name, Salesperson-name, Amount)
CUSTOMER (Name, City, Industry-type)

An instance of these relations is shown in Figure 9.25. Use the data in those tables for the following problems.

9.24   Give an example of the product of SALESPERSON and ORDER.

FIGURE 9.25
Sample data for questions 9.24
through 9.28

Name	Age	Salary
Abel	63	120,000
Baker	38	42,000
Jones	26	36,000
Murphy	42	50,000
Zenith	59	118,000
Kobad	27	34,000

SALESPERSON

Number	Cust-name	Salesperson-name	Amount
100	Abernathy Construction	Zenith	560
200	Abernathy Construction	Jones	1800
300	Manchester Lumber	Abel	480
400	Amalgamated Housing	Abel	2500
500	Abernathy Construction	Murphy	6000
600	Tri-City Builders	Abel	700
700	Manchester Lumber	Jones	150

ORDER

Name	City	Industry-type
Abernathy Construction	Willow	B
Manchester Lumber	Manchester	F
Tri-City Builders	Memphis	B
Amalgamated Housing	Memphis	B

CUSTOMER

9.25   Show an example of

SALESPERSON[Name, Salary]
SALESPERSON[Age, Salary]

Under what conditions will SALESPERSON [Age, Salary] have fewer rows than SALESPERSON?

9.26   Show an example of a select on SALESPERSON Name, on SALESPERSON Age, on both SALESPERSON Name and Age.

9.27   Show an example of an equijoin and a natural join of SALESPERSON and ORDER where Name of SALESPERSON equals Salesperson-name of ORDER.

9.28 Show relational algebra expressions for:

a. The names of all salespeople
b. The names of all salespeople having an ORDER row
c. The names of salespeople not having an ORDER row
d. The names of salespeople having an order with ABERNATHY CON-STRUCTION
e. The ages of salespeople having an order with ABERNATHY CON-STRUCTION
f. The city of all CUSTOMERS having an order with salesperson JONES

GROUP II QUESTIONS

9.29 Suppose you have the task of explaining to management the tasks required for implementing a relational database system. Prepare a three-page report to management that discusses the nature of the activities and the time and cost risks associated with each.

9.30 Obtain access to a DBMS product that has a graphical interface (Paradox and R:BASE for DOS are examples). Process the queries expressed as relational algebra in this chapter with this product. Compare and contrast the two approaches. Which do you prefer? Which would an end-user prefer? Explain your answer and any differences in preferences.

Structured
Query Language —SQL

Structured Query Language, or SQL, is the most important relational data manipulation language in use today. It has been endorsed by the American National Standards Institute (ANSI) as the language of choice for manipulating databases. It is the data access language used by many commercial DBMS products including DB2, SQL/DS, ORACLE, INGRES, SYBASE, SQL Server, dBASE IV, R:BASE, and others.

Because of its popularity, SQL has become the standard language for information interchange among computers. Since there is a version of SQL that will run on almost any computer and operating system, computer systems may exchange data by passing SQL requests and responses to each other. This role for SQL is likely to increase in the future.

The development of SQL began at IBM's San Jose research facilities in the mid-1970s under the name SEQUEL. Several versions of SEQUEL were released, and the product was renamed SQL in 1980. Since then, IBM has been joined by many other vendors in developing products for SQL, and development continues. The American National Standards Institute also maintains a continuing interest in SQL and periodically, updated versions of the SQL standard are published.

- QUERYING A SINGLE TABLE
- QUERYING MULTIPLE TABLES
- CHANGING DATA

This chapter discusses the core of SQL as described in the 1986 ANSI standard.[1] Keep in mind that the constructs and allowed expressions in a particular implementation of SQL (say, for example, in INGRES or SQL Server) may differ in minor ways from the ANSI standard. This situation exists in part because many of the DBMS products were developed before there was agreement on the standard. It also exists because vendors added capabilities to their products to gain a competitive advantage. From a marketing perspective, simply supporting the ANSI standard may be judged as not enough.

SQL commands can be used interactively as a query language, or they can be embedded in application programs. In the latter case, they are processed by a precompiler as described in Chapter 9. Thus, SQL is *not* a programming language (like COBOL); rather, it is a *data sublanguage,* or a *data access language,* that is embedded in other languages.

In this chapter, we will present interactive SQL statements. Adjustments and modifications are needed when embedding these statements into programs as you will see in the next chapter. Also, here we are only concerned with data manipulation statements. There are also SQL commands for data definition and control. You will see examples of them in the context of the DBMS product DB2 in the next chapter.

Querying a Single Table

First, we consider SQL facilities for manipulating a single table. To follow custom, all SQL statements will be shown in capital letters. At times, SQL expressions will be indented. This is done for clarity; in SQL, the position of expressions is arbitrary. Finally, to provide reference numbers for text discussion, each SQL example is numbered and placed in parentheses. These numbers are not part of SQL; they are inserted for discussion purposes only.

---

[1] American National Standards Institute, Inc., *American National Standard for Information Systems—Database Language—SQL.* ANSI Publication X3.135–1986. A second version of this standard is currently (1991) in draft and under review.

Furthermore, SQL is a transform-oriented language. It accepts one or more relations as input and produces a single relation as output. The result of every SQL query is a relation; even if the result is a single number, that number is considered to be a relation with a single row and a single column. Thus, SQL, like relational algebra, is *closed.*

SAMPLE DATA

To facilitate the discussion of SQL, we will use the same set of six relations used to illustrate relational algebra in the previous chapter. The structure of those relations is shown in Figure 10.1 and sample data for three of them appears in Figure 10.2.

PROJECTIONS USING SQL

To form a projection with SQL, we name the relation to be projected and list the columns to be shown in the format of an SQL SELECT command. To illustrate, the projection STUDENT [SID, Name, Major] is specified with the following SQL statements:

```
SELECT      SID, NAME, MAJOR
FROM        STUDENT
```
(1)

The keywords SELECT and FROM are always required. The columns to be obtained are listed after the keyword SELECT. The table to be used is listed after the keyword FROM. The result of this projection for the data in Figure 10.2 is

100	JONES	HISTORY
150	PARKS	ACCOUNTING
200	BAKER	MATH
250	GLASS	HISTORY
300	BAKER	ACCOUNTING
350	RUSSELL	MATH
400	RYE	ACCOUNTING
450	JONES	HISTORY

Do not confuse the keyword SELECT with the relational algebra operator selection. SELECT is an SQL verb that can be used to perform a relational algebra projection, selection, and to specify other actions. Selection is the relational algebra operation of obtaining a subset of rows from a table.

Consider another example,

```
SELECT      MAJOR
FROM        STUDENT
```
(2)

1. JUNIOR (Snum, Name, Major)
2. HONOR-STUDENT (Number, Name, Interest)
3. STUDENT (SID, Name, Major, Grade-level, Age)
4. CLASS (Name, Time, Room)
5. ENROLLMENT (Student-number, Class-name, Position-number)
6. FACULTY (FID, Name, Department)

FIGURE 10.1
Relations used for SQL examples

The result of this operation is the following list of rows:

HISTORY
ACCOUNTING
MATH
HISTORY
ACCOUNTING
MATH
ACCOUNTING
HISTORY

As you can see, this list contains duplicate rows, and consequently, in a strict sense, this list is not a relation. In the day-to-day world, however, most people would call it a relation with duplicate rows. SQL does not automatically eliminate duplicates because such removal can be very time consuming and in many cases is not desired or necessary.

If it is necessary to be certain that duplicate rows be removed, then the qualifier DISTINCT must be specified as follows:

(3)

```
SELECT DISTINCT MAJOR
FROM    STUDENT
```

The result of this operation is the relation:

HISTORY
ACCOUNTING
MATH

SID	Name	Major	Grade-level	Age
100	JONES	HISTORY	GR	21
150	PARKS	ACCOUNTING	SO	19
200	BAKER	MATH	GR	50
250	GLASS	HISTORY	SN	50
300	BAKER	ACCOUNTING	SN	41
350	RUSSELL	MATH	JR	20
400	RYE	ACCOUNTING	FR	18
450	JONES	HISTORY	SN	24

a. STUDENT relation

Student-number	Class-name	Position-number
100	BD445	1
150	BA200	1
200	BD445	2
200	CS250	1
300	CS150	1
400	BA200	2
400	BF410	1
400	CS250	2
450	BA200	3

b. ENROLLMENT relation

Name	Time	Room
BA200	M-F9	SC110
BD445	MWF3	SC213
BF410	MWF8	SC213
CS150	MWF3	EA304
CS250	MWF12	EB210

c. CLASS relation

FIGURE 10.2
Sample data used for SQL examples

SELECTIONS USING SQL

The relational algebra selection operator is also performed with the SQL SELECT command. An example is the following:

```
SELECT      SID, NAME, MAJOR, GRADE-LEVEL, AGE          (4)
FROM        STUDENT
WHERE       MAJOR = 'MATH'
```

The SELECT expression specifies the names of all columns of the table. FROM specifies the table to be used and the new phrase, WHERE, provides the condition(s) for the selection. The format SELECT—FROM—WHERE is the fundamental structure of SQL statements. The following is an equivalent form of query example 4:

```
SELECT      *                                           (4a)
FROM        STUDENT
WHERE       MAJOR = 'MATH'
```

The asterisk (°) means that all columns of the table are to be obtained. The result of both queries (4 and 4a) is:

| 200 | BAKER | MATH | GR | 50 |
| 350 | RUSSELL | MATH | JR | 20 |

We can combine selection and projection as follows:

```
SELECT      NAME, AGE                                   (5)
FROM        STUDENT
WHERE       MAJOR = 'MATH'
```

The result is

| BAKER | 50 |
| RUSSELL | 20 |

Several conditions can be expressed in the WHERE clause. For example, the expression

```
SELECT      NAME, AGE                                   (6)
FROM        STUDENT
WHERE       MAJOR = 'MATH'
      AND   AGE > 21
```

obtains the following:

| BAKER | 50 |

The conditions in WHERE clauses can refer to a set of values. To do this, the keyword IN or NOT IN may be used. Consider:

```
SELECT      NAME                                          (7)
FROM        STUDENT
WHERE       MAJOR IN ['MATH', 'ACCOUNTING']
```

Notice that multiple values can be placed inside the brackets. This expression means "Present the names of students who have either a math or an accounting major." The result is

PARKS
BAKER
BAKER
RUSSELL
RYE

The expression

```
SELECT      NAME                                          (8)
FROM        STUDENT
WHERE       MAJOR NOT IN ['MATH', 'ACCOUNTING']
```

will cause the names of students other than math or accounting majors to be presented. The result is

JONES
GLASS
JONES

The expression MAJOR IN means that the value of the Major column can equal *any* of the listed majors. This is equivalent to the logical OR operator. The expression MAJOR NOT IN means the value must be different from *all* of the listed majors.

SORTING

The rows of the result relation can be sorted by the values in one or more columns. Consider the following example:

```
SELECT      NAME, MAJOR, AGE                              (9)
FROM        STUDENT
WHERE       MAJOR = 'ACCOUNTING'
ORDER BY    NAME
```

This query will list the accounting majors in ascending sequence by value of name. The result is

BAKER	ACCOUNTING	41
PARKS	ACCOUNTING	19
RYE	ACCOUNTING	18

More than one column can be chosen for sorting. If so, the first column listed will be the major sort field, the next column the next major sort field, and so on. Columns can also be declared to be ascending (ASC) or descending (DESC) as shown in the next statement:

```
SELECT      NAME, MAJOR, AGE                              (10)
FROM        STUDENT
WHERE       GRADE-LEVEL IN ['FR', 'SO', 'SN']
ORDER BY    MAJOR ASC, AGE DESC
```

The result is

BAKER	ACCOUNTING	41
PARKS	ACCOUNTING	19
RYE	ACCOUNTING	18
GLASS	HISTORY	50
JONES	HISTORY	24

ORDER BY can be combined with any of the SELECT statements.

SQL BUILT-IN FUNCTIONS

SQL provides five built-in functions:[2] COUNT, SUM, AVG, MAX, and MIN. COUNT and SUM sound similar but are different. COUNT computes the number of rows in a table; SUM totals numeric columns. AVG, MAX, and MIN also operate on numeric columns. AVG computes the average value, MAX and MIN obtain the maximum and minimum values of a column in a table.

The query expression

```
SELECT      COUNT(*)                                      (11)
FROM        STUDENT
```

---

[2]Sometimes built-in functions are referred to as **aggregate functions** to distinguish them from program language built-in functions such as substring.

counts the number of STUDENT rows and displays this total in a table having a single row and single column as follows:

```
┌─────────┐
│    8    │
└─────────┘
```

With the exception of GROUP BY (considered later), built-in functions cannot be intermixed with column names in the SELECT statement. Thus,

```
SELECT      NAME, COUNT (*)
```

is not allowed.

Consider the expressions:

```
SELECT      COUNT (MAJOR)                                        (12)
FROM        STUDENT

SELECT      COUNT (DISTINCT MAJOR)                               (13)
FROM        STUDENT
```

Expression 12 counts all majors, including duplicates. Expression 13 counts only unique majors. The results are:

```
┌─────────┐
│    8    │                                                      (12)
└─────────┘

┌─────────┐
│    3    │                                                      (13)
└─────────┘
```

The special functions can be used to request a result, as in the above examples. In most implementations of SQL, and in the ANSI standard SQL, the built-in functions *cannot* be used as part of a WHERE clause.

BUILT-IN FUNCTIONS AND GROUPING

To increase their utility, built-in functions can be applied to groups of rows within a table. Such groups are formed by collecting rows (logically, not physically) that have the same value of a specified column. For example, students can be grouped by major. This means one group will be formed for each value of MAJOR. For the data in Figure 10.2, there will be a group of HISTORY majors, a group of ACCOUNTING majors, and a group of MATH majors.

The SQL keyword GROUP BY instructs the DBMS to group together rows that have the same value of a column. Consider:

```
SELECT      MAJOR, COUNT (*)                                     (14)
FROM        STUDENT
GROUP BY    MAJOR
```

The result of this expression is

HISTORY	3
ACCOUNTING	3
MATH	2

The rows of the STUDENT table have been logically grouped by the value of MAJOR. Then the COUNT function sums the number of rows in each group. The result is a table having two columns, the major name and the sum. Thus, for subgroups, both columns and built-in functions can be specified in the SELECT statement.

In some cases, we do not want to consider all of the groups. For example, we might form groups of students having the same major and then wish to consider only those groups that have more than two students. In this case, we use the SQL HAVING clause to identify the subset of groups we want to consider.

Suppose we want to list the majors that have more than two students and the count of students in each of those majors. The following SQL statements will obtain this result:

```
SELECT      MAJOR, COUNT (*)                          (15)
FROM        STUDENT
GROUP BY    MAJOR
HAVING      COUNT (*) > 2
```

Here, groups of students having the same major are formed. Then, groups having more than two students are selected. (Other groups are ignored.) The major and the count of students in these selected groups are produced. The result is

HISTORY	3
ACCOUNTING	3

For even greater generality, WHERE clauses can be added as well. Doing so, however, creates the possibility of ambiguity. Consider the following example:

```
SELECT      MAJOR, AVG (AGE)                          (16)
FROM        STUDENT
WHERE       GRADE-LEVEL = 'SN'
GROUP BY    MAJOR
HAVING      COUNT (*) > 1
```

The result of this expression will be different depending on whether the WHERE condition is applied before or after the HAVING condition. To eliminate this ambiguity, the SQL standard specifies that WHERE clauses are to be applied first. Thus, in the above operation, senior students are selected. Then groups are formed, then the groups are selected by the HAVING condition, and then the result is presented. In this case, the result is

HISTORY	37

(Query 16 is not valid for all implementations of SQL. For many implementations, the only attributes that can appear in the SELECT phrase of a query with GROUP BY are those attributes that appear in the GROUP BY phrase and built-in functions of those attributes. Thus, in query 16, only MAJOR and built-in functions of MAJOR would be allowed.)

Querying Multiple Tables

In this section we extend the discussion of SQL to include operations on two or more tables. The STUDENT, CLASS, and ENROLLMENT data in Figure 10.2 will be used to illustrate these SQL commands.

RETRIEVAL USING SUBQUERY

Suppose we need to know the names of students enrolled in the class BD445. If we know that students with SIDs of 100 and 200 are enrolled in this class, then the following will produce the correct names:

```
SELECT     NAME                                          (17)
FROM       STUDENT
WHERE      SID IN [100, 200]
```

Usually, we will not know the SIDs of students in a class. We do have a facility, however, for determining those SIDs. Consider the expression:

```
SELECT     STUDENT-NUMBER                                (18)
FROM       ENROLLMENT
WHERE      CLASS-NAME = 'BD445'
```

The result of this operation is

100
200

These are the student numbers we need. Now, combining expressions 17 and 18, we obtain the following:

```
SELECT     NAME                                          (19)
FROM       STUDENT
WHERE      SID   IN
```

(continued on next page)

```
(SELECT      STUDENT-NUMBER
FROM         ENROLLMENT
WHERE        CLASS-NAME ='BD445')
```

Observe that the second SELECT, called the subquery, is enclosed in parentheses.

It may be easier to understand these statements if you work from the bottom and read up. The last three statements obtain the student numbers for people enrolled in BD445. The first three statements produce the names for the two students selected. The result of this query is

JONES
BAKER

This strategy can be very useful. Realize, however, that for this operation to be semantically correct, SID and STUDENT-NUMBER must arise from the same domain.

This strategy can be applied to three or even more tables. For example, suppose we want to know the names of the students enrolled in classes on Monday, Wednesday, and Friday at 3 o'clock (denoted MWF3 in our data). First, we need the names of classes that meet at that time:

```
SELECT     CLASS.NAME                            (20)
FROM       CLASS
WHERE      TIME = 'MWF3'
```

(Since we will be dealing with three different tables, we will qualify column names with table names to avoid confusion and ambiguity. Thus CLASS.NAME refers to the column NAME in the relation CLASS.)

Now we obtain the identifying numbers of students in these classes with the expression:

```
SELECT     ENROLLMENT.STUDENT-NUMBER             (21)
FROM       ENROLLMENT
WHERE      ENROLLMENT.CLASS-NAME IN
    (SELECT    CLASS.NAME
    FROM       CLASS
    WHERE      TIME = 'MWF3')
```

This yields:

100
200
300

which are the numbers of the students in class MWF3. Now, to obtain the names of those students, we specify:

```
SELECT      STUDENT.NAME                                    (22)
FROM        STUDENT
WHERE       STUDENT.SID IN
    (SELECT      ENROLLMENT.STUDENT-NUMBER
    FROM         ENROLLMENT
    WHERE        ENROLLMENT.CLASS-NAME IN
        (SELECT     CLASS.NAME
        FROM        CLASS
        WHERE       CLASS.TIME = 'MWF3'))
```

The result is

JONES
BAKER
BAKER

This strategy works well as long as the attributes in the answer come from a single table. If, however, the result comes from two or more tables, we have a problem. For example, suppose we want to know the names of students and the names of their classes. Say we need SID, student name, and class name. In this case, the results come from two different tables (STUDENT and ENROLLMENT) and the subquery strategy will not work. We need to be able to join the tables together.

JOINING WITH SQL

To produce the names of every student's classes, we need to join the STUDENT table with the ENROLLMENT table. The following statements will do this:

```
SELECT      STUDENT.SID, STUDENT.NAME,
            ENROLLMENT.CLASS-NAME                          (23)
FROM        STUDENT, ENROLLMENT
WHERE       STUDENT.SID = ENROLLMENT.STUDENT-NUMBER
```

Recall that a join is the combination of a product operation, followed by a selection, followed (usually) by a projection. In expression 23, the FROM statement expresses the product of STUDENT and ENROLLMENT. Then, the WHERE statement expresses the selection. The meaning is "Select from the product of STUDENT and ENROLL-MENT those rows in which SID of STUDENT equals STUDENT-NUMBER of ENROLLMENT." Finally, after the selection, the projection of student number, name, and class name is taken. The result is

100	JONES	BD445
150	PARKS	BA200
200	BAKER	BD445
200	BAKER	CS250
300	BAKER	CS150
400	RYE	BA200
400	RYE	BF410
400	RYE	CS250
450	JONES	BA200

The WHERE clause can contain qualifiers in addition to those needed for the join. For example:

```
SELECT      STUDENT.SID, ENROLLMENT.CLASS-NAME          (24)
FROM        STUDENT, ENROLLMENT
WHERE       STUDENT.SID = ENROLLMENT.STUDENT-NUMBER
    AND     STUDENT.NAME = 'RYE'
    AND     ENROLLMENT.POSITION-NUMBER = 1
```

The additional qualifiers here are STUDENT.NAME = 'RYE' and ENROLL-MENT.POSITION-NUMBER = 1. This operation will list the student number and class name of all students named RYE who were first to enroll in a class. The result is:

400	BF410

When data is needed from more than two tables, we can follow a similar strategy. In the following example, three tables are joined:

```
SELECT      STUDENT.SID, CLASS.NAME, CLASS.TIME,
            ENROLLMENT.POSITION-NUMBER                  (25)
FROM        STUDENT, ENROLLMENT, CLASS
WHERE       STUDENT.SID = ENROLLMENT.STUDENT-NUMBER
    AND     ENROLLMENT.CLASS-NAME = CLASS.NAME
    AND     STUDENT.NAME = 'BAKER'
```

The result of this operation is

200	BD445	MWF3	2
200	CS250	MWF12	1
300	CS150	MWF3	1

COMPARISON OF SQL SUBQUERY AND JOIN

Join can be used as an alternate way of expressing many subqueries. For example, in expression 19, we used a subquery to determine the students enrolled in the class BD445. We can also use a join to express this query as follows:

```
SELECT      STUDENT.NAME                                    (26)
FROM        STUDENT, ENROLLMENT
WHERE       STUDENT.SID = ENROLLMENT.STUDENT-NUMBER
   AND      ENROLLMENT.CLASS-NAME = 'BD445'
```

Similarly, the query "What are the names of the students in class MWF at 3?" can be expressed as:

```
SELECT      STUDENT.NAME                                    (27)
FROM        STUDENT, ENROLLMENT, CLASS
WHERE       STUDENT.SID = ENROLLMENT.STUDENT-NUMBER
   AND      ENROLLMENT.CLASS-NAME = CLASS.NAME
   AND      CLASS.TIME = 'MWF3'
```

Although join expressions can substitute for many subquery expressions, they cannot substitute for all of them. Subqueries that involve EXISTS and NOT EXISTS (discussed in the next section) cannot be represented by joins.

Similarly, subqueries cannot be substituted for all joins. When using a join, the displayed columns may come from any of the joined tables; when using a subquery, the displayed columns may come only from the table named in the FROM expression in the first SELECT.

For example, suppose we want to know the names of classes taken by undergraduates. We can express this as a subquery:

```
SELECT      DISTINCT CLASS-NAME                             (28)
FROM        ENROLLMENT
WHERE       STUDENT-NUMBER IN
   (SELECT      SID
   FROM         STUDENT
   WHERE        GRADE-LEVEL NOT = 'GR')
```

or as a join:

```
SELECT      DISTINCT ENROLLMENT.CLASS-NAME                  (29)
FROM        ENROLLMENT, STUDENT
WHERE       ENROLLMENT.STUDENT-NUMBER = STUDENT.SID
   AND      STUDENT.GRADE-LEVEL NOT = 'GR'
```

However, if we want to know both the names of the classes and the grade levels of the undergraduate students, then we must use a join. A subquery will not suffice because the desired results arise from two different tables. The names of the classes are stored in ENROLLMENT, and the names of the students are stored in STUDENT. The following will obtain the correct answer:

```
SELECT      DISTINCT ENROLLMENT.CLASS-NAME,
            STUDENT.GRADE-LEVEL                              (30)
FROM        ENROLLMENT, STUDENT
WHERE       ENROLLMENT.STUDENT-NUMBER = STUDENT.SID
    AND     STUDENT.GRADE-LEVEL NOT = 'GR'
```

The result will be

BA200	SO
CS150	SN
BA200	FR
BF410	FR
CS250	FR
BA200	SN

EXISTS AND NOT EXISTS

EXISTS and NOT EXISTS are logical operators; their value is either true or false depending on the presence or absence of rows that fit qualifying conditions. For example, suppose we want to know the student numbers of students enrolled in more than one class.

```
SELECT      DISTINCT STUDENT-NUMBER                         (31)
FROM        ENROLLMENT A
WHERE       EXISTS
    (SELECT     *
    FROM        ENROLLMENT B
    WHERE       A.STUDENT-NUMBER = B.STUDENT-NUMBER
        AND     A.CLASS-NAME NOT = B.CLASS-NAME)
```

In this example, the query and the subquery both refer to the ENROLLMENT table. To prevent ambiguity, these two uses of ENROLLMENT have been assigned a different name. In the first FROM statement, ENROLLMENT is assigned the temporary and arbitrary name A. In the second FROM statement, it is assigned another temporary and arbitrary name, B.

The meaning of the subquery expression is this: Find two rows in ENROLLMENT having the same student number, but different class names. (This means the student is taking more than one class.) If two such rows exist, then the logical value of EXISTS is true. In this case, present the student number in the answer. Otherwise, the logical value of the EXISTS is false; do not present that SID in the answer.

Another way of viewing this query is to imagine two separate and identical copies of the ENROLLMENT table. Call one copy Table A and the other copy Table B. We will compare each row in A with each row in B. First, consider the first row in A and the first row in B. In this case, since the two rows are identical, both the STUDENT-NUMBERs and the CLASS-NAMEs will be the same. Do not display the SID.

Now, consider the first row in A and the second row in B. If the STUDENT-NUMBERs are the same and the CLASS-NAMEs are different, then display the STUDENT-NUMBER. Essentially, we are comparing the first row of ENROLLMENT with the second row of ENROLLMENT. For the data in Figure 10.2, neither the STUDENT-NUMBERs nor the CLASS-NAMEs are the same.

We continue comparing the first row of A with each row of B. If the conditions are ever met, we print the STUDENT-NUMBER. When all of the rows in B have been examined, we move to the second row of A. It is compared to all of the rows in B (actually, if we are considering the nth rows in A, then only rows greater than n need be considered in B).

The result of this query is

200
400

To illustrate the application of NOT EXISTS, suppose we want to know the names of students taking all classes. Another way of expressing this query is to say we want the names of students such that there are no classes that the student did not take. The following expresses that statement:

```
SELECT      STUDENT.NAME                                      (32)
FROM        STUDENT
WHERE       NOT EXISTS
     (SELECT    *
     FROM       ENROLLMENT
     WHERE      NOT EXISTS
          (SELECT    *
          FROM       CLASS
          WHERE      CLASS.NAME = ENROLLMENT.CLASS-NAME
          AND        ENROLLMENT.STUDENT-NUMBER =
                     STUDENT.SID))
```

This query has three parts. In the bottom part, we try to find classes the student did take. The middle part determines if any classes were found that the student did not take. If not, then the student is taking all classes, and the student's name is displayed.

This query may be difficult to understand. If you have trouble with it, use the data in Figure 10.2 and follow the query instructions. The answer, for that data, is that no student is taking all classes. You might try to change the data so that a student does take all classes. Another approach for understanding this query is to attempt to solve it by a means other than NOT EXISTS. The problems you encounter will help you understand why NOT EXISTS is necessary.

A final example combines many SQL concepts, and illustrates the power of this data sublanguage. Suppose we want to know the names of graduate students taking classes only with other graduate students.

```
SELECT      A.NAME                                             (33)
FROM        STUDENT A
WHERE       STUDENT.GRADE-LEVEL = 'GR'
    AND     NOT EXISTS
    (SELECT     *
    FROM        ENROLLMENT B
    WHERE       STUDENT.SID = B.STUDENT-NUMBER
        AND     B.CLASS-NAME IN
        (SELECT     C.CLASS-NAME
        FROM        ENROLLMENT C
        WHERE       B.CLASS-NAME = C.CLASS-NAME
            AND         C.STUDENT-NUMBER IN
            (SELECT     D.SID
            FROM        STUDENT D
            WHERE       C.STUDENT-NUMBER = D.SID
                AND     D.GRADE-LEVEL NOT = 'GR')))
```

The meaning of this query is "Present the names of students where there is no row in ENROLLMENT that matches the student with a class which is one of the classes that are matched with students who have a grade level other than graduate." The result of this query is

```
JONES
```

The last three queries are complicated. Do not assume from this that SQL is complicated. Actually, compared to the alternatives, SQL is simple; these last three queries are difficult because we are solving queries that are logically quite complex. For most day-to-day problems, SQL queries are far more simple and straightforward.

Changing Data

SQL has provisions for changing data in tables by inserting new rows, deleting rows, and modifying values in existing rows. SQL also has facilities for changing data structure. However, we will not consider changing data structure until we study DB2 in the next chapter.

INSERTING DATA

Rows can be inserted into a table one at a time or in groups. To insert a single row, we state:

```
INSERT      INTO ENROLLMENT                                  (34)
            VALUES (400, 'BD445', 44)
```

If we do not know all of this data, say we do not know Position-number, we could say:

```
INSERT      INTO ENROLLMENT                                  (35)
            (STUDENT-NUMBER, CLASS-NAME)
            VALUES (400, 'BD445')
```

Position-number could then be added later. Note that this causes the value of Position-number to be null. A null value indicates that the value is missing—it is not the same as blanks or zeros. Unfortunately, some implementations of SQL do not discriminate between nulls and blanks or zeros. This lack leads to ambiguity in the database data. For example, is a blank to be interpreted as a null value or as a real value that happens to be blank?

We can also copy rows in mass from one table to another. For example, suppose we want to fill the JUNIOR table that was defined in Figure 9.14.

```
INSERT      INTO JUNIOR                                      (36)
      VALUES
      (SELECT      SID, NAME, MAJOR
      FROM         STUDENT
      WHERE        GRADE-LEVEL = 'JR')
```

This example, and all of the SQL SELECT expressions developed in the previous two sections, can be used to identify rows to be copied. This feature provides quite powerful capabilities.

DELETING DATA

As with insertion, rows can be deleted one at a time or in groups. The following example will delete the row for student number 100:

```
DELETE     STUDENT                                          (37)
WHERE      STUDENT.SID = 100
```

Note that if student 100 is enrolled in classes, this delete will cause an integrity problem. The ENROLLMENT rows having STUDENT-NUMBER = 100 will have no corresponding STUDENT row. We addressed such integrity problems in Chapter 6.

Groups of rows can be deleted as shown in the following two examples. These examples will delete all enrollments for accounting majors as well as all accounting majors.

```
DELETE     ENROLLMENT                                       (38)
WHERE      ENROLLMENT.STUDENT-NUMBER IN
      (SELECT      STUDENT.SID
      FROM         STUDENT
      WHERE        STUDENT.MAJOR = 'ACCOUNTING')


DELETE     STUDENT                                          (39)
WHERE      STUDENT.MAJOR = 'ACCOUNTING'
```

The order of these two operations is important. If the order were reversed, none of the ENROLLMENT rows would be deleted because the matching STUDENT rows would have already been deleted.

MODIFYING DATA

Rows can also be modified one at a time or in groups. The keyword SET is used to change a column value. After SET, the name of the column to be changed is specified and then the new value or way of computing the new value. Consider two examples:

```
UPDATE      STUDENT                                          (40)
SET         POSITION-NUMBER = 44
WHERE       SID = 400

UPDATE      STUDENT                                          (41)
SET         POSITION-NUMBER = MAX(POSITION-NUMBER) + 1
WHERE       SID = 400
```

In operation 41, the value of the column will be calculated using the MAX built-in function. Some implementations of SQL may not allow the built-in function to be used as an argument in the SET command, however.

To illustrate mass updates, suppose the name of a course has been changed from BD445 to BD564. In this case, to prevent integrity problems, both the ENROLLMENT and the CLASS tables need to be changed.

```
UPDATE      ENROLLMENT                                       (42)
SET         CLASS-NAME = 'BD564'
WHERE       CLASS-NAME = 'BD445'

UPDATE      CLASS
SET         CLASS-NAME = 'BD564'
WHERE       CLASS-NAME = 'BD445'
```

As stated in Chapter 2, mass updates are quite dangerous. The user is given great power—power which, when used correctly, can rapidly accomplish the task at hand, but when used incorrectly, can cause serious problems.

Summary

SQL is today's most important relational data manipulation language. It has become the standard for information exchange among computers, and its popularity continues to grow. SQL statements that operate on a single table include SELECT, SELECT with WHERE, with GROUP BY, and with GROUP BY and HAVING. SQL built-in functions of COUNT, SUM, AVG, MAX, and MIN can also be used.

Operations on two or more tables involve retrieval using subquery and joins and EXISTS and NOT EXISTS. Subqueries and joins can perform many of the same operations, but they do not totally substitute for one another. Subqueries require that the attributes retrieved arise from a single relation; joins do not. On the other hand, some queries are possible with EXISTS and NOT EXISTS that are impossible with joins.

SQL statements for data modification include INSERT, DELETE, and UPDATE commands, which are used to add, remove, and change data values.

This chapter presented the basic SQL commands in generic form. In the next chapter you will see how these commands are used to process a database using a commercial DBMS product.

GROUP I   QUESTIONS

The questions in this group refer to the following three relations:

SALESPERSON (Name, Age, Salary)
ORDER (Number, Cust-name, Salesperson-name, Amount)
CUSTOMER (Name, City, Industry-type)

An instance of these relations is shown in Figure 10.3. Use the data in those tables and show SQL statements to display or modify data as indicated in the following questions:

10.1   Show the ages and salaries of all salespeople.

10.2   Show the ages and salaries of all salespeople (duplicates omitted).

10.3   Show the names of all salespeople less than thirty years old.

10.4   Show the names of all salespeople having an order with ABERNATHY CONSTRUCTION.

10.5   Show the names and salary of all salespeople not having an order with ABERNATHY CONSTRUCTION, in ascending order of salary.

10.6   Compute the number of orders.

10.7   Compute the number of different customers having an order.

10.8   Compute the average age of a salesperson.

10.9   Show the name of the oldest salesperson.

10.10 Compute the number of orders for each salesperson.

10.11 Compute the number of orders for each salesperson, considering only orders having an amount exceeding 500.

10.12 Show the names and ages of salespeople having an order with ABERNATHY CONSTRUCTION (use subquery).

FIGURE 10.3
Sample data for Group I questions

Name	Age	Salary
Abel	63	120,000
Baker	38	42,000
Jones	26	36,000
Murphy	42	50,000
Zenith	59	118,000
Kobad	27	34,000

SALESPERSON

Number	Cust-name	Salesperson-name	Amount
100	Abernathy Construction	Zenith	560
200	Abernathy Construction	Jones	1800
300	Manchester Lumber	Abel	480
400	Amalgamated Housing	Abel	2500
500	Abernathy Construction	Murphy	6000
600	Tri-City Builders	Abel	700
700	Manchester Lumber	Jones	150

ORDER

Name	City	Industry-type
Abernathy Construction	Willow	B
Manchester Lumber	Manchester	F
Tri-City Builders	Memphis	B
Amalgamated Housing	Memphis	B

CUSTOMER

10.13   Show the names and ages of salespeople having an order with ABERNATHY CONSTRUCTION (use join), in descending order of age.

10.14   Show the age of salespeople having an order with a customer in MEMPHIS (use subquery), in descending order of age.

10.15   Show the age of salespeople having an order with a customer in MEMPHIS (use join).

10.16   Show the industry type and ages of salesperson of all orders for companies in MEMPHIS.

10.17   Show the names of salespeople having two or more orders.

10.18   Show the names and ages of salespeople having two or more orders.

10.19   Show the names and ages of salespeople having an order with all customers.

10.20   Show an SQL statement to insert a new row into CUSTOMER.

10.21   Show an SQL statement to insert a new name and age into SALESPERSON; assume salary is undetermined.

10.22   Show an SQL statement to insert rows into a new table, HIGH-ACHIEVER (Name, Age), where, to be included, a salesperson must have a salary of at least 100,000.

10.23   Show an SQL statement to delete customer ABERNATHY CONSTRUCTION.

10.24   Show an SQL statement to delete all orders for ABERNATHY CONSTRUCTION.

10.25   Show an SQL statement to change the salary of salesperson JONES to 45,000.

10.26   Show an SQL statement to give all salespeople a 10 percent pay increase.

10.27   Assume salesperson JONES changes name to PARKS. Show SQL statements to make appropriate changes.

GROUP II QUESTIONS

10.28   Obtain information on relational calculus. Show how the example queries 1 through 33 would be processed using relational calculus.

10.29   Obtain information on the DBMS product Paradox. Show how queries 1 through 33 would be processed using Paradox.

10.30   Obtain information on the DBMS product INGRES. Show how queries 1 through 33 would be processed using INGRES.

10.31   Obtain information about the DBMS product SQL Server or SYBASE (the two are closely related). How does this product's DML differ from SQL? How does it differ from INGRES? What are the strengths of these products? the weaknesses?

10.32   Obtain a copy of any of the relational products mentioned above, or any other relational product. Store the data in Figure 10.2 using this product. Process the queries 1 through 33 using this DBMS.

Relational Implementation with DB2

The prior two chapters addressed the implementation of relational databases. Chapter 9 discussed the processes and tasks involved in such implementation and developed a foundation of relational processing by discussing relational algebra. Chapter 10 presented SQL, the most important relational data manipulation language.

Chapter 11 brings the discussion of those two chapters together by presenting the implementation of an example database using the DBMS product, DB2. We begin by considering some of the information problems faced by the marketing department of a manufacturing company. We then outline the features and functions of an information system that would solve those problems. This information system includes a relational database, and we define both the objects and the relations that need to be stored in the database.

Next, we present an overview of the IBM relational DBMS called Database2 or, more frequently, DB2. We examine not only the data definition and data manipulation features of DB2, but also features that support concurrent processing, backup and recovery, and database security.

- CASE STUDY: KDK APPLIANCES
- DB2: THE PRODUCT
- RELATIONAL IMPLEMENTATION USING DB2

Finally, we present portions of the relational application developed for the manufacturing company. These portions include interactive DB2 queries and a COBOL program that contains embedded DB2 commands.

This chapter is long. It includes a case, a description of the features and functions of DB2, and an application of DB2 to the case situation. Although a shorter case or a simpler product could have been chosen, this would not be appropriate. Long as it may seem, the case is actually much shorter and less complicated than most real-life business applications.

Similarly, DB2 is typical of mainframe DBMS products. These products are designed to provide fast performance with high reliability while processing hundreds of concurrent transactions per minute. This means they are complicated and thus require considerable expertise and knowledge on the part of systems and database administrators. Unlike microcomputer DBMS products, they are not designed to be easy to use and install. Instead, they are designed for high performance. This chapter provides the only exposure you will have to such products in this text. Read this chapter, in part, to gain an appreciation for the difference between a DBMS for personal applications and one for large organizational applications.

In truth, many important and useful features and functions of DB2 have been omitted in this discussion. You can learn about them in the publications *DB2 System and Database Administration Guide* and *DB2 Application Programming Guide,* both published by IBM.

CASE STUDY: KDK APPLIANCES

KDK Appliances manufactures major kitchen appliances, such as refrigerators, ranges, microwave ovens, and dishwashers. The company markets its products to independent dealers, who then sell to the public. Currently, its market is primarily the northeastern United States, but it plans to develop new sales regions in the Midwest and Canada soon.

Each sales region is serviced by several salespeople. Salespeople call on dealers and explain KDK's product line, dealer training program, incentives, and local advertising programs. It is possible for one dealer to work with more than one KDK salesperson.

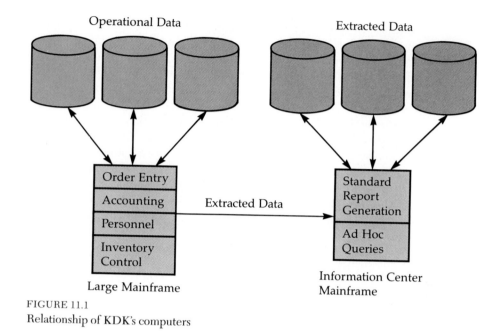

FIGURE 11.1
Relationship of KDK's computers

KDK has a large mainframe computer that handles all order processing, inventory control, personnel, and accounting functions. Stored within the mainframe are files and databases that track sales and other data to meet various reporting requirements.

In addition to the large mainframe computer, KDK has a smaller mainframe computer in its Information Center. This smaller mainframe processes extracts of operational data that are periodically downloaded (copied) from the large mainframe. No updating of data takes place in the Information Center. Rather, all updating is accomplished by the carefully controlled programs running on the large mainframe (see Figure 11.1).

The Information Center exists to support planning and analysis functions. It is staffed by operations personnel as well as by systems administrators, database administrators, and systems analysts. These people support the functional business personnel who perform business studies. The Information Center uses the IBM relational product DB2. It has installed additional programs to provide online concurrent access, but those programs are not within the scope of discussion of this chapter.

PROBLEMS

The marketing department plays a key role in the success of the company's plans to expand. The marketing department presently employs eight product managers (PMs), each responsible for a particular line of products (one for refrigerators, one for ranges, and so forth). PMs, as part of their duties, develop an annual product plan for each major product (a major product being, for example, a particular refrigerator model or a specific type of microwave oven). The product plan establishes, among other things, the sales goals for the product and the budget for marketing. Marketing expenses include advertising, dealer training, salesperson training, dealer promotions, and so forth.

To make wise decisions regarding the use of marketing dollars, PMs want to access data stored in the computer. They need to know, for example, product sales by region and by salesperson. They also need to know the effect some aspect of marketing (say, advertising) has had on product sales. All the PMs know that the information they need can be produced from data stored in the Information Center computer.

Instant response time is not vital, because the PMs usually need quarterly, monthly, or weekly summaries of data. For example, instant access to a particular order is not important to a PM. (In contrast, consider how important response time is when performing the order entry function on KDK's large operational mainframe.)

All of the PMs are either familiar with SQL or willing to learn it. None is a programmer, though, and none has the time or the interest to learn COBOL. Typical of the questions that a PM wants answered are

- Which dealers participated in our shared advertising program this month?
- What was the total sales figure for product #45678 during March? How does that compare to sales for April?

KDK Appliances sponsors a co-op advertising program. KDK employs several agencies to develop advertising campaigns for various media, including newspapers (daily or weekly), periodicals (weekly or monthly), television, and radio. Much of KDK's advertising is shared with dealers. This means that in addition to the advertising copy promoting a specific KDK product, a dealer's name, address, and logo appear in the ad (see Figure 11.2). Thus, although KDK products are the central focus of the ad, a local dealer can share the benefits by sharing the cost of the ad.

Some dealers take advantage of this arrangement, whereas others do not. The share costs (percentages of the cost borne by KDK and the dealer) vary from one ad to another and from one dealer to another. Sales and marketing personnel establish the share costs for each ad.

OVERVIEW OF THE SOLUTION

After studying these problems and discussing them with several of the product managers, one of the systems analysts proposed that KDK develop a database system on the Information Center's computer, which already contains the data needed to answer most of the product managers' questions. The data would be periodically extracted from KDK's operational mainframe computer. (The frequency depends on how up-to-date the data needs to be. The analyst suggested that they begin downloading data once a week. If that proves unsatisfactory, downloading can be done more or less frequently.)

Some of the information that PMs need is highly predictable. For example, each PM needs a monthly report summarizing his or her product's sales by region, by dealer, and by salesperson. The analyst decided to write application programs in COBOL to produce those reports. The programs will be run on a regular schedule.

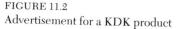
FIGURE 11.2
Advertisement for a KDK product

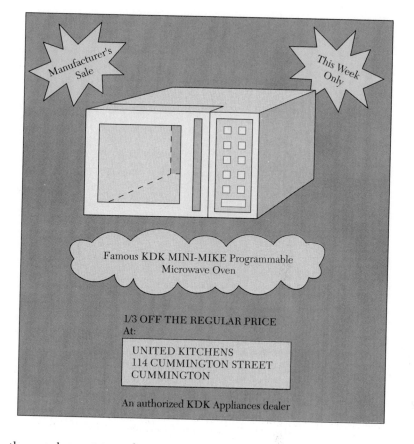

In addition to the regular anticipated reports, the analyst suggested that each PM learn how to use SQL to make simple ad hoc queries. Complex queries will be handled by Information Center personnel as needed.

DATABASE SECURITY PRECAUTIONS

Because the Information Center handles extracts of data for all divisions of the company, certain security precautions must be taken to protect the data and to ensure the privacy of proprietary information. First, the Information Center systems analysts must be authorized by the company's database administrator to extract sales and other data from the operational database on the large mainframe. Second, because the operational database on the large mainframe contains vast amounts of private data (such as employee salaries), only the data necessary for the assessment of product sales will be extracted.

Third, because many employees use Information Center terminals to perform queries, this database will be made available to PMs only. All other employees (except for Information Center personnel) will be prevented from using it. Fourth, PMs will be authorized to use only this database. They will have no access to databases that have been established for other user departments. The Information Center will assign each PM an identification number that will serve as a password for access to the database.

Finally, data will only be downloaded from the mainframe computer. No updates will be made to the extracted data and no data will be sent back to the large mainframe. The extracted data will be merely a snapshot of the data in the operational database, a work copy that can be destroyed when the PMs are finished with it.

OBJECT DEFINITIONS

To develop the proposed system, the analyst needed first to identify the objects in which the PMs were interested. To start, the analyst and PMs examined reports, transactions, and other entities. Let us first consider the reports and identify the underlying objects needed to construct them.

PRODUCT SALES SUMMARY Reports

Figure 11.3 shows three examples of product sales summaries the PMs need each month. Figure 11.3a is a sample PRODUCT SALES SUMMARY BY SALESPERSON report. It contains data about products (product number, name, description, price), salespeople (name), and sales (total units sold by each salesperson). This suggests the existence of PRODUCT, SALESPERSON, and SALE objects. We will not be sure until all reports, transactions, and so forth have been examined.

The PRODUCT SALES SUMMARY BY DEALER report (Figure 11.3b) contains data about products (product number, name, description, price), dealers (name), and sales (total units sold to each dealer). Thus, in addition to the objects mentioned above, it is likely that a DEALER object will exist as well.

The third summary report, PRODUCT SALES SUMMARY BY REGION (Figure 11.3c), contains data about products (product number, name, description, price), regions (region number), and sales (total units sold in each region). Now, in addition to the potential objects already identified—PRODUCT, SALESPERSON, SALE, and DEALER—another possible object is found: REGION.

DEALER ACTIVITY SUMMARY Report

Figure 11.4 shows an example of the DEALER ACTIVITY SUMMARY report. It contains data about dealers (dealer number, name address, telephone number), sales (invoice number, data, invoice total), and advertisements (advertisement name, date, cost, and dealer's share). We have already identified DEALER and SALE (an invoice is the record of sale) as potential objects. The DEALER ACTIVITY SUMMARY report suggests a few more attributes of these objects, such as dealer address, telephone number, and invoice number. This report also suggests that advertisements are possible objects.

FIGURE 11.3
PRODUCT SALES SUMMARY
reports

PRODUCT SALES SUMMARY BY SALESPERSON

- -

Product Number: 87224

Name/Description: Mini-Mike Programmable compact microwave
                  oven
Price: $194.99

SALESPERSON	UNITS SOLD
John Eberle	280
Margaret Gosselin	200
Hans Jensen	50
TOTAL	530

a. SALES SUMMARY BY SALESPERSON report

PRODUCT SALES SUMMARY BY DEALER

- -

Product Number: 87224

Name/Description: Mini-Mike Programmable compact microwave
                  oven
Price: $194.99

DEALER	UNITS SOLD
Lisbon Furniture and Appliances	30
Parks Department Store	200
United Kitchens	50
Gem Appliances	100
Rich Appliance Co.	100
Sounds Terrific	50
TOTAL	530

b. SALES SUMMARY BY DEALER report

PRODUCT SALES SUMMARY BY REGION

- -

Product Number: 87224

Name/Description: Mini-Mike Programmable compact microwave
                  oven
Price: $194.99

REGION	UNITS SOLD
2	200
5	330
TOTAL	530

c. SALES SUMMARY BY REGION report

FIGURE 11.4
DEALER ACTIVITY SUMMARY
report

DEALER ACTIVITY SUMMARY

#6644   (617) 479-5555
J&S Department Store
75 Rock Road
Plymouth, MA 02787

- -

Purchases to Date

Invoice #	Date	Total
1013	01/02/88	15349.81
1071	02/01/88	22467.00
1296	03/02/88	18949.37
1380	04/01/88	36755.29
	TOTAL	93620.47

- -

Advertising to Date

Ad Name	Date	Ad Cost	Dealer's Share (%)
Ultra	03/10/88	250.00	67
Free Time	02/15/88	400.00	67
St. Paddy's Sale	03/14/88	600.00	67
Ultra	03/15/88	250.00	60

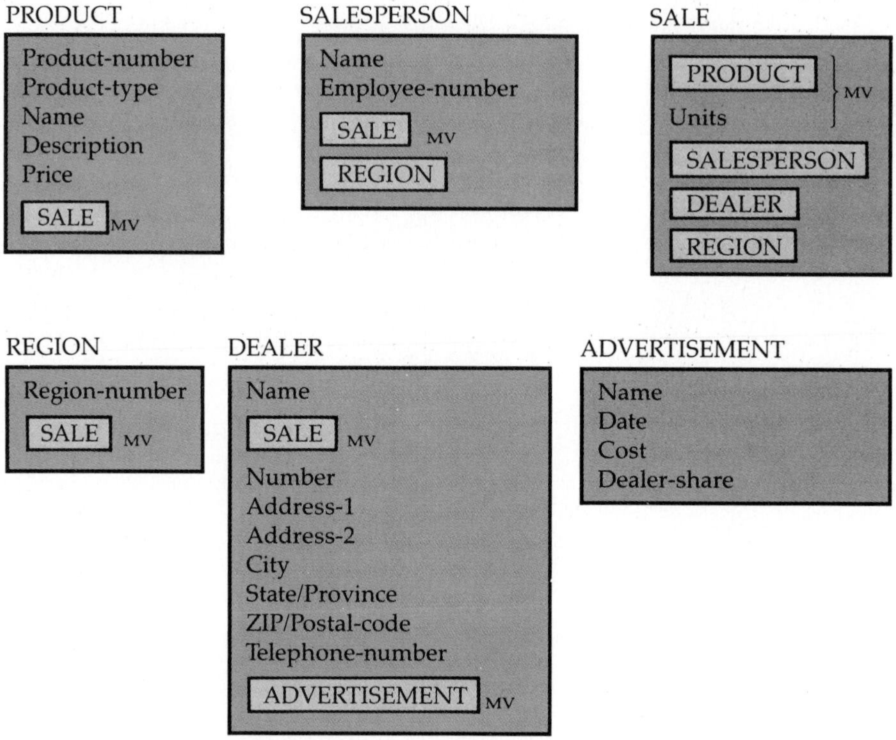

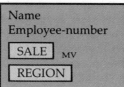

PRODUCT

Product-number
Product-type
Name
Description
Price
[SALE] MV

SALESPERSON

Name
Employee-number
[SALE] MV
[REGION]

SALE

[PRODUCT] } MV
Units
[SALESPERSON]
[DEALER]
[REGION]

REGION

Region-number
[SALE] MV

DEALER

Name
[SALE] MV
Number
Address-1
Address-2
City
State/Province
ZIP/Postal-code
Telephone-number
[ADVERTISEMENT] MV

ADVERTISEMENT

Name
Date
Cost
Dealer-share

FIGURE 11.5
Preliminary sketch of KDK's objects

```
INVOICE 1001                                     02/01/91
SOLD TO:                           SALES REP:  #5762
Lisbon Furniture and Appliances               Paula Jasinski
692 S. Ellington Rd.
South Windsor, CT   06114


      Number    Name              Price       Qty     Extended-price
1     80911     Kitchen Valet    $1,699.99     2      $ 3,399.98
2     87755     Mity-Mike          344.99     20        6,899.80
3     93861     E. Range-white     679.99     15       10,199.85
4
5
6
                                            TOTAL     $20,499.63
```

FIGURE 11.6
Product manager's view of invoice

Figure 11.5 illustrates our findings so far. The potential objects are PRODUCT, SALESPERSON, SALE (or INVOICE), REGION, DEALER, and ADVERTISEMENT. This is by no means a complete and final list. These objects are only the beginning of our investigation. Study the object diagrams in Figure 11.5 carefully, making sure you understand them before continuing.

Sales Invoice Document

Product managers derive much information about product sales from one important document: the sales invoice. An invoice for each sale is completed by a salesperson. An *actual* invoice captures many details about the dealer, the product(s) sold, and the dollar amounts of the transaction, discounts, credits, balance due, and shipping charges. All invoice details are entered into KDK's large operational mainframe computer. Keep in mind, however, that PMs need only a subset of the data on an actual invoice. An invoice as viewed by a product manager is illustrated in Figure 11.6. It contains data about the invoice (number, sale date, total), salesperson (number, name), dealer (name, address), and items sold (line item number, product number, name, price, quantity sold, extended price).

It is easy to see that what we have just described as an *invoice* is an embellishment of what we have been calling a *sale*. Because the PMs are more likely to use the term *invoice* than *sale* (this was discovered by talking to the PMs), we will modify the object diagrams from Figure 11.5, replacing the SALE object with the updated INVOICE object. The results are shown in Figure 11.7.

Advertising

We noted earlier that KDK advertises its products to consumers in various media, such as print and television. An ad that can be run in, say, a newspaper is referred to as an *ad-*

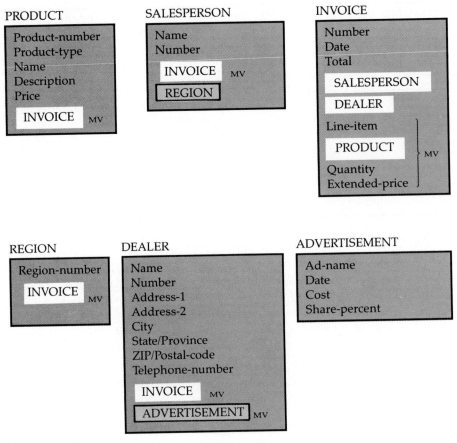

FIGURE 11.7
Modified sketch of KDK's objects, replacing SALE with INVOICE

copy. Each ad-copy is given a title by the advertising agency that developed it. When a particular ad-copy is actually run in a newspaper on a certain date at a certain cost, it is referred to as an *advertisement.* Thus, an ad-copy called "Free Time" emphasizing the time-saving features of various KDK appliances might be run in several newspapers over a period of three or four months. Each instance it is run is called an advertisement.

As we already noted, each advertisement may be shared by a local appliance dealer, as long as the dealer agrees to share the cost of the ad. Because each ad-copy can target several products, and because each advertisement can be shared by a dealer, product managers need to track various aspects of advertising. After all, a large portion of each PM's budget is devoted to advertising.

The underlying objects in the advertising portion of the system, then, are AD-COPY and ADVERTISEMENT. The object diagrams for them are illustrated in Figure 11.8. Note that this more complete definition of the ADVERTISEMENT object replaces the one seen in Figure 11.7.

FIGURE 11.8
Object diagrams for advertising
portion of KDK database

AD-COPY

Ad-name
Agency
First-run-date
PRODUCT   MV

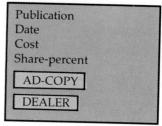

ADVERTISEMENT

Publication
Date
Cost
Share-percent
AD-COPY
DEALER

Final Version

Using object diagrams like the ones we developed in Figures 11.7 and 11.8, the analyst reviewed his understanding of the problems with the PMs. This gave each of the PMs the opportunity to correct or confirm what the analyst had done.

One point the analyst raised during this review concerned the REGION object. The analyst wanted to be sure the PMs did not need any data about a region. When the product managers concurred that they needed no additional data, the analyst decided to drop the REGION object. Thus modified, the object diagrams seemed acceptable, and the analyst proceeded with the next step, translating the object definitions into relation definitions.

RELATION DEFINITIONS

The Information Center analyst at KDK Appliances followed the guidelines you learned in Chapter 7 for transforming objects into relations. We will first examine the INVOICE object.

INVOICE

INVOICE is a hybrid object because the line-item composite group contains an object property. Thus, the INVOICE object will be represented by several relations. One will contain general information about an invoice. Another will contain the line items associated with the invoice. The relations have a one-to-many relationship and both relations are mandatory (see Figure 11.9). The formats of the two relations are

INVOICE (<u>Number</u>, Date, Salesperson.Number, Dealer.Number, Total)
LINE-ITEM (<u>Invoice.Number</u>, <u>Line-item-number</u>, Product.Number,
      Quantity, Extended-price)

An example of the INVOICE and LINE-ITEM relations is shown in Figure 11.10. Notice that the key for INVOICE (Invoice.Number) is part of the key for LINE-ITEM. This must be done because INVOICE has a composite.

Three foreign keys appear in the INVOICE and LINE-ITEM relations, namely Salesperson.Number, Dealer.Number, and Product.Number. These keys are needed to estab-

FIGURE 11.9
Relationship between INVOICE
and LINE-ITEM

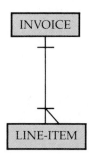

Number	Date	Salesperson. Number	Dealer. Number	Total
10982	03/12/91	8555	2425	38549.05
75214	03/12/91	1755	4528	60472.95
63911	03/15/91	5762	6178	12249.92
41200	03/18/91	5762	6644	147997.70

INVOICE relation

Invoice. Number	Line-item-number	Product. Number	Quantity	Extended-price
10982	001	14365	50	14999.50
10982	002	74961	30	17999.70
10982	003	87033	15	5549.85
75214	001	87214	25	4874.75
75214	002	87224	100	25999.00
75214	003	87033	80	29599.20
63911	001	56271	3	3749.97
63911	002	80911	5	8499.95
41200	001	15965	200	129998.00
41200	002	74961	30	17999.70

LINE-ITEM relation

FIGURE 11.10
Sample data in INVOICE and LINE-ITEM relations

lish the one-to-many relationships between DEALER and INVOICE, between SALES-PERSON and INVOICE, and between PRODUCT and INVOICE. Consider these objects.

DEALER and SALESPERSON

The DEALER object in Figure 11.7 is a compound object because it contains multivalued object properties, namely INVOICE and ADVERTISEMENT. There is a 1:N relationship in both cases.

Similarly, the SALESPERSON object in Figure 11.7 is a compound object. It has a 1:N relationship with INVOICE. In Figure 11.11 we have added the DEALER and SALESPERSON relations to the diagram from Figure 11.9. The relationships between SALESPERSON and INVOICE and between DEALER and INVOICE are mandatory-to-optional. This means that an invoice must be associated with a salesperson and a dealer, but that a salesperson or a dealer does not have to have any invoices. The relation formats are

> DEALER (<u>Number</u>, Name, Address-1, Address-2, City, State/Province,
>   ZIP/Postal-code, Telephone)
> SALESPERSON (<u>Number</u>, Name, Region)

Sample data for the DEALER and SALESPERSON relations is shown in Figure 11.12. Following the guidelines established in Chapter 7, the 1:N relationship between DEALER and INVOICE is represented by placing the key field of DEALER (Dealer.Number) in the INVOICE relation. Similar comments hold for the relationship between SALESPERSON and INVOICE.

PRODUCT

Another object in Figure 11.7 is PRODUCT. According to the object diagram, an N:1 relationship exists between a product and an invoice. More specifically, an N:1 relationship exists between a line item and a product. A certain product—say, a dishwasher—

FIGURE 11.11

Result of adding DEALER and SALESPERSON relations to Figure 11.9.

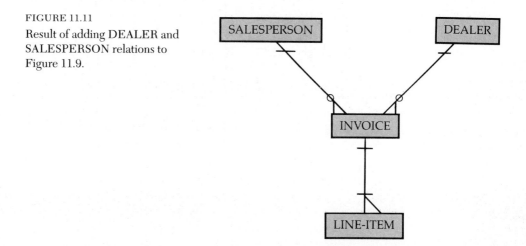

SALESPERSON relation

Number	Name	Region
1043	Ronald Hunt	1
2711	John Eberle	5
8555	Margaret Gosselin	2
5762	Paula Jasinski	4
1755	Hans Jensen	5
6042	Lawrence Smithers	1
2814	Maxine Whittier	3

SALESPERSON relation

DEALER relation

Number	Name	Address-1	Address-2	City	State	ZIP	Phone
6178	Gem Appliances	1005 Farmington Ave.	-0-	W. Hartford	CT	06754	(203) 555-4312
2425	S. K. Lafferty	Prestige Park	Building 43	E. Hartford	CT	06832	(203) 555-6789
6624	Rich Appliance Co.	17 Whiting Street	Suite 4143	New Britain	CT	06588	(203) 555-6609
0212	Lisbon Furniture & Appliances	692 Ellington Road	-0-	South Windsor	CT	06551	(203)677-4582
9356	Gallo's Appliance Outlet	P.O. Box 344	264 Park Road	W. Hartford	CT	06431	(203) 549-6772
4516	United Kitchens	114 Cummington Street	-0-	Cummington	MA	07231	(617) 438-0065
9101	Parks Department Store	21 Main Street	-0-	Worcester	MA	07488	(617) 756-2295
6644	J & S Department Store	75 Rock Road	-0-	Plymouth	MA	02787	(617) 555-9734
4528	Sounds Terrific	1433 W. Northeast Highway	Suite 5678	Boston	MA	07665	(617) 885-4000

DEALER relation

FIGURE 11.12
Sample data for SALESPERSON and DEALER relations

FIGURE 11.13

PRODUCT relation added to
diagram in Figure 11.11

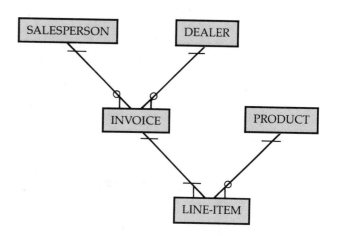

can be found on line items from various invoices issued to many different dealers. This
can be represented relational as shown in Figure 11.13.

The relational format for the PRODUCT relation is

PRODUCT (<u>Number</u>, Name, Description, Price)

The 1:N relationship between PRODUCT and LINE-ITEM has been established by
placing Product.Number in the LINE-ITEM relation. Sample data for the PRODUCT
relation can be found in Figure 11.14.

ADVERTISEMENT and AD-COPY

Two more objects, ADVERTISEMENT and AD-COPY (see Figure 11.8), need to be
transformed into relations. A dealer can share the cost of several advertisements, but any
advertisement features at most one dealer. Thus, a 1:N relationship exists between dealer
and advertisement.

Similarly, one ad-copy can be run several times in many newspapers. Consequently, a
1:N relationship exists between an ad-copy and an advertisement. Adding these relations
to the ones in Figure 11.13, we arrive at the result in Figure 11.15.

The next relationship we need to incorporate is the one between PRODUCT and
AD-COPY. Each product can be featured in several ads, and each ad can specify several
products. Thus, we have an N:M relationship between PRODUCT and AD-COPY.

Recall from Chapter 7 that many-to-many relationships are incorporated into a relation model by establishing an intersection relation containing only keys from the two
other relations. In this case, an intersection relation called PRODUCT-AD is defined.
Each row contains a product number and an ad-name. The PRODUCT-AD relation is
added to the ones from Figure 11.15. The result is found in Figure 11.16.

The formats for these three new relations are

AD-COPY (<u>Ad-name</u>, Agency, First-run-date)
ADVERTISEMENT (<u>Publication</u>, <u>Date</u>, <u>Ad-name</u>, Cost, Share-percent,
       Dealer.Number)
PRODUCT-AD (<u>Ad-Name</u>, <u>Product.Number</u>)

Type/number	Name	Description	Price
392761	Electric range—white	Electric range	$299.99
393861	Electric range—white	Electric range; self-clean; window	$679.99
393863	Electric range—toast	Electric range; self-clean; window	$689.99
393867	Electric range—avocado	Electric range; self-clean; window	$689.99
370351	Gas range—white	Gas range; 21-inch	$279.99
370353	Gas range—toast	Gas range; 21-inch	$289.99
374961	Gas range—white	Gas range; 36-inch; continuous clean	$599.99
374963	Gas range—toast	Gas range; 36-inch; continuous clean	$599.99
374976	Gas range—avocado	Gas range; 36-inch; continuous clean	$599.99
380551	Fifth-burner kit	Gas range 5th burner to replace griddle	$19.99
787214	Mini-mike	Compact microwave oven	$194.99
787224	Mini-mike	Programmable compact microwave oven	$259.99
787755	Mity-mike	Programmable solid-state full-size microwave oven	$344.99
787033	Mity-mike	#87755 with carousel	$369.99
415965	Ultra wash	Electronic dishwasher	$649.99
414365	Dishwasher	18-inch; 2-level dishwasher	$299.99
417375	Dishwasher—P	Dishwasher-portable	$409.99
416037	Dishwasher—sp	Space saver dishwasher	$249.99
556681	Porcelain-plus	Refrigerator; porcelain-on-steel; 25.8 cu ft	$1,599.99
556271	Quiet Cold	Frost-free refrigerator; ice maker	$1,249.99
580911	Kitchen Valet	Refrigerator; all-electronic; customized panels	$1,699.99
580922	KDK Limited Edition	Refrigerator; frost-free; special use compartments	$2,549.99
593252	Mini-fridge	Compact refrigerator	$99.00
593286	Mini-fridge	Compact refrigerator/freezer	$174.99
594605	Compact-fridge	3.6 cu ft compact refrigerator	$219.99
594911	Compact-fridge	#94605 with push-button defrost	$299.99

FIGURE 11.14
Sample data for PRODUCT relation

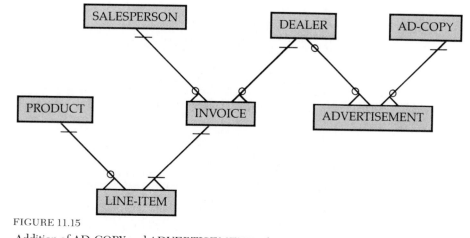

FIGURE 11.15

Addition of AD-COPY and ADVERTISEMENT relations to those in Figure 11.13

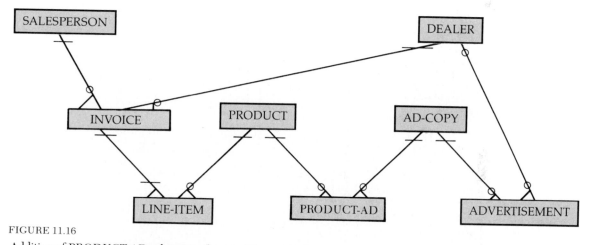

FIGURE 11.16

Addition of PRODUCT-AD relation to those in Figure 11.15

Sample data for the **AD-COPY** and **ADVERTISEMENT** relations appears in Figure 11.17 and for **PRODUCT-AD** in Figure 11.18.

KDK CASE SUMMARY

All of the objects identified earlier can be constructed from data stored in the relations we defined. Reports summarizing product sales on various criteria (such as salesperson, region, and dealer), reports analyzing advertising, and much more can be readily extracted from the database.

Ad-name	Agency	First-run-date
Dishwashers	On-Target Ads	03/10/91
Free Time	Haskins	02/15/91
Microwaves	On-Target Ads	03/12/91
Presidents	Haskins	02/03/91
Ranges	On-Target Ads	02/01/91
St. Paddy's Sale	J&J Marketing	03/12/91
The Bachelor	J&J Marketing	01/04/91
The Fridge	Haskins	02/01/91
Ultra	J&J Marketing	03/10/91
Working Woman	Haskins	03/01/91

AD-COPY relation

Publication	Date	Ad-name	Cost	Share%	Dealer.Num
Herald	02/01/91	Ranges	300.00	25.	6644
Free Press	02/01/91	Ranges	320.00	33.	6178
Free Press	02/03/91	Presidents	450.00	50.	4528
Sentinel	02/15/91	Free Time	400.00	33.	6178
Herald	02/17/91	Free Time	350.00	50.	6178
Herald	02/19/91	Ranges	300.00	40.	4516
Sentinel	03/10/91	Dishwashers	400.00	50.	9101
Times	03/10/91	Ultra	250.00	33.	6644
Courier	03/11/91	Ultra	280.00	40.	0212
Sentinel	03/12/91	Working Woman	500.00	40.	9356
Times	03/14/91	St. Paddy's Sale	600.00	33.	6644
Times	03/14/91	The Bachelor	550.00	25.	4516
Herald	03/15/91	Ultra	250.00	40.	6644

ADVERTISEMENT relation

FIGURE 11.17
Sample data for AD-COPY and ADVERTISEMENT relations

Ad-name	Product.Number		Ad-name	Product.Number
Dishwashers	17375		Ranges	93861
Dishwashers	16037		Ranges	93863
Dishwashers	14365		Ranges	93867
Free Time	70351		Ranges	74967
Free Time	16037		Ranges	74963
Free Time	92761		Ranges	80551
Microwaves	87033		St. Paddy's Sale	15965
Microwaves	87224		St. Paddy's Sale	93867
Microwaves	87755		St. Paddy's Sale	94605
Microwaves	87214		St. Paddy's Sale	74967
Presidents	93286		The Bachelor	15965
Presidents	80551		The Bachelor	87755
Presidents	93861		The Bachelor	93867
Presidents	74961		The Fridge	56681
Presidents	80922		The Fridge	80922
Presidents	14365		Ultra	15965
Presidents	93252		Working Woman	93867
Ranges	92761		Working Woman	87033
Ranges	74961		Working Woman	87755

FIGURE 11.18
Sample data for PRODUCT-AD relation

The next step is to actually implement the database structure: define tables, fields, and constraints; assign passwords; establish security procedures; and allocate file space. Following that, the analyst will test the database structure by downloading some sample data from the mainframe and making various queries. Finally, when no errors are found in testing, KDK can download sales data from the mainframe computer and begin to use the newly established database in the Information Center.

Some programs need to be written in COBOL and tested before they can be used to produce the product managers' reports. Inquiries can be made against the database using SQL. The relational database product used in the Information Center at KDK Appliances is DB2, which we will examine next.

DB2: The Product

Database2 (DB2) is IBM's relational database management system for large mainframe computers that run IBM's MVS operating system. Another popular IBM DBMS, called IMS/DB, is based on the hierarchical (DL/I), rather than the relational, model. IMS/DB is an older, and therefore more established, database product that was already firmly installed in many companies before the development of the relational model. To allow its customers flexibility in their choice of DBMS products, IBM designed DB2 to coexist with DL/I. Thus, DB2 allows the same application program to access both DL/I and DB2 database data. User organizations can take advantage of the newer relational product without having to abandon or convert all of their hierarchical applications. You will study DL/I in Chapter 12.

KEY FEATURES

DB2 uses SQL to perform all database operations: data definition, data access, data manipulation, and authorization functions. Recall from Chapter 10 that SQL is a high-level language used for relational database processing. DB2 is one product that incorporates this flexible and powerful language.

SQL statements can be entered by a user at a computer terminal. This mode employs an interactive terminal interface called DB2I. SQL statements can also be embedded in application programs written in assembler language, COBOL, PL/I, and FORTRAN. Later in this chapter we will present examples of both interactive commands and COBOL programs containing SQL instructions.

DB2 is well suited for the multi-user environment. It allows users to dynamically create and modify tables, views, and other database structures, to dynamically define and modify database security parameters, and to execute various database utilities online. Most functions can be performed—within certain limits—even while other users are employing the database.

Especially important in the multi-user environment is the mechanism for recovery in the event of a system failure. DB2 includes built-in features for such important services as activity logging and recover, thus facilitating failure recovery. And because DB2 is just one of several subsystems that may be in operation at the time of a system failure, its recovery features are coordinated with those of other subsystems that may be present, such as CICS or other CCPs.

DB2 enables a person—database designer, database administrator, or end-user—to define and manipulate various **constructs.**[1] Constructs include databases, tables, views, and indexes, to name a few. In the next section, we will examine DB2 constructs and learn some SQL data definition (DDL) statements.

---

[1]IBM uses the term *object* instead of *construct*. In this book, we have been using the term *object* to refer to semantic objects—things in the users' work environment. To avoid confusion, we will use the word *construct* where IBM uses *object*.

DB2 DATA DEFINITION LANGUAGE

In this section we will briefly describe each DB2 construct to help you envision the DB2 environment. DB2 constructs include resources that application programmers (and sometimes end-users) need to understand, such as tables and views, as well as resources that database designers and DBAs need to understand, such as storage groups and table spaces. We will also present SQL statements to define several objects for KDK Appliances' Information Center database.[2]

The DB2 constructs we will examine are tables, views, table spaces, indexes, index spaces, databases, and storage groups. Although a few other DB2 constructs exist, they are not important to our discussion and therefore will not be presented.

Tables

Like all products based on the relational model, DB2 stores data in what the user sees as **tables** with rows and columns. You can use SQL to retrieve and change data in a table, to insert and delete rows, and to add new columns to an existing table.

Views

A DB2 **view** is a virtual table. It is derived from one or several base tables and is not physically stored in the database (although table data is). Views can be accessed and manipulated much like tables, using many of the same SQL data manipulation statements used for tables. Often a user cannot tell whether he or she is processing a table or a view. Examples of a base table and a view of it are illustrated in Figure 11.19.

Database users, including application programmers and end-users, need to know only about tables and views. Database designers and DBAs need to understand not only tables and views, but also physical database storage. This includes table spaces, indexes, index spaces, data bases, and storage groups.

Table Spaces

A **table space** is a collection of one or more VSAM data sets, or files, used to store database data on magnetic disk. Thus, tables are stored in table spaces (see Figure 11.20). A table space can hold approximately 64 billion bytes of data, although that size is not practical.

Table spaces are DB2's recoverable units. If the database system crashes, the table spaces will be recovered, not the databases or individual tables. Perhaps you can see why huge table spaces (such as 64 billion bytes of data), although theoretically possible, are in reality seldom defined. Recovery of a table space that large would be very difficult and time consuming.

---

[2]DB2 allows separate passwords for *system administrators* and *database administrators*. A system administrator can access and change constructs for all databases on the DB2 system. A database administrator is restricted to a particular database.

FIGURE 11.19
Example of base table and view

Name	Salary	Hire-date	Office	Extension
Walker	21800	12/88	321	246
Berg	36500	10/85	411	647
Dean	42900	02/91	308	795
Hsiu	36500	09/88	307	581
Cameratta	40000	03/83	419	669

a. EMPLOYEES (base table)

Name	Office	Extension
Walker	321	246
Berg	411	647
Dean	308	795
Hsiu	307	581
Cameratta	419	669

b. EMPLOYEE-DIRECTORY (view of EMPLOYEES)

A table space can be either a **simple table space** or a **partitioned table space.** A simple table space can hold one or more tables, whereas a partitioned table space holds exactly one table.

The DBA would probably define a partitioned table space for a very large table. Each partition would then contain a part of the table based on the range of values in one or more columns. For example, each partition might contain taxpayer data based on Social Security Number. Partitions are independent of one another and can be reorganized and recovered individually.

Simple table spaces might contain several small, related tables. For example, the DBA might establish one table space for each user department and use each table space to store all tables pertinent to a particular department. Some applications require exclusive use of a table, so they issue a LOCK TABLE statement. When this happens, the entire table space is locked, preventing other tables in it from being accessed. If separate table spaces "belong" to individual user departments, it is less likely that one user will interfere with another user's processing by locking him or her out.

Indexes

Indexes are used to reduce table access time. An index places table data in logical sequence, regardless of its physical sequence. Multiple indexes can be defined for a single table. Consider the table in Figure 11.21a. (In this example, rows are numbered to represent relative locations within the table. In practice, record addressing is far more

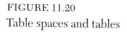

FIGURE 11.20
Table spaces and tables

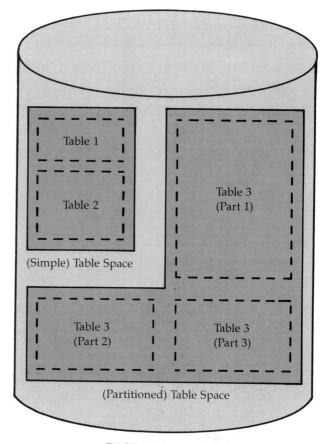

DASD (Disk) Volume

complex, as discussed in Appendix B.) The rows might be stored in the sequence in which they appear in the figure. Now suppose that a user frequently needs to access the data by customer name. Use of the index illustrated in Figure 11.21b makes finding a specific name, and the location of that row in the CUSTOMER table, very fast because the index is arranged in alphabetical order on Name.

Similarly, suppose another user frequently accesses the table by customer number. The index in Figure 11.21c would be useful in that case. That index also ensures unique customer numbers; we will learn how later in this chapter. Of course, the table in Figure 11.21 is very small, so the effect of using an index could be insignificant. In fact, using indexes on such a small table would probably downgrade performance. Not only does index searching require time, but every addition or deletion to the CUSTOMER table would also require updates to the indexes. But if the table included, say, 800,000 records, then indexes would improve processing time.

Subject to concurrent processing restrictions, indexes can be defined at any time. An index is a physical construct, completely separate from the table to which it is related. As

FIGURE 11.21
Indexes on CUSTOMER table

Row#	Cust#	Name	Credit-limit	ZIPcode
1	10	Smith	3000	06413
2	20	Jones	3000	95060
3	30	Whittaker	2000	07814
4	40	Murphy	3000	62200
5	50	Wang	3000	08142
6	60	Youngblood	2000	62200
7	70	Jones	2000	95060

a. CUSTOMER table

Name	Row#
Jones	2
Jones	7
Murphy	4
Smith	1
Wang	5
Whittaker	3
Youngblood	6

b. INDEX on Name

Cust#	Row#
10	1
20	2
30	3
40	4
50	5
60	6
70	7

c. Index on Cust#

mentioned, DB2 automatically maintains an index once it is created. In fact, after an index has been defined for a table, DB2 decides without any direction from a user or a programmer when, if ever, to use it. In other words, once an index has been defined, neither a user nor an application programmer actually references it.

Index Space

An **index space** is an area of disk storage in which DB2 stores an index (see Figure 11.22). When an index is created, DB2 automatically allocates an index space for it.

Data Bases

IBM uses the term **data base** (two words) to define a collection of DB2 tables and indexes and the storage areas that hold them. Of course, several DB2 data bases can exist on the same computer system. DB2 is designed to use a data base as an operational unit.

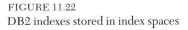

FIGURE 11.22
DB2 indexes stored in index spaces

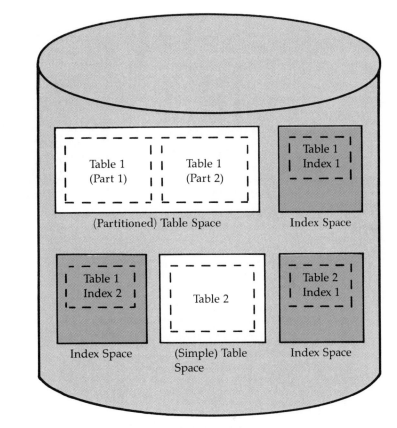

DASD (Disk) Volume

This means that it can *start* a data base (make it available), *stop* a data base (make it unavailable), and assign *authorization* to use a data base (allow users to access the data).

Of course, users and application programmers do not deal directly with data bases any more than they deal with table spaces or indexes. Users and application programmers refer only to tables and views. They are shielded from needing to know anything about the underlying database structures.

Storage Groups

A **storage group** is a group of disk volumes on which DB2 allocates space for user databases (see Figure 11.23). DB2 manages its own data set allocation unless the system administrator overrides this feature. This means that DB2 keeps track of available disk space and locates tables, indexes, and other database constructs in that space. It also releases disk space for use when it becomes available, such as when an index or a table is dropped. The system administrator can also define, locate, and delete data sets. Sometimes this is done when tuning, or optimizing, the database system.

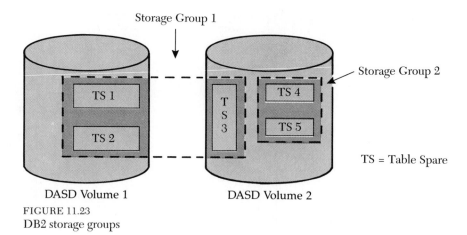

FIGURE 11.23
DB2 storage groups

USING DB2 TO CREATE TABLES, VIEWS, AND INDEXES

SQL data definition language (DDL) as implemented in DB2 allows us to define various DB2 constructs. In this section and the ones that follow, we will illustrate SQL DDL by defining several constructs—tables, views, and indexes—for the Information Center database at KDK Appliances.

Defining a Table

DB2 employs the SQL CREATE statement to define constructs. In Chapter 10 we examined only the data manipulation functions of SQL. In this chapter we will add data definition statements as well. Before defining a table, you should decide on the names of all the columns, their data types and lengths, and whether you wish to allow null values.

Allowable DB2 data types for field values are summarized in Figure 11.24. A **null value** is a field value that is unknown or not applicable. A null value is different from a zero or a blank value. For example, a customer balance of zero is different from an unknown customer balance. You can prohibit null values from specific columns when you create a table. For example, a key column should not be allowed to have null values.

Consider the SALESPERSON relation for which sample data appears in Figure 11.12. The following CREATE statement defines it:

```
CREATE TABLE SALESPERSON
        (NUMBER        CHAR (4)         NOT NULL,
         NAME          CHAR (20)        NOT NULL,
         REGION        DECIMAL (1))
```

This statement creates the PRODUCT relation for the sample data shown in Figure 11.14:

```
CREATE TABLE PRODUCT
        TYPE            CHAR (1)        NOT NULL,
        NUMBER          CHAR (5)        NOT NULL,
        NAME            CHAR (25)       NOT NULL,
        DESCRIPTION     CHAR (50),
        PRICE           DECIMAL (7,2)   NOT NULL)
```

Defining a View

The CREATE statement can also be used to define a view. It includes a SELECT statement that specifies the view. The following CREATE statement defines for the PRODUCT relation a view that includes only product numbers and prices:

```
CREATE VIEW PRICELIST
     AS    SELECT     NUMBER,    PRICE
           FROM       PRODUCT
```

Now the view, PRICELIST, can be manipulated in exactly the same way as a table. Data is retrieved from a view using the same SQL statements we use for a table. If the view is a subset of rows or columns of a single table, it can be used to update base table data. However, views that are the result of a join operation cannot be used to update table data.

This next statement creates a view that contains only those rows in the PRODUCT relation for refrigerators (the Type field contains a 5):

```
CREATE VIEW REFRIGERATORS
     AS    SELECT     *
           FROM       PRODUCT
           WHERE      TYPE  =  '5'
```

By specifying SELECT ∘ we include all of the columns. By specifying WHERE TYPE = '5' we include only rows for refrigerators. This view can be used to update base table data.

Consider a third view. Assume that KDK wants one particular user to have only restricted access to the DEALER and ADVERTISEMENT relations (see Figures 11.12

INTEGER	31-bit signed binary values
SMALLINT	15-bit signed binary values
FLOAT	Floating point values
DECIMAL(p,q)	Packed decimal values of p (1 to 15) digits; a number of decimal places (q) to the right of the decimal point may be specified
CHAR(n)	Fixed length text data n (1 to 254) characters long
VARCHAR(n)	Variable length text data up to n (1 to 32674) characters

FIGURE 11.24
Some allowable DB2 data types

and 11.17). This user should be able to access only those dealers who have participated in shared advertising. We might define an appropriate joined view like this:

```
CREATE VIEW ACTIVEDEALER
        AS    SELECT     DEALER.NUMBER, DEALER.NAME,
                         TELEPHONE, ADVERTISEMENT.DATE,
                         COST, SHARE-PERCENT
              FROM       DEALER, ADVERTISEMENT
              WHERE      DEALER.NUMBER =
                         ADVERTISEMENT.DEALER-NUMBER
```

Since this view is based on a join, it cannot be used to update base table data.

Defining an Index

Indexes are usually defined and dropped by the DBA, or system administrator. As mentioned earlier, neither users nor application programmers ever reference an index. DB2 decides when to use an index and which one to use.

One reason to use an index, as described in the previous section, is to increase processing speed. Several indexes can be defined for one table, theoretically allowing rapid access on many different fields.

Another reason for defining an index on a table, however, is that an index can force the uniqueness of values of a column (or multiple columns). For example, the dealer number in KDK's DEALER relation must be unique (although dealer name, address, ZIP, and so forth do not need to be unique). The way to establish the uniqueness of the dealer number field is to issue this CREATE statement:

```
CREATE     UNIQUE INDEX XDEALER
           ON DEALER (DLRNUM)
```

In the next example, since UNIQUE is not specified, the resulting index might include duplicate telephone numbers. Incidentally, the index value is assumed to be ascending (ASC) unless otherwise specified (DESC):

```
CREATE     INDEX XDLRPHONE
           ON DEALER (PHONE DESC)
```


Using DB2 to Change a Table

Often when we design a database, we are unable to anticipate *all* of the user's needs. And even if we could, user needs change over time. As a result, we sometimes need to modify our database design. Notice that we are not talking about changing the data stored in tables (that happens all the time, of course), but rather the structure of tables themselves.

DB2 offers two ways to modify table specifications: by dropping and then re-creating the table and by using the ALTER statement. The ALTER statement can be used only for adding a column to an existing table and for changing validation routines.

To remove a column, change a column's data type or length, or change whether null values are allowed, you must drop the table and re-create it. We will see how to drop a table in the next section. For now, just know that when you drop a table, you lose the table data as well as all views and indexes based on the table. To do this, you would follow these steps:

1. Define a new table with all the changes and a different name.
2. Copy table data from the old table to the new one.
3. Define all indexes on the new table.
4. Drop the old table (this loses all the view of it, too).
5. Restore the original table name as a view of the new table. This allows applications that once referenced the old table to remain unchanged because the new view is processed exactly the same as the old table.
6. Define views like the ones defined for the old table. These can be exact duplicates of the old views because you can base a view on another view, just as you can base a view on a table. (Of course, if a view contains a column that has just been dropped, then the view is no longer valid.)
7. Authorize users to use the new table and views.

Clearly, this type of database modification is done only by a DBA or someone who is authorized by the DBA.

The second option for changing a table design uses the ALTER statement. With it we can add a column to an existing table. For instance, suppose we wanted to add a salary column to the SALESPERSON relation. The following statement would accomplish this:

```
ALTER      TABLE SALESPERSON
           (ADD SALARY DECIMAL (7,2))
```

Using DB2 to Delete Tables and Views

Periodically, the DBA needs to eliminate tables from the database. Users are rarely authorized to do this, because they could inadvertently delete data they do not realize is needed by another user. In the previous section, we saw how the DBA might need to delete a table in order to change its structure.

Deleting a table erases not only the table, but also all dependent views and indexes. Thus, dropping a table should not be done hastily.

To delete the ADVERTISEMENT table from its database, KDK's DBA would issue the following DROP statement:

```
DROP TABLE ADVERTISEMENT
```

The table and all its data would be deleted from the table space, and all indexes and views associated with it would also be erased.

The DROP statement can be used to delete views. The DBA might authorize a user to create views and then delete them when they are no longer useful. It is unlikely that a user would be authorized to drop views that might be used by anyone else, however. That responsibility (and control) should remain with the DBA. We could delete the ACTIVEDEALER view by issuing this statement:

```
DROP      VIEW ACTIVEDEALER
```

Any applications that used that view (or views based on that view) would no longer work.

DB2 Creation Facilities Summary

DB2 allows the DBA or user to define, modify, and delete various database constructs—tables, views, table spaces, indexes, index spaces, data bases, and storage groups. Users and application programmers are concerned only with tables and views. In addition to tables and views, the DBA and database designers need to understand the underlying physical structures and database storage.

DB2 DATA MANIPULATION LANGUAGE: SQL

Some differences exist in DB2 statements for the interactive user and for the application programmer. The differences exist because of differences in the user's and the programmer's environments. The interactive user wants results to be immediately displayed on a screen. The application programmer wants the DBMS to place values in columns and rows into program variables. We will address these issues in this section.

Interactive Data Manipulation

Interactive DB2, or DB2I, supports all of the SQL statements described in Chapter 10. The format is the same as shown in that chapter, and we will not repeat the discussion here. The user simply types the commands as shown in Chapter 10 at the DB2I prompt.

Accessing DB2 from COBOL Application Programs

DB2 application programs can be written in COBOL, PL/I, FORTRAN, C, and assembler language. SQL statements can be embedded in programs written in any of these languages. The examples used in this text will be embedded in COBOL programs.

As shown in Figure 11.25, all application programs that access DB2 must first be processed by the DB2 **precompiler.** The precompiler analyzes program source statements and processes those that are flagged SQL statements (you'll see how later). The precompiler inserts into the program required **table formats,** which are already written in the host language and stored on disk. It also builds for each SQL statement a **data base request module,** or DBRM, which it stores for later use. And the precompiler replaces SQL statements with host-language call statements to access the DBRMs. As illustrated in Figure 11.25, the modified source code is then input to a standard language compiler for normal compilation.

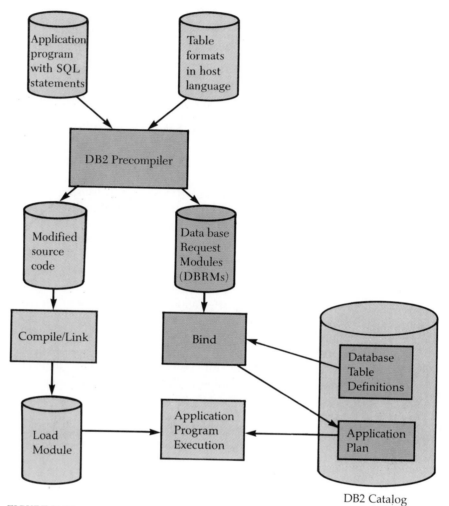

FIGURE 11.25
Steps in application program development with DB2

The Bind process uses the DBRMs, database table definitions, available indexes, and other database data to determine the access paths for each SQL request. It stores these in the database catalog as an **application plan,** which is loaded when the first SQL call is executed.

For the DB2 precompiler to recognize statements intended for it, all SQL statements are embedded in keywords. Specifically, every SQL statement is preceded by the keywords EXEC SQL and followed by the keyword END-EXEC. In COBOL, the keyword END-EXEC is followed by a period unless the SQL statement is located in an IF statement. The general format of a DB2 SQL statement in a COBOL program is

```
EXEC SQL   statement        END-EXEC
```

Only one statement can be included between the keywords. Multiple SQL statements require multiple EXEC SQL ... END-EXEC statements.

DB2 SQL statements are embedded in the DATA DIVISION and the PROCE-DURE DIVISION.

SQL Statements in the DATA DIVISION

Two types of statements are embedded in the DATA DIVISION. The first describes data items that are used to pass **database data** between the application program and DB2. The second type describes **system data** that is shared by the application program and DB2.

Figure 11.26 shows part of a COBOL program that processes the SALESPERSON table defined earlier. The DATA DIVISION includes data item definitions for all three columns of SALESPERSON. These columns have been renamed. NAME is now SALESPERSON-NAME, NUMBER is SALESPERSON-NUM, and REGION is SALES-REGION. The correct correspondence of names will be established in the PRO-CEDURE DIVISION.

The data types and lengths of data items do match, although COBOL uses a different vocabulary than SQL does. For example, when we created the table using SQL, we defined SPNUM as CHAR(4). The equivalent COBOL definition for SALESPERSON-NUM is PICTURE X(4).

All data items that DB2 and the application program share are grouped together. This enables the precompiler to identify them. (We show these statements in the WORK-ING-STORAGE SECTION, but they could be located elsewhere in the DATA DIVI-SION.) The group of data item definitions is preceded by the DB2 keywords BEGIN

```
DATA DIVISION.
WORKING-STORAGE SECTION.
EXEC SQL   BEGIN DECLARE SECTION     END-EXEC.
01    SALESPERSON.
      05    SALESPERSON-NUM        PICTURE X(4).
      05    SALESPERSON-NAME       PICTURE X(20).
      05    SALES-REGION           PICTURE 9   COMP-3.
EXEC SQL   END DECLARE SECTION     END-EXEC.
EXEC SQL   INCLUDE SQLCA   END-EXEC.
PROCEDURE DIVISION.
      MOVE '5762' TO SALESPERSON-NUM.
      EXEC SQL
           SELECT NAME, REGION
           INTO :SALESPERSON-NAME,  :SALES-REGION
           FROM SALESPERSON
           WHERE NUMBER = :SALESPERSON-NUM
      END-EXEC.
```

FIGURE 11.26
SQL statements embedded in COBOL program

DECLARE SECTION and is terminated with the message END DECLARE SEC-
TION. In Figure 11.26, the definition of SALESPERSON is found in the DECLARE
SECTION.

As you just learned, the DECLARE SECTION is used to define data items that will
be used to transfer database data between the application program and DB2. In addition
to database data, the application program and the DBMS also need to share system data.
For example, after each SQL statement is executed, DB2 sets a return code that indicates whether an error occurred. Both DB2 and the application program need access to
this return code.

System data is defined in the program with the DB2 SQL message INCLUDE
SQLCA (which stands for SQL Communications Area). When the precompiler processes this INCLUDE message, it inserts the data definitions seen in Figure 11.27a into
the application program.

For brevity, Figure 11.27b describes only a few of the data items in SQLCA. Knowing
all of them would contribute little to your understanding of DB2. The one data item that
you need to understand is SQLCODE.

SQLCODE is set by DB2 after each SQL command is executed. If the command is
executed normally, SQLCODE is set to zero. If an unusual but normal condition occurs,
SQLCODE is set to a positive value. For example, end of data is indicated by the value
100. If an abnormal, unexpected condition occurs, SQLCODE is set to a negative value.
Insufficient VSAM file space is an example of an abnormal unexpected event.

SQL Statements in the PROCEDURE DIVISION

SQL statements in the PROCEDURE DIVISION instruct DB2 to perform some action.
For example, the SELECT statement in Figure 11.26 will cause DB2 to extract from the
database the name and region of salesperson 5762 and to place those values in the data
items called SALESPERSON-NAME and SALES-REGION. This SQL statement is
almost identical to the format followed when writing interactive SQL commands. The
exception is the INTO clause that tells DB2 the name of the **host variable** (or variables)
into which DB2 will place the value(s) it obtains from the database.

One problem for the DB2 precompiler is distinguishing between data names defined
in the database and those defined locally within the application program. If all names are
unique, then it can process the statements correctly. However, it is impossible to guarantee that the application programmer will always choose data names not already used
in the database. Consequently, a colon (:) precedes the names of program variables used
within any embedded SQL statement.

As stated in Chapter 9, COBOL (as well as many other programming languages) is
designed to process data one record at a time. A typical COBOL program retrieves one
record, processes it, retrieves the next one, processes it, and so forth, until all the records
have been handled. DB2, however, processes tables. That is to say, a DB2 SELECT
statement always returns a table of data. (Sometimes the table contains only one row, as
in the example in Figure 11.26.) This distinction between COBOL file processing and
DB2 relation processing is important for the application programmer who might be
tempted to think that SQL statements correspond to simple READ and WRITE statements. They do not.

```
01      SQLCA.
        05      SQLCAID         PICTURE  X(8).
        05      SQLCABC         PICTURE  S9(9)  COMPUTATIONAL.
        05      SQLCODE         PICTURE  S9(9)  COMPUTATIONAL.
        05      SQLERRM
                49    SQLERRML  PICTURE  S9(4)  COMPUTATIONAL.
                49    SQLERRMC  PICTURE  X(70).
        05      SQLERRP         PICTURE  X(8).
        05      SQLERRD         OCCURS  6  TIMES
                                PICTURE  S9(9)  COMPUTATIONAL.
        05      SQLWARN.
                10    SQLWARN0  PICTURE  X(1).
                10    SQLWARN1  PICTURE  X(1).
                10    SQLWARN2  PICTURE  X(1).
                10    SQLWARN3  PICTURE  X(1).
                10    SQLWARN4  PICTURE  X(1).
                10    SQLWARN5  PICTURE  X(1).
                10    SQLWARN6  PICTURE  X(1).
                10    SQLWARN7  PICTURE  X(1).
        05      SQLEXT          PICTURE  X(8).
```

a. COBOL description of SQLCA

Data-item	Content
SQLCODE	Return code. Set by DB2 after each command. Zero indicates successful operation. Positive value indicates normal condition (such as end of data). Negative value indicates abnormal error.
SQLERRM	Error message. Set when SQLCODE is less than 0.
SQLERRP	Name of DB2 routine detecting error. Set when SQLCODE is less than 0.
SQLERRD	DB2 system status.
SQLWARN	Warning flags. Set for conditions such as data-item truncation (receiving data-item too small), null values encountered when processing SUM, AVG, MIN, or MAX, recovery from deadlock, and so forth.

b. Content of selected SQLCA data-items

FIGURE 11.27
DB2 Communications Area

The application programmer would be better served by thinking of DB2 as a vehicle for retrieving an entire input data set, or pseudofile, from the database. Then the data is processed one row at a time. To do this, we define a **cursor** within the application program.

A cursor is a pointer that operates on a SELECT statement. The cursor indicates the row to be processed within the pseudofile generated by the SELECT statement. In Figure 11.28, for example, the cursor CURRENT is defined to operate on the SELECT statement that will retrieve the names of all salespeople in region 5. In subsequent state-

```
PROCEDURE DIVISION.
      .
      .
      .
    MOVE 5 TO SALES-REGION.
    EXEC SQL DECLARE CURRENT CURSOR FOR
         SELECT NAME FROM SALESPERSON
         WHERE REGION = : SALES-REGION
    END EXEC.
      .
      .
      .
    EXEC SQL OPEN CURRENT END-EXEC.
    EXEC SQL FETCH CURRENT INTO : SALESPERSON-NAME END-EXEC.
    PERFORM PROCESS-FETCH UNTIL SQLCODE NOT = 0.
    EXEC SQL CLOSE CURRENT END-EXEC.
      .
      .
      .
PROCESS-FETCH.
    (Instructions to process SALESPERSON-NAME go here.)
    EXEC SQL FETCH CURRENT INTO : SALESPERSON-NAME END-EXEC.
```

FIGURE 11.28
Use of cursor to sequentially process a set of database records

ments the program uses CURRENT to sequentially process the retrieved rows. As you can see in Figure 11.28, the logic is simply sequential file processing logic: the cursor is opened (similar to opening a file), the first row is fetched (similar to a read), and then a loop is executed to process the rest of the data (similar to processing an entire file). Processing stops when SQLCODE is returned with a value of 100, indicating end of data. For now we will ignore other types of error processing.

The format of the FETCH statement is

```
FETCH cursor-name INTO dataname(s)
```

The datanames in the FETCH statement must match the column names identified in the SELECT statement where the cursor is defined.

More details about the programming techniques used with DB2 will appear in the example in the last section of this chapter.

DB2 CONCURRENT PROCESSING

Because DB2 allows concurrent processing, it must provide facilities to control and limit interference between users. This is done via locks.

Two types of locks employed by DB2 are shared locks and exclusive locks. When an application reads database data, DB2 acquires a **shared lock** on the data. A shared lock allows other applications to read the same data. However, applications that wish to modify that data need to wait until the lock has been released. This ensures that everyone has access to the most current data.

When an application needs to modify data (DB2 knows this by analyzing the SQL statements in the application), DB2 acquires an **exclusive lock** on the data. An exclusive lock prevents all other applications from accessing the data. When the application is finished with the data, the lock is released, thereby giving other applications access to the updated data. If DB2 did not acquire exclusive locks, it would be possible for a second application to use the old version of the data while it was in the process of being updated by the first application. This would compromise the integrity of the stored data.

In addition to choices about the type of lock, DB2 offers options regarding the **level,** or **locksize.** The two locking units in DB2 are table spaces and pages. (Recall that a table space is an area of disk storage in which one or several base tables are stored. Table spaces are made up of **pages,** 4k-byte blocks of disk space. Pages generally contain parts of tables.) Although you might expect DB2 to apply locks to tables or even to rows within tables, this is not the case. When an exclusive lock is acquired for a table space, no application can access the data in *any* table stored in that table space.

When establishing a new database, the DBA can specify the lock level within a table space. This is done via the LOCKSIZE option of the CREATE TABLESPACE command. The format is

```
LOCKSIZE = ANY | PAGE | TABLESPACE
```

If the DBA specifies TABLESPACE, then locks (either shared or exclusive) will be applied to the entire table space in which a referenced table resides. This option improves the performance of the application, but in doing so it can seriously delay other applications needing access to something in that table space.

If the DBA selects PAGE, then locks initially are applied at the page level (DB2 may escalate to the table level if it detects poor performance). Locking at the page level results in fewer conflicts than does locking at the table space level, but more resources are required to administer it.

Finally, if the DBA specifies ANY, then DB2 selects the appropriate level, depending on the number of pages that may be required to fulfill an application's needs. If only a few pages may be referenced, then page-level locks will be applied. On the other hand, if many pages may be required, then table-space-level locks will be applied. ANY is the default value for the LOCKSIZE option. Thus, the DBA does not need to specify the LOCKSIZE option when creating a table space. By default, DB2 can be allowed to select the proper level of locking based on the type of SQL request and the number of pages involved.

As mentioned, locks are completely transparent to end-users and application programmers. All necessary locking and unlocking is performed automatically by DB2.

COMMIT and ROLLBACK

All DB2 table data modifications must be either committed or discarded. When a change is committed, it is final and becomes part of the actual database data. When a commitment occurs, all page locks placed on that data are released and the updated data is made available to other applications. A commitment is automatically executed when an application terminates normally. It can also be explicitly invoked with the SQL COMMIT statement.

Sometimes DB2 table modifications need to be discarded. This occurs, for example, when an end-user wants to terminate a transaction in the middle. To discard the changes, the application program issues an SQL ROLLBACK statement. This statement returns the tables to their original state (the state after the most recent COMMIT), thus eliminating any pending updates to the table. At that point, all page locks are released and other applications have access to the unchanged data.

DB2 and the Deadlock

When two or more applications are deadlocked, DB2 resolves the problem by examining the number of log records each application has written. DB2 terminates the application(s) with the fewest log records since the last commitment. The more active application is selected to continue processing. (See Chapter 14 for a more comprehensive discussion of deadlock.)

DB2 BACKUP AND RECOVERY

DB2 stores before and after images of all database changes on a log. Changes are written to the log before they are written to the database. DB2 periodically checks itself. When checkpoints occur, all changes residing in system buffers are written to the database and a checkpoint record is written to the log. Thus, at the time of a checkpoint, the log and DB2 databases are synchronized.

DB2 can recover from a system failure by first applying all before images created since the most recent checkpoint and then applying all after images of committed transactions. As a result, all committed changes can endure the crash. Transactions that were in progress at the time of the crash need to be restarted.

Databases are stored on disks and are therefore vulnerable to physical damage. Should disk damage occur, the database must be re-created from backup copies. This means the user organization must periodically save the database. In DB2, this is done via utility programs that copy table spaces (that is, the physical storage areas that contain table data). DB2 includes an option that allows the user organization to make backup copies of only those pages in a table space that have been modified since the latest backup was done. This option can save much time because unchanged pages are not copied unnecessarily.

DB2 SECURITY

DB2 provides security mechanisms to protect the database. One such mechanism is views. Another allows the DBA to assign processing capabilities to particular users.

Views

Views provide data security at the field level. Recall that a view is a subset of columns, rows, or both derived from one or more base tables. To prevent a user from accessing any data in a base table except the fields he or she needs to access, the DBA simply defines a view of the table and authorizes the user to access the view (but not the base table). We discussed how to use SQL to create a view earlier in this chapter, so the following two examples are presented without further explanation.

The user of this view of KDK's DEALER table is given access only to dealer names and telephone numbers:

```
CREATE VIEW DLRPHONES
       AS SELECT NAME, TELEPHONE
       FROM DEALER
```

The user of this view is given access to dealer records only in the state of Massachusetts:

```
CREATE VIEW MASSDLRS
       AS SELECT *
       FROM DEALER
       WHERE STATE/PROVINCE = 'MA'
```

DB2 Resources

DB2 is able to control access to various database resources, including tables, views, databases, utility programs, the DB2 catalog, and table spaces. Because DB2 users (both end-users and application programmers) access only tables and views, we will just discuss DB2's control over them. Though not shown here, system administrators and database administrators have access to all database resources.

DB2 can control access to data in tables and views. Users can be authorized to issue SELECT, INSERT, DELETE, and UPDATE statements against a table or view. Also, the columns that may be updated can be specified. The use of the ALTER command to change a table definition can also be restricted.

Identifying Users

Because DB2 is used in the MVS environment, many users can access it concurrently from a variety of other subsystems, such as IMS and CICS transaction managers, TSO, and batch jobs. Although you need not understand all these subsystems, it is important to realize that each has a means of identifying authorized users. For instance, TSO terminal users have a log-on ID that identifies them, a batch job has a special parameter on the job card, and IMS users have a sign-on ID or a logical terminal name (thus the equipment, not the person, is authorized to access the system). Other systems have similar authorization IDs.

DB2 uses the connecting subsystem's ID as the identifier for the DB2 user. DB2 assigns capabilities to access certain resources to authorization IDs. Explicit authorization is accomplished by means of the SQL GRANT statement. The format is

```
GRANT capability resource-list
TO authorization-ID-list
(WITH GRANT OPTION)
```

The capabilities likely to be granted to users are the following:

- ALTER   The definition of the specified tables may be altered.
- DELETE   Rows may be deleted from the specified tables or views.
- INSERT   Rows may be inserted into the specified tables or views.
- SELECT   Rows may be selected from the specified tables or views.
- UPDATE The values for the specified list of columns within the specified tables or views may be updated.

The resource list for most users is simply the names of tables or views for which they will have the specified capabilities. The authorization-ID list is the list of user IDs to whom the specified authorization is being granted. The authorization-ID list can also be the keyword PUBLIC, which grants the authority to all users. Here are some examples that illustrate the GRANT command:

- All users are allowed to look at the DEALER table:

```
GRANT SELECT ON TABLE DEALER TO PUBLIC
```

- An application program can insert new records into the ADVERTISEMENT table:

```
GRANT INSERT ON TABLE ADVERTISEMENT TO PROG87
```

- A user known by the ID TERM 14 is allowed to access the view DLRPHONES:

```
GRANT SELECT ON VIEW DLRPHONES TO TERM 14
```

- Two users are allowed to change table definitions for the DEALER and SALES-PERSON tables:

```
GRANT ALTER ON TABLE DEALER, SALESPERSON TO USER5,
USER7
```

- An application program is allowed to delete SALESPERSON records:

```
GRANT DELETE ON TABLE SALESPERSON TO PERS000
```

When the DB2 database is installed, the system administrator is given total control over all resources. He or she may grant authority to or revoke authority from any other individual including DBAs. This is done via the GRANT statement. Of course, the resources and capabilities available to the system administrator include many options besides those just described.

The GRANT statement contains an optional clause: WITH GRANT OPTION. When used, this clause enables the grantee to give others the same capabilities over the same resources. Thus, one can pass along authorization to others. Consider this example:

```
GRANT SELECT ON AD-COPY TO MURPHY WITH GRANT OPTION
```

This gives Murphy permission to read the AD-COPY table and allows her to authorize other users to do the same.

In addition to explicit authorization conveyed by the GRANT command, the creator of a construct is automatically given full authority WITH GRANT OPTION over that construct. This cannot be revoked unless the construct itself is deleted from the database.

If authority is revoked (by means of the REVOKE command), it has a cascading effect. This means that not only is the specified privilege revoked from the named authorization ID, but also from anyone else to whom that authorization ID granted that privilege. Suppose user A were granted authority to read a table with the GRANT option and subsequently granted that privilege to user B. When user A is transferred to another department and his authority to read the table is revoked, user B's authority stemming from the GRANT is also automatically revoked. The following illustrates the sequence of events:

1. DBA:

   ```
   GRANT SELECT ON TABLE PRODUCT TO USERA WITH GRANT
   OPTION
   ```

   (User A can now read the PRODUCT table.)

2. User A:

   ```
   GRANT SELECT ON TABLE PRODUCT TO USERB
   ```

   (Users A and B can now read the PRODUCT table.)

3. DBA:

   ```
   REVOKE SELECT ON TABLE PRODUCT FROM USERA
   ```

   (Neither user A nor user B can read the PRODUCT table.)

Relational Implementation Using DB2

In this section we will illustrate the implementation of KDK's Information Center database using DB2. A summary of KDK's database design appears in Figures 11.29 and 11.30.

First we will create the database using interactive DB2 commands. Then we will illustrate several online queries that product managers (or Information Center personnel) might execute. Finally, we will present an application program that produces one of the standard reports needed by the PMs.

CREATING THE DATABASE STRUCTURE

Interactive DB2 statements to create the database structure (KDKICB) presented in Figures 11.29 and 11.30 are shown in Figure 11.31. As you can see, the statements are straightforward. Having completed the design earlier, we need only to specify the format of each table and column using DB2.

INVOICE	(<u>Number</u>, Date, Total, Salesperson.Number, Dealer.Number)
LINE-ITEM	(<u>Invoice.Number</u>, <u>Line-item-number</u>, Product.Number, Quantity, Extended-price)
DEALER	(<u>Number</u>, Name, Address-1, Address-2, City, State/Province, ZIP/Postal-code, Telephone)
SALESPERSON	(<u>Number</u>, Name, Region)
PRODUCT	(<u>Number</u>, Name, Description, Price)
AD-COPY	(<u>Ad-name</u>, Agency, First-run-date)
ADVERTISEMENT	(<u>Publication</u>, <u>Date</u>, <u>Ad-name</u>, Cost, Share-percent, Dealer.Number)
PRODUCT-AD	(<u>Ad-name</u>, Product.Number)

FIGURE 11.29

Summary of relations for KDK Appliances' Information Center database

Keep in mind that this database will be used for queries only—it will be neither updated nor altered. It is a snapshot of corporate operational data downloaded from the mainframe database for analysis by the product managers. All updates are done to the operational data in a carefully controlled environment. Therefore, other than authorizing each PM to access (SELECT) the tables, no other authority will be granted. No one needs to alter, delete, or update any of the data. And because all the PMs are given access to all the columns in all the tables, no views are necessary.

EXAMPLES OF INTERACTIVE QUERY

Figure 11.32 shows four sample queries of KDK's Information Center database. The first one lists the names of dealers who shared advertising with KDK during the month of March. The DB2 word DISTINCT eliminates duplicate names from the list. The name of a dealer who shared more than one ad with KDK would appear several times in the list, but we will print it only once.

This example employs the subquery technique. Recall from Chapter 10 that subqueries allow us to narrow the scope of our search through the database by qualifying one level of query with another. Read from the bottom up, the first example in Figure 11.32 begins by building a list of numbers for dealers who shared with KDK the cost of advertising during March. Then, moving up to the next SELECT statement, it extracts dealer names from the DEALER table for all the dealers whose numbers appeared in the first list. Finally, the DISTINCT option causes the DBMS to eliminate duplicate names.

The second example in Figure 11.32 also employs the subquery technique, only this time it is more complex. Once again we will interpret the statement by reading it from the bottom up. We begin by building a list of product numbers for refrigerators (Type = '5'). Then we build a list of invoice numbers that have line items for any of those products. Next, we extract dealer numbers for all of those invoices occurring in March, and finally we build a list of dealer names, eliminating duplicates. This is the list of dealers who purchased refrigerators during March.

FIGURE 11.30

Table descriptions for KDK's
Information Center database

INVOICE	
Number	Char (4)
Date	Numeric YYMMDD
Total	Numeric 9999.99
Salesperson. Number	*
Dealer. Number	*
LINE-ITEM	
Invoice. Number	*
Line-item-number	Numeric 999 positive integer
Product. Number	*
Quantity	Numeric 999 positive integer
Extended-price	Computed numeric 9(6).99
DEALER	
Number	Char(4)
Name	Char(45)
Address-1	Char(25)
Address-2	Char(25)
City	Char(15)
State/Province	Char(2)
ZIP/Postal-code	Char(10)
Telephone	Char(10)
SALESPERSON	
Number	Char(4)
Name	Char(20)
Region	Numeric 9
PRODUCT	
Type	Numeric 9
Number	Char(5)
Name	Char(25)
Description	Char(50)
Price	Numeric 99999.99
AD-COPY	
Ad-name	Char(15)
Agency	Char(30)
First-run-date	Numeric YYMMDD
ADVERTISEMENT	
Publication	Char(10)
Date	Numeric YYMMDD
Ad-name	*
Cost	Numeric 9999.99
Share-percent	Numeric 999.99
	E.g., 30% is 30.00
Dealer. Number	*
PRODUCT-AD	
Ad-name	*
Product.number	*

*Definitions for foreign keys are shown in the foreign relations.

```
CREATE    TABLE        INVOICE
          (NUMBER                      CHAR(4)          NOT NULL,
          DATE                         DECIMAL(6)       NOT NULL,
          TOTAL                        DECIMAL(7,2)     NOT NULL,
          SALESPERSON-NUMBER           CHAR(4)          NOT NULL,
          DEALER-NUMBER                CHAR(4)          NOT NULL)
CREATE    TABLE        LINE-ITEM
          (INVOICE-NUMBER              CHAR(4)          NOT NULL,
          LINE-ITEM-NUMBER             DECIMAL(3)       NOT NULL,
          PRODUCT-NUMBER               CHAR(5)          NOT NULL,
          QUANTITY                     DECIMAL(3)       NOT NULL,
          EXTENDED-PRICE               DECIMAL(8,2)     NOT NULL)
CREATE    TABLE        DEALER
          (NUMBER                      CHAR(4)          NOT NULL,
          NAME                         CHAR(45)         NOT NULL,
          ADDRESS-1                    CHAR(25),
          ADDRESS-2                    CHAR(25),
          CITY                         CHAR(15)
          STATE/PROVINCE               CHAR(10),
          ZIP/POSTAL-CODE              CHAR(10),
          TELEPHONE                    CHAR(10))
CREATE    TABLE        SALESPERSON
          NUMBER                       CHAR(4)          NOT NULL,
          NAME                         CHAR(20)         NOT NULL,
          REGION                       DECIMAL(1)).
CREATE    TABLE        PRODUCT
          (TYPE                        CHAR(1)          NOT NULL,
          NUMBER                       CHAR(5)          NOT NULL,
          NAME                         CHAR(25)         NOT NULL,
          DESCRIPTION                  CHAR(50),
          PRICE                        DECIMAL(7,2)     NOT NULL)
CREATE    TABLE        AD-COPY
          (AD-NAME                     CHAR(15)         NOT NULL,
          AGENCY                       CHAR(30),
          FIRST-RUN-DATE               DECIMAL(6))
CREATE    TABLE        ADVERTISEMENT
          (PUBLICATION                 CHAR(10)         NOT NULL,
          DATE                         DECIMAL(6)       NOT NULL,
          AD-NAME                      CHAR(15)         NOT NULL,
          COST                         DECIMAL(6,2)     NOT NULL,
          SHARE-PERCENT                DECIMAL(5,2),
          DEALER-NUMBER                CHAR(4))
CREATE    TABLE        PRODUCT-AD
          (AD-NAME                     CHAR(15)         NOT NULL,
          PRODUCT-NUMBER               CHAR(5)          NOT NULL)
```

FIGURE 11.31

Interactive DB2 statements to create tables for KDK's Information Center database

```
1.    List the dealers who participated in shared advertising during the month of March:
      SELECT DISTINCT NAME FROM DEALER
            WHERE DEALER.NUMBER IN
            SELECT DEALER-NUMBER
                FROM ADVERTISEMENT
                WHERE ADVERTISEMENT.DATE BETWEEN 880301 AND 880331
2.    List the dealers who purchased refrigerators (product type = 5) in March:
      SELECT DISTINCT NAME FROM DEALER
            WHERE DEALER.NUMBER IN
                SELECT DEALER-NUMBER FROM INVOICE
                WHERE DATE BETWEEN 880301 AND 880331
                    AND INVOICE.NUMBER IN
                        SELECT INVOICE-NUMBER FROM LINE-ITEM
                        WHERE LINE-ITEM.PRODUCT-NUMBER IN
                            SELECT NUMBER FROM PRODUCT
                            WHERE TYPE = '5'
3.    List the products that were advertised in March:
      SELECT NUMBER, NAME, DESCRIPTION FROM PRODUCT
            WHERE PRODUCT.NUMBER IN
                SELECT DISTINCT PRODUCT-NUMBER FROM PRODUCT-AD
                WHERE PRODUCT-AD.AD-NAME = ADVERTISEMENT.AD-NAME
                    AND ADVERTISEMENT.DATE BETWEEN 880301 AND 880331
4.    Print the total sales for product #94605 for the month of March. Then print it for the
      month of April:
      CREATE VIEW PRODUCTSALES
            (DATE, PRODUCT, EXTENDED-PRICE)
            AS SELECT DATE, PRODUCT-NUMBER, EXTENDED-PRICE
                FROM INVOICE, LINE-ITEM
                WHERE LINE-ITEM.INVOICE-NUMBER = INVOICE.NUMBER
                    AND LINE-ITEM.PRODUCT-NUMBER = '94605'
      SELECT SUM(EXTENDED-PRICE) FROM PRODUCTSALES
            WHERE DATE BETWEEN 880301 AND 880331
      SELECT SUM(EXTENDED-PRICE) FROM PRODUCTSALES
            WHERE DATE BETWEEN 880401 AND 880430
```

FIGURE 11.32
Sample interactive DB2 queries against KDK's database

The third illustration in Figure 11.32 extracts data from several tables in order to give the user the desired results. Product names and descriptions come from the PRODUCT table. Advertisements, which are dated, are stored in the ADVERTISEMENT table. But advertisements are not directly associated with any product—they are associated with advertising copy by means of the Ad-name column. Similarly, products are not associated directly with an advertisement, but with advertising copy by means of the Ad-name column in the PRODUCT-AD table.

We begin by joining the PRODUCT-AD table and the ADVERTISEMENT table, matching on Ad-name. Then we extract unique (distinct) product numbers, and only for advertisements that ran in March. Finally, we extract from the PRODUCT table the name and description for each product number we have identified.

The fourth example of a query in Figure 11.32 begins by building a view (the join of two tables) and then selecting total sales figures from the view. The view is made up of sales data for product #94605. This data is taken from the INVOICE table (date) and the LINE-ITEM table (product number, extended price). Having established this subset of the larger base tables, we can ask DB2 to calculate the two sales totals by invoking the SUM built-in function in the SELECT statement. Two SELECT statements are needed, of course, one for each month.

APPLICATION PROGRAM EXAMPLE

Figure 11.33 presents a COBOL program that prints the report shown in Figure 11.3c, titled PRODUCT SALES SUMMARY BY REGION. In this section we will examine the COBOL program, noting the placement of DB2 commands. Although this example is written in COBOL, SQL can also be embedded in PL/I, FORTRAN, and assembler language programs.

Looking at the WORKING-STORAGE SECTION of the DATA DIVISION, we find the definition of variables that will hold data values as they are retrieved by DB2 from the database. These variables are defined following the SQL message BEGIN DECLARE SECTION. Notice that each SQL statement is surrounded by the precompiler keywords EXEC SQL and END-EXEC.

Within the DECLARE SECTION we have defined a sale record, made up of six fields. Later, in the PROCEDURE DIVISION, you will see that the data for this sale record is found in four different database tables. The words END DECLARE SECTION signal the precompiler that part of the program is complete.

The next instruction in the WORKING-STORAGE SECTION directs the precompiler to copy SQLCA into the COBOL program. Again, this is a list of parameters shared by the DBMS and the application program. The most significant field in SQLCA is SQLCODE, as described earlier.

The remainder of the WORKING-STORAGE SECTION defines work areas and report formats to be used by the program. These are normal COBOL entries that are unaffected by the presence of DB2.

In the PROCEDURE DIVISION we find a mixture of SQL statements and ordinary COBOL instructions. The first sequence of instructions in the PROCEDURE DIVISION defines a cursor (C-1) that will be used to retrieve data from the database. The SELECT statement on which the cursor operates is lengthy, but it is easily understood. To print the report seen in Figure 11.3, we need a set of sales records containing product numbers, names and descriptions, prices, quantities sold, and regions. Those pieces of data are found in several different database tables, so in the SELECT statement we specify to DB2 the sources of the data (the four tables) and the links it needs to follow in order to retrieve the correct data

```
WHERE LINE-ITEM.INVOICE-NUMBER = INVOICE.NUMBER, etc.
```

```
IDENTIFICATION DIVISION.
PROGRAM-ID.   DB2-EXAMPLE.
ENVIRONMENT DIVISION.
CONFIGURATION SECTION.
SPECIAL-NAMES.
     (special names go here)
INPUT-OUTPUT SECTION.
FILE-CONTROL.
     SELECT     (SELECT statements for non-database files go here)
DATA DIVISION.
FILE SECTION.
     FD          (FDs for non-database files go here)
WORKING-STORAGE SECTION.
*
*     DECLARE VARIABLES FOR USE WITH DB2
*
     EXEC SQL   BEGIN DECLARE SECTION     END-EXEC.
 01  SALE-RECORD.
     05   PRODUCT-NUMBER     PICTURE X(05).
     05   PRODUCT-NAME       PICTURE X(25).
     05   PRODUCT-DESC       PICTURE X(50).
     05   QUANTITY-SOLD      PICTURE S999        COMP-3.
     05   UNIT-PRICE         PICTURE S9(5)V99    COMP-3.
     05   SALE-REGION        PICTURE S9          COMP-3.
     EXEC SQL   END DECLARE SECTION     END-EXEC.
*    REQUEST DB2 TO COPY INTO COBOL PROGRAM
*    DEFINITIONS FOR DB2 COMMUNICATIONS AREA.
*
     EXEC SQL   INCLUDE SQLCA              END-EXEC.
*
*    DEFINE NON-DATABASE VARIABLES
*
 77  PRODUCT-NUMBER HOLD     PICTURE X(5).
 77  REGION-HOLD             PICTURE X.
 77  SUM-UNITS-THIS-REGION   PICTURE 999         COMP-3 VALUE 0.
 77  SUM-UNITS-THIS-PRODUCT  PICTURE 99999       COMP-3 VALUE 0.
 01  PAGE-HEADER-1.
     05   FILLER            PICTURE X(24)  VALUE SPACES.
     05   FILLER            PICTURE X(31)
          VALUE 'PRODUCT SALES SUMMARY BY REGION'.
     05   FILLER            PICTURE X(25)  VALUE  SPACES.
 01  GROUP-1.
     05   FILLER            PICTURE X(16)
          VALUE 'PRODUCT NUMBER: '.
```

FIGURE 11.33

COBOL program to produce PRODUCT SALES SUMMARY BY REGION report

```
      05     PRODUCT-NUMBER-OUT   PICTURE X(05).
      05     FILLER               PICTURE X(59)   VALUE SPACES.
01  GROUP-2.
      05     FILLER               PICTURE X(16)
             VALUE 'DESCRIPTION: '
      05     NAME-OUT             PICTURE X(25).
      05     FILLER               PICTURE X(39)   VALUE SPACES.
01  GROUP-3.
      05     FILLER               PICTURE X(16)   VALUE SPACES.
      05     DESCRIPTION-OUT      PICTURE X(50).
      05     FILLER               PICTURE X(14)   VALUE SPACES.
01  GROUP-4.
      05     FILLER               PICTURE X(16)
             VALUE 'PRICE: '
      05     PRICE-OUT            PICTURE $(6).99.
      05     FILLER               PICTURE X(55)   VALUE SPACES.
01  COLUMN-HEADERS.
      05     FILLER               PICTURE X(30)   VALUE SPACES.
      05     FILLER               PICTURE X(24)
             VALUE 'REGION        UNITS SOLD'.
      05     FILLER               PICTURE X(26)   VALUE SPACES.
01  REGION-TOTAL-LINE.
      05     FILLER               PICTURE X(32)   VALUE SPACES.
      05     REGION-OUT           PICTURE X.
      05     FILLER               PICTURE X(13)   VALUE SPACES.
      05     UNITS-SOLD-OUT       PICTURE ZZ9.
      05     FILLER               PICTURE X(31)   VALUE SPACES.
01  PRODUCT-TOTAL-LINE.
      05     FILLER               PICTURE X(36)   VALUE SPACES.
      05     FILLER               PICTURE X(08).
             VALUE   'TOTAL'
      05     TOTAL-OUT            PICTURE ZZZZ9.
      05     FILLER               PICTURE X(31)   VALUE SPACES.
PROCEDURE DIVISION.
    EXEC SQL
        DECLARE C-1 CURSOR FOR
        SELECT PRODUCT.NUMBER, PRODUCT.NAME,
               PRODUCT.DESCRIPTION, LINE-ITEM.QUANTITY,
               PRODUCT.PRICE, SALESPERSON.REGION
        FROM PRODUCT, SALESPERSON, LINE-ITEM, INVOICE
        WHERE LINE-ITEM.INVOICE-NUMBER = INVOICE.NUMBER
          AND INVOICE.SALESPERSON-NUMBER = SALESPERSON.NUMBER
          AND LINE-ITEM.PRODUCT-NUMBER = PRODUCT.NUMBER
        ORDER BY PRODUCT.NUMBER, SALESPERSON.REGION
    END-EXEC.
    OPEN OUTPUT REPORT-FILE.
    EXEC SQL  OPEN C-1       END-EXEC.
```

FIGURE 11.33 *continued*

```
        EXEC SQL   FETCH C-1 INTO :SALE-RECORD    END-EXEC.
        MOVE PRODUCT-NUMBER TO PRODUCT-NUMBER-HOLD.
        MOVE SALE-REGION TO REGION-HOLD.
        PERFORM ISSUE-HEADERS.
        PERFORM PROCESS-AND-FETCH UNTIL SQLCODE = 100.
        EXEC SQL   CLOSE C-1 END EXEC.
        PERFORM ISSUE-REGION-TOTAL.
        PERFORM ISSUE-PRODUCT-TOTAL.
        CLOSE REPORT-FILE.
        EXIT PROGRAM.
 *
   PROCESS-AND-FETCH.
        IF PRODUCT-NUMBER NOT EQUAL PRODUCT-NUMBER-HOLD
        THEN PERFORM ISSUE-REGION-TOTAL
             PERFORM ISSUE-PRODUCT-TOTAL
        ELSE
             IF REGION-NUMBER NOT EQUAL REGION-HOLD
             THEN PERFORM ISSUE-REGION-TOTAL
             ELSE NEXT SENTENCE.
        ADD QUANTITY-SOLD TO SUM-UNITS-THIS-REGION.
        ADD QUANTITY-SOLD TO SUM-UNITS-THIS-PRODUCT.
        EXEC SQL   FETCH C-1 INTO :SALE-RECORD    END-EXEC.
   ISSUE-REGION-TOTAL.
        MOVE SUM-UNITS-THIS-REGION TO UNITS-SOLD-OUT.
        MOVE REGION-HOLD TO REGION-OUT.
        MOVE REGION-TOTAL-LINE TO (printer record goes here).
        PERFORM WRITE-LINE.
        MOVE 0 TO SUM-UNITS-THIS-REGION.
        MOVE SALE-REGION TO REGION-HOLD.
   ISSUE-PRODUCT-TOTAL.
        MOVE SUM-UNITS-THIS-PRODUCT TO TOTAL-OUT.
        MOVE PRODUCT-TOTAL-LINE TO (printer record goes here).
        PERFORM WRITE-LINE.
        MOVE 0 TO SUM-UNITS-THIS-PRODUCT.
        MOVE PRODUCT-NUMBER TO PRODUCT-NUMBER-HOLD.
        PERFORM ISSUE-HEADERS.
   ISSUE-HEADERS.
        MOVE PAGE-HEADER-1 TO (printer record goes here).
        PERFORM WRITE-NEW-PAGE.
        MOVE PRODUCT-NUMBER TO PRODUCT-NUMBER-OUT.
        MOVE GROUP-1 TO (printer record goes here).
        PERFORM WRITE-LINE.
        MOVE PRODUCT-NAME TO NAME-OUT.
        MOVE GROUP-2 TO (printer record goes here).
        PERFORM WRITE-LINE.
        MOVE PRODUCT-DESC TO DESCRIPTION-OUT.
```

FIGURE 11.33 *continued*

```
      MOVE GROUP-3 TO (printer record goes here).
      PERFORM WRITE-LINE.
      MOVE UNIT-PRICE TO PRICE-OUT.
      MOVE GROUP-4 TO (printer record goes here).
      PERFORM WRITE-LINE.
      MOVE COLUMN-HEADERS TO (printer record goes here).
      PERFORM WRITE-LINE.
  WRITE-NEW-PAGE.
      (instructions for printing line at top of page go here)
  WRITE-LINE.
      (instructions for writing a line go here).
```

FIGURE 11.33 *continued*

Finally, we state that the rows (records) need to be made available to the program sorted by region number within product number.

Having established the cursor, we now have a conceptual pseudofile that contains all the newly constructed sales records in the desired sequence. The rest of the program follows ordinary sequential file processing logic, testing for two control level breaks (one on region number, the other on product number).

First we open the output report file. Then we issue SQL statements to prepare the database data to be processed:

```
OPEN C-1
```

We use the cursor to retrieve the first database row in the sale pseudofile

```
FETCH C-1 INTO :SALE-RECORD
```

placing the data values into the fields we defined in the DECLARE SECTION above. The word SALE-RECORD is preceded by a colon (:) to help the precompiler distinguish it from words it expects to find defined in the database tables. This FETCH SQL statement effectively reads the first sale record from the pseudofile.

The next instruction sequence saves the product number and region values in work areas and writes the first set of report headers. Ready to process the first record, then, we go into a loop called PROCESS-AND-FETCH. Note that we will remain in this program loop until no more "sale records" are left in the database (UNTIL SQLCODE = 100). When that eventually happens, we close the cursor, releasing those resources to other users of this database, and terminate our program normally.

Within the main program loop, PROCESS-AND-FETCH, we find only one SQL statement. The last command in the loop is

```
FETCH C-1 INTO :SALE-RECORD
```

This instruction, like an ordinary COBOL READ, presents to the program the next sequential row from the pseudofile, replacing the one just processed. As already mentioned, the loop will be executed until all appropriate data has been retrieved from the database.

The remaining COBOL paragraphs contain no SQL statements. They are used simply to format and produce the SALES SUMMARY report and would be no different if a sequential input file had been used.

You should note that because KDK Appliances' Information Center database is being used exclusively for analyzing data, no database changes are illustrated. If changes to table data were made in an application program, then either the COMMIT SQL statement would be invoked whenever a change were to be made permanent (perhaps after each valid record update), or the ROLLBACK SQL command would be invoked if the program discovered an error partway through an update. Also, a COMMIT would automatically be invoked when the program terminated. However, COMMITS are unnecessary in this sample program because it does not update the database.

Summary

KDK Appliances, a manufacturing company, needed to analyze sales data from its operational database. The most effective and least disruptive way to do this was to download sales data from the operational database onto a smaller mainframe computer located in the company's Information Center. Then the snapshot of the operational data could be studied by product managers, so they would have the timely data they needed to make decisions and to plan marketing strategies. KDK Appliances chose Database2 (DB2) as its relational database management system.

After identifying various objects that the product managers needed, we developed a relational database design. First we drew a set of object diagrams. Then we converted them into relation diagrams. With the design completed, we turned to the database management system DB2 for implementation.

DB2 is an IBM product used to process relational databases on large computers operating under MVS. DB2 uses the language SQL to define, access, and manipulate data and to grant authorizations. SQL statements can be issued interactively or they can be embedded into application programs written in COBOL, PL/I, FORTRAN, and assembler language.

DB2 allows a person to define various database constructs, such as tables, views, table spaces, indexes, index spaces, data bases, and storage groups. Users, both online end-users and application programmers, refer only to tables and views. The database administrator, or someone performing other system functions, is concerned with physical database storage and organization and thus deals with other DB2 constructs as well.

Database constructs can be defined, modified, and deleted. DB2 includes SQL statements to perform all those functions.

SQL data manipulation language as implemented in DB2 includes all the relational functions we studied in Chapter 10. In addition to reading a database, we can insert records, update stored data, and delete rows from a table. The SQL statements for these four functions are SELECT, INSERT, UPDATE, and DELETE.

When SQL statements are embedded in an application program, the entire program must first be processed by the DB2 precompiler. The precompiler finds all SQL statements (indicated in COBOL by the keywords EXEC SQL . . . END-EXEC) and translates them into equivalent host-language instructions. It builds database request modules, stores them on disk, and inserts call statements into the program to access them. Thus, the application programmer needs to know little about the inner workings of the database management system. The precompiler effectively shields the programmer from it.

In order to process a multiple-row query, the application programmer needs to define a cursor—a pointer that acts on a SELECT statement. Although the SELECT statement does not actually generate a file, you can imagine that a cursor defines a pseudofile in which DB2 will store the rows it retrieves. Then the set of retrieved rows can be processed one at a time as if in a sequential file.

DB2 handles the potential problems of concurrent processing by using locks on portions of a database. Shared locks allow multiple concurrent access to the same data. But if any application needs to modify data, DB2 acquires an exclusive lock. No other application can access data that has an exclusive lock on it. When the lock is released, all applications have access to the updated data. The exclusive lock ensures the integrity of the data.

DB2 can lock either table spaces (which might include several tables) or pages (which contain tables or parts of tables). Locking pages causes less interference with other concurrent users but costs more to administer. Trade-offs like these are common in information processing.

DB2 logs all database changes before they are committed, or written, to the database. Database modifications that are not yet committed can be backed out by issuing the ROLLBACK command. This might be necessary if a processing error is detected or a system failure occurs. The system log enables DB2 to recover data in the event of a system crash. It applies all before images of the database since the latest checkpoint. Then it applies all after images of committed transactions (they had been logged). Any transactions that were in progress at the time of the crash need to be restarted.

DB2 security consists of granting to certain identifiable users the ability to perform certain functions on certain database resources. One way to restrict access to database table data is to define views (or subsets) of the tables and authorize users to reference them, but not the base tables. This approach protects data at the field level.

DB2 allows the database administrator to control end-users' and application programmers' use of the SELECT, UPDATE, INSERT, DELETE, and ALTER commands to specified tables and views. Authorization is performed by means of the GRANT statement. When DB2 is installed, only one person is given the authority to GRANT. This privilege can be passed on to other administrators and even to users. Privileges that can be granted can also be rescinded by means of the REVOKE command. In this way, the DBA can exercise control over database access.

This chapter concluded with illustrations of KDK's Information Center database as implemented in DB2. We first established the database structure and then performed some online queries against it. We also presented a COBOL program that produces one of the many sales analysis reports needed by product managers.

|||||||||||||||||||||||||

GROUP I   QUESTIONS

11.1   Why did **KDK** Appliances decide only to download sales data from the operational mainframe computer? What effect does that decision have on the processing privileges product managers will eventually be granted on the Information Center database?

11.2   Why does the INVOICE as defined for the Information Center database contain fewer fields than the actual invoice used for operational processing?

11.3   What is the purpose of the PRODUCT-AD relation?

11.4   Describe two modes of DB2 access.

11.5   Define each of these terms: *table, view, base table.* Describe their relationships to one another.

11.6   How can a view be used for database security?

11.7   Which database constructs are referenced by users and application programmers?

11.8   Explain the relationship between data base, storage group, table space, page, index space, table, and index.

11.9   Write the DB2 SQL statements that create a table, an index, and a view. Assume the table contains customer name, address, and account number. Build an index on account number. Assume the view presents unique customer names.

11.10 Show the DB2 statement that adds to the table a column for the customer's age.

11.11 Write the DB2 statement(s) that would add these records to the customer table you changed in question 11.10:

```
Mike Thompson, Madison, #456, 45
Paul Hand, New Haven, #722, 20
Karen Munroe, Gales Ferry, #076, 27
```

11.12 Show the DB2 statements needed to drop the table, index, and view defined in question 11.9.

11.13 Explain the role of the DB2 precompiler.

11.14 How does the precompiler know which instructions are SQL instructions and which belong to the host language?

11.15 Explain the role of a cursor in DB2 processing.

11.16 Explain the difference between a shared lock and an exclusive lock.

11.17 Why is an exclusive lock required when data is going to be modified?

11.18   What two lock sizes are allowed in DB2? What is the advantage of each over the other?

11.19   What is the purpose of the COMMIT statement? What is the purpose of the ROLLBACK statement?

11.20   How does DB2 handle a deadlock?

11.21   Explain how DB2 can recover from a system crash. Explain how DB2 can recover from database damage.

11.22   Explain the role of the GRANT statement. How can GRANT authority be given to another user?

11.23   Explain the role of the REVOKE statement. What is the cascade effect of the REVOKE statement?

GROUP II QUESTIONS

11.24   Locate a company that is using DB2. Determine how long it has had the system, why it chose DB2, and how well DB2 has worked out. Has productivity improved as a result of using DB2? Does the company use DB2 interactively, or is it used in application programs, or both? Do users do any of their own programming using DB2? Do users develop any online inquiries using DB2? Does the company have an information center? If possible, get a copy of an application program. Explain the meaning of each embedded SQL statement. How does DB2 identify the application program as an authorized user? How often does this company back up its database? Does it copy the entire database or does it back up only pages changed since the previous backup? Has this company ever had to recover the database? What problems, if any, did it experience? Has performance ever been a problem? If so, what did the company do to improve it? Explain whether you believe that DB2 has been an effective DBMS for that company.

11.25   Locate a company that has a relational DBMS other than DB2. Answer the questions in 11.24 for this DBMS.

11.26   Write an application program to produce the PRODUCT SALES SUMMARY BY SALESPERSON report illustrated in Figure 11.3a.

11.27   Write an application program to produce the DEALER ACTIVITY SUMMARY report illustrated in Figure 11.4.

PART V

Database Implementation with Hierarchical and Network Data Models

Part V considers the implementation of databases using DBMS products based on the hierarchical and network data models. Unlike the relational model, which can be used for both transaction and ad hoc processing, these models are used primarily for transaction processing applications.

Chapter 12 summarizes the characteristics of transaction processing and then presents Data Language/I, a data model developed by IBM and the sole surviving hierarchical data model. Chapter 13 then presents the CODASYL DBTG data model, the most important network model. The CODASYL DBTG model was used for the design of the interface of a dozen or so DBMS products in the early to mid-1970s.

Today, databases structured according to the hierarchical and network models are far less common than those structured according to the relational model. Still, however, there are thousands of such databases and most of them are used for large, organizational database processing. Because of this installed base, these models are important. Also, in the course of your career, you may be called upon to convert a hierarchical or network database to a relational database. If so, knowledge of these models will be quite important to you.

Transaction Processing and Data Language/I

The previous three chapters were concerned with database implementation using the relational model. We focused on that model because most databases today are structured according to the relational model. As described, the relational model can support all types of databases including operational transaction processing systems, decision support and other ad hoc processing systems, and personal database systems. The relational model is thus robust in the range of its application.

There are, however, two important classes of DBMS products besides the relational model. Such DBMS products are used, nearly exclusively, for transaction processing systems that support organizational operations. They are seldom used for decision support or other ad hoc processing and never used for personal database applications.

One of these classes, the hierarchical data model, represents data in the form of hierarchies or trees. Data Language/I is the sole surviving member of this class. We will address Data Language/I in this chapter. The second class is the network model; it represents data in terms of one-to-many relationships. The most important version of the network model is the CODASYL DBTG model. We will address that model in the next chapter.

- TRANSACTION PROCESSING
- DATA LANGUAGE/I
- DL/I DATA MANIPULATION LANGUAGE

The hierarchical and network models arose during the very earliest period of database processing, prior to the commercial viability of the relational model. Their chief importance lies in the multitudes of existing information systems that are based on them. Few new information systems are developed using these models.[1] Thus, these models will be important to you primarily because you may be called upon to maintain existing information systems based on them, or because you may participate in the conversion of a database using one of these models to the relational model.

We begin by discussing the characteristics of transaction processing and by surveying its history. Then we will discuss the nature of databases that support transaction processing. After this overview, we will consider the hierarchical data model as implemented in IBM's Data Language I, or *DL/I*. We will discuss the components of DL/I and then show how these components are used to represent the various types of objects you have studied. Finally, we present the DL/I data manipulation language commands and illustrate their use.

We are discussing transaction processing here because it is the chief application of both DL/I and the CODASYL DBTG data models. This does not mean, however, that products based on the relational model cannot support transaction processing. They can, as you saw for DB2 in Chapter 11.

Transaction Processing

To understand transaction processing systems, consider the needs of a flourishing business. Goods are purchased and sold. Clients come and go. Money is earned and spent. Time passes. At some point, somebody (perhaps an owner, a tax agent, an employee, or an auditor) asks, "What is the state of the business?," or "How much money did we make last month?," or "What were your travel expenses in 1991?," or "How much have I contributed to the stock option plan?" We could answer these questions by taking the person

---

[1] Few does not mean none. Some organizations, particularly those that have made a substantial investment in systems based on one of these models, continue to develop new, nonrelational systems. This is, however, a small percent of the new databases being developed today.

on a tour of the company, saying, "Here's the business, see for yourself!" Such a response would be unhelpful if not downright ludicrous. The person wants a report of the measurement of some *aspect* of the business's operation, not a tour of the entire enterprise.

To provide more realistic answers to questions like these, businesses maintain accounting and operational records. They gather names, inventory goods, count money, and so forth, and then they store these measurements. In some businesses, records of these measurements (or a portion of them) are stored in an **operational database.**

Such a database is a **model** of a user's model of operational aspects of the business. This model represents conditions within the organization. Business, however, is dynamic and conditions change. As they do, the model must be changed as well. Otherwise, over time the model will come to bear little resemblance to the business.

A **transaction** is the representation of an event in the business. Examples are orders, receipts, transfers, and the like. A transaction processing application accepts the transaction data and processes it in accordance with rules embedded in its logic. During processing, the program modifies the operational database in accordance and produces records of the transaction, which are sometimes called **real outputs.**

The term *real output* is used to differentiate between program outputs that are changes to database data and program outputs that are communicated, in some way, to the business environment. An example of a real output is the confirmation of a hotel reservation.

This distinction is important because outputs to a database can be readily changed if they are in error. Real outputs, once they have been communicated, are difficult to change. Normally, compensating transactions must be processed to change real outputs. In the case of a hotel reservation confirmation, if an error is made, a change or revocation of the reservation will need to be generated and communicated to the customer. The role of a transaction processing application is illustrated in Figure 12.1.

CHARACTERISTICS OF TRANSACTION PROCESSING

Transaction processing applications differ in character from other applications you have studied in this text. First, transaction processing applications support basic business operations. They are used to service teller lines at banks, for credit card authorizations, to make hotel reservations, and the like. *Fast performance* with *quick response time* is critical. Business cannot afford to have customers waiting long for the transaction processing system to respond. The turnaround time from the input of the transaction to the production of real outputs must be a few seconds or less.

Transaction processing systems must also be *reliable.* Perhaps nothing is more frustrating to business employees and customers than being unable to complete a sale or other business transaction because "the computer is down." To be effective, the failure rate of a transaction processing application must be very low. Furthermore, when the system does fail, quick and accurate recovery is essential. Comprehensive backup and recovery including transaction logging, rollback, and rollforward (see Chapter 14) are mandatory for most transaction processing applications.

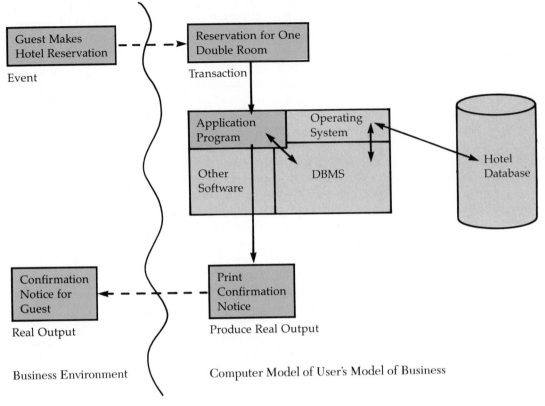

FIGURE 12.1
Role of transaction processing application program

Unlike other types of database applications, *flexibility is less important* for transaction processing applications. In fact flexibility is sometimes undesirable. Transaction processing is standardized processing. Businesses want every transaction to be processed the same way regardless of the clerk, the customer, or the time of day. If transaction processing applications were flexible, too many opportunities for nonstandard operations would exist.

Additionally, business operations change slowly. For example, commercial airlines cannot frequently change the way they accept airline reservations. The social system of travel agents, customers, and employees is too large and therefore cannot adapt readily to change.

Since transaction processing supports business operations, *control* is important. For example, in order to prevent an employee from defrauding the company by creating bogus purchase orders and then authorizing their payment (and stealing the cash), a company might distribute duties and responsibilities among employees. In this case, some employees may have authority to issue purchase orders while other employees authorize payments. For the sake of control, these two activities must be performed by different employees. In such an environment, a transaction processing application that

FIGURE 12.2
Characteristics of transaction
processing systems

- Fast performance with quick response time
- Reliable processing
- Quick and accurate recovery
- Controlled processing
- Restricted views of database for application programs
- Data protected via DBMS security mechanisms
- Equipment usually located in closed environment

FIGURE 12.2
Characteristics of transaction
processing systems

supports purchasing should enforce this separation of duties and authorities by allowing purchasing agents access to only purchasing data and payment clerks access to only payment data.

Furthermore, transaction processing applications usually have a *restricted view of the database.* There is no need, for example, for an order entry program to have access to accounts payable data. If both order data and payables data are stored in the database, then better control will result if the view of the order entry program is restricted to order data. Thus, transaction processing subsets of the database are often defined, and the scope of the database available to a transaction program is restricted to a particular subset. A subset is called an **application view,** or **subschema.**

As stated, an operational database is a model of the business or organization. As such, it is a valuable asset and needs to be *protected.* Only authorized users should have access to the database, and they should be able to perform only authorized actions. Most transaction-processing-oriented DBMS products provide security facilities. The DBA must ensure that applications take advantage of those facilities and must supplement them with programs and manual procedures where necessary.

Finally, the environment of typical transaction processing applications differs substantially from that of personal and ad hoc or decision support database applications. Because of the importance of reliability and control, the computers that support transaction processing usually reside in a *closed and controlled environment.* Access to such environments is monitored and only authorized personnel are allowed for authorized purposes. The characteristics of transaction processing systems are summarized in Figure 12.2.

DATABASES FOR TRANSACTION PROCESSING

Database processing began with transaction processing applications. In the early and mid-1960s, many efforts at data integration failed. Systems designers knew that file processing was inadequate and that some type of data modeling that facilitated the definition and processing of record relationships was needed. Many approaches and techniques were attempted. Over time, these fell into three major categories.

Three Data Models

By the early 1970s, three different methods of modeling data were generally recognized: the hierarchical data model, the network data model, and the relational data model. The **hierarchical data model** represents data relationships using hierarchies, or trees. All data relationships must be transformed into hierarchies before they can be defined in the database. We will illustrate this model in the next sections of this chapter.

As you will see, although it is possible to transform any object structure into hierarchies, the transformation is sometimes contrived. The most important and popular database product based on the hierarchical data model is **Data Language I,** or DL/I, which was developed and is marketed by IBM. We will present an overview of DL/I in later sections of this chapter.

The **network data model** readily represents one-to-many relationships. Therefore it can be used to directly represent all object types we discussed in Chapter 7, except many-to-many compound objects. Such objects must be transformed into one-to-many relationships, just as we have done for the relational model in previous chapters. The most important network data model is the CODASYL DBTG (Conference on Data Systems Languages, Data Base Task Group) model. We will illustrate the use of this model in Chapter 13.

The **relational data model** is the third major data model, one which you have studied throughout this text. As you have already learned, this model was defined in 1970 but had little practical significance until relational DBMS products became available in the early 1980s. However, development of the relational model during the 1970s and 1980s has contributed much to the understanding and theory of data modeling. Furthermore, as you have seen in previous chapters, the relational model is a useful tool for logical database design and for the implementation of databases that are directly processed by end-users.

Predefined Relationships

Both the hierarchical and the network data models require that relationships be predefined. That is, all relationships must be anticipated and defined before implementing the database. Adding new relationships to an existing database is more difficult with these two models than it is using the relational model. The reason for this concerns the method used for representing relationships.

Unlike the relational model, in which relationships are established by data values, the hierarchical and network models represent relationships by means of separate **data structures,** such as indexes and linked lists (see Appendix B). These data structures must be established by the DBMS before the relationships can be represented. Consider the ramifications of this approach.

For transaction processing applications, the representation of relationships in data structures has two advantages over storing relationships within the data. First, performance is likely to be better (at least with currently available technologies). When relationships are predefined, data structures can be selected for and tuned to the workload. Most relational DBMS products cannot begin to match the performance of well-tuned hierarchical and network DBMS products.

The second advantage is control. For transaction processing applications, the restriction that relationships be predefined can be very desirable. Transaction processing needs to be standardized. Most organizations do not want users of transaction processing applications to be able to perform ad hoc processing of data. Furthermore, requirements for most transaction processing applications evolve slowly. In most cases, ample time is available to adjust the database structure as new requirements emerge. Consequently, what is generally viewed as an advantage of relational database processing is often regarded as unnecessary or undesirable for transaction processing. Of course, more and more transaction processing is being performed on relational databases.

Implementing Databases for Transaction Processing

The process of implementing a database structured according to the hierarchical and network models must be extended from that described in previous chapters. As shown in Figure 12.3, we begin by defining reports, forms, and form-processing logic. From these we define objects, and then we transform object definitions into a relational database design. If we were using a relational database, we would then develop applications and implement them as shown in Chapters 8 and 11. But if the database is to be organized using either the hierarchical or network data models, we must perform an additional step. We must first convert the relational design to a hierarchical or network database design. This process will be illustrated later in this chapter and in the next chapter.

Keep in mind that although we will describe the use of the hierarchical and network data models for transaction processing, relational DBMS products can be used for trans-

FIGURE 12.3
Steps in database design

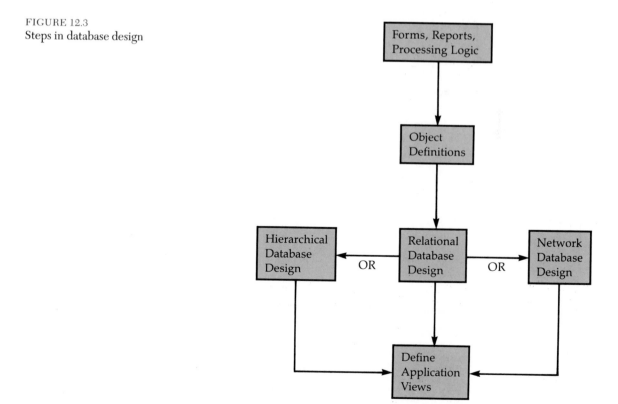

action processing as well. In some microcomputer database applications, particularly those involving multi-user processing on LANs, relational DBMS products are used for transaction processing. Here, however, the workload is considerably less than it is in most minicomputer or mainframe transaction processing applications. In any case, Figure 12.3 shows that relational database designs can be used for databases implemented with any of the three models.

The last step in Figure 12.3 concerns the identification of application views. As stated, control and security are important for transaction processing applications, and an application's view of data is often restricted to a portion of the database. In designing this view, the designer must determine the objects an application needs to access and views of those objects. Once the views have been defined, then the database can be physically designed, and the database and views can be created. We will consider this topic further as we discuss the hierarchical and network data models.

Data Language/I

IBM developed DL/I in the 1960s as an outgrowth of data processing needs in the aerospace industry. A joint development project was undertaken by IBM and North American Aviation. DL/I is a language for processing a database. The most popular implementation of DL/I is IMS, or Information Management System, which is IBM's primary transaction-processing-oriented DBMS. Actually, IMS is both a communications processor and a database management system, so it would be more correct to say that DL/I is implemented in IMS/DB, which is the database portion of IMS. DL/I uses hierarchies (trees) to represent relationships. This means that the users' objects must be transformed into tree representations before they can be processed using DL/I.

In DL/I terms, fields are grouped into **segments,** and segments are the nodes of tree structures. Recall from Chapter 7 that a **tree** is a collection of records and relationships such that each record has at most one parent, and all relationships are one-to-many from parent to child. (Throughout this discussion, we will use the DL/I term *segment* rather than record or row.) DL/I refers to a particular tree structure (a collection of related segments) as a **data base record.** (*Data base* is two words in DL/I.) A sample STUDENT data base record is sketched in Figure 12.4. The forked line notation used throughout this text is not part of DL/I notation, but it is used here for consistency. Each

FIGURE 12.4
STUDENT data base record

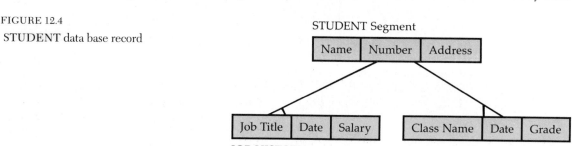

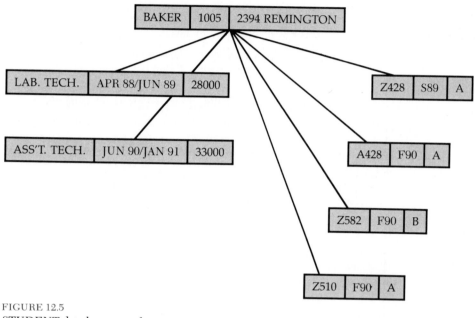

FIGURE 12.5
STUDENT data base record occurrence

FIGURE 12.6
FACULTY data base record

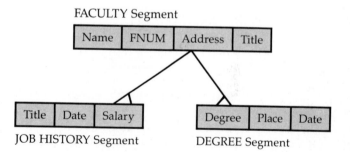

STUDENT segment has Name, Number, and Address fields. Also, under each STUDENT segment are a variable number of JOB HISTORY and CLASS segments. An occurrence of the STUDENT data base record is shown in Figure 12.5.

In DL/I, a **data base** is composed of data base records. These records can be occurrences of the same record type or of several different record types. For example, a DL/I data base could consist of occurrences of the STUDENT data base record in Figure 12.4 and the FACULTY data base record in Figure 12.6. The data base would comprise all occurrences of each data base record type. Figure 12.7 summarizes DL/I data structures.

Data base records are defined via a **data base description.** In the DBMS product IMS, a set of assembly-language macro instructions indicates the structure of each data base record. (Note that this is different from the relational language SQL you studied earlier. SQL includes both data definition and data manipulation statements. DL/I is for

Data Structure	Description
Field	Smallest unit of data
Segment	Group of fields; segments must be related by hierarchical structure; each segment has a sequence field used for logical ordering
Data base record	Hierarchically structured group of segments
Data base	Collection of data base record occurrences of one or more data base record types

FIGURE 12.7
Summary of DL/I data structures

STUDENT segment description
- DBD   NAME = STUDB
- SEGM   NAME = STU, BYTES = 61
- FIELD   NAME = SNAME, BYTES = 30, START = 1
- FIELD   NAME= (NUM,   SEQ), BYTES=11, START=31
- FIELD   NAME=ADDR, BYTES=20, START=42

JOB HISTORY segment description
- SEGM   NAME = JOBHIST, PARENT = STU, BYTES = 47
- FIELD   NAME = JOBTITLE, BYTES = 30, START = 1
- FIELD   NAME = (JDATE, SEQ), BYTES = 11, START = 31
- FIELD   NAME = SALARY, BYTES = 6, START = 42

CLASS segment description
- SEGM   NAME = CLASS, PARENT = STU, BYTES = 10
- FIELD   NAME = (CNAME, SEQ), BYTES = 5, START = 1
- FIELD   NAME = CDATE, BYTES = 4, START = 6
- FIELD   NAME = GRADE, BYTES = 1, START = 10

FIGURE 12.8
Data base description for STUDENT data base record of Figure 12.4

data manipulation only. This reflects DL/I's age; it arose before having a convenient means of data definition was judged important.) Figure 12.8 depicts a portion of the data base description for the STUDENT data base record in Figure 12.4. The format of this description is unique to IMS.

Each segment description is headed by a SEGM macro that names the segment, shows its total length, and gives the name of the parent, if there is one. The first segment, or **root,** has no parent. Each field within a segment is represented by a FIELD macro that indicates the field name, length, and starting position in the segment. One field within each segment is designated the **sequence field.** This field is used to order occurrences of a given segment type. The order is a logical one; it appears to the application program that segments are in order by the sequence field, but the physical ordering of segments may be different.

In Figure 12.8, the STUDENT segment is named STU and is 61 bytes long. The STU record is composed of an SNAME field in bytes 1 through 30, a NUM field in bytes 31 through 41, and an ADDR field in bytes 42 through 61. (DL/I uses uppercase letters, so all names are shown in capitals.) The sequence field for STU segments is NUM.

JOB HISTORY segments are called JOBHIST and are composed of JOBTITLE, JDATE, and SALARY fields. CLASS segments are called CLASS and have CNAME, CDATE, and GRADE fields.

The data base description is assembled and can be stored in object form in a library to be called into main memory when needed. Consequently, each application programmer need not perform the time-consuming process of writing the data base description for his or her program.

REPRESENTATION OF OBJECTS IN DL/I

This section will illustrate the representation of objects using DL/I. We begin with a discussion of one method by which trees are represented in physical storage. Next we will show how a simple network can be decomposed into trees with duplication and then how to eliminate that duplication. After that, we will present a set of objects illustrating the object types we discussed in Chapter 7, and we will show how to represent this set of objects so they can be processed by DL/I. Finally, we will define the DL/I terms *logical data base record* and *physical data base record* and show examples of each.

Physical Representation of Trees

In order to appreciate the way in which DL/I eliminates data duplication, you must first understand how trees are represented in physical storage. We will present the essence of one technique in this section. See Appendix B for more information.

Figure 12.9 presents object diagrams of three objects used in a university library. TITLE contains data about a particular book title as well as two object properties, PUBLISHER and COPY. PUBLISHER contains data about a publisher and its salesperson as well as the object property TITLE. COPY contains data about a copy of a TITLE as well as a multivalued property, Due-date. This repeating property contains all of the dates on which that book copy has been due.

These three objects can be represented by the hierarchical data structure shown in Figure 12.10a. Each rectangle is defined as a DL/I segment. Sample data for this hier-

TITLE   PUBLISHER   COPY

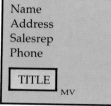

FIGURE 12.9

Three objects used by university library

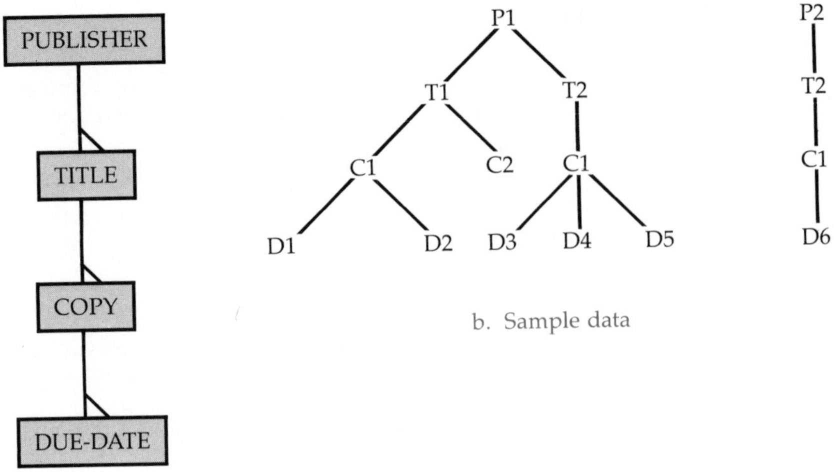

b. Sample data

a. Hierarchy of
   objects

FIGURE 12.10

Hierarchical data structure

FIGURE 12.11

Child and twin pointer
representation of hierarchy in
Figure 12.10

Record Number	Key Data	Nonkey Data	Pointers Child	Pointers Twin
1	P1	· · ·	2	12
2	T1	· · ·	4	3
3	T2	· · ·	6	0
4	T1 C1	· · ·	7	5
5	T1 C2	· · ·	0	0
6	T2 C1	· · ·	9	0
7	T1 C1 D1	· · ·	0	8
8	T1 C1 D2	· · ·	0	0
9	T2 C1 D3	· · ·	0	10
10	T2 C1 D4	· · ·	0	11
11	T2 C1 D5	· · ·	0	0
12	P2	· · ·	13	0
13	T3	· · ·	14	0
14	T3 C1	· · ·	15	0
15	T3 C1 D6	· · ·	0	0

archy is shown in Figure 12.10b. Since this is a hierarchy, it can be represented by DL/I in a straightforward fashion.

There are many ways in which a tree like the one in Figure 12.10 can be represented in physical storage. In fact, IMS supports several different methods. One technique, illustrated in Figure 12.11, is called the **child and twin pointer** method.

Figure 12.11 assumes that each segment is stored in a separate physical record. This is unrealistic, but convenient for our purposes. In practice, many segments would be blocked into a single physical record. However, because dealing with blocking and unblocking would not contribute to your understanding of the topic at hand, we have chosen to omit it and simplify the illustration. Each record is addressed by its relative position in the file. For example, the record containing the segment for PUBLISHER P2 is located at address 12.

Each record in Figure 12.11 has three sections. One contains the key of the segment, one contains nonkey data, and one contains two pointers, or addresses of other related segments. The first pointer is a **child pointer.** If a segment has any children, this pointer will contain the address of the record holding the first child segment. If the segment has no children, this pointer will be zero.

The second pointer is a **twin pointer.** If a segment has any siblings (segments of the same type having the same parent segment), this pointer will contain the address of the record holding the next sibling segment. If there are none (or no more), this pointer will be zero. Examine Figure 12.11 and be certain you understand how the pointers represent the tree in Figure 12.10. For practice, follow the pointers from P1, through T2, to the due date D5.

This data structure will allow records to be inserted and deleted without reorganizing the file. The pointers are simply changed. See Appendix B for more information about this process. We will come back to this example to illustrate how duplicated data can be eliminated. But now, let us consider the transformation of simple networks into trees.

Transforming Simple Networks into Trees

Figure 12.12a shows an expansion of the library objects shown in Figure 12.9. The PUBLISHER and TITLE objects are the same. The COPY object is the same except a STUDENT object property has been added to it. The fourth object is STUDENT. It represents students who check out copies of titles.

The design of a data base that represents these four objects is shown in Figure 12.12b. Observe this data structure is *not* a hierararchy because COPY has two parents of different types, TITLE and STUDENT. In fact, this structure is a **simple network.**

Since this structure is not a hierarchy, it cannot be *directly* represented in DL/I. It must first be transformed into a hierarchy. Figure 12.13a shows such a transformation. Two trees have been generated, one for each parent of COPY. Observe that in doing this, the data of COPY and of all of its children has been duplicated. This is shown in Figure 12.13b.

In general, it is always possible to transform a simple network into trees, although there will be some data duplication. For every node that has two parents, create two trees. We will show more examples later in this chapter.

Complex Networks

In Chapter 7 you learned that three types of data structures are based on binary record relationships: trees, simple networks, and complex networks. A relational design, however, includes only two of these types, namely trees and simple networks. Complex networks are eliminated from relational designs because the only objects that generate

FIGURE 12.12
Representation of objects with
simple network

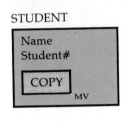

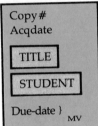

a. Four objects used by university library

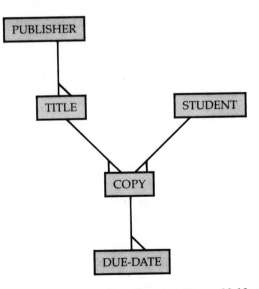

b. Simple network for objects in Figure 12-12a

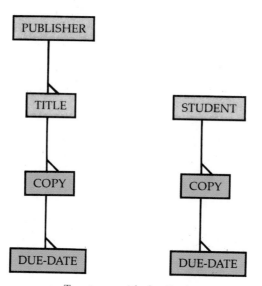

a. Two trees with duplication

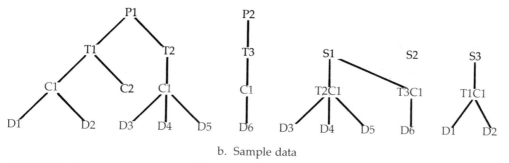

b. Sample data

FIGURE 12.13
Representing simple network with trees

them, M:N compound objects, are represented in a relational design as simple networks containing an intersection relation. See Chapter 7 for a review of this representation.

Thus, if you follow the process illustrated in Figure 12.3, producing the relational design before turning to DL/I, complex networks will already have been transformed into simple networks. Hence, you need to know only how to transform simple networks into trees.

Eliminating Data Duplication

We eliminate data duplication by storing the data once and representing all subsequent references to that data by pointers. In Figure 12.14a, the PUBLISHER/TITLE/COPY/ DUE-DATE tree will be stored intact, as shown in Figure 12.11. In contrast, the STU-DENT/COPY/DUE-DATE tree is not stored in that form. The children segments of

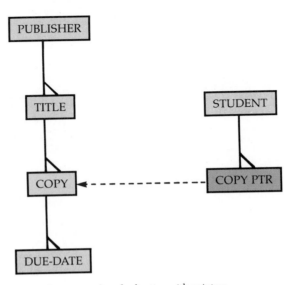

a. Eliminating data duplication with pointers

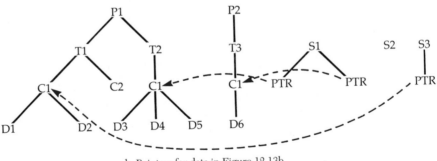

b. Pointers for data in Figure 12.13b

FIGURE 12.14
Child and twin pointer representation of simple network

STUDENT contain **pointers** to data rather than data. This is illustrated in Figure 12.14b.

Figure 12.14c shows how these structures can be stored using the child and twin pointer scheme. The first fifteen records of this file are the same as those in Figure 12.11. These records represent the PUBLISHER/TITLE/COPY/DUE-DATE tree. Records 16 through 21 represent the STUDENT/COPY/DUE-DATE tree. Observe that the nonkey data fields of COPY children (such as T2, C1) have been replaced by pointers to segments containing actual COPY data.

Using this strategy, both trees can be represented without duplicating the COPY or DUE-DATE data. The strategy is not without risk, however. The possibility exists that **fragments,** or children segments that become logically detached from a parent, will be created. For instance, suppose a STUDENT segment is linked to a COPY of a TITLE.

FIGURE 12.14, *continued*

Record Number	Key Data	Nonkey Data	Pointers Child	Twin
1	P1	. . .	2	12
2	T1	. . .	4	3
3	T2	. . .	6	0
4	T1 C1	. . .	7	5
5	T1 C2	. . .	0	0
6	T2 C1	. . .	9	0
7	T1 C1 D1	. . .	0	8
8	T1 C1 D2	. . .	0	0
9	T2 C1 D3	. . .	0	10
10	T2 C1 D4	. . .	0	11
11	T2 C1 D5	. . .	0	0
12	P2	. . .	13	0
13	T3	. . .	14	0
14	T3 C1	. . .	15	0
15	T3 C1 D6	. . .	0	0
16	S1	. . .	19	17
17	S2	. . .	0	18
18	S3	. . .	21	0
19	T2 C1	PTR = 6	0	20
20	T3 C1	PTR = 14	0	0
21	T1 C1	PTR = 4	0	0

c. Child and twin pointer representation of simple network

Now suppose that the TITLE segment and its children segments (COPY and DUE-DATE) are deleted from the data base. The COPY pointer under the STUDENT segment now points to an invalid location and is therefore a fragment. Similarly, a student may not check out a book until the copy has been stored in the PUBLISHER, TITLE, COPY, DUE-DATE hierarchy.

Such dynamic constraints are unlike constraints we have encountered before. The relationship between STUDENT and COPY is optional-to-optional, but once a student is related to a COPY segment, that segment cannot be deleted. Neither can a STUDENT segment be related to a COPY segment that has not already been entered. Because such constraints are not enforced by IMS, that task falls to the application programmer.

This situation is unfortunate because, if application programs are incorrectly written so that the constraints are not enforced or are enforced incorrectly, then fragments will exist in the database. The fragments will be difficult to detect until user errors occur. Further, the presence of one fragment creates the suspicion that more may exist—a suspicion that is exceedingly difficult to investigate.

DL/I Representation of the Library Example

To illustrate the transformation of a relational design to DL/I, consider the expanded set library objects shown in Figure 12.15. This group contains one example of most of the object types described in Chapter 7, namely composite objects; 1:1, 1:N, and M:N com-

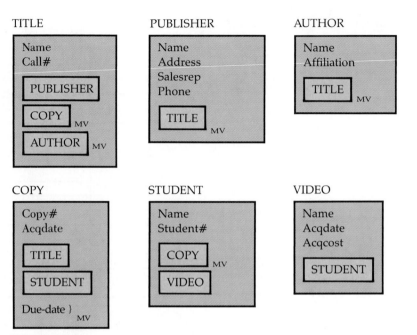

FIGURE 12.15
Six objects used by university library

FIGURE 12.16
Relational design for objects in
Figure 12.15

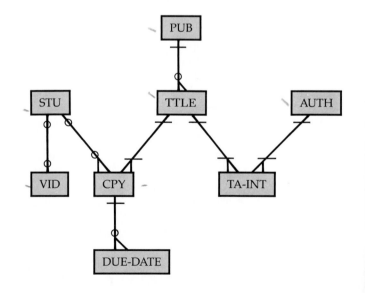

pound objects; and association objects. COPY is a composite object because it contains Due-date as a multivalued nonobject property. The 1:1 compound objects are STUDENT and VIDEO (students are allowed to check out only one videocassette at a time). The 1:N compound objects are PUBLISHER and TITLE. The M:N compound objects are AUTHOR and TITLE, because an author can write many books and a book can be written by many authors. The association object is COPY which documents the relationship between a TITLE and the STUDENT who checks it out.

A relational design for these objects is shown in Figure 12.16. Observe there is one relation for each object. The names of the relations are slightly different from the object names to differentiate the two. In addition to these six relations, the relation DUE-DATE represents that repeating group in the COPY object, and the intersection relation TA-INT represents the M:N relationship between TITLE and AUTHOR. To be certain you understand this design, identify which relations compose each object.

The relational design in Figure 12.16 is not a hierarchy because two relations, CPY and TA-INT, have more than one parent. Therefore, we must create two trees for each of these relations, a total of four trees. This has been done in Figure 12.17a, (only three trees appear because the middle tree in this figure holds two of them). Consider CPY first. Since both TTLE and STU are parents of CPY, we need to construct one tree for each of them. Thus you will see in Figure 12.17a the STU/CPY/DUE-DATE tree (part of the leftmost tree in that figure) and the PUB/TTLE/CPY/DUE-DATE tree (part of the middle tree). STU also has a child VID which we can add under STU without causing a problem, completing that tree.

Now consider the TA-INT relation in Figure 12.16. The purpose of TA-INT is to represent many titles for a given author and many authors for a given title. Thus, we want a tree with AUTH as parent and TTLE as child, and a tree with TTLE as parent and AUTH as child. This representation is also shown in Figure 12.17a. AUTH/TTLE/CPY/DUE-DATE is shown as a separate tree. The TTLE/AUTH relationship has been represented within the PUB/TTLE/CPY/DUE-DATE tree by adding the AUTH relation under TTLE. Thus, Figure 12.17a actually shows four trees (two for each of the relations that have two parents), but two of the trees have been combined under the common parent TTLE.

The trees in Figure 12.17a have considerable data duplication. We can eliminate that duplication with pointers, as shown in Figure 12.17b. Concerning CPY, we must choose either to put the data under TTLE and the pointers under STU or to put the pointers under TTLE and the data under STU. The choice between the two depends on the workload and the type of physical data structure used to store the trees. As a general rule, the data should be stored as part of the tree that is used most frequently. However, the particulars of this depend on specific features of IMS and are not relevant to the discussion here.

LOGICAL AND PHYSICAL RECORDS

DL/I divides a data base into physical and logical constructs. The terms **physical data base** (PDB) and **physical data base record** (PDBR) are used to describe the data as it exists in data storage. The terms **logical data base** (LDB) and **logical data base rec-**

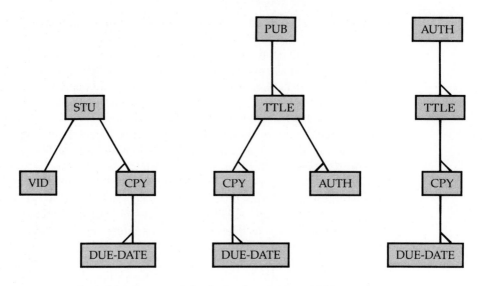

a. Logical data base records for the data base in Figure 12.16

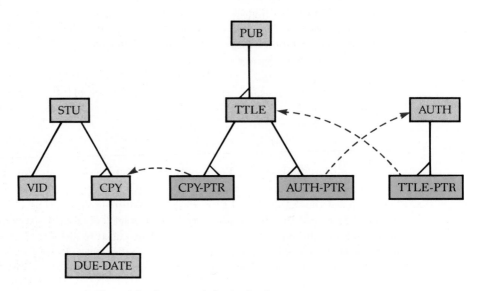

b. Physical data base records for the data base in Figure 12.16

FIGURE 12.17
Representing hierarchies for DL/I processing

ord (LDBR) are used to describe the data as it appears to the application programs that process it. LDBRs differ from PDBRs in either of two ways. An LDBR may be a subset of a PDBR, or an LDBR may contain portions of two or more PDBRs and represent tree structures that are not present in the PDBRs. The trees sketched in Figure 12.17a are LDBRs. They represent data as it appears to an application program. Conversely, the trees sketched in Figure 12.17b are PDBRs.

To understand LDBRs that are subsets of PDBRs, consider the PDBR STU/CPY/VID/DUE-DATE tree in Figure 12.17b. Personnel at the video checkout desk need not have access to CPY and DUE-DATE data. The application that checks out videocassettes requires only STU and VID data. To meet this need, the data base developers would define an LDBR containing only STU/VID. This LDBR is a subset of the STU/CPY/VID/DUE-DATE PDBR. All three of the LDBRs in Figure 12.17a are examples of LDBRs that contain relationships not present in the PDBRs. Consider the LDBR AUTH/TTLE/CPY/DUE-DATE. The PDBR that represents this tree is AUTH/TTLE-PTR. Clearly the LDBR is *constructed* from data in two PDBRs. The data base developer defines PDBRs and LDBRs using macro instructions similar to those shown in Figure 12.8. The specifics of these instructions are beyond the scope of this text.

APPLICATION VIEWS

For reasons of control, application programs are generally not allowed to access the entire data base. Instead, they are given access to **views** of objects. With DL/I, a view of an object is represented by an LDBR. Thus, an application view in DL/I consists of the definition of one or more LDBRs.

Consider the university library applications. The video checkout desk needs access to STUDENT and VIDEO data. Thus, an LDBR consisting of STU/VID would be defined for application programs that support the video checkout station. The book checkout desk needs access to STUDENT and COPY data, so an LDBR consisting of STU/CPY would be defined for applications that support this function. The acquisitions desk needs access to PUBLISHER, TITLE, COPY, and DUE-DATE (to be able to determine how frequently copies are used) data, so an LDBR with only this data would be defined for programs serving that department. Similarly, LDBRs would be defined for the reference desk, the overdue fines collection clerk, and so forth.

The prevention of fragments needs to be carefully considered when defining these LDBRs and their processing. Because of the way that networks are represented, dynamic constraints can exist in addition to normal relationship constraints (M-M, M-O, and so forth). As discussed in the section on the elimination of data duplication, data that is pointed to from one PDBR must be deleted with great care. Otherwise, pointers to the addresses vacated by the deleted data will become invalid. Because IMS does not provide facilities for defining and enforcing such dynamic constraints, they must be enforced by application programs. Unfortunately, the constraints may not be apparent to programmers who see only a particular LDBR's view of the data base.

Additionally, as you will see in the next section, an application program can actually delete data that is not visible in its LDBR. Since this is the case, the application programmer needs to be told which operations can be performed on data in each view. Further, with IMS, processing rights and authorities that limit allowable actions can be defined for each LDBR. As discussed in Chapter 14, these authorities need to be carefully thought out during the data base design stage.

DL/I Data Manipulation Language

DL/I processes data in segments. DL/I statements can retrieve, update, insert, and delete segments. Unlike SQL, which can be used interactively or can be embedded in application programs, DL/I statements *must* be embedded in application programs. DL/I is not an interactive query language. (Keep in mind that DL/I was one of the earlier database languages, used exclusively for transaction processing by information systems professionals not by end-users.)

Using DL/I, the application programmer defines an input/output (I/O) work area that is shared by the application program and the DBMS product. To insert or update a segment, the application program places new data in the work area; the DBMS takes the data from there to modify the data base. When the DBMS retrieves data from the data base, it places the data in the work area for the program to access. System status data, such as completion flags and error flags, is also placed in the work area by the DBMS so the application program can examine it.

The DL/I syntax presented in this section is general; it could apply to almost any programming language. Unlike DB2, IMS does not have a precompiler. DL/I commands are executed by calling a DBMS subroutine from the host program. The parameters of a data base subroutine call specify the command type, search criteria, and other data. The format of data base subroutine calls depends on the host language. We will present only the DL/I commands—we will not be concerned with programming language particulars. To illustrate the DL/I data manipulation commands, consider the LDBR in Figure 12.18. The LDBR is based on the PUB/TTLE/AUTH-PTR/CPY-PTR PDBR in Figure 12.17b.

FIGURE 12.18
Sample LDBR for data base in
Figure 12.17b

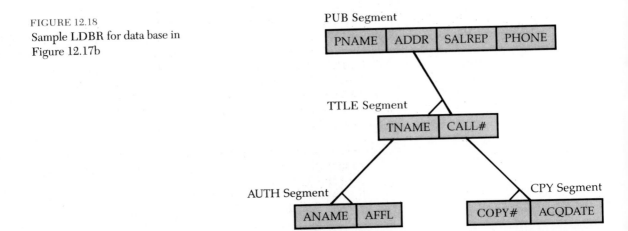

GET UNIQUE (GU)

This command is used to read a particular segment into the I/O work area. For example, the statement

```
GU    PUB (SALREP = 'JONES')
```

will cause the first PUB segment with the SALREP value of JONES to be placed into the I/O work area. Thus, if the occurrences in Figure 12.19 are the first ones in the data base, then the segment P2,NYC,JONES,(212)555-1776 will be placed in the work area. The following statements will cause the first AUTH with name A3 of TTLE T2 to be placed in the work area:

```
GU    PUB
      TTLE (TNAME = 'T2')
      AUTH (ANAME = 'A3')
```

If no such segment exists, the DBMS will set an appropriate return code in the work area.

The DBMS will search for the desired segment by starting at the first occurrence of the LDBR, at the first T2 occurrence of the TTLE segment (assuming there could be more than one), and at the first A3 occurrence of the AUTH segment (again assuming there could be more than one). The order of the segments is determined by the sequence fields in each segment (see Figure 12.8). For this LDBR, assume the following sequence fields:

Segment	Sequence Field
PUB	PNAME
TTLE	TNAME
AUTH	ANAME
CPY	COPY#

Thus, to find the first occurrence of AUTH A3 in TTLE T2, segments will be examined in the following order: P1 (PUB) segment, T1, T2 (TTLE segments), and finally A2, A3 (AUTH segments). The segment read into the work area will be A3.

The qualifying data after the GU command is called a **segment search argument** (SSA). In general, an SSA is the name of a segment, optionally followed by a condition. As shown, there can be one SSA for each segment in the hierarchical path for the segment to be retrieved.

GET NEXT (GN)

This command is used to read the next segment. Next implies that there be a current segment to start from, so it is necessary to indicate a current segment before issuing a GN command. For example, the statements

```
GU    PUB
      TTLE (TNAME = 'T1')
GN    TTLE
```

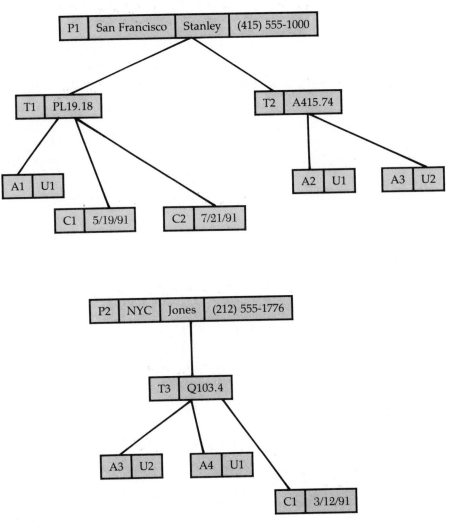

FIGURE 12.19
Two occurrences of the LDBR in Figure 12.18

will cause the first TTLE segment in the data base with TNAME field equal to T1 to be placed in the I/O work area. This establishes a current position. (There would most likely be some program instructions to process that segment following the GU command, but we have omitted them.) The GN statement reads the next TTLE segment. For the occurrence in Figure 12.19, the T1 segment will be read first, followed by the T2 segment. If a subsequent GN TTLE command is executed, the DBMS will attempt to find another TTLE segment under the current PUB segment. There is none for this occurrence, so it will search under the next PUB segment (P2) and read the T3 occurrence of TTLE.

A third execution of GN TTLE will cause the DBMS to look for the next TTLE segment. Since there are no more in the P2 occurrence of PUB, the DBMS will search the next LDBR occurrence for a TTLE segment and, if it finds one, will place it in the work area. The search will continue to the end of the data base if necessary. If no TTLE segment remains in the data base, appropriate status data will be set.

When the GN statements are executed, the DBMS selects the next occurrence of the segment named. If there is no such occurrence under the current parent, the DBMS switches to the next parent. The application program may need to know, however, when the DBMS selects a segment from a new parent. For example, if the second GN TTLE statement is executed as discussed in the preceding paragraph, the program may need to know that a new PUB segment has been retrieved.

To provide this information, when a segment is read, data about the path leading to the segment is placed in the work area. IMS places the *fully concatenated key* of the retrieved segment in the work area. This key is the concatenation of all sequence fields of segments leading to the segment along with the sequence field of the segment. For example, the fully concatenated key for the A4 AUTH segment is P2 T3 A4. After the second GN TTLE command is executed as described above, the DBMS will return the key P2 T3 and the application program will be able to detect the new PUB segment by the change in PUB sequence field in the key. Now consider another example. The commands

```
GU    PUB
      TTLE (TNAME = 'T1')
GN    TTLE (CALL #> 'P')
```

will cause the T1 TTLE segment to be read, followed by the next TTLE segment with a call number starting with a letter beyond P in the collating sequence. Consequently T3 will be read next. The important point here is that sequential retrieval can be either *qualified* (with a condition after the segment name) or *unqualified* (with no condition).

Another type of sequential retrieval command requests the next segment regardless of its type. For example, the commands

```
GU    PUB
      TTLE (TNAME = 'T1')
GN
```

will cause the T1 segment of TTLE to be read, followed by the A1 AUTH segment. A subsequent GN command will read the C1 CPY segment.

As an aside, this LDBR does not include DUE-DATE segments (or, as sometimes expressed in DL/I, this LDBR *is not sensitive to* DUE-DATE segments). When the GN commands are executed, no DUE-DATE data is presented to the application program. It is automatically skipped by the DBMS. IMS never presents to an application data to which the application is not sensitive.

GET NEXT WITHIN PARENT (GNP)

This command sequentially retrieves segments under one parent. When all segments under that parent have been read, end-of-data status is returned to the program. For example, when the commands

```
GU    PUB
      TTLE (TNAME = 'T1')
GNP   TTLE
            GNP   TTLE
```

are executed, the T1 and T2 segments of P1 will be read. The second GNP command will not return data; rather, it will cause the end-of-data status flag to be set. Contrast this with the statements

```
GU    PUB
      TTLE (TNAME = 'T1')
GN    TTLE
GN    TTLE
```

Here, the second GN command will retrieve the T3 TTLE segment.

GET HOLD COMMANDS

The three commands Get Hold Unique (GHU), Get Hold Next (GHN), and Get Hold Next within Parent (GHNP) operate exactly as the Get counterparts except that they inform the DBMS to prepare for a change or deletion of the retrieved segment. They are used in conjunction with Replace and Delete commands. When the application program replaces or deletes a segment, it must first issue one of the forms of the Get Hold commands for that segment. The DBMS will retrieve the segment and "hold" it. Then the Replace or Delete command can be issued.

REPLACE (REPL)

The Replace command is used to modify data within a segment. For example, the commands

```
GHU   PUB
      TTLE (TNAME = 'T2')
```

(here the application program changes TTLE data)

```
REPL
```

will cause the DBMS to retrieve the T2 TTLE segment and to replace that segment with the changed data. (In this example, and in several that follow, we will show program processing in lowercase letters. The syntax of the commands to execute this logic is language dependent and will be omitted.)

As another example, suppose it is desired to set the acquisition date of all copies of all titles to 1/1/91. The following instruction sequence will accomplish this:

```
GHU   PUB
      TTLE
      CPY
DOWHILE data remains
      Set ACQDATE = '1/1/91'
      REPL
      GHN CPY
END-DO
```

The GHU command obtains the first CPY segment in the data base, and the GHN command obtains all subsequent ones.

Another example is to change the acquisition date to 1/1/91 only for those titles that were published by a publisher located in NYC. The programming logic for this process appears in Figure 12.20. This requires the use of both GHN and GHNP commands as follows:

```
GU    PUB (ADDR = 'NYC')
      (set status-1 = 1 if data exists; 0 otherwise)
DOWHILE status-1 = 1
      GHNP TTLE
           CPY
      (set status-2 = 1 if data exists; 0 otherwise)
      DOWHILE status-2 = 1
           (set ACQDATE = '1/1/91')
           REPL
           GHNP  TTLE
                 CPY
           (set status-2 = 1 if data exists; 0 otherwise)
      END-DO
      GN    PUB (ADDR = 'NYC')
      (set status-1 = 1 if data exists; 0 otherwise)
END-DO
```

The GU command attempts to find the first publisher located in NYC. If one exists, the loop is executed for that publisher. The program attempts to obtain the first CPY within that publisher. If one exists, its ACQDATE is changed and it is replaced. The program attempts to read the next CPY within the current publisher parent. If one exists, it, too, is changed and replaced, and so forth. When there is no CPY within the current publisher parent, then the program attempts to obtain the next publisher in NYC. If one exists, the outer loop is repeated again.

DELETE (DLET)

Delete operates in conjunction with the Get Hold commands in a manner similar to Replace. The commands

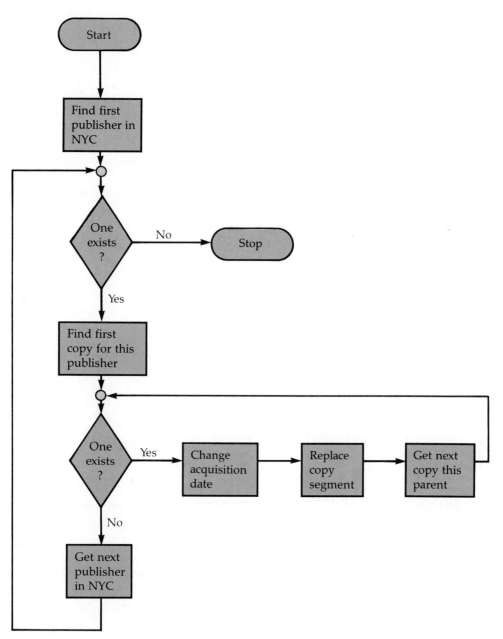

FIGURE 12.20
Logic required to change acquisition dates for NYC publishers

```
GHU    PUB (PNAME = 'P1')
       TTLE (TNAME = 'T1')
       AUTH (ANAME = 'A1')
DLET
```

will delete the A1 segment under T1 and P1 from the data base. When a segment is deleted, any subordinate segments are also deleted (including ones invisible to the application). Thus the commands

```
GHU    PUB (PNAME = 'P1')
       TTLE (TNAME = 'T1')
       CPY (COPY# = 1)
DLET
```

will delete not only the C1 copy segment under T1 and P1, but also all of the DUE-DATE segments under that copy. Thus, subordinate segments to which the application is not sensitive will be deleted.

Deletion of invisible data is dangerous and not recommended. In order to prevent it from happening, the database administrator, database designers, and application programmers must communicate clearly with one another. Standards need to be established and enforced. Designs need to be reviewed carefully. Otherwise, application programmers will write application code that appears to them to be correct, but that in fact is causing errors—errors that the programmers had no possibility of knowing might exist.

INSERT (INSRT)

Insert is used to create a new segment. For example, the statements (instructions to place new AUTH data in I/O work area)

```
INSERT    PUB (PNAME = 'P1')
          TTLE (TNAME = 'T2')
          AUTH
```

will insert a new AUTH segment into the data base. Since the AUTH sequence field is ANAME, the new segment will be logically inserted in order of that field. For example, if the new value of ANAME is A4, then the new AUTH segment will be inserted logically as the last AUTH segment under the T2 parent.

DL/I DATA MANIPULATION COMMAND SUMMARY

Figure 12.21 summarizes the DL/I data manipulation commands. All of these commands operate on the logical structure of the data as seen by an application program. Since the physical structure of the data may be quite different from the logical structure, the DBMS must translate the logical activity into actions on the physical data structures. The application is independent of the physical structures and is freed from maintaining them.

Name	Function
Get Unique (GU)	Retrieve a particular segment
Get Next (GN)	Retrieve the next segment
Get Next within Parent (GNP)	Retrieve the next segment under a particular parent
Get Hold Unique (GHU)	Similar to above commands, but used to obtain a segment to be modified or deleted
Get Hold Next (GHN)	
Get Hold Next within Parent (GHNP)	
Replace (REPL)	Used in conjunction with Get Hold commands to modify or delete a segment
Delete (DLET)	
Insert (INSRT)	Insert a new segment

FIGURE 12.21
Summary of DL/I data manipulation commands

Summary

DBMS products based on the hierarchical and network data models are used to support transaction processing systems. They are seldom used for decision support or other ad hoc systems, and they are never used for personal database systems. These products arose during the earliest years of database processing and their importance lies in the multitudinous existing databases that are structured according to them. Few new databases are constructed with them. Their chief importance to you lies in maintenance of existing applications or in conversion of databases to the relational model.

An operational database is a model of important aspects of a business. Transaction processing applications update such databases to keep them current. Transactions, which are representations of business events, are processed both to change the data and to generate real outputs. Real outputs cannot be undone in the case of error. Rather, compensating transactions must be generated.

Transaction processing applications differ in character from decision support or personal applications. Transaction processing systems must demonstrate fast response time. They should not fail often, and when they do, they must be recovered quickly and accurately. Unlike decision support applications, transaction processing applications do not need to be flexible—in fact, because business processing is standardized processing, flexibility may be undesirable. Control, however, is very important. One means of control is the use of views that restrict a database system user's view of the data. Another form of control is placing the computer equipment in a closed environment.

Three data models evolved to support transaction processing: the hierarchical data model, the network data model, and the relational data model. The sole surviving hierarchical data model is the IBM language DL/I. The most important network model is the CODASYL DBTG data model, which will be discussed in the next chapter.

Both the hierarchical and network data model require that relationships be predefined. This requirement exists because relationships are carried in data structures such as linked lists; they are not carried in the data as is done with the relational model.

Although predefinition reduces flexibility, it does have two advantages: better performance and greater control.

When developing databases based on the hierarchical or network data models, we must add an additional step to the development process. During implementation, the DBMS-independent relational design must be converted to the hierarchial or network design.

DL/I uses terminology substantially different from the relational model. In DL/I a row or record is called a segment. A segment is a group of fields. One field in the segment is designated as the sequence field; it is used to logically order the segments. A tree is made up of several related segments. An instance of a tree is a data base record (DL/I spells data base as two words). Data base records are defined via a data base description. A data base is comprised of data base records of one or more types.

DL/I is hierarchical; the segments in a data base record can have at most one parent. Thus, in order to represent networks (relationships in which a child has more than one parent), the network must be decomposed into trees with data duplication. The duplication is then eliminated through the use of pointers or other data structures. The child and twin pointer scheme illustrated in this chapter is one example.

DL/I uses the term *physical data base record* (or PDBR) to refer to physically stored data and the term *logical data base record* (or LDBR) to refer to application views of data. An LDBR differs from a PDBR in one of two ways: it may be a subset of a PDBR or it may contain portions of two or more PDBRs. An application view is a set of one more LDBRs.

DL/I statements to retrieve, modify, insert, and delete segments must be embedded in application programs; thus, DL/I cannot be used interactively. DL/I data base requests are actually accomplished by issuing subroutine calls from the application program. IMS, the product in which DL/I is implemented, does not include a precompiler.

Basic DL/I commands are Get Unique, Get Next, Get Next within Parent, Get Hold Unique, Get Hold Next, Get Hold Next within Parent, Replace, Delete, and Insert. Each of these commands operates on an LDBR.

GROUP I QUESTIONS

12.1 Explain the difference in the range of application of DBMS products based on the hierarchical, network, and relational models.

12.2 Explain how a database is a model of an organization.

12.3 What is a transaction?

12.4 What is a real output? Why is the distinction between real outputs and other outputs important?

12.5 Summarize the basic characteristics of a transaction processing application.

12.6 Why is flexibility not desirable in a transaction processing system?

12.7   Summarize the nature of the three data models that arose to support transaction processing systems.

12.8   Describe the advantages of the fact that relationships in a hierarchical or network data model must be predefined.

12.9   How must the implementation process be extended when developing databases based on the hierarchical and network models?

12.10   Define the DL/I terms *field, segment, data base record,* and *data base.*

12.11   What DL/I structure corresponds to a node on a tree?

12.12   How are DL/I data base records defined? Does DL/I include data definition language as well as data manipulation language?

12.13   Describe the child and twin pointer scheme and illustrate with an example other than the one in this text.

12.14   Why must simple networks be transformed into trees before they can be stored for processing by DL/I?

12.15   Why, if you follow the data base design process described in this text, do you not need to transform complex networks into trees before storing them for DL/I processing?

12.16   How does DL/I eliminate data duplication, even though logically more than one tree contain the same (duplicate) data?

12.17   What is the danger in deleting a segment that is being pointed to by another segment in the data base?

12.18   How can an application program delete data to which it is not sensitive?

12.19   What is the difference between a physical data base record and a logical data base record? In what two ways does an LDBR differ from a PDBR?

12.20   What is an application view? What is its role?

GROUP II QUESTIONS

12.21   Consider the following organizational chart.

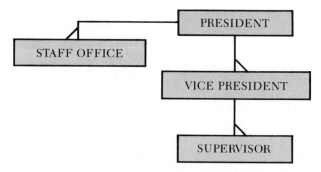

a. Sketch an occurrence of this structure.
b. What in this example constitutes a DL/I segment? a data base record? the data base?

12.22 Assume each segment in question 12.21 has Name, Address, Employee-number, and Salary fields. Write a data base description similar to the one in Figure 12.8 for this data base.

12.23 Sketch the hierarchical structure and logical pointers necessary to model the following data base records in DL/I:

a.
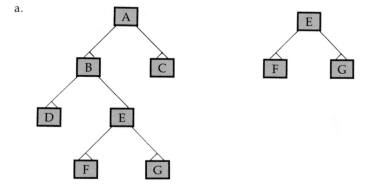

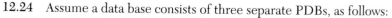

b.
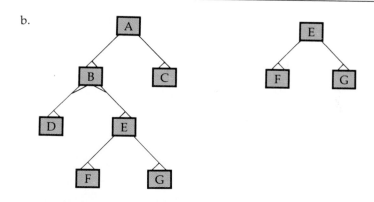

12.24 Assume a data base consists of three separate PDBs, as follows:

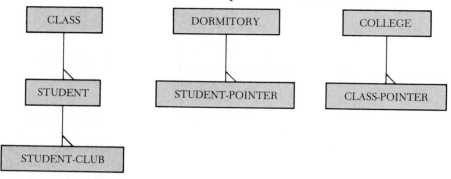

Describe the LDBR required to respond to the following requests:

a. Obtain the names of all students in a class taught by the College of Business.
b. Obtain the name of every student club that has at least one member living in Green Dormitory.

The data following question 12.29 pertains to questions 12.25 through 12.29. Sequence fields are underlined.

12.25 Describe the results of the following retrievals:

```
a. GU    FACTORY
         PRODUCT (COST = 40)
         PART
b. GU    FACTORY
         WREHOUSE (NAME = 'W2')
         DISTRBTR
c. GU    FACTORY
         PRODUCT (COST = 40)
         PART (NUM-REQ = 24)
   GN    PART
   GN    PART
   GN    PART
   GN    PART
d. GU    FACTORY
         PRODUCT (COST = 40)
   GNP   PART
   GNP   PART
```

12.26 What will happen when the last GN PART statement is executed in question 12.25c? How will the user be able to detect this?

12.27 What will happen if another GNP PART statement is executed immediately after those in question 12.25d?

12.28 Show the DL/I statements needed to specify the following actions:

a. Delete the | PRT6 | 24 | segment under PRD2.
b. Delete all data about warehouse W3.
c. Delete all data about factory F1.
d. Delete all products costing more than $45.

12.29 Show the DL/I statements needed to perform the following modifications and additions. In doing so, explain actions that must be performed by language-unique commands as well:

a. Modify PRD2 to show a cost of $85.
b. Modify the cost of all products to be 10 percent greater.
c. Add distributor D11 to warehouse W2 and distribute D14 to warehouse W3.

d. Add to factory F1: PRD4, COST $105, with parts PRT2, 26 required, and PRT4, 31 required.

e. Change the cost of PRD1 to $45 and add PRT6, 21 required to it.

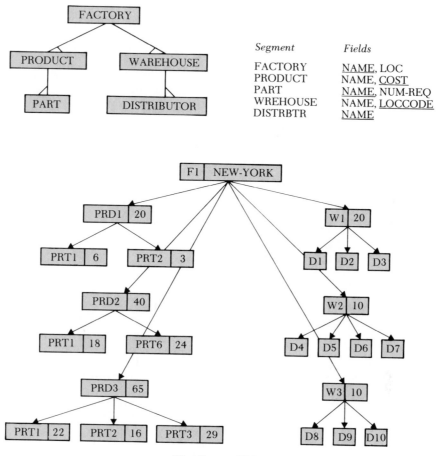

Segment	Fields
FACTORY	NAME, LOC
PRODUCT	NAME, COST
PART	NAME, NUM-REQ
WREHOUSE	NAME, LOCCODE
DISTRBTR	NAME

First Factory PDBR

CODASYL DBTG Model

In this chapter we will introduce a third data model that is frequently used to build databases to support transaction processing. The network data model derives its name from the fact that simple networks can be represented directly, without the transformations required for the hierarchical data model. Although at one time there were several varieties of network models, the only one of consequence today is the CODASYL DBTG data model.

We will begin with a brief history of this model and then discuss its features and functions, starting with the data definition components. Next, we will illustrate how these components are used to represent each of the object types discussed in this text. After that, application views, or subschemas as they are called in the DBTG model, will be presented. Finally, the DBTG data manipulation language will be discussed in the context of the library database introduced in Chapter 12.

- HISTORY OF THE CODASYL DBTG DATA MODEL
- CODASYL DBTG DATA DEFINITION LANGUAGE
- A SCHEMA DEFINITION FOR THE LIBRARY DATABASE
- CODASYL DBTG DATA MANIPULATION LANGUAGE
- CODASYL DBTG MODEL AS A MODEL

History of the CODASYL DBTG Data Model

The CODAYSL DBTG data model was developed by a group known as the CODASYL (Conference on Data Systems Languages) Data Base Task Group (hence the name CODASYL DBTG). The CODASYL committee is best known as the group that developed the standards for COBOL. The popularity and effectiveness of COBOL is due, in large measure, to the presence of COBOL language standards. The CODASYL data model evolved over several years, and quite a few transaction-oriented DBMS products are based on this model. However, the CODASYL data model never enjoyed the same degree of acceptance as the COBOL specification.

Several reasons account for the lack of wide acceptance of the DBTG model. First, as you will see, this model is complex and incohesive. For example, a statement in a schema definition can combine with a seemingly unrelated operation in an application program to produce strange and unexpected results. Designers and programmers must be very careful when building DBTG databases and applications. Second, the model has a decidedly COBOL flavor to it (for an example, skip ahead to Figure 13.18). This similarity has been an issue in organizations where COBOL is not the language of choice. Further, the development of the CODASYL database model was heavily politicized; the committee had to contend with the tendency to include everyone's favorite idea. Finally, in fairness to this model, it originated very early in the history of database technology. Many important concepts were included in this model, but mistakes were also made. Some people believe the model was developed too soon—before the essential concepts of database technology were known and had been explored.

The history of the CODASYL model is complex. Three different versions were developed, and although the data model was twice submitted to the American National Standards Institute (ANSI) for consideration as a national standard, it was never accepted. Instead, in August 1986, the relational model and SQL were recognized as the national database standard.

The basic functions and features of the three versions of the CODASYL model are the same. Most of the commercial DBMS products based on this model are based on the earliest one, developed in 1971. Later models, in 1978 and 1981, changed some of the language and syntax (the 1971 model had inappropriately used COBOL reserved words), added features to support the definition of constraints, and made other changes. The discussion in this chapter will adhere to the 1981 model, but where it is important to know how earlier models differ from this version, concepts from the earlier models will also be presented.

Strictly speaking, only the 1971 version was called the CODASYL *DBTG* model. In subsequent versions, the DBTG was dropped. Common industry practice, however, refers to all versions of this model as the DBTG model, and we will follow that practice.

As you read this chapter, keep in mind that you are learning about a *model*. This model was used as the basis for the design of a number of transaction-oriented DBMS products such as IDMS/R, IDS, DMS-170, and others. The developers of these products conformed to the model to greater and lesser degrees. You will not find a product that exactly fits the CODASYL DBTG model (of any version). However, the core features and functions of these products conform to the basic philosophy and orientation of this model.

The DBTG model (1971) introduced the terms **data definition language** (DDL) and **data manipulation language** (DML). As you know from earlier discussions in this text, the DDL is the language used to describe the structure of the database, and the DML is the language used to describe the processing of the database. Recall that DL/I, discussed in Chapter 12, does not include a DDL. Thus, the CODASYL model was an improvement over the earlier database products that included only data manipulation facilities.

CODASYL DBTG Data Definition Language

The 1981 version of the CODASYL model provides three different types of database view. The **schema** is the complete logical view of the database. It is the entire database as viewed by the database administrator or other humans. A **subschema** is a view of the database as it appears to an application program. A subschema is a subset of the database, and, in the 1978 and 1981 models, a subschema is allowed to have records that are constructed by joining records in the schema. This is similar to a view composed of relation joins as discussed in Chapter 11.

The **data structure description** is the third type of view. This description maps schema records, fields, and relationships to physical storage. It is the view of the database as it appears in physical storage. Because data structure descriptions were introduced in the second (1978) version of the model, they are not widely used. As it is unlikely that you will ever encounter them, we will omit them from our discussion.

As shown in Figure 13.1, users interact with the database via an application program (no interactive query language exists). One or more users can execute a single program. Each user has a **user working area** (UWA). This area contains database and control data for a particular user (it is similar to the DL/I input-output work area described in Chapter 12). The execution of a program by one of the users is called a **run-unit.** In Figure 13.1 there are three run-units for Application Program A. As shown in this figure, application programs view the database through a subschema. Programs may share subschemas, or each may have its own.

DATA DEFINITION CONSTRUCTS

This section describes the basic constructs for defining databases using the CODASYL model. Database designers use these constructs to define schemas and subschemas. Here and for the rest of this chapter, we will present the essence of the DDL and DML concepts and commands. The discussion is not intended to be an exhaustive study of all options and formats. Our goal is to help you understand the concepts behind the CODASYL model.

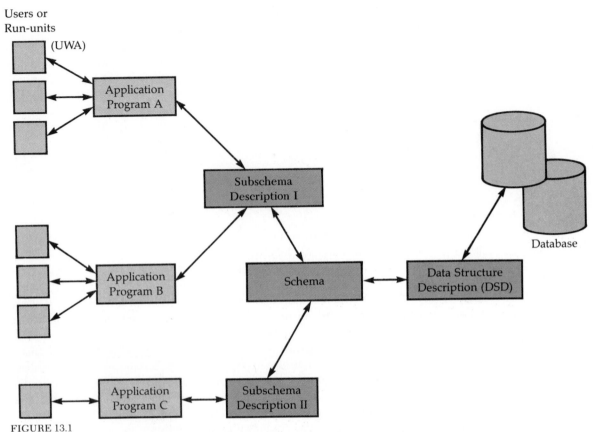

FIGURE 13.1

CODASYL DBTG program/data view relationships

The three fundamental building blocks of DBTG data definition are data-items, records, and sets. A fourth construct, area, was present in early editions of the model but has since been dropped.

Data-items

A **data-item** is a field. It corresponds to an attribute or column in the relational model. Data-items have names and formats. Examples of data-items are Name, Character 25; Address, Character 40; Amount, Fixed 6.2. Although data-items arise from domains, the domain concept is not recognized by the DBTG model.

Records

A **record** is a collection of data-items. Figure 13.2 shows several examples of DBTG records. Unlike the relational model, this model allows **vectors,** which are repetitions of a data-item (like GPA in Figure 13.2b), and it allows repeating groups, such as the data-

Name	Number	Address	Age	Sex

a. Record composed of data-items

Data-items   Vector Data-aggregate

Name	Student Number	Freshman GPA	Sophomore GPA	Junior GPA	Senior GPA

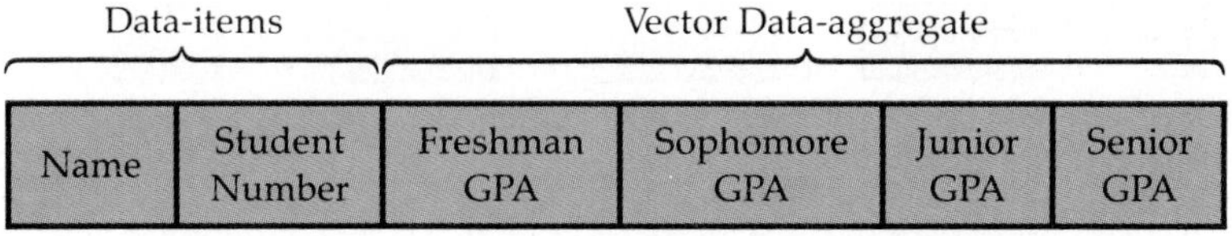

b. Record composed of data-items and a vector data-aggregate

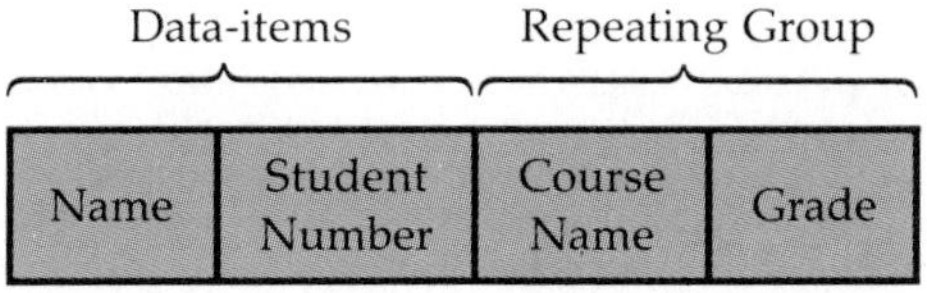

Data-items   Repeating Group

Name	Student Number	Course Name	Grade

c. Record with repeating group

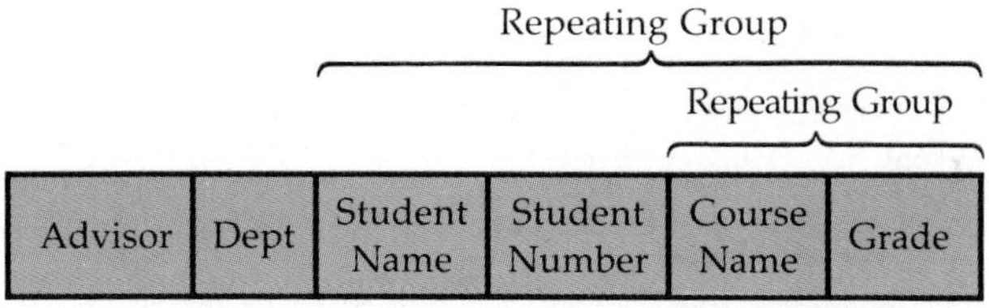

Repeating Group

Repeating Group

Advisor	Dept	Student Name	Student Number	Course Name	Grade

d. Record with nested repeating group

FIGURE 13.2
CODASYL DBTG record types

items Course Name and Grade in Figure 13.2c. Although such repeating groups are allowed, they are unnecessary and generally not recommended. Repeating groups were developed to represent composite objects. A better way of representing them is with two record types and a set, as shown in the next section.

Sets

A **set** is a one-to-many relationship between records. Sets have *owners* and *members*. The owner of a set is the parent. In Figure 13.3, ACCOUNTING is the owner of one set and MARKETING is the owner of another set. Members of a set are the children in the one-to-many relationship. In Figure 13.3, Jones, Parks, and Williams are the members of the set owned by ACCOUNTING.

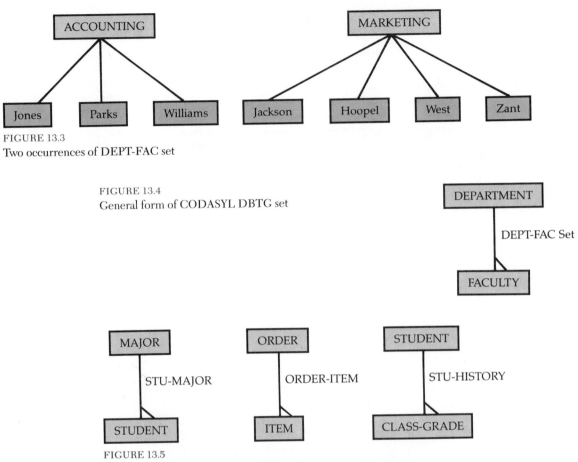

FIGURE 13.3
Two occurrences of DEPT-FAC set

FIGURE 13.4
General form of CODASYL DBTG set

FIGURE 13.5
Example of CODASYL DBTG sets

Figure 13.3 shows two occurrences of a general structure. These occurrences represent instances of a one-to-many relationship between DEPARTMENT and FACULTY records. Figure 13.4 is a generalized representation of this relationship. The general structure, such as the one in Figure 13.4, is called the *set*, and examples of the structure, such as those in Figure 13.3, are called *instances*, or *occurrences*, of the set.

To define a set, we specify a set name and identify the type of record that will be the owner and the type (or types) of records that will be the members. For example, in Figure 13.5, the set STU-MAJOR has MAJOR owner records and STUDENT member records. The set ORDER-ITEM has ORDER owner records and ITEM member records. The set STU-HISTORY has STUDENT owner records and CLASS-GRADE member records.

The DBTG model has specific rules regarding set definition. First, a set can have only one type of record as owner. However, one or more record types can be members. Figure 13.6a shows the set ACTIVITY; the owner record is CLUB, and the member records are

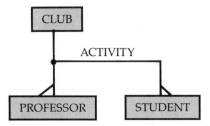

a. Set with two member record types

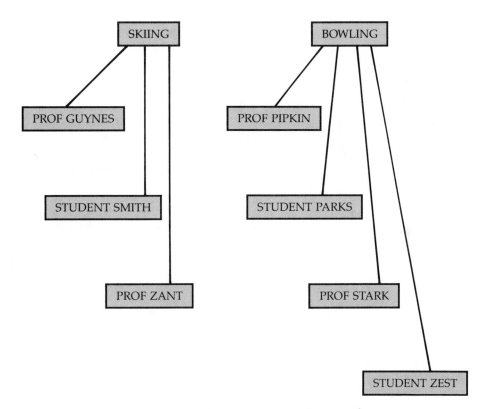

b. Occurrences of set with two member record types

FIGURE 13.6
Set with two member record types and example occurrences

PROFESSOR and STUDENT. Figure 13.6b shows two instances of this set. Both PROFESSOR and STUDENT records are members of the SKIING and BOWLING clubs.

According to the DBTG model, a member record can belong to only one instance of a particular set. Stated equivalently, a record may not have two parents in the same set. This means, in Figure 13.6, that Professor Guynes can only have the SKIING parent record. He may not have BOWLING as well. Furthermore, Professor Pipkin can only have the BOWLING record as parent. She may not have SKIING as well. If faculty members are allowed to belong to more than one club, then a DBTG set cannot be used to represent this relationship. In fact, if faculty members were allowed to belong to two clubs, then this would be an instance of an M:N relationship. We will discuss the representation of such relationships in the next section.

Although a record cannot have two owners in the *same* set, a record may have two owners if they are in *different* sets. For example, a professor may have one ACTIVITY owner and one JOB-TITLE owner. Figure 13.7 extends Figure 13.6 to allow this possibility. Professor Guynes, for example, has both SKIING and FULL PROFESSOR records as parents.

The restrictions on set membership just described mean that a set can readily be used to represent 1:1 and 1:N relationships. This means that DBTG sets can directly represent

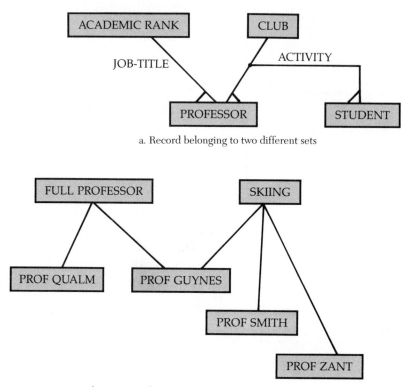

a. Record belonging to two different sets

b. Instance of set structure in Figure 13.7a

FIGURE 13.7

Example of two-owner record in different sets

- A set is a collection of records.
- There are an arbitrary number of sets in the database.
- Each set has one owner record type and one or more member record types.
- Each owner record occurrence defines a set occurrence.
- There are an arbitrary number of member record occurrences in one set occurrence.
- A record may be a member of more than one set.
- A record may not be a member of two occurrences of the same set.

FIGURE 13.8
Summary of set characteristics

composite objects, 1:1 and 1:N compound objects, association objects, and any hybrid objects that do not include an M:N compound object. M:N compound objects cannot be represented because M:N relationships cannot be represented directly with DBTG sets. The characteristics of sets are summarized in Figure 13.8.

Areas

Until 1981 the CODASYL DBTG model included a fourth data definition construct called *area* (1971), or *realm* (1978). This fourth construct referred to a collection of records and sets that could be allocated to a physical entity such as a file, disk, or similar physical storage unit. All versions of the DBTG model were indefinite about how records or sets were to be placed into areas (alias realms). The decision regarding the use of this construct was left to DBMS product designers.

In 1981 the area (realm) construct was deleted from the CODASYL model because it was considered a physical construct and therefore inappropriate for a schema or subschema description. Consequently, we will not consider this construct further in this chapter.

CODASYL DBTG REPRESENTATION OF OBJECTS

The process for developing a database according to the CODASYL DBTG model is similar to that used for developing DL/I databases. It differs only in the last step. We collect forms, reports, and other evidence of users' views, develop a data model, convert the data model to a DBMS-independent relational design, and then, finally, convert the relational design to a CODASYL DBTG design.

To illustrate this conversion we will use the six objects defined for the library in Chapter 12. The relations that underlie these objects are summarized in Figure 13.9.

Composite Objects

To represent a composite object in the DBTG model, we define two record types and a set. One record type represents the object and the second represents the composite group of attributes within the object. The set represents the relationship.

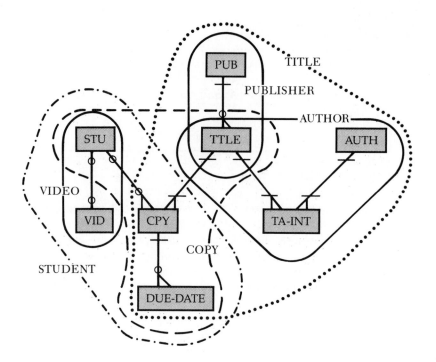

Object	Entry Point	Relations Involved
PUBLISHER	PUB	PUB, TTLE
TITLE	TTLE	TTLE, PUB, TA–INT, AUTH, COPY, DUE–DATE
AUTHOR	AUTH	AUTH, TA–INT, TTLE
COPY	CPY	CPY, DUE–DATE, STU, TTLE
STUDENT	STU	STU, VID, CPY, DUE–DATE
VIDEO	VID	STU, VID

FIGURE 13.9

Underlying objects and relational design for library database

Consider the composite group DUE-DATE within the COPY object in Figure 13.9; it consists of the multivalued attribute DUE-DATE. The relational representation of CPY and DUE-DATE is shown in Figure 13.10a, and the DBTG representation is shown in Figure 13.10b. Observe that the one-to-many relationship is represented by a CODA-SYL DBTG set. (The representation of the STU and TTLE relationships will be shown in Figure 13.14.) As discussed in Chapter 4, the oval indicates an optional relationship; a hash mark indicates a mandatory relationship.

One important difference between the relational representation and the DBTG representation is that in the relational representation, the relationship from DUE-DATE to CPY is carried in the foreign key (Call#, Copy#). In the CODASYL representation, the relationship is not carried in the data. The foreign key (Call#, Copy#) does *not* appear in the DUE-DATE record. When a DUE-DATE record is created, the record itself is inserted into a particular instance of the HISTORY set. From that point on, the DBMS is responsible for maintaining that association, by means of physical location, pointers, or some other method. Unlike the relational model, the relationship is carried in **overhead data** maintained by the DBMS and not in the data itself.

The set in Figure 13.10b is sometimes called an **information bearing set,** since it carries the information about which DUE-DATE records belong to which CPY records. Database practitioners disagree about the desirability of information bearing sets. On one hand, information bearing sets reduce the amount of data duplication (Title and Copy# in this case).

On the other hand, use of information bearing sets can be risky. If, for some reason, the overhead structure is lost or becomes suspect, there is no way of determining which DUE-DATE records belong to which CPY records. Also, some people believe that burying data in overhead structures is philosophically wrong. That data, some believe, should be visible to the user and not hidden only to be known by the DBMS.

Examples can be constructed to support both positions. If the composite key is large, so that there is considerable duplication of data, a strong case can be made for information bearing sets. Otherwise there is little harm in carrying the duplicate key data along, and this redundancy does improve the reliability of the database. We will show both types in this and the next chapter.

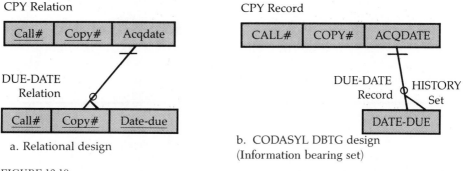

CPY Relation

| Call# | Copy# | Acqdate |

DUE-DATE Relation

| Call# | Copy# | Date-due |

a. Relational design

CPY Record

| CALL# | COPY# | ACQDATE |

DUE-DATE Record   HISTORY Set

| DATE-DUE |

b. CODASYL DBTG design (Information bearing set)

FIGURE 13.10

Representation of composite object

FIGURE 13.11

Representation of 1:1 compound object

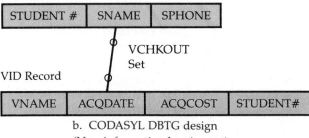

a. Relational design

b. CODASYL DBTG design
(Non-information bearing set)

1:1 Compound Objects

To represent a 1:1 compound object, we define a record for each object and a set for the relationship. Since the relationship is 1:1, it is arbitrary which record is the parent and which is the child. In general, performance will probably be better if the record more frequently used as the entry point is the parent (the actual answer depends on the workload, the DBMS, and the supporting data structures). Thus, if it is more common for student data to be accessed followed by video, then STU should be the parent. If more frequently video data should be accessed followed by student, then VID should be the parent.

These comments pertain to the frequency with which the *relationship* is used. VID may be accessed by itself, without accessing STU, or the reverse. What matters is identifying the record most frequently accessed first whenever the relationship is processed.

Figure 13.11 shows the relational representation of the STUDENT and VIDEO objects (13.11a) as well as a DBTG representation (13.11b). Observe that VCHKOUT is a non-information bearing set since STUDENT# is carried as a data-item of VID.

The DBTG model provides no direct means to limit the number of child records that can belong to a set (in this case, a student is allowed only one videocassette at a time). However, we can require the STUDENT# data-item in VID to be unique, thereby limiting the number of videos for a student to one. You will see an example of this in the next section.

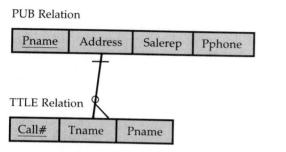

a. Relational design

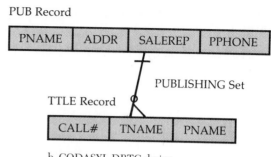

b. CODASYL DBTG design
(Non-information bearing set)

FIGURE 13.12
Representation of 1:N compound object

1:N Compound Objects

We represent a 1:N compound object by defining two record types and a set. Each object is stored in a record and the set represents the relationship. The record on the 1 side of the relationship is the parent and the record on the N side is the child. Stated differently, the record having the foreign key in the relational design is the child record of the set in the DBTG design.

Figure 13.12 shows the DBTG representation of the PUBLISHER and TITLE objects from Figure 13.9. PUB is the parent of the PUBLISHING set and TTLE is the child.

Since PNAME is included in the TTLE record, PUBLISHING is a non-information bearing set. One advantage of this arrangement is that, if a report or form requires TTLE data plus the name of the publisher, then including PNAME in TTLE saves DBMS processing. The appropriate PUB record need not be accessed to obtain the name. If, however, the report or form requires data besides Pname, say, Phone, then the lookup will be necessary.

M:N Compound Objects

M:N compound objects cannot be represented directly in the DBTG model. They must be converted to simple networks with intersection data as is done with the relational model. Figure 13.13a shows the relational representation of the TITLE and AUTHOR objects from Figure 13.9. TA-INT has been created to represent the M:N relationship.

The DBTG representation of the simple network consists of three records and two sets as shown in Figure 13.13. One record is defined for each object and a third for the intersection data. The sets represent the M:N relationship.

To find all of the authors of a given book, the program would access all of the TA-INT children in the T-A set, and for each child record, obtain the A-T parent. To find all of the titles written by a particular author, the program would access all of the TA-INT children of the A-T set, and for each one, obtain the T-A parent.

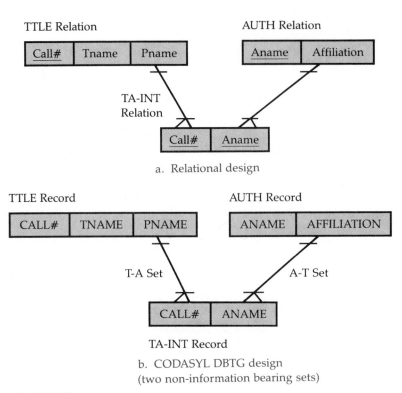

a. Relational design

b. CODASYL DBTG design
(two non-information bearing sets)

FIGURE 13.13
Representation of M:N compound object

The intersection record of an M:N object *never* contains data beyond the identities of the related records. If it did, then we would call it an association object, not an M:N compound object.

The sets shown in Figure 13.13 are non-information bearing sets. If information bearing sets were to be used here, the records would have no data whatsoever, only pointers or other overhead. There is nothing wrong with that fact; it simply indicates that the function of an intersection record is to represent the relationship. If the relationship is carried in information bearing sets, there is no need for data.

Association Objects

Figure 13.14 shows the DBTG representation of the association object COPY, with its associate objects STUDENT and TITLE. To define the association object COPY, we define one record for each object, and two sets: one for the 1:N relationship between COPY and TITLE, and one for the 1:N relationship between COPY and STUDENT.

This structure is similar to the one in Figure 13.13 except that the record that is the child of the two sets is itself an object; it is seen by the user as an entity that establishes the relationship between two other objects. We would have discovered this during design, when we might have found a form or report about copies. That fact would have told us that eventually a program would need to access the CPY record as an entry point.

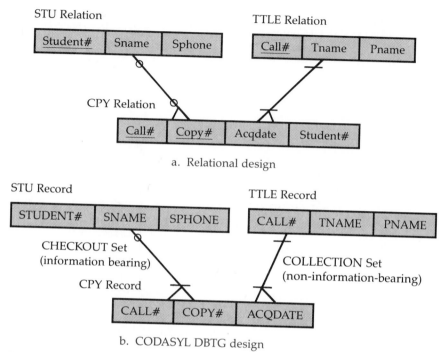

FIGURE 13.14
Representation of association object

Conversely, the TA-INT record in Figure 13.13 is not an independent object. No program will ever access TA-INT as an entry point. Rather, TA-INT is used as a bridge between related TITLE and AUTHOR records. Stated in another way, CPY will contain data of its own, TA-INT will not.

In this example, CHECKOUT is an information bearing set, but COLLECTION is not information bearing. The decision to structure these sets in this manner is arbitrary. Since Call# is part of the key of CPY, it is already carried in data and not by the set. But since Student# is not part of the key, that relationship can be carried by the set. On the other hand, Student# could have been placed in the CPY record, making COLLEC-TION a non-information bearing set. There is no compelling reason to choose one way or the other—they both work. (Contrast this with the relational model, in which relationships *must* be carried in the data—information bearing sets do not exist.)

DBTG SET ORDERING

According to the DBTG model, member records of a set can be ordered in a variety of ways. Figure 13.15 lists the possibilities. If the set order is FIRST, then when new records are placed in a set occurrence, they will be placed in the first position. Subsequently, when the set members are accessed, the new record will be the first one retrieved. This placement is logical, supported by underlying data structures. The physical placement is unknown and unimportant except to the DBMS itself. If the set order

FIGURE 13.15
CODASYL DBTG set member
ordering options

FIRST
LAST
NEXT
PRIOR
SYSTEM DEFAULT
SORTED

FIGURE 13.16
Set ordering for library database

Set Name	Order
PUBLISH	Sorted by TNAME
T-A	System default
A-T	System default
COLLECTION	Sorted by COPY#
CHECKOUT	Last
VCHKOUT	Last (but immaterial)
HISTORY	Last
TITLE-SEQ	Sorted by TNAME

is LAST, then new records will be placed in the last position. In this case, set members will be ordered chronologically, by time in the database.

If the order is NEXT, then new members will be placed in the next position after the most recently accessed member record of the set. To use this option, at least one set record must have already been accessed to establish a position. The new record is placed immediately after that most recently accessed record. If the most recently accessed record of the set were the owner, then the new record would be placed at the start of the set members. If the order is PRIOR, then the new record will be inserted just prior to the most recently accessed set record. If that record is the owner, then the new record will be placed at the end of the set.

If the set is ordered by SYSTEM DEFAULT, then the database designer is stating that the order is immaterial to applications. The DBMS can determine the order. Finally, set members can be SORTED on the value of a data-item they contain. If so, then the name of the data-item is identified in a separate KEY clause (as we will illustrate). Figure 13.16 shows the set ordering we will use for sets in the library database.

As long as records belong to sets, they can be ordered within the set. For some applications, however, the entire file of records needs to be sorted, regardless of the sets to which records of the file might belong. To satisfy this need, the DBTG provides system sets.

A **system set** is a special set that has only one occurrence for each type of record. That occurrence is owned by the DBMS. To provide sequential processing, the set is defined as an ordered set based on one or more data-items in the record. Thus, if TTLE records are to be sorted by Call#, a system set having TTLE records as members and ORDER of Call# would be created. We have called this system set TITLE-SEQ in Figure 13.16. TTLE records can then be processed in Call# order.

SET MEMBERSHIP

The DBTG model provides a group of commands to put records into set occurrences, to take records from set occurrences, and to move records around within set occurrences. We will discuss these commands in the section on the DML. However, the allowable commands depend on the definition of **set membership.** Set membership involves two concepts: getting members into set occurrences, and once in, getting members out.

Set Insertion Status

When we define a set in the schema we must give it an **insertion status,** either AUTO-MATIC or MANUAL. If insertion status is AUTOMATIC, then whenever a member record is created, the DBMS automatically inserts the record into the set. If the insertion status is MANUAL, then a member record is not put into a set occurrence until the application program executes a special command, CONNECT.

Set Retention Status

Additionally, when a set is defined in the schema, it must be given a **retention status.** This status can be FIXED, MANDATORY, or OPTIONAL. If FIXED, then once a record is placed in a set occurrence, it must remain in *that* occurrence of the set. To change its set membership, the record must be deleted from the database and recreated.

If the retention status is MANDATORY, then once a record is placed in a set occurrence, it must always belong to a set occurrence; however, the occurrence need not be the initial one. Thus MANDATORY sets require that once a record is put into a set occurrence, it must stay in *some* occurrence of the set. A special command, RECON-NECT, is used to move a member record from one occurrence to another, as you will see.

Finally, if the retention status is OPTIONAL, then member records can be removed, inserted, and moved from set occurrence to set occurrence without restriction. Figure 13.17 summarizes the interaction of set insertion and retention status.

CONSTRAINTS

The DBTG model provides partial support for domain, intra-, and inter-relation (record) constraint enforcement. The DBTG support for constraint enforcement has evolved over time within different versions of the model. We will show the capabilities of the 1981 model here. Because the DBTG model was evolving at the same time that the need for constraint enforcement was becoming apparent, constraint enforcement was not thoroughly developed.

Domain Constraints

The DBTG model does not recognize the concept of domain. Thus, data-items are inde-pendently defined to have a particular physical appearance and particular constraints. If

Retention status

	FIXED	MANDATORY	OPTIONAL
AUTO-MATIC	DBMS puts record in set at time of creation. Once in, it cannot be taken out.	DBMS puts record in set at time of creation. It can be moved to another occurrence with RECONNECT.	DBMS puts record in set at time of creation. It can be disconnected, reconnected, or connected.
MANUAL	Application program puts record into set. Once in, it cannot be taken out.	Application program puts record into set. It can be moved to another occurrence with RECONNECT.	Application program puts record into set. It can be disconnected, reconnected, or connected.

Insertion status

FIGURE 13.17
Set insertion and set retention status

two or more data-items are based on the same domain, it is up to the database developer to know this and to ensure that the physical descriptions and constraints are defined in the same way.

The manner in which data-item formats are defined is rather open-ended. Various versions of the model provide a variety of data-items and formats for data-item specification. Basically, the model includes the common data formats, such as CHARACTER, FIXED, CURRENCY, DATE, TIME, and so forth. Additionally, the length of data-items and the number of places to the right of the decimal point (where appropriate) can also be specified.

In addition to format descriptions, the 1981 DBTG provides a means to limit allowed data-item values. This is done via the CHECK statement in the schema definition. Here are some examples of CHECK statements:

```
CHECK IS NOT EQUAL 0
CHECK IS LESS THAN 500
CHECK IS NOT NULL
```

The first two CHECK statements enforce range restrictions on allowable values. The last one ensures the existence of a value in a mandatory field, such as a key field. CHECK statements are located in the schema definition next to the data-item that they limit. Examples are shown in the next section. (See Figure 13.18).

Intrarecord Constraints

The DBTG model supports one type of intrarelation constraint: **uniqueness.** Record instances can be defined to be unique based on one or more data-items, considered singly or as composites. For example, suppose the record type TTLE contains the data-item TNAME. (As with DL/I, the DBTG model does not support lowercase letters.

```
SCHEMA NAME IS LIBRARY
     RECORD NAME IS PUB
          DUPLICATES ARE NOT ALLOWED FOR PNAME
          PNAME                         TYPE IS    CHARACTER    10
                                        CHECK IS   NOT NULL

          ADDRESS                       TYPE IS    CHARACTER    25
          SALPSN                        TYPE IS    CHARACTER    20
          PPHONE                        TYPE IS    FIXED        10


     RECORD NAME IS TTLE
          DUPLICATES ARE NOT ALLOWED FOR CALL#
          DUPLICATES ARE NOT ALLOWED FOR TNAME
          CALL#                         TYPE IS    CHARACTER    8
                                        CHECK IS   NOT NULL
          TNAME                         TYPE IS    CHARACTER    50
                                        CHECK IS   NOT NULL
          PNAME                         TYPE IS    CHARACTER    10
                                        CHECK IS   NOT  NULL
     RECORD NAME IS CPY
          DUPLICATES ARE NOT ALLOWED FOR CALL#, COPY#
          CALL#                         TYPE IS    CHARACTER    8
                                        CHECK IS   NOT NULL
          COPY#                         TYPE IS    FIXED        2
                                        CHECK IS   NOT NULL
          ACQDATE                       TYPE IS    DATE


     RECORD NAME IS AUTH
          DUPLICATES ARE NOT ALLOWED FOR ANAME
          ANAME                         TYPE IS    CHARACTER    30
                                        CHECK IS   NOT NULL
          AFFILIATION                   TYPE IS    CHARACTER    30


     RECORD NAME IS TA-INT
          DUPLICATES ARE NOT ALLOWED FOR CALL#, ANAME
          CALL#                         TYPE IS    CHARACTER    8
                                        CHECK IS   NOT NULL
          ANAME                         TYPE IS    CHARACTER    30
                                        CHECK IS   NOT NULL     7


     RECORD NAME IS STU
          DUPLICATES ARE NOT ALLOWED FOR STUDENT#
          STUDENT#                      TYPE IS    FIXED        10
                                        CHECK IS   NOT NULL
          SNAME                         TYPE IS    CHARACTER    30
          SPHONE                        TYPE IS    FIXED
```

FIGURE 13.18
Library schema definition

```
RECORD NAME IS VID
        DUPLICATES ARE NOT ALLOWED FOR VID#, VCOPY#
        DUPLICATES ARE NOT ALLOWED FOR STUDENT#
        VID#                        TYPE IS    FIXED        5
                                    CHECK IS   NOT NULL
        VCOPY#                      TYPE IS    FIXED        2
                                    CHECK IS   NOT NULL
        VNAME                       TYPE IS    CHARACTER   40
        STUDENT#                    TYPE IS    FIXED       10


RECORD NAME IS DUE-DATE
        DATE-DUE                    TYPE IS    DATE
                                    CHECK IS   NOT NULL


SET NAME IS PUBLISH
        OWNER IS PUB
        ORDER IS SORTED BY DEFINED KEYS
        MEMBER IS TTLE
        INSERTION IS AUTOMATIC, RETENTION IS FIXED
        KEY IS ASCENDING TNAME
        SET SELECTION IS BY VALUE OF PNAME


SET NAME IS T-A
        OWNER IS TTLE
        ORDER IS SYSTEM DEFAULT
        MEMBER IS TA-INT
        INSERTION IS AUTOMATIC, RETENTION IS FIXED
        CHECK IS CALL# IN TTLE = CALL# IN TA-INT
        SET SELECTION IS BY VALUE OF CALL#


SET NAME IS A-T
        OWNER IS AUTH
        ORDER IS SYSTEM DEFAULT
        MEMBER IS TA-INT
        INSERTION IS AUTOMATIC, RETENTION IS FIXED
        CHECK IS ANAME IN AUTH = ANAME IN TA-INT
        SET SELECTION IS BY VALUE OF ANAME


SET NAME IS COLLECTION
        OWNER IS TTLE
        ORDER IS BY DEFINED KEYS
        MEMBER IS CPY
        INSERTION IS AUTOMATIC, RETENTION IS FIXED
        KEY IS ASCENDING COPY#
        SET SELECTION IS STRUCTURAL CALL# = CALL#
```

FIGURE 13.18 *continued*

```
SET NAME IS CHECKOUT
        OWNER IS STU
        ORDER IS LAST
        MEMBER IS CPY
        INSERTION IS MANUAL, RETENTION IS OPTIONAL
        SET SELECTION IS BY VALUE OF STUDENT#

SET NAME IS VCHKOUT
        OWNER IS STU
        ORDER IS LAST
        MEMBER IS VID
        INSERTION IS MANUAL, RETENTION IS OPTIONAL
        SET SELECTION IS BY VALUE OF STUDENT#

SET NAME IS HISTORY
        OWNER IS CPY
        MEMBER IS DUE-DATE
        ORDER IS LAST
        INSERTION IS AUTOMATIC, RETENTION IS FIXED
        SET SELECTION IS BY VALUE OF CALL#, COPY#

SET NAME IS TITLE-SEQ
        OWNER IS SYSTEM
        ORDER IS SORTED BY DEFINED KEYS
        MEMBER IS TTLE
        INSERTION IS AUTOMATIC, RETENTION IS FIXED
        KEY IS ASCENDING TNAME
```

FIGURE 13.18 *continued*

Data-items will be shown in capitals letters for this model.) The following statement can be inserted in the schema to ensure that duplicate titles are prohibited:

```
DUPLICATES NOT ALLOWED FOR TNAME
```

Such statements are located in the schema in the section defining the record having the constraint. Consider another example involving the record CPY which contains the data-items CALL# and COPY#. The statement

```
DUPLICATES NOT ALLOWED FOR CALL#, COPY#
```

states that the composite (CALL#, COPY#) must be unique. There may be records having duplicate CALL# values (for different copies of the same book), and there may be records having duplicate COPY# values (for copy numbers of different titles), but the combination of a particular call number with a particular copy number must be unique.

Consider the difference in the DUPLICATE statement for CPY (immediately above) and the following two statements for TTLE:

```
DUPLICATES NOT ALLOWED FOR TNAME
DUPLICATES NOT ALLOWED FOR CALL#
```

The two statements for TTLE define uniqueness for data-items independently. The single statement for CPY defines uniqueness for the composite (CALL#, COPY#).

Interrecord Constraints

The DBTG model provides partial support for the definition of interrecord constraints, or referential integrity, through two facilities. One is via the definition of set retention status and the second is a version of the CHECK command.

Consider Figure 13.17 in light of the four types of binary record relationships (M-M, M-O, O-M, and O-O). If the retention status of a set member is either FIXED or MANDATORY, then that record will always be in a set, and hence it will always have a parent. Thus, either of these two values of retention status can be used to enforce the parent side of M-M or M-O constraints. Further, defining a set as OPTIONAL means a parent may or may not exist and thus can be used to define the parent side of O-M or O-O constraints.

Set insertion status does not facilitate the definition of interrecord constraints. In fact, some database practitioners find it to be more confusing than helpful. AUTOMATIC/FIXED and AUTOMATIC/MANDATORY definitions provide for consistent enforcement of M-x (meaning either M-M or M-O) constraints. MANUAL/FIXED and MANUAL/MANDATORY provide such enforcement once the record is placed in a set. However, MANUAL insertion status allows a child record to be stored in the database before the parent is stored.

Set insertion and retention status concern a child record's requirement for a parent. They do not consider a parent record's requirement for a child. Thus, insertion and retention status do not concern the enforcement of x-M constraints. Unfortunately, such constraints must be enforced by application programs.

The 1981 model provided a version of the CHECK statement that enforces values in foreign keys. As such, it can only be used for non-information bearing sets (sets in which the key of the parent is stored as a foreign key in the child record).

For example, consider the TTLE and CPY records discussed above. CALL# in CPY is a foreign key from TTLE. The following CHECK statement, placed in the set definition portion of the schema, will enforce a match between the key and the foreign key:

```
CHECK IS CALL# IN TTLE = CALL# IN CPY
```

This statement, which is associated with a set, say COLLECTION, makes sense only if CALL# is located in both records. With this statement, whenever a record is placed into a set occurrence, the values of CALL# must match. This is another way of enforcing an M-x constraint.

Perhaps you are beginning to get a feel for the inconsistent and eclectic nature of this model. Such a CHECK statement leans in the direction of interrelation constraints in the relational model. Yet, its presence is somewhat confusing laid on top of the rest of the DBTG model. Such is the nature of emerging technology.

A Schema Definition for the Library Database

Figure 13.18 presents a schema definition for the library database design shown in Figure 13.9. There are many ways that the DBTG model could be used to represent this database; Figure 13.18 is one of them. It shows options that another database designer might not have chosen. With this model, there can be several feasible definitions for the database because it is so open-ended.

The schema definition has two major parts. The first concerns the definition of record structures and the second the definition of sets.

RECORD DEFINITIONS

Examine the definition of the PUB record in Figure 13.18. The first statement declares that values of PNAME must be unique. Following that, the data-items are described. Notice the CHECK statement that enforces the domain constraint that PNAME may not be null.

The definition of TTLE is next. Here, two different statements declare that both TNAME and CALL# are to be unique. Since these statements are separate, they imply that value of TNAME and values of CALL# must each be unique. As stated previously, this is different from declaring that a composite group be unique. An example of composite data-item uniqueness occurs in the definition of the next record, CPY. The DUPLICATES statement in that record declares that the composite (CALL#, COPY#) must be unique.

The remaining record definitions are similar. One unusual statement appears in the definition of VID. In that record, STUDENT# is required to be unique. Since a set is defined with STU as parent and VID as child, this relationship would normally be one-to-many. The same value of STUDENT# could appear in many different instances of VID. With the declaration that STUDENT# be unique, however, the same STUDENT# can appear in only one VID record. Thus, this declaration turns what would normally be a one-to-many relationship into the one-to-one relationship required in the design.

SET DEFINITIONS

Continue to refer to Figure 13.18. One set is defined for each one-to-many relationships shown in Figure 13.9. The first set, PUBLISH, represents the relationship between PUB and TTLE. The owner record of this set is PUBLISH and the member record is TTLE. Records within the set are to be maintained in sorted order of TNAME. This is defined by two statements in the set definition. The first, ORDER IS SORTED BY DEFINED KEYS, indicates the order is to be kept by a value of one or more data-items within the member record. The particular data-item is then identified by the statement, KEY IS ASCENDING TNAME. The fourth statement in the set definition specifies the set insertion and retention status. AUTOMATIC, FIXED was chosen here because every book must have a publisher, and the publisher of a book cannot change.

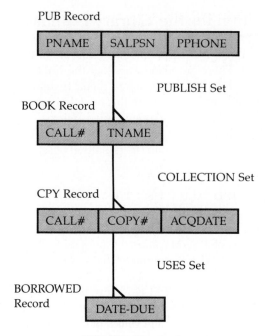

a. PURCHASE subschema

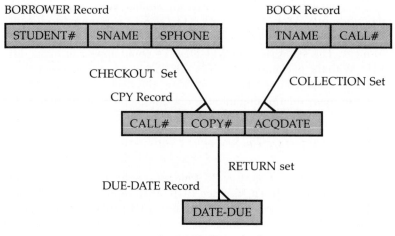

b. BORROW subschema

FIGURE 13.19
Sample of subschema structures

The last statement in the set definition specifies how the DBMS is to identify a particular set occurrence when it needs one. There are several situations in which this is necessary as you will see when we discuss the DML. Here is one instance: Since the insertion status of TTLE is AUTOMATIC, when a new TTLE record is created, the DBMS must insert it into an instance of the PUBLISH set. The question is, which instance of that set? The SET SELECTION statement indicates how the DBMS is to identify such a set instance. This particular statement indicates the DBMS is to use the value of PNAME to identify a PUB record. The new TTLE record is to be inserted into the set occurrence owned by that PUB record.

The remaining sets are also defined in Figure 13.18. The sets T-A and A-T represent the M:N relationship between titles and authors. Both of these sets are non-information bearing since they contain the keys of their parents. The order of these sets is SYSTEM DEFAULT. This means the application developers are unconcerned about the order of member records within the set. Other statements are similar to those for PUBLISH except that these sets include a CHECK clause.

Consider the set T-A. The CHECK clause in this set definition informs the DBMS to enforce the constraint that the values of CALL# in TTLE and TA-INT must match. Since the insertion status is AUTOMATIC, the retention status is FIXED, and the set selection is by value of CALL#, this CHECK clause is redundant. Unless the DBMS code is in error, it should be impossible for nonmatching values of CALL# to ever occur in the same set.

Observe that the set insertion and retention status, the SET SELECTION, and the CHECK statements interact. To determine the impact of any one of these three statements, you must consider the other two. This interaction, which is used to enforce interrecord constraints, is, unfortunately, complicated and sometimes a bit mysterious. This interaction requires that both the database designer and the application programmer know and remember the action of these statements. If the programmer does not understand this interaction, unanticipated results may occur.

The COLLECTION set represents the one-to-many relationship between TTLE and CPY. It is similar to the other set definitions except for the SET SELECTION statement. This SET SELECTION statement is a combination of SET SELECTION and a CHECK statement. It indicates that the DBMS is to preserve the interrecord constraint that owner and member records in this set always have the same CALL# value. When the DBMS needs a set occurrence for some reason, it is to select the one that will enable this constraint to be maintained. Further, no data-item changes that would violate this constraint are to be allowed. This statement is equivalent to the combination of CHECK and SET SELECTION statements shown in the definitions for the sets T-A and A-T. Such a statement can only be used for non-information bearing sets.

The CHECKOUT set is similar to other sets except that its INSERTION STATUS is MANUAL and RETENTION is OPTIONAL. Records are placed into this set by application programs and they can be removed without restriction. This is appropriate since copies of books can be checked out and returned dynamically. The order of this set is LAST. This means the member records will occur in the set in chronological order. The book checked out first will be the first record in the set.

CHECKOUT and the next set, VCHKOUT, are the only sets in this database that have MANUAL and OPTIONAL status. The other records and sets represent more permanent conditions. Authors of book titles, for example, do not change. In this database, only the allocations of students to books or videos change.

The last set is a system set. It contains all of the TTLE records in the database. The purpose of this set is to provide a logical ordering of TTLE records by CALL#.

The schema definition we just reviewed includes the major facilities of the 1981 DBTG DDL. It differs from earlier versions primarily in that it includes CHECK clauses and that keys and SET SELECTION statements are handled slightly differently. If you understand these statements in this schema, however, you should have little trouble understanding statements in schema definitions of DBMS products based on other versions of the DBTG model.

SUBSCHEMA DEFINITIONS

Application programs do not access the database schema directly. Instead, they view the database via subschemas. These subschemas are basically subsets of the schema. (The 1981 model does allow the definition of virtual records via joins of actual records. One implementation of this model, the product IDMS/R licensed by Cullinet, makes extensive use of this feature.)

Unfortunately, there is currently no accepted DBTG standard for subschema descriptions. The 1981 schema language is incompatible with the 1978 subschema language (the last date for which a subschema standard was published). Work was never finished to reconcile these two because industry interest in this model waned as the relational model gained popularity. We will show here a subschema as typically implemented in a commercial DBTG product.

SUBSCHEMAS FOR THE LIBRARY DATABASE

To illustrate the definition and use of CODASYL DBTG subschemas, we will consider two subschemas for the library database. Figure 13.19a shows the structure of the PURCHASE subschema, used by application programs in the purchasing department. The second subschema, BORROW, is shown in Figure 13.19b. BORROW is used by the checkout desk when books are loaned.

PURCHASE Subschema

The general format of a subschema description is shown in Figure 13.20. Each subschema description has three divisions. The TITLE DIVISION contains the name of the subschema, the MAPPING DIVISION contains alias descriptions, and the STRUCTURE DIVISION indicates the records, data-items, and sets in the schema that are present in the subschema.

```
TITLE DIVISION.
(subschema name)
MAPPING DIVISION.
ALIAS SECTION.
(alternate names for records, sets, or data-items)
STRUCTURE DIVISION.
RECORD SECTION.
(records and data-items that are to appear in the subschema)
SET SECTION.
(sets to appear in the subschema)
```

FIGURE 13.20

Format of subschema description, 1978 specification

Figure 13.21a presents a subschema description for PURCHASE. In the MAPPING DIVISION, the record TTLE is renamed BOOK and the record DUE-DATE is renamed BORROWED. Additionally, the set HISTORY is renamed USES and the data-item DATE-DUE is named USE-DATE. The application program that accesses this subschema must use these aliases rather than the names in the schema description. AD is a keyword that stands for *alias definition*.

The RECORD SECTION of this subschema redefines the PUB record to omit the ADDRESS data-item. All of the data-items in BOOK, CPY, and BORROWED are to be present in the PURCHASE subschema. Finally, in the SET SECTION, the sets PUB-LISH, COLLECTION, and USES are declared to be included in PURCHASE. SD is a keyword that stands for *set definition*.

BORROW Subschema

The subschema BORROW is defined in Figure 13.21b. The structure of the description is the same as that for PURCHASE. BORROW includes BOOK (alias for TTLE), BOR-ROWER (alias for STU), CPY, and DUE-DATE records. The sets included are COL-LECTION, CHECKOUT, and RETURN (alias for HISTORY).

These figures present the essence of the CODASYL DBTG model's facility for sub-schema description. In the next chapter we will see how these concepts were implemented in an actual DBMS product. For now, we will use both the schema and sub-schema descriptions to illustrate the DML commands.

CODASYL DBTG Data Manipulation Language

This section presents the essence of the DBTG DML. First, we discuss general concepts and then we consider single-record processing. Finally, we discuss DML processing of several records using sets.

FIGURE 13.21
Sample of subschema definitions
for library database

```
TITLE DIVISION.
SS PURCHASE WITHIN LIBRARY.
MAPPING DIVISION.
ALIAS SECTION.
AD      RECORD TTLE IS BOOK.
AD      RECORD DUE-DATE IS BORROWED.
AD      SET HISTORY IS USES.
AD      DATE-DUE IS USE-DATE.
STRUCTURE DIVISION.
RECORD SECTION.
01      PUB.
            05          PNAME     PIC X(10).
            05          SALPSN    PIC X(20).
            05          PHONE     PIC 9(10).
01      BOOK ALL.
01      CPY ALL.
01      BORROWED ALL.
SET SECTION.
SD      PUBLISH.
SD      COLLECTION.
SD      USES.
```

a. PURCHASE subschema definition

```
TITLE DIVISION.
SS BORROW WITHIN LIBRARY.
MAPPING DIVISION.
ALIAS SECTION.
AD      RECORD TTLE IS BOOK.
AD      RECORD STU IS BORROWER.
AD      SET HISTORY IS RETURN.
STRUCTURE DIVISION.
RECORD SECTION.
01      BOOK.
            05          TNAME     PIC X(50).
            05          CALL#     PIC X(8).
01      BORROWER ALL.
01      CPY ALL.
01      DUE-DATE ALL.
SET SECTION.
SD      COLLECTION.
SD      CHECKOUT.
SD      RETURN.
```

b. BORROW subschema description

GENERAL DML CONCEPTS

Most CODASYL DBTG data manipulation commands have two steps. First, a FIND command is issued to identify the record to be acted upon. The FIND command does not read or otherwise process the indicated record. It simply identifies a record for the DBMS to locate. After a record has been identified, a second DML command can be issued to perform an operation on it. Typical patterns are FIND, GET;[1] or FIND, MODIFY; or FIND, ERASE.

The only DML command that does not follow this pattern is STORE. Since this command inserts a new record into the database, there is nothing to be found before it is executed.

As stated, every DBTG run-unit (a particular user connected to a particular program) has a user working area (UWA). The records in the subschema are stored in the UWA. For the PURCHASE subschema, there are four records in the UWA: PUB, BOOK, CPY, and BORROWED. For the BORROW subschema they are BOOK, BORROWER, CPY, and DUE-DATE. The UWA contains other data as well. In particular, it contains currency indicators and special registers.

Currency Indicators

Currency indicators are place markers. When the program issues a FIND command, a record is found and its identity is stored in a special variable called a **currency indicator.** Subsequently, when a GET, MODIFY, ERASE, or other command is issued, the DBMS references the currency indicator to determine which record to act upon. Also, currency indicators are used as reference points for sequential processing commands such as FIND NEXT or FIND PRIOR. We will discuss these statements later.

Several currency indicators exist. Every record type and set type in the subschema has its own currency indicator. These indicators identify the most recently processed record of a type or in a set. Also, the run-unit itself has a currency indicator that identifies the most recently processed record of any type. For the PURCHASE subschema, there are currency indicators for PUB, BOOK, CPY, and BORROWED records; for PUBLISH, COLLECTION, and USES sets; and for the run-unit that is processing the subschema. For the BORROW subschema there are indicators for BOOK, BORROWER, CPY, and DUE-DATE records; for COLLECTION, CHECKOUT, and RETURN sets; and for the run-unit that is processing this subschema.

Initially, all of these currency indicators are null, indicating that no record has been accessed. As records are processed, the DBMS updates currency indicator values.

The currency indicators can be envisioned as variables in a table. Figure 13.22 lists the currency indicators for the BORROW subschema, as it is processed. The top row shows the initial status of all the currency indicators. The indicator in the first column is

---

[1]Because the combination FIND, GET is so common, some products have defined a special command for the combination. IDMS/R, for example, defines the OBTAIN command as the combination FIND, GET. The options and syntax of OBTAIN are the same as for FIND.

Currency Indicator for:

Statement	RUN-UNIT	BOOK	BORROWER	CPY	DUE-DATE	COLLECTION	CHECKOUT	RETURN
Initial	NULL	NULL	NULL	NULL	NULL	NULL	NULL	NULL
FIND BORROWER with STUDENT # = 150	BORROWER 150	NULL	BORROWER 150	NULL	NULL	NULL	BORROWER 150	NULL
FIND CPY R726.8.L, COPY 3	CPY R726.8.L COPY 3	NULL	BORROWER 150	CPY R726.8.L COPY 3	NULL	CPY R726.8.L COPY 3	CPY R726.8.L COPY 3	CPY R726.8.L COPY 3

FIGURE 13.22
Currency indicators for the BORROW subschema

the current of run-unit (the most recently processed record of any type). Indicators in other columns refer to the record and set types as listed.

The FIND command sets currency indicator values. For example, when a FIND command is executed to FIND the BORROWER record with STUDENT# equal to 150, the current of run-unit, current of BORROWER, and current of CHECKOUT are all set to point to the record for BORROWER 150. (See the second row in Figure 13.22.) If a FIND command were then issued to locate the CPY record with CALL# equal to "R726.8.L" and COPY# equal to "3", then the current of run-unit, current of CPY, current of CHECKOUT, current of COLLECTION, and current of RETURN would be set to point the CPY record having "R726.8.L", COPY "3". The modified currency indicators are shown in the third row. Notice that current of BORROWER is unaffected by the second FIND command.

Special Registers

Special registers are also kept in the UWA. Unlike machine registers (you might remember them from a systems architecture or assembly language course), these "registers" are simply data fields in which the DBMS places system information for the application program to access, such as return codes and error messages. For example, after execution of a DML command, the DBMS places a return code in a register called DB-STATUS. If the command is executed without problems, it sets DB-STATUS to zero. Other values of DB-STATUS indicate an error or an unusual situation. One common use of DB-STATUS is to signal end-of-data.

Other special registers are DB-SET-NAME, DB-DATA-NAME, and DB-RECORD NAME. The first two are set only when an error occurs. The DBMS places the names of the record and the data-item it was processing at the time of the error in these registers. DB-RECORD-NAME is set when an error occurs and also whenever a FIND or STORE command has been executed. This data is useful when the application program is processing records in a set that has more than one record type as members.

DBTG DML FOR SINGLE-RECORD PROCESSING

The following examples show how FIND is used in conjunction with other commands to process the database. The commands will be shown in pseudocode form. The particular syntax of each of these commands depends on the language in which they are embedded and on the particular implementation of the DBTG model.

Suppose we want to read the BORROWER record for STUDENT# 150. The following commands will do this:

```
MOVE ''150'' TO STUDENT# IN BORROWER
FIND ANY BORROWER USING STUDENT#
GET BORROWER
```

The FIND command sets the current of run-unit, current of BORROWER, and current of CHECKOUT to point to the record for student 150. Then the GET command places the record into the BORROWER record area in the UWA. GET always operates on the current of run-unit record.

Suppose we want to read all of the CPY records for a book having the call number R726.8.L:

```
MOVE ''R726.8.L'' TO CALL# IN CPY
FIND ANY CPY USING CALL#
DOWHILE DB-STATUS = 0
        GET CPY
        (process CPY data)
        FIND DUPLICATE CPY USING CALL#
END-DO
```

DB-STATUS is used here to control loop processing. This code assumes that DB-STATUS will be set to a value other than zero only at end of data. A more sophisticated (and appropriate) algorithm would examine the value of DB-STATUS to ensure that no other condition or error occurred. We will defer that level of detail until the next chapter.

The first FIND specifies that ANY record could qualify. The next FIND specifies DUPLICATE. This keyword means the desired record must have the same value of CALL# that the current of CPY contains.

To illustrate the elimination of records, suppose we want to delete all CPY records of the book having the call number R726.8.L60:

```
MOVE ''R726.8.L'' TO CALL# IN CPY
FIND FOR UPDATE ANY CPY USING CALL#
DOWHILE DB-STATUS = 0
        ERASE CPY
        FIND FOR UPDATE DUPLICATE CPY USING CALL#
END-DO
```

The logic is similar to that for the GET. However, the ERASE command is used in this example. Also, the words FOR UPDATE are added to the FIND command. These keywords inform the DBMS that an update is to occur. The DBMS will lock the record for the run-unit. This is similar to the DL/I GET HOLD commands described in the previous chapter.

To illustrate the modification of records, suppose the BORROWER with STUDENT# of 150 changes her name to WILLIS:

```
MOVE ''150'' TO STUDENT# IN BORROWER
FIND FOR UPDATE ANY BORROWER USING STUDENT#
GET BORROWER
IF DB-STATUS = 0
    THEN MOVE ''WILLIS'' TO SNAME IN BORROWER
         MODIFY SNAME
    ELSE do error processing
END-IF
```

In this case, the MODIFY statement indicates that only the SNAME data-item has been changed. If no data-item is listed, the DBMS is to assume that the entire record (or this subschema's view of it) has been changed.

To *create* a new record, we first build it in the UWA and then issue a STORE command. The following statements insert a BORROWER record into the database:

```
MOVE ''2000'' TO STUDENT# IN BORROWER
MOVE ''CALBOM'' TO SNAME IN BORROWER
MOVE ''5258869'' TO PHONE IN BORROWER
STORE BORROWER
```

After the STORE command, the new record is the current of run-unit, current of BORROWER, and current of CHECKOUT.

Although not shown, the program should examine DB-STATUS to determine if the command executed successfully. Actually, DB-STATUS should be examined after every DBMS command. In these examples, and in the following, we will sometimes omit this examination and subsequent error processing. This omission simplifies the discussion. Remember, however, that actual application programs need to examine DB-STATUS after every command and do appropriate error processing.

PROCESSING MULTIPLE RECORDS WITH SETS

Set are used to process records by relationship. Three commands are used to insert and remove records from sets. Several different formats of the FIND command are then used to process records within sets.

Inserting and Removing Records from Sets

The DBTG model provides three commands for processing set members: CONNECT, DISCONNECT, and RECONNECT. The first command places a record into a set, the second removes a record from a set, and the third changes set membership.

The allowed use of these commands depends on the set insertion and retention status. The insertion status governs the use of CONNECT, while the retention status governs the use of DISCONNECT and RECONNECT.

If the insertion status is AUTOMATIC, then CONNECT is unnecessary, at least when the record is created. (If the set retention status is OPTIONAL, then the record may be removed from its initial set assignment and later placed in a new set using CONNECT.) If the insertion status is MANUAL, then CONNECT must be used to place the record into a set.

If the retention status is FIXED, then DISCONNECT and RECONNECT are invalid. If the retention status is MANDATORY, then RECONNECT is valid but DISCONNECT is not. If the retention status is OPTIONAL, then both of these commands are valid.

The COLLECTION and CHECKOUT sets in the BORROW subschema represent the two extremes. COLLECTION is AUTOMATIC/FIXED, and CHECKOUT is MANUAL/OPTIONAL. None of these commands is valid for COLLECTION. Since the insertion status is AUTOMATIC, CONNECT is unnecessary. Since the retention status is FIXED, neither DISCONNECT nor RECONNECT is valid.

On the other hand, all of these commands are necessary and valid for CHECKOUT. CONNECT must be used to place a record into CHECKOUT, and both RECONNECT and DISCONNECT may be then used.

CONNECT places the current of the member record type into the current of the set. To illustrate its operation, suppose student 150 wishes to check out copy 2 of the book with call number of R726.8.L. The following statements will accomplish this:

```
MOVE ''R726.8.L'' to CALL#
MOVE ''2'' TO COPY#
FIND ANY CPY USING CALL#, COPY#
MOVE ''150'' TO STUDENT#
FIND ANY BORROWER USING STUDENT#
CONNECT CPY TO CHECKOUT
```

The first FIND command establishes copy 2 of R726.8.L as the current of CPY. The second FIND then establishes student 150 as the current of the CHECKOUT set. The copy is then placed in the set with CONNECT. Since the SET SELECTION clause is BY VALUE OF STUDENT#, the second FIND command is not actually necessary. If it were not there, the DBMS would use the value of STUDENT# to determine the set occurrence for the CONNECT command.

DISCONNECT operates similarly. The current of member record type is removed from the current of set. The following commands take copy 2 of R726.8.L from the set owned by student 150:

```
MOVE ''R726.8.L'' to CALL#
MOVE ''2'' TO COPY#
FIND ANY CPY USING CALL#, COPY#
MOVE ''150'' TO STUDENT#
FIND ANY BORROWER USING STUDENT#
DISCONNECT CPY FROM CHECKOUT
```

As with CONNECT, the second FIND statement is unnecessary since the SET SELECTION is BY VALUE OF STUDENT#.

RECONNECT operates by disconnecting the current of a record type from its occurrence in a set and connecting it into the current occurrence of that same set. For example, the following commands reassign copy 2 of book R726.8.L from student 150 to student 400:

```
MOVE ''R726.8.L'' to CALL#
MOVE ''2'' TO COPY#
FIND ANY CPY USING CALL#, COPY#
MOVE ''400'' TO STUDENT#
```

```
FIND ANY BORROWER USING STUDENT#
RECONNECT CPY TO CHECKOUT
```

The first FIND command establishes the current of CPY. The next one establishes student 400 as the current of CHECKOUT. The record is then moved from student 150's set occurrence to student 400's set occurrence.

As stated, when the set insertion status is AUTOMATIC, the DBMS connects records into sets when they are created. An appropriate record must be available to serve as parent at the time the new record is created. For example, when a new CPY record is created, it will automatically be inserted into a COLLECTION set. The appropriate BOOK record must exist in the database:

```
MOVE ''PS477.5C'' TO CALL# IN CPY
MOVE ''3'' TO COPY# IN CPY
MOVE ''11/14/87'' TO ACQDATE IN CPY
STORE CPY
```

When the STORE command is executed, CPY will automatically be inserted into the COLLECTION set occurrence of which PS477.5C is the parent. If this BOOK does not exist, an error will occur.

The new CPY record is connected to the appropriate set because of the STRUCTURAL SET SELECTION statement in the definition of COLLECTION. This statement means, when necessary, find a parent record of COLLECTION that will make the CALL# in the child record equal to the CALL# in the parent record. Since the insertion status of COLLECTION is AUTOMATIC, the DBMS must find such a parent when the STORE is executed.

Processing of a MANDATORY set is similar except that once a record is placed in a set (either MANUAL or AUTOMATIC, depending on its insertion status), only the RECONNECT command may be used. DISCONNECT is not allowed.

Set Membership and ERASE Commands

If a record owns a set occurrence, then special considerations apply when the record is deleted. The application program can request that all children (and children of children, and so forth) be erased when the record is erased, or it can be more selective.

Suppose we want to delete a BOOK record and all of the CPY and DUE-DATE records that pertain to this book. The following statements will accomplish this for the book whose call number is Q360.C33:

```
MOVE ''Q360.C33'' TO CALL#
FIND FOR UPDATE ANY BOOK USING CALL#
ERASE ALL BOOK
```

The keyword ALL in the above ERASE command directs the DBMS to erase all CPY records (and all DUE-DATE records belonging to the set owned by CPY).

If ALL is not specified in the ERASE command, then the result depends on the retention status of the owned sets. If the retention status is FIXED, then the ERASE will be successful and all owned children records will be erased as well. If the retention status is MANDATORY, then the ERASE will be disallowed. If it were allowed, the remaining child records would be fragments. Their retention status is MANDATORY, and they must reside in a set. If the DBMS were to erase their parent, it would not know what to do with the fragments.

If the retention status is OPTIONAL, then the ERASE will be allowed and any child records will be disconnected from the set. However, they will remain in the database.

Using Sets for Record Retrieval

Once records have been placed in sets, set membership can be used to retrieve records by relationships. Or, in the terminology of this text, sets and set membership can be used to construct objects from records.

Suppose we want to process a view of the STUDENT object that contains both BOR-ROWER and CPY records. Say we want to retrieve the call numbers of all the books on loan to student 400. The following statements will do this:

```
MOVE ''400'' TO STUDENT#
FIND ANY BORROWER USING STUDENT#
FIND FIRST CPY WITHIN CHECKOUT
DOWHILE DB-STATUS = 0
     GET CPY
     (process CPY record to display CALL#)
     FIND NEXT CPY WITHIN CHECKOUT
END-DO
```

The first FIND command establishes the current of BORROWER as well as the current of CHECKOUT. The next FIND command then sets the current of CPY to the first record in the set owned by the BORROWER with STUDENT# of 400. The first record is then processed and the next one identified with the FIND NEXT command. In addition to FIND FIRST and FIND NEXT, this model also provides FIND LAST and FIND nth, where n is the ordinal position of the record in the set. This last option is useful only if the set members are ordered in some manner.

Suppose we want not only the call numbers of all books on loan to student 400, but also the titles. Titles are stored in TTLE records, and therefore we must retrieve the owner of each CPY record. Thus, we start with student, find a CPY record owned by that student, find the parent of that record, and then repeat for the next CPY record owned by that student. This can be done as follows:

```
MOVE ''400'' TO STUDENT#
FIND ANY BORROWER USING STUDENT#
FIND FIRST CPY WITHIN CHECKOUT
DOWHILE DB-STATUS = 0
     GET CPY
     FIND OWNER WITHIN COLLECTION
```

```
        GET TTLE
        (process CPY and TTLE records to display CALL#
and
          title)
        FIND NEXT CPY WITHIN CHECKOUT
    END-DO
```

The FIND OWNER statement establishes the owner of the CPY record as the current of run-unit.

CODASYL DBTG Model as a *Model*

The CODASYL DBTG model is a rich, comprehensive, and complicated model. Because of its long history and the many different versions, committees, companies, and people involved, it is inconsistent and difficult to comprehend. As a model, however, it is rich enough to enable the expression of database designs and application program logic for transaction processing databases and applications.

You may think of this situation as analogous to using pseudocode for specifying program logic. Pseudocode is vague in some ways, but it is entirely serviceable for the expression of program logic. Of course, when the logic is expressed in a programming language, the vagueness is replaced with statements that have one and only one interpretation to the language compiler. So it is with this model. The DBTG model can be used to express designs and logic, and, within the parameters of the model, the statements can mean what you want them to mean. Once the database is implemented, however, and a particular DBMS product is used, then the statements available and their function and meaning will become exact.

Summary

Like the hierarchical data model, the network data model is the basis for many DBMS products that perform transaction processing. The most significant network data model is known as the CODASYL DBTG data model, named after the committee that developed it. The most significant difference between the network data model and the hierarchical data model is that simple networks can be represented directly in the network model. Thus, it was an improvement over the earlier hierarchical model.

The history of the CODASYL DBTG data model is a long one. Essentially, many people were involved in the development of the model, and its many options and formats reflect the views of so many participants. It is a rich but not very cohesive model.

The DBTG model introduced the concept of both a data definition and a data manipulation language for DBMS products. Unlike DL/I, which includes no database definition facilities, products based on the DBTG model include both languages.

A schema is a logical view of the entire database as seen by the database administration. A subschema is a subset of the database, like a view in the relational model. A subschema is the application program's view of the database.

All user interaction with the database is accomplished via application programs (there is no interactive query language in the model). An application program can be run by one or more users. Each user has his or her own user work area for passing data to and from the DBMS.

The building blocks used for DBTG data definition are data-items (or fields), records (collections of data-items), and sets (a set is a one-to-many relationship between records). These building blocks can be used to represent all of the object types we have discussed in this text: composite, compound, and association. When defining the database, it is a straightforward step to transform the relational database definition into the DBTG database definition.

When defining DBTG sets, we specify various options such as how the members will be ordered, how members will be placed in a set occurrence (insertion status), and how, if at all, a member can be removed from a set occurrence (retention status). These options allow us to enforce some database constraints. However, the DBTG model does not provide complete and comprehensive facilities for constraint enforcement.

Among the constraints the DBTG model does enforce are domain constraints (allowable values and mandatory existence), intrarecord constraints (uniqueness, both of individual data-item values and of composite data-item values), and interrecord constraints (referential integrity, by means of set retention status and via the CHECK command).

The DBTG model also provides a data manipulation language. Generally, database accesses are accomplished in two steps: the first step is used to identify the record to be acted upon, and the second step performs some operation. The DBTG FIND statement is used to identify a record. When executed, the FIND statement sets the value of one or more currency indicators.

A currency indicator is a place marker; it points to the most recently identified record in a record type, set, or run-unit. Each execution of a FIND may modify one or several of these place markers. After a currency indicator is set, a subsequent instruction can access the record to which it is pointing.

Special registers are data-items in the user work area whose values are set by the DBMS to report on the status of the system. They can be accessed by the application program. Special registers are used to indicate error conditions, end-of-data, the name of the most recently processed record, and so forth.

DBTG commands are available to read, insert, modify, and delete database records. DBTG DML can be used to access and process individual database records and to process sets. The syntax shown in this chapter is generic. Exact syntax varies by DBMS product.

‖‖‖‖‖‖‖‖‖‖‖‖‖‖‖‖‖‖‖

GROUP I QUESTIONS

13.1 Explain the relationship between user, run-unit, application program, subschema, schema, database, and DBMS.

13.2 Define *data-item*. How are data-items related to domains? How are domains defined using the DBTG model?

13.3 Define *record* as used in the DBTG model.

13.4 Define the following terms and explain their purpose: *set, owner, member, set occurrence*.

13.5 Give an example of a set structure. Sketch two occurrences of this set.

13.6 Consider the following tree: School districts have schools, and schools have pupils (one record type) and teachers (another record type). Teachers have past assignments. Show a DBTG representation of this tree and illustrate two occurrences.

13.7 Consider the following simple network: Fathers have children and teachers teach children. Show a DBTG representation of this simple network. Describe two occurrences.

13.8 Consider the following complex network: Children have many hobbies, and a hobby is enjoyed by many children. Show a DBTG representation of this complex network. Describe two occurrences.

13.9 List the DBTG currency indicators and describe situations in which each would be used.

13.10 Explain how most DBTG DML operations are executed in two steps.

For questions 13.11 through 13.16, provide pseudocode similar to that in this chapter. Refer to the following schema:

SALESPERSON with data-items NAME, AGE, SALARY
ORDER with data-items NUMBER, CUST-NAME, SALESPERSON-NAME, AMOUNT
CUSTOMER with data-items NAME, CITY, INDUSTRY-TYPE
SET SALE with owner SALESPERSON and member ORDER
SET PURCHASE with owner CUSTOMER and member ORDER

13.11 Retrieve:

a. Customer with name ABC CONSTRUCTION
b. Order with number 12345
c. All orders for customer ABC CONSTRUCTION

13.12 Delete all orders for salesperson PARKS.

13.13   Change the industry type of ABC Construction to type J (assume INDUSTRY-TYPE is a character data-item).

13.14   Store a new SALESPERSON record: name is CURTIS, age is 39, salary is 65,000.

13.15   Change the name of customer ABC Construction to SoftSystems. Make changes to ORDER records as well, assuming the retention status of PURCHASE is

   a. OPTIONAL
   b. MANDATORY
   c. FIXED

13.16   Assume that both SALE and PURCHASE are MANUAL, OPTIONAL sets.

   a. Create an ORDER record and place it in the correct set occurrences of PURCHASE and SALE.
   b. Change the name of a customer in an ORDER record and RECONNECT it to the correct occurrence (assume the record is already in an occurrence).
   c. Remove all ORDERs for customer JONES from sets to which they belong.

GROUP II QUESTIONS

13.17   Modify Figure 13.10b to make it a non-information bearing set. Modify Figures 13.11b, 13.12b, 13.13b to make all sets information bearing ones. Modify Figure 13.14b to make CHECKOUT a non-information bearing set, and COLLECTION an information bearing set. Are any of these reversals impossible to carry out? Why?

13.18   Compare and contrast the DBTG model with the relational model. Which model is easier to understand? Which do you think would be easier to use? For what applications would the DBTG model be preferred to the relational model? For what applications would the relational model be preferred to the DBTG model?

13.19   Locate in your community a company that uses a CODASYL DBTG DBMS. Interview personnel and determine how schemas and subschemas are designed. If possible, obtain a copy of a schema, subschema, and application program. Compare these to the concepts described in this chapter.

Administration

Part VI considers the subjects of data administration and database administration. As you will learn, the difference in these two topics concerns scope. The scope of data administration concerns is wide; it encompasses data throughout the entire organization. The scope of database administration is narrower; it is oriented to a particular database rather than to the organization as a whole. Chapter 14, the sole chapter in this part, also includes a discussion of reliability and security—two important concerns of database administration.

Data Administration and Database Administration

Data is an important organizational asset. Consequently, organizations must establish policies, procedures, standards, and similar management structures to ensure that the data is both protected and
well utilized. Data administration and database
administration are two organizational functions that
have these responsibilities. We begin by describing
the need for data administration—a group that takes
an organizationwide view of the importance and role
of data. We discuss the challenges of data administration and then describe the basic data administration functions.

The following section concerns database administration. This function, which is oriented to a particular database rather than to the organization as a
whole, is concerned with the management of database structure, activity, and the DBMS itself.

Next we discuss database reliability and security.
Providing reliability is particularly difficult (and
important) in multi-user environments. We discuss
some of the problems that can occur and solutions
to those problems. Solutions can be *proactive* (preventing the problems) and *reactive* (responding to
failure). Finally, we present a model of security and
describe several types of database security schemes.

- DATA AS AN ORGANIZATIONAL ASSET
- DATA ADMINISTRATION
- DATABASE ADMINISTRATION
- DATABASE RELIABILITY
- DATABASE SECURITY

As you will see, the first half of this chapter concerns broad management issues; the second half concerns specific techniques and technology. The combination of subjects having these two different natures may seem odd; it does, however, reflect the nature of these functions. Data administration and database administration require both management and diplomacy skills and also high levels of technical competency.

Because of this dual nature, when you meet someone with the title data administrator or database administrator, it is often difficult to know the nature of his or her work. The person could be management oriented and concerned with the large issues of effective data usage in the organization. Or, the person could also be technically oriented and narrowly focused on the details of database design and implementation, DBMS tuning, and the like. As you read this chapter, keep these differences in mind.

Data as an Organizational Asset

An organization's data is as much of a resource as are its plant, equipment, and financial assets. Data is time consuming and expensive to acquire, and it serves an important role not only in an organization's operations and management, but also in product quality and delivery. Further, data often serves to establish and maintain the organization's competitive advantage. For example, consider the value of a customer list to a mail-order company or of price and volume histories to a stock brokerage.

Because of this value, organizational data needs to be managed as other organizational assets are. In recognition of this need, many organizations have established offices of data administration and database administration. The purpose of these offices is to guard and protect the data and also to ensure that the data is utilized effectively.

In some ways, data administration is to data what the controller is to money. The responsibility of a controller is not only to ensure that financial assets are protected and accounted for, but also to ensure that they are well used. Storing an organization's money in a vault will protect it, but the money will be poorly utilized. It must be invested in ways that facilitate the organization's goals and objectives.

Similarly, with data administration, simply protecting the data is not enough. Data administration and database administration must also take steps to increase the utility the organization receives from its data.

Data Administration

The terms **data administration** and **database administration** are both used in industry. In some cases the terms are considered synonymous; in other cases a distinction is made. In this text, we make the following distinction: We use the term *data administration* to refer to an organizationwide function whose scope of activity spans all of the organization. The term *database administration* refers to a function that is specific to a particular database. The scope of database administration includes the database and the systems that process that database. Sometimes the term *global database administration* is used instead of *data administration.*

NEED FOR DATA ADMINISTRATION

To understand the need for data administration, consider the analogy of a university library. The typical university library contains hundreds of thousands of books, journals, magazines, government reports, and so forth. These resources provide no utility while they are on the bookshelves. To be useful, they must be made available to people who have an interest and need in their contents.

Clearly, the library must have some means for describing its collection so that potential users can determine what's available. At first glance, this might seem like a trivial problem. You might say, "Well, build a card catalog." But much work must be done to be able to do just that. How are the library's works to be identified? How are they to be described? Even more basic, what constitutes a work? How can we accommodate different ways of identifying works (ISBN, Dewey decimal system, government report number, and so on)? How do we help people find things that they may not know exist?

Other complications arise. Suppose the university is so large that several libraries are needed. In this case, how are the collections to be managed as one resource to the university? Further, some departments will maintain their own libraries. Are these to be made part of the university system? Further, many professors have extensive personal libraries. Should these be part of the system?

CHALLENGES OF DATA ADMINISTRATION

The library analogy does not go far enough; organizational data administration is considerably more difficult than library administration. For one, it is not at all clear what constitutes a work in an organization. Libraries have books, periodicals, and so forth. Organizational data occurs in myriads of formats. Organizations have traditional data records, but they also have documents, spreadsheets, graphics and illustrations, technical drawings, audio files, and so forth. How is this potpourri to be described? What are the basic categories of organizational data? These questions are important because their answers determine how the data will be organized, managed, protected, and accessed.

Furthermore, most organizations have many names for the same thing. A telephone number can be described as a Phone-Number, Phone#, Telephone#, Employee-phone, Dept-phone, and so forth. Which of these names is preferred? When a graphic designer places a telephone number on a new form, what label should she use? When a programmer writes a new program, what name should he use for the program variable that holds telephone number? Clearly, there are economies in using the same name, at least for many applications.

Additionally, there are many ways of representing the data element. A phone number can be represented as a ten-digit integer, a ten-digit text field, a thirteen-digit text field in the form *(nnn)nnn-nnnn,* a twelve-digit text field in the form *nnn-nnn-nnnn,* or in still other formats. Which of these should be allowed? Which, if any, should be the standard?

Such differences between organizational data and the library materials are miniscule, however, when compared to the next difference: People must be able to change organizational data.

In contrast, consider what would happen at the library if people checked out books, wrote in them, tore out pages, added pages, and then put the books back on the shelves. Or, even worse, suppose someone checked out three books, made changes in all three, checked them back in, and told the librarian: "Either change all of these or none of them."

This analogy is simplistic though. Unlike the description in the previous paragraph, when people change data, they do not immediately change the data in the database. Instead, they read a copy of the data into the application program, change it there, and then attempt to replace the official copy of the data with their changed copy. Since, in multi-user systems, several people may be doing this at the same time, it is readily possible for users' activities to interfere.

In addition to all of these operationally oriented challenges, there are additional challenges from organizational issues. For example, data can mean organizational power; hence changes in data control can mean changes in power. Thus, behind the tasks of data administration lie all sorts of political issues. A discussion of these is beyond the scope of this text, but they are important nonetheless.

The challenges for data administration are summarized in Figure 14.1.

FUNCTIONS OF DATA ADMINISTRATION

Because of the challenges just described, data administration is a complex activity. To guard and protect the data while at the same time increasing the data's utility to the organization, a number of different functions or tasks must be accomplished. As shown in Figure 14.2, these activities can be grouped into several different categories.

Marketing

First and foremost, data administration has the responsibility for declaring its existence and selling its services to the rest of the organization. Employees need to know that data administration exists. They need to know that there are policies, standards, and guide-

FIGURE 14.1
Challenges of data administration

- Many types of data exist.
- Basic categories of data are not obvious.
- The same data can have many names.
- The same data can have many descriptions and formats.
- Data is changed—often concurrently.
- Political-organizational issues complicate operational issues.

FIGURE 14.2
Functions of data administration

Marketing
- Communicate existence of data administration to organization.
- Explain reason for existence of standards and policies.
- Describe services provided in a positive light.

Data Standards
- Establish standard means for describing data items. Standards include name, definition, description, processing restrictions, and so forth.
- Establish data proponents.

Data Policies
- Establish organizationwide data policy. Examples are security, data proponency, and distribution.

Forum for Data Conflict Resolution
- Establish procedures for reporting conflicts.
- Provide means for hearing all perspectives and views.
- Have authority to make decision to resolve conflict.

Return on Organization's Data Investment
- Focus attention on value of data investment.
- Investigate new methodologies and technologies.
- Take proactive attitude about information management.

lines that pertain to organizational data. They need to know the reasons for these, and they need to be given reasons to respect and follow data administration rules, guidelines, and restrictions.

As Vinden[1] points out, data administration must be, in the final analysis, a service function, and the users must perceive it that way. Thus, data administration activities

---

[1]Robin J. Vinden, *Data Dictionaries for Database Administrators* (Blue Ridge Summit, Pa.: TAB Books, 1990), 18.

must be communicated to the organization in a positive, service-providing light. Employees need to believe that they have something to gain from data administration. Otherwise, the function becomes all cost and no benefit to the users, and it will be shunned.

Data Standards

For organizational data to be managed effectively, it must be organized in some coherent fashion. If each department, function, or employee were to pick a different definition for what constitutes a data item or for the means by which data items are to be named or described, chaos would result. It would be impossible to even compile an inventory of data, let alone to manage it.

Consequently, many organizations decide that important data items will be described in a standard way. For example, data administration may determine that every data item of importance to the organization will be described by a standard name, definition, description, set of processing restrictions, and proponent.

Once this structure is determined, the next question is, who sets the values of these standard descriptions? For example, who decides the standard name or standard processing restrictions?

In most organizations, the data administration group does *not* determine the standard descriptions. Instead, each item is assigned a **data proponent,** which is a department or other organizational unit that is in charge of the management of that data item. The proponent is given the responsibility for establishing and maintaining the official organizational definitions for data items assigned to it. Even though the data administration group may be the proponent of some data items, most proponents arise from other departments.

You may, in your career, encounter the term *data owner.* This term is generally used in the same way that the term *data proponent* is used in this text. We avoid the term here because it implies a degree of propriety that does not exist. Both legally and practically, the organization is the one and only owner of the data. Although some group or groups have a legitimate claim to a greater degree of authority over particular data than others, these groups do *not* own that data. Hence, the term *data proponent* will be used instead.

To summarize, the foundation of data administration is a system of data standards. The data administration group has the responsibility for working with users and management to develop a workable system. Further, these standards must be documented and communicated to the organization by some effective means. Procedures for assessing compliance with standards and for encouraging the following of standards must also be developed.

Data Policies

Another group of data administration functions concerns data policies. To illustrate the need for such policy, consider first data security. Every organization has data that is proprietary or sensitive. Data administration has the responsibility for developing a security system to protect that data. Questions like the following need to be addressed: What security schemes should exist? Does the organization need a multilevel security system similar to that of the military? Or, would a simpler system suffice?

The security policy must also address questions such as what is required for someone to have access to sensitive data? What agreements must they sign to do so? What about employees of external agents? Can sensitive data be copied? How are employees to be trained with regard to security? What happens when security procedures are violated? These questions exemplify the issues that must be addressed.

A second type of data policy concerns data proponency and processing rights. What does being a data proponent mean? What rights does the proponent have that other groups do not? Who establishes proponency and how can it be changed?

A third example of the need for data policy concerns data distribution. This policy addresses the following questions: Can official data be distributed on more than one computer? If so, which, if any, is *the official* copy? What processing is allowed on distributed data? Can data that has been distributed be returned to the official data store? If so, what checks must exist to validate it before accepting it? You will learn about the need for other elements of the data distribution policy in the next two chapters.

Forum for Data Conflict Resolution

To be effective, organizational data must be shared. But humans have difficulty sharing. Consequently, the organization must be prepared to address disputes regarding data proponency, processing restrictions, and other matters.

The first responsibility of data administration in this regard is to establish procedures for reporting conflicts. When one user or group has needs that conflict with another's, the groups need a way to make their conflict known in an orderly manner. Without open disclosure, the conflict can degenerate into unproductive carping of one group with another.

Once the conflict has become known, established procedures should allow all involved parties to present their case. Data administration staff, perhaps in conjunction with involved data proponents, then must make a decision. The foregoing scenario assumes, however, that the organization has granted data administration the authority to make and enforce the resulting decision.

Data administration provides a forum for the resolution for such conflict. The scope of this forum is the entire organization. As you will see, database administration also provides forums for conflict resolution. The scope of those forums, however, is restricted to a particular database.

Increasing the Return on the Organization's Data Investment

A final function for data administration is to focus on the need to increase the organization's return on its data investment. Data administration is the department that asks questions like, "Are we getting what we should be getting from our data resource? If so, can we get more? If not, why not? Is it all worthwhile?"

This focus involves all of the other functions described: it includes marketing, establishing standards or policy, conflict resolution, and so forth. Sometimes this function also involves investigating new techniques for storing, processing, or presenting data, new methodologies, new technology, and the like.

Successful fulfillment of this role requires a *proactive* attitude about information management. In such a mode, the relevant questions are how can we use information to increase our market position, our economic competitiveness, and our overall net worth? Data administration must work closely with the organization's planning and development departments to anticipate rather than just react to the need for new information requirements.

Database Administration

Whereas the scope of activity for data administration is the entire organization, the scope of activity for *database* administration is restricted to a particular database and the systems that process it. Database administration operates within the framework provided by data administration to facilitate the development and use of a particular database and its applications. The acronym **DBA** is used to refer both to the function *database administration* and to the job title *database administrator.*

Chapter 1 defined three levels of database: personal, workgroup, and organizational. The database administration function exists at all three of these levels; however, it varies in complexity. Database administration is considerably simpler for personal than for workgroup applications, and database administration for workgroup applications is, in turn, considerably simpler than for organizational applications. But the tasks and functions exist at all three levels.

Often personal database administration is done on an informal basis. For example, individuals follow simple procedures for backing up their database, and they keep minimal records for documentation. In this case, the person who uses the database performs the DBA functions.

More administration is required for workgroup applications, and typically one or two individuals fulfill this function on a part-time basis. They mix database administration tasks in with their other job duties. In this case, there are one or two part-time DBAs.

At the organizational level, database administration responsibilities are often too time consuming and too varied to be handled even by a single full-time person. Supporting a database with dozens or hundreds of users requires considerable time as well as both highly technical knowledge and keen diplomatic skills. Usually an office of database administration is developed. The manager of the office is often known as the *database administrator.* Consequently, in this case, the acronym *DBA* refers either to the office or to the manager, depending on context.

In the following discussion, we will describe DBA functions for the administration of a large, organizational database. Functions for workgroup and personal databases are similar, but simpler.

The overall responsibility of the DBA is to facilitate the development and use of the database within the context of guidelines set out by data administration. Usually this means balancing the conflicting goals of protecting the database and maximizing its availability and benefit to users.

The DBA is responsible for the development, operation, and maintenance of the database and its applications. Specific functions of database administration can be grouped in the following categories:

- Management of the database structure
- Management of data activity
- Management of the DBMS
- Establishing the database data dictionary
- Providing for database reliability
- Providing for database security

We will consider each of these functions in turn. The last two functions are more complicated than the others, so they will be described in some detail.

MANAGEMENT OF DATABASE STRUCTURE

Management of structure includes participating in the initial database design and implementation as well as control and management of changes to the database. Ideally, the DBA is involved early in the development of the database and its applications. The DBA participates in the requirements study, helps to evaluate alternatives, including the DBMS to be used, and has a crucial role in the design of the database structure. For large, organizational applications, the DBA will most likely be a manager who supervises the work of technically oriented database design personnel.

Once the database has been designed, it is implemented using the DBMS product and the database data is created. The DBA participates in the development of procedures and controls to ensure high integrity and quality of the database data.

User requirements will change, users will find better ways to accomplish their goals, database technology will change, and DBMS vendors will upgrade their products. All changes to the database structure or procedures need to be carefully managed. Change to the database structure is usually an evolutionary—not revolutionary—process.

Configuration Control

After a database and its applications have been implemented and are in use, requests for changes are inevitable. For example, requests can arise from new requirements or they can be the result of inadequate understanding of requirements.

In any case, changes must be made with regard to the entire database community. The DBA must consider the ramifications of the change on all database application users, because the impact of changes is seldom felt by only one application. In some cases, the DBA may decide that even though a particular change has a negative effect on a user, it is in the best interests of the company to make it. The DBA must carefully explain such a decision to the user group.

Effective database administration means that procedures and policies exist by which users can register the need for change, the entire community can discuss the impacts of the change, and a decision can be made to implement or not implement the proposed change.

Because of the size and complexity of a database and its applications, changes will sometimes have unexpected results. The DBA must be prepared to repair a database and to gather sufficient information to diagnose and correct the problem that caused the damage. The database is most vulnerable to failure after a change.

Documentation

The final responsibility of the DBA in the management of database structure is documentation. It is extremely important to know what changes have been made, how they were made, and when they were made. A change to the database structure may cause an error that does not manifest itself for six months. Without proper documentation of the change, diagnosis of the problem is next to impossible. Dozens of job reruns may be required to identify a point where certain symptoms first occurred. For this reason, it is also important to maintain a record of test procedures and test runs made to verify a change. If standardized test procedures, test forms, and record-keeping methods are used, the recording of test results does not have to be time consuming.

Although maintaining documentation is tedious and unfulfilling, the effort pays off when disaster occurs and the documentation is the difference between solving and not solving a major (and costly) problem. Today, also, a number of products are emerging that ease the burden of documentation. Many CASE tools, for example, can be used to maintain documentation of logical database designs. Data dictionaries also provide documentation assistance. Other products that read and interpret the database data structures maintained by popular DBMS products are available.

Another reason for maintaining good documentation of changes to the database structure is to allow proper use of historical data. If, for some reason, marketing wants to analyze three-year-old sales data which has been in the archives for two years, it will be necessary to know what structure was current at the time the data was last active. Records that show the changes to structure can be used to answer the question. A similar situation arises when a six-month-old backup copy of data must be used to repair a damaged database (this should not occur, but sometimes it does). The backup copy can be used to reconstruct the database to the state it was in at the time of the backup. Then, transactions and structural changes can be applied in chronological order to eventually restore the database to a current state.

Figure 14.3 summarizes DBA responsibilities for the management of database structure.

MANAGEMENT OF DATA ACTIVITY

The DBA protects the data but does not process it. The DBA is not a user of the system. Consequently, the DBA does not manage *data values*. Rather, the DBA manages *data activity*. The database is a shared resource, and the DBA provides standards, guidelines,

FIGURE 14.3
Summary of DBA responsibilities
for the management of database
structure

> **Participate in Database and Application Development**
> - Assist in requirements stage and evaluation of alternatives.
> - Play an active role in database design and creation.
> - Develop procedures for integrity and quality of database data.
>
> **Facilitate Changes to Database Structure**
> - Seek communitywide solutions.
> - Assess impact on all users.
> - Provide configuration control forum.
> - Be prepared for problems after changes are made.
> - Maintain documentation.

control procedures, and documentation to ensure that users work in a cooperative and complementary fashion when processing database data.

Because of the high degree of interrelated activity, database processing must be standardized processing. Providing database standards is one aspect of managing data activity. Every database field must have a standard name and format. Every database record must have a standard name, format, and standardized access strategies. Every database file must have a standard name and standardized relationships with other files. The DBA establishes these standards in a manner that satisfies the majority of the collective needs of all database users.

When organizations have an effective data administration function, many of these standards will already exist. In this case, the DBA extends and amplifies the existing organizational standards and ensures that those standards are reflected and enforced by the database standards. The database standards will be more detailed and particular to the needs of users of the particular database.

Once established, the details of standardization are recorded in the DBMS **data dictionary.** Then both systems developers and users can query the dictionary to determine exactly what data is being maintained, what the names and formats of data items are, and what relationships exist.

Another aspect of managing data activity is the establishment of data proponency, access, and modification rights. Since the data is a shared resource, problems occur regarding processing rights. The DBA, together with the relevant data proponents, considers each shared data item and determines the access and modification rights of particular applications and users.

This activity is undertaken with regard for the greater communitywide benefit rather than the benefit of one particular application, group, or user. Once processing rights have been determined, they can be implemented by the DBMS, by applications that process the database via the DBMS, or by both.

As you will learn later in this chapter, problems can occur when two or more user groups are authorized to modify the same data. One such problem, called the **lost**

update problem, occurs when the work of one user is overwritten by the work of a second user.

The DBA is responsible for identifying possibilities for such problems and for developing procedures and standards for avoiding them. This involves ensuring that the facilities of the DBMS are used properly by both programmers and users. It also may involve establishing processing schedules and other manual procedures. For example, in some cases the DBA may restrict types of activities by user groups to certain periods of the day to avoid concurrency problems that can degrade overall system performance.

Another important concern for the DBA in the management of data activity is development of recovery techniques and procedures. Although, as you will learn, the DBMS performs one part of the recovery process, people play a critical role. The DBA must anticipate failures and develop standardized procedures for handling them. Users must know what to do while the system is down, and what to do first when the system is made available. The operations staff must know how to initiate a database recovery process, which backup copies of the database to use, how to schedule the rerunning of lost work (other systems are using the computer resources, too, and priorities need to be established and enforced), and so on. If a communications control program is in use (a likely situation in an online multi-user database environment), the recovery of its processing must be coordinated with database recovery. All of these problems are the responsibility of the DBA.

Finally, the DBA is responsible for publishing and maintaining documentation about data activity. This includes documentation about database standards, data retrieval and access rights, recovery procedures, and policy enforcement. Good documentation is especially important because it is needed by diverse user groups throughout the organization. As with all documentation, keeping it current is a major and unpopular task.

Many DBMS products provide utility services to assist in the management of data activity. Some systems record the names of users and application programs that access (or are authorized to access) objects in the database. In this case, the DBMS data dictionary can be queried to determine which programs can access a particular record and what actions each can take. Figure 14.4 summarizes DBA responsibilities for the management of data activity.

FIGURE 14.4

Summary of DBA responsibilities
for the management of data activity

- Establish database standards consistent with data administration standards.
- Establish and maintain data dictionary.
- Establish data proponencies.
- Work with data proponents to develop data access and modification rights.
- Develop, document, and train staff on backup and recovery procedures.
- Publish and maintain data activity standards documentation.

MANAGEMENT OF THE DBMS

In addition to managing data activity and database structure, the DBA must manage the DBMS itself. The DBA should compile and analyze statistics about system performance and identify potential problem areas. Keep in mind that the database is serving many user groups. The DBA needs to investigate all user complaints about system response time, accuracy of data, ease of use, and so forth. If changes are needed, the DBA must plan and implement them.

The DBA must periodically (and continually) monitor user activity on the database. DBMS products include features that collect and report statistics. Some of these reports may indicate, for example, which users have been active, which files and perhaps which data items have been used, and which access methods have been employed. Error rates and error types can also be captured and reported. The DBA analyzes this data to determine whether a change to the database design is needed to improve performance or ease the users' tasks. If so, the DBA will make the change.

The DBA should analyze run-time statistics on database activity and performance. When a performance problem is identified (either by a report or by a user complaint), the DBA must determine whether a modification to the database structure or system is appropriate. Examples of possible structure modifications are establishing new keys, purging data, deleting keys, and establishing new relationships between objects.

When the vendor of the DBMS being employed announces new product features, the DBA must consider them in light of the overall needs of the user community. If the DBA decides to incorporate new DBMS features, users need to be notified and trained in their use. Thus, the DBA must manage and control change to the DBMS as well as to the database structure.

Other changes to the system for which the DBA is responsible vary widely, depending on the DBMS product as well as other software and hardware in use. For example, changes to other software (such as the operating system or a communications control program) may mean that some DBMS parameters must be modified. Thus, the DBA must tune the DBMS product to other software in use.

DBMS options are initially chosen when little is known about how the system will perform in the particular user environment. Consequently, operational experience and performance analysis over a period of time may indicate a change is necessary. Even if performance seems acceptable, the DBA may want to alter the options and observe the effect on performance. This process is referred to as tuning, or optimizing, the system.

Figure 14.5 summarizes the DBA's responsibilities for DBMS product management.

ESTABLISHMENT OF THE DATABASE DATA DICTIONARY

A DBMS data dictionary is an important tool for the database administrator. A data dictionary is actually a user-accessible catalog of data about the database. Its importance can be demonstrated by the following problem: Suppose a development team creates a data-

FIGURE 14.5
Summary of DBA responsibilities
for the management of the DBMS
product

- Generate database application performance reports.
- Investigate user performance complaints.
- Assess need for changes to database structure or application design.
- Modify database structure.
- Evaluate and implement new DBMS features.
- Tune the DBMS.

base consisting of 20 tables and 300 columns. Seventy-five application programs process this database on a regular basis.

Suppose that adhering to a new tax law requires changes in the way that employee taxes are calculated and in the formats of the data fields that are used. Before modifying either data or programs, the manager of data processing needs to assess the impact of these changes (in order to allocate people and testing facilities, to develop user training, and so forth). The manager needs to know which programs reference which data items.

If a data dictionary is in place, then a simple query (just like a query against data) can provide the answer to the manager's question. If there is no cross-referencing mechanism in place, then each application program needs to be studied (usually by application programmers) to determine whether it references the data items in question. Obviously, the first of the approaches is much faster and probably much more accurate.

Data dictionaries are not new. In fact, many data processing managers developed their own cross-referencing systems long before databases became popular. Now, however, many DBMS products include an integrated data dictionary option. As you saw in Chapter 11, IBM incorporates a user-accessible catalog in its DB2 relational database product. Other manufacturers offer similar options.

Some data dictionaries are active and some are passive. An active data dictionary is one whose entries are automatically modified by the software whenever changes are made to the database structure. Passive data dictionaries, in contrast, need to be updated separately when database changes are made; otherwise, they will not accurately reflect the state of the database. Active data dictionaries usually cost more, but they assure currency; they are not available with every DBMS product. Passive data dictionaries are less expensive than active ones, but more effort is required to keep them up-to-date. Either type of data dictionary, however, greatly aids the DBA in recording and tracking data names, formats, relationships, and cross-references.

Database Reliability

An important category of responsibilities for the DBA concerns database reliability. Here, the DBA is responsible for ensuring that programs and procedures are developed so as to provide for reliability of the data in light of the reality of machine malfunctions, program bugs, and human errors.

For single-user, personal databases, little is required. Procedures should be developed to periodically save copies of the database data and to keep records of processing since the save so that work can be duplicated, if necessary.

In the multi-user environment, the situation is more complicated. First, users process the database concurrently, and there is always the possibility that one user's work may interfere with another's. Additionally, recovery after failure is more complicated. Simply reprocessing the transactions is undesirable, not only because of the duplication of manual work involved, but also because, in a multi-user environment, it is possible that the results of the reprocessing may differ from the original results. If so, the documents (confirmation of orders, for example), generated during the first processing may be incorrect.

First we will consider control of concurrent processing and then address backup and recovery.

CHARACTERISTICS OF MULTI-USER PROCESSING

In a multi-user environment, users submit work in units called **transactions.** They are also known as **atomic transactions** and **logical units of work** (LUWs). A transaction is a series of actions to be taken on the database such that either all the actions are done successfully or none of them are and the database remains unchanged. For example, suppose a transaction to enter a customer order includes the following actions:

1. Change the customer record with the new order data.
2. Change the salesperson record with the new order data.
3. Insert a new order record into the database.

Suppose the last step failed, perhaps because of insufficient file space. Imagine the confusion that would take place if the first two changes were applied, but not the third one. The customer might receive an invoice for an item never received, and a salesperson might receive a commission on an item never sent to the customer.

Figure 14.6 compares the results of performing these activities as a series of independent steps (Figure 14.6a) and as an atomic transaction (Figure 14.6b). Notice that when the steps are done atomically and one fails, no changes are applied to the database. Defining a series of steps as a transaction is an important aspect of concurrency control.

Concurrent processing happens when two transactions are interleaved, which is common in the multi-user environment. In almost all cases (the exception concerns certain, very rare, special-purpose hardware), the CPU of the machine processing the database executes only one instruction at a time. Rather than devote all CPU time to a single transaction until it is completed, then starting on the next one, and so forth, the operating system instead switches CPU services among waiting tasks so that some portion of each of them is accomplished in a given period of time.

This switching among tasks happens so quickly that two people seated at terminals side-by-side, processing the same database, may believe that their two transactions are processed simultaneously. In reality, the two transactions are interleaved. The CPU performs instructions for one task, then switches to the second, then back to the first, and so forth. Though humans cannot perceive that interleaving has taken place, it has.

492

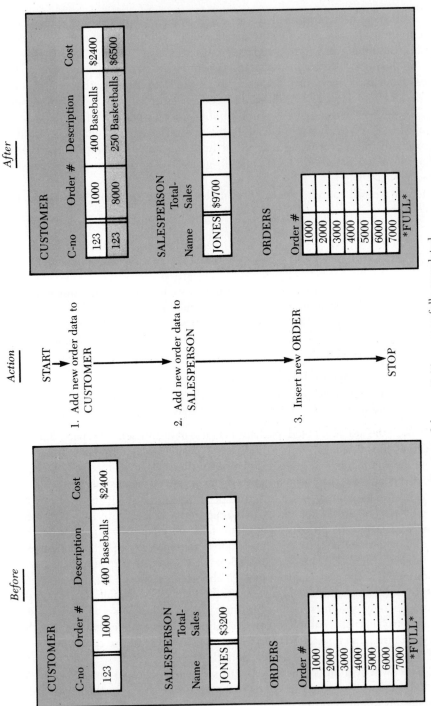

FIGURE 14.6
Comparison of results of applying serial actions versus a multiple-step transaction

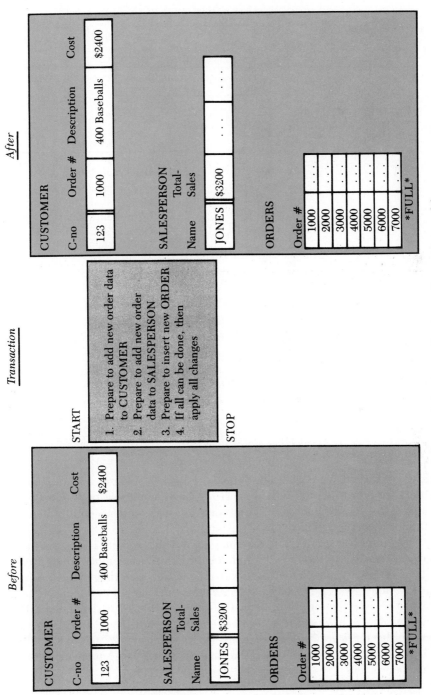

Before

CUSTOMER

C-no	Order #	Description	Cost
123	1000	400 Baseballs	$2400

SALESPERSON

Name	Total-Sales		
JONES	$3200	. . .	. . .

ORDERS

Order #
1000
2000
3000
4000
5000
6000
7000

FULL

Transaction

START

1. Prepare to add new order data to CUSTOMER
2. Prepare to add new order data to SALESPERSON
3. Prepare to insert new ORDER
4. If all can be done, then apply all changes

STOP

After

CUSTOMER

C-no	Order #	Description	Cost
123	1000	400 Baseballs	$2400

SALESPERSON

Name	Total-Sales		
JONES	$3200	. . .	. . .

ORDERS

Order #
1000
2000
3000
4000
5000
6000
7000

FULL

b. No change made because entire transaction not successful

FIGURE 14.6 *continued*

493

FIGURE 14.7
Example of concurrent processing
of two users' tasks

User A	User B
1. Read item 100 2. Change item 100 3. Write item 100	1. Read item 200 2. Change item 200 3. Write item 200

Order of processing at CPU

1. Read item 100 for A
2. Read item 200 for B
3. Change item 100 for A
4. Write item 100 for A
5. Change item 200 for B
6. Write item 200 for B

Figure 14.7 shows two concurrent transactions. User A's transaction reads item 100, changes it, and rewrites the item in the database. User B's transaction takes the same actions, but on item 200. The CPU processes user A until it encounters an I/O interrupt, a signal that control can be passed to another task. The operating system shifts control to user B. The CPU now processes user B until an interrupt occurs, at which point the operating system passes control back to A. To the users, processing appears to be simultaneous; in reality, it is interleaved, or concurrent.

Lost Update Problem

The concurrent processing illustrated in Figure 14.7 poses no problems because the users are processing different data. However, suppose that both users want to process item 100. Let's say, for example, that user A wants to order 5 units of item 100 and user B wants to order 3 units of the same item.

Figure 14.8 illustrates the problem. User A reads the item 100 record into a user work area. According to the record, there are 10 items in inventory. Then user B reads the item 100 record into another user work area. Again, according to the record there are 10 in inventory. Now user A takes 5, decrements the count of items in its user work area to 5, and rewrites the record for item 100. Then user B takes 3, decrements the count in its user work area to 7, and rewrites the item 100 record. The database now shows, incorrectly, that there are 7 items 100 in inventory. To review: we started with 10 in inventory, user A took 5, user B took 3, and the database shows that 7 are in inventory. Clearly, we have a problem.

Both users obtained current data from the database. However, when user B read the record, user A already had a copy that it was about to update. This situation is called the

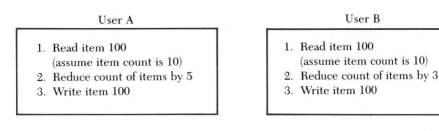

FIGURE 14.8
Lost update problem

lost update problem or the **concurrent update problem.** There is another, similar problem called the **inconsistent read problem** that you will learn about in Chapter 16.

One remedy for the inconsistencies caused by concurrent processing is to prevent multiple applications from having copies of the same record when the record is about to be changed. This approach is called **resource locking.**

RESOURCE LOCKING

To prevent concurrent processing problems, data that is retrieved for update must not be shared among users. (In this sense, the term *user* refers to the user of the DBMS, not necessarily the end-user. Thus, a user can be either a person seated at a terminal using the DBMS query/update facility or an application program that calls the DBMS for service.)

To prevent such sharing, the DBMS can place **locks** on data that is retrieved for update. Figure 14.9 shows the order of processing using a lock command. User B's transaction must wait until user A is finished with the item 100 record. Using this strategy, user B can read the item 100 record only after user A has completed the modification. In this case, the final item count stored in the database will be 2, as it should be. (We started with 10, A took 5, and B took 3, leaving 2.)

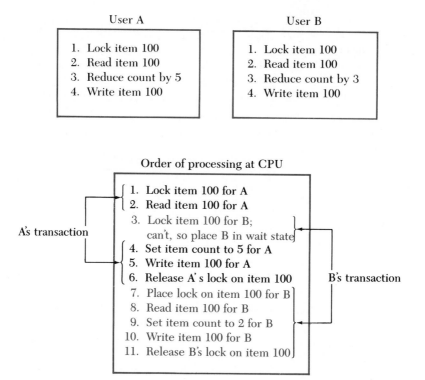

FIGURE 14.9
Concurrent processing with explicit locks

Lock Terminology

Locks can be placed either automatically by the DBMS or by command issued to the DBMS from the application program or query user. Locks placed by the DBMS are called **implicit locks**; those placed by command are called **explicit locks.**

In the example above, the locks were applied to rows of data. Not all locks are applied at this level. Some DBMS products lock at the page level, some at the table level, and some at the database level. The size of a lock is referred to as the **lock granularity.** Locks with large granularity are easy for the DBMS to administer but cause frequent conflict. Locks with small granularity are difficult to administer (there are many more details for the DBMS to keep track of and check), but conflict is less frequent.

Locks also vary by type. An **exclusive lock** locks the item from access of any type. No other transaction can read or change the data. A **shared lock** locks the item from change but not from read. Other transactions can read the item as long as they do not attempt to alter it.

Serializable Transactions

However the DBMS and application program accomplish locking, they must ensure that the database suffers from no anomalies due to concurrent processing. Stated more formally, when two or more transactions are processed concurrently, the results in the database should be logically consistent with the results that would have been achieved had the transactions been processed in any arbitrary serial fashion. A scheme for processing concurrent transactions in this way is said to be **serializable.**

Serializability can be achieved by a number of different means. One way is to process the transaction using **two-phased locking.** With this strategy, transactions are allowed to obtain locks as necessary, but once the first lock is released, no other lock can be obtained. Transactions thus have a **growing phase,** in which locks are obtained, and a **shrinking phase,** in which locks are released. The rationale for two-phased locking is discussed in Chapter 16.

A special case of two-phased locking is used with a number of popular DBMS products, including DB2. With it, locks are obtained throughout the transaction, but no lock is released until the COMMIT or ROLLBACK command is issued. This strategy is actually more restrictive than two-phase locking requires, but it is easier to implement.

In general, the boundaries of a transaction should correspond with the definition of the object it is processing. Following the two-phase strategy, rows of each relation in the object are locked as needed. Changes are made, but the data is not committed to the database until all of the object has been processed. At this point, changes are made to the actual database and all locks are released.

Consider an order entry transaction that involves an object CUSTOMER-ORDER which is constructed from data in the CUSTOMER table, the SALESPERSON table, and the ORDER table. To ensure that the database will suffer from no anomalies due to concurrency, the order entry transaction begins by issuing all of its locks (on CUSTOMER, SALESPERSON, and ORDER) and concludes by applying all database changes and then releasing all of its locks.

Many DBMS products employ the two-phase locking strategy. One example is IBM's DB2 relational database product. The DB2 COMMIT command applies all database changes and then releases all locks. Thus, by definition, COMMIT ends a transaction. Refer to Chapter 16 for more information on this subject.

Deadly Embrace

While locking solves one problem, it introduces another. Consider what might happen if two users want to order two items from inventory. Suppose A wants to order some paper, and if she can get the paper, she wants to order some pencils. Further, suppose that user B wants to order some pencils, and if he can get the pencils, he wants to order some paper. The order of processing could be as shown in Figure 14.10.

What has happened? Users A and B are locked in the **deadly embrace** in a condition known as **deadlock.** Each is waiting for a resource which the other person has locked. There are two common ways of solving this problem: prevent deadlock from occurring or allow deadlock to occur and then break it.

Preventing deadlock can be accomplished in several ways. One is to only allow users to have one lock at a time. In essence, users must lock all the resources they want at once. If user A in the illustration had locked both the paper and the pencil records at the beginning, then the embrace would never have occurred.

The other strategy is to allow the deadlock to occur, detect it, and then break it. Unfortunately, there is only one way to break deadlock: kill one of the transactions. If the

FIGURE 14.10
Deadlock

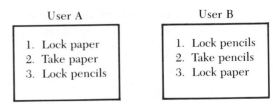

User A

1. Lock paper
2. Take paper
3. Lock pencils

User B

1. Lock pencils
2. Take pencils
3. Lock paper

Order of processing at CPU

1. Lock paper for user A
2. Lock pencils for user B
3. Process A's requests; write paper record
4. Process B's requests; write pencil record
5. Put A in wait state for pencils
6. Put B in wait state for paper

situation in Figure 14.10 has occurred, one of the two transactions must be aborted. When that happens, the lock will be released and the other transaction can process the database unhindered. Obviously any changes the killed transaction has made to the database must be undone. We will discuss the techniques for this in the next section.

DATABASE RECOVERY

Computer systems, database oriented or not, can fail. Hardware fails. Programs have bugs. Human procedures have errors and people make mistakes. All of these can and do occur in database processing applications.

When a database becomes inoperable, especially an online system, several problems must be addressed. First, from the business standpoint, business functions must continue. For example, customer orders, financial transactions, and packing lists must be completed manually. Later, when the computer is running again, the data can be entered. Second, computer operations personnel must as quickly as possible restore the system to a usable state, as close as possible to what it was when the system crashed. Third, users must know what to do when the system becomes available again. Some work may need to be reentered, and users must know how far back they need to go.

Performing recovery may be exceedingly difficult. It is impossible simply to fix the problem and resume processing where it was interrupted. Even if no data is lost during a failure (which assumes that all types of memory are nonvolatile—an unrealistic assumption), the timing and scheduling of computer processing is too complex to be accurately re-created. Enormous amounts of overhead data and processing would be required for the operating system to be able to restart processing precisely where it was interrupted. It is simply not possible to roll back the clock and put all the electrons in the same configuration they were in at the time of the failure. Thus, two approaches are possible: recovery via reprocessing, and recovery via rollback/rollforward.

Recovery via Reprocessing

Since processing cannot be resumed precisely at a precise point, the next best alternative is to go back to a known point and reprocess the workload from there. The simplest form of this type of recovery is to periodically make a copy of the database (called a **database save**) and to keep a record of all transactions that have been processed since the save. Then, when failure occurs, the operations staff can restore the database from the save and reprocess all transactions.

Unfortunately, this simple strategy is normally unfeasible. First, reprocessing transactions takes the same amount of time as processing them in the first place. If the computer is heavily scheduled, the system may never catch up.

Second, when transactions are processed concurrently, events are asynchronous. Slight variations in human activity, such as a user inserting a floppy disk more slowly, or a user reading an electronic mail message before responding to an application prompt, may change the order of the execution of concurrent transactions. Thus, whereas customer A got the last seat on a flight during the original processing, customer B may get the last seat during reprocessing. For these reasons, reprocessing is seldom a viable form of recovery for concurrent processing systems.

Recovery via Rollback/Rollforward

A second approach is to periodically make a copy of the database (the database save) and to keep a log of the changes made by transactions against the database since the save. Then, when failure occurs, one of two methods can be used. Using **rollforward,** the database is restored to the save and all valid transactions since the save are reapplied. (We are not reprocessing the transactions; the application programs are not involved in the rollforward. Instead, the processed changes, as recorded in the log, are reapplied.)

The other method is **rollback.** Here, we undo changes made by erroneous or partially processed transactions by undoing the changes they have made to the database. Then, valid transactions that were in process at the time of the failure are restarted.

Both of these methods require that a **log** be kept of transaction results. The log contains a record of data changes in chronological order. Transactions are written to the log before they are applied to the database. If the system crashes between the time a transaction is logged and the time it is applied, then at worst there is a record of an unapplied transaction. If transactions were applied before they were logged, then it would be possible (as well as undesirable) to change the database but have no record of the change were the system to crash in the meantime. If this happened, an unwary user might reenter an already completed transaction.

When a failure occurs, the log is used to both undo and redo transactions, as shown in Figure 14.11. To undo a transaction, the log must contain a copy of every database record (or page) before it was changed. Such records are called **before images.** A transaction is undone by applying before images of all its changes to the database.

To redo a transaction, the log must contain a copy of every database record (or page) after it was changed. These records are called **after images.** A transaction is redone by applying after images of all its changes to the database. Possible data items of a transaction log are shown in Figure 14.12a.

FIGURE 14.11
Undo and redo transaction
procedures

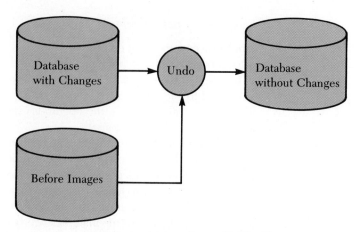

a. Removing database changes (Roll back)

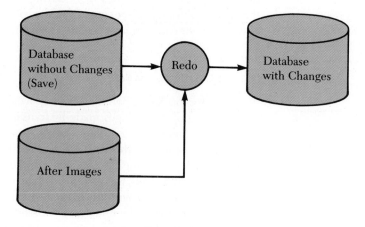

b. Reapplying database changes (Roll forward)

For this example log, each transaction has a unique name for identification purposes. Further, all images for a given transaction are linked together with pointers. One pointer points to the previous change made by this transaction (the reverse pointer), and the other points to the next change made by this transaction (the forward pointer). A zero in the pointer field means this is the end of the list. The DBMS recovery subsystem uses these pointers to locate all records for a particular transaction. Figure 14.12b shows an example of the linking of log records.

Other data items in the log are the time of the action, the type of operation (START marks the beginning of a transaction; COMMIT terminates a transaction, releasing all locks that were in place), the object acted upon such as record type and identifier, and finally, the before and after images.

Given a log with both before and after images, the undo and redo actions are straightforward (to describe, anyway). To undo the transaction in Figure 14.13, the recovery

Transaction ID	Type of Operation							
Reverse Pointer	Object							
Forward Pointer	Before Image							
Time	After Image							

a. Possible data items of a log record

Relative
Record
Number

	Transaction ID	Reverse Pointer	Forward Pointer	Time	Type of Operation	Object	Before Image	After Image
1	OT1	0	2	11:42	START			
2	OT1	1	4	11:43	MODIFY	CUST 100	(old value)	(new value)
3	OT2	0	8	11:46	START			
4	OT1	2	5	11:47	MODIFY	SP AA	(old value)	(new value)
5	OT1	4	7	11:47	INSERT	ORDER 11		(value)
6	CT1	0	9	11:48	START			
7	OT1	5	0	11:49	COMMIT			
8	OT2	3	0	11:50	COMMIT			
9	CT1	6	10	11:51	MODIFY	SP BB	(old value)	(new value)
10	CT1	9	0	11:51	COMMIT			

b. Log instance for three transactions

FIGURE 14.12
Transaction log

processor simply replaces each changed block with its before image. When all before images have been restored, the transaction is undone.

To redo a transaction, the recovery processor starts with the version of the database at the time the transaction started and applies all after images. This action assumes that an earlier version of the database is available from a database save. If it is necessary to restore a database to its most recent save and then reapply all transactions, much processing time may be required. To minimize this problem, DBMS products provide a facility called **checkpoint.**

A checkpoint command provides a point of synchronization between the database and the transaction log. To perform a checkpoint, the DBMS refuses to accept any new requests, it finishes processing outstanding requests, and it empties its buffers. The DBMS then waits until the operating system notifies it that all outstanding write requests to the database and to the log are complete. At this point, the log and the database are synchronized. A checkpoint record is then written to the log. When the database needs to be recovered, after images only for transactions that started after the checkpoint need to be applied.

FIGURE 14.13
Example of recovery strategy

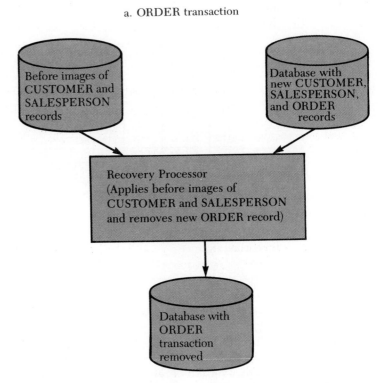

Accept order data from terminal
Read CUSTOMER and SALESPERSON records
Change CUSTOMER and SALESPERSON records
Rewrite CUSTOMER record
Rewrite SALESPERSON record   } (Log records written here)
Insert new ORDER record

****CRASH****

a. ORDER transaction

Before images of CUSTOMER and SALESPERSON records

Database with new CUSTOMER, SALESPERSON, and ORDER records

Recovery Processor
(Applies before images of CUSTOMER and SALESPERSON and removes new ORDER record)

Database with ORDER transaction removed

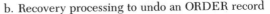

b. Recovery processing to undo an ORDER record

Checkpoints may be inexpensive operations, and often it is feasible to take three or four checkpoints per hour (or more). In this way, no more than fifteen or twenty minutes of processing will need to be recovered. Some DBMS products automatically checkpoint themselves, making human intervention unnecessary.

As you can imagine, the ability to restore the database system to a usable state is critical in most situations. (It might not be so critical in a single-user environment, for example. First, only one individual is inconvenienced, and second, the system is probably not so heavily scheduled that reprocessing large volumes of work is unfeasible.) Although

DBMS products include some of the recovery features we have discussed, remember that people play a vital role in backup and recovery. The DBA needs to establish procedures for computer center personnel and users to follow in the event of a system crash.

Database Security

Database processing can provide far greater productivity than other types of processing. Unfortunately, however, such processing also increases company vulnerability. With a database, company data—a valuable resource—will be centralized and readily accessible. In fact, DBMS products are designed to maximize this accessibility.

This situation is terrific for the authorized user. But, unfortunately, DBMS products are also easy for unauthorized users—and criminals—to use. Recognizing the problem of unauthorized use, most DBMS vendors have incorporated security features into their products. To the extent possible, these features allow only identifiably authorized users (people or programs) to access the data, and they can restrict types of processing on the data.

All of the users (and programmers) who are authorized to access a database system do not have complete access to all of the data. Some users have access to more data than other users, and some individuals have more extensive processing rights as well. For example, some users can modify or delete records, but other users cannot. In the database environment, users do not all enjoy the same privileges.

In *Database Security and Integrity*, Fernandez, Summers, and Wood[2] developed a model of database security. Their model is essentially a table of processing permissions, or **authorization rules.** As shown in Figure 14.14, the table has four columns representing subjects, entities, actions, and authorization constraints.[3] A row in this table indi-

Subject	Entity	Action	Authorization Constraint
PGM OE104J	ORDER Record	Insert	Amount less than $500,000
Sally Smith	ORDER Record	Read	None
Payroll Dept	EMPLOYEE Record	Read	Hourly workers
Payroll Dept	EMPLOYEE Record	Modify	Hourly workers
Payroll Dept	EMPLOYEE Record	Insert	Hourly workers
Payroll Supv	EMPLOYEE Record	Delete	Hourly workers
Payroll Supv	Read Permission of EMPLOYEE Records	Grant	To payroll personnel

FIGURE 14.14
Sample of authorization rules

---

[2]E. B. Fernandez, R. C. Summers, and C. Wood, *Database Security and Integrity* (Reading, Mass.: Addison-Wesley, 1981).

[3]Actually, Fernandez, Summers, and Wood use the term *object* rather than entity. We use the term *entity* here so as to distinguish between semantic objects and the items referred to in this security model.

cates that the named subject has permission to take the indicated action on the listed entity, subject to the stated authorization constraints. Thus, row 1 indicates that the program OE104J is authorized to insert ORDER records as long as the amount of the order is less than $500,000.

Although no DBMS product provides security in the form of this model, the model is an effective framework for understanding security capabilities and can aid the DBA when determining processing rights and responsibilities among users. The following discussion amplifies the four columns in the model.

SUBJECTS

A **subject** is any identifiable user or user group that can process the database. Examples of subjects are particular people (Sally Smith), groups of people (everyone in the payroll department), people operating in particular roles (a teller executing deposit transactions), application programs, and remote computers.

Determining whether someone who claims to be a subject really is that subject is difficult. People can be identified by fingerprints, voice prints, and passwords, to name a few. Passwords are by far the most commonly used identifiers in a computer environment. Computer equipment is identified by hardware configuration (say, the line connected to port 4) and by the presence or absence of specialized signals. Programs are usually identified by name, position in memory, or specialized protocol.

In the database environment, the subject desiring access to an entity provides his/her/its identifier (name or password, for example). For verification, the DBMS looks up the name of the entity and other data in a table, and if it is found, allows the subject access to the entity.

ENTITIES

The second column of the security table in Figure 14.14 contains entities, the database units to be protected by security. Examples of entities (using relational terminology) are databases, relations, rows, attributes, views, the DBMS, programs, transactions, knowledge of status (for example, the existence or nonexistence of an attribute), and the like.

The term *granularity,* which was used to refer to the size of locks, is also sometimes used to refer to the size of security entities. A security system that allows access to (or prevents access from) only the entire database as a unit has large granularity. A security system that allows access to or prevents access from a particular attribute has small granularity.

Small-granularity security systems allow close control over data. User access can be limited to the data needed to perform a function. On the other hand, security systems with small granularity require more overhead to administer. If a DBMS must check authorization every time a user accesses any attribute of any row, then processing will be slow and expensive.

Choosing the granularity of a security system involves a trade-off between closely tailored security and processing efficiency. As security increases, efficiency decreases. Although the DBMS enforces the security that is put in place, the DBA is responsible for determining what security is needed in the first place.

ACTIONS

The action column in Figure 14.14 identifies what the subject can do to the entity. Possibilities include reading, inserting, deleting, modifying, creating, destroying, and granting. Inserting and creating sound similar, but they differ as follows: inserting means adding data to an existing structure; creating means building the structure. Thus a subject can insert a row (record) or create (the structure of) a table. Similarly, deleting means removing data, and destroying means eliminating data and structure.

The grant action means to bestow a permission (such as permission to modify data) on another subject. In Figure 14.14 the last row of the table specifies that the payroll supervisor has authority to grant to payroll personnel permission to read employee records.

Usually the DBA is given sweeping grant authority by the DBMS. That is to say, when the DBMS is installed, someone needs to be identified to the system to grant authority to all other individuals. This is usually the DBA. Furthermore, some DBMS products automatically assign grant authority to anyone who creates a new table. They, in turn, can then grant permissions to perform actions on that table to whomever they choose. This constitutes ownership of that data.

AUTHORIZATION CONSTRAINTS

Authorization constraints specify limitations on permissions concerning subject, entity, and action. Several examples of authorization constraints are shown in Figure 14.14. For example, the payroll department can process EMPLOYEE records for hourly workers. If this table constituted all the authorization constraints on the database (highly unlikely), then it would be clear that the payroll department could process records *only* for hourly workers—not for supervisory or executive employees.

SECURITY IN DBMS PRODUCTS

No commercial DBMS provides as general a security capability as that shown in Figure 14.14. DBMS products generally offer a subset of capabilities. The DBA needs to determine security requirements and augment the capabilities of the DBMS product in areas where it is lacking.

In this section we will consider a number of different approaches to security that are taken by commercial DBMS products.

Subject-oriented Security

With subject-oriented security, subjects are defined to the DBMS, and each subject is allocated permissions. Prior to allowing a subject to perform a database action, the DBMS confirms that the subject has such authority. If the subject does not have permission, then the DBMS disallows the user request. The table in Figure 14.15 illustrates permissions that have been assigned to one subject. In this case the subject is a program. The table tells us that all ORDER transactions are authorized to read CUSTOMER, SALESPERSON, and ORDER records. ORDER transactions may insert only ORDER records. They may modify all three types of records. ORDER transactions are not authorized to delete any data, nor can they grant any rights to other subjects.

Entity-oriented Security

Another approach to security defines authorizations from the standpoint of entities. In this case, each entity has an authorization matrix. The matrix shows what actions can be taken by various subjects on that entity. Most often the subjects are defined by passwords. For example, in Figure 14.16 subjects who can provide the password SESAME can read, insert, modify, and delete SALESPERSON records. People who supply the password ABALONE can read SALESPERSON records but take no other action.

Combination of Subject- and Entity-oriented Security

Some DBMS products provide both subject- and entity-oriented security. In this case, both subjects and entities have authorization matrices.

FIGURE 14.15
Subject-oriented security example:
permissions granted to program
processing ORDER transactions

Entities

		CUSTOMER Records	SALESPERSON Records	ORDER Records
Actions	Read	Y	Y	Y
	Insert	N	N	Y
	Modify	Y	Y	Y
	Delete	N	N	N
	Grant	N	N	N

FIGURE 14.16
Entity-oriented security example:
permissions granted for
SALESPERSON records

Entity: SALESPERSON Record

		Subjects Who Know Password SESAME	Subjects Who Know Password ABALONE
Actions	Read	Y	Y
	Insert	Y	N
	Modify	Y	N
	Delete	Y	N
	Grant	N	N

Constraints via Programmable Exits

Constraints on authorization rules are not generally supported by DBMS products. However, some DBMS products have an indirect way of enforcing authorization constraints. These DBMS products will exit to (call) user-written programs whenever a specified action is performed on a specified entity. The program can then provide the logic to enforce the constraint. It should be noted that end-users do not generally write such programs; they are usually developed by professional programmers. Consider an example.

Suppose no order in excess of $50,000 is to be accepted after 3:00 PM on a Friday or the day before a holiday. Instead, such orders are to be referred to a supervisor. In this case, the database designer specifies that whenever an ORDER record is created a special program is to be called. This program will determine if the above conditions are true. If so, the program will disallow the insert and send a message to a supervisor.

User exits provide a great deal of flexibility. They can be employed to supplement capabilities of a DBMS or to compensate for deficiencies in a particular DBMS product. Their advantage is flexibility and increased control and security. But exits to user-written routines have disadvantages as well. For instance, the user organization must develop and test these routines. Such routines add overhead to the system. They may need to be dynamically loaded (copied into computer memory from disk storage each time they are needed) and therefore degrade system performance.

In terms of security, then, a DBMS includes facilities for identifying subjects and allowing them to access the database, for restricting the actions subjects can perform, for restricting entities that a subject can access, and for allowing user-developed routines to be incorporated into normal processing. Thus, the *operation* of a security system is one function of the DBMS. However, as described earlier, establishing the *policies and administration* of a security system is a function of data administration or database administration.

Summary

Data is an important organizational asset and must be administered so as to guard and protect it while at the same time maximizing its usefulness to the organization. The functions of data administration and database administration exist to serve this need.

The scope of data administration is the entire organization. Data administration is responsible for determining what data is to be protected and for establishing data standards, policies, proponents, and other managerial guidelines and constraints to ensure data quality and usefulness. Functions of data administration include marketing its services, setting data standards and policies, providing a forum for conflict resolution, and taking other measures to increase the return that the organization receives from its data investment.

The scope of database administration is a particular database and the applications that process that database. Functions include managing the database structure, establishing frameworks to manage data activity, and managing the DBMS software. Additionally, the database administration is responsible for establishing and managing the database data dictionary.

The database management system includes features that are essential in a multi-user environment. Although the primary functions of a DBMS are to store, retrieve, and modify data, other features include controlling concurrent processing, providing backup and recovery services, and providing facilities to establish an appropriate level of database security.

Concurrent updates can be a problem if two users attempt to modify the same record at once. When this happens, anomalies can occur in the database. DBMS products solve this problem by applying locks on resources whenever the data might be changed. Locks prevent other users from accessing a record until the transaction is completed and the lock is released.

Concurrent processing can also be a problem if two users each lock resources the other one needs. This situation, called deadlock, can be resolved by the DBMS by terminating one of the transactions and undoing any changes it made to the database.

In the event of a system failure, the database must be restored to a usable state as quickly as possible. Any transactions in progress at the time of the crash must be reapplied, and any processing that was done manually while the system was down must be entered. Recovery can be accomplished by straightforward reprocessing or by rollback/rollforward. The latter strategy is almost always preferred.

Transaction logs must be maintained to ensure that all lost work is reapplied. Checkpoints can be taken more frequently than database saves. Although they require some overhead, checkpoints minimize the amount of reprocessing that needs to be done in the event of a failure.

Database security means allowing only authorized subjects to perform authorized actions on specified entities, subject to any managerial constraints. Once established by the DBA, many of these access and processing rights are enforced by the DBMS. Constraints that are not enforced by the DBMS can be enforced by user-written subroutines.

GROUP I   QUESTIONS

14.1   Describe the two purposes of data administration and database administration.

14.2   Explain the difference in the terms *data administration* and *database administration*.

14.3   How is the data administrator analogous to the company controller?

14.4   Explain the necessity of data administration. What is likely to happen if there is no data administration function?

14.5   Summarize the marketing function of data administration.

14.6   Summarize the data standards function of data administration.

14.7 What is a data proponent? What functions does a data proponent serve? What is the difference between a data proponent and a data owner?

14.8 Summarize the data policy function of data administration.

14.9 Explain the need for a forum for data conflict resolution.

14.10 What might data administration do to help increase an organization's return on its data investment?

14.11 Describe the need for database administration. What is likely to happen if there is no database administration function.

14.12 Explain how database administration is likely to vary among personal, workgroup, and organizational databases.

14.13 Summarize the DBA's responsibilities for management of database structure.

14.14 What is configuration control? Why is it necessary for databases to have it?

14.15 Describe two situations in which database system documentation plays a major role.

14.16 Summarize the DBA's responsibilities for management of database activity. What are data access and modification rights? Why are they important?

14.17 Summarize the DBA's responsibilities for management of DBMS software.

14.18 What is the function of a data dictionary? Explain the difference between a passive and an active data dictionary.

14.19 Define *transaction, atomic transaction,* and *logical unit of work.*

14.20 What is concurrent processing? Under what conditions is concurrent processing a problem?

14.21 Describe the lost update problem.

14.22 Explain the difference between explicit and implicit locks.

14.23 Define *lock granularity.* What general statements can be made about the differences between large and small lock granularity?

14.24 Explain the difference between an exclusive and a shared lock.

14.25 Define *serializability.*

14.26 What is a two-phase locking, and how can it be used to prevent the lost update problem?

14.27 What is the deadly embrace?

14.28 Describe two ways a DBMS can handle the deadly embrace.

14.29 Explain how a database can be recovered by reprocessing. Why is database recovery by reprocessing usually not feasible?

14.30   Define *rollback* and *rollforward.*

14.31   Why is it important to write to the log before changing the database?

14.32   Describe the rollback process. Under what conditions is rollback more appropriate than rollforward?

14.33   Describe the rollforward process. Under what conditions is rollforward more appropriate than rollback?

14.34   Why is it usually advantageous to take frequent checkpoints of a database?

14.35   Define *subject, object, action,* and *authorization constraint* as they apply to database security.

14.36   How does a DBMS implement subject-oriented security?

14.37   How does a DBMS implement object-oriented security?

14.38   Explain the use of programmable exits for security.

GROUP II QUESTIONS

14.39   Interview the DBA of a local company. Determine whether a data dictionary system is in use. Is it integrated with the DBMS? If so, what are the advantages and disadvantages? If not, ask why the company chose that type of data dictionary. Find out if the dictionary system is active or passive. Why was that type of data dictionary chosen?

14.40   Interview the manager of a local small business that uses a microcomputer DBMS. Is there a DBA? If not, determine who in the company performs each of the DBA's functions. Also determine if any of the DBA's functions are not being performed. Why are they not being performed? Find out what support the DBA (or people performing the DBA's functions) receives from the DBMS (for example, run-time statistics or a data dictionary).

14.41   This discussion of database administration in this chapter assumed an organizational database. Explain how you think the tasks of database administration would change for a workgroup database. How would the scope of the functions change? Would any of the functions described in this chapter be unnecessary? Would any new functions be required?

PART VII

Distributed Processing

Part VII, the last part of this text, considers distributed processing. Chapter 15 introduces the subject and then focuses on the structure and processing characteristics of two distributed architectures: resource sharing and client-server systems. These architectures involve distributed *application* processing.

Chapter 16 then considers distributed *database* processing. It describes the characteristics and components of distributed database systems and presents four processing goals for the distributed DBMS (DDBMS). The chapter specifically addresses two difficult issues in distributed processing—concurrency control and failure recovery.

Chapter 15 presents distributed processing as it is being done now. Chapter 16 presents the hopes and difficulties that exist for the implementation of distributed processing as many would like it to be done in the future. Today, the leading edge of the commercial application of distributed processing lies in between the discussions in these two chapters.

Resource Sharing and Client-Server Architectures

This chapter introduces the subject of distributed processing. The first section describes a number of multi-user processing architectures and introduces client-server, resource sharing, and distributed database systems. After that introduction, the resource sharing and client-server architectures are described in more detail. Distributed databases are addressed in the next chapter.

Both resource sharing and client-server architectures have increased in popularity as more organizations have installed local area networks. As you will learn, for database application processing, the client-server architecture has important advantages over the resource sharing architecture and is becoming prevalent for such applications. Consequently, pay particular attention to understanding client-server systems.

- MULTI-USER DATABASE PROCESSING ARCHITECTURES
- RESOURCE SHARING OF DOWNLOADED DATA
- DISTRIBUTING APPLICATIONS VIA CLIENT-SERVER SYSTEMS
- EMERGENCE OF TWO TYPES OF DBMS

Multi-user Database Processing Architectures

Multi-user database systems are supported by a number of different systems architectures. Classically, teleprocessing systems were the most common. As the price of CPUs has fallen, however, it has been economically feasible to employ more than one computer; this addition has resulted in a number of new multi-user database architectures. Three important new architectures are client-server, resource sharing, and distributed database. We will discuss each of these types in this section, after reviewing the structure of teleprocessing systems.

TELEPROCESSING SYSTEMS

The classical approach for supporting a multi-user database system is teleprocessing. With teleprocessing systems, there is one computer and one CPU. All processing is accomplished by this single computer.[1]

Figure 15.1 shows a typical teleprocessing system. Users operate dumb terminals (or microcomputers that emulate dumb terminals) that transmit transaction messages and data to the centralized computer. The communications control portion of the operating system receives the messages and data and routes them to the appropriate application program. Programs, in turn, call on the DBMS for services. The DBMS uses the data management portion of the operating system to process the database. When a transaction is completed, results are returned to the users at the dumb terminals via the communications control portion of the operating system.

Figure 15.1 shows n users that submit transactions that are processed by three different application programs. Since there is little intelligence at the users' end (that is, the dumb terminals), all commands for formatting the screen must be generated by the CPU and transmitted over the communications lines. This means the users' interface is generally character oriented and primitive. Systems like this are called teleprocessing systems since all inputs and outputs are communicated over a distance (*tele-* means distance) to the centralized computer for processing.

Historically, teleprocessing systems have been the most common architecture for multi-user database systems. However, as the price-performance ratio of computers has fallen, and, in particular, with the advent of the microcomputer, other architectures that employ multiple computers have begun to be used.

CLIENT-SERVER SYSTEMS

Figure 15.2 presents a schematic of one of them, called the **client-server architecture.** Unlike teleprocessing, which involves a single computer, the client-server architecture

---

[1]In some teleprocessing systems, special-purpose computers are used as communication front-ends and concentrators. While, in a strict sense, these are computers, they are used only to process the communications control portion of the operating system. They have no direct role in applications or database processing and we will ignore them in this discussion.

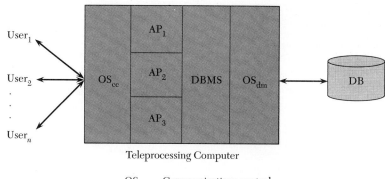

Teleprocessing Computer

OS_{cc} = Communications control
             portion of operating system

OS_{dm} = Data management portion of
             operating system

FIGURE 15.1
Relationships of programs in a teleprocessing system

involves multiple computers connected in a network. Some of the computers process application programs and are designated as *clients.* Another computer is designated as the *server,* and it is given the task of processing the database.

Figure 15.2 shows an example. Here, each of n users has his or her own application processing computer. In this figure, user$_1$ processes AP$_1$ and AP$_2$ on computer 1. User$_2$ processes AP$_2$ on computer 2 and user$_n$ processes AP$_2$ and AP$_3$ on computer N. Additionally, another computer is used as the database server.

There are many options as to computer type. The client computers could, in theory, be mainframes, minis, or microcomputers. Because of cost, however, in almost all cases the client computers are microcomputers. Similarly, any type of computer could be the server, but again, because of cost, the server is most often a microcomputer. The clients and server are generally connected together using a local area network (LAN).

Although it is exceedingly rare for client computers to be anything other than micros, there are some situations in which the server is a mini or mainframe. This occurs when considerable power is required from the server, or where, for political or organizational reasons, it is deemed inappropriate to locate the database on a microcomputer.

The system in Figure 15.2 has a single server. This need not always be the case. There may be multiple servers that process different databases or that provide other services on behalf of the clients. For example, in an engineering consulting firm, one server might process the database while a second server provides support for computer-assisted design graphics.

If there are multiple database processing servers, then each one must process a different database for the system to be considered a client-server system. When two servers process the same database, the system is no longer called a client-server system; rather

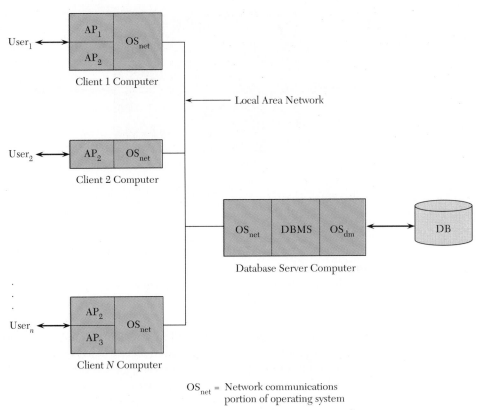

OS$_{net}$ = Network communications portion of operating system

OS$_{dm}$ = Data management portion of operating system

FIGURE 15.2
Client-server architecture

it is called a distributed database system (introduced later in this section and discussed in Chapter 16).

Figure 15.3 summarizes the roles for the client and the server. As listed, the client computer manages the user interface. It accepts data from the user, processes application logic, and generates requests for database services. Clients then transmit those requests to the server and receive results, which are then formatted for the user.

The server accepts client requests, processes them, and returns a response to the client. While doing this, the server performs database integrity checking, maintains the database overhead data, and provides concurrent access control. The server also performs recovery and optimizes query/update processing.

A client-server system places the application processing closer to the user. One advantage of this is increased performance. Several CPUs are processing applications in parallel. In addition, communications costs are reduced. Only requests for DBMS processing and responses to those requests need to be sent over the communications network. This means there is less communications traffic than in teleprocessing.

FIGURE 15.3
Roles for client and server
computers

Client Roles	Server Roles
Manage the user interface	Accept database request from clients
Accept data from the user	Process database requests
Process application logic	Format results and transmit to client
Generate database requests	Perform integrity checking
Transmit database requests to server	Maintain database overhead data
	Provide concurrent access control
Receive results from server	Perform recovery
Format results	Optimize query/update processing

Because multiple computers process applications, and because those computers only need the server for database processing, the users' interface can be much more elaborate. Sophisticated menus and forms are possible with different colors, type fonts, and type sizes. Graphical user interfaces are becoming common for client-server applications.

One disadvantage of client-server systems concerns control. The client computers operate simultaneously and hence they process applications in parallel. This introduces the possibility of the lost update and other multi-user control problems. These problems are more severe than in teleprocessing systems because the computers process in parallel. Multiple operating systems that direct multiple CPUs must coordinate their processing over communications media. This differs from teleprocessing where all activity is governed by a single, local operating system. A later section of this chapter will address concurrency control in the client-server architecture.

RESOURCE SHARING SYSTEMS

A second multi-computer architecture is shown in Figure 15.4. This architecture, called **resource sharing,** distributes not only the application programs but also the DBMS out to the processing computers. In this case, the *server* is a file server and not a database server. If you compare Figures 15.1, 15.2, and 15.4, you will see that in each step more software is moved to the users' computers. Almost all resource sharing systems employ local area networks of microcomputers.

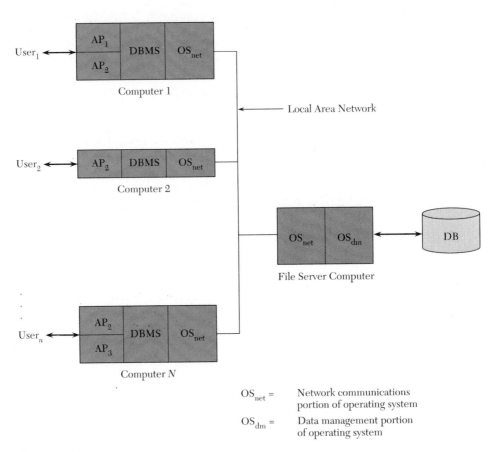

FIGURE 15.4
Resource sharing architecture

The resource sharing architecture was developed before the client-server architecture and, in many ways, it is more primitive than the client-server. With resource sharing, the DBMS on each user computer sends requests to the data management portion of the operating system on the file server for file-level processing. This means that considerably more traffic crosses the LAN than with the client-server architecture.

To understand this statement, consider the processing of a query to obtain the Name and Address of all rows in the CUSTOMER table where Zip equals 98033. In a client-server system, the application program would send the SQL command:

```
SELECT NAME, ADDRESS
FROM   CUSTOMER
WHERE ZIP = 98033
```

The server would respond with all qualifying Names and Addresses.

In a resource sharing system, the DBMS is on the local computer. Therefore, no program on the file server is capable of processing SQL or any similar language. All such processing must be done on the user computer. Therefore, the DBMS must send a request to the file server to transmit the entire CUSTOMER table. Furthermore, if that table has indices or other overhead associated with it, then the overhead structures must be transmitted as well.

As you can see, with resource sharing, much more data needs to be transmitted across the LAN. Furthermore, while one user computer is processing a request, it locks large portions of the database. Put differently, with resource sharing, a very high level of lock granularity is required. As a consequence, throughput is reduced.

Because of these problems, resource sharing systems are seldom used for transaction-oriented multi-user database processing. Too much data needs to be locked and transmitted for each transaction. An attempt to use this architecture for transaction processing would result in very slow performance.

There is, however, one database application for which this architecture makes sense: the query processing of downloaded, extracted data. If one or more users need access to large portions of the database for producing reports or answering queries, then it can make sense to have a server that downloads large sections of data. In this case, the downloaded data is not updated and not returned to the database. You will see examples of the processing of extracted data later in this chapter.

Resource sharing systems are also used for nondatabase applications. Resource sharing LANs are frequently used for applications that require large, fast disks for the storage of large single-user files, large spreadsheets, and the like. They are also used to share expensive printers, plotters, and other peripheral equipment.

DISTRIBUTED DATABASE SYSTEMS

A fourth alternative, shown in Figure 15.5, is a called a distributed database system. With this alternative, the database itself is distributed. In Figure 15.5, the database (or a portion of it) is stored on all N computers. As shown in this figure, computers 1, 2, and N process both applications and the database. Computer 3 processes the database, only.

In Figure 15.5, the dashed line around the files indicates that the database is composed of all of the segments of the database on all N computers. These computers may be physically located in the same facility, on different sides of the world, or somewhere in between.

Distributed Processing Versus Distributed Database Processing

Consider Figures 15.1, 15.2, 15.4, and 15.5 again. The resource sharing, client-server, and distributed database architectures all differ from teleprocessing in an important way: they all involve the use of multiple computers for applications or DBMS processing. Because of this characteristic, most people[2] would say that all three of these architectures

---

[2]The term *most people* is used because these definitions are not standardized. There are products sold as distributed DBMS that do not have the capabilities defined here. I believe the definitions used here conform to what most information systems professionals mean. The distinctions are valid, in any case. A rose would smell as sweet by any other name.

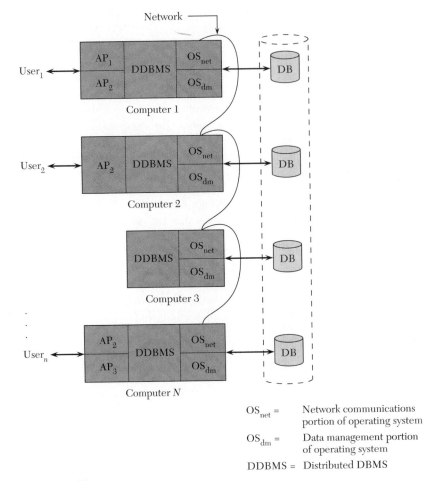

FIGURE 15.5
Distributed database architecture

are examples of **distributed systems.** The term arises because applications processing has been distributed among several computers.

Observe, however, that the database itself is distributed only in the architecture shown in Figure 15.5. Neither the client-server nor the resource sharing architectures involve distributing the database to multiple computers. Consequently, most people would not refer to the resource sharing or client-server architectures as **distributed database systems.**

When resource sharing systems are used to process downloaded, extracted data, they fall into a grey area. Strictly speaking, because the data is downloaded, it is distributed, and such a system should be called a distributed database system. On the other hand, downloaded data is seldom updated, as you will learn later in this chapter. Since that is the case, the data is not truly distributed.

Types of Distributed Databases

There are a number of types of distributed database systems. To understand them, first consider Figure 15.6a, which shows a nondistributed database. This example database has four pieces, W, X, Y, and Z. All four pieces of these segments are located on a single database and there is no data duplication. Now consider the distributed alternatives in Figures 15.6b–d.

Figure 15.6b shows the first distributed alternative. Here, the database has been partitioned into two pieces; W and X are stored on computer 1 and Y and Z are stored on computer 2. In Figure 15.6c, the entire database has been replicated on two computers. Finally, in Figure 15.6d, the database has been partitioned and a portion (Y) has been replicated.

Comparison of Distributed Database Alternatives

These alternatives are summarized on a continuum in Figure 15.7. The alternatives are arranged in increasing degree of distributed, from left to right. The nondistributed database is shown on the leftmost point of the continuum and the partitioned, replicated database on the rightmost point. In between these extremes are a database that is partitioned and the partitions are allocated to two or more computers, and a database that is not partitioned, but each entire database is replicated on two or more computers.

Characteristics of the alternatives on this continuum are listed in Figure 15.7. Alternatives toward the right provide an increase in parallelism, an increase in independence, an increase in flexibility, and an increase in availability. On the other hand, those alternatives also involve greater expense, greater complexity, greater difficulty of control, or greater risk to security.

Of these advantages, one is particularly significant to future business professionals. Alternatives on the right of Figure 15.7 provide increased flexibility and hence can be better tailored to the organizational structure and the organizational process. A highly decentralized manufacturing company, for example, in which plant managers have wide latitude in the their planning, can never be well satisfied by an organizational information system with the structure of Figure 15.6a. The structure of the information system architecture and the structure of the company fight with one another. Thus, alternatives on the right-hand side can provide a better and more appropriate fit to the organization than those on the left.

Of the disadvantages, the greatest is difficulty of control and the resulting potential loss of data integrity. Consider the database architecture in Figure 15.6d. A user connected to computer 1 can read and update a data item in partition Y on computer 1 at the very same time that a different user connected to computer 2 can read and update that data item in partition Y on computer 2.

For reasons you will learn in the next chapter, the strategies used to control concurrent processing for a database on one computer do not work, in the general case, for those on multiple computers. In time, new algorithms and technology may be developed, but for now, it is not possible to allow unrestricted concurrent processing of a partitioned, replicated database. Instead, if this architecture is to be used, restrictions must be placed on processing as you will learn in Chapter 16.

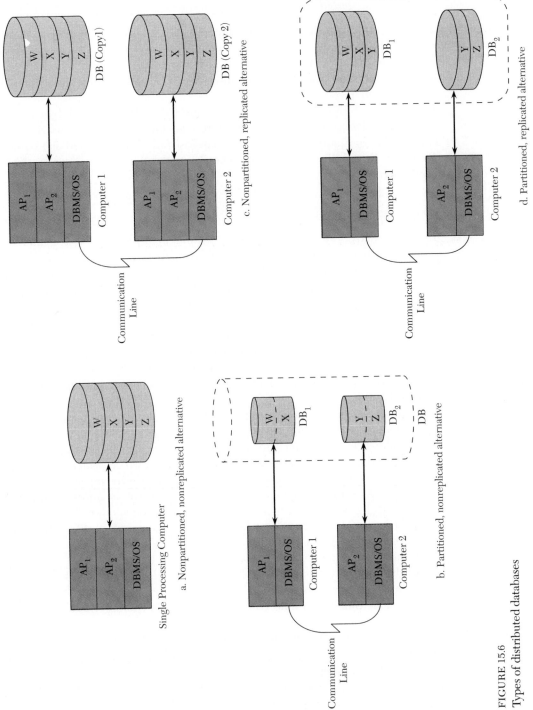

FIGURE 15.6
Types of distributed databases

FIGURE 15.7

Continuum of database distribution alternatives

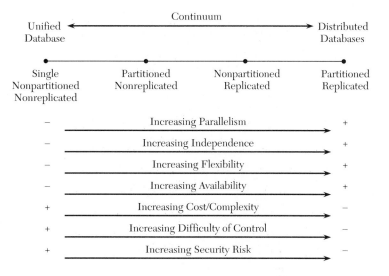

In the remainder of this chapter, we will discuss two of the architectures described here. First we will examine the use of resource sharing for the processing of downloaded data. Then we will study a client-server database system that supports a multi-user transaction-based application.

Resource Sharing of Downloaded Data

The number of applications involving downloaded data has increased dramatically in recent years as the processing power of microcomputers has increased. At first, bulk data was shared between computers by transferring it on magnetic media such as a diskette. This approach was slow and cumbersome since it involved handling physical media. This style of sharing changed as microcomputers became integrated into the corporate communications network. Today, many organizations process downloaded data using resource sharing LAN-based systems.

When data is transferred in bulk from one computer to another, database administration tasks change significantly, both in character and in complexity, and developers and users need to be aware of this. We will discuss these problems after describing the processing of downloaded data in more detail and presenting an example.

ROLE OF RESOURCE SHARING

The resource sharing architecture is not suited for transaction processing of multi-user databases. Too much of the database must be locked and transmitted for such an application to make sense. Resource sharing can be effective, however, for query and reporting from downloaded data.

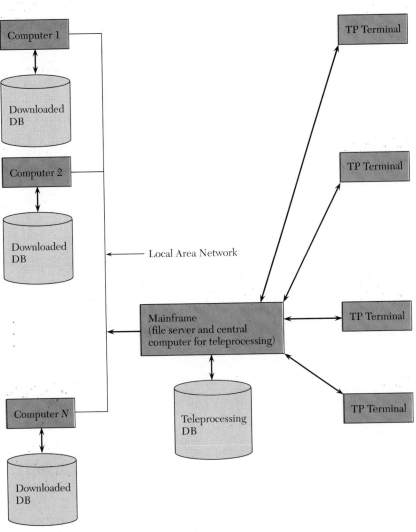

FIGURE 15.8
Resource sharing of downloaded data with mainframe as file server

Figures 15.8 and 15.9 show two different alternatives that illustrate the use of resource sharing for processing downloaded data. In Figure 15.8, a local area network connects microcomputers together with a file server. In this example, the file server is actually a mainframe computer which is, itself, the center of a teleprocessing system that supports a multi-user transaction-oriented database application. The transaction users process transactions against the database stored on the mainframe.

Periodically, say once per week, decision support users employ their microcomputers to obtain an **extract** of the transaction processing database. This extract is obtained from the mainframe with the understanding that the data will never be returned. Additionally, if changes are made to the data, the understanding is that such changes are not official.

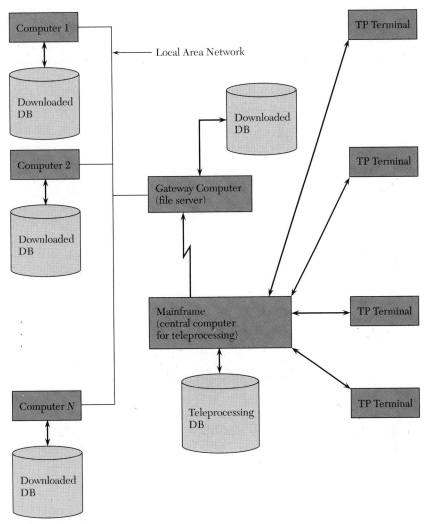

FIGURE 15.9
Resource sharing of downloaded data with gateway micro as file server

Official changes must be submitted for processing by users connected to the transaction processing application.

Figure 15.9 shows an alternative resource sharing architecture. Here, the decision support users also employ microcomputers on a LAN, but the LAN's file server is changed from the mainframe to another micro. In this case, the micro serves as a gateway to the teleprocessing system on the mainframe.

The file server in Figure 15.9 periodically obtains a copy of all of the data that is of interest to any of the decision support users that it supports on the LAN. When one of these users requests data, the file server transmits it to the user from its own files. In this way, the workload on the mainframe computer is reduced because the mainframe is required to deal only with the LAN file server and not individually with each micro on the LAN.

Either of these architectures make sense only if the decision support users need not make official changes to the data and can live with data that is not up-to-date. Additionally, this structure can probably only be justified if the decision support users make extensive use of the data they obtain. This would occur if the users require sophisticated reports that are time consuming to prepare or if they need the data for extensive ad hoc query processing.

UPDATING DOWNLOADED DATA

In some rare situations, the applications processing downloaded data are allowed to update and return the data to the source database. When this is done, manual procedures must ensure that lost update and inconsistent read problems do not occur when the data is returned. Either of these could happen if the applications on the source database and the distributed application are allowed to update the same data. Manual procedures must control processing so that this cannot occur. Such processing is risky and, as stated, it is consequently rare.

EXAMPLE: UNIVERSAL EQUIPMENT

Universal Equipment Co. manufactures and sells heavy equipment for the construction industry. Its products include bulldozers, graders, loaders, drilling rigs, and the like. Every product is assigned to a product manager in the marketing department who is responsible for product planning, advertising, marketing support, development of sales support material, and so forth. Each product manager is assigned a group of two or three related products.

Advertising is the product managers' largest budget item. They therefore want to be able to measure the effectiveness of ads they run. Universal's ads always contain a mail-in card to request information. The cards have a preprinted number unique to each ad appearance, so this number can be used to identify the ad that generated a particular lead. To facilitate lead tracking, the marketing department has developed a microcomputer database application that is used by the product managers.

Database Structure

Figure 15.10a shows the objects processed by this application. AD represents an advertisement. AD-APPEARANCE is the occurrence of a particular ad in a particular publication. PRODUCT represents a particular product such as a bulldozer. PRODUCT contains two repeating groups, one on quotas and one on sales. The groups are multivalued because sales quotas are assigned for each quarter and because product sales are recorded on a weekly basis.

The view of PRODUCT is quite simple. The complete PRODUCT object actually contains more properties, such as AD. But because the other relationships are not

FIGURE 15.10
Objects and relations to support
Universal product marketing
database

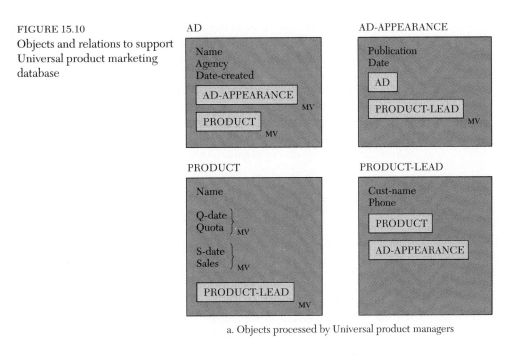

a. Objects processed by Universal product managers

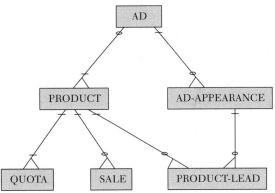

b. Relational structure to support objects in Figure 15.10a

needed for the product managers' application, we will omit them. The database structure that supports these objects is shown in Figure 15.10b.

Download Process

Product managers are assigned a microcomputer that is connected to other micros through a local area network in Universal's Marketing Department. To obtain sales and product-lead data, the micros call on a file server which serves as a gateway to Universal's mainframe (transaction processing computer). The architecture is similar to that shown in Figure 15.9.

Every Monday, a key user in the marketing department runs a program developed by Universal's MIS Department that updates the SALES, QUOTA, and PRODUCT-LEAD tables on the file server's database with data from the corporation's mainframe database. This program adds to the database the data from the previous week and also makes corrections. Product and sales data are imported for all related products to enable product managers to do comparative studies.

Once the data has been downloaded to the file server, each product manager can obtain the data of interest to him or her from that server. Controls exist to ensure that product managers do not obtain data for which they are not authorized access.

POTENTIAL PROBLEMS IN PROCESSING DOWNLOADED DATABASES

Importing data presents several potential problems, including coordination, consistency, access control, and computer crime.

Coordination

First consider **coordination,** using the PRODUCT-LEAD and AD-APPEARANCE tables for illustration. The PRODUCT-LEAD table is updated from data on the mainframe (leads are handled by sales personnel, and they are recorded on the mainframe). But the AD-APPEARANCE table is updated "locally" by the key user in the marketing department. This user obtains the data from reports prepared by the advertising manager and the advertising agency.

This situation could cause problems when an ad is run for the first time in a new issue or publication. For example, it could happen that the ad generates leads that are recorded on the mainframe database before the AD-APPEARANCE data is stored on the file server. When those leads are downloaded, the program importing the data will have to reject the lead data. Such data violates the constraint that a PRODUCT-LEAD must have an AD-APPEARANCE parent.

Thus the activities of local updating and downloading must be carefully coordinated. The key user needs to insert AD-APPEARANCE data before importing data from the mainframe. Similar coordination problems can occur when updating SALES and QUOTA data.

Consistency

The second potential problem of downloaded data concerns **consistency.** Each of the product managers receives downloaded SALES and QUOTA data which they are not supposed to change. But what might happen if a product manager *did* change the data? In this case, the data in that product manager's database might be inconsistent with data in the corporate database, with the file server's data, and possibly with data in other product managers' databases. The reports produced by that product manager could disagree with other reports. If several product managers update data, much inconsistent data could be generated.

Clearly, this situation calls for strict control on the part of the DBA. The database should be designed so that data cannot be updated. If this is not possible—say the microcomputer database product will not enforce such a restriction, and the costs of writing programs to enforce it are considered prohibitively high—then the solution to this problem is education. Product managers need to be aware of the problems that will occur if they change data, and they need to be directed not to do so.

Access Control

A third potential problem is more difficult **access control.** When data is transferred to several computer systems, access control becomes more difficult. At Universal, for example, SALES and QUOTA data may be sensitive. For example, the vice president of sales may not want the sales personnel to learn about upcoming sales quotas until the annual sales meeting. But, if fifteen product managers have copies of this data in their databases, it can be difficult to ensure that the data will be kept confidential until the appropriate time.

Further, the file server receives all SALES and QUOTA data. This file server is supposed to be downloaded in such a way that a product manager receives only the SALES and QUOTA data for the products that he or she manages. Product managers can be quite competitive with one another, however, and they may wish to find ways of obtaining data for each other's products. Making this data accessible on the file server in the marketing department may create management problems.

Computer Crime

The fourth potential problem, increased potential for **computer crime,** is closely allied to that of access control. Whereas access control concerns inappropriate but legal activity, crime concerns illegal actions. Data on the corporate mainframe can be very valuable. Universal Equipment's sales and quota data, for example, is of great interest to competitors.

When data is downloaded in bulk to the file server and then to one or many microcomputers, illegal copying becomes difficult to prevent. A diskette is easily concealed. Further, employees sometimes have modems with which they access work computers from off-site locations. In these situations, the copying of data over the telephone is nearly impossible to detect or prevent.

Increased risk of computer crime is an important potential problem of downloaded databases. In fact, this disadvantage alone might prohibit such a system from being developed, even though it would otherwise be an excellent solution.

The potential problems of downloaded databases are summarized in Figure 15.11.

Distributing Applications via Client-Server Systems

As described previously, with client-server database systems, application programs are distributed to the client computers and the database is processed by the server computer

FIGURE 15.11
Issues and potential problems of
downloaded data applications

FIGURE 15.11
Issues and potential problems of
downloaded data applications

> ***Coordination***
> - Downloaded data must conform to database constraints.
> - Careful timing of updates to local and downloaded data are
>   required.
>
> ***Consistency***
> - In general, downloaded data should not be updated.
> - Applications need features to prevent updating.
> - Users need education on potential problems.
>
> ***More Difficult Access Control***
> - Data may be replicated on many computers.
> - Procedures to control data access are more complicated.
>
> ***Increased Potential for Computer Crime***
> - Illegal copying is difficult to prevent.
> - Diskettes and access via modem are easy to conceal.
> - Risk may prevent the development of downloaded data
>   applications.

as shown in Figure 15.2. Unlike resource sharing, the DBMS program resides on the
database server and is not distributed to client computers. To better understand such
systems, consider the following example.

EXAMPLE: LEGACY SYSTEMS

Legacy Systems is a microcomputer software publisher. Legacy has more than thirty
products and an installed base of over 100,000 customers. In addition to its software
products, Legacy also sells extended customer support. The customer support department uses a client-server system to keep track of customers and their queries.

The customer support department operates as follows: When customers call for service, the customer support personnel first ask for the customer's contract number. This
number consists of two parts, the customer number and the license number for a particular product. These numbers are then verified against Legacy's records before service is
provided.

Customer support personnel create a record of each call. Such records are needed so
that when the customer calls again, Legacy personnel have a record of what has tran-
spired (the customer may be assigned a different support representative each time he or
she calls). Additionally, while assisting a customer, the support representatives often generate action items for departments within Legacy. For example, the representatives
sometimes direct sales personnel to ship a replacement copy of a software product to a
customer.

Legacy Client-Server Network

Legacy has installed a local area network of twenty-one microcomputers in the customer
support department. One micro is the database server and the other twenty micros pro-

FIGURE 15.12
Database structure for Legacy
application

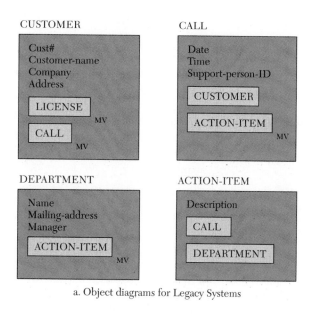

a. Object diagrams for Legacy Systems

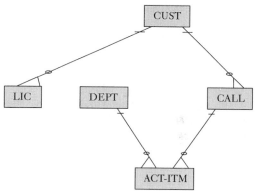

b. Relational structure to support objects in Figure 15.12a

cess client application programs. There are two types of programs: the Customer Support application and the Customer Processing application. The Customer Support application is used by customer support representatives while they are serving customers. The Customer Processing application is used to record new licenses, to produce mailing labels for newsletters and license renewal requests, and to update customer and other data. Each of the twenty application micros can process either application.

Database Structure

Figure 15.12a shows the four objects that need to be processed to support these applications. The CUSTOMER object contains multiple occurrences of the CALL and LICENSE objects. CALL contains CUSTOMER and multiple occurrences of the object

ACTION-ITEM. ACTION-ITEM contains CALL and DEPARTMENT as well as data about the action to be taken. Finally, DEPARTMENT contains data about Legacy departments as well as multiple occurrences of ACTION-ITEM.

ACTION-ITEM is an association object establishing the relationship between CALL and DEPARTMENT. The structure of the database supporting these objects is shown in Figure 15.12b.

Legacy defines a customer as any entity having a license for one of its products. Hence, a customer may be an individual, a corporation, or some other organization. As shown in Figure 15.12a, each CUSTOMER object has potentially many LICENSEs and many CALLs.

PARALLEL APPLICATION PROCESSING

Unlike teleprocessing, where the processing of the DBMS and all applications occurs on one machine, with client-server applications, the multiple computers operate in parallel. For the Legacy system, each of the twenty client computers can be processing applications in parallel while the server processes database requests, also in parallel. Thus, a client-server system has the potential for greater throughput than a teleprocessing system.

Figure 15.13 shows the processing of four transactions on two client computers and one server. Observe that while the client computers must wait for data to be processed by the server, they do not need to wait for each other. For all but database activity, the two computers operate in parallel.

There is a limitation, however. Since there is only one database server, application programs cannot process an action against the database simultaneously. The database actions will be serialized on the database server.

Additionally, because a CUSTOMER can be an organization, it is possible that two customer support representatives may be dealing with the same CUSTOMER object at the same time. Two people who work for the same company, for example, may call about two different licenses on two different products. This means that client-server systems

FIGURE 15.13
Parallel processing on client-server system

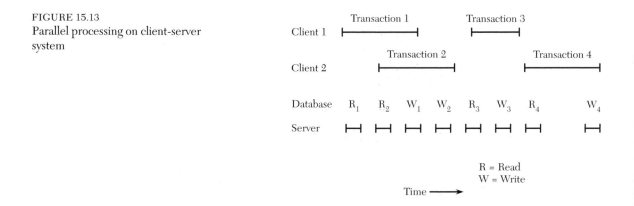

must provide for some type of locking and they must allow for deadlock and other problems. We will examine these issues later in this section.

DATABASE INTEGRITY

With the client-server architecture, all database processing is consolidated on a single computer. Such consolidation provides an opportunity to achieve a high degree of data integrity. Since every database request is processed by the server, if database constraints are defined to the server, it can consistently apply them.

To understand the desirability of this, consider Figure 15.14. In Figure 15.14a, integrity checking is not performed by the server. Instead, application programs on the client computers are required to check constraints during processing. In Figure 15.14b, integrity checking is performed by the DBMS on the server.

If you compare these two figures you will see why server constraint checking is preferred. If the clients check constraints, then the checking logic must be included in every application program. This is not only wasteful and inefficient, it is error-prone. Application programmers may understand the constraints differently and they may make errors when programming them. Further, whenever a new application is developed, all of the constraint checking must be duplicated.

Additionally, not all data changes are made via application programs. Users can make changes through a query/update language, and data can be imported in mass. Seldom are constraints checked for data changes from these sources.

If the server performs constraint checking, then constraints need only be defined, verified, and validated once. Further, data changes from all sources will be checked for integrity. It will not matter whether a change is submitted by an application program or a query/update process or is imported. Regardless of the source, the DBMS will ensure that constraints are not violated.

TRIGGERS

A **trigger** is an application procedure that is invoked by the DBMS automatically when some event occurs. For example, in an inventory application, a trigger could be written to generate an order whenever the quantity of an item on hand falls below a certain threshold value.

To implement a trigger, the developer writes the trigger code and informs the DBMS of the existence of the trigger and the conditions under which the trigger should be invoked. Later, when those conditions come into existence, the DBMS calls the trigger. In a client-server system, the triggers reside on and are invoked by the server.

Triggers, while very useful, can also be problematical. When triggers exist, a user can cause activity on the database that he or she does not expect or even know about. A telemarketing person in order entry, for example, might want to reserve stock for a hot prospect. If the user does not know of the existence of the trigger, he or she may generate a dummy order to hold the stock. Later, if the prospect decides not to purchase, the user

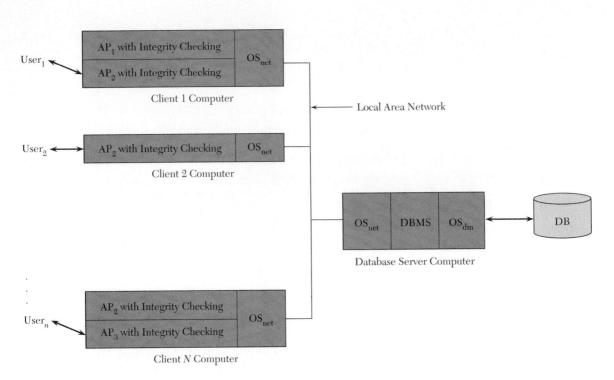

a. Application integrity checking

FIGURE 15.14
Client-server integrity checking

may return the stock to inventory. Meanwhile, unknown to the user, the trigger has generated orders for more of the product—orders which are unnecessary and which the user would not have generated had he or she known about them.

Additionally, in a multi-user environment, trigger procedures sometimes need to invoke locks. The transaction that causes the event that invokes the trigger may have already obtained locks that conflict with the trigger. In this situation, a transaction can unknowingly come into deadlock with itself.

Finally, triggers can cascade and even form a closed loop. They cascade when one trigger creates a condition that causes another trigger to be invoked which creates a condition that causes a third trigger to be invoked, and so on. Triggers form loops when they cascade back to themselves. If this occurs, the DBMS must have some means of preventing an infinite loop.

In truth, both DBMS-enforced constraint checking and triggers could be done by DBMS products in teleprocessing systems. There is no special characteristic of client-server systems that means only they can have centralized constraint checking and triggers. In practice, however, it turns out that these capabilities are more common on client-server DBMS products. This is so because such products are newer than teleprocessing-oriented DBMS products, and centralized constraint checking and triggers are relatively new ideas.

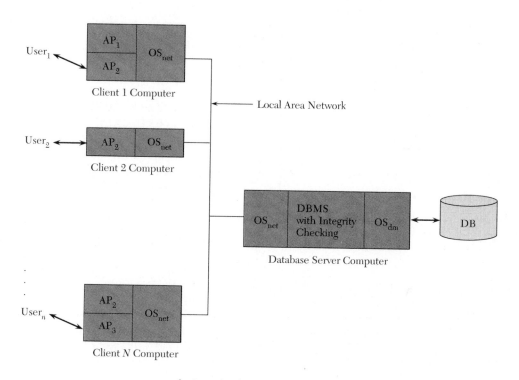

b. Centralized integrity checking

FIGURE 15.14, *continued*

CONCURRENT PROCESSING CONTROL

One of the challenges in the development of client-server applications is to gain the maximum degree of parallelism on the client computers while providing protection against problems such as lost updates and inconsistent reads. We will present two strategies for simultaneous processing control in this section.

To illustrate concurrent processing control for client-server applications, consider the transaction logic shown in Figure 15.15, a transaction processed by customer support representatives at Legacy Systems. The support representative obtains the customer and license data from the customer and uses it to read the appropriate row in CUST. Then, the representative answers the customer's questions, updates CUST data, and stores a new row in CALL. Finally, if the call results in an action item for one of Legacy's departments, a new row in ACT-ITM is stored.

Since several representatives could potentially process the same customer data, it is necessary to protect against the lost update and inconsistent read problems. There are two major ways in which this can be done.

Control via Implicit Locking

The first strategy is the same as that used in traditional teleprocessing systems. This strategy is similar to that shown for DB2 in Chapter 11. To implement this strategy, the

FIGURE 15.15
Logic of the CALL transaction

```
START TRANSACTION
READ CUST DATA
IF VALID
        THEN ANSWER CUSTOMER'S QUESTIONS
             UPDATE CUST DATA
             STORE CALL DATA
             IF NEED LEGACY ACTION
                 THEN STORE ACT-ITM DATA
             END-IF
             COMMIT TRANSACTION
        ELSE ROLLBACK TRANSACTION
END-IF
```

DBMS places locks implicitly on each DBMS command executed after the START TRANSACTION. These locks are then held until either a COMMIT or ROLLBACK command is issued.

For the logic in Figure 15.15, an implicit lock is placed on CUST data when it is read at the start of the transaction. The lock is held until either COMMIT or ROLLBACK is issued. If the CUST data is valid, the customer's questions will be answered and a new CALL record will be stored. CUST data is also updated. Finally, if necessary, a new ACT-ITM row is created. Both the new CALL and the new ACT-ITM records will be locked until the COMMIT command is issued.

Figure 15.16 shows the time required for processing two CALL transactions. In Figure 15.16a, the transactions process different CUST data so there is no data conflict. Client 2 waits while the server processes client 1's CUST data request, but after that, both clients process in parallel to the end of the transactions.

Figure 15.16b shows the situation for two transactions that attempt to process the same row in CUST. In this case, client 2 waits for data until client 1 has finished processing its CALL transaction.

Such waiting may be problematical. If the customer talking to the support representative on client 1 has many questions, then the CUST data will be locked a long time— several minutes or more. Also, if the user has much data to enter about the call or about an action item, this, too, will extend client 2's wait. Also, it might be that the user at client 2 can process his or her CALL transaction much faster than the user at client 1. If so, it is possible the user on client 2 could read the data, change it, and replace it while the user on client 1 talks to the customer.

These problems become even more severe if the DBMS does not support row-level locking. Some DBMS products, for example, lock a page (a block of rows) rather than a row, and some even lock the entire table.

If locking is performed at such large levels of granularity, then implicit locks can result in appreciable and *unnecessary* delays. The situation depicted in Figure 15.17 assumes page-level locking. Two transactions are processing two different CUST rows that happen to lie in the same page. In this case, client 2 must wait for client 1 to finish, even

FIGURE 15.16
Locking on client-server system

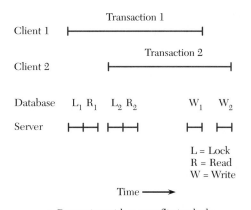

a. Processing with nonconflicting locks

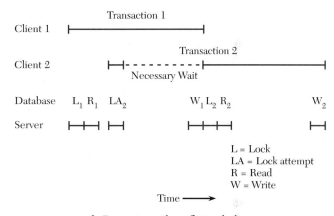

b. Processing with conflicting locks

though the two transactions are processing different rows. Again, the delay may be substantial. In this case, it is also unnecessary.

Control via Delayed Locking

A second strategy for control in distributed applications is to defer the locking until the last possible moment. With this style, as much of the transaction is processed as possible before any locks are placed. Then, the locks are obtained and held very briefly. To use this strategy, the DBMS must not apply any locks implicitly. Instead, the application program must place the locks.

Consider Figure 15.18 which shows the CALL transaction logic using delayed locks. As shown, CUST data is read without any lock and without starting any transaction. A copy of the data, as read, is stored as OLD-CUST. Then, the customer is serviced and CUST data is modified in memory. CALL data is created in memory as is ACT-ITM data, if appropriate.

At this point all of the time-consuming aspects of the transaction have been completed and the user has keyed in all of the data, so the transaction is started and a lock is

FIGURE 15.17

Page-level lock processing of nonconflicting data requests on the same page

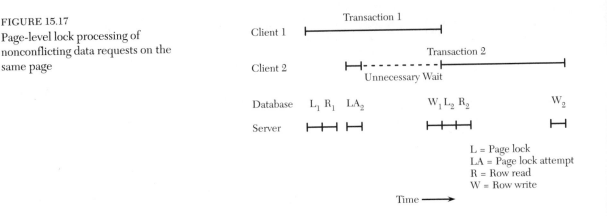

```
READ CUST DATA
SAVE A COPY OF CUST DATA AS OLD-CUST
IF VALID
     THEN ANSWER CUSTOMER'S QUESTIONS
          CHANGE CUST DATA IN MEMORY
               -DO NOT WRITE TO DATABASE
          CREATE CALL DATA
               -DO NOT WRITE TO DATABASE
          IF NEED LEGACY ACTION
               THEN CREATE ACT-ITM DATA
                     -DO NOT WRITE TO DATABASE
          END-IF
          START TRANSACTION
          LOCK CUST DATA
          READ CUST DATA
          IF CUST DATA = OLD-CUST
               THEN UPDATE CUST
                     STORE CALL
                     IF ACTION
                          THEN WRITE ACT-ITM
                     END-IF
                     COMMIT TRANSACTION
               ELSE ROLLBACK TRANSACTION
                     INFORM USER DATA WAS CHANGED
                     RESTART TRANSACTION
          END-IF
     END-IF
```

FIGURE 15.18

Logic of the CALL transaction using delayed locks

obtained on the CUST data. CUST data is reread. If the data just read is the same as OLD-CUST, then no other user has changed the data since the customer service call was started. In this case, the data is updated and stored, locks are released, and the transaction is committed.

If CUST data does not equal OLD-CUST, then someone has changed CUST while the call was in process. In this case, the user is informed that CUST data has been changed by another user, and the user reapplies changes to CUST. This latter actions requires the user to repeat some work, but this should not be too much of a problem since it should occur infrequently.

With delayed locks, the locks are held for very short periods of time. This reduces required waiting. Also, if two transactions are processing the same data in parallel, the one that finishes first will be the one whose changes are committed to the database. The faster transaction will not need to wait for the slower transaction to finish.

Finally, the delayed locking strategy is particularly appropriate if the DBMS locks at a level higher than row. Two users processing different rows in the same page or table, for example, will be able to process nearly in parallel. Since the locks are held for such a short period of time, the users will minimize their interference. Figure 15.19 shows the situation for the two transactions shown in Figure 15.17. Unlike implicit locking, there is almost no delay.

The problem with delayed locking is that transactions may need to be processed twice or even several times. Furthermore, the logic is more complicated, and this scheme therefore places a greater burden on the application programmer or client portion of the DBMS, or both.

RECOVERY

Recovery in client-server systems is accomplished in the same way that it is done in teleprocessing. The server computer keeps a log of changes to the database. Periodically, the database is backed up to tape or another medium. When failures occur, the server DBMS can perform both rollback and rollforward.

The description here, however, assumes a full-featured server DBMS. Not all products that are advertised as server DBMS products are able to support locking, constraint

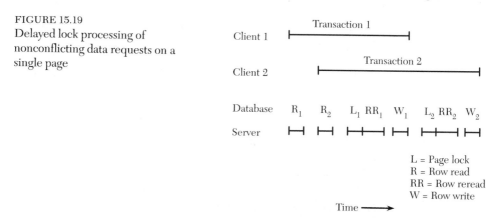

FIGURE 15.19
Delayed lock processing of nonconflicting data requests on a single page

checking, backup, and recovery as described here. As with any other product, the buyer needs to be certain to check for these features and functions.

Emergence of Two Types of DBMS

As client-server systems evolve, they are tending to split DBMS products into two separate categories of product. The first category is server DBMS products, which are similar to mainframe DBMS products. They offer a complete set of features for multi-user database processing. The capabilities of a server DBMS are similar to those of a mainframe DBMS. Currently, the most popular server DBMS is SQL Server developed by the Sybase Corporation and licensed by Microsoft.

The second category of products evolved from personal computer DBMS products. Although they are advertised as DBMS products, in the context of a client-server system, they are actually application generators. In Figure 15.2, such a product would operate on client computers. Popular products that fall into this category are Paradox and DataEase.

DBMS products that operate on the client side tend to focus on providing features and functions that ease application development and provide an easy-to-use front-end to applications. DBMS products that operate on the server side tend to focus on providing features and functions for fast performance, concurrency control, integrity, and the like. This product differentiation will probably continue in the future.

Summary

The classical approach for supporting a multi-user database system is teleprocessing. As computers have become less expensive, however, other architectures have been developed; among them are client-server systems, resource sharing systems, and distributed database systems.

With teleprocessing, users operate dumb terminals or micros that emulate dumb terminals. The communications control program, application programs, DBMS, and operating system are all processed by a single, centralized computer. Because all processing is done by a single computer, the user interface of a teleprocessing system is usually simple and primitive.

A client-server system consists of a network of computers, most often connected via a local area network. In nearly all cases, the user computers, called clients, are microcomputers, and in most cases, the server computer is also a micro, although minis and mainframes can be used in this role. Application programs are processed on the client computer; the DBMS and the data management portion of the operating system reside on a server. A client-server system can have multiple servers. If so, each server processes a different database. Systems in which two or more servers process the same database are called distributed database systems.

Client computers manage the user interface; they accept data from the user, process application logic, generate requests for database services, and process the data received.

Server computers process the database. While doing so, the server performs database integrity checking, maintains overhead data, and provides concurrent access control and related functions.

Client-server systems place the application closer to the user. The result is increased performance and more sophisticated interfaces for users. One disadvantage of client-server systems is control; because of parallel processing, conflicts due to concurrency are more difficult to manage.

Resource sharing systems also involve networks of computers, and, like client-server architectures, they most frequently consist of micros connected via local area networks. The chief difference between resource sharing systems and client-server systems is that the server computer provides fewer services for the user computers. The server, which is called a *file* server and not a *database* server, provides access to files and other resources. As a consequence, both the DBMS and the application programs must be distributed to the users' computers.

Resource sharing involves considerably more data transmission than client-server systems, and it requires that locks be obtained on large groups of data and held for long periods of time. Thus, resource sharing typically provides less throughput than client-server applications.

With a distributed database system, multiple computers process the same database. There are several types of distributed databases: partitioned, nonreplicated; nonpartitioned, replicated; and partitioned, replicated. In general, the greater the degree of partitioning and replication, the greater the flexibility, independence, and reliability. At the same time, expense, control difficulty, and security problems increase. Distributed databases are discussed in the next chapter.

Resource sharing is used infrequently for multi-user, transaction processing systems. It can be used, however, for the query and reporting of downloaded data. In this case, data is extracted from an operational database and placed on the file server. Microcomputers on the resource sharing network then obtain copies of the data for query and report processing. Such downloaded data is almost never changed and returned to the original data source. Potential problems of the processing of downloaded data include coordination, consistency, access control, and increased potential for computer crime.

Client-server systems are often used for multi-user transaction-processing applications. Such systems can provide high performance because of the parallel processing that is done among client and server computers. Additionally, integrity can be improved by placing integrity and constraint checking on the server. Triggers can cascade and form loops, however, so they need to be implemented with care.

Concurrent processing control is as important with client-server systems as it is with other types of multi-user systems. Two styles are possible. Implicit locks are similar to the locks employed with traditional database applications; they are similar to the locking described for DB2 in Chapter 11.

With delayed locking, the second style, as much of the transaction as possible is processed before obtaining a lock. Then, locks are obtained and data is reread. If there has been no change in the data, the transaction is committed to the database as processed. If there has been a change, the transaction is reprocessed as necessary. Delayed locking is especially useful when locking is done at a level of granularity larger than a row at a time and when transactions are likely to be lengthy because of slow human processing.

Recovery in client-server systems is similar to recovery in teleprocessing database systems.

As client-server systems evolve, they are forcing the definition of two categories of DBMS. Server DBMS products are very much like the mainframe and minicomputer DBMS products that have been used for years. They provide DBMS services on the operating system and file management interfaces. Client DBMS products are extensions of personal DBMS products used on microcomputers. They provide an easy-to-use user interface that is also easy to develop. Client DBMS products are in many ways, application development systems.

||||||||||||||||||||||||||||||||

GROUP I   QUESTIONS

15.1   Sketch the essential architecture of a teleprocessing system. Name and identify the computer(s) and programs involved. Explain which computer processes which programs.

15.2   Why is the users' interface on teleprocessing applications generally character oriented and primitive?

15.3   Sketch the essential architecture of a client-server system. Name and identify the computer(s) and programs involved. Explain which computer processes which programs.

15.4   What types of processing hardware are used with client-server systems?

15.5   How many servers can a client-server system have? What restriction exists about server use?

15.6   Explain why client-server systems can have fast performance.

15.7   How do typical user interfaces on client-server systems differ from user interfaces on teleprocessing systems?

15.8   Describe an important disadvantage of client-server systems.

15.9   Sketch the essential architecture of a resource sharing system. Name and identify the computer(s) and programs involved. Explain which computer processes which programs.

15.10   Explain how the processing of the following SQL query would differ between a client-server system and a resource sharing system:

```
SELECT   STUDENT-NAME, CLASS-NAME
FROM     STUDENT, GRADE
WHERE    STUDENT.S# = GRADE.S#
AND      GRADE = 'A'
```

Assume the database contains two tables as follows:

STUDENT (<u>S#</u>, Student-name, Student-phone)
GRADE (<u>Class#</u>, <u>S#</u>, Grade)

Also assume that the keys have indices.

15.11   Explain why resource sharing systems are seldom used for multi-user transaction processing applications.

15.12   Sketch the essential architecture of a distributed database system. Name and identify the computer(s) and programs involved. Explain which computer processes which programs.

15.13   Explain how distributed database systems differ from client-server systems.

15.14   Describe three types of distributed database systems. Explain how they differ in terms of flexibility and control.

15.15   Sketch two alternative systems that could be used to facilitate the processing of downloaded data.

15.16   Why is it generally unwise to allow the updating of downloaded data? If such updating is allowed, what precautions must be taken?

15.17   Describe potential coordination problems for processing downloaded data.

15.18   Describe potential consistency problems for processing downloaded data.

15.19   Describe potential access control problems for processing downloaded data.

15.20   Describe potential problems of computer crime when processing downloaded data.

15.21   Explain why it is desirable to place integrity and constraint checking on the server in a client-server system. What efficiencies result?

15.22   What is a trigger and what is its purpose? What problems can occur when using triggers?

15.23   Describe how to control concurrency in a client-server system using implicit locking. First define the logic of a transaction and then show how that logic would apply to a client-server system that has three clients and a single database server.

15.24   Describe how to control concurrency in a client-server system using delayed locking. Use the same transaction logic and system as you used in answering question 15.23.

15.25   How does recovery differ in a client-server system from that in a teleprocessing system?

15.26   Describe two categories of DBMS products that are emerging from client-server systems.

GROUP II QUESTIONS

Questions 15.27 through 15.29 concern the following example: Consider a database having the following five tables:

- SP (<u>SP#</u>, SP-name, Region, Total-sales-made)
- CUST (<u>Cust#</u>, Cust-name, Cust-phone, Balance)
- ORDER (<u>Order#</u>, Order-date, SP#, Cust#, Amount)
- LINE-ITEM (<u>Order#</u>, <u>Line-item#</u>, Item#, Qty, Extended-price)
- INVENTORY (<u>Item#</u>, Description, Unit-price, Quantity-on-hand)

Assume that the following transactions exist:

- T_1 Add/change/delete a row in CUST
- T_2 Add/change/delete a row in INVENTORY
- T_3 Add a new order by creating a new row in ORDER, new rows in LINE-ITEM, decrementing Quantity-on-hand in INVENTORY, adding Amount of ORDER to Balance in CUST, and adding Amount of ORDER to Total-sales-made in SP. Ensure that sufficient stock is in inventory for each item ordered. Do not allow any backorders.

Further assume that the organization has three users in the order processing department. Each of these three users is authorized to process transactions of type T_3. Only one of them is authorized to process transactions of type T_2 and the other two users are authorized to process transactions of type T_3.

15.27   Sketch the architecture of a teleprocessing system to process these three transactions against this database. Explain the programs that would be required. Develop pseudocode or a flowchart of the logic to process transaction T_3. Also describe an example of a concurrent processing problem that could occur in this system and explain how to prevent that problem.

15.28   Sketch the architecture of a client-server system to process these three transactions against this database. Explain the programs that would be required and show where they would reside. Develop pseudocode or a flowchart of the logic to process transaction T_3. Explain what data would need to be transmitted across the LAN to process this transaction. Also describe an example of a concurrent processing problem that could occur in this system and explain how that problem could be prevented using the delayed locking strategy. Discuss advantages and disadvantages of this system as compared to the teleprocessing system described in your answer to question 15.27.

15.29   Sketch the architecture of a resource sharing system to process these three transactions against this database. Explain the programs that would be required and show where they would reside. Develop pseudocode or a flowchart of the logic to process transaction T_3. Explain what data would need to be transmitted across the LAN to process transactions of this type. Also describe an example of a concurrent processing problem that could occur in this system and explain how that problem could be prevented using locks. What level of granularity of lock would be required? Discuss advantages and disadvantages of this system as compared to the client-server solution in question 15.28.

Distributed Database Processing

We conclude this textbook with a discussion of distributed database processing. This chapter will describe the characteristics and components of distributed database systems and present four processing goals for the distributed DBMS (DDBMS). Finally, we will consider two difficult issues in distributed processing— concurrency and failure/recovery—in detail.

Before proceeding, be aware that this knowledge about distributed database processing continues to evolve, and by no means are we dealing with a mature discipline. As Bernstein and Goodman wrote about one aspect of distributed processing, "Distributed concurrency control, by contrast [with nondistributed], is in a state of extreme turbulence. More than 20 concurrency control algorithms have been proposed for DDBMSs, and several have been, or are being, implemented. These algorithms are usually complex, hard to understand, and difficult to prove correct (indeed, many are incorrect)."[1] Although this quotation, from two of the most prominent researchers in this discipline, was published in 1981, it continues to be true today.

In short, many of the problems have been identified, but few *robust* solutions are known. Further,

- OVERVIEW
- COMPONENTS OF DISTRIBUTED DATABASE SYSTEMS
- FOUR GOALS FOR A DISTRIBUTED DBMS
- DISTRIBUTED CONCURRENCY CONTROL
- FAILURE TRANSPARENCY

---

[1]Philip A. Bernstein and Nathan Goodman, "Concurrency Control in Distributed Database Systems," *Computing Surveys* 13(June 1981), 185.

the subject is exceedingly complex and research activities are splintered on different facets of the problems. Additionally, much of the work has been theoretical and important implementation issues have been ignored. For example, several of the engineers of R°, a DDBMS prototype implementation, wrote the following regarding the production of log records: "The discussions of commit protocols in the literature are very vague, if there is any mention at all, about this crucial (for correctness and performance) aspect of the protocols."[2]

At the same time, end-users, equipped with microcomputers and local databases, are increasing the pressure on the MIS department to provide some form of distributed processing. The resource sharing and client-server systems described in Chapter 15 are the first indications of this pressure. In response to this opportunity, vendors of DBMS products have begun to announce so-called DDBMS products. Most of these products leave substantial numbers of distributed database processing problems unsolved. As your career progresses, however, these offerings will improve, and over time, true distributed DDBMS products will be developed.

Your goal in reading this chapter should be to understand the nature of distributed database processing, its advantages and disadvantages, design considerations for distributed database systems, and the major problems that need to be overcome. Such knowledge will provide a foundation for this complicated subject that is likely to grow and evolve tremendously during your career.

Overview

Distributed database processing is database processing in which the execution of transactions and the retrieval and updating of data occur across two or more independent and usually geographically separated computers. Figure 16.1 shows a distributed database system involving four computers.

---

[2]C. Mohan, B. Lindsay, and R. Obermarck, "Transaction Management in the R° Distributed Database Management System," *Transactions on Database Systems* 11(December 1986), 378.

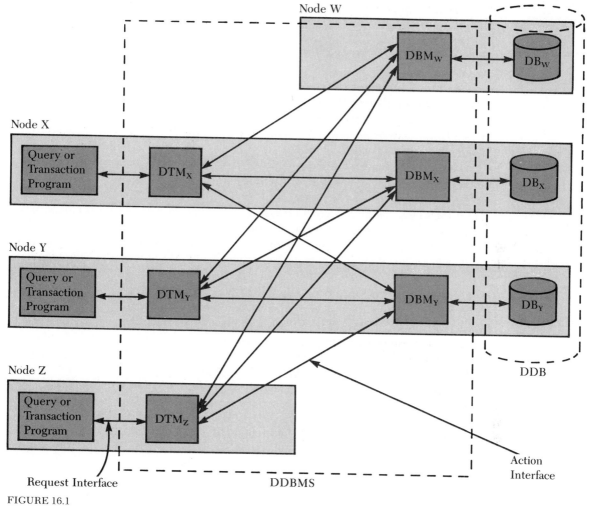

FIGURE 16.1
Distributed database architecture

The **distributed database management system** (DDBMS) consists of the collection of distributed transaction and database managers on all computers. As shown, this DDBMS is a generic schematic. It represents a collection of programs that operate on different computers. These programs may all be subsystems of a single DDBMS product that is licensed from a single vendor. Or, these programs may be a collection of programs from disparate sources; some may be licensed from vendors and some may be written in-house. The point of this figure is to illustrate the functions that must be served to accomplish distributed database processing.

A **distributed transaction manager** (DTM) is a program that receives processing requests from query or transaction programs and translates them into actions for the database managers. As you will see, an important function of the DTM is to coordinate and control these actions. Depending on the nature of the application and the DDBMS, the DTM may be provided as part of the DDBMS; or, it may be developed in-house by the organization that implements the distributed system; or, in less sophisticated applications, some of its function may even be performed by people following manual procedures.

A **database manager** (DBM) is a program that processes some portion of the distributed database. It retrieves and updates user and overhead data in accordance with action commands received from the DTMs. The DBM may be a subset of a DDBMS product, or it may be a commercial nondistributed DBMS. In some cases, the DDBMS may contain different DBMS products.

A **node** is a computer that executes either a DTM, a DBM, or both. A **transaction node** processes a DTM, and a **database node** processes a DBM and its database.

For the example shown in Figure 16.1, node W is a database node running DBM_W and storing DB_W. Node X is both a transaction and database node with DTM_X, DBM_X, and DB_X. Similarly, node Y is both a transaction and database node. Node Z is a transaction node, only.

Query or transaction programs communicate with DTMs via requests. These requests are similar to the requests for DBMS action that you have already studied. Example requests are SELECT EMPLOYEE WHERE E# EQ 123 or STORE DUE-DATE. Such requests operate on logical constructs, however. The query or application program is not referring to any particular physical instance of the construct.

DTMs communicate with DBMs via actions to be executed on specific data instances. Thus, if the new occurrence of DUE-DATE is to be stored in DB_X and DB_Y, then the DTM will translate the *request* STORE DUE-DATE into two *actions;* one will direct DBM_X to store the new data and the second will direct DBM_Y to store this data.

In principle, requests and actions could differ in terms of their level of abstraction as well. For example, a request could be expressed in terms of an object and be translated into actions expressed in terms of the distributed composite relations or files. To date, no such DDBMS exists, however.

ADVANTAGES OF DISTRIBUTED PROCESSING

There are four advantages of distributed database processing. First, it can result in *better performance* than centralized processing. Data can be located close to the point of use so that communication time is shorter. Also, several computers operating simultaneously can yield more processing throughput than a single computer.

Second, replicated data *increases reliability*. When a computer fails, replicated data can be obtained from other computers. Users are not dependent on the availability of a sole source for their data. A third advantage is that distributed systems are more *easily scaled in size*. Additional computers can be added to the network as the number of users or their processing workload expands. The addition of a new, smaller computer is often easier and cheaper than upgrading a single, centralized computer. Further, if the workload decreases, a reduction in the size of the network can also be readily accomplished.

Finally, distributed systems are more *readily tailored to the structure of the users' organization*. Figure 16.2 shows the organization of a geographically distributed manu-

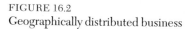

FIGURE 16.2
Geographically distributed business

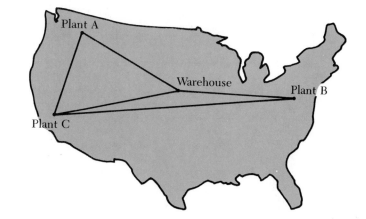

facturer. The general managers of each plant have considerable authority and latitude in the operation of their facilities. If these plants were dependent on a single, centralized computer, then the system architecture would conflict with the operational philosophy and policy of the company. Even in more centralized organizations, distributed processing provides greater flexibility to fit the structure than does centralized processing.

DISADVANTAGES OF DISTRIBUTED PROCESSING

Oddly enough, the first two disadvantages of distributed databases are the same as the first two advantages. First, *performance can be worse* for distributed processing than for centralized processing. Depending on the nature of the workload, the network, the DDBMS, and the concurrency and failure strategies used, the advantages of local data access and multiple processors can be overwhelmed by the coordination and control tasks required. This situation is especially likely when the workload calls for a large number of concurrent updates on replicated data that must be widely distributed.

Second, distributed database processing *can be less reliable* than centralized processing. Again, depending on the reliability of processing computers, the network, the DDBMS, the transactions, and error rates in the workload, a distributed system can be less available than a centralized one. Both of these disadvantages indicate that distributed processing is no panacea. Although it holds the promise of better performance and greater reliability, this promise is not guaranteed.

A third disadvantage is *increased complexity,* which often translates into *high construction and maintenance expense.* Since there are more hardware components, there is more to learn about and there are more interfaces that can fail. Additionally, as you will see, concurrency control and failure recovery can be exceedingly complicated and difficult to implement. Often a greater burden is placed on programmers and on operations personnel. This means more experienced (and expensive) personnel are required.

Finally, distributed database processing is *difficult to control.* A centralized computer resides in a controlled environment with closely supervised operations personnel. Processing activities can be monitored (though with difficulty). In a distributed system, processing computers often reside in the users' work areas. Physical access is frequently

FIGURE 16.3
Advantages and disadvantages of distributed database processing

Advantages	Disadvantages
Better performance	Worse performance
Increased reliability	Decreased reliability
Easily scaled in size	Increased complexity
Readily tailored to organization structure	Higher costs
	Difficult to control

uncontrolled; operations procedures are sometimes lax and performed by people who have little appreciation or understanding of the importance of the procedures. Finally, in the event of a disaster or catastrophe, recovery can be far more difficult to synchronize than with a centralized system. The advantages and disadvantages of distributed database processing are summarized in Figure 16.3.

Components of Distributed Database Systems

As stated, this is a confusing topic. Much of the confusion exists because so many different types of processing fall under the term *distributed database processing* and can fit into the general architecture of Figure 16.1. For example, consider the system in Figure 16.4a. This system conforms to the architecture shown in Figure 16.1, where the nodes are specified to be mainframe computers. For this system, the processing is most likely based on equality of cooperating colleagues. Each database node (W, X, and Y) has authority to insert, modify, delete, and read any data throughout the network. Further, the data is coordinated among the computers in as close to real time as possible.

Now consider Figure 16.4b. Here, node W is a mainframe, nodes X and Y are minicomputers, and node Z is a microcomputer. In this instance, the processing rules could be the following: Only node W can modify the database. Nodes X and Y, which have copies of data on node W, are authorized for read-only access, and node Z may only obtain data from node Y. No attempt is made to keep the data current in real time. Instead, once each day, nodes X and Y are refreshed from node W, and once each week, node Z is refreshed from node Y.

Figure 16.4c shows a third instance of the architecture in Figure 16.1. Here node W is a mainframe and nodes X, Y, and Z are microcomputers attached to a local area network. Node X is a gateway to the mainframe; it obtains all of the database data that X, Y, and Z need from W and stores it on its own database. Suppose that node Y needs frequent access to some of the data but processes this data on a read-only basis. When either nodes X or Z make changes to data, they do it to the copy on W. Periodically, W refreshes X's database with data that has been changed.

These three examples all conform to the general architecture in Figure 16.1, but they are entirely different. They each have their own set of capabilities, and they each have their own set of problems. To bring order to this complexity, consider the following five components of a distributed database system: hardware, programs, data, procedures, and personnel.

HARDWARE

As shown in Figure 16.4, processing nodes can consist of many different types of hardware. In some distributed systems (Figure 16.4a), all of the nodes are homogeneous. In others (Figure 16.4b and c), they are heterogeneous. Differences in processing speeds and storage capacities need to be considered when determining the processing authorities of the nodes.

PROGRAMS

The principal program that we need to consider in a distributed database system is the DDBMS. The DDBMS architecture shown in Figure 16.1 is generic. The DTMs and DBMs can be subsystems of a single DDBMS product that is licensed from one vendor. Alternatively, and, at present, more commonly, the DDBMS is an amalgam of programs developed in-house and products obtained from various software vendors. In many cases, the DTMs are written in-house and the DBMs are commercial DBMS products.

Consider the examples in Figure 16.4. In the first example, all of the computers are the same class of machine (mainframe), and the company with this system could elect to license a DDBMS that is a single product. If so, the DTMs and DBMs would be provided by the vendor as subsystems of the DDBMS. Each DTM would expect to be communicating with only the DBM that is provided by the vendor. R°, a prototype DDBMS developed by IBM, is an example of such a product. In truth, such DDBMS products are rare.

Now consider Figure 16.4b. This system involves a mixture of hardware types, and it is unlikely that any commercial DDBMS product would work across all of them. It would be possible for the DBMs to be versions of a single commercial DBMS product, however, as long as that product runs on all classes of hardware. Oracle, for example, runs on mainframes, minicomputers, and microcomputers. The DTMs, however, are not part of the commercial product. Instead, they would be application programs written in-house that access the product on a foreign computer and download the data. Or, alternatively, several DBMS products could be used as DBMs as described next.

Figure 16.4c shows a mainframe communicating with a local area network of microcomputers. In this case, the DBM could be a single product as in the case above, or it could be a mixture of products. If a mixture, then the DBM on node W might be a mainframe DBMS product like DB2, and the DBMs on nodes X, Y, and Z could be

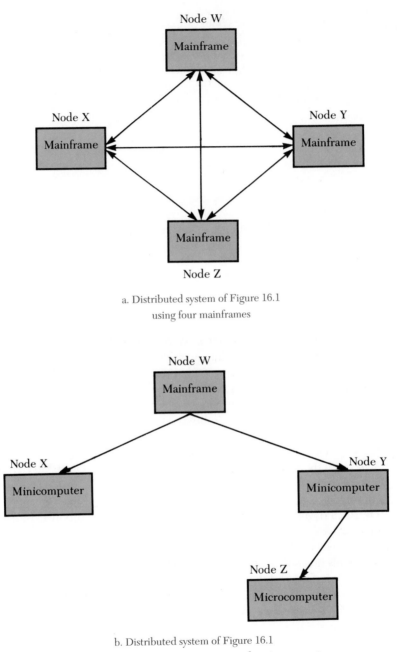

a. Distributed system of Figure 16.1
using four mainframes

b. Distributed system of Figure 16.1
using a mainframe, two minicomputers, and a microcomputer

FIGURE 16.4
Three instances of architecture in Figure 16.1

FIGURE 16.4, *continued*

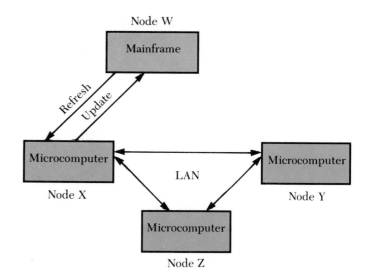

c. Distributed system of Figure 16.1 using a mainframe, LAN, and three
microcomputers

multi-user LAN versions of a microcomputer DBMS such as Paradox or DataEase. It is
possible that an extract program, which obtains data from the database on node X, would
be provided by the microcomputer DBMS vendor. Thus, the DDBMS can be a single
product, or it can be an amalgam of different programs and products.

DATA

One of the key characteristics of a distributed database system is whether or not the data
is **replicated.** A distributed database can be nonreplicated, partially replicated, or fully
replicated. If it is nonreplicated, then one and only one copy of each data item exists.
Data items are assigned to particular nodes and they may only reside at their assigned
node. Any application needing access to the data item must obtain it from the officially
designated node.

A partially replicated database contains some data items that are duplicated and some
that are not. A system directory indicates whether a data item is replicated and where
the data item is stored. A fully replicated distributed database is one in which the entire
database is duplicated on two or more nodes. A node either has all of the database or
none of it.

PROCEDURES

There are a multitude of procedural components of distributed database systems. The
first group of procedures concerns **processing rights.** Which nodes can do what to
which data? In the simplest distributed systems, data is nonreplicated, and only the node

that stores the data can update it. (Actually, in the very simplest system, no data is updated at all. Data is obtained from a foreign source and processed as read-only data. Such a situation is rare, however.) In more complicated situations, any node can issue an update request for any data item on its own or any other node. If the data item is replicated, all copies are changed.

In the design of a distributed system, the developers must determine processing rights. In doing so, they must consider the requirements, the capabilities of the hardware and programs, the control of concurrency, and other factors.

Another component of procedures concerns **data currency.** How up-to-date must the data be? Does every node need the most current value of all of the data items it accesses? Can some databases be allowed to become out of date? In 16.4a, all nodes have access to the most current data. In Figures 16.4b and 16.4c, some of the nodes are processing historical data. In general, the more current the replicated data, the more expensive the system. Enormous numbers of processing cycles will be devoted to control and coordination for the system in Figure 16.4a. Powerful and expensive CPUs will be required to process this network.

Closely related to the issues of processing rights and currency is the issue of **data flow.** Who updates whom? In Figure 16.4b, node W updates data on nodes X and Y, whereas in Figure 16.4c, node X updates data on node W. Such flows are determined by the requirements and the processing rights of the nodes.

Another procedural component concerns **control.** In the case of conflicting processing requests, which node resolves the conflict? In general, authoritarian control (usually implemented in systems like those in Figures 16.4b and 16.4c) is easier to implement than schemes based on equality (usually implemented in systems like that in Figure 16.4a).

In fact, for distributed systems like the one in Figure 16.4a, control can be distributed and diffused throughout the network. No single node need be in charge. Control decisions can be made by any of the nodes depending on the control issue and the state of the system. This situation allows for greater flexibility, but it is far more complex.

PERSONNEL

Distributed systems vary considerably in the demands they place on people. Systems with a sophisticated and powerful DDBMS, place few special demands on users. In fact, users do not know they are processing distributed data. They simply access their applications, and all distributed processing is taken care of for them by the DDBMS. For less sophisticated systems, users must become involved: The less sophisticated the DDBMS, the greater the role that must be taken by people.

Consider the system in Figure 16.4b. Users at nodes X and Y may need to invoke one or more programs to cause data to be downloaded from the mainframe. Similarly, the users at node Z may need to manually start programs to bring data down from node Y. Depending on the design of the system, the users may also bear the responsibility for inspecting processing reports to determine that the data was received without error and that the correct data was transmitted.

In very primitive distributed systems, the users may even bear some of the responsibilities of the DTM. For example, in some systems users make data changes on the local database and then manually cause these changes to be made for replicated data on other nodes. In the most primitive systems, users employ the NIKE method (they put on their sneakers and run down the hall carrying diskettes of data changes from computer to computer).

Four Goals for a Distributed DBMS

Traiger et al. defined four goals for a distributed DBMS.[3] These goals provide an excellent framework for a survey of the issues, problems, and solutions proposed for distributed databases. Each of the goals involves an aspect of **transparency.**

In a distributed database system, transparency means that query facilities and transaction programs are isolated from the management of the distributed database, so that they realize the advantages of distributed processing without having to become involved in the particulars of the database distribution. Programmers and users can then focus on the nature and logic of the information problem they need to solve and not be forced to deal with matters that more properly belong to the DDBMS. (To simplify the discussion, for the balance of this chapter, we will refer to query users and transaction programs simply as *transactions.*)

Specifically, transactions need access to the database via a DDBMS that provides the following four types of transparency: **data location, data replication, concurrency,** and **failure.** This means that, in the ideal, the transaction is not even aware that the data is distributed. All four of these distribution issues are handled behind the scenes. We will consider each transparency goal in turn.

LOCATION TRANSPARENCY

Transactions need to be independent of the location of a particular data item. If they are not, then location issues greatly complicate transaction logic. Consider the manufacturing company sketched in Figure 16.2. Suppose the inventory manager wants to move three refrigerators from plant A to plant B; as a consequence, two inventory records need to be modified. Suppose the data involved is not replicated, but it may be stored on a computer at either facility. If the program that processes this transaction is not transparent to the location of the data, it will need to consider four cases: both records at A, one at A and one at B, one at B and one at A, and both at B. Obviously, the logic of the transaction is confounded by the need to consider the data's location. The logic would be much more complicated for a more sophisticated example, and in any case, such considerations are unnecessary and inappropriate for an *application* program.

---

[3]Irving L. Traiger, Jim Gray, Cesare A. Galtieri, and Bruce G. Lindsay, "Transactions and Consistency in Distributed Database Systems," *Transactions on Database Systems* 7(September 1982), 323–342.

Location transparency can be provided if the distributed transaction managers (DTMs in Figure 16.1) have the responsibility for determining the location of data and issuing actions on the appropriate DBMs. This can be accomplished if DTMs have access to directories of data locations. In this way, if data is moved, only the DTM need be involved. All transactions are isolated from the change in location.

REPLICATION TRANSPARENCY

Transactions are transparent to replication if they can process without knowledge of how many times, or even if, data is replicated. The transaction can act as if all data is stored only once on a single node. With replication transparency, new duplicates can be created or existing duplicates eliminated without any impact on the end-user's transaction or query processing.

To provide replication transparency, the transaction managers must translate transaction processing requests into actions for the database managers. Reads are straightforward. The DTM selects one of the nodes that stores the data and issues an action to read it. To facilitate the selection, the DTM may keep statistics about the time required to read data from various nodes. It selects the node with the best performance. Writing replicated data is more involved. The DTM must issue a write action for every DBM that stores a copy of that data.

This discussion assumes that every DTM has an accurate and up-to-date copy of a directory that indicates data locations. Interesting problems arise when we consider what happens when the directory must be changed to account for new data copies or elimination of data copies. Clearly, coordination is critical. All directories must be installed in such a manner that no DTM thinks data is available before it is (in the case of reads) and that every DTM knows that data is available when it is (in the case of writes). Otherwise, a DTM may request data that is not yet available or fail to issue a write on a DBM when data has become available. See Bernstein and Goodman[4] for more information about directory processing.

CONCURRENCY TRANSPARENCY

Many transactions involving the distributed database can be in execution at the same time. In spite of this, the results of a transaction must remain the same. The DDBMS provides concurrency transparency if the results of all concurrent transactions are logically consistent with the results that would have been obtained if the transactions had been executed one at a time, in some arbitrary serial order. Stated in other terms, the

---

[4]Philip A. Bernstein and Nathan Goodman, "An Algorithm for Concurrency Control and Recovery in Replicated Distributed Databases," *Transactions on Database Systems* 9(December 1984), 596–615.

logic of transactions processed concurrently with other transactions must be the same as it would have been if the transaction had been processed alone.

Two major strategies have been developed to provide concurrency control. One, called **distributed two-phase locking,** is an extension of the concurrency control mechanism we discussed in Chapters 14 and 15. A second method is called **timestamp ordering.** Both of these techniques have been implemented in DDBMS products. Distributed two-phase locking is more common and we will discuss it further in the next section.

FAILURE TRANSPARENCY

The fourth goal for the DDBMS is to provide failure transparency. This means that transactions are correctly processed in spite of transaction, DDBMS, network, and computer failures. Stated in terms of Chapter 14, in spite of failure, transactions will be **atomic.** Either all of a transaction will be processed or none of it will be. Further, once the results of transactions have been committed, they will be permanent.

Failure transparency is the most difficult of the four goals. Part of the problem is that there are so many types of failure. On one end of the spectrum is a node that never fails, sometimes called a **perfect node.** On the other end is a node that fails in a totally unknown manner. Such a node may communicate garbage over the network or, because of its failure, may send validly formatted but inappropriate actions over the network. Such a node is called an **insane node.**

Another type of failure involves nodes that become malevolent—meaning that the node has the express purpose of performing unauthorized activity or of intentionally causing harm. It is even possible to consider failures in which nodes conspire with each other to subvert the distributed system. Such failures are sometimes called **Byzantine failures.**

In between the extremes of perfect nodes and insane nodes are **sane nodes.** A sane node is a node that can fail, but only in a defined and known way. The simplest example of a sane node is one that is either perfect or it fails to respond at all.[5]

Another reason that failure transparency is so difficult is that concurrency control is so complicated. In a sense, concurrency control problems are solved at the expense of failure recovery. It is as if a bubble of air under the carpet has been pushed from one corner only to reappear in another. The concurrency control mechanisms work as long as no failure occurs at certain times or states of the distributed database (or as long as recovery can be guaranteed to proceed in a certain manner, and so forth). In the general case of partitioned, replicated databases, many theoretical and practical implementation problems still remain to be solved. We discuss failure transparency in more detail later in this chapter.

---

[5]Hector Garcia-Molina, Frank Pittelli, and Susan Davidson, "Applications of Byzantine Agreement in Database Systems," *Transactions on Database Systems* 11(March 1986), 27–47.

Distributed Concurrency Control

In this section and the next, we will consider some of the technical issues involved in developing DDBMS products that provide concurrency and failure transparency. This section discusses the nature of the concurrency control problem in distributed databases and presents the essential concepts of one fundamental concurrency control method. The next section discusses failure transparency.

These two sections contain the most technical discussions in this text. Your goal in reading them should be to understand the issues involved in providing robust concurrency control and failure/recovery. Strive to attain knowledge from these sections that will enable you to be an informed consumer when evaluating DDBMS products. Understand the problems these products need to overcome. With this knowledge, when vendors make claims regarding capabilities of their DDBMS products, you will be able to ask pertinent questions that reveal the potential limitations of those products.

Distributed databases face the same concurrency problems as do centralized databases. The problems and their solutions are more complicated, however, because several independent computers and potentially replicated data exist. We begin with a discussion of the anomalies that can occur if processing is not controlled appropriately. These anomalies are similar to those described in Chapter 14 for centralized processing. We will approach them somewhat more formally, however, to establish terminology needed to address this more difficult problem. The discussion in this section follows the organization set out by Bernstein and Goodman.[6]

CONCURRENT PROCESSING ANOMALIES

Figure 16.5a illustrates the first anomaly, sometimes called the **lost update anomaly.** Suppose the transactions in this example occur in the business of the distributed manufacturer in Figure 16.2. Assume the transactions process the same nonreplicated data item that is stored on a computer at plant A. The transactions could arise from the same DTM or from different DTMs. Each transaction is reducing the quantity on hand for some item in inventory. (In these examples, we need not consider the identity of the item.)

The nomenclature, $r_1(N_A)$ means a read by transaction number 1 of the value of N that is stored at plant A. The arrow and value indicate the value read. Similarly, $w_1(N_A)$ means a write from transaction 1 of a value of N to the computer at plant A. The arrow and value indicate the value written.

As you can see from this example, w_1 is lost. The write from transaction 2 overlays it. We described this problem for non-distributed systems in Chapter 14.

---

[6]Philip A. Bernstein and Nathan Goodman, "Concurrency Control in Distributed Database Systems," *Computing Surveys* 13(June 1981), 185–221.

FIGURE 16.5
Examples of anomalies due to
concurrency

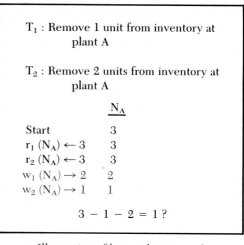

T_1 : Remove 1 unit from inventory at
       plant A

T_2 : Remove 2 units from inventory at
       plant A

	N_A
Start	3
$r_1 (N_A) \leftarrow 3$	3
$r_2 (N_A) \leftarrow 3$	3
$w_1 (N_A) \rightarrow 2$	2
$w_2 (N_A) \rightarrow 1$	1

$$3 - 1 - 2 = 1 ?$$

a. Illustration of lost update anomaly

T_3 : Move 4 units from warehouse (W)
       to plant B

T_4 : Count number of units at A, B, and W

	N_A	N_B	N_W
Start	3	1	6
$r_3 (N_W) \leftarrow 6$	3	1	6
$w_3 (N_W) \rightarrow 2$	3	1	2
$r_4 (N_W) \leftarrow 2$	3	1	2
$r_3 (N_B) \leftarrow 1$	3	1	2
$r_4 (N_A) \leftarrow 3$	3	1	2
$r_4 (N_B) \leftarrow 1$	3	1	2
$w_3 (N_B) \rightarrow 5$	3	5	2

b. Illustration of inconsistent
read anomaly

A second anomaly is shown in Figure 16.5b. This anomaly, sometimes called the **inconsistent read anomaly** occurs when one transaction reads a data item while another one writes it. In this example, one transaction (T_3) is moving four units from the warehouse to plant B while another transaction (T_4) is counting the total number of units at plants A and B and the warehouse. Although there are a total of ten units in the three locations, T_4 concludes there are only six. This occurs because T_4 reads N_W after T_3 decrements the units, but reads N_B before T_3 adds them.

SERIAL AND SERIAL-EQUIVALENT EXECUTIONS

The situations illustrated in Figure 16.5 are judged to be anomalies because they generate results that the users do not expect. More specifically, they generate results that are logically inconsistent with the results that would have been produced if the transactions had been executed one at a time, or serially.

Figure 16.6 shows two serial executions: one of T_1 followed by T_2 and a second of T_3 followed by T_4. In both cases the results are logically consistent with what the users would expect.

Serial executions, even though they generate consistent results, prohibit concurrency and result in poor performance. Thus, a goal of concurrency control is to allow concurrency but in such a way that the results of the concurrent execution are logically consistent with those of a serial execution.

Equivalent Executions

An execution of transactions that is not serial but that generates the same results as a particular serial execution is said to be *equivalent to the serial execution*. Figure 16.7 shows an execution of T_3 and T_4 that is equivalent to a serial execution of T_3 followed by T_4.

More formally, two executions of a series of transactions are said to be **equivalent** if two conditions are met: (1) each read in the two executions reads data item values produced by the same write in both executions, and (2) the final write of a data item is the same in both executions.[7] If you examine Figure 16.7, you will find that both of these conditions are met.

These conditions make sense intuitively. They imply that the transactions receive the same inputs in both executions, and that the final data item values are the same.

Definitions

Before proceeding, we need to define a number of terms. Two operations **conflict** if they operate on the same data item and at least one of the operations is a write. From this it follows that there are two types of conflict. **Read-write conflict** occurs when one

---

[7]Philip A. Bernstein and Nathan Goodman, "Concurrency Control in Distributed Database Systems," *Computing Surveys* 13(June 1981), 185–221.

FIGURE 16.6
Examples of serial executions

Serial Execution of $T_1 T_2$	Serial Execution of $T_3 T_4$
$r_1 (N_A) \leftarrow 3$	$r_3 (N_W) \leftarrow 6$
$w_1 (N_A) \rightarrow 2$	$w_3 (N_W) \rightarrow 2$
$r_2 (N_A) \leftarrow 2$	$r_3 (N_B) \leftarrow 1$
$w_2 (N_A) \rightarrow 0$	$w_3 (N_B) \rightarrow 5$
	$r_4 (N_A) \leftarrow 3$
	$r_4 (N_W) \leftarrow 2$
	$r_4 (N_B) \leftarrow 5$

FIGURE 16.7
Nonserial execution of T_3, T_4 that is equivalent to a serial execution of T_3, T_4

$r_3 (N_W) \leftarrow 6$
$r_3 (N_B) \leftarrow 1$
$r_4 (N_A) \leftarrow 3$
$w_3 (N_W) \rightarrow 2$
$r_4 (N_W) \leftarrow 2$
$w_3 (N_B) \rightarrow 5$
$r_4 (N_B) \leftarrow 5$

FIGURE 16.8
Intertransaction conflicts in T_1, T_2, T_3, T_4

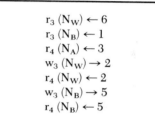

T_1 : $r_1 (N_A)$
$\quad\quad w_1 (N_A)$

T_2 : $r_2 (N_A)$
$\quad\quad w_2 (N_A)$

T_3 : $r_3 (N_W)$
$\quad\quad w_3 (N_W)$
$\quad\quad r_3 (N_B)$
$\quad\quad w_3 (N_B)$

T_4 : $r_4 (N_A)$
$\quad\quad r_4 (N_W)$
$\quad\quad r_4 (N_B)$

operation is a read and the other is a write. **Write-write conflict** occurs when both operations are writes.

Figure 16.8 shows the intertransaction conflicts in the transactions T_1 through T_4. For example, $r_1(N_A)$ has a read-write conflict with $w_2(N_A)$, and $w_1(N_A)$ has a write-write conflict with $w_2(N_A)$. Other conflicts are shown by the arrows. Notice that in addition to these conflicts, there are conflicts within transactions. Such conflicts are assumed to be managed by the logic within the transaction program and need not concern the DDBMS.

Figure 16.8 shows a particular **execution** of the transactions T_1 through T_4. This execution is an ordered sequence of requests to DTMs. We will call an ordered sequence of requests a **schedule.**

The schedule in Figure 16.8 is one of many possible schedules. Schedules that are equivalent to serial schedules are called **consistent schedules.** For example, consider the serial execution T_1 followed by T_2 followed by T_3 followed by T_4. Any schedule that is equivalent to this serial execution is said to be a consistent schedule of that schedule.

We will label the requests according to the transaction that generates them. Thus, REQ_i refers to a request that arises in the processing of T_i. In Figure 16.8, for example, both $r_2(N_A)$ and $w_2(N_A)$ will be referred to as REQ_2.

Serialization

The following is a paraphrase of a fundamental theorem of serialization: Suppose we have a serial list of ordered transactions, $T_1, T_2, \ldots, T_n$. Call this ordered list **T.** A particular schedule, **S,** is a consistent schedule of **T,** if for any two conflicting requests, say REQ_i and REQ_j arising from distinct transactions T_i and T_j, respectively, REQ_i precedes REQ_j in **S** if and only if T_i precedes T_j in **T.**[8]

To understand this theorem first realize that it is concerned only with the order of *conflicting* requests. This theorem says that for the schedule to be consistent with **T,** the order of conflicting requests must mirror the order of the transactions that spawn them. By implication, it also says that we need not be concerned with the order of nonconflicting requests.

Figure 16.9 shows a consistent but nonserial execution of the serial execution T_1 followed by T_2 followed by T_3 followed by T_4. Observe that the order of conflicting requests does, in fact, mirror the order of the transactions.

Serialization in Distributed Systems

So far, this discussion pertains to centralized teleprocessing as much as it does to distributed processing. We can focus the discussion on distributed processing in the following way. The order of conflicting requests must mirror the order of the transactions no matter where they are processed and no matter how many times they are processed. Figure 16.10a shows a consistent, concurrent schedule of the transactions from Figure 16.8. These transactions are processed on two nodes without replication. Figure 16.10b shows a consistent concurrent schedule of these transactions where the node B data is replicated.

The discussion in the previous paragraph implies that all nodes agree on a single order for the transactions. In fact, they may not. Two nodes may each determine that its transactions should be next. As you will see, this situation creates other problems; to solve

---

[8]Philip A. Bernstein and Nathan Goodman, "Concurrency Control in Distributed Database Systems," *Computing Surveys* 13(June 1981), 185–221.

FIGURE 16.9

Consistent, nonserial schedule of
T_1, T_2, T_3, T_4

$r_3 (N_W)$
$r_1 (N_A)$
$r_3 (N_B)$
$w_3 (N_W)$
$r_4 (N_W)$
$w_1 (N_A)$
$w_3 (N_B)$
$r_2 (N_A)$
$r_4 (N_B)$
$w_2 (N_A)$
$r_4 (N_A)$

FIGURE 16.10

Examples of distributed consistent
schedules

Node Storing A & B Data	Node Storing W Data
$r_1 (N_A)$	
$r_3 (N_B)$	$r_3 (N_W)$
$w_3 (N_B)$	$w_3 (N_W)$
$w_1 (N_A)$	$r_4 (N_W)$
$r_2 (N_A)$	
$r_4 (N_B)$	
$w_2 (N_A)$	
$r_4 (N_A)$	

a. Consistent concurrent schedule of
T_1, T_2, T_3, T_4 on two nodes

Node Storing A & B Data	Node Storing B & W Data
$r_1 (N_A)$	
$r_3 (N_B)$	$r_3 (N_W)$
$w_3 (N_B)$	$w_3 (N_B)$
$w_1 (N_A)$	$w_3 (N_W)$
$r_2 (N_A)$	$r_4 (N_W)$
$r_4 (N_B)$	
$w_2 (N_A)$	
$r_4 (N_A)$	

b. Consistent schedule with replicated data

them, at times it will be necessary to abort a transaction in progress and back out its changes.

The fundamental theorem formalizes the objectives of concurrency control mechanisms. Somehow, these mechanisms must ensure that conflicting requests are processed in the order of the transactions that generate them. There are many ways in which the requirements of this fundamental theorem could be met. We consider one in the next section.

CONCURRENCY CONTROL USING DISTRIBUTED TWO-PHASE LOCKING

The most common method of enforcing the constraints of the fundamental theorem of serialization is called **distributed two-phase locking.** Using this method, DTMs are required to hold locks before reading and writing data. Specifically, before reading a data item, the DTM must have been granted a read lock by the DBM from which the data is read. Before updating a data item, a DTM must have been granted a write lock from every DBM that stores that data item.

Growing and Shrinking Phases

Locks are granted with the following restrictions. A read lock may be granted as long as no other transaction holds a write lock on the data item. A write lock may be granted as long as no other transaction has a lock, of either type, on the data item. Thus, read locks may be shared with reads but not writes, and write locks may not be shared at all. (If a lock cannot be granted, the transaction is placed into a wait state until either the lock is granted or the transaction is aborted.) Finally, once a DTM releases a lock, it may never be granted another lock. It can only release locks from that point.

The term *two-phase* arises from this last restriction. Eswaran et al.[9] proved that the read and write locks described will generate consistent schedules if and only if transactions process in two phases. During the first phase, they are allowed to acquire locks but may not release any. This is called the growing phase. As soon as a transaction releases a lock, a point called the **locked point,** transactions enter the shrinking phase. During this second phase, transactions may release locks but may not acquire them.

If locks are held until the transaction issues an END or similar request, then the growing phase is the entire length of the transaction. The shrinking phase occurs after the END is issued. This processing method, described for DB2 in Chapter 11, meets the two-phase restriction. In fact, it is more restrictive than necessary. By Eswaran's proof, processing can continue after the locked point; the only limit is that no more locks can be granted. Holding all locks until the commit point and then releasing them is thus sufficient but not necessary for the production of consistent schedules.

[9]K. P. Eswaran, J. N. Gray, R. A. Lorie, and I. L. Traiger, "The Notion of Consistency and Predicate Locks in a Database System," *Communications of the ACM* 19(November 1976) 624–633.

Distributed Locking

For distributed databases, each DBM must include a subsystem that grants and releases locks. Furthermore, the DTMs must be programmed to incorporate the rules we described. The DTM can issue a read request as soon as it obtains a single read lock. It must, however, obtain write locks from all nodes that store the data item before it issues the write commands.

To understand distributed locking, consider the cases of read-write conflict, write-read conflict, and write-write conflict.

For read-write conflict, suppose a data item, A, resides on nodes X, Y, and Z, and that transaction T_5 holds a read lock for A on X. If another transaction, say T_6, wants to update A, it must obtain a write lock for A on X, Y, and Z. The DBMs on Y and Z will issue the lock without delay. The DBM on X will not grant the lock, however, until T_5 finishes. Thus, read-write conflicts are avoided.

Now consider write-read. Suppose T_6 holds a write lock for A on X, Y, and Z. If T_7 wants to read A, it will need to obtain a read lock on one of X, Y, or Z. None of the DBMs on these nodes will grant the lock, however, until T_6 releases the locks. Thus, write-read conflicts are avoided.

Finally, consider write-write conflicts. Suppose T_8 holds a write lock for A on X, Y, and Z, and T_9 wants to update A. T_9 must wait until all of the write locks have been released and it obtains a write lock for A on X, Y, and Z. Thus, write-write conflicts are avoided.

To show that this strategy generates consistent schedules, it is also necessary to show that the order of locks remains the same as for a serial schedule. This is done in the Eswaran proof, and it is what gives rise to the need for the growing and shrinking phases.

DISTRIBUTED DEADLOCK PROCESSING

The disadvantage of controlling concurrency with locking is that deadlock can result. Figure 16.11 shows a deadlock situation among three transactions running on three different nodes, A, B, and W. Each node holds a data item, N, which is a count of the

FIGURE 16.11
Distributed deadlock example

Node A	Node B	Node W
$r_1 (N_A)$	$r_2 (N_B)$	$r_3 (N_W)$
$r_1 (N_B)$	$r_2 (N_W)$	$r_3 (N_A)$
$w_1 (N_A)$-Wait	$w_2 (N_B)$-Wait	$w_3 (N_W)$-Wait

FIGURE 16.12
Example of wait-for graph

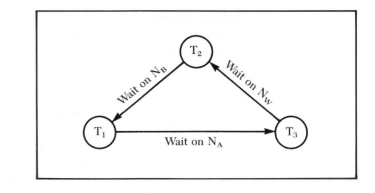

number of units of something in inventory at that site. T_1 is attempting to transfer units from A to B, T_2 is attempting to transfer units from B to W, and T_3 is attempting to transfer units from W to A.

To make the transfer, each transaction first reads the data at the two sites involved. T_1, for example, reads both N_A and N_B. Before reading, it obtains a read lock on these two items. When T_1 attempts to write N_A, it must obtain a write lock on it. It must wait, however, because T_3 holds a read lock on that data item.

If you examine the locks carefully, you will find that T_1 is waiting on T_3, T_3 is waiting on T_2, and T_2 is waiting on T_1. This situation is diagrammed in the wait-for graph in Figure 16.12. In this graph, the nodes (circles) represent transactions and the edges (lines connecting the circles) represent waits. A **deadlock** situation exists whenever there is a cycle or path from a node back to itself.

As with centralized processing, there are two fundamental strategies for dealing with deadlock. One is to be careful in the placement of locks and disallow waiting that can lead to a deadlock situation. This strategy is called **deadlock prevention.** The second strategy is to place locks without restriction, but then to detect deadlock when it occurs. This strategy is called **deadlock detection.**

Deadlock Prevention

With deadlock prevention schemes, the lock managers in the DBMs are careful in allowing waiting to occur. When a transaction, T_i, attempts to place a lock that conflicts with a lock held by a second transaction, T_j, the lock manager evaluates the situation and does not allow waiting if the potential for deadlock exists.

If there is such potential, the lock manager can either deny T_i's request, or it can abort T_j and approve the request. If the request is denied, the strategy is called **nonpreemptive.** In this case, T_i must be aborted and restarted. If T_j is aborted, the strategy is called **preemptive.** In this case, T_j is restarted.

There are several varieties of both strategies. The simplest nonpreemptive strategy is not to allow waiting at all. If a transaction, T_i, requests a lock that conflicts with a lock held by another transaction, it is automatically aborted and restarted. This strategy simplifies lock processing but causes many restarts.

Another strategy is to assign priorities to transactions and to allow the transaction with the higher priority to have precedence. Thus, when T_i requests a lock on a resource held by T_j, the response will be nonpreemptive if the priority of T_i is less than or equal to T_j; it will be preemptive otherwise. As with all types of priority scheduling, there is the danger that low priority transactions will never be allowed to complete.

A third strategy considers the age of transactions. Each transaction is assigned a unique birth time. When a lock conflict arises, the relative ages are considered. In **wait-die** strategy, when T_i requests a lock on data held by T_j, T_i is allowed to wait if it is younger than T_j. Otherwise it is aborted. This is a nonpreemptive strategy.

Wound-wait is a preemptive strategy. Here, when T_i requests a lock on data held by T_j, if T_i is older than T_j, T_i is allowed to wait. Otherwise T_j is preempted and restarted. In both cases, it is important that transactions keep their original birth time when they are restarted.

As with centralized database processing, it is also possible to prevent deadlock by having transactions request all locks in an agreed on order. This restriction violates concurrency transparency, however, because it forces application programmers to consider concurrency issues when developing programs.

Deadlock Detection

With deadlock detection strategies, waiting is allowed without restriction. All lock requests are accepted; if locks conflict, transactions are allowed to wait.

There are two major ways in which deadlock is detected. One involves time-outs. Transactions are allowed to wait a certain period of time for a resource to be freed. When the waiting time exceeds this amount, deadlock is presumed to exist, and one of the transactions involved in the lock is aborted and restarted. One problem with this strategy is that waits can result from causes other than deadlock, especially in a distributed system. Transactions may be aborted and restarted unnecessarily.

The second approach for detecting deadlock is more precise. With it, wait-for graphs like the one in Figure 16.12 are constructed. The graphs are searched for cycles. If cycles are found, a deadlock exists and one or more transactions are aborted and restarted. Data structures for representing graphs and algorithms for identifying cycles are well-known.[10]

The problem with identifying cycles in a distributed database, however, is that wait-for graphs require knowledge of all locks in the distributed system. No single lock manager possesses all of this data. Several methods exist to provide it. In one method, a particular node is identified as the global deadlock detector. All lock managers periodically send their lock data to this global lock manager. This node constructs the global wait-for graph and determines if deadlocks exist. If they do, it causes appropriate transactions to be terminated and restarted. See Bernstein and Goodman[11] for a summary of other deadlock detection schemes.

---

[10]A. V. Aho, E. Hopcroft, and J. D. Ullman, *The Design and Analysis of Computer Programs* (Reading, Mass.: Addison-Wesley, 1975).

[11]Philip A. Bernstein and Nathan Goodman, "Concurrency Control in Distributed Database Systems," *Computing Surveys* 13(June 1981), 185–221.

CONCURRENCY CONTROL IN R°

To date, the best known and most successful lock processing DDBMS is R°, an operational, prototype implementation developed by the IBM Almaden Research Center. It supports distributed partitioned databases but no redundancy. Concurrency is controlled by distributed two-phase locking. No attempt is made to prevent deadlock. Instead, deadlock is detected by algorithms on the distributed nodes.

In R°, each node is responsible for determining its own local deadlocks. There is no global deadlock detector. Instead, deadlock detection is shared among the nodes. Nodes are programmed to detect the possibility of a global deadlock and to send lock information to nodes that are managing transactions that may be blocked. Further, each node also has the responsibility of processing potential global lock data that is sent to it. Proponents of R° assert that the algorithm is such that only a single node will detect a particular global deadlock. When detected, only local transactions are aborted.

Failure Transparency

The fourth goal for a DDBMS is to provide transparency to failure. As we have seen, failures arise from a variety of sources. Sane nodes fail predictably. Insane nodes fail unpredictably and can broadcast validly formatted but inappropriate actions. Malicious, Byzantine-type failures are caused by nodes that intend to deceive.

In this discussion we will assume the easiest type of failure. In particular, we assume that nodes are not only *sane* but also that when they fail, they do nothing at all. Insane nodes and Byzantine-type failure are beyond the scope of this discussion.

Additionally, we will assume that the distributed system is partitioned cleanly. If node A is unable to communicate with node B, we assume that node B is unable to communicate with node A as well.

As stated previously, failure transparency should provide *atomic* transactions. Either all of a transaction should be processed or none of it should. Further, once committed, the effects of a transaction should be permanent.

In reality, such atomicity cannot be reached in all cases, even for sane failures. If too much of the network fails, or if critical portions fail at critical times, then recovery with guaranteed atomicity may not be possible. The recovery manager of SDD-1, a prototype DDBMS, recognizes this fact with the definition of system **catastrophes.**[12] Catastrophes occur when too many components fail. Recovery from a catastrophe requires manual intervention and may result in a database containing fragments of transactions.

The discussion in this section assumes that a log is kept of transaction activities so that it is possible to back out a transaction any time prior to the commit point. Also, at times it is important that the DDBMS be guaranteed that a log record will survive a failure. In these cases, we will use the term *force-write*. This term means that the DDBMS issues

---

[12]M. Hammer and D. Shipman, "Reliability Mechanisms for SDD-1: A System for Distributed Databases," *Transactions on Database Systems* 5(December 1980), 431–466.

FIGURE 16.13
Inconsistency generated by
inopportune node failure

r_1 (X_A) - with read lock on X_A
r_2 (Y_D) - with read lock on Y_D
A fails
D fails
W_1 (Y_C) - with write lock on
            available copies of Y
W_2 (X_B) - with write lock on
            available copies of X
A recovers
D recovers
Database is now inconsistent

the write command and waits for the operating system to confirm that the record has been written to nonvolatile storage before continuing.

NEED FOR DIRECTORY MANAGEMENT

In a distributed database, each DTM maintains a directory of the location(s) of data items. The processing of these directories is crucial, particularly in a system with replication. To understand why, consider the situation shown in Figure 16.13.

This distributed replicated database has four nodes, labeled A–D. Data item X is stored on nodes A and B, and item Y is stored on nodes C and D. Transaction 1 reads the copy of X on A (first obtaining a read lock), and transaction 2 reads the copy of Y on D (also with a read lock). Then node A fails followed by node D. Next transaction 1 writes Y on all nodes that contain Y. To do so, it must first obtain a write lock on those nodes. The only such node is C, since node D has failed. Consequently, transaction 1 is able to write Y, even though transaction 2 has a read lock on it. Similarly, transaction 2 writes X on all nodes that contain X. The only such node is B, since node A has failed. Hence transaction 2 obtains a write lock on B, and writes X on B, even though transaction 1 has a write lock on it.

When nodes A and D subsequently recover, the database is in an inconsistent state. The values of X differ on nodes A and B and the values of Y differ on nodes C and D.

The inconsistency arose because the transaction managers were unable to detect locks held by failed nodes. The situation can be correctly processed if the directories are themselves subject to careful locking procedures. Such procedures are presented in a discussion of the **available copies algorithm.**[13] (This reference is also the source of this example.)

A discussion of this algorithm is beyond the scope of this text. You should be aware of this type of anomaly, however, when you review DDBMS products.

---

[13]Philip A. Bernstein and Nathan Goodman, "An Algorithm for Concurrency Control and Recovery in Replicated Distributed Databases," *Transactions on Database Systems* 9(December 1984), 596–615.

COMMITMENT IN DISTRIBUTED DATABASE SYSTEMS

In nondistributed systems, transaction atomicity is accomplished by delaying changes to the database until the transaction is committed or aborted. For distributed systems, committing data changes is more complicated.

The Commitment Problem in Distributed Systems

To begin, consider the following generic summary of the distributed commitment process: Every transaction is allocated a private workspace during its processing. As the transaction progresses, updates are made in the private workspace, but they are not committed to the database. When the transaction finishes, if all nodes holding updates for the transaction are able to commit them to their respective databases, then the changes are made. Otherwise the transaction and all of its changes are aborted.

Consider a distributed system like that shown in Figure 16.1. When a DTM issues an update request to a DBM, the DBM places the updated data in a private workspace that it maintains for that transaction. (For the first such update action, it creates the private workspace.) The DBM does not write the update in the database, however. If a DTM issues a read request for a data item that the transaction has changed, the DBM provides the updated value from the private workspace. This much is straightforward. When, however, the transaction finishes, and the DTM sends out commit actions, a complication arises.

Suppose three DBMs hold changes in behalf of a particular transaction. What if in the process of committing, one of them discovers that it cannot commit its changes? Unless something is done, only two of three of the DBMs will update their databases. Clearly, this result is unacceptable.

Two-phase Commitment

To solve this problem, distributed commitment is broken into a two-stage process called **two-phase commitment.**[14] With this method, the DTM that is processing a transaction first sends out a pre-commit action to all DBMs holding updated data for that transaction. This pre-commit action informs the DBMs that the transaction is finished, and it asks the DBMs to respond YES or NO, according to whether or not they can commit the changes on data they store. If all DBMs respond YES, then the DTM sends out a commit action; otherwise the DBM issues an abort action to all DBMs and restarts the transaction.

When a DBM receives the pre-commit action, it ensures that it can make the changes (depending on the form of concurrency control involved, the DBM may be unable to make the changes—resolution of deadlock is a case in point). If the DBM can make the

---

[14]Observe that the standard vocabulary of database technology includes both the terms *two-phase commitment* and *two-phase locking.* Do not confuse these terms. Two-phase commitment pertains only to distributed database processing. Two-phase locking pertains to both distributed and nondistributed database processing.

FIGURE 16.14
Summary of two-phase commit

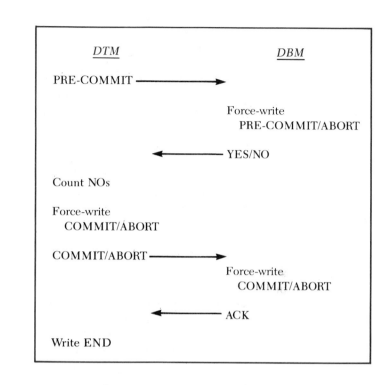

changes, then it force-writes log records saying that it can commit the changes. These changes are not written to the database, however. Next, the node responds YES to the DTM. Finally, when the DTM issues the commit action, the DBM updates the database.

This discussion does not consider cases in which either the DTM or the DBMs fail after the pre-commit action is accepted by the DBM. To understand what happens in this case, we need to be more specific. To do this, consider the example situation in Figure 16.14 (adapted from an article by Mohan, Lindsay, and Obermarck).[15] In studying this example, recall that a transaction can be committed only if all DBMs involved are able to commit. A NO vote by any DBM is a veto.

Two-phase Commit Processing Without Failure

When the DBM receives the pre-commit action, it determines whether it can commit the transaction. If it can, it force-writes a PRE-COMMIT record on the log and sends a YES message back to the DTM. If the DBM is unable to commit the transaction, it force-writes an ABORT record on the log and sends a NO message. If it sends a NO, the DBM is guaranteed that the transaction will be aborted, and it can therefore forget about that transaction.

---

[15]C. Mohan, B. Lindsay, and R. Obermarck, "Transaction Management in the R* Distributed Database Management System," *Transactions on Database Systems* 11(December 1986), 378–396.

When the DTM has received responses from all DBMs, it examines the votes. If any node responded NO, then the DTM force-writes an ABORT record in its log, aborts the transaction, and sends ABORT actions to all DBMs that voted YES (it need not send actions to those which voted NO because they have already assumed the transaction will fail). If all DBMs voted YES, then the DTM force-writes a COMMIT record to its log and sends COMMIT actions to all DBMs.

If the DBMs receive an ABORT action, they force-write ABORT records on their logs and abort the transaction. If the DBMs receive a COMMIT action, they force-write COMMIT records on their logs and commit the transaction. In either case, the DBMs send an acknowledgment to the ABORT or COMMIT action sent by the DTM.

Once the DTM receives ACKs from all DBMs, it writes an END record in its log and forgets the transaction.

Two-phase Commit Processing Under Failure

Now consider what happens when either the DTM or a DBM fails at various points in this process. If a DBM fails and, during recovery, finds part of a transaction in its log, with neither a PRE-COMMIT nor an ABORT record, then it can ignore that transaction. The node failed in the middle of the transaction, and therefore the DTM cannot have received a YES from this node. The transaction will have been aborted. If it finds an ABORT record in its log, it can ignore the transaction for similar reasons.

If the DBM finds a PRE-COMMIT record without a COMMIT, then it does not know what to do. It knows that it voted YES, but it does not know the outcome of the vote by other DBMs. Therefore, in this case, the DBM must ask the DTM for information about this transaction. Once it receives a response (whether an ABORT or COMMIT) from the DTM, it can process as under normal conditions. Finally, if the DBM finds both PRE-COMMIT and COMMIT records in the log, then it knows the transaction should have been committed, and it ensures that it was by applying after images as described in Chapter 14.

Now consider DTM failures. If the DTM fails before sending any PRE-COMMIT actions, it aborts the transaction. It knows that all DBMs will (eventually) abort it as well, so it need take no other action. (Here, by the way, is a case of something falling through the crack between failure/recovery issues and concurrency control issues. There may be locks on data items on the DBMs. Those locks will stay in place until either a deadlock situation forces the DBM to abort the transaction, until the DBM fails and its recovery processor notices the incompleted transaction, or until a utility program cleans up the log. It would be better for the DTM to send ABORT actions for such a transaction during recovery so that DBMs can release their locks. There is nothing in the **failure processing** algorithm, however, that necessitates this.)

If the DTM finds a COMMIT record in its log with no corresponding END, then it failed before all of the acknowledgments were received, and it periodically sends COMMIT actions to the DBMs that did not acknowledge. Once it receives all such acknowledgments, it writes the END to the log. If the DTM finds an ABORT record in its log with no corresponding END, then it sends ABORT actions to all DBMs that have not acknowledged and writes an END to the log.

Review Figure 16.14 and ensure that you understand how this algorithm provides transaction atomicity with regard to these types of failure. In actuality, the situation is somewhat more complicated than described here, but this discussion should give you the gist of two-phased commitment. If you consider that failures can occur in the middle of failure recovery, and that, especially for replicated data, directory processing needs to be considered as well, you can can begin to sense how difficult failure transparency can be. See Mohan, Lindsay, and Obermarck[16] for more information about two-phased commitment.

CONSISTENCY IN PARTITIONED NETWORKS

The final failure issue we will consider concerns distributed database processing in partitioned networks. A **partition** is a subnetwork that is created when nodes become disconnected due to node or communication line failure. Figure 16.15a shows a distributed network; Figure 16.15b shows the network that is broken into two partitions because of a failure of node E.

When a partition occurs, if data is not replicated, then the consequences, though undesired, are straightforward. A transaction can operate if all of the data it reads and writes is located on nodes in the partition in which the transaction is initiated. Otherwise, the transaction must wait until the network is recovered. For the example in Figure 16.15b, transactions initiated in Partition I can run if the data they read and write is located on nodes A, B, C, or D. Transactions initiated in Partition II can run if the data they read and write is located on nodes F, G, or H.

As mentioned earlier, organizations often choose to replicate data to increase reliability and performance. When data is replicated, processing during a partition must be carefully controlled, and recovery is considerably more difficult. If the network in Figure 16.15 supports order entry, and if inventory data is stored in both partitions, then it would be possible to sell the same last item to two different customers. Furthermore, once the network is recovered, the two separately processed collections of inventory data must be combined to produce a single, consistent collection.

CORRECTNESS VERSUS AVAILABILITY IN PARTITIONED NETWORKS

A wide variety of anomalies can occur when processing replicated data in a partitioned network. Figure 16.16 illustrates two of them. In the first example, nodes A and H, in two different partitions, both sell diamond necklaces. They begin with the same count of four. Node A sells three necklaces while node H sells two to one customer and one to a

[16]C. Mohan, B. Lindsay, and R. Obermarck, "Transaction Management in the R° Distributed Database Management System," *Transactions on Database Systems* 11(December 1986), 378–396.

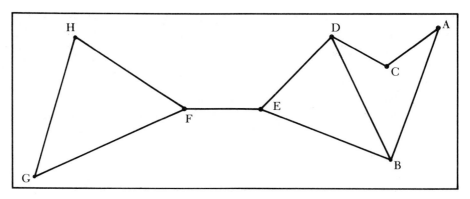

a. Sample distributed network

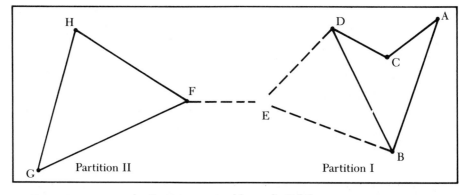

b. Partitions caused by node E failure

FIGURE 16.15
Sample partitions

second customer. At the point of recovery, the records in both nodes indicate there is one necklace remaining. In fact, a total of six necklaces were sold when only four were available to begin. Further, at recovery, A and H have the same item count. This example shows the recovery process must do more than ensure that data items from separate partitions have the same value.

In the second example, processing in two partitions violates a constraint. A customer's credit limit is $5000, and starting balance is $4500. Node A sells the customer $400 worth of goods and node H sells the customer $300. After recovery, the customer's balance is $5200, $200 in excess of the credit limit.

[17]S. B. Davidson, H. Garcia-Molina, and D. Skeen, "Consistency in Partitioned Networks," *Computing Surveys* 17(September 1985), 341–370.

FIGURE 16.16
Anomalies due to partitions

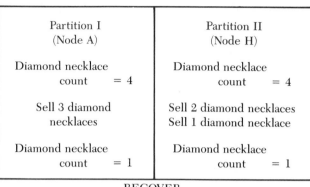

Partition I (Node A)	Partition II (Node H)
Diamond necklace count = 4	Diamond necklace count = 4
Sell 3 diamond necklaces	Sell 2 diamond necklaces Sell 1 diamond necklace
Diamond necklace count = 1	Diamond necklace count = 1

RECOVER

a. Update anomaly due to partition

Partition I (Node A)	Partition II (Node H)
Cust 100 credit limit = $5000	Cust 100 credit limit = $5000
Cust 100 balance = $4500	Cust 100 balance = $4500
Sell $400 of goods to Cust 100	Sell $300 of goods to Cust 100
Cust 100 balance = $4900	Cust 100 balance = $4800

RECOVER:
Recompute Cust 100 balance = $5200

b. Constraint violation due to partition

As Davidson, Garcia-Molina, and Skeen[17] have pointed out, processing in partitioned networks involves a trade-off between the poles of correctness and availability. Absolute correctness is easiest to provide if no processing of replicated data is allowed during a partition. One could argue, however, that in that case, why bother to replicate the data at all? Improved performance during nonpartitions would be the only reason.

On the other extreme, availability is greatest if no restrictions are made on the processing of replicated data during partitions. For some applications, this is feasible. Since airlines overbook flights, what difference does it make if occasionally, during partitions, the same seat is sold to different customers? Both the airlines and the passengers prefer high availability of reservations data to absolute correctness. The world banking system takes a different attitude on this matter, however. Once again we come back to the need for an understanding of system requirements.

FIGURE 16.17
Precedence graph combined for
two partitions

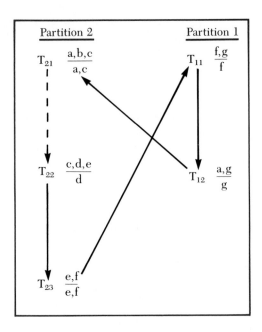

STRATEGIES FOR PROCESSING PARTITIONED REPLICATED DATA

Many different strategies have been proposed for the processing of replicated data in partitioned networks. The article just cited (by Davidson, Garcia-Molina, and Skeen) provides an excellent survey of many. Here we will discuss one of the leading strategies called the **optimistic protocol.**

This strategy uses graphs (like the wait-for graphs in Figure 16.12) to keep track of dependencies among data changes. While the network is partitioned, changes are allowed without restriction (hence the name *optimistic*), and **precedence graphs** are kept that indicate which transactions have read and written which data. During recovery, the graphs of all partitions are combined and analyzed. If inconsistencies have developed, some transactions are rolled back and their changes eliminated.

Figure 16.17 shows an example of a combined precedence graph involving two partitions (this figure is adapted from Figure 5 in another Davidson article[18]). The meaning of this figure is as follows: T_{ij} is transaction number j running in partition number i. The dotted arrows indicate that a transaction wrote a data item that was read by a subsequent transaction. A solid arrow indicates that a transaction read a data item that was later changed by another transaction. The data items read by a transaction are above the line next to the transaction; the items written are shown below that line. Thus, T_{11} read items f and g and wrote item f.

---

[18]S. B. Davidson, "Optimism and Consistency in Partitioned Distributed Database Systems," *Transactions on Database Systems* 9(September 1984), 456–482.

Davidson has proved that the database is consistent if and only if there are no cycles in the precedence graph. The graph in Figure 16.17 contains cycles (arrows that come back to a node) and therefore this database will be inconsistent. There are actually several inconsistencies here. For one, T_{11} reads an old value of data item f. The item had been changed by T_{23} but T_{11} was unaware of the change because of the partition in the network.

The strength of this strategy is its robustness. It will detect all inconsistencies, and there is sufficient data available to be able to correct the database via rollback.

There are two important disadvantages, however. For one, logs must be kept of all read and write activity. Although Davidson does not say so, it would appear that many, if not all, of these log writes must be forced. This need will generate a significant performance problem.

Second, roll back completed, committed transactions violate transaction atomicity. With this strategy, committed changes are not necessarily permanent. For the data in Figure 16.17, T_{22} may need to be rolled back after real outputs have been generated by the transaction. Customers may have been promised diamond necklaces that cannot be delivered. The fact that the customer will later receive an apology and explanation that the necklace did not exist at the time of the sale may not be much consolation.

In spite of these disadvantages, the optimistic protocol strategy shows promise for networks that require consistent and correct processing in spite of partitions in the network.

Summary

Distributed database processing is database processing in which the execution of transactions and the retrieval and updating of data occur across two or more independent and usually geographically separated computers. The distributed DBMS (DDBMS) consists of the collection of distributed transaction managers (DTMs) and database managers (DBMs) on all computers. The DTMs receive processing requests and translate them into actions for the DBMs. Coordination and control are important DTM functions. The DBMs process some portion of the distributed database in accordance with action requests from the DTMs.

Advantages of distributed database processing are better performance, increased reliability, more readily sized to requirements, and tailored to organization structures. Disadvantages are worse performance, reduced reliability, increased complexity, high construction and maintenance costs, and difficulty in control. The character, capabilities, and performance of distributed systems depend on the hardware used, the functionality of the DDBMS, the degree of data replication, the types of procedures, and the tasks required of the users of the system.

Four goals for a DDBMS are location, replication, concurrency, and failure transparency. In theory, location and replication transparency are not too difficult to provide. The problems of concurrency and failure transparency are more difficult; robust solutions are only beginning to be found, even in theory. Robust practical solutions do not yet exist.

The control of concurrent processing for distributed database systems is a difficult problem. If processing is not controlled, problems such as the lost update and inconsistent read anomalies can occur. Distributed processing transactions need to be processed in such a manner that nonserial, concurrent executions of transactions have the same impact on the database as serial, nonconcurrent executions would have.

For both distributed and nondistributed processing, transactions must lock resources in a two-phased process. During the first phase, the growing phase, locks are acquired. As soon as the first lock is released, the growing phase is terminated and no more locks can be acquired. Releasing all locks at the end of a transaction meets this criterion but is more restrictive than necessary.

Distributed systems perform locking using a distributed two-phase locking strategy. Distributed deadlock can occur; it must either be prevented or resolved by aborting one of the transactions. R° is a prototype DDBMS developed by IBM that implements distributed two-phase locking.

Failure transparency is difficult to provide. For one, there are too many types of failure. Limited transparency can be provided for sane node failures. Data directories must be part of the locking and recovery mechanisms for distributed failure/recovery.

Update commitment is more complicated for distributed than for nondistributed processing. The commit process must be broken into two phases. During the first phase, nodes declare the ability to commit. During the second phase, they perform actions to commit. Two-phased commit processing must include forced writes and acknowledgment between nodes.

A network is partition if it is broken into two or more pieces by a failure of some type. Processing in partitioned networks can create integrity problems. Correctness and availability are trade-offs in a partitioned network. One strategy for providing integrity in partitioned networks uses precedence graphs. This strategy may at times require that committed transactions be de-committed, which is undesirable, but at present, unavoidable, at least for this type of processing.

GROUP I QUESTIONS

16.1 Define *distributed database processing*.

16.2 Describe the difference between a DBMS and a DDBMS. Explain how it is possible for a DDBMS to contain DBMS products.

16.3 What is the function of the distributed transaction manager?

16.4 What is the function of the database manager?

16.5 Define *node, transaction node,* and *database node*.

16.6 Explain the difference between a request and an action.

16.7 Summarize the advantages of distributed database processing.

16.8   Summarize the disadvantages of distributed database processing.

16.9   Explain how the choice of node hardware affects the character of the distributed system. Show two alternative systems that conform to the design in Figure 16.1. Use Figure 16.4 as an example.

16.10   Explain the difference between a DTM that is provided as part of a DDBMS and a DTM that is developed in-house.

16.11   Define the terms *nonreplicated, partially replicated,* and *fully replicated* databases.

16.12   Explain how processing rights can vary from one distributed system to another.

16.13   How does the degree of data currency affect the design of a distributed database system?

16.14   Discuss the difference in control philosophies between the systems in Figure 16.4a and 16.4b.

16.15   Explain this statement: "The less sophisticated the DDBMS, the greater the role that must be taken by people."

16.16   Define and describe *location transparency.*

16.17   Define and describe *replication transparency.*

16.18   Define and describe *concurrency transparency.*

16.19   Define and describe *failure transparency.*

16.20   What is a sane node?

16.21   Define and give an example of the *lost update anomaly.*

16.22   Define and give an example of the *inconsistent read anomaly.*

16.23   What is a serial execution? What is an execution of transactions that is equivalent to a serial execution?

16.24   Describe and explain the two conditions required for two executions to be equivalent.

16.25   Define *read-write, write-read,* and *write-write* conflict.

16.26   Define *schedule, serial schedule,* and *consistent schedule.*

16.27   Summarize the processing of two-phase locking.

16.28   Give an example of a distributed deadlock.

16.29   What are the two primary means of dealing with distributed deadlock?

16.30   Explain the meaning of the wait-for graph in Figure 16.12.

16.31   Explain the processing problem depicted in Figure 16.13.

16.32 Why is it necessary to break distributed commitment into two phases?

16.33 Explain the commit processing illustrated in Figure 16.14.

16.34 Define *partitioned network*.

16.35 Explain the problems illustrated in Figure 16.16.

16.36 Explain how processing in partitioned networks involves a trade-off between correctness and availability.

16.37 How can a precedence graph be used to determine if the processing of a partitioned database is consistent?

GROUP II QUESTIONS

16.38 Contact a corporation that has installed a distributed database system. Interview the developers and users. Map the system components into the architecture of Figure 16.1. Did the company procure a DDBMS or did it assemble the equivalent of a DDBMS from other software components? What software serves the role of the DTMs? of the DBMs? Identify the components of the distributed system. What has the company's experience been? What problems and pitfalls have been encountered? What were important factors that lead to successes?

16.39 Contact a vendor of a commercial DDBMS. What hardware does the system operate with? Map the architecture of the DDBMS into the scheme in Figure 16.1. What components are the DTMs? What components are the DBMs? What claims does the vendor make regarding location, replication, concurrency, and failure transparency? How does the product control concurrent processing? Is two-phase locking used? If not, what technique is employed? What failure/recovery mechanisms are used? Is two-phase commit employed? What happens when the network is partitioned? Determine the number of installations of the product, and, if possible, the number of actual systems in use. What factors does the vendor believe lead to success? What problems and pitfalls are the most serious?

File Organization

Computer data is stored on peripherals called secondary storage devices. These storage devices can be divided into two broad categories: sequential and direct access. Sequential devices require that data be accessed in the sequence in which it was entered. Thus, before processing the fifth record in a sequential file, a program would first need to access the first, second, third, and fourth records. Direct access storage devices allow a program to access any record directly without accessing any preceding or succeeding records.

Sequential devices such as tape units and keyboards do not have a significant impact on database applications. They are used, for example, for obtaining instructions or for archiving database data. But the database itself, including application data, overhead data, and meta-data, is stored on direct access storage devices, typically on disk.

In this appendix we will describe various formats used to store data on direct access storage devices. We will also examine various means of processing disk files. This background may help you understand better how a DBMS works.

- DIRECT ACCESS STORAGE DEVICES
- BASIC FILE ORGANIZATIONS

Direct Access Storage Devices

The most common type of direct access storage device (DASD) is conventional, or hard disk. Most such disks consist of stacks of disk surfaces that are mounted on a spindle. Other, smaller disks, such as floppy disks, consist of one disk that is written on one or two sides.

FIXED DISKS

A *fixed disk* (Figure A.1) is a set of disk surfaces mounted on a spindle and enclosed inside a disk unit. Such devices are sometimes called a *disk pack* or *disk tower*. In some computer systems the fixed disks are permanently installed. This is usually the case for personal computers, for example. In other cases, the fixed disks can be removed from the disk unit. Removable, fixed disks are found on minicomputers and mainframes.

With a disk, data is recorded in concentric circles, or *tracks*. The number of surfaces on a disk pack as well as the number of tracks on a recording surface depend on the type of disk. For example, the IBM 3350, a disk unit used with older IBM systems, has 16 disks per pack, 30 surfaces per pack (the top and bottom surfaces are not used), and 555 tracks per recording surface.

Data is read from or written to a disk by read/write heads. In most disk units, the heads are attached to access arms that can move to position the heads at any track on the recording surface of a disk. When the access arms are fixed in a position, data can be read from or written to one track on each recording surface. The collection of these tracks is called a *cylinder*. Note that the 3350 has 555 cylinders, and each cylinder has 30 tracks. A disk pack and read/write heads of a smaller disk unit are shown in Figure A.1.

Not all disk units have movable read/write heads. Some units have fixed heads. Fixed-head units have one read/write head per cylinder and consequently are more expensive than movable-head units of a similar size. They may be faster, however, because no time is spent moving the read/write heads to the correct track. Some disk devices even have a combination of fixed heads on some cylinders and movable heads on others.

OTHER DIRECT ACCESS HARDWARE

In addition to conventional, hard disk storage units, three other types of direct access media are commonly used. One is called a *diskette, floppy disk*, or sometimes just *floppy*. This medium is similar to hard disk storage, but diskettes have only one disk instead of a stack of them. Further, this disk is flexible, hence the term *floppy* (Figure A.2). One or both sides of the disk can be recorded on, depending on the type of diskette.

Early diskettes were 5¼ inches across and were enclosed in a flexible case. More recent floppy disks are 3½ inches across and are enclosed in a hard plastic case. Either type of disk is processed similarly to fixed disks. There are only one or two tracks per cylinder, however.

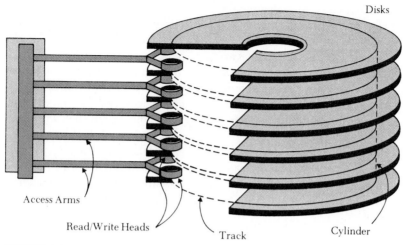

FIGURE A.1
Disk pack with access arms

FIGURE A.2
Floppy disk

Another commonly used direct access medium is CD-ROM (compact disk, read-only memory). With this medium, data is not recorded magnetically; rather it is recorded in small holes in the disk surface disk. This technology is similar to that used for stereo system compact disks. The major advantage of CD-ROMs is high capacity. Since CD-ROM devices are read only, however, they have limited use in database applications.

A number of companies have attempted to build compact disk systems that allow writing. WORM (write once, read many) devices allow for one write on a surface. Unlimited writing of compact disks is not yet possible. When such writing does become possible, compact disk technology will become more important for database applications.

Another type of DASD is actually a hybrid, or combination of tape and disk technology. It is called a *mass storage device.* Data is stored on small rolls of magnetic tape and then moved, or *staged,* to a direct access storage device when needed. After the data is processed, it is moved from disk back to the small rolls of tape.

DIRECT ACCESS DATA FORMATS

The formats of data on certain IBM DASD products are described in this section. We have chosen these devices because they are typical and because these devices are commonly used in database applications.

Key and No-key Formats

The format of data on IBM DASD depends on whether the records are written with or without keys. Here, the term *key* means an identifier that is external to the record (not embedded) and which the operating system uses to locate a particular record. Embedded keys that are not used by the operating system to access records are not included in this definition of key. We will discuss them in the section on direct file organization later in this appendix.

Figure A.3 features the no-key format. The index point is a special mark on the track that indicates the start of the track. Note that a track is a circle; the two index points shown are actually the same point. The Gs in this figure represent gaps in the data on the track that are necessary for correct timing of activities.

To illustrate the use of these gaps, suppose the control unit of the disk is searching for the start of a track. When the index point is detected, a signal is sent from the disk to the control unit; the control unit then performs certain activities and responds with a signal to the device to read the next field (home address). While these actions occur, the disk is rotating. When the disk receives the signal to read home address, the disk has already rotated past the index point. Consequently, there must be a gap between the home address and the index point. Other gaps are necessary for similar reasons. They are of different lengths, depending on the length of delay between the processing of data fields.

The home address area as well as the count and data areas of the track descriptor record are used by the system to specify the address of the track (cylinder and track numbers), whether the track is operative or defective, and if defective, which alternate

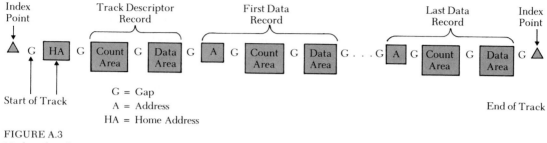

FIGURE A.3
No-key data format

track has been used as a replacement. These data fields normally concern the operating system but not its users.

The next three groups (A, count area, and data area) constitute one data record. These groups repeat on the track for each data record. The A field is a 2-byte address marker that enables the control unit to sense the beginning of a record.

The count area is pictured in detail in Figure A.4. The flag field is used by the system to indicate the condition of the track and other information used by the control unit. The cylinder number (2 bytes), head number (2 bytes), and record number (1 byte) form the unique record identifier. KL is the key length, which is always zero for the no-key data format. DL is the length of the data area that follows. The cyclic check field is used to check for errors in reading and writing.

The important concept here is that the unique record identifier and the length of the data area precede each data record. The control unit knows exactly how much data to read from the count area because the area is always 11 bytes long. It refers to the DL field in the count area to obtain the length of the data area. Thus the control unit has the length of a data area before reading it.

The data format of keyed records is very similar to that of no-key records. The only differences are that a key area precedes the data area of every data record and the key-

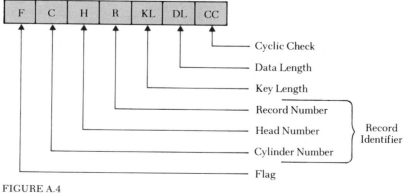

FIGURE A.4
Count area

length field in the count area is not zero. It contains the length of the key area (Figure A.5).

Fixed Block Architecture

Several years ago, vendors (notably IBM) developed a new disk type based on *fixed block architecture* (FBA). These devices do not use the record formats shown in Figures A.3 through A.5. Rather, data is stored in fixed-size containers or blocks. The IBM 3370, an example of a FBA device, stores data in 512-byte blocks. Data is packed into these fixed-size containers like furniture is packed into shipping crates.

The IBM 3370 has two sets of read/write heads per disk pack. Since these heads can operate simultaneously, data can be processed much faster. However, data that appears to the programmer to be stored contiguously (physically next to each other) may in fact be stored by the two sets of heads on completely separated parts of the disk. Thus, with these devices, a logically sequential file may not be physically sequential at all.

With traditional devices it is possible to access records by physical position. The cylinder, track, and record number can be used to identify a record. With FBA this is no longer possible. Instead, blocks are accessed by block number; this number is translated into a physical location.

Consequently, when data is stored on fixed block devices, programs have no control over the physical location of data. This lack of control can result in inefficiencies. On the other hand, separating programs from knowledge of physical data locations creates device independence. Data can be moved from one device to another without any impact on programs.

Record Blocking

As Figures A.3 through A.5 show, there is a considerable amount of overhead for each data record. One way to reduce this overhead is to make the physical records larger by grouping several logical records into one physical record. This process is called *record blocking*. For example, suppose the logical data records are 100 bytes long. Any number of them can be blocked together. If we group eight, we form a block of records 800 bytes long. Record blocking reduces the amount of overhead information per track, and consequently reduces the total amount of space for the file. It also increases the complexity of the input/output (I/O) task. Either the application program or the operating system must block records before writing them and deblock them when reading.

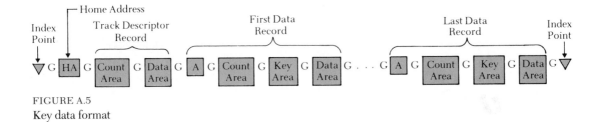

FIGURE A.5
Key data format

Basic File Organizations

A DBMS must interface with the operating system to perform I/O. More generally, any program, whether a DBMS or not, must do this. The portion of the operating system that does I/O is often referred to as the *data management access methods* (or just *access methods*). Figure A.6 shows the relationship of the operating system user (DBMS or application program), the access methods, and the secondary storage device on which data is stored.

Many access methods have been developed. Each has a particular *file organization* and *access technique* (or techniques). Strictly speaking, the file organization is the structure of the file; the access technique is the way the file structure is manipulated. Commonly, however, this distinction is not made, in which case file organization describes not only structure but also access technique. We will use the latter, more common definition.

There are three important types of file organization: sequential, indexed sequential, and direct. Sequential file processing is used by DBMS for producing log files and archive database copies. Indexed sequential files, as such, are not used by DBMSs. The *techniques* of indexed file processing, however, are used. To explain, no DBMS processes the database using the operating system's indexed sequential file organization. Many DBMSs, however, create their own version of indexed files. So, if you learn indexed sequential file processing, you will accomplish two objectives: you will learn a type of file processing, and you will learn a technique used by the DBMS itself.

Finally, direct organization, or a variant closely akin to direct organization, is used by all DBMSs to organize the database itself. Therefore, learning direct organization will help you to understand how DBMS products operate.

SEQUENTIAL FILE ORGANIZATION

Sequential file organization is the simplest of the three file organizations to be discussed. Records are written to a file in sequence. Once a sequential file is created, records can be added to the end of the file. It is not possible to insert records in the middle of the file without rewriting the file. Also, it is generally not possible to modify an existing record without rewriting the file. Records are usually read in sequence. With some systems, it is possible to start this sequential reading at any record location; there is no requirement to start at the beginning of the file.

FIGURE A.6
Access method interfaces

588

INDEXED SEQUENTIAL FILE ORGANIZATION

The indexed sequential file organization allows both sequential and random processing. Sequential processing can start at the beginning of the file or at any other record in the file. Random processing is accomplished by specifying the key-field value for the desired record. This record is found via indexes.

The following discussion presents the actions taken by the operating system. Application programs are not involved with the details that follow. Rather, the application program issues a command, for example, to read a particular record or insert a new record. Finding space, updating indexes, and so forth are all done by the operating system.

Indexed sequential files are composed of three areas. The *prime area* contains records of the file. When the file is created or reorganized, all records reside in the prime area. The second area of an indexed sequential file is the *overflow area.* Records are placed in the overflow area when additions to the file cannot be fitted into the prime area. The *indexes* are located in the third area of an indexed sequential file. These indexes are used to locate a particular record for random processing.

File Indexes

To understand the processing of an indexed sequential file, consider an example wherein four data records fit on a track. Figure A.7 shows the first five tracks of that file. Note that each record has a unique key and that records are in order by key.

Suppose it is necessary to read record 79. One way to access this record is to sequentially read the records in the file until record 79 is found. This may be a very slow process. A faster way of finding record 79 is to use the track index (Figure A.8). The track index contains the value of the highest key on each track. To locate the track that contains record 79, it is necessary only to find in the track index the first track that contains a record with a key greater than or equal to 79. In this case, that is track 4. The highest key of track 3 is 75, and the highest key of track 4 is 82. Therefore, if record 79 exists, it must

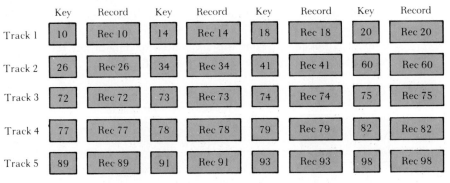

FIGURE A.7
Five tracks of an indexed sequential file

FIGURE A.8
Track index

Track Number	Highest Key on Track
1	20
2	60
3	75
4	82
5	98

be on track 4. Consequently, the next step is to read sequentially track 4 to find record 79. It is because of the combination of using an index and then reading sequentially that this access method is called indexed sequential.

Using the track index does not eliminate sequential searching; it just reduces the magnitude of the task. Instead of searching a large file of records, we are able to search a table that points toward the desired record location.

If the file is long, then it may occupy many cylinders on the disk. To increase efficiency, a *cylinder index* is used, in addition to the track indexes. This index shows the value of the highest key on each cylinder of the file. Thus, if the file occupies twenty cylinders, there will be twenty entries in the cylinder index. Now to find a given record it is necessary to search the cylinder index to determine which cylinder the record is on, then to search the track index for that cylinder to determine the proper track. Then that track is searched to find the correct record. For brevity, Figure A.9 assumes there are only five tracks per cylinder. In common practice there are more, depending on the device.

If the file is very large, searching the cylinder index might be time consuming. In this case, it might be desirable to break the cylinder into parts and create a master index on the parts of the cylinder index. For example, the cylinder index might be broken into parts having twenty entries each. The master index has the highest key in each part.

To find a particular record, it is necessary to search the master index to find the correct part of the cylinder index, then search that part of the cylinder index to locate the cylinder on which the record resides. Following that, it is necessary to search the track index for that cylinder, and then to sequentially read the track in order to find the record itself (Figure A.10).

Indexed Sequential File Processing

When an indexed sequential file is created, all records are written into the prime area in sequence by key. The indexes are generated at this time. We have already seen how records can then be retrieved from the file. The process of updating a record (sometimes referred to as *update-in-place*) is similar to the retrieval process. The indexes are used to find the desired record, and the new version of the record is written on top of the old one.

Cylinder Index

Cylinder	Highest Key
1	98
2	184
3	278
.	.
.	.
.	.

Track Index for Cylinder 1

Track	Highest Key
1	20
2	60
3	75
4	82
5	98

Track Index for Cylinder 2

Track	Highest Key
1	107
2	122
3	148
4	163
5	184

Track Index for Cylinder 3

Track	Highest Key
1	201
2	210
3	223
4	259
5	278

Assume desired record has key value 248.

1. Search cylinder index to find correct cylinder. Cylinder 2 has highest key of 184; cylinder 3 has 278. Therefore, cylinder 3 must contain the record.

2. Search track index for cylinder 3 to find track. Track 3 has highest key of 223; track 4 has 259. Therefore, track 4 must contain the record.

3. Search track 4 for the desired record.

FIGURE A.9
Search of cylinder and track indexes

A deletion from the file is also straightforward. The indexes are used to find the desired record, and a special mark is inserted into the record to indicate that it has been deleted. Even though the record may be physically present, subsequent attempts to read the record will result in an error. The program that performs the access must check for the special mark that indicates deletion.

Insertions to an indexed sequential file are quite troublesome because the key order of the file must be maintained. To illustrate, assume that it is necessary to insert record 55 into the file depicted in Figure A.7. The only way that key sequence can be preserved is for record 55 to replace record 60 on the file. But what happens to record 60? Clearly it is undesirable to put 60 on top of 72, put 72 on top of 73, and so on, completely rewriting the remainder of the file. The answer is that record 60 is put into an overflow area and pointers are set up to ensure that record 60 can be found during subsequent processing. Doing this requires extension to the track index. If we compare Figure A.11 to A.8, we see that two fields have been added to each index entry. The first word holds the highest key in the overflow area for this track. The second word holds the address of the first overflow area or is null if there is none.

Master Index

Parts of Cylinder
Index

Track Indexes

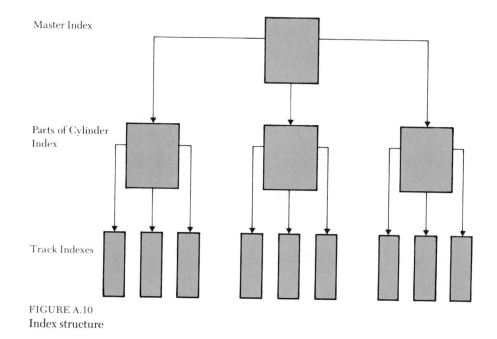

FIGURE A.10
Index structure

When record 55 is inserted into the file, it replaces record 60, which is written into the overflow area, and the track index is modified accordingly. The results of these operations appear in Figure A.12. Note that a new field has been attached to record 60 in the overflow area. This field is used to point to the next record in the overflow area. In this case it is null.

Now suppose record 24 is to be inserted into the file. A key value of 24 is greater than the last key on track 1, but less than the first key on track 2. Therefore, record 24 will be added to track 2. All records on track 2 are moved over one place, and record 55 is bumped into the overflow area. The file now appears as in Figure A.13. Record 55 is the first record in the overflow area, and a pointer (address) to record 60 has been added to record 55.

If record 57 were added to the file, it would be inserted into the overflow area and the address in record 55 would be modified to point to record 57 (Figure A.14). The prime area and track index would remain the same.

FIGURE A.11
Complete track index

Track Number	Highest Key on Track	Highest Key in Overflow	Address of First Overflow Record
1	20	20	Null
2	60	60	Null
3	75	75	Null
4	82	82	Null
5	98	98	Null

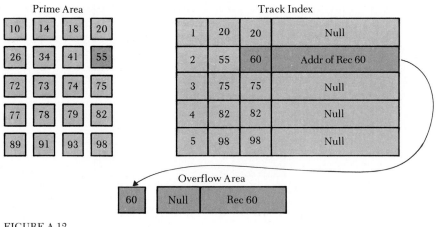

FIGURE A.12
Addition of record 55

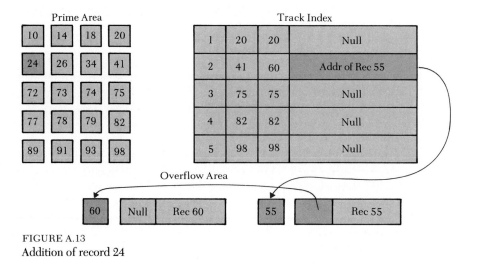

FIGURE A.13
Addition of record 24

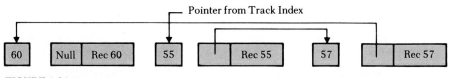

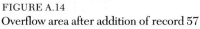

FIGURE A.14
Overflow area after addition of record 57

It should be clear from this discussion that insertions in indexed sequential files are indeed troublesome. If there have been many insertions, it usually takes a long time to find a record. At some point, processing becomes prohibitively inefficient. Then the entire file must be reformatted. Reformatting means creating a new file with all the records in key sequence in the prime area. The operating system vendor usually supplies such reformatting utilities.

DIRECT FILE ORGANIZATION

Direct file organization is used primarily for random processing, although sequential reading is possible. (Note that the word *random* here means processing a specific record, usually identified by its key field. It does not mean processing records arbitrarily. The term *direct* is more appropriate, if less frequently used, to describe the manipulation of direct files.)

Direct file organization differs from indexed sequential file organization in that records are in no particular order on the file. Thus sequential reading may present records in apparently nonsensical order. The programmer has greater flexibility with direct than with indexed sequential organization, but the programming task is more complex.

Direct organization is the fundamental organization of almost every database. DBMS products usually do their database I/O using direct organization. Typically, when other features such as indexes are needed, the DBMS provides them on top of the operating system's direct access methods.

Records are identified in one of several ways. One method is to specify the *relative track* and *relative record number* of a desired record. Relative track means track number relative to the start of the file. Relative record number means record number relative to the start of the track. A second method of identifying a record is by *relative track* and *key* (in this case, records must have keys). A third method is by *relative block address;* this is the block number (physical record number) of the desired record relative to the start of the file. The last way is by *physical address.* This could be the actual cylinder, head, and track record number on the device, or it could be a block address and displacement within the block (FBA devices). In general, physical addresses change if the file is moved to another volume or device.

Unlike indexed sequential organization, where each record is identified to the system by its key, direct organization does not support any particular correspondence between record content and file address. It is left to the programmer to establish a way of correlating records to file locations.

Address Computation

Perhaps the easiest way of addressing records is to use a field or portion of a field as a relative block address. For example, suppose an inventory file has records with Part-number fields. If part number are unique, say if they start with 1 and run consecutively in steps of 1 up to the number of parts in inventory, then the part number can be used as the relative block address of the record in the file. Unfortunately, such part numbers are very rare.

A second approach, sometimes referred to as a *hashing scheme,* is to perform some sort of arithmetic operation on a field of the record and to use the result as an address. For example, in a file of students, each record may have a student number. If these student numbers do not start with 1 and run consecutively in increments of 1, they are not suitable for use as addresses. Addresses can be created, however, by using only the last few digits of the student number. This is sometimes referred to as the *division/ remainder* method because taking the last few digits is equivalent to dividing by a number and using the remainder. For example, taking the last five digits is equivalent to dividing by 100,000 and using the remainder.

The problem with a hashing scheme is that the generated addresses may not be unique. Students with numbers 4363570 and 8263570 will both have address 63570. This situation is referred to as a *collision* and the resulting addresses, 63570, are called *synonyms.*

There are techniques for processing synonyms, but even so, it is always desirable to minimize them. Analysis of records may show that the last five digits are not the best ones to use. Perhaps using the second, fourth, and last three digits would lead to fewer synonyms.

Another type of hashing scheme is *folding,* in which a key is split into parts. The parts are added, and the sum or part of the sum is used as an address. Folding can be combined with the division/remainder method. The parts of the key are added together and the sum is divided by a number; the remainder is the calculated address. This scheme is generally effective, because every character in the key participates in the hashing calculation. See Figure A.15.

A third approach for addressing a direct file is to use a cross-reference list or table. The table has keys in one column and file addresses in another (Figure A.16). To find a record, the key column is searched for a match on the desired key value. If a match is found, the address is taken from the corresponding address column. That address may be any of the four types mentioned previously. The indexes of an indexed sequential file are an extension of this concept.

A variation of this technique is often used in database systems. Consider a database of employee information. Assume there are three database record types: employee SALARY, employee PERSONAL data, and employee CHILD. Further, assume all three types reside on the same physical file with one database record per block. This means that relative block addresses are also relative record addresses.

Figure A.17 shows the relationships of the SALARY, PERSONAL, and CHILD records. To find employee information, the database system maintains a cross-reference table like that in Figure A.18. The first column has Employee-number, the second the relative block address of the physical record containing the SALARY record for that employee, and the third the relative block address of the PERSONAL record.

The cross-reference table for the CHILD records is within the PERSONAL records. The first 200 bytes of each PERSONAL record contain personal data and the last 40 bytes contain space for up to ten 4-byte relative block addresses of CHILD records. One such record is shown in Figure A.19. In this example, then, part of the cross-reference table is carried with the data.

Key:	412483	Key:	715823408
Add:	412 + 483	Add:	715 + 823 + 408
		Divide sum:	1946/1000
Address:	895	Address:	946

a. Folding   b.   Folding with Division/Remainder

FIGURE A.15
Hashing methods for addressing records

FIGURE A.16
Cross-reference table

Key	Address (Relative Block Type)
123	1
241	8
618	6
723	4
1841	5
1981	2
2318	7
2742	3
.	.
.	.
.	.

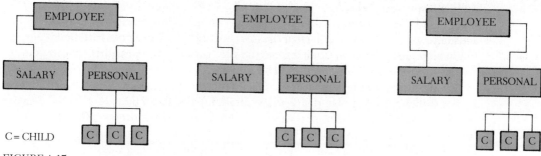

C = CHILD

FIGURE A.17
EMPLOYEE data structure

FIGURE A.18
Employee cross-reference table

Employee- number	SALARY Record Address	PERSONAL Record Address
100	4	12
130	5	9
180	11	6
240	8	7
260	3	2
300	10	1

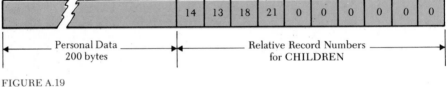

|← Personal Data →|← Relative Record Numbers →|
| 200 bytes | for CHILDREN |

| 14 | 13 | 18 | 21 | 0 | 0 | 0 | 0 | 0 | 0 |

FIGURE A.19
PERSONAL record

Direct File Processing

Because of the flexibility inherent in direct file organization, there are many ways to process such files. A method that typifies processing using hash addressing schemes is illustrated here. Another method not using hash addressing is discussed in Appendix B.

Consider a database of fixed-length student database records. (Fixed-length records are all the same number of bytes. *Variable-length* records can be different lengths within a file.) There is one database record in each block. Assume there are 16,000 database records to be processed randomly by student number. The division/remainder method is used to generate relative block addresses. Finally, assume the file is to be 80 percent full, which means that the total size of the file will be 20,000 records. The reason for having 4000 unused records will soon be evident.

Assume student numbers have six digits. One way to create a relative block address from a student number is to divide the student number by 20,000 and take the remainder. The result will range from 0 to 19,999. Since we want addresses from 1 to 20,000 we will add 1 to this remainder. This procedure will generate synonyms, so it is necessary to find a method for processing them. We establish the following rules:

1. To insert a record:

   a. If the calculated address is empty, insert the record at that address.
   b. If the calculated address is full, do not insert the record at that address. Increment the calculated address by 1. Repeat steps a and b up to ten times.

    c. If steps a and b have been repeated ten times and the record still has not been inserted, print the message FILE TOO DENSE and stop.

2. To find a record (for retrieval, updating, or deletion):

    a. Read the record at the calculated address.
    b. If this is the desired record, stop. If not, increment the calculated address by 1. Repeat steps a and b up to ten times.
    c. If steps a and b have been repeated ten times and the record has not been found, print the message RECORD NOT FOUND and stop.

These rules assume that empty or unused records can be identified. One way to indicate empty records is to insert a special mark into the first byte of each one before any data records are loaded. The mark must be one that cannot be confused with valid data. A bit combination that does not have a character representation may be a good choice. When a record is deleted, this special mark can be inserted into the record.

    The purpose of the limit of ten repetitions is to prohibit searching all the way through the file. Such searching would be extremely expensive. This means that the file cannot be 100 percent full because if the last empty record number is, say, 18,000, and the generated address for a record is 5, the empty record will not be found. We accept this situation because we do not want to read from record 5 to 18,000 to find the record.

    The number ten is arbitrary here. We could say fifteen or twenty, but this could result in slower processing. Note that if the message FILE TOO DENSE is written, it means that too many synonyms have been generated in one area. The file should be made larger and the address computation modified.

    Actually, for this type of processing, 80 percent density is high; 60 percent might be more realistic. Note that the fewer synonyms there are (or the better the hashing scheme is), the more dense the file can be.

    Many hashing schemes are possible. The one we used in this illustration is very simple. It could be expanded, for example, to include blocked records. When records are blocked, several data records are placed together in one physical record. Thus, several synonyms can be stored in the same block. In this case, records are stored away from the calculated address only when the block becomes full. This strategy can reduce the number of extra reads. Another extension uses a hash function to generate the first location but then uses linked lists (see Appendix B) to represent alternate locations.

    As mentioned earlier, direct files are the ones most heavily used in database systems. Therefore, an understanding of direct file organization and direct file processing can be useful background for a database student. It should be noted, however, that it is the DBMS, not the programmer, that interfaces with the access method. As illustrated in Figure A.20, if direct files are used in a file processing system, the programmer is responsible for performing the address calculation, managing collisions, locating synonyms, and possibly other related tasks. In a database system, however, the user (which can be an application programmer or an end-user employing online query facilities) merely indicates which record is desired and the DBMS handles the preliminary I/O tasks. Ultimately, of course, it is the access methods of the operating system that interface with the direct files stored on disk (refer back to Figure A.6).

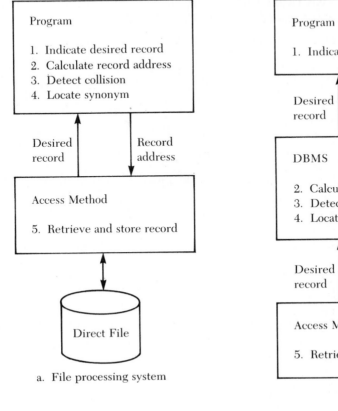
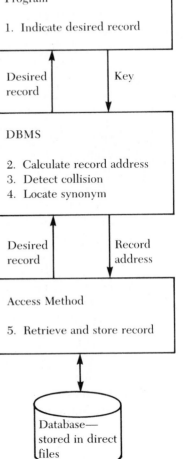

a. File processing system

b. Database application

FIGURE A.20
Direct file processing responsibilities

Summary

There are three fundamental ways in which data is stored on direct access storage devices. Each of the basic file organizations—sequential, indexed sequential, and direct—has certain advantages and disadvantages when compared with the others. If you are involved in developing a file processing system, you will need to select the appropriate file organization for that application. However, for database processing, direct files are currently the most widely used.

With direct file processing, different types of data records can be stored in the same file. Their locations are determined not by arrival sequence (as in sequential files) nor by key sequence (as in indexed sequential files). Instead, an address is determined for each record based on some programmer-defined scheme. This address might be the physical address (cylinder, head, and record number), or relative record number (the 1st, 2nd, or 200th record in the file), or some other means of locating the record in the file.

Related records, although probably physically separate from one another on the file, can be logically connected together via cross-reference tables and by pointers embedded into data records themselves. Other techniques that were not discussed in this appendix can also be used to connect related records.

Although a knowledge of direct file processing is helpful background information for the database student (and in many cases for the database practitioner), remember that it is the DBMS, not the database user, that interfaces with the operating system in order to locate records in the database. This complex task is not the responsibility of the end-user or the application programmer.

GROUP I   QUESTIONS

A.1   Suppose an indexed sequential file has twelve unblocked fixed-length records, arranged three per track. If the key of the first record is 5, that of the second is 10, and so on in increments of 5, sketch the prime area. Sketch the track index.

A.2   For the file described in A.1 sketch the prime and overflow areas after each of the following actions occurs:

a. Record 22 is inserted.
b. Records 22 and 16 are inserted.
c. Records 22, 16, and 21 are inserted.

A.3   If the STUDENT file considered in this appendix is 60 percent dense, how many records should the file contain?

A.4   How must the hashing scheme be modified for the STUDENT file if it is 60 percent dense?

A.5   If records A, B, and C are synonyms, which record should be closest to its calculated address? How should the input file be sorted prior to loading the file?

A.6   Construct a hashing scheme different from the one described in this appendix.

A.7   Explain how the index of an indexed sequential file can be considered an extension of cross-reference-list addressing on a direct file.

A.8   Describe a method for processing synonyms that is different from the one described in this appendix.

GROUP II QUESTIONS

A.9   Write a program to create and process an indexed sequential file of STUDENT records. Assume the records have a 6-byte Student-number, which is the key, a 20-byte Name field, and a 4-byte Major field. You should load the file, dump it sequentially, and then randomly insert, delete, replace, and read records. Finally, dump the file sequentially. Be sure your program can detect efforts to insert a record that is already on the file or to delete or replace one that is not on file.

A.10   Write a program to create and maintain a direct file of STUDENT records. Assume the records have a 6-byte Student-number, a 20-byte Name field, and a 4-byte Major field. Create 100 empty records on the direct file and use a hash-addressing scheme on the Student-number field. The file is too dense if a record cannot be inserted in one of the three records past its calculated address. Insert, delete, read, and replace records. Be sure your program can detect efforts to insert a record that is already there or to replace or delete one that is not on the file.

A.11   Investigate any commercial DBMS product. Determine what kind of file organization is used to store and manipulate database data. How does the file organization differ from the basic ones described in this appendix? How is it similar?

Data Structures
for Database Processing

The file organization methods presented in Appendix A are by themselves inadequate for database processing. Sequential files are, of course, wholly inappropriate for storing data. Indexed sequential files are seldom used by DBMS products because the assumptions behind them are much too limiting. Direct files are used by almost all DBMS products because of their versatility. However, even direct files, by themselves, cannot provide the services needed by database users. To provide these services, DBMS products build and maintain specialized data structures. These data structures are the topic of this appendix.

We begin by discussing flat files and some of the problems that can occur when such files need to be processed in different orders. This leads to a discussion of three data structures that address such problems: sequential lists, linked lists, and inverted lists (or indexes).

Next we illustrate how each of the binary relationships discussed in Chapter 7—trees, simple networks, and complex networks—are represented using various data structures. Finally, we explore how to represent and process multiple keys.

Although a thorough knowledge of data structures is not required to use most DBMS products, this kind of background is essential to the database

- FLAT FILES
- REPRESENTING BINARY RELATIONSHIPS
- SECONDARY-KEY REPRESENTATIONS

administrator and the systems programmer working with a DBMS. Knowing the fundamental data structures will also help you to evaluate and compare database products.

Flat Files

A *flat file* is a file that has no repeating groups. Figure B.1a shows a flat file; Figure B.1b shows a file that is not flat because of the repeating field, Item. A flat file can be stored as a sequential, indexed sequential, or direct file.

Flat files have been used for many years in commercial processing. They are usually processed in some predetermined order, say in ascending sequence on a key field.

PROCESSING FLAT FILES IN MULTIPLE ORDERS

Sometimes users want to process flat files in ways that are not readily supported by the file organization employed. Consider, for example, the ENROLLMENT records in Figure B.1a. To produce student schedules, the records must be processed in Student-number sequence. But to produce class rosters, the records need to be processed in Class-number sequence.

The records, of course, can be stored in only one physical sequence. They can be in order, for example, on Student-number or on Class-number, but not both at the same

Enrollment Record

Student-number	Class-number	Semester

Invoice Record

Invoice-number	Item(s)

Sample Data

200	70	88S
100	30	89F
300	20	89F
200	30	88S
300	70	88S
100	20	88S

Sample Data

1000	10	20	30	40
1010	50			
1020	10	20	30	
1030	50	90		

a. A flat file

b. A non-flat file

FIGURE B.1
Examples of flat and nonflat files

time. The traditional solution to the problem of processing records in different orders is to sort the records in student order, process the student schedules, then sort the records in class order, and produce class rosters.

For some applications, such as a batch-mode system, this solution is cumbersome but effective. But suppose both orders need to exist simultaneously. Suppose two concurrent users have different views of the ENROLLMENT records. What do we do then?

One solution is to create two copies of the ENROLLMENT file and sort them as shown in Figure B.2. Since the data is listed in sequential order, this data structure is sometimes called a *sequential list*. Sequential lists are usually stored as sequential files. We mentioned in the introduction to this appendix that sequential files are never employed to store database data. It follows, then, that the sequential list is not a data structure used in database organization.

This is so because maintaining several orders by keeping multiple copies of the same sequential list is usually not effective. The duplicated sequential list creates the potential for data integrity problems. Fortunately, there are other data structures that allow us to process records in different orders, and which do not require duplication of data. They include *linked lists* and *inverted lists* or *indexes*. Before we discuss these structures, we need to clarify how we will be presenting record addressing.

A NOTE ON RECORD ADDRESSING

Usually the DBMS creates large physical records, or blocks, on its direct access files. These physical records are used as containers for logical records. There are typically many logical records per physical record. We will assume, realistically, that each physical record is addressed by its relative record number (RRN). Thus a logical record might be assigned to physical record number 7 or 77 or 10,000. The relative record number is the logical record's physical address. If there is more than one logical record per physical record, the address will also need to specify where the logical record is within the phys-

Student-number	Class-number	Semester
100	30	89F
100	20	88S
200	70	88S
200	30	88S
300	20	89F
300	70	88S

a. Sorted by Student-number

Student-number	Class-number	Semester
300	20	89F
100	20	88S
100	30	89F
200	30	88S
200	70	88S
300	70	88S

b. Sorted by Class-number

FIGURE B.2
ENROLLMENT data stored as sequential lists

ical record. Thus the complete address for a logical record might be relative record number 77, byte location 100. This means the record begins in byte 100 of block 77.

To simplify illustrations in this text, we assume that there is only one logical record per physical record. Consequently, we will not be concerned with byte offsets within blocks. This is unrealistic, but it simplifies the discussion.

MAINTAINING ORDER WITH LINKED LISTS

Linked lists can be used to keep records in logical order that are not necessarily in physical order. To create a linked list a field is added to each data record. The *link* field holds the address (in our illustrations the relative record number) of the *next* record in logical sequence. For example, Figure B.3 shows the ENROLLMENT records expanded to include a linked list; this list maintains the records in Student-number order. Notice that the link for the numerically last student in the list is zero.

Figure B.4 shows ENROLLMENT records with two linked lists: one list maintains the Student-number order and the other list maintains the Class-number order. Two link fields have been added to the records, one for each list.

When insertions and deletions are done, linked lists have a great advantage over sequential lists. For example, to insert the ENROLLMENT record for student 200 and class 45, both of the lists in Figure B.2 would need to be rewritten. For the linked lists in Figure B.4, however, the new record could be added to the physical end of the list; only the values of two link fields need to be changed to place the new record in the correct sequences. These changes are shown in Figure B.5.

Also, when a record is deleted from a sequential list a gap is created. A record can be deleted from a linked list simply by changing values of the link, or *pointer* fields. In Figure B.6, the ENROLLMENT record for student 200, class 30 has been logically deleted. No other record points to its address, so it has been effectively removed from the chain, even though it still exists physically.

There are many linked list variations. We can make the list into a *circular list* or *ring*, by changing the link of the last record from zero to the address of the first record in the list. Now we can reach every item in the list starting at any item in the list. Figure B.7a shows a circular list for the Student-number order. Also, a *two-way linked list* has links in both directions. In Figure B.7b, a two-way linked list has been created for ascending and descending student order.

Records ordered using linked lists cannot be stored on a sequential file. Some type of direct access file organization is needed to be able to use the link values. Thus either indexed sequential or direct file organization is required for processing linked lists. As mentioned in Appendix A, DBMS products nearly always use direct organizations.

MAINTAINING ORDER WITH INVERTED LISTS

Logical record order can also be maintained using *inverted lists,* or as they are sometimes called, *indexes.* An inverted list is simply a table that cross-references record addresses

FIGURE B.3
ENROLLMENT data in Student-number order using a linked list

Relative Record Number	Student-number	Class-number	Semester	Link
1	200	70	88S	4
2	100	30	89F	6
3	300	20	89F	5
4	200	30	88S	3
5	300	70	88S	0
6	100	20	88S	1

Start of list = 2

FIGURE B.4
ENROLLMENT data in two orders using linked lists

Relative Record Number	Student-number	Class-number	Semester	Student Link	Class Link
1	200	70	88S	4	5
2	100	30	89F	6	1
3	300	20	89F	5	4
4	200	30	88S	3	2
5	300	70	88S	0	0
6	100	20	88S	1	3

Start of student list = 2
Start of class list = 6

FIGURE B.5
ENROLLMENT data after insertion of new record (in two orders using linked lists)

Relative Record Number	Student-number	Class-number	Semester	Student Link	Class Link
1	200	70	88S	4	5
2	100	30	89F	6	7
3	300	20	89F	5	4
4	200	30	88S	7	2
5	300	70	88S	0	0
6	100	20	88S	1	3
7	200	45	88S	3	1

Start of student list = 2
Start of class list = 6

FIGURE B.6
ENROLLMENT data after
deletion of student 200, class 30 (in
two orders using linked lists)

Relative Record Number	Student-number	Class-number	Semester	Student Link	Class Link
1	200	70	88S	7	5
2	100	30	89F	6	7
3	300	20	89F	5	2
4	200	30	88S	7	2
5	300	70	88S	0	0
6	100	20	88S	1	3
7	200	45	88S	3	1

Start of student list = 2
Start of class list = 6

FIGURE B.7
ENROLLMENT data sorted by
Student-number using circular and
two-way linked lists

Relative Record Number	Student-number	Class-number	Semester	Link
1	200	70	88S	4
2	100	30	89F	6
3	300	20	89F	5
4	200	30	88S	3
5	300	70	88S	2
6	100	20	88S	1

Start of list = 2

a. Circular linked list

Relative Record Number	Student-number	Class-number	Semester	Ascending Link	Descending Link
1	200	70	88S	4	6
2	100	30	89F	6	0
3	300	20	89F	5	4
4	200	30	88S	3	1
5	300	70	88S	0	3
6	100	20	88S	1	2

Start of ascending list = 2
Start of descending list = 5

b. Two-way linked list

with some field value. For example, in Figure B.8a you can see that the ENROLLMENT records are stored in no particular order. Figure B.8b shows an inverted list on Student-number. In this list the Student-numbers are arranged in sequence; each entry in the list points to a corresponding record in the original data.

As you can see, the inverted list is simply an index on Student-numbers. To process ENROLLMENT sequentially on Student-number, we simply process the inverted list sequentially, obtaining ENROLLMENT data by reading the records indicated by the pointers. Figure B.8c shows another inverted list for ENROLLMENT. This one maintains Class-number order.

To use an inverted list, the data to be ordered (here ENROLLMENT) must reside on an indexed sequential or direct file. The inverted lists, however, can reside on any type of file. In practice, almost all DBMS products keep both the data and the indexes on direct files.

If you compare the linked list with the inverted list you will notice the essential difference between them. With a linked list, pointers are stored along with the data. Each

Relative Record Number	Student-number	Class-number	Semester
1	200	70	88S
2	100	30	89F
3	300	20	89F
4	200	30	88S
5	300	70	88S
6	100	20	88S

a. ENROLLMENT data

Student-number	Relative Record Number
100	2
100	6
200	1
200	4
300	3
300	5

b. Inverted list on Student-number

Class-number	Relative Record Number
20	3
20	6
30	2
30	4
70	1
70	5

c. Inverted list on Class-number

FIGURE B.8
ENROLLMENT data and corresponding inverted lists

record contains a link field containing a pointer to the address of the next related record. With an inverted list, pointers are stored in indexes, separate from the data. Thus the data records themselves contain no pointers. Both techniques are used by commercial DBMS products.

B-TREES

A special application of the concept of inverted lists, or indexes, is called a *B-tree*. A B-tree is a multilevel index that allows both sequential and direct processing of data records. It also guarantees a certain level of efficiency in processing because of the way the indexes are structured.

A B-tree is an index that is made up of two parts, the sequence set and the index set (using IBM's VSAM terminology—VSAM file organization is based on B-trees). The *sequence set* is an inverted list containing an entry for every record in the file. The index is in physical sequence, usually by primary key value. This arrangement allows sequential access to the data records: simply process the sequence set in order, obtaining the data records to which each entry points.

The *index set* is an index pointing to groups of entries in the sequence set inverted list. This arrangement provides rapid direct access to records in the file. It is the index set that makes B-trees unique. An example of a B-tree appears in Figure B.9. An occurrence of this structure can be seen in Figure B.10.

Notice that the bottom row in Figure B.9, the sequence set, is simply an inverted list. It contains an entry for every record in the file (although both the data records and their addresses have been omitted for brevity). Also notice that the sequence set entries are in groups of three. The entries in each group are physically in sequence, and each group chains to the next one via a linked list. This can be seen clearly in Figure B.10.

Now examine in Figure B.9 the index set above the sequence set. The top entry contains two values, 45 and 77. By following the leftmost link (to RRN2), we can access all the records whose key field values are less than or equal to 45; by following the middle pointer (to RRN3), we can access all the records whose key field values are greater than 45 and less than or equal to 77; and by following the rightmost pointer (to RRN4), we can access all the records whose key field values are greater than 77.

Similarly, at the next level there are two values and three pointers in each index entry. Each time we drop to another level, we narrow our search for a particular record. For example, if we continue to follow the leftmost pointer from the top entry, and then we follow the rightmost pointer from there, we can access all records whose key field value is greater than 27 and less than or equal to 45. We eliminated all that were greater than 45 at the first level.

B-trees are by definition balanced. That is to say that all the data records are the exact same distance from the top entry in the index set. This aspect of B-trees guarantees performance efficiency. However, the algorithms for inserting and deleting records are more complex than those for ordinary trees (which can be unbalanced), because several index entries might need to be modified when records are added or deleted to keep all records the same distance from the top index entry.

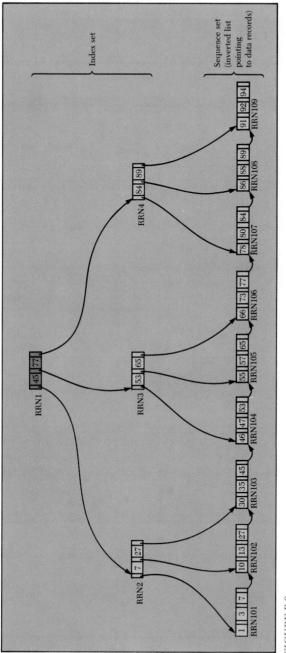

FIGURE B.9
General structure of simple B-tree

RRN	Link1	Value1	Link2	Value2	Link3	
1	2	45	3	77	4	
2	101	7	102	27	103	Index Set
3	104	53	105	65	106	
4	107	84	108	89	109	

.
.
.

	R1	Addr1	R2	Addr2	R3	Addr3	Link	
101	1	Pointer to 6	3	Pointer to 8	7	Pointer to 12	102	
102	10	. . .	13	. . .	27	. . .	103	
103	30	. . .	35	. . .	45	. . .	104	Sequence Set
104	46	. . .	47	. . .	53	. . .	105	(Addresses of
105	55	. . .	57	. . .	65	. . .	106	data records
106	66	. . .	73	. . .	77	. . .	107	are omitted)
107	78	. . .	80	. . .	84	. . .	108	
108	86	. . .	88	. . .	89	. . .	109	
109	91	. . .	92	. . .	94	. . .	0	

FIGURE B.10
Occurrence of the B-tree in Figure B.9

SUMMARY OF DATA STRUCTURES

Figure B.11 summarizes techniques for maintaining ordered flat files. Three supporting data structures are possible. Sequential lists can be used, but data must be duplicated to maintain several orders. Because sequential lists are not used in database processing, we will not consider them further. Both linked lists and inverted lists can be used without data duplication. B-trees are special applications of inverted lists.

As shown in Figure B.11, sequential lists can be stored using any of the three file organizations discussed in Appendix A. In practice, however, they are usually kept on sequential files. Additionally, while both linked and inverted lists can be stored using either indexed sequential or direct files, DBMS products almost always store them on direct files.

Representing Binary Relationships

In this section we will examine how each of the logical record relationships discussed in Chapter 7—trees, simple networks, and complex networks—can be represented using linked lists and inverted lists. First, we will review the three record relationships.

FIGURE B.11
Summary of data structures and
data organizations used for ordered
flat files

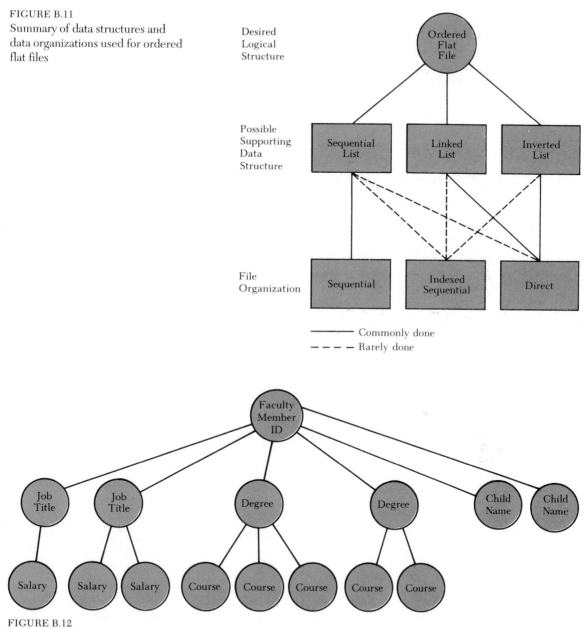

FIGURE B.12
Occurrence of a faculty member record

REVIEW OF RECORD RELATIONSHIPS

Records can be related in three ways. A *tree* relationship is one in which there are one or more one-to-many relationships, but each child record has only one parent. The occurrence of faculty data shown in Figure B.12 illustrates a tree. There are several 1:N relationships, but any child record has only one parent. Figure B.13 shows a general schematic of this structure.

A *simple network* is a collection of records and 1:N relationships among them. What distinguishes a simple network from a tree is the fact that in a simple network a child can have more than one parent as long as the parents are different record types. The occurrence of a simple network of students, advisors, and major fields of study in Figure B.14 is represented schematically in Figure B.15.

A *complex network* is also a collection of records and relationships. In a complex network, however, the relationships are many-to-many instead of one-to-many. The relationship between students and classes is a complex network. An occurrence of this relationship can be seen in Figure B.16. The general schematic is in Figure B.17.

We saw earlier that we can use linked lists and inverted lists to process records in orders different from the one in which they are physically stored. We can also use those same data structures to store and process the relationships among records.

REPRESENTING TREES

We can use sequential lists, linked lists, and inverted lists to represent trees. In using sequential lists, we duplicate much data. Furthermore, sequential lists are not used by DBMS products to represent trees. Therefore we will discuss only linked lists and inverted lists.

Linked List Representation of Trees

Figure B.18 shows a tree structure in which VENDOR records are parents and INVOICE records are children. Figure B.19 shows two occurrences of this structure. In

FIGURE B.13
Schematic of faculty member tree structure

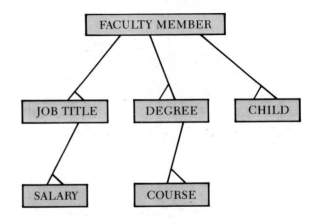

FIGURE B.14
Occurrence of simple network

FIGURE B.15
General structure of a simple network

FIGURE B.16
Occurrence of complex network

FIGURE B.17
Schematic of a complex network

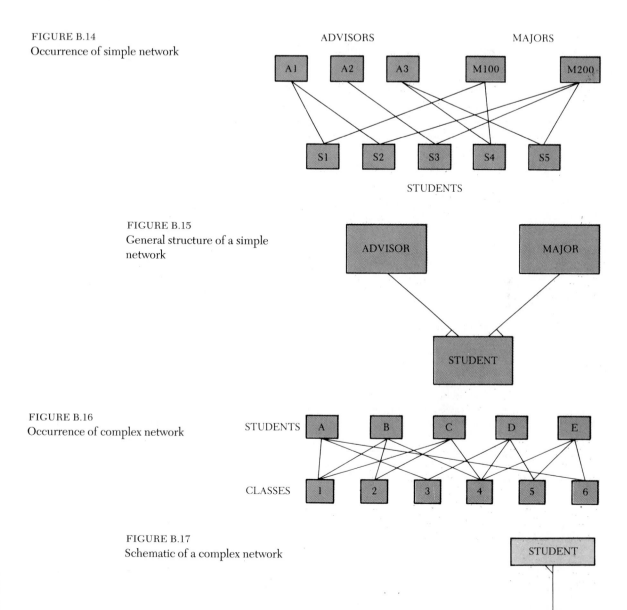

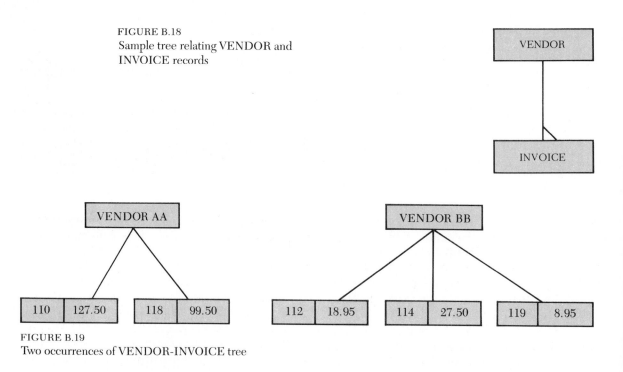

FIGURE B.18
Sample tree relating VENDOR and
INVOICE records

FIGURE B.19
Two occurrences of VENDOR-INVOICE tree

FIGURE B.20
File representation of trees in
Figure B.19

Record Number	Record Contents	
1	VENDOR AA	
2	VENDOR BB	
3	118	99.50
4	119	8.95
5	112	18.95
6	114	27.50
7	110	127.50

Figure B.20, all of the VENDOR and INVOICE records have been written to a direct access file. VENDOR AA is in relative record number 1 (RRN1), and VENDOR BB is in relative record number 2. The INVOICE records have been stored in subsequent slots as illustrated. Note that these records are not stored in any particular order, nor do they need to be.

Our problem is that we cannot tell from this file which invoices belong to which vendors. To solve this problem with a linked list, we will add a pointer field to every record. In this field we will store the address of some other related record. For example, we will place in VENDOR AA's link field the address of the first invoice belonging to it. This is RRN7, which is INVOICE 110. Then we will make INVOICE 110 point to the next invoice belonging to VENDOR AA, in this case RRN3. This slot holds INVOICE 118. To indicate that there are no more children in the chain, we insert a 0 in the link field for RRN3.

FIGURE B.21
Tree occurrences represented by
linked lists

Relative Record Number	Record Contents		Link Field
1	VENDOR AA		7
2	VENDOR BB		5
3	118	99.50	0
4	119	8.95	0
5	112	18.95	6
6	114	27.50	4
7	110	127.50	3

This technique is shown in Figure B.21. If you examine the figure carefully you will see that a similar set of links has been used to represent the relationship between VENDOR BB and its invoices.

The structure in Figure B.21 is much easier to modify than a sequential list of the tree. For example, suppose we add a new invoice, say number 111, to VENDOR AA. To do this, we just add the record to the file and insert it into the linked list. Physically, the record can be placed anywhere. But where should it be placed logically? For this example, let's assume the children are to be kept in ascending order on invoice number. In that case, we need to make INVOICE 110 point to INVOICE 111 (at RRN8), and we need to make INVOICE 111, the new invoice, point to INVOICE 118 (at RRN3). This modification is shown in Figure B.22.

Similarly, deleting an invoice is easy. If INVOICE 114 is deleted, we simply modify the pointer in the invoice that is now pointing to INVOICE 114. In this case, it is INVOICE 112 at RRN5. We will give INVOICE 112 the pointer that INVOICE 114 had before deletion. In this way, INVOICE 112 will point to INVOICE 119 (see Figure B.23). We have effectively cut one link out of the chain and welded together the ones it once connected.

FIGURE B.22
Insertion of INVOICE 111 to file
in Figure B.21

Relative Record Number	Record Contents		Link Field	
1	VENDOR AA		7	
2	VENDOR BB		5	
3	118	99.50	0	
4	119	8.95	0	
5	112	18.95	6	
6	114	27.50	4	
7	110	127.50	8	
8	111	19.95	3	← Inserted Record

FIGURE B.23
Deletion of INVOICE 114 from
file in Figure B.22

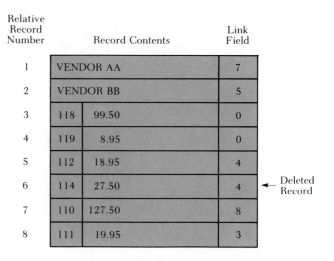

Relative Record Number	Record Contents		Link Field	
1	VENDOR AA		7	
2	VENDOR BB		5	
3	118	99.50	0	
4	119	8.95	0	
5	112	18.95	4	
6	114	27.50	4	← Deleted Record
7	110	127.50	8	
8	111	19.95	3	

Inverted List Representation of Trees

A tree structure can readily be represented using inverted lists. The technique is to store each one-to-many relationship as an inverted list. These lists are then used to match parents and children.

Using the VENDOR and INVOICE records as shown in Figure B.21, we see that VENDOR AA (in RRN1) owns INVOICEs 110 (RRN7) and 118 (RRN3). Thus RRN1 is the parent of RRN7 and RRN3. We can represent this fact with the inverted list shown in Figure B.24. The list simply associates a parent's address with the addresses of each of its children.

If the tree has several 1:N relationships, then several inverted lists will be required, one for each relationship. For the structure in Figure B.13, five inverted lists are needed.

REPRESENTING SIMPLE NETWORKS

As with trees, simple networks can also be represented using linked lists and inverted lists.

FIGURE B.24
Inverted list representation of
VENDOR-INVOICE relationship

Parent Record	Child Record
1	7
1	3
2	5
2	6
2	4

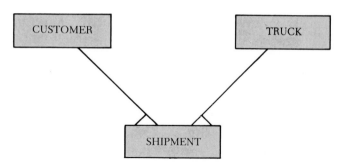

Linked List Representation of Simple Networks

Consider the simple network in Figure B.25. It is a simple network because all the relationships are 1:N and SHIPMENT records have two parents of different types. Each SHIPMENT has a CUSTOMER parent and a TRUCK parent. The relationship between CUSTOMER and SHIPMENT is 1:N because a customer can have several shipments. The relationship from TRUCK to SHIPMENT is 1:N because one truck can hold many shipments (assume shipments are small enough to fit in one truck or less). An occurrence of this network is shown in Figure B.26.

In order to represent this simple network with linked lists, we need to establish one set of pointers for each 1:N relationship. In this example, that means there will be one set of pointers to connect CUSTOMERs with their SHIPMENTs, and another set of pointers to connect TRUCKs with their SHIPMENTs. Thus a CUSTOMER record will contain one pointer (to the first SHIPMENT it owns), a TRUCK record will contain one pointer (to the first SHIPMENT it owns), and a SHIPMENT record will have two pointers, one for the next SHIPMENT owned by the same CUSTOMER, and one for the next SHIPMENT owned by the same TRUCK. This scheme is illustrated in Figure B.27.

FIGURE B.26
Occurrence of simple network in
Figure B.25

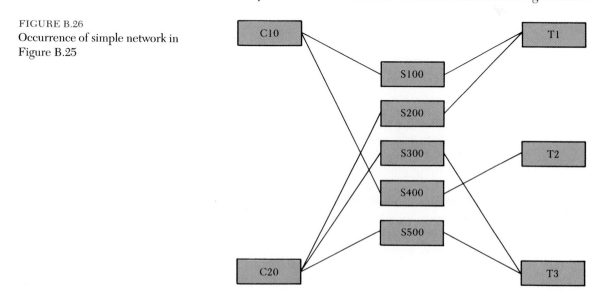

FIGURE B.27

Representation of simple network
with linked lists

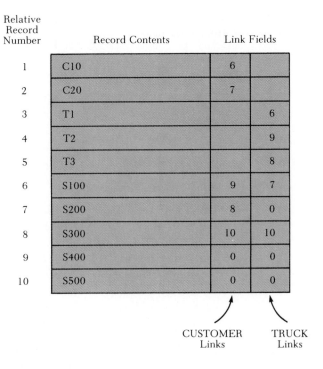

Relative Record Number	Record Contents	Link Fields	
1	C10	6	
2	C20	7	
3	T1		6
4	T2		9
5	T3		8
6	S100	9	7
7	S200	8	0
8	S300	10	10
9	S400	0	0
10	S500	0	0

CUSTOMER Links   TRUCK Links

Inverted List Representation of Simple Networks

A simple network has at least two 1:N relationships. Each relationship can be represented using an inverted list, as illustrated in our discussion of trees.

For example, consider the simple network shown in Figure B.25. This network has two 1:N relationships, one between TRUCK and SHIPMENT, and one between CUSTOMER and SHIPMENT. We can store each of these relationships in an inverted list. Figure B.28 shows the two inverted lists needed to represent the example in Figure B.26. Records are loaded into the same positions as in Figure B.27.

REPRESENTING COMPLEX NETWORKS

Complex networks can be physically represented in a variety of ways. They can be decomposed into trees or simple networks, and these simpler structures can then be represented using one of the techniques we just described. Alternatively, they can be represented directly using inverted lists. Linked lists are not used by any DBMS product to directly represent complex networks.

In practice, complex networks are nearly always decomposed into simpler structures. Therefore we will consider only representations using decomposition.

A common approach to representing complex networks is to reduce them to simple networks and then to represent the simple networks with linked lists or inverted lists as discussed in the previous section. Note, however, that a complex network involves a rela-

FIGURE B.28

Representation of simple network
with inverted lists

Customer Record	Shipment Record
1	6
1	9
2	7
2	8
2	10

Truck Record	Shipment Record
3	6
3	7
4	9
5	8
5	10

tionship between two records, whereas a simple network involves relationships among three records. Thus, to decompose a complex network into a simple one we need to create a third record type.

The record that is created when a complex network is decomposed into a simple one is called an *intersection record*. Consider the student-class complex network. An intersection record will contain a unique key from a STUDENT record and a unique key from a corresponding CLASS record. It will contain no other application data, although it might contain link fields.

The general structure of this relationship is shown in Figure B.29. Assuming the record names are unique (such as S1, S2, C1, and so forth), an instance of the STUDENT-CLASS relationship is illustrated in Figure B.30.

Notice that the relationship from STUDENT to intersection record is 1:N, and the relationship from CLASS to intersection record is also 1:N. Thus we have created a simple network that can now be represented with the linked list or inverted list techniques shown previously. A file of this occurrence using the linked list technique is shown in Figure B.31.

SUMMARY OF RELATIONSHIP REPRESENTATIONS

Figure B.32 summarizes the representations of record relationships. Trees can be represented using sequential lists (although we did not discuss this approach), linked lists, and inverted lists. Sequential lists are not used in DBMS products. A simple network can

FIGURE B.29

Decomposition of complex network
to simple network

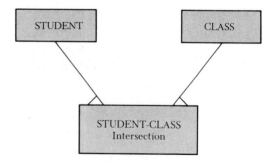

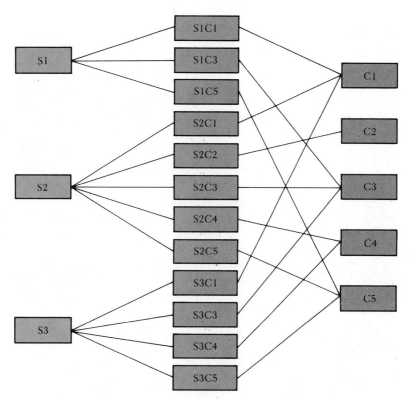

FIGURE B.30
Instance of STUDENT-CLASS relationship showing intersection records

be decomposed into trees and then represented, or it can be represented directly using either linked or inverted lists. Finally, a complex network can be decomposed into a tree or a simple network (using intersection records), or it can be represented directly using inverted lists.

Notice that sequential file organization is used only for storing sequential lists. Consequently, it is seldom used for database processing. Similarly, indexed sequential file organization is never used. Direct file organization is used by almost all DBMS products.

Secondary-Key Representations

In many cases the word *key* indicates a field (or fields) whose value uniquely identifies a record. This is usually called the *primary key*. Sometimes, however, applications need to access and process records by a *secondary key*, one that is different from the primary key. Secondary keys might be unique (such as a professor's name), or they might be non-unique (such as a customer's zip code). In this section we will use the term *set* to refer to

FIGURE B.31

Occurrence of network in Figure B.30

Relative Record Number	Record Contents	Link Fields	
1	S1	9	
2	S2	12	
3	S3	17	
4	C1		9
5	C2		13
6	C3		10
7	C4		15
8	C5		11
9	S1C1	10	12
10	S1C3	11	14
11	S1C5	0	16
12	S2C1	13	17
13	S2C2	14	0
14	S2C3	15	18
15	S2C4	16	19
16	S2C5	0	20
17	S3C1	18	0
18	S3C3	19	0
19	S3C4	20	0
20	S3C5	0	0

STUDENT Links   CLASS Links

all records having the same value of a non-unique secondary key. For example, there is a set of records having the zip code 98040.

In Appendix A we discussed using keys to associate records with particular file locations. For example, we might apply a hashing algorithm to a key in order to generate a relative record address. Clearly, only one record key can be used for this purpose. The key used for this is the primary key. Secondary keys can be used to identify records, but they must reference the physical location determined by the primary key.

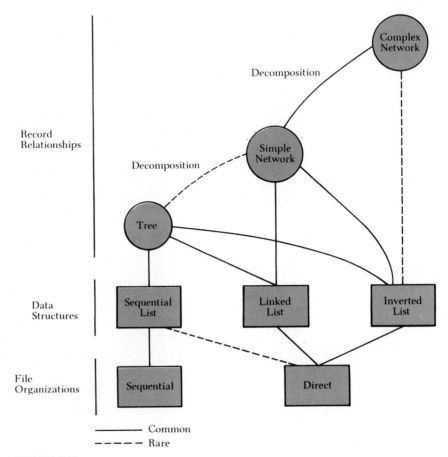

FIGURE B.32
Record relationships, data structures, and file organizations

Some DBMS products do not use key values to determine record locations at all. Instead, the DBMS assigns records to locations in accordance with available space and other considerations known only to the DBMS. For these systems there are no primary keys. Every key is considered a secondary key and is processed using one of the techniques in this section.

Both linked and inverted lists are used to represent secondary keys. As you will see, linked lists are practical only for non-unique keys. Inverted lists, however, can be used for both unique and non-unique key representations. We will discuss the linked list representation first.

LINKED LIST REPRESENTATION OF SECONDARY KEYS

Consider an example of CUSTOMER records as shown in Figure B.33. The primary key is Account-number, and there is a secondary key on Credit-limit. Possible Credit-limit

FIGURE B.33
CUSTOMER record

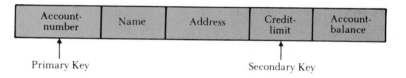

values are 500, 700, and 1000. Thus there will be a set of records for the limit of 500, a set for 700, and a set for 1000.

To represent this key using linked lists we will add a link field to the CUSTOMER records. Inside this link field we will create a linked list for each set of records. Figure B.34 shows a database of eleven customers; for brevity, only Account-number and Credit-limit are shown. A link field has been attached to the records. Assume one database record occupies one physical record on a direct file using relative record addressing.

Three pointers need to be established so we know where to begin each linked list. These are called *heads*, and they are stored separate from the data. The head of the $500 linked list is RRN1. Record 1 links to record 2, which in turn links to record 7. Record 7 has a zero in the link position, indicating that it is the end of the list. Consequently, the $500 credit limit set consists of records 1, 2, and 7. Similarly, the $700 set contains records 3, 5, and 10, and the $1000 set contains relative records 4, 6, 8, 9, and 11.

To answer a query like "How many accounts in the $1000 set have a balance in excess of $900?," the $1000 set linked list can be used. In this way, only records in the $1000 set need to be read from the file and examined. The advantage of this approach is not readily apparent in this small example. Suppose, however, there are 100,000 CUSTOMER records and only 100 of them are in the $1000 set. If there is no linked list, all 100,000 records must be examined. With the linked list, only 100 records need to be examined, namely the ones in the $1000 set. Using the linked list saves 99,900 reads.

Relative Record Number	Link	Account-Number	Credit-Limit	Other Data	
1	2	101	500		HEAD-500 = 1
2	7	301	500		HEAD-700 = 3
3	5	203	700		HEAD-1000 = 4
4	6	004	1000		
5	10	204	700		
6	8	905	1000		
7	0	705	500		
8	9	207	1000		
9	11	309	1000		
10	0	409	700		
11	0	210	1000		

FIGURE B.34
Representing Credit-limit secondary key using linked list

Linked lists are not an effective technique for every secondary-key application. In particular, if the records are processed nonsequentially in a set, linked lists are inefficient. For example, if it is often necessary to find the 10th or 120th or nth record in the $500 Credit-limit set, processing will be slow. Linked lists are inefficient for direct access.

Also, if the application requires that secondary keys be created or destroyed dynamically, the linked list approach is undesirable. Whenever a new key is created, a link field must be added to every record. This often requires reorganization of the database—a time-consuming and expensive process.

Finally, if the secondary keys are unique, each list has a length of one and a separate linked list exists for every record in the database. Since this situation is unworkable, linked lists cannot be used for unique keys.

For example, suppose the CUSTOMER records contain another unique field, say Social-security-number. If we attempt to represent this unique secondary key using a linked list, every Social-security-number will be a separate linked list. Further, each linked list will have just one item in it, the single record having the indicated Social-security-number.

INVERTED LIST REPRESENTATION OF SECONDARY KEYS

A second technique for representing secondary keys uses an inverted list. One inverted list is established for each secondary key. The approach varies depending on whether key values are unique or non-unique.

Unique Secondary Keys

Suppose the CUSTOMER records in Figure B.33 contain Social-security-number (SSN) as well as the fields shown. To provide key access to the CUSTOMER records using SSN we simply build an inverted list on the SSN field. Sample CUSTOMER data is shown in Figure B.35a, and a corresponding inverted list is illustrated in Figure B.35b. The inverted list shown uses relative record numbers as addresses. It would be possible to use Account-numbers instead, in which case the DBMS would locate the desired SSN in the inverted list, obtain the matching Account-number, and then hash to the record itself.

Non-unique Secondary Keys

Inverted lists can also be used to represent non-unique secondary keys. However, because each set of related records can contain an unknown number of members, the entries in the inverted list are of variable length. For example, Figure B.36 shows the inverted list for the Credit-limit sets for the CUSTOMER data. The $500 set and the $700 set each have three members, so there are three account numbers in each entry. The $1000 set has five members, so there are five account numbers in that entry.

FIGURE B.35

Representing unique secondary key with inverted lists

Relative Record Number	Account-number	Credit-limit	Social Security Number (SSN)
1	101	500	000-01-0001
2	301	500	000-01-0005
3	203	700	000-01-0009
4	004	1000	000-01-0003

a. Sample CUSTOMER data (with SSN)

SSN	Relative Record Number
000-01-0001	1
000-01-0003	4
000-01-0005	2
000-01-0009	3

b. Inverted list for SSN secondary key

In reality, representing and processing non-unique secondary keys are complex tasks. Several different schemes are used by commercial DBMS products. One method that is typical uses a values table and an occurrence table. Each values table entry consists of two fields. The first field has a key value. For the CUSTOMER Credit-limit key, the values are 500, 700, and 1000. The second field of the values table entry is a pointer to the occurrence table.

The occurrence table contains record addresses. Addresses of records having a common value in the secondary-key field appear together in the table. Figure B.37 shows the values and occurrence tables for the Credit-limit key.

To locate records having a given value of the secondary key, the values table is searched for the desired value. Once the given key value is located in the values table, the pointer is followed to the occurrence table to obtain the addresses of records having that key value. These addresses are used to obtain the desired records.

FIGURE B.36

Inverted list for Credit-limit key in Figure B.33

Credit-limit	Account-number				
500	101	301	705		
700	203	204	409		
1000	004	905	207	309	210

FIGURE B.37
Values and occurrence tables for
Credit-limit key in Figure B.33

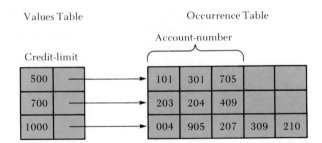

When a new record is inserted into the file, the DBMS must process each secondary-key field. For non-unique keys, it must ensure that the new record key value is in the values table; if so, it adds the new record address to the appropriate entry in the occurrence table. If not, it must insert new entries in the values and occurrence tables.

When a record is deleted, its address must be removed from the occurrence table. If no addressees remain in the occurrence table entry, the corresponding values table entry must also be deleted.

When the secondary-key field of a record is modified, the record address must be removed from one occurrence table entry and inserted in another. If the modification is a new value for the key, an entry must be added to the values table.

The inverted list approach to representing secondary keys overcomes objections stated for the linked list approach. Direct processing of sets is possible. For example, the third record in a set can be retrieved without processing the first or second ones. Also, it is possible to dynamically create and delete secondary keys. No changes are made to the records themselves; the DBMS just creates additional values and occurrence tables. Finally, unique keys can be processed efficiently.

The disadvantages of the inverted list approach are that it requires more file space (the table use more overhead than pointers) and that the DBMS programming task is more complex. Note that the *application programming* task is not necessarily any more or less difficult—but it is more complex to write DBMS software that processes inverted lists than it is to write software that processes linked lists. Finally, modifications are usually processed more slowly because I/O is required to access and maintain the values in the occurrence tables.

Summary

Specialized data structures are used for database processing. A flat file is a file that contains no repeating groups. Flat files can be ordered using sequential lists (physically placing the records in the sequence in which they will be processed), linked lists (attaching to each data record a pointer to another logically related record), and inverts lists (building a table, separate from the data records, containing pointers to related records). B-trees are special applications of inverted lists.

Sequential lists, linked lists, and inverted lists (or indexes) are fundamental data structures. (Sequential lists, however, are seldom used in database processing.) These data structures can be used to represent record relationships as well as secondary keys.

The three basic record relationships—trees, simple networks, and complex networks—can be represented using linked lists and inverted lists. Simple networks can be decomposed into trees and then represented; complex networks can be decomposed into simple networks containing an intersection record and then represented.

Secondary keys are used for accessing the data on some field besides the primary key. Secondary keys can be unique or non-unique. Non-unique secondary keys can be represented with both linked lists and inverted lists. Unique secondary keys can be represented only with inverted lists.

||||||||||||||||||||||||||||||||

GROUP I   QUESTIONS

B.1   Define *flat file*. Give an example (other than one in this text) of a flat file and an example of a file that is not flat.

B.2   Show how sequential lists can be used to maintain the file from question B.1 in two different orders simultaneously.

B.3   Show how linked lists can be used to maintain the file from question B.1 in two different orders simultaneously.

B.4   Show how inverted lists can be used to maintain the file from question B.1 in two different orders simultaneously.

B.5   Define *tree* and give an example structure.

B.6   Give an occurrence of the tree from question B.5.

B.7   Represent the occurrence from question B.6 using linked lists.

B.8   Represent the occurrence from question B.6 using inverted lists.

B.9   Define *simple network* and give an example structure.

B.10   Give an occurrence of the simple network from question B.9.

B.11   Represent the occurrence from question B.10 using linked lists.

B.12   Represent the occurrence from question B.10 using inverted lists.

B.13   Define *complex network* and give an example structure.

B.14   Give an occurrence of the complex network from question B.13.

B.15   Decompose the complex network from question B.14 into a simple network, and represent an occurrence of it using inverted lists.

B.16   Explain the difference between primary and secondary keys.

B.17   Explain the difference between unique and non-unique keys.

B.18   Define a *file containing a unique secondary key.* Represent an occurrence of that file using an inverted list on the secondary key.

B.19   Define a *non-unique secondary key* for the file in question B.18. Represent an occurrence of that file using a linked list on the secondary key.

B.20   Perform the same task as in question B.19, only use an inverted list to represent the secondary key.

GROUP II QUESTIONS

B.21   Develop an algorithm to produce a reporting listing the IDs of students enrolled in each class using the linked list structure in Figure B.4.

B.22   Develop an algorithm to insert records into the structure in Figure B.4. The resulting structure should resemble the one in Figure B.5.

B.23   Develop an algorithm to produce a report listing the IDs of students enrolled in each class using the inverted list structure shown in Figures B.8a, b, and c.

B.24   Develop an algorithm to insert a record into the structure in Figure B.8a, being sure to modify both of the associated inverted lists in Figures B.8b and c.

B.25   Develop an algorithm to delete a record from the structure in Figure B.34, which shows a secondary key represented with a linked list. If all records for one of the Credit-limit categories (say, $1000) are deleted, should the associated head pointer also be deleted? Why or why not?

B.26   Develop an algorithm to insert a record into the structure shown in Figure B.34. Suppose the new record has a Credit-limit value different than the ones already established. Should the record be inserted and a new linked list established? Or should the record be rejected? Who should make that decision?

GLOSSARY

Action/Object Menu. A system of menus in which the topmost menu refers to actions and the lower level menus refer to objects on which those actions are taken.

After image. A record of a database entity (normally a row or a page) after a change. Used in recovery to perform rollforward.

AI. Artificial Intelligence.

Analysis paralysis. The situation that results when the development team becomes mired in creating requirements documentation. In large projects, the requirements may take so long to develop that, by the time they are understood and documented, they have changed and must be redone.

Anomaly. Undesirable consequence of a data modification. Used primarily in discussions of normalization. With insertion anomalies, facts about two or more different themes must be added to a single row of a relation. With a deletion anomaly, facts about two or more themes are lost when a single row is deleted.

Application. A business computer system that processes a portion of a database to meet a user's information needs. Consists of menus, forms, reports, and application programs.

Application meta-data. Data dictionary data about the structure and contents of application menus, forms, and reports.

Application program. A custom-developed program for processing a database. Can be written in a standard procedural language such as COBOL, C, or BASIC, or it can be written in a language unique to the DBMS.

Association object. An object that represents the combination of at least two other objects and contains data about that combination. Often used in contracting and assignment applications.

Atomic transaction. A group of logically related database operations that are performed as a unit. Either all of the operations are performed or none of them are.

Attribute. 1) Column of a relation. Also called column, field, and data-item. Also called logical transaction. 2) Less common, a synonym for property in an entity or semantic object.

Base table. In relational implementations, the table from which relational views are defined.

Before image.   A record of a database entity (normally a row or a page) prior to a change. Used in recovery to perform rollback.

Binary relationship.   A relationship between exactly two entities or objects.

Bottom-up database design.   The process of designing a database that works from the detailed and specific to the general. Quick, but may result in a database design that is too narrow in scope.

Boyce-Codd normal form.   A relation in third normal form in which every determinant is a candidate key.

Buffer.   An area of memory used to hold data. For a read, data is read from a storage device into a buffer; for a write, data is written from the buffer to storage.

Built-in function.   In SQL, any of the functions COUNT, SUM, AVG, MAX, or MIN.

Byzantine failure.   Intentional node or network failure caused by malevolent nodes, perhaps acting as a conspiracy.

Call.   A programming language statement that passes control to an external subroutine for a service. The expectation is that control will be passed back. Examples include CALL, GOSUB, and BAL.

Candidate key.   An attribute or group of attributes that identifies a unique row in a relation. One of the candidate keys is chosen to be the primary key.

Cardinality.   In a binary relationship, the maximum or minimum number of elements allowed on each side of the relationship. The maximum cardinality can be 1:1, 1:N, N:1, and N:M. The minimum cardinality can be Optional:Optional, Optional:Mandatory, Mandatory:Optional, and Mandatory:Mandatory.

Cartesian product.   A relational operation on two relations, A and B, producing a third relation, C, such that C contains the concatenation of every row in A with every row in B.

CCP.   Communications control program. A program that controls and administers transactions requests and responses in a teleprocessing system. The CCP routes transactions to the correct application programs and returns responses to the correct user terminal.

Checkboxes.   In a GUI environment, an element of the user interface in which a user can select one or more items from a list. Items are selected by clicking on them.

Checkpoint.   The point of synchronization between a database and a transaction log. All buffers are force-written to external storage. This is the standard definition; this term is sometimes used in other ways by DBMS vendors.

Child.   A row, record, or node on the many side of a one-to-many relationship.

Child and twin pointer scheme.   In DL/I, a technique used to represent segment relationships of a data base record in storage.

Client computer.   A microcomputer on a local area network with client/server architecture. In a database application, the client computer processes database application programs. Requests for actions on the database are sent to the database computer.

Client/server architecture.   The structure of a local area network in which one microcomputer performs services on behalf of other microcomputers. For a database system, the server computer, which is called a database server, processes the DBMS, and client computers process the application programs. All database activity is processed by the database server.

COBOL.   Common Business Oriented Language. The most widely used third generation language for business applications.

CODASYL. Conference on Data Systems Languages. A non-profit committee of vendor, user, and academic personnel who established and now maintain the conventions for COBOL. The DBTG, or DataBase Task Group, developed a network model which was popular in the 1970s and early 1980s, but which is fading from use.

Column. A logical group of bytes in a row of a relation or a table. The meaning of a column is the same for every row of the relation.

Command. A statement input to a database application by which users specify the activity to be performed. *Contrast* with **Menu.**

Commit. A command issued to the DBMS to make database modifications permanent. Once the command has been processed, the changes are written to the database and to a log in such a way that they will survive system crashes and other failures. Usually used at the end of an atomic transaction. *Contrast* with **Rollback.**

Communications Control Program. *See* **CCP.**

Complex network. A collection of entities, objects, or relations and their relationships in which at least one of the relationships is complex (many-to-many).

Compound object. An object that contains at least one other object.

Composite group. A group of properties in a semantic object that is multi-valued.

Composite key. A key having more than one attribute.

Composite object. An object having at least one multivalued property or property group. So named because the key of the relation that represents the multivalued property or group will be a composite key.

Computed value. A column of a table that is computed from other column values. Values are not stored but are computed when they are to be displayed.

Concurrency transparency. In a distributed database system, the condition in which application programs do not know and do not need to know if data is being concurrently processed. The DDBMS organizes update activities so that the results produced when concurrent processing is underway are consistent with the results that would occur if there were no concurrent processing.

Concurrent processing. In teleprocessing applications, the sharing of the CPU among several transactions. The CPU is allocated to each transaction in round robin or in some other fashion for a certain period of time. Operations are performed so quickly that they appear to users to be simultaneous. In local area network and other distributed applications, the term is used to refer to the (possibly simultaneous) processing of applications on multiple computers.

Constraint. A rule on the allowed values of attributes whose truth can be evaluated. Usually does not include dynamic rules such as "SalesPersonPay can never decrease" or "Salary now must be greater than Salary last quarter".

CPU. Central Processing Unit. The portion of the computer hardware that processes arithmetic and logic instructions. Term usually includes main memory as well.

Currency indicator. In the CODASYL DBTG model, a variable which identifies the most recently accessed record or set. There are currency indicators for run-unit, record-type, and set.

Cursor. An indicator of the current position or focus. 1) On a computer screen, a blinking box or underscore that indicates the position into which the next entry will be made. 2) In a file or embedded SQL SELECT, the identity of the next record or row to be processed.

Data access language. *See* **data sub-language.**

Data administration.   The enterprise-wide function that concerns the effective use and control of the organization's data assets. Can be an individual but more often is a group. Specific functions include setting data standards and data policies and providing a forum for conflict resolution. *See* **database administrator.**

Data base record.   In DL/I, a hierarchical collection of segments. See logical data base record and physical data base record.

Data dictionary.   A user-accessible catalog of both database and application meta-data. An active data dictionary is a dictionary whose contents are updated by the DBMS automatically whenever changes are made to the database or application structure. A passive data dictionary is one whose contents must be manually updated when changes are made.

Data dictionary and database administration subsystem.   A collection of programs within the DBMS used to access the data dictionary and to perform database administration functions such as maintaining passwords, performing backup and recovery, and other similar functions.

Data-item.   1) A logical group of bytes in a record. Usually used with file processing. 2) In the context of the relational model, a synonym for attribute.

Data model.   1) a model of the users' data requirements expressed in terms of either the E-R model or the Semantic Object model. Sometimes called a users' data model. 2) a language for describing the structure and processing of a database; *see* **hierarchical data model, network data model,** and **relational data model.**

Data owner.   Same as **data proponent.**

Data proponent.   In the context of data administration, a department or other organizational unit in charge of managing a particular data item.

Data structure diagram.   A graphical display of tables (files) and their relationships. Tables are shown in rectangles; relationships are shown by lines. A many relationship is shown with a fork on the end of the line. Optional relationships are depicted by ovals; mandatory relationships are shown with hash marks.

Data sub-language.   A language for defining and processing a database that is intended to be embedded in programs written in another language—in most cases, a procedural language such as COBOL, C, or BASIC. A data sub-language is an incomplete programming language; it contains only constructs for data access.

Database.   A self-describing collection of integrated records.

Database administrator.   The individual or group responsible for establishing policies and procedures to control and protect a database. Works within guidelines set by Data Administration to control database structure, manage data change activities, and maintain DBMS programs.

Database machine.   Special purpose CPU that is designed specifically for processing a database. Sometimes called backend machine because it resides between the operating system and the data. Not commercially successful and seldom used today.

Database server.   On a local area network with client/server architecture, the microcomputer that runs the DBMS and processes actions against the database on behalf of the client computers.

Dataflow diagram.   A graphical display by systems developers that illustrates business processes and the data interfaces. Shows the flow of the system from the perspective of data.

DB2.   Data Base 2. A relational DBMS developed and licensed by IBM for use on mainframe computers.

DBA.   *See* **Database administrator.**

DBM.   Database Manager. In a DDBMS, software that processes some portion of a distributed database in accordance with action requests received from distributed transactions managers (DTMs).

DBMS.   Database Management System. A set of programs used to define, administer, and process the database and its applications.

DBMS engine.   A DBMS subsystem that processes logical I/O requests from other DBMS subsystems. It submits physical I/O requests to the operating system.

DBTG.   1) A subcommittee of CODASYL that developed the DBTG network data model. 2) A network data model which models data as records and record relationships as sets. Only simple networks can be directly represented. Fading in popularity, but still in use on mainframe computers.

DDBMS.   Distributed database management system. 1) The collection of DTMs and DBMs on all computers that process a distributed database (*see* Chapter 16). 2) A commercial DBMS product that has been modified to allow for processing of a distributed database.

DDL.   Data Definition Language. The portion of a data model that is used to define the structure of the database, views, and subschemas.

Deadlock.   A condition that can occur during concurrent processing in which each of two (or more) transactions is waiting to access data the other transaction has locked. Also called the *deadly embrace.*

Deadly embrace.   *See* **Deadlock.**

Definition tools subsystem.   The portion of the DBMS program that is used to define and change the database structure.

Degree.   For relationships in the E-R model, the number of entities that participate in the relationship. In almost all cases, relationships are of degree 2.

Deletion anomaly.   In a relation, the situation in which the removal of one row of a table deletes facts about two or more themes.

Determinant.   One or more attributes that functionally determine another attribute or attributes. In the functional dependency $(A, B) \longrightarrow C$, the attributes (A, B) are the determinant.

Difference.   A relational algebra operation performed on two union-compatible relations, A and B, that produces a third relation, C. Each row in C will be present in A but not in B.

Distributed database.   A database that is stored on two or more computers. Distributed data can be partitioned or not-partitioned, replicated or not-replicated.

Distributed database application.   A business computer system in which the execution of transactions and the retrieval and updating of data occurs across two or more independent and usually geographically distributed computers.

Distributed two-phase locking.   Two-phase locking in a distributed environment. Locks are obtained and released across all nodes on the network. *See* **two-phase locking.**

DL/I.   Data Language I. A data model developed by IBM in the late 1960s for defining and processing hierarchical databases. The IBM DBMS product IMS is based on DL/I. IMS is still in widespread use on mainframes, but such databases are slowly being replaced by relational databases.

DML.   Data Manipulation Language. The portion of a data model used to describe the processing of a database.

Domain.   1) The set of all possible values an attribute can have. 2) A description of the format (data type, length) and the semantics (meaning) of an attribute.

Domain/key normal form.   A relation in which all constraints are logical consequences of domains and keys.

Download.   Copying database data from one computer to another, usually from a mainframe or mini to a microcomputer or LAN.

DSD.   *See* **Data Structure Diagram.**

DSS.   Decision Support System. An interactive computer-based facility for assisting decision making, especially for semi-structured and unstructured problem situations. Often includes a database and query/update facility for processing ad hoc requests.

DTM.   Distributed Transaction Manager. In a DDBMS, software that receives processing requests from users or application programs and translates them into DBM actions requests. A DTM can send requests to DBMs on nodes different from its own.

Encapsulated Data.   Data that is contained within a program or object that is not visible or accessible to other programs or objects.

Entity.   1) A distinct thing that is of importance to a user that needs to be represented in a database. 2) In the E-R model, entities are restricted to things that can be represented by a single table. *Also see* **strong entity, weak entity,** and **existence dependent entity.**

Entity class.   A set of entities of the same type, e. g., EMPLOYEE and DEPARTMENT.

Entity instance.   A particular occurrence of an entity, e. g., Employee 100 and the Accounting Department.

Entity-relationship diagram.   A graphic used to represent entities and their relationships. Entities are normally shown in squares or rectangles and relationships are shown in diamonds. The cardinality of the relationship is shown inside the diamond.

Entity-relationship model.   Constructs and conventions used to create a model of the users' data (*see* **data model**). The things in the users' world are represented by entities and the associations among those things are represented by relationships. Results are usually documented in an E-R Diagram.

Entry-point relation.   Used with regard to the relations that represent an object. The entry-point relation is the relation whose key is the same as the key of the object it represents. The entry point relation is normally the first relation processed. Also, the name of the entry point relation is normally the same as the name of the object.

Equijoin.   The process of joining relation A containing attribute A1 with B containing attribute B1 to form a relation C such that, for each row in C, A1 = B1. Both A1 and B1 will be represented in C.

E-R Diagram.   *See* **entity-relationship diagram.**

Existence dependent entity.   Same as **weak entity.** An entity that cannot appear in the database unless an instance of one or more other entities also appears in the database. A subclass of existence dependent entities are ID-dependent entities.

Export.   A function of the DBMS which writes a file of data in bulk. The file is intended to be read by another DBMS or program.

Extract.   A portion of an operational database downloaded to a LAN or microcomputer for local processing. Extracts are created to reduce communications cost and time when querying and creating reports from data created by transaction processing.

Failure transparency. In a distributed database system, the condition in which application programs are isolated from failure.

Field. 1) A logical group of bytes in a record. Used with file processing. 2) In the context of the relational model, synonym for **attribute.**

File processing system. An information system in which data is stored in separate files. There is no integrated data dictionary. The format of files is usually stored in application programs.

File server. In a local area network , a microcomputer which contains a file which it processes on behalf of other microcomputers on the network. This term is normally used for the resource sharing architecture. *See* **client computer, client/server architecture, database server,** and **resource sharing architecture.**

First normal form. Any table that fits the definition of relation.

Flat file. A file that has only a single value in each field. The meaning of the columns is the same in every row.

Force-write. A write of database data in which the DBMS waits for acknowledgement from the operating system that the after-image of the write has been successfully written to the log.

Foreign key. An attribute that is a key of one or more relations other than the one in which it appears.

Form. 1) A display on a computer screen used to present, enter, and modify data. Also called a data entry form or panel. 2) A paper document used in a business system to record data, usually about a transaction. Forms are analyzed in the process of building a data model.

Forms generator. A portion of the Application Development Subsystem that is used to create a data entry form without having to write any application program code.

Fourth normal form. A relation in third Boyce-Codd normal form in which every multi-valued dependency is a functional dependency.

Fragment. A row in a table (or record in a file) in which a required parent or child is not present. For example, a row in a LINE-ITEM table for which no ORDER row exists.

Fully concatenated key. In DL/I, a composite of the sequence fields of a segment and the sequence fields of all of its parents. The root occupies the leftmost position in the concatenated key. The segment occupies the rightmost position.

Functional dependency. A relationship between attributes such that one attribute or group of attributes determines the value of another. The expression $X \longrightarrow Y$ is read "X determines Y" or "Y is functionally dependent on X." It means, given a value of X, we can determine the value of Y.

Generalization hierarchy. A set of objects or entities of the same logical type that are arranged in a hierarchy of logical sub-types. For example, EMPLOYEE has subtypes ENGINEER and ACCOUNTANT. ENGINEER has the subtypes ELECTRICAL ENGINEER and MECHANICAL ENGINEER. Subtypes inherit characteristics of their supertypes.

Generalization object. An object that contains subtype objects. The generalization object and its subtypes all have the same key. Subtype objects inherit properties from the generalization object.

Granularity. The size of database resource that can be locked. Locking the entire database is large granularity; locking a column of a particular row is small granularity.

Graphical user interface. An interface having windows, graphical symbols, pop-down menus, and other structures that are often manipulated with a mouse pointer. Popular graphical user interface products are Windows from Microsoft and the Macintosh System Software from Apple.

GUI. *See* **graphical user interface.**

HAS-A relationship. In the E-R model, a relationship between two entities of different logical types. EMPLOYEE HAS-A(n) AUTO. *Contrast* with **IS-A.**

Hierarchical data model. A data model that represents all relationships using hierarchies or trees. Network structures must be decomposed into trees before they can be represented by a hierarchial data model. DL/I is the only surviving hierarchical data model.

Hierarchy. *See* **Tree.**

Host variable. A variable in an application program into which a DBMS places a value from the database.

Hybrid object. An object that contains a mixture of object types. Often, composite/compound or generalization/composite/compound.

ID-dependent entity. An entity that cannot logically exist without the existence of another entity. An APPOINTMENT, for example, cannot exist without a CLIENT to make the appointment. The ID-dependent entity always contains the key of the entity on which it depends. Such entities are a subset of a weak entity.

Import. A function of the DBMS which reads an entire file of data in bulk.

IMS. Information Management System. A transaction processing system developed and licensed by IBM. It includes IMS/DC, a communications control program, and IMS/DB, a DBMS that implements the DL/I data model.

Inconsistent read. An anomaly that occurs in concurrent processing in which transactions execute a series of reads inconsistent with one another. Can be prevented by two-phase locking and other strategies.

Index. Overhead data used to improve access and sorting performance. Indexes can be constructed for a single column or for groups of columns. Especially useful for columns used for control breaks in reports and for columns used to specify conditions in joins.

Index space. An area of disk storage in which DB2 stores an index.

Information bearing set. In the CODASYL DBTG data model, a set in which the relationship between records is not represented in data values. The relationship is recorded in overhead data created and processed by the DBMS. The relationship is not visible in data. *Contrast* with **Non-information bearing set.**

Insane node. A node which fails in an unexpected manner. Such a node may transmit garbage across the network or may accidentally transmit invalid transactions that appear valid. *Contrast* with **Byzantine failure** and **sane node.**

Insertion anomaly. In a relation, the condition that exists when, to add a complete row to a table, one must add facts about two or more logically different themes.

Insertion status. In the CODASYL DBTG model, a rule that determines how records are to be placed into sets. Records can be placed automatically by the DBMS or manually by the application program.

Inter-relation constraint. A restriction that requires the value of an attribute in a row of one relation to match the value of an attribute found in another relation. For example, Cust# in ORDER must equal Cust# in CUSTOMER.

Intersection. A relational algebra operation performed on two union compatible relations, A and B, forming a third relation, C, such that C contains only rows that appear in both A and B.

Intersection relation. A relation that is used to represent a many-to-many relationship. It contains the keys of the relations in the relationship. When used to represent many-to-many compound objects, it has no non-key data. When used to represent entities having a many-to-many relationship, it may have non-key data if the relationship has data.

Intra-relation constraint.   A restriction on data values within a relation. For example, in PART (Part#, P-name, Units), the rule that if Part# starts with a 1, then Units must equal Pounds.

I/O.   Input/Output. The process within the operating system that reads and writes data from and to peripheral storage devices.

IS-A relationships.   In the E-R model, a relationship between two entities of the same logical type. ENGINEER IS-A(n) EMPLOYEE; both of these entities are employees and are of the same logical type. *Contrast* with **HAS-A relationships.**

Join.   A relational algebra operation on two relations, A and B, that produces a third relation, C. A row of A is concatenated with a row of B to form a new row in C if the rows in A and B meet restrictions about their values. For example, A1 is an attribute in A and B1 is an attribute in B. The join of A with B where A1< B1 will result in a relation C having the concatenation of rows in A and B in which the value of A1 is less than the value of B1. *See* **equijoin** and **natural join.**

Key.   1) A group of one or more attributes that identifies a unique row in a relation. Since relations may not have duplicate rows, every relation has at least one key, which is the composite of all of the attributes in the relation. Sometimes called *logical key.* 2) With some relational DBMS products, an index on a column used to improve access and sorting speed. Sometimes called *physical key.*

LAN.   Local Area Network. A group of microcomputers connected to each other via communications lines within close proximity, usually less than a mile. *See* **resource sharing** and **client/ server architectures.**

LDBR.   *See* **logical data base record.**

List box.   In a GUI environment, an element of the user interface in which a list of choices is presented in a rectangle. The user moves the cursor to shade the item to be selected from the list.

Location transparency.   In a distributed database system, the condition in which application programs do not know and do not need to know where data is located. The DDBMS finds data, wherever it is located, without involvement on the part of the application program.

Lock.   The process of allocating a database resource to a particular transaction in a concurrent processing system. The size of the resource locked is known as the lock granularity. With an *exclusive lock,* no other transaction may read or write the resource. With a *shared lock,* other transactions may read the resource, but no other transaction may write it.

Log.   A file that contains a record of database changes. The log contains before images and after images.

Logical data base record.   In DL/I, a hierarchy of segments as perceived by an application program. Such a structure may or may not exist physically; it may be materialized from other structures using pointers and other overhead data.

Logical unit of work.   A group of logically related database operations that are performed as a unit. Either all of the operations are performed or none of them are. Same as **atomic transaction.** Term used with the DBMS DB2.

Lookup.   The process of obtaining related data by using the value of a foreign key. For example, when processing a row of ORDER (Order#, Ord-Date, Cust#, . . .), using the value of Cust# to obtain the related value of Cust-Name from CUSTOMER (Cust#, Cust-Name, . . .).

LUW.   *See* **logical unit of work.**

Mask.   A format used when presenting data in a form or report.

Materialization.   1) The physical appearance of data in a form or report. 2) The appearance of a view of a semantic object in a form or report.

Member.   In the CODASYL DBTG model, a record type that is on the many side of a one-to-many or set relationship.

Menu.   A list of options presented to the user of a database (or other) application. The user selects the next action or activity from a list. Actions are restricted to those in the list. *Contrast* with **Command.**

Meta-data.   Data about the structure of data in a database stored in the **data dictionary.** Meta-data is used to describe tables, columns, constraints, indexes, and so forth. *Compare* to **application meta-data.**

Method.   A program attached to an object-oriented-programming (OOP) object. Methods can be inherited by lower level OOP objects.

Modeless processing.   In a database application, the characteristic of inferring the mode of the user's processing from the user's actions. For example, on entering a key field, if the value exists in the database, inferring that an update is to occur; if the value does not exist in the database, inferring that an insert is to occur.

Modem.   Modulator-demodulator. A device used to convert digital signals to analog signals and the reverse. Most often used to communicate over telephone lines.

Multivalued dependency.   A condition in a relation with three or more attributes in which independent attributes appear to have relationships they do not have. Formally, in a relation R (A, B, C), having key (A, B, C) where A is matched with multiple values of B (or of C, or both), B does not determine C, and C does not determine B. For example, in the relation EMPLOYEE (Emp#, Emp-skill, Dependent-name), where an employee can have multiple values of Emp-skill and Dependent-name. Emp-skill and Dependent-name do not have any relationship, but they appear to in the relation.

Natural join.   A join of a relation A having attribute A1 with relation B having attribute B1 where A1 equals B1. The joined relation, C, contains either column A1 or B1, but not both. *Contrast* with **equijoin.**

Natural language interface.   An interface to an application program or DBMS by which users can enter requests in the form of standard English or other language.

Network data model.   A data model which supports at least simple network relationships. The CODASYL DBTG, which supports simple network relationships but not complex relationships, is the most important network data model.

Node.   1) An entity in a tree. 2) A computer in a distributed processing system.

Non-information bearing set.   In the CODAYSL DBTG model, a set in which the child record type contains the key of the parent record type. The set ownership is implied by the value of the key in the child record instances.

Non-object property.   A property of a semantic object that is a simple value and not an object.

Normal form.   A rule or set of rules governing the allowed structure of relations. The rules involve attributes, functional dependencies, multi-valued dependencies, domains, and constraints. The most important normal forms are 1NF, 2NF, 3NF, Boyce-Codd NF, 4NF, 5NF, and Domain/key normal form.

Normalization.   The process of evaluating a relation to determine if it is in a specified normal form and of converting it into relations that are in that specified normal form, if necessary.

Null value.   A value that has either unknown or not applicable. A null value is not the same as a zero or blank, although in most commercial DBMS products, null values are represented by zeros or blanks.

Object. 1) A semantic object. 2) A structure in an object-oriented program that contains an encapsulated data structure and methods. Such objects are arranged in a hierarchy so that objects can inherit methods from their parents. 3) In DB2, a term used to refer to data bases, tables, views, indexes and other structures. 4) In security systems, a unit of data that is protected by a password or by other means.

Object diagram. A portrait-oriented rectangle that represents the structure of a semantic object.

Object instance. The occurrence of a particular semantic object, i.e., the SALESPERSON semantic object having LastName equal to Jones.

Object property. A property of a semantic object that is, itself, an object.

Object view. The portion of a semantic object that is visible to a particular application. A view consists of the name of the semantic object plus a list of the properties that are visible in that view.

Option button. In a GUI environment, an element of the user interface in which the user can select an item from a list. Clicking on one button de-selects the button that is currently pressed (if any). Operates like radio buttons in a car radio. Same as radio button (*see* **radio button**) but introduced under a different name to avoid litigation among vendors.

Orphan. Any row (record) that is missing its parent in a mandatory one-to-many relationship.

Overhead data. Meta-data that is created by the DBMS to improve performance, for example, indexes and linked lists.

Owner. 1) In the CODASYL DBTG model, a record type that is on the one side of a one-to-many or set relationship. 2) In the context of data administration, a department or other organizational unit that is in charge of the management of a particular data item.

Page. A unit of disk storage. In DB2, a 4K block of contiguous disk space. Used to hold database, data dictionary, and overhead data.

Panel. A display on a computer screen used to present, enter, and modify data. Same as form.

Parent. A row, record, or node on the one side of a one-to-many relationship.

Partition. 1) A portion of a distributed database. 2) The portion of a network that is separated from the rest of the network during a network failure.

PDBR. *See* **physical data base record.**

Perfect node. A node that never fails. Such nodes exist only theoretically and are used only in the study of failure/recovery techniques.

Pervasive key. In a database application, a key that performs the same function throughout the application. The meaning of the key always remains the same.

Physical data base record. In DL/I, a hierarchy of segments that as it is stored in data base files.

PL/I. Programming Language I. A third generation programming language promulgated by IBM.

Pointer. An address to an instance of a data structure. Often, the address of a record in a directly addressed file.

Pop-down list box. In a GUI environment, a list box which appears when the user selects an icon that represents the box.

Precompiler. A program that translates the database access commands of a particular DBMS product. Such commands are embedded in an application program normally written in a third-generation language. The commands are translated into data structures and calls to DBMS processing routines in the syntax of the third generation language.

Primary key.   A candidate key that is selected to be the key of a relation.

Processing interface subsystem.   That portion of the DBMS routines that executes commands for processing the database. It accepts input from interactive query programs and from application programs written in standard languages or in DBMS specific languages.

Processing rights and responsibilities.   Organizational policies regarding which groups can take which actions to specified data-items or other collections of data.

Product.   A relational operation on two relations, A and B, producing a third relation, C, such that C contains the concatenation of every row in A with every row in B. Same as Cartesian product.

Projection.   A relational algebra operation performed on a relation, A, that results in a relation, B, where B has a (possibly improper) subset of the attributes of A. Projection is used to form a new relation that reorders the attributes in the original relation or to form a new relation that has only some of the attributes from the original relation.

Program/data independence.   The condition that exists when the structure of the data is not defined in application programs. It is defined in the database and application programs obtain it from the DBMS. In this way, changes can be made to data structures and not necessarily require changes to application programs.

Property.   A characteristic of an entity or semantic object.

Proponent.   *See* **data proponent.**

Prototype.   A quickly-developed demonstration of an application or portion of an application.

QBE.   Query by Example. A style of query interface, first developed by IBM but now used by other vendors, that allows users to express queries by providing examples of the results they seek.

R°.   An experimental distributed database management system developed by IBM. It allows the database to be partitioned, but not replicated.

Radio button.   In a GUI environment, an element of the user interface in which the user can select one item from a list. Clicking on one button de-selects the button that is currently pressed (if any). Operates like radio buttons in a car radio.

Real output.   An output that is transmitted to the client of an information system such as an order confirmation. When produced in error, such outputs cannot be changed by recovering the database. Instead, compensating transactions must be executed.

Record.   1) A group of fields pertaining to the same entity. Used in file processing systems. 2) In the context of the relational model, synonym for row and tuple.

Recursive relationship.   A relationship among entities, objects, or rows of the same type. For example, where CUSTOMERs refer other CUSTOMERs, the relationship *refers* is recursive.

Referential integrity.   The condition in a database in which all inter-relation constraints are satisfied.

Relation.   A two-dimensional array containing single-valued entries and no duplicate rows. The meaning of the columns is the same in every row. The order of the rows and columns is immaterial. Same as **table.**

Relational data model.   A data model in which data is stored in relations and relationships between rows are represented by data values.

Relational database.   A database consisting of relations. Usually, such a database is structured according to the principles of normalization. In practice, relational databases contain relations having duplicate rows. Most DBMS products include a feature to remove duplicate rows when necessary and appropriate. Such removal is not performed as a matter of course because it can be time-consuming and expensive.

Relational schema. A set of relations with inter-relation constraints.

Relationship. An association between two entities, objects, or rows of relations.

Replicated data. In a distributed database, data that is stored on two or more computers.

Replication transparency. In a distributed database system, the condition in which application programs do not know and do not need to know whether data is replicated. If it is replicated, the DDBMS ensures that all copies are updated consistently without involvement on the part of the application program.

Report. An extraction of data from a database. Reports can be printed, displayed on a computer screen, or stored as a file. Part of a database application. *Compare* with **form.**

Resource sharing architecture. The structure of a local area network in which one microcomputer performs file processing services on behalf of other microcomputers. In a database application, each user computer contains a copy of the DBMS which forwards input/output requests to the file server. Only file I/O is processed by the file server; all database activity is processed by the DBMS on the user's computer.

Retention status. In the CODASYL DBTG model, a rule that states whether or not a record must exist in a set. If FIXED, a record may never be removed from its original set. If MANDA-TORY, a record must be a member of a set, once it is placed into a set. If OPTIONAL, a record may or may not reside in a set.

Rollback. The process of recovering a database in which before images are applied to the database to return to a prior checkpoint or other point in which the database is logically consistent.

Rollforward. The process of recovering a database by applying after images to a saved copy of the database to bring it to a checkpoint or other point in which the database is logically consistent.

Root. The topmost record, row, or node in a tree. The root has no parent.

Row. A group of columns in a table. All of the columns in a row pertain to the same entity. Synonymous with **tuple** and **record.**

Run-unit. In the CODASYL DBTG model, the execution of an application program by a user. Several run-units may be utilizing the same application program concurrently.

Sane node. A node which fails only in a known and anticipated fashion.

Schema. A complete logical view of the database.

Screen. *See* **form.**

Second normal form. A relation in first normal form in which all non-key attributes are dependent on all of the key.

Segment. In DL/I, a collection of fields that is a node in a data base record.

Segment search argument. An expression in a DL/I that indicates the segment or segments on which the command is to be applied.

Selection. A relational algebra operation performed on a relation, A, producing a relation, B, such that B contains only the rows in A that meet restrictions specified in the selection.

Semantic object model. Constructs and conventions used to create a model of the users' data. The things in the users' world are represented by semantic objects (sometimes called objects). Relationships are modeled within the objects. Results are usually documented in object diagrams.

Sequence field. In DL/I, a field that is used to logically order segments of a given type under a given parent. The order can be ascending or descending.

Set. In the CODASYL DBTG model, a structure that represents a one-to-many relationship among records. The parent record type is called the set *owner* and the child record type(s) is called the set *member*.

Sibling. A record or node that has the same parent as another record or node.

Simple network. 1) A set of three relations and two relationships such that one of the relations, R, has a many-to-one relationship with the other two relations. Rows in R have two parents, and the parents are of different types. 2) Any set of tables and relationships containing the structure defined in 1).

Simple object. An object that contains no repeating properties and no object properties.

SQL. Structured Query Language. A language for defining the structure and processing of a relational database. Used as a stand alone query language and also embedded in application programs. Accepted as a national standard by the American National Standards Institute. Developed by IBM.

Strong entity. In the entity-relationship model, any entity whose existence in the database does not depend on the existence of any other entity. *See also* **weak entity** and **ID-dependent entity.**

Subschema. A subset of a database that is processed by one more applications. Also called an *application view.* Used primarily with the CODASYL DBTG model.

Subtype. In generalization hierarchies, an entity or object that is a sub-species or sub-category of a higher level type. ENGINEER is a subtype of EMPLOYEE.

Supertype. In generalization hierarchies, an entity or object that logically contains subtypes. EMPLOYEE is a supertype of ENGINEER, ACCOUNTANT, and MANAGER.

System set. In the CODASYL DBTG model, a set that is owned by the DBMS. Used for sequential processing of all of the records of a given type.

Table space. In DB2, a collection of one or more VSAM data sets, or files, used to store database data on magnetic disk.

Third normal form. A relation in second normal form that has no transitive dependencies.

Top-down database design. The process of designing a database that works from the general to the specific. Resulting databases can serve the overall needs of the organization; the danger is that they may never be completed. *See* **bottom-up design** and **analysis paralysis.**

Transaction. 1) An atomic transaction. 2) The record of an event that occurs in the business world.

Transitive dependency. In a relation having a least three attributes, R(A, B, C), the situation in which A determines B, B determines C, and B does not determine A.

Tree. A collection of records, entities, or other data structures in which each element has at most one parent except for the topmost element which has no parent.

Trigger. A procedure invoked when a specified condition exists in the data of a database. For example, when Quantity-on-Hand of an item reaches 0 (or some specified amount), a procedure could be triggered to order more of the item.

Tuple. Synonym for **row.**

Twin. A record or node that has the same parent as another record or node.

Two-phase commitment. In distributed database systems, a process of commitment among nodes in which the nodes first vote on whether they can commit a transaction. If all nodes vote yes, the transaction is committed. If any node votes no, then the transaction is aborted. Required to prevent inconsistent processing in distributed databases.

Two-phase locking. The procedure by which locks are obtained and released in two phases. During the growing phase, locks are obtained. During the shrinking phase, locks are released. Once a lock is released, no other lock will be granted that transaction. Such a procedure ensures consistency in database updates in a concurrent processing environment.

Union. A relational algebra operation performed on two union compatible relations, say A and B forming a third relation, say C, such that C contains every row in both A and B, minus any duplicate rows.

Union compatible. Two tables have the same number of attributes and where the attributes in corresponding columns arise from the same domain.

User work area. In the CODASYL DBTG model, an area of main memory that contains data values pertaining to a particular run-unit.

UWA. *See* **user work area.**

VAR. Value Added Reseller. A person, company, or group which develops database applications and resells them to other companies. The VAR adds value to the DBMS product by building the application.

View. 1) The subset of a database that can be processed by an application. 2) An object view.

Weak entity. In the entity-relationship model, an entity whose existence in the database depends on the existence of another entity. *See also* **ID-dependent entity** and **strong entity.**

Window dressing. The fixed text, lines, boxes, and other graphical symbols, and the positions of such text and graphical symbols that are used in a form or report. A materialization of an object is a view of the object plus the window dressing.

WYSIWIG. What you see is what you get. A term used with form and report generators in which the DBMS recreates exactly what the developer types on the screen during form and report development.

BIBLIOGRAPHY

||||||||||||||||||||||||||||||

Agostic, M. & Johnson, R.G. "A Framework of Reference for Database Design." In *ACM Data Base,* Vol. 15, No. 4, Summer, 1984, pp. 3–9.

Aho, A.V., Hopcroft, E., & Ullman, J.D. *The Design and Analysis of Computer Programs.* Addison-Wesley, 1975.

ANSI X3. *American National Standard for Information Systems—Database Language—SQL.* ANSI, 1986.

ANSI X3H2. *Proposed American National Standard for a Data Definition Language for Network Structured Databases.* American National Standards Institute, 1981.

ANSI X3H2. *Overview of DBCS/Programming Language Interface.* American National Standards Institute, 1982.

Astrahan, M.M., et al. "System R: Relational Approach to Database Management." In *Transactions on Database Systems*, Vol. 1, No. 2, June 1976.

Astrahan, M.M., et al. "System R: A Relational Database Management System." In *Computer,* Vol. 12, No. 5, May 1979.

Astrahan, M.M., et al. "A History and Evaluation of System R," *IBM Research Report* RJ2843, June 1980.

Atre, S. *Data Base: Structured Techniques for Design, Performance, and Management.* John Wiley, 1980.

Banerjee, J. "Data Model Issues for Object-Oriented Applications." In *ACM Transactions on Office Information Systems*, Vol. 5. No. 1, January 1987.

Bernstein, P.A., & Goodman, N. "Concurrency Control in Distributed Database Systems." In *Computing Surveys*, Vol. 13, No. 2, June 1981.

Bernstein, P.A., & Goodman, N. "An Algorithm for Concurrency Control and Recovery in Replicated Distributed Databases." In *Transactions on Database Systems*, Vol. 9, No. 4, December 1984.

Bernstein, P.A., Rothnie, J.B., & Shipman, D.W. *Distributed Data Base Management.* IEEE Catalog No. EHO 141-2, 1978.

Blaha, M., Premerlani, W.J., & Rumbaugh, J.E. "Relational Database Design Using an Object-Oriented Methodology." In *Communications of the ACM,* Vol. 31, No. 4, April, 1988, pp. 414–427.

Blasgen, M.W., et al. "System R: An Architectural Overview." In *IBM Systems Journal,* Vol. 20, No. 1, January 1981.

Boehm, B.W. *Software Engineering Economics.* Prentice-Hall, 1981.

Bohl, M. *Introduction to IBM Direct Access Storage Devices.* Science Research Associates, 1981.

Boulanger, D. & March, S.T. "An Approach to Analyzing the Information Content of Existing Databases." In *ACM Data Base,* Vol. 20, No. 2, Summer, 1989, pp. 1–8.

Boyce, R.F., et al. "Specifying Queries as Relational Expressions: SQUARE." In *Communications of the ACM,* Vol. 18, No. 11, November 1975.

Bray, O.H. *Distributed Database Management Systems.* Lexington Books, 1982.

Britton-Lee Corporation. *IDM 500.* Britton-Lee, 1982.

Browning, D. "Data Managers and LANs." In *PC Tech Journal,* Vol. 5, No. 5, May 1987.

Carlson, D.A. & Ram, S. "An Architecture for Distributed Knowledge Based Systems." In *ACM Data Base,* Vol. 22, No. 1/2, Winter/Spring, 1991.

Cashing, D.L. *A Programmer's Guide to File Processing.* PWS-Kent, 1991.

Chamberlin, D.D., et al. "SEQUEL 2: A Unified Approach to Data Definition, Manipulation, and Control." In *IBM Journal of Research and Development,* Vol. 20, No. 6, November 1976.

Chen, P. "The Entity-Relationship Model: Toward a Unified View of Data." In *ACM Transactions on Database Systems,* Vol. 1., No. 1, March 1976.

Chen, P. *The Entity-Relationship Approach to Logical Data Base Design.* QED Information Sciences, Data Base Monograph Series, No. 6, 1977.

Chen, P. *Entity-Relationship Approach to Information Modeling.* E-R Institute, 1981.

Chorfas, D.N. *Databases for Networks and Minicomputers.* Petrocelli, 1982.

Chu, W.W., & Chen, P.P. *Centralized and Distributed Data Base Systems.* IEEE Catalog No. EHO 154-5, 1979.

CINCOM Systems Incorporated. *TOTAL Reference Manual.* CINCOM Systems, 1982.

CODASYL. *Data Base Task Group Report, 1971.* Association for Computing Machinery, 1975.

CODASYL COBOL Committee. *COBOL Journal of Development,* 1978.

CODASYL Data Base Administrators Working Group. *Data Structure Definition,* 1978.

CODASYL Data Description Language Committee. *DDL Journal of Development,* 1978.

Codd, E.F. "A Relational Model of Data for Large Shared Databanks." In *Communications of the ACM,* Vol. 13, No. 6, June 1970.

Codd, E.F. "Extending the Relational Model to Capture More Meaning." In *Transaction on Database Systems,* Vol. 4, No. 4, December 1979.

Codd, E.F. "Relational Database: A Practical Foundation for Productivity." In *Communications of the ACM,* Vol. 25, No. 2, February 1982.

Cullinet Corporation. *IDMS/R COBOL Programmer's Reference Manual.* Cullinet Corp., 1986.

Cullinet Corporation. *IDMS/R Logical Record Facility.* Cullinet Corp., 1986.

Cullinet Corporation. *IDMS/R Systems Overview.* Cullinet Corp., 1986.

Date, C.J. *An Introduction to Database Systems,* Fifth Edition. Addison-Wesley, 1990.

Davidson, S.B. "Optimism and Consistency in Partitioned Distributed Database Systems." In *Transactions on Database Systems,* Vol. 9, No. 3, September 1984.

Davidson, S.B., Garcia-Molina, H., & Skeen, D. "Consistency in Partitioned Networks." In *Computing Surveys,* Vol. 17, No. 3, September 1985.

DeMarco, T. *Structured Analysis and System Specification.* Yourdon Press, 1978.

Dolan, K. *Business Computer Systems Design.* Mitchell, 1983.

Ellzey, R.S. *Data Structures for Computer Information Systems.* Science Research Associates, 1982.

Elson, M. *Data Structures.* Science Research Associates, 1975.

Embley, D.W. "NFQL: The Natural Forms Query Language." In *ACM Transactions on Database Systems,* Vol. 14, No. 2, June, 1989, pp. 168–211.

Eswaran, K.P., Gray, J.N., Lorie, R.A., & Traiger, I.L. "The Notion of Consistency and Predicate Locks in a Database System." In *Communications of the ACM,* Vol. 19, No. 11, November 1976.

Ewing, J.J. "An Object-Oriented Operating System Interface." In *Conference Proceedings from the Object-Oriented Programming Systems, Languages and Applications, ACM SIGPLAN,* Vol. 21, No. 11, November 1986.

Fagin, R. "Multivalued Dependencies and a New Normal Form for Relational Databases." In *Transactions on Database Systems,* Vol. 2, No. 3, September 1977.

Fagin, R. "A Normal Form for Relational Databases that Is Based on Domains and Keys." In *Transactions on Database Systems,* Vol. 6, No. 3, September 1981.

Fernandez, E.B., Summers, R.C., & Wood, C. *Database Security and Integrity.* Addison-Wesley, 1981.

Flavin, M. *Fundamental Concepts of Information Modeling.* Yourdon Press, 1981.

Freedman, D.P., & Weinberg, G.M. *Walkthroughs, Inspections, and Technical Reviews* (3rd Ed.). Little, Brown, 1982.

Garcia-Molina, H., Pittelli, F., & Davidson, S. "Applications of Byzantine Agreement in Database Systems." In *Transactions on Database Systems,* Vol. 11, No. 1, March 1986.

Garnto, C. & Watson, H.J. "An Investigation of Database Requirements for Institutional and Ad Hoc DSS." In *ACM Data Base,* Vol. 16, No. 4, Summer, 1985, pp. 3–9.

Gray, J., et al. "The Recovery Manager of the System R Database Manager." In *Computing Surveys,* Vol. 13, No. 2, June 1981.

Hammer, M., & McLeod, D. "Database Description with SDM: A Semantic Database Model." In *Transactions on Database Systems,* Vol. 6, No. 3, September 1981.

Hammer, M., & Shipman, D. "Reliability Mechanisms for SDD-1: A System for Distributed Databases." In *Transactions on Database Systems,* Vol. 5, No. 4, December 1980.

Hawryszkiewycz, I.T. *Database Analysis and Design.* Science Research Associates, 1984.

Herlihy, M. "Dynamic Quorum Adjustment for Partitioned Data." In *Transactions on Database Systems,* Vol. 12, No. 2, June 1987.

Higa, K. & Liu Sheng, O.R. "An Object-Oriented Methodology for Database/Knowledgebase Coupling: An Implementation of the Structured Entity Model in Nexpert System." In *ACM Data Base,* Vol. 20, No. 1, Spring, 1989, pp. 24–29.

Honkanen, P. "The Integrity Problem, and What Can Be Done about It Using Today's DBMSs." In *ACM Data Base,* Vol. 20, No. 3, Fall, 1989, pp. 21–27.

Hubbard, G.U. *Computer-Assisted Data Base Design.* Van Nostrand Reinhold, 1981.

IBM Corporation. *SQL/Data System General Information.* IBM Document GH24-5012-0, 1981.

IBM Corporation. *SQL/Data System Planning and Administration.* IBM Document SH24-5014-1, 1982.

IBM Corporation. *SQL/Data System Application Programming.* IBM Document SH24-5018-1, 1982.

IBM Corporation. *System/38 Control Program Facility Concepts.* IBM Publication Number GC21-7729, 1982.

IBM Corporation. *System/38 Installation Manual-Conversion Planning.* IBM Publication Number GC21-7732, 1982.

IBM Corporation. *IBM Database 2 Relational Concepts.* IBM Document GG24-1581, 1983.

IBM Corporation. *IBM Database 2 Concepts and Facilities Guide.* IBM Document GG24-1582, 1983.

IBM Corporation. *IBM Database 2 SQL Usage Guide.* IBM Document GG24-1583, 1983.

IBM Corporation. *IBM Database 2 V1 R2 Release Guide.* IBM Document GG24-1702-0, 1986.

Iivari, J. "Object-oriented Information Systems Analysis." In *Proceedings of the Twenty-Fourth Annual Hawaii International Conference on Systems Sciences, Vol. II.* IEEE Computer Society Press, 1990, pp. 205–218.

Inmon, W.H. *Effective Data Base Design.* Prentice-Hall, 1981.

Jackson, M.A. *Principles of Program Design.* Academic Press, 1975.

Johnson, L.F., & Cooper, R.H. *File Techniques for Data Base Organization in COBOL.* Prentice-Hall, 1981.

Kapp, D., & Leben, J.F. *IMS Programming Techniques.* Van Nostrand Reinhold, 1978.

Kim, W. "On Optimizing an SQL-Like Nested Query." In *Transactions on Database Systems,* Vol. 7, No. 3, September 1982.

Knuth, D.E. *The Art of Computer Programming: Fundamental Algorithms.* Addison-Wesley, 1968.

Knuth, D.E. *The Art of Computer Programming: Sorting and Searching.* Addison-Wesley, 1973.

Kroenke, D.M. "Developing Object-Oriented Database Applications on Microcomputers." In *Proceedings of the Second International Conference on Computers and Applications,* Beijing, June 1987.

Kulkarni, U.R. & Jain, H.K. "Using Semantic Knowledge in Partitioning and Allocation of Data in Distributed Databases." In *Proceedings of the Twenty-Fourth Annual Hawaii International Conference on Systems Sciences, Vol. II.* IEEE Computer Society Press, 1990, pp. 146–154.

Kydd, C.T. "Understanding the Information Content of MIS Management Tools." In *MIS Quarterly,* September, 1989.

Lamport, L. "Time, Clocks, and the Ordering of Events in a Distributed System." In *Communications of the ACM,* Vol. 21, No. 7, July 1978.

Litwin, W., & Abdellatif, A. "Multidatabase Interoperability." In *Computer,* Vol. 19, No. 12, December 1986.

Lum, V.Y., Yuen, P.S.T., & Dodd, M. "Key to Address Transform Techniques: A Fundamental Performance Study on Large Existing Formatted Files." In *Communications of the ACM,* Vol. 14, No. 4, April 1971.

Lyon, J.K. *The Database Administrator.* John Wiley, 1976.

Maier, D., Nordquist, P., & Grossman, M. "Displaying Database Objects." In *Proceedings of the 1st International Conference on Expert Database Systems.* Benjamin-Cummings, 1985.

Maier, D., Stein, J., Otis, A., & Purdy, A. "Development of an Object-Oriented DBMS." In *Conference Proceedings from the Object-Oriented Programming Systems, Languages and Applications, ACM SIGPLAN,* Vol. 21, No. 11, November 1986.

Martin, J. *Computer Data-Base Organization.* Prentice-Hall, 1975.

Mohan, C., Lindsay, B., & Obermarck, R. "Transaction Management in the R° Distributed Database Management System." In *Transactions on Database Systems,*Vol. 11, No. 4, December 1986.

Nolan, R.L. *Managing the Data Resource Function.* West Publishing, 1974.

Oracle Corporation. *ORACLE.* Oracle Corp., 1991.

Orenstein, J.A. "Spatial Query Processing in an Object-Oriented Database System." In *ACM SIG-MOD International Conference on Management of Data, 1986,* Vol. 15, No. 2, June 1986.

Orr, K.T. *Structured Systems Development.* Yourdon Press, 1977.

Orr, K.T. *Structured Requirements Definition.* Ken Orr & Associates, 1981.

Ozsu, M.T. & Valduriez, P. *Principles of Distributed Database Systems.* Prentice-Hall, 1990.

Page-Jones, M. *The Practical Guide to Structured Systems Design.* Yourdon Press, 1980.

Palmer, I. *Data Base Systems: A Practical Reference.* QED Information Sciences, 1975.

Peters, L.J. *Software Design: Methods and Techniques.* Yourdon Press, 1981.

Potter, W.D. & Trueblood, R.P. "Traditional, Semantic, and Hyper-Semantic Approaches to Data Modeling." In *IEEE Computer,* June, 1988, pp. 53–63.

Putnam, L.H. *Software Cost Estimating and Life-Cycle Control: Getting the Software Numbers.* IEEE Catalog No. EHO 165-1, 1980.

Reisner, P. "Human Factor Studies of Database Query Languages: A Survey and Assessment." In *Computing Surveys,* Vol. 13, No. 1, March 1981.

Schaeffer, H. *Data Center Operations.* Prentice-Hall, 1981.

Shipman, D. "The Functional Data Model and the Data Language DAPLEX." In *ACM Transactions on Database Systems,* Vol. 6, No. 1, January, 1987.

Skarra, A.H., & Zdonik, S.B. "The Management of Changing Types in an Object-Oriented Database." In *Conference Proceedings from the Object-Oriented Programming Systems, Languages and Applications, ACM SIGPLAN,* Vol. 21, No. 11, November 1986.

Stonebreaker, M.R., et al. "The Design and Implementation of INGRES." In *Transactions on Database Systems,* Vol. 1, No. 3, September 1976.

Sybase Corporation. *SYBASE SQL Server: Technical Overview.* Sybase, 1989.

Thro, E. *The Database Dictionary.* Microtrend Books, 1990.

Traiger, I.L., Gray, J., Galtieri, C.A., & Lindsay, B.G. "Transactions and Consistency in Distributed Database Systems." In *Transactions on Database Systems,* Vol. 7, No. 3, September 1982.

Tsichritzis, D.C., & Lochovsky, F.H. *Data Models.* Prentice-Hall, 1982.

Ullman, J.D. *Principles of Database Systems.* Computer Science Press, 1980.

Vetter, M., & Maddison, R.N. *Database Design Methodology.* Prentice-Hall International, 1981.

Warnier, J.D. *Logical Construction of Systems.* Van Nostrand Reinhold, 1981.

Weinberg, V. *Structured Analysis.* Yourdon Press, 1978.

Wellesley Software. *Learning SQL.* Prentice-Hall, 1991.

Welty, C., & Stemple, D.W. "Human Factors Comparison of a Procedural and a Nonprocedural Query Language." In *Transactions on Database Systems,* Vol. 6, No. 4, December 1981.

Wiederhold, G., "Views, Objects, and Databases." In *Computer,* Vol. 19, No. 12, December 1986.

Woelk, D., Kim, W., & Luther, W. "An Object-Oriented Approach to Multi-Media Databases." In *ACM SIGMOD International Conference on Management of Data, 1986,* Vol. 15, No. 2, June 1986.

Yourdon, E., & Constantine, L.L. *Structured Design.* Prentice-Hall, 1979.

Zaniolo, C., & Melkanoff, M.A. "A Formal Approach to the Definition and the Design of Conceptual Schemata for Database Systems." In *Transactions on Database Systems,* Vol. 7, No. 1, March 1982.

Zdonik, S.B. & Maier, D. (Eds.). *Reading in Object-Oriented Database Systems.* Morgan Kaufmann Publishers, 1990.

Zhao, L. & Robers, S.A. "An Object-Oriented Data Model for Database Modeling, Implementation and Access." In *The Computer Journal,* Vol. 31, No. 2, February, 1988, pp. 116–124.

Zloof, M.M. "Query by Example." In *Proceedings of the National Computer Conference,* AFIPS, Vol. 44, May 1975.